The Path to Victory

The Path to Victory

THE MEDITERRANEAN THEATER
IN WORLD WAR II

DOUGLAS PORCH

Farrar, Straus and Giroux

New York

Farrar, Straus and Giroux
19 Union Square West, New York 10003

Copyright © 2004 by Douglas Porch
Distributed in Canada by Douglas & McIntyre Ltd.
Printed in the United States of America
First edition, 2004

Owing to limitations of space, all acknowledgments for permission to reprint
previously published material can be found on pages 797–798.

Library of Congress Cataloging-in-Publication Data
Porch, Douglas.
The path to victory : the Mediterranean theater in World War II / Douglas
Porch.— 1st ed.
      p.   cm.
Includes bibliographical references and index.
ISBN 0-374-20518-3 (alk. paper)
1. World War, 1939–1945—Campaigns—Mediterranean Region.
2. Mediterranean Sea—Strategic aspects. 3. Mediterranean Region—History—
20th century.   I. Title.

D766.P67 2004
940.53182'2—dc22

2003060845

EAN: 978-0-374-20518-8

Designed by Robert C. Olsson

www.fsgbooks.com

1   3   5   7   9   10   8   6   4   2

For Françoise

CONTENTS

PREFACE

This book counts several points of origin. The first is a lifelong fascination for the Mediterranean that springs from its rich history, the mosaic of peoples who live along its coasts, and the stunning beauty of its land and seascapes. A second motivating factor has been my students at the Naval Postgraduate School, many of whom serve with the U.S. Mediterranean fleet and in peacekeeping missions in Bosnia or Kosovo, or who are natives of Mediterranean nations. They challenge one to understand the importance of the Mediterranean as a maritime highway, a geographic link between and among continents and oceans.

The "Joint and Combined" emphasis of U.S. military education encourages the study and practice of the interaction between air, sea, and land power in a multifaceted operational environment. While the combination of these three forms of warfare are conditions for victory in all theaters, their efficient interaction was especially vital in the Mediterranean theater in World War II. This requires that one consider the Mediterranean theater as a geographic and strategic whole, rather than as a sequence of discrete campaigns. The Mediterranean was more than the sum of its parts. Those who fought there had to engage over the sweep of a theater that offers a particularly complex series of operational as well as strategic challenges. The extreme variations in geography, not to mention forms of warfare, especially from 1943 when Italy signed an armistice and insurgency warfare kicked in on the northern shore of the Mediterranean, put pressure on generals and admirals constantly to reconfigure and adapt their armies, navies, and air forces to new conditions. As in the Pacific, victory or defeat in World War II Mediterranean campaigns came down to who fought more efficiently in a three-dimensional setting. But the land component in the Mediterranean was far larger than in the island-hopping Pacific campaigns. A military force that mastered one or even two forms of warfare, but was deficient in a third, found itself at a severe disadvantage. Initially the Axis united German proficiency in land and air warfare with Italian sea power to command the "central position" in the Mediterranean. This allowed Rommel to run circles around the British in the Western Desert. But Axis air and naval power proved to be wasting assets. And while the Wehrmacht remained formidable right up to the last days of the war, years of Mediterranean fighting had shorn it of offensive capability, reducing it to desperate defensive campaigns in the mountains of Italy and the forests of the Balkans.

Finally, victory was determined not only by *how* one fought, but *where* one fought. War is never conducted in a political vacuum, but is, as Clausewitz reminds us, "politics by other means." In the politically complex, even volatile Mediterranean world, this famous dictum could almost be stood on its head. German and "Anglo-Saxon" generals particularly detested fighting in the Mediterranean, where every strategic decision, every coalition, every invasion proposal was prickly with political consequence. The British commander in the Middle East, General Archibald Wavell, resisted fighting in politically fractured Greece, Syria, and Iraq. French and Italian politics meant sleepless nights for Allied commanders right up to war's end. Meanwhile, it could be said that the Axis failed to exploit its political opportunities in the Arab world and seriously mismanaged the political dimensions of its occupation of the Balkan Peninsula and Greece, with significant military consequences.

This book, therefore, is a work of synthesis, one that attempts to meld the histories of the individual campaigns in North Africa, Greece and Crete, the Horn of Africa, Syria and Iraq, Tunisia, and Sicily and Italy, and the histories of the air and sea wars and the insurgencies fought out on, above, and around the seas. But this work aspires to be more than a litany of battles. I have examined the interrelationship of these campaigns in the context of a Mediterranean theater and a Mediterranean strategy to better assess the importance of the Mediterranean in its relationship to the larger war. Historians have not, on the whole, been kind to the Allied Mediterranean effort. From its inception, the Mediterranean was an "encounter" theater, a place where Italian and British interests intersected. Churchill opted to fight there to protect the corridor to the British empire, to demonstrate that London meant to fight to the knife against the Axis, to emphasize his distance from Chamberlain's failed appeasement policies, to attract U.S. support, and possibly to redeem a Mediterranean strategy that had foundered at Gallipoli in World War I. As a consequence, Hitler was forced to intervene to rescue Mussolini. American strategy was grafted onto the original British investment at Roosevelt's insistence, over the protests of his secretary of war and his chief of staff, who argued that intervention in the Mediterranean attacked no German center of gravity, and therefore constituted a wasteful diversion of American assets for the benefit of the "British empire machine."

The consequence of this Allied stumble into a poorly thought-out and "opportunistic" Mediterranean strategy was a dreadful slogging match in a theater in which the British and subsequently the Americans were outgeneraled and outfought around the shores of a sea of trifling strategic importance. British historian John Ellis complained that "the Mediterranean is consistently over-emphasized in most English studies of the war . . . the whole campaign barely merits an extended footnote." While the Mediterranean did constitute a strategic diversion, "the overall impression, indeed, is of a remarkable lack of direction in Mediterranean planning, with key decisions taken off the cuff, simply because no one, least of all on the American side, could think of anything better to do."[1] Corelli Barnett called the Allied Mediterranean strategy a "cul-de-sac . . . mere byplay in the conclusion of a war that had been won in mass battles on the Eastern and Western Fronts."[2] The Allies paid a heavy price for their opportunism because, by September 1943, their Mediterranean commitments had been funneled into the blind alley of the Italian Peninsula. This led to the foreseeable consequence, once preparations for the invasion of

Northwestern Europe got under way, of the two regions' being treated as rival, rather than complementary, theaters. David Kennedy has called the Italian campaign "a slogan not a strategy," and condemned that battleground as "a grinding war of attrition whose costs were justified by no defensible military or political purpose."[3] Others, while offering a more balanced assessment of the Italian campaign, nevertheless consider the Mediterranean portion of Allied grand strategy to have been a "failure" because, much as in World War I, the Mediterranean competed with, rather than complemented, the main Western Front.[4] British historian John Keegan compares Italy to Wellington's campaign against Napoleonic forces in Spain, one in which the soldiers' "sense of purpose and stoutness of heart" are all the more to be admired "because of the campaign's marginality." "Their war was not a crusade," he writes, "but, in almost every respect, an old-fashioned one of strategic diversion on the maritime flank of a continental enemy, the 'Peninsular War' of 1939–45."[5]

This work argues that while the Mediterranean was not the *decisive* theater of the war, it was the *pivotal* theater, a requirement for Allied success. None of the Mediterranean theater's staunchest advocates at the time—Churchill, Harold Alexander, nor Mark Clark—ever argued that the Mediterranean should or could replace the Eastern Front or Northwestern Europe in importance. However, they did believe that the Mediterranean was a vital prelude to the invasion of Northwestern Europe, and that it played a significant role in the defeat of the Axis. This book seeks to explain how significant that contribution actually was to Allied victory. In the process, it assesses the relationship of the peripheral Mediterranean theater with the main Eastern and Western Fronts. My argument is that it was impossible for the Western Allies to transition successfully from Dunkirk to Operation Overlord without passing through the Mediterranean. That theater was critical in forging the Anglo-American alliance, in permitting Allied armies to acquire fighting skills, audition leaders and staffs, and evolve the technical, operational, tactical, and intelligence systems required to invade Normandy successfully in June 1944. Overlord was rehearsed in North Africa, Sicily, and Italy. By 6 June 1944, the

Mediterranean had worn down and ultimately dismembered the Axis. The "Peninsular War of 1939–45" became Hitler's hematoma, much as its "old-fashioned" 1808–14 counterpart had created an ulcer for Napoleon over a century earlier. It bought time for Roosevelt to build up American forces so that he could impose Washington's primacy in the Western Alliance, and therefore to shape postwar Europe according to U.S., rather than British or European, priorities.

To factor the Mediterranean out of World War II is to imagine a disaster of epic proportions, and a military outcome in the European theater far different from an unconditional surrender of Germany. Some who fault the Mediterranean strategy, like American historian Robert Love, blame it for delaying the invasion of Northwestern Europe, which, had it been carried out in 1943, would have brought an earlier end to the Reich and preempted Stalin's land grab in Eastern Europe. Love blames a combination of Churchill's imperial ambitions and Roosevelt's "vacillation" for "a wasteful, peripheral strategy in the Mediterranean" that allowed the Russians to overrun Eastern Europe and gave the Germans a bonus two years to strengthen their Atlantic defenses.[6] At best, Italy was a *pis aller*, a series of "hesitant and flawed" operations that gave Hitler the leisure to organize his criminal war against European civilians.[7] The sad truth is that Sledgehammer/Roundup, the planned invasion of northern France in 1942 or 1943, would certainly have collapsed in bloody disaster against a strongly entrenched German army, backed by a powerful Luftwaffe, with German wolf packs prowling among the Allied fleet supporting the invasion. Defeat would have throttled the Western Alliance, as U.S. strategy would have veered toward the Pacific. The political fortunes of Churchill and Roosevelt, not to mention Charles de Gaulle, perhaps even the stability of British and American democracy, would have been compromised. Hitler would have solidified his hold on the Continent, resistance movements would have become demoralized, and Stalin might have sought to cut the best deal he could with the invader. Postwar Europe, including its Mediterranean frontier, would certainly have been a far different place. Therefore, my argument is that the Mediterranean was vital to Allied success precisely because it forced the postponement of a premature invasion of Northern Europe.

This book owes its inception to my colleague at the Naval Postgraduate School, Professor Daniel Moran, who pointed out that beyond the multivolume British official histories of the Mediterranean War, no single-volume work exists that treats World War II in the Mediterranean as a theater in its own right, rather than as a series of discrete campaigns. I want to thank my agent Michael Congdon for encouraging me to pursue this idea and for his constant advice and support. John Glusman at Farrar, Straus and Giroux has, as always, proved an exacting editor, but one of patience and faith. Carlo D'Este, whose histories of the American forces and generals who fought in the Mediterranean must make him the dean of Mediterranean military historians, kindly agreed to read the manuscript. Any errors or inaccuracies that remain are, of course, my responsibility. It is traditional for authors to thank their families. I should like to conform to that practice, especially in the case of my wife, Françoise, who spent many weekends at home because her husband was otherwise unavailable for more social activities.

The Path to Victory

A Strategist's Nightmare

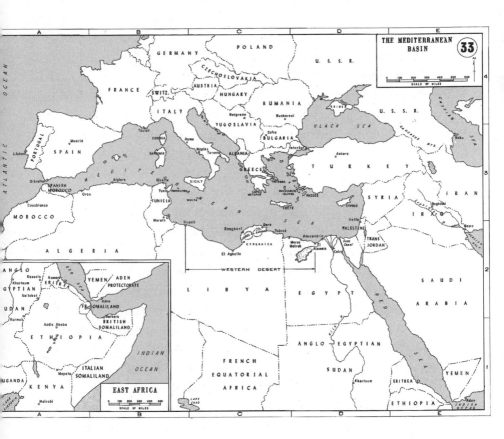

A LTHOUGH THE MEDITERRANEAN is an ancient seat of conflict, it does not lend itself easily to battle. Its purpose and geography confuse the most able strategists. Few since the Romans have envisioned the inland sea as an organizing principle buckled at Gibraltar against outside intrusion. This is because no one since the Romans has been strong enough to dominate it. The result is that the races that reside on the Mediterranean's shores, peoples who nurture quarrels as an ancient birthright, adopt a proprietary but parochial attitude toward their neighborhoods. For them, the Mediterranean is a segmented lake, a discrete sequence of basins and channels whose islands, coasts, and hinterlands they struggle to control. Everyone searches for an ally, and an opportunity, to settle a score, to seize a marginal advantage in the millennial quarrel with their neighbor. The Mediterranean "in all ages seems to have taught only catastrophe and violence . . . a lesson in anarchy, without shade or sequence . . ." The author of those words, Henry Adams, was writing of Sicily. But his observation appears a fitting commentary on the entire sea.[1]

The strategy adopted by each of the belligerents was shaped in great part by their vision of that sea. The fortunes of the Mediterranean, writes the French historian of that sea in the sixteenth century, Fernand Braudel, "are often easier to read on its outer margins than at the very heart of its bewildering activity."[2] In World War II, it was the nations on the margins—Germany, the United States, and Great Britain—who dictated the fortunes of the Mediterranean. The first two powers were reluctant interventionists, unable to discern strategic benefit in a sea that, to them, appeared only to offer boundless opportunities for indecisive engagements. Unlike its adversaries—and even some of its allies—London never ceased to view the Mediterranean as "a single geo-strategic unit."[3] Nor was it merely a lake contained by three continents. Only an imperial, maritime power was afforded the luxury to view the Middle Sea as a highway, a crimp in the earth's crust that folds, bends, and twists from the Azores to Bombay. Since the seventeenth century Britain had been active in the Mediterranean, fighting French and Spaniard to ensure that its shortest route to India was preserved. The opening of the Suez Canal in 1868 began what many saw as the dawn of Britain's Mediterranean hegemony[4] over a segment of a geostrategic puzzle, a maritime link that London had to control to survive. If the growth of Italian naval power in the interwar years opened an Italian bid to appropriate the central position in the Mediterranean, India occupied the central position in Britain's world-view, a key link with the antipodes and a strategic objective in its own right. Landsmen like Hitler viewed the Mediterranean as a glacis that protected the southern approaches to his European fortress. Mussolini barked that the inland sea, dominated by France and Great Britain, incarcerated Italy's ambitions, preventing its "march to the oceans." However, those with a nautical imagination—and a command of maritime history—saw offensive possibilities in the sea, as if it were a sequence of intersecting rivers that followed shorelines, coiled around promontories, and filtered through archipelagoes.

Skeptics complain that the Mediterranean had scant value to Axis or Allies in World War II.[5] Anglo-Saxon historiography especially, the argument continues, has exaggerated the Mediterranean's significance for at least three reasons: First, until June 1944, the Mediterranean was virtually the only place where Western Allied and Axis ground forces were locked in combat. Therefore, there is a tendency to equate El Alamein with Stalingrad as the twin turning points of the war, when, in fact the two battles are hardly comparable in either scale or significance. Second, the tendency to write off the desert conflict in particular as a gladiatorial contest between Generals Erwin Rommel and Bernard Montgomery has discouraged basic questions about the significance of events as opposed to their undeniable drama.[6] Third, the popularity of counterfactual history among English-speaking historians encourages speculation about strategic alternatives, paths not taken by the major combatants that might have altered the outcome of the war. The Mediterranean offers one area where strategic imagination can be exercised unchecked by more prosaic considerations of logistics and material strength. "German historians, who are brought up to view the practice of counter-factual history as time-wasting speculation . . . have invariably come to the conclusion that for the Third Reich the Mediterranean could never have been more than a strategic dead end," writes German historian Klaus Schmider.[7]

Even before the war began, the Mediterranean was fast becoming a backwater of declining strategic and economic significance. The creation of a fragile and volatile system of neophyte states amid the wreckage of the Ottoman Empire in 1922, in the words of historian David Fromkin, had merely substituted the "Middle Eastern Question" for the "Eastern Question," which had troubled European diplomacy for much of the nineteenth century. The difference was that, unlike the pre–World War I decades, Great Britain now lacked the confidence or the energy to impose a modernizing vision on the confusion of ancient tribes that peopled the region.[8] The Abyssinia crisis of 1935 focused British attentions on the need to defend the home islands and Singapore at the expense of the Mediterranean, which, it was argued, could be effectively closed off by air power.[9] By 1938, less than 9 percent of the total value of British imports flowed through Suez, while soldiers claimed that the defense of Suez was a luxury that Britain might no longer be able to afford.[10] However, the counterargument is that the Mediterranean was increasing in both relative economic and strategic importance before the war began, and continued to increase thereafter. Two things intervened to reverse the waning fortunes of the Mediterranean in British strategic calculations: first, the arrival in the Admiralty in 1938 of "a group of convinced Mediterraneanists" led by deputy chief of naval staff Vice-Admiral Andrew Cunningham, who argued that Britain had more political and economic interests in the Mediterranean than in the Far East. Cunningham believed that should war occur, the Royal Navy, together with its French ally, would be far more likely to gain success against Italy than against Germany or Japan at the war's outset.[11] Therefore, while the Mediterranean may have been an encounter theater in World War II, and Allied strategy there utterly opportunistic, as American military strategists like George Marshall argued at the time and historians like John Ellis have claimed since, Mediterranean combat was guided by a strong sense of London's estimate of the Mediterranean's value. Second, opportunism that displays a suppleness able to capitalize on the enemy's strategic mistakes constitutes a strength, not a weakness.

The 1938 discovery of oil in Saudi Arabia and Kuwait reinforced Cunningham's view of the strategic importance of older fields in Iran and Iraq, and hence of the Mediterranean's strategic value. The prohibition on British merchant shipping through the Mediterranean from April 1940, combined with the shipping shortage, made it prohibitively expensive to send Iranian oil 18,000 miles around the Cape of Good Hope to London, requiring the British Isles to fight the war with American, not Middle Eastern, oil.[12] Nevertheless, the lack of oil was a serious disadvantage to the Axis, which had to ship this precious commodity via a circuitous and tenuous passage from Ploesti in Romania through the Black Sea, the Turkish Straits, the Aegean, and across the Adriatic to Italy. From Italy, Axis tankers had to run the Maltese gauntlet to Tripoli or, in 1943, Tunis and Bizerte. The sacrifice of three-quarters of the Italian merchant fleet in an attempt to supply Axis forces in North Africa cast Mussolini into a deep depression in the spring of 1943. "My illness has a name," he insisted, "—convoys."[13] The absence of natural oil deposits forced Germany to rely on synthesization of oil from coal. But from 1942, once stocks plundered in Europe were exhausted, the Axis lived in a perpetual oil crisis. Nevertheless, the relatively meager output of Middle Eastern oil fields compared to those of the Caucasus or North America, the feasibility and costs of conquering them, and the time lag in developing an infrastructure to ensure an abundant flow, meant that the Middle East never became a strategic objective worth the German investment.[14]

Egypt and Suez, indeed the entire Mediterranean, was defended for military, not economic, reasons. When London contemplated withdrawing the fleet from the Mediterranean in 1940, Cunningham argued strongly that such an action would tip the region into the enemy camp, a view supported by Churchill, who saw the Mediterranean as the "carotid artery of Empire."[15] Although American chief of staff George Marshall characterized the British decision to fight in the Mediterranean as a "prestige" strategy that was "fundamentally unsound,"[16] strategically the British, and ultimately the Americans, had little to lose by fighting there, and much to gain. This made the Mediterranean, especially the Eastern Mediterranean, the perfect battlefield for the British. Defeat in the Mediterranean would probably not mean the defeat of Britain, while victory there would sustain morale, undermine Italy, encourage American aid, overextend Axis forces, protect Middle Eastern oilfields, draw the French back into the war, keep Spain on the sidelines, and contain the Arab penchant for creative anarchy. The Mediterranean did not so much compete with the Eastern Front as complement it by drawing off some Axis forces, showing Allied solidarity with the Soviet struggle, and, from 1943, offering a more direct route for war matériel to reach the USSR. A minimal Allied outlay in advisers and matériel in Greece and the Balkans required the Germans to invest significant resources in repression. Until the Normandy invasion of June 1944, the Mediterranean offered the optimum point where the concentration of manpower reserves of the British empire—Australia, New Zealand, South Africa, and India— might be amalgamated with the industrial resources of the United States.

Furthermore, unlike their adversaries, the British in the Eastern Mediterranean wallowed in oil. In 1934, an oil pipeline had reached Haifa from the Mosul field in Iraq. This reduced the volume of crude oil shipped through the Canal by 68 percent and further lessened the commercial importance of Suez.[17] Haifa was transformed into the "Singapore of the Middle East"—the most modern harbor in the Levant, which included an oil dock, an air terminal, and a light naval base. An oil refinery, completed in June 1940, became the principal source of fuel for the fleet, supplied by a regular tanker service between Haifa and Alexandria. Additional oil was transported by tanker from the Abadan refinery to capacious bunkering stations at Suez.[18] Lack of fuel caused Italian battleships to idle in port and Rommel's offensives in the Western Desert literally to run out of gas. While Luftwaffe pilots went untrained for lack of fuel,[19] the British spigot of energy flowed with such prodigality that British soldiers in the Western Desert cleaned their uniforms with petrol because it was more plentiful than water.[20]

Another advantage held by the Allies in the Mediterranean stemmed from the fact that combat there required a complex interaction of land, naval, and air forces unparalleled in any other theater.[21] This handed the trump in the Mediterranean to the British and ultimately to the Allies. The Royal Navy was the link service, the sine qua non of Mediterranean conflict, for the simple reason that the campaign there was an amphibious one. Also, the fleet bought time for the British army and the RAF in the Mediterranean to achieve a measure of combat effectiveness that would enable it to compete with the enemy. Navies increasingly found it impossible to operate without air cover in the Mediterranean. A new phase in the Mediterranean war came in May 1941, when land-based aircraft forced the Royal Navy to abandon the evacuation of Crete as too costly.[22] Nevertheless, air forces, though important, were no substitute for naval power there. The Mediterranean was as much an "island-hopping" campaign as was the Pacific. Islands form the keys to the control of that sea— Malta, Corsica, Crete, Cyprus. But in the Mediterranean, as Braudel notes, even continental land masses are islands. Greece, Italy, the Iberian Peninsula, Asia Minor are "islands the sea does not surround," self-contained worlds severed from the European continent by mountains. The Balkans were segregated by mountains into ethnic islands. North Africa, an island surrounded by Sahara and sea, separates into more islands. The Maghreb, the series of mountainous ridges that runs from Tunis to Casablanca, is called the Djezirat el Moghreb— "Island of the Setting Sun"—by the Arabs. The 1940 defeat of France made French North Africa even more of an island, cut off from its political as well as geographical base, and hence a target for Operation Torch in November 1942. The Western Desert was an island, independent for strategic purposes of the African continent to which it belongs. How the Germans and Italians believed they could win in the desert until they mastered the sea lanes leading to it offers irrefutable testimony to their failure to internalize the Mediterranean's strategic geography. Nor does it stretch the concept of insularity too much to claim that status for Syria, in 1941 severed both geographically and politically from its base. Italy can be visualized as a series of islands suited to amphibious assault—Sicily, Salerno, Naples, Anzio-Rome and Livorno-Pisa-Florence, the Po Valley. And Italy could be bypassed to attack the "island" of southern France.

Of Britain's three services, the Royal Navy was best prepared for war in 1940. The navy had trained hard in the interwar years to shed its Great War reputation for inflexibility and lack of initiative. From the beginning of the war in operations off Calabria, to shunting convoys to Malta, to protecting and supporting amphibious operations, the Royal Navy proved extremely adept at integrating the various fleet elements for operational success. This was especially the case when naval operations were guided by Ultra intelligence. Technologically, the development of sonar (Asdic), radar, and aerial torpedoes gave it the upper hand over its adversaries at Cape Matapan and Taranto—even at Mers el-Kébir. Its ship handling against enemy surface fleets was exemplary, in part because captains and admirals were trusted to use their judgment and not micromanaged.[23]

The Royal Navy in the Mediterranean also benefited for much of the war from the leadership of Admiral Sir Andrew Bourne Cunningham. When war was declared in the Mediterranean in June 1940, "ABC" was a fifty-eight-year-old acting admiral and commander of the Mediterranean fleet. When war correspondent Alan Moorehead met Cunningham dressed in a white shirt, shorts, and kneesocks, sitting in his sea cabin aboard his flagship *Warspite* in Alexandria harbor in December 1940, "he was obviously enjoying life." And no wonder, as the Royal Navy had just sunk three Italian battleships swinging at anchor at Taranto. A Scot with round, red-veined cheeks and tropical blue eyes, Cunningham exemplified the Royal Navy's attempt to break away from the Great War mold of risk-averse leadership. His slight frame seemed to radiate energy, at no time more than when he sortied his fleet.[24] He rapidly established a reputation as an aggressive commander determined to bring the Italian fleet to battle, a fighting instinct that he communicated to his fleet captains. Cunningham's victories at Cape Matapan and Taranto were masterstrokes of technological and operational surprise. He displayed a Nelsonian keenness to close with the enemy, wagering victory against more modern and often faster Italian ships on the courage of his crews and the superior seamanship of his captains. And while not celebrated as a strategist, Cunningham understood instinctively that the war would not be won unless all services cooperated, which greatly enhanced his standing with his fellow service chiefs.[25]

Despite Cunningham's achievement, he was more respected than loved in the fleet. Like many upper-class British commanders, he lacked the common touch when dealing with his sailors. Cunningham's "courage and tenacity" speeches—"swinging the lead" in naval parlance—usually drew negative reviews below decks, especially in the wake of ship losses that rattled morale. Many interpreted the attitude of steely resolve Cunningham invariably projected in the face of adversity as evidence that he failed fully to appreciate how far ships had been made vulnerable by land-based aircraft.[26] Nor was the

Cunningham-Churchill chemistry ever perfectly calibrated. In some ways this is surprising. Churchill, after all, was a navy man on a permanent quest to find commanders like Cunningham who possessed the indefinable "Nelson touch" that the Royal Navy valued in its commanders. Had Cunningham been in Jellicoe's shoes in 1916, it is quite possible to speculate that the High Seas Fleet would never have escaped to home waters at the conclusion to the Battle of Jutland. For months in 1941 and 1942, Cunningham was practically the only one of Churchill's commanders who delivered success, and at a time in the war when British victories were scarce. In some ways, however, Cunningham was more like World War I first sea lord Admiral Jackie Fisher, whom Churchill first admired and then broke with in the aftermath of the failed Gallipoli campaign of 1915. Cunningham was a man much happier on the bridge of his flagship than in an office. Montgomery complained that Cunningham's obvious talent for big-fleet actions did not extend to the preparation of joint operations with the army, in which he was "out of his depth." Like Fisher, he possessed a wicked temper that sapped all initiative from his staff. His combative personality, low tolerance for Churchill's tendency to meddle in operational decisions, and eventually the support of the supreme Allied commander General Dwight Eisenhower, made him almost immune from criticism and control.[27] Churchill had opposed Cunningham's nomination as first sea lord in October 1943, but gave in when confronted by Cunningham's universal support in the navy. Cunningham reciprocated Churchill's disesteem. His replies to the prime minister's eccentric strategic projects were spare, even terse. He complained that time with Churchill was usually "wasted . . . What a drag on the wheel of war this man is."[28]

While the Royal Navy's strengths were unique, its weaknesses were shared by its enemies. Its most serious weakness was the lack of an air arm, so that, like the Italians, the Royal Navy was obliged to rely on the cooperation of an independent air force. The only planes Cunningham commanded directly in June 1940 were a handful of lightly armed flying boats at Malta and Alexandria and seventeen lumbering Swordfish torpedo-reconnaissance biplanes, made even slower when long-range gas tanks were fitted on them, which flew off the twenty-year-old carrier *Eagle* to provide reconnaissance in the immediate vicinity of his ships. The Royal Navy's lack of air cover became critical once the Germans intervened in force in the Mediterranean in early 1941. Despite the benefit of Asdic, the Royal Navy also demonstrated early weaknesses in antisubmarine warfare, in part because it had been difficult to test its techniques outside of real-war conditions.

A final problem for the navy was one always difficult to manage in the Mediterranean—concentration of force. France's surrender in June 1940 gave the Italians unrestricted domination of the central Mediterranean. Italian ships and planes operating out of Sardinia, Naples, and Taranto in southern Italy, Palermo in Sicily, Corfu, Rhodes, Tripoli, and Cyrenaica forced Cunningham to divide his forces between Gibraltar and the Near East, while at the same time fight to preserve Malta, his only outpost in the central Mediterranean. Gibraltar was in the process of modernization in 1940. But however modern it became, it was always a base whose survival depended on Spanish good will. The fall of Gibraltar would have made it extremely difficult for the British to operate in the Western Mediterranean and to supply Malta. It would also have allowed the Italians to concentrate their naval forces against British naval strength in the Eastern Mediterranean.[29] Gibraltar also shared an open bay with Algeciras, where Franco turned a blind eye to the Italian spies, and on occasion Italian special forces, who operated with impunity. In the central Mediterranean, Malta had been the Mediterranean fleet's home port, the place where most of its repair docks had been located. However, the 1938 Czechoslovak crisis accentuated Malta's vulnerability should Italy declare war. Locating a substitute port in the Eastern Mediterranean for docking or repair was far from obvious. Famagusta on Cyprus was three hundred miles from Suez, too close to Turkey, and required considerable time and investment to make ready. Haifa and Port Said could only accommodate "light" forces. This left Alexandria as the only harbor large enough to berth a fleet.

In 1939 "Alex" was a cosmopolitan but dust-blown city on the fringe of the Nile Delta. Even by the exceptional standards of Mediterranean port cities, Alexandria plumbed new depths of squalor. Hawkers of watermelons, fish, and almonds pushed carts past cafes full of hookah-sucking men, through streets teeming with plaintive beggars, thieving children, dignified camels, and piles of fetid rubbish. The city's numerous bordellos and significant foreign communities, many of whose members seemed to be in the pay of one secret service or another, made Alexandria a permanent conspiracy against military discipline and security. But from a nautical perspective, that was only the start of Alexandria's problems. The harbor was difficult to enter in foul weather and vulnerable to attack from the sea and the air. Oil storage was precariously close to the harbor, so that fuel might spread over the surface of the water and immolate the entire fleet in an attack. British ships sailing toward the Italian mainland nine hundred miles away quickly found themselves beyond the range of land-based air cover. Above all, Egypt, indeed, the entire Near East, appeared vulnerable simultaneously to invasion and insurrection. Nevertheless, despite the obvious basing shortcomings of Alexandria, in the year and a half before the outbreak of war, docks and repair facilities, tugs, lighters, and naval stores were shifted there from Malta.[30] On 8 April 1939, following Italy's invasion of Albania, the Mediterranean fleet departed Valetta harbor for Egypt.

But Britain's strengths also composed its vulnerabilities. The problem from a strategic perspective with viewing the Mediterranean as a river is that it is a rather long one, running over two thousand miles from Gibraltar to Suez. Initially, as war loomed, this seemed not to pose an insurmountable problem. There was always the hope, increasingly forlorn, that Italy might stay neutral. From a strategic perspective, neutrality seemed very much in Rome's interests, for every step toward belligerency increased Italian insecurity. Three-fifths of Italy's imports of coal and oil in peacetime flowed through Suez or Gibraltar. Mussolini's conquest of Ethiopia from 1935 cast part of his army beyond Suez, in the process putting "a noose round his own neck" that "left the end hanging out for anyone with a navy to pull."[31] "Most blockadeable Italy" was, therefore, threatened by a maritime siege that the Germans would prove able only to mitigate, not alleviate, by land.[32] After the Munich crisis of September 1938, however, hopes for Italian neutrality required a case of almost terminal optimism to sustain. Still, the high cards in the Mediterranean were held

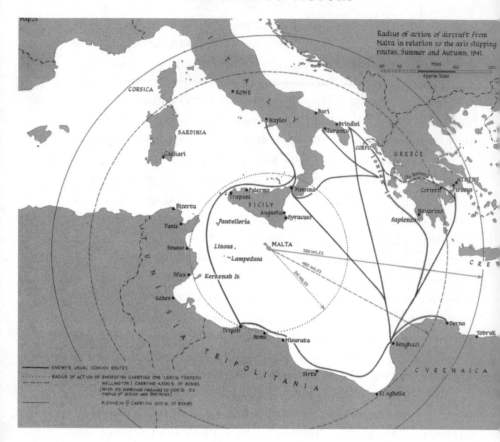

Radius of action of aircraft from Malta in relation to the axis shipping routes, Summer and Autumn, 1941.

by the Anglo-French alliance. The French at Mers el-Kébir, the port of Oran in Algeria, and the British at Gibraltar could dominate the sea's western basin. The central Mediterranean could be contested from Bizerte, Tunis, Corsica, and Toulon. Indeed, so precarious was Malta's position and so superfluous was it to requirements that the Admiralty took minimal steps to fortify it against an Italian invasion. France's (temporary) elimination from the war in 1940 overnight transformed Malta from a sacrificial citadel to an unsinkable aircraft carrier astride the route from Italy to North Africa. Malta was the only place in the central Mediterranean where bombers flying from Gibraltar to Suez could refuel. Valetta's Grand Harbor, a two-and-a-half-mile-long azure incision in Malta's northern coast, supplied the only haven for British ships in a long stretch of otherwise hostile Axis sea. Malta's problem was that while it lay eleven hundred miles from Gibraltar and nine hundred miles from Egypt, Valetta was only twenty minutes' flying time from Sicily.

Malta's importance to Allied success in the Mediterranean was a subject of intense debate during the war, and has continued to divide historians since.[33] Axis strategists considered Suez, not Malta, the more valuable prize. However, the island's heroism made it a constant focus of British propaganda,[34] and with good reason. Siege was a condition familiar to the Maltese—indeed, war was that island's raison d'être. As travel writer Paul Theroux notes, Malta glories in war because it is only then that this parched, tawny rock eighteen miles long and eight miles wide reveals its value.[35]

Called the "Lock of the Mediterranean" since 1530 when Charles V ordered the Knights of Saint John of Jerusalem, expelled from Rhodes by Turkish power, to garrison it, Malta resides at the confluence of the "streams" of Mediterranean nautical activity. The island sits like a cork centered in the hourglass between the great eastern and western basins of that sea. It also barred the north-south route across the Sicilian channel that connected Mussolini to his African empire. Malta was the way station between Gibraltar and Suez. From Malta, British ships might sail up the Ionian coast of Greece, past Corfu and the Albanian shore into the Adriatic, the frontier that separates Italian, Slav, and Greek. Or the sea route from Malta might filter through the Aegean past the Turkish Straits into the Black Sea and the heart of Southeastern Europe. This route offered possibilities that tantalized British Prime Minister Winston Churchill, and encouraged some of his most egregious miscalculations in the Mediterranean—in two world wars! So, Malta was transformed by France's defeat into Britain's bantam Mediterranean double. An island besieged, suffering, enduring.

It was Britain's good fortune that this most vulnerable outpost was inhabited by a people who acquiesced in their geography as their fate. The stone-choked soil, after centuries of serving foreign masters as a Christian presidio off an Islamic shore, bred a population both devoutly Catholic and politically compliant. The British fleet arrived in Malta in 1800 to displace Napoleon's navy, and remained. Malta's strategic value increased with the opening of the Suez Canal in 1869, and it subsequently became headquarters for the Royal Navy's prestigious Mediterranean fleet. The shipyard, nestled beneath the harbor cliffs, provided work for artisans, mechanics, and stevedores. Quarrymen sectioned the ocher stone that made Valetta one of the most handsome of the Mediterranean's capitals. Most of Malta's quarter-million inhabitants were illiterate, scratching a living from a soil bleached of nutrients by centuries of erosion and deforestation. Or they emigrated. Malta depended on Italy and Libya for 70 percent of its food, fertilizers, and animal fodder; 95 percent of the island's other economic requirements came by sea. Political power lay in the hands of an elite of Anglo-Maltese families. However, Italian influence began to infect the island in the 1920s, encouraged by some intermarriage and the intrusion of Italian words into Malta's Semitic language. When the pro-Italian Nationalist Party came to power in the early 1930s, the British suspended the constitution and reimposed direct rule. A policy of vigorous Anglicization ensued: the use of Italian words was forbidden in the law courts while the island's two Italian schools closed their doors. Mussolini's 1935 invasion of Abyssinia swept away the residue of pro-Italian sentiment on the island. When war broke out in 1940, Maltese loyalties were staunchly British. The result was a popular stoicism and patience during the war that became admired as a model of unostentatious heroism.[36]

The two outer pillars of Britain's position in the Mediterranean, Gibraltar and Suez, appeared to be as vulnerable as Malta in 1940. Everything about Gibraltar was incongruous—its appearance, its geographic position, the fact that it survived as a British enclave at all. To those sailing into Gibraltar from the west, the Atlantic chill surrendered to a breeze that was "land-based and fragrant" as one passed Cape Trafalgar and glided toward the entrance to the Mediterranean.[37] However, Gibraltar's distant promise of voluptuousness proved an empty one. The town had the appearance of a down-at-heel British seaside resort transported into a blistered, south Iberian landscape. The houses, pancaked against the saffron face of "the Rock," looked as if designed for Brighton or Blackpool, down to the lace curtains in the windows. Even the town's promenade exuded a hybrid odor of lavender and fish-and-chips.

With the fall of France, Gibraltar remained the only Western Allied stronghold on the continent of Europe. Most of its twenty thousand inhabitants were evacuated to Britain. Work began on twenty-five miles of tunnels bored into the rock to house ammunition dumps and workshops. The debris was used to extend the airstrip, which eventually could accommodate six hundred planes, into the sea. Beyond the harbor crowded with nests of tankers, merchantmen, and destroyers assembling for convoys to Malta, lay what British sailors prosaically called "the Gut," a mile-wide sleeve of current flowing into the Mediterranean from west to east. To the south loomed the Atlas Mountains and Africa beyond.

While Gibraltar had been a British colony since 1704, its continued attachment to the crown had been placed in serious jeopardy by the confluence of the 1939 Republican defeat in the Spanish Civil War and Hitler's victory in the West in May–June 1940. The great fear in London was that General Francisco Franco would take advantage of momentary Franco-British weakness to resolve outstanding Spanish claims on Gibraltar and seize the African empire that, in his view, the industrial countries had denied Spain.

Franco was a difficult man to read. Even in retrospect, historians disagree on his true intentions. This is explained in part because everyone searched for more subtlety than the man actually possessed. In fact, Franco was cautious rather than complex. He lacked Mussolini's flamboyance and reserved his Hitler-like venom for his Spanish Republican adversaries. He possessed a soldier's insistence on "fidelity and obedience" from those who served him. Long years of campaigning in the Moroccan Rif had created a man of minimal needs—he ate simply and quickly, detested ostentation, and valued plain living. Even as leader of Spain, he traveled with his toilet articles in a metal biscuit box. He loathed liberals, Communists, and Freemasons, whom he treated as he had recalcitrant soldiers of the Spanish Legion—with great brutality. In the final phases of the Spanish Civil War, for instance, so possessed had he been by vindictiveness against his Republican enemies that he refused international supplications to allow them to surrender honorably. Instead, he permitted his Falangists to exact horrendous reprisals. It was said that Franco signed death sentences while sipping his morning coffee. His allegiances, like his needs, were straightforward. Portraits of Queen Isabella and religious articles spread around his living quarters spoke to his Catholic faith and his dedication to the unity, grandeur, and independence of Spain.

But Franco's caution was driven by more than personality. The truth was that the Spanish dictator's lack of a solid base in Spain limited his strategic options. While Hitler and Mussolini led political parties, Franco was essentially a loner, a general of no political experience, to whom conservative Spaniards of various allegiances had turned in a time of national crisis. While he had earned great prestige in the Civil War, Franco lacked the charisma to rally men once united in opposition against the Republic around a single vision for Spain's future. Falangists, led by their spokesman Ramón Serrano Suñer, pressed Franco to join in the remaking of Spain, and of Europe, on the fascist model. Others, like General Count Gomez Jordana, the minister of foreign affairs for much of the war, favored the Allies. Supporters of Spain's two deposed royal houses reached out to the army and the church, and quarreled with the Falangists. Franco kept changing personnel so that no group would have a strong figure to rally behind. Thus, for the moment, Franco played for time. Operating on the Gallician peasant principle that "a closed mouth catches no flies," Franco fomented confusion about his intentions by allowing those around him to speak freely, in the firm conviction, of course, that they were merely expressing the Caudillo's views. Madrid accordingly produced a cacophony of statements and a puzzlement of initiatives that baffled Franco cognoscenti in both camps. Nevertheless, as the momentum in Europe clearly shifted to the Axis, on 12 June 1940 Spain switched from neutrality to "nonbelligerency." Two days later, Spanish troops occupied the international port of Tangier. German U-boats began to resupply in Spanish harbors. Franco was on the ladder, the Spaniards said. It was simply impossible to know whether he would climb toward war or descend toward neutrality.[38]

One key to the maintenance of Spanish neutrality and the preservation of Gibraltar lay two thousand miles away at Suez. Franco was able to resist German demands to seize Gibraltar with the argument that it made no sense to close the western entrance to the Mediterranean so long as the British held open a back door in Egypt.[39] Therefore, the fates of Britain's far-flung Mediterranean outposts were linked. Unfortunately, Britain's strategic position at Suez seemed hardly more secure. The British protectorate over Egypt had been abolished in 1922. However, for Britain, imperial habits proved hard to shake. Sovereignty was hedged by clauses that allowed Britain to retain supervisory powers over the courts and finances, and to protect "imperial communications." The economic power of Egypt's significant foreign community, with its comparatively extravagant lifestyle and exemption from many local laws, was deeply resented in the impoverished country. Britain continued to occupy the Sudan and Egypt continued to claim it. Finally, tempestuous relations between the British-appointed King Fuad I and the nationalist Wafd Party lent a perpetual volatility to Egyptian politics.

None of this was particularly vexing to London until the 1935 Italian invasion of Ethiopia. London considered closing the Suez Canal to Italian traffic, but backed down because it was illegal, because it would violate Egyptian sovereignty, because France opposed it, and because closure would set a poor precedent for the future. Nevertheless, both Egypt and Britain felt threatened by the expansion of Italian power beyond the canal. Rome reinforced Libya with three divisions. Fifty-one percent of the passengers coming through the canal in that year were Italian soldiers bound for Ethiopia. Members of the substantial Italian community at Port Said, some of the younger members wearing black shirts, gathered on the breakwater to sing the Fascist anthem "Giovinezza" and shout *"Duce! Duce!"* at passing Italian troopships. Wealthier Italian expatriates subscribed gold and jewelry to pay canal fees, buy oil, or supply provisions for the troops. The 1936 death of King Fuad prodded London and Cairo to unite against a common Italian threat. An April 1936 Anglo-Egyptian treaty of alliance recognized the strategic importance of the canal to Britain, but also claimed it as an integral part of Egypt. Article 8 of the treaty stipulated that British forces would guard the canal, but would gradually with-

draw to the Canal Zone and Alexandria until, by 1956, all British occupation of Egypt would formally end. Restrictions on British force
levels, which would not exceed ten thousand troops, three thousand
airmen, and four hundred pilots, reinforced the notion of Egyptian
sovereignty. Egypt would now have its own army independent of
British control, and a military academy opened to youth of all social
backgrounds. The British inspector general of the army was replaced
by an Egyptian, military intelligence was confided to local hands, and
Egyptian attachés named to foreign embassies. Special provisions protecting foreigners—called "capitulations"—were abolished, handing
the Egyptian government complete control over courts and taxation.
Britain sponsored Egypt's entry into the League of Nations in 1937.
The Egyptian government undertook to improve roads and port facilities and assist British forces in the event of war. The question of the
Sudan was shelved.[40]

For a nation accustomed to alien oversight, these British concessions should have been hailed as significant steps toward complete
freedom from foreign control. However, the rise of Italian power in
the Mediterranean combined with new forces in Egyptian politics to
unsettle the turbulent but manageable triangular relationship between
the British, the Palace, and the Wafd. By 1939, Egypt and its canal had
become the link in a unified Middle East Command. The number of
British troops in Egypt was growing, not diminishing, as the 1936 treaty
stipulated. Nor were they withdrawing from the Nile Delta to Alexandria and the Canal Zone as envisaged. This buildup should have reassured Cairo, also threatened by Italian assertiveness in the Eastern
Mediterranean. However, it strengthened Egyptian belief that "their"
canal, so prized by both sides, was illegally occupied.[41] This feeling
stoked volatile Egyptian nationalism that, when combined with the
tempestuous personality of the new king, hurled Anglo-Egyptian relations into disarray. When sixteen-year-old Farouk, then a cadet at
RMA Woolwich, succeeded the autocratic Fuad in 1936, the British
hailed the dawn of a new era in Anglo-Egyptian relations. Alas, Farouk
proved to be both immature and dissolute. The young monarch gratu-
itously and repeatedly insulted British ambassador Sir Miles Lampton,
keeping him waiting for royal audiences and surrounding himself with

Italian advisers. When the British objected, the monarch countered by conferring Egyptian citizenship on the Italians. To Churchill's great fury, Egypt did nothing to curtail Axis intrigue and spying on important British installations at Alexandria and in the Canal Zone. Farouk also created his own secret police, and founded a fascist-style youth movement to rival the Wafd Blue Shirts.[42]

The Wafd Party was increasingly marginalized, as a nationalist-inspired intellectual and business elite criticized them as old-fashioned, in thrall to the landed gentry, out of touch with Egypt's problems, and tainted by association with the British — in short, irrelevant. Worse, by ensuring British backing for the Wafd, the 1936 treaty was seen as the major impediment to land reform ardently desired by many *fellah*, who, in 1942 as Rommel approached the delta, imagined that a German victory would result in land redistribution.[43] More sinister was the Ikhwan, or Moslem Brotherhood, which emerged as a stealth challenger to Wafd domination in the 1930s. These xenophobic fundamentalists began gradually to infiltrate universities and through them the teaching profession, the officer corps, and the professional classes in general. By 1946, Ikhwan counted one million adherents, a well-armed militia, and militants prepared to carry out political assassinations to help their organization to power.[44]

The Ikhwan's intensity sprang from Egyptian outrage over Arab-Zionist conflict in Palestine. In the dark days of 1917, as Russia teetered on the brink of revolution and the U-boat war raged around British shores, British Foreign Secretary Lord Balfour declared that "HM's Government views with favour the establishment in Palestine of a national home for the Jewish people, and will use their best endeavours to facilitate the achievement of this object." The goal of the British government was a short-term one: to rally the support of Jews, especially American Jews, to the Allied cause. It was also timed to coincide with the British invasion of Palestine under General Edmund Allenby, whose army contained a symbolic contingent of five thousand Jews.

Although the Balfour declaration had insisted that "nothing shall be done which may prejudice the civil and religious rights of existing non-Jewish communities in Palestine," friction between newcomers and established residents quickly escalated as the Jewish population in Palestine soared from 55,000 in 1918 to 161,000 a decade later. Once they had forced the door of the British mandate, the Zionists had no intention of retreating before their goal of a Jewish state. They bought up Arab land to establish agricultural communities, founded the city of Tel Aviv, and flooded into Jerusalem and Haifa. The Arab community fought back. Anti-Jewish riots and attacks on Jewish settlers began in 1920, and became a permanent feature of Jewish-Arab relations thereafter. British attempts to temporize between the two communities foundered on the rocks of Zionist militancy and Arab intransigence. White paper succeeded white paper. British restrictions on Jewish immigration collapsed as the triumph of Hitler and rising anti-Semitism provoked a wave of Jewish emigration toward Palestine from Germany, Hungary, Poland, and Romania. By 1935, 375,000 Jews lived in Palestine, and more were on the way.

This volatile situation needed only a spark to ignite, and that was supplied by Amin al-Husseini, the grand mufti of Jerusalem. On the surface, al-Husseini's delicate features and gentle manner, accentuated by his deep blue eyes, trim goatee, and soothing voice, made him appear the embodiment of moderation and restraint. In fact, he was a thug who spewed anti-British and anti-Semitic venom and organized squads of hit men to eliminate his political enemies and attack Jewish settlements. Nominally, the position of grand mufti should not have provided a platform for rabble rousing. The job description called for a legal expert, a jurist who issued interpretations of Koranic law. It was the post for a thoughtful man, an adjudicator. That is precisely why the approval of al-Husseini's April 1921 election under dubious circumstances proved to be such a dreadful mistake on the part of Sir Herbert Samuels, British high commissioner of Palestine. It was also surprising, because in the process, Samuels reanimated al-Husseini's hitherto languishing fortunes. An ex–Ottoman officer turned schoolteacher, al-Husseini had been sentenced by the British to ten years in prison for his part in orchestrating the 1920 anti-Jewish riots in Jerusalem. Samuels not only pardoned al-Husseini and allowed him to stand for office. He actually validated al-Husseini's election, even though he came fourth among the candidates, miscalculating that al-Husseini's low vote indicated a lack of influence.[45]

Al-Husseini's fortunes stalled in the 1920s, because his influence was checked by the "National Party," because Jewish immigration dipped, and because Samuels was replaced as high commissioner by the no-nonsense Viscount Plummer of Messines, who had commanded the British Second Army in the Great War. But the 1930s proved to be his decade. Jewish immigration surged, sharpening Arab-Jewish tensions. Likewise, the same factors that had marginalized the Wafd in Egypt made the National Party appear unresponsive to the recrudescence of Islamic fundamentalism. A rising Palestinian middle class, ironically an offspring of economic activity stimulated by Jews, looked to the mufti for political leadership. As head of the Moslem Council, the mufti made appointments to Moslem schools and courts, and controlled significant trust funds that he used, among other things, to spread his message in Iraq and Syria, and to purchase arms. Finally, the mufti also benefited from the downturn in Britain's international fortunes. From 1938, Germany, Italy, and even Spain stoked the glowing embers of Arab nationalism with radio broadcasts, "cultural" subsidies, and anti-Semitic articles that the mufti translated and distributed through Moslem schools. Palestinian Arabs imitated fascist political organizations and praised German racial laws, failing to appreciate that Hitler was Zionism's best recruiting sergeant, one who actually exacerbated their problems. Rather, they dreamed of the day when Italy and Germany would eject Britain, and with them the Jews, from the Middle East.

Nothing the British did to resolve tensions in Palestine worked. After a year of killings, strikes, and tax boycotts, in 1937 London proposed the partition of Palestine between Jew and Arab. This simply stoked an already raging conflagration. Moslems rioted from Tunis to Bombay, Hitler promised to underwrite an Arab revolt with arms, and attacks on Jewish settlements and British troops who tried to protect them escalated. In October 1938, Palestine boiled over with rebellion. Twenty thousand British soldiers struggled to keep order as Moslem militants turned much of Jerusalem into a no-go area. Moderate

Arab leaders who urged compromise were assassinated by the mufti's thugs. Arab belligerency stoked Jewish determination to resist. Young Jewish militants like Moshe Dayan brought the Haganah ("Defense"), founded in the 1920s, out into the open to cooperate with the British, hard pressed for manpower. Indeed, Jewish "guards" organized and trained by Scots Captain Orde Wingate led reprisal raids against the mufti's supporters as far away as Syria and Lebanon. But the solution to the crisis, London realized, was political. So, in 1938, in an attempt to appease the Arabs, the British backed off partition and slapped severe restrictions on Jewish immigration. This simply enraged the Zionists, who charged that London had signed the death warrant of European Jewry. They began to organize clandestine immigration, enlist all able-bodied men and women in the Haganah, and spin off even more militant groups like the Irgun, which initiated a bombing campaign against British official buildings.[46]

Thus, on the edge of war, the outposts that anchored Britain's position in the Mediterranean were sunk into fragile foundations. Malta lay hostage to Mussolini as Gibraltar was to Franco. The Middle East in 1940 was a ticking social, ideological, and political time bomb. The repeated requirements during the war to intervene in Middle Eastern politics in Egypt, Palestine, Syria, Iraq, Iran, and Afghanistan to bolster Britain's short-term military interests in effect stored up humiliations and resentments that ultimately destroyed the basis for the British presence there.[47] Probably the only country where the Arab population was pro-Allies was Libya, and more specifically Cyrenaica, where the harsh Italian campaign of conquest left bitter scars and sent fourteen thousand refugees to Egypt.[48] Even in French North Africa, the Moslem population seethed with bitterness. When the Axis forces flooded into Tunisia in November 1942 to counter Operation Torch, the Allied landings in Morocco and Algeria, the Germans were overwhelmed by Arabs demanding to enlist in their forces.[49] The mere appearance of Axis tanks in Egypt might have brought about the collapse of Britain's position in the Middle East, deprived it of oil, and made communication with India and the Far East immensely more difficult. The elimination of France had drastically reduced Britain's naval advantage, as well as turned valuable bases in North Africa and Syria into potentially hostile territory. With this dreary strategic prospect, Britain slithered reluctantly into war in the Mediterranean.

THE AXIS FAILURE TO EXPLOIT
BRITISH VULNERABILITIES

Historians have made three arguments to deprecate the importance of the Mediterranean in the opening years of the war. The first is that even had the Axis concentrated against Britain in the Mediterranean in 1940–41, Britain could not have been defeated because its center of gravity ultimately resided in the United States. The second point is that Axis conflicts of interest were so great in the Mediterranean in 1940–41 that they could never have coalesced on a single strategic plan. Therefore it is nonsense to talk about missed Axis opportunities when there were none to miss. Finally, the Mediterranean was never a substitute for Operation Barbarossa in Hitler's mind. Barbarossa, the invasion of the Soviet Union, was central to Hitler's political program.[50] Rommel never had a chance, even in 1942 when he knocked on the door of the Nile Delta. Logistically, he was desperately overstretched. But also, strategically the drive toward the Nile, the Middle East, and ultimately India would work only if it was coordinated with a Japanese advance on India from the east. But Axis leaders failed to cooperate to achieve strategic objectives. Tokyo's war in Asia and the Pacific was as much a "parallel war" as Mussolini's breakout into the Mediterranean. The remarkable thing about Rommel is how much he achieved with such a paltry logistical base, made inadequate both because of the huge demands of the Eastern Front and because Hitler's goal in the Mediterranean was to bolster Mussolini, not overwhelm the British position there. Speculation about a grand Axis link-up in India or Iran is sheer fantasy.[51] The year 1942 "was Germany's last chance to deal the Soviet Union a crippling blow and thus eliminate permanently at least one of the three main adversaries [Great Britain, the United States, and the Soviet Union] ranged against it," writes German historian Klaus Schmider. For this reason, "there can be no argument with Hitler's logic: should Rommel be able to rush the British position in the Nile delta, so much the better; but no success in the Middle East could be a possible substitute for victory over the

Red Army." Even had the British been driven beyond the Nile, Torch would have redressed the balance in the Allies' favor in November 1942 and forced Rommel to retreat.[52]

To suggest that the Mediterranean was a dramatic but otherwise marginal sideshow is to misunderstand the role that theater played in Churchill's vision for victory. Churchill considered defeat in the Mediterranean a disaster second only to the invasion and conquest of the British Isles.[53] Britain's leaders—Churchill, Eden, and Macmillan— had invested their political reputations in the Middle East, which they saw as the base of Britain's position as a great power, and had decided to defend it at the expense of Singapore. The surest way to incite a prime ministerial temper tantrum, Major General Sir John Kennedy, Britain's director of military operations, discovered in April 1941, was to suggest that the price of holding Egypt may have exceeded the benefits. Puce with rage, Churchill shouted that talk of surrendering Egypt was tantamount to "defeatism." "War is a contest of wills," an implacable Churchill bellowed at the DMO. "It is pure defeatism to speak as you have done."[54] In Churchill's mind, the Mediterranean became the epicenter of Britain's resurrection, the genesis of victory, the place where Chamberlain's appeasement strategy was buried and Britain's determination and valor were showcased to friend and foe alike. The failure of Churchill's Mediterranean strategy would have flattened British spirits, exhausted his political capital, and breathed new life into Halifax and the appeasers.

John Ellis argues that British histories of World War II are far too preoccupied with Mediterranean events. But one need only look at the place the Middle Eastern theater retains in the British memory of World War II to comprehend its psychological importance to the wartime generation. The Middle East was Britain's last independent military show. It produced the famous Eighth Army and Britain's only hero-general of the war.[55] Nor was support for Britain in the United States firm in the summer of 1940. Isolationists counted powerful advocates in Congress and in the America First Committee, a vocal public platform. Britain would have to demonstrate its worthiness as a potential ally through its resolve to fight on before it could win American trust and support. The Mediterranean, together with the Battle of Britain, offered Churchill early opportunities to exhibit Britain's qualities—and shortcomings—as a potential ally. Many of Churchill's strategic choices, like the surprise attack on the French fleet at Mers el-Kébir that astonished the world, and the controversial decision to support Greece in May 1941, were taken with one eye fixed on the impact they would have on U.S. opinion.

Nor is a strategic choice merely about damage one might inflict on the enemy. It is also about eliminating opportunities for the enemy to do mischief to you. With a dollop of strategic vision, the Axis might have recognized that an early offensive posture in the Mediterranean offered an excellent preventive defense, because it would remove the Mediterranean as a potential strategic option for the Allies. Although Churchill boasted after Dunkirk of attacking the Reich with bombers and "setting Europe ablaze" with internal rebellion, realistically the Mediterranean offered the only place where Britain was able to continue the war at a relative advantage. Virtually the only road back into the war for Britain, and eventually France, ran through the Mediterranean. The United States eventually became Britain's source of strength. But where was that strength to be directed? The Mediterranean was the only place where, in the short term, the United States would be able to apply force against the Axis, in particular against Italy, the weaker partner. Closing off the Mediterranean would have offered "blockadeable" Italy a protective cocoon. Furthermore, a theory of victory for the Axis in the Mediterranean was not difficult to imagine. It only required them to convert Britain's tenuous advantages there into vulnerabilities—shut down Gibraltar and Malta and "set the Middle East ablaze." This would not necessarily defeat Britain, but it would mean that the only way back into the war for Churchill, and eventually Roosevelt, was across the Channel. And that would prove a difficult task against an Axis unshaken by defeats in the Mediterranean, even with American assistance.

The second argument against Axis success in the Mediterranean is that the Axis missed no strategic opportunities in 1940–41 for the simple reason that German and Italian interests in the Mediterranean were too divergent to enable them to cooperate in plucking the fruits of France's fall and Britain's weakness. The Axis was a *mésalliance*, in which the two partners sometimes cooperated on a military level but seldom on an economic or political plane. It was an operational rather than a strategic coalition.[56] This is, of course, true. But Axis failure to cooperate to achieve a coherent strategy was not foreordained. Strategy, after all, is about making choices. The option of devising a coherent and rational strategic vision was opened to the Axis, as it was to the Allies, had they wished to choose it. In fact, there were voices in the German camp, including Hitler himself, who urged Mussolini to build on his momentum in North Africa and even offered to help Rome to do so. One of those voices was Kriegsmarine commander-in-chief Grand Admiral Erich Raeder. In the autumn of 1940, Raeder proposed to follow up on the defeat of France to close down Britain in the Mediterranean before the United States could enter the war. At first, Hitler seemed alight with the prospect of a "detour through the Mediterranean and Africa on the way to world empire."[57] But he soon cooled on the idea for a number of reasons: he regarded the Mediterranean as Mussolini's sphere of influence and became confused and disheartened by the political complexities of trying to craft alliances there. Finally, when placed in the bureaucratic context of German interservice rivalry, Raeder's proposal offered an outrageous fantasy requiring vast German fleets to command a measureless world empire, "navalism run amuck." The reveries of the Kriegsmarine invited the derision of the other services: "These people dream in continents," army chief of staff Franz Halder said of his nautical colleagues.[58]

Hitler's rejection of Raeder's South Plan throws light on the third argument: that Hitler eschewed a Mediterranean option because it conflicted with his plan to attack the Soviet Union. Again, this is correct to a point. What it ignores, however, is the question of timing. Britain's resistance in the Mediterranean and in the Battle of Britain in August–September 1940 actually confirmed, and possibly accelerated, Hitler's decision to attack the USSR, because it persuaded him that the USSR was "Britain's sword on the Continent."[59] He reasoned that British setbacks in the Mediterranean would not end British resistance. That would only come once London was convinced that Moscow was unable to help them in a war against Germany. In this context, Hitler saw the South Plan for what it was—an attempt to dissuade, or at the very least delay, his decision for Barbarossa. Like the American generals whom he would later confront, Hitler realized that once assets were committed to a peripheral theater, it became difficult to extract them for other purposes. Therefore, the Mediterranean would be "postponed" until after Barbarossa. In doing so, Hitler inverted what should have been his priorities. By attacking in the Mediterranean with a weak force that was not configured for combat in a maritime environment, Hitler chose to fight on Britain's terms. For that he would pay a high price.

CHAPTER ONE

1940: War Comes to the Mediterranean

B ENITO MUSSOLINI was the son of a village schoolteacher and an intermittently employed blacksmith and bar owner. Adolf Hitler's father was a minor Austrian civil servant. From an early age, both men combined aversion to hard work with an attraction to extreme political ideas. Each was a loner, socially awkward, with neither friends nor a sense of humor; in short, immature, crippled personalities, failures in life lifted by circumstance and cunning into tragic prominence.

Pictures of Mussolini as a middle-aged dictator show a man with a receding hairline, brows arched above eyes that appear fixed on some distant object, jaw locked in an expression of pensive resolve. Mussolini invariably strove to create the effect of a man firmly in control of Italy's destiny. But those closest to him searched in vain for evidence of an inner core of beliefs, a node of conviction beyond an opportunistic search for personal advantage. His career consisted of an extravagant quest for notoriety on the political margins. Those who knew him as a young man noted that his reputation as a brawler, his reluctance to make eye contact, his obsessive womanizing, and his tendency to dress alternatively as a tramp and as a dandy offered testimony to the absence of any fixed self-image.

Mussolini had failed as a teacher and labor organizer when, in 1912 at the age of twenty-nine, he unexpectedly grabbed the editorship of a small-circulation, underfunded Socialist newspaper called *Avanti!* This gave Mussolini the platform to contrive a name for himself as a crusader against poor working conditions and a supporter of strikes and demonstrations. He credited his editorials for the Socialist success in the 1913 elections. However, he broke with his party over the issue of neutrality in 1914, resigned from *Avanti!*, and started his own paper, *Il Popolo d'Italia*. By December 1914 he had taken over a group of dissident, prowar Socialists who called themselves the *Fascisti*, and began to preach Italy's need for a "really great war" that would bring territorial aggrandizement and showcase the mettle of the Italian people. He railed against neutralist politicians and rejoiced in 1915 when King Vittorio Emanuele signed a declaration of war against Austria without consulting Parliament.

Mussolini's war service consisted of a tedious but unexceptionable routine of inconclusive skirmishes fought from waterlogged, lice-infected trenches. Invalided out of the army as a sergeant in June 1917 after a grenade launcher exploded during a training exercise, wounding him severely, he returned to find *Il Popolo d'Italia* fallen on hard times. But he managed to build it up with subsidies from arms manufacturers seduced by his scathing denunciations of antiwar Socialists, whom he blamed for the defeatism that gripped Italy in the wake of its crushing October 1917 defeat at Caporetto. He also found time to plot with disaffected politicians and General Luigi Cadorna, fired as Italian commander-in-chief after Caporetto, to overthrow the government. And while any rabble-rouser might have done the same, Mussolini's genius was to foresee, while the war still raged, that returning soldiers would offer a pool of disaffected men vulnerable to his rants. Having worked assiduously to bring a reluctant Italy into the war, Mussolini now labored as diligently to foment dissatisfaction with its outcome. He insisted that the Italian victory at Vittorio Veneto in October 1918 was responsible for the collapse of the Central Powers. For this reason, Italy should be rewarded at the peace table with her "natural frontiers" to include Trieste, the Italian Tyrol, Fiume, and most of Dalmatia. His demands constituted a setup for dashed expectations.

Like many European countries, Italy emerged from the war with wounded political institutions, a weak economy, an unemployed mass of demobilized soldiers, and a people disoriented by the enormity of their sacrifices for trifling gain. When Mussolini held the first meeting of the Fascist movement in March 1919, only about fifty supporters appeared. From 1920, however, he began to gather adherents by championing Italian advancement in the Balkans and the theme, to which he would frequently return, that Italy must dominate both the Adriatic and the Mediterranean. In the extremely violent elections of 1921, the Fascists picked up thirty-five parliamentary seats. Mussolini pioneered terror tactics against his political enemies of such violence that many of his own followers were shocked. But these methods attracted ambitious and ruthless thugs to Fascist ranks, men willing to lay waste to Socialist-led municipal governments and trade union headquarters. Meanwhile, governments came and went, presided over by politicians of indifferent ability who were either powerless or unwilling to rein in the Fascists, whom they saw as useful antidotes to the Socialists.

In 1922 the Socialists called a general strike to protest Fascist violence. Mussolini unleashed his followers to smash their printing presses, shatter their picket lines, and occupy Socialist-run municipalities, all in the name of defending public order against the revolutionary threat. Realizing that Italy's weak government and factious Parliament would not act against him, Mussolini began to organize his insurrection, "to take by the throat the miserable political class that governs us." On the night of 27–28 October 1922, groups of Fascists began to occupy telephone exchanges and government offices. The king, timid and confused by contradictory advice, failed to sign an order authorizing martial law. Instead, on 29 October, Vittorio Emanuele named the thirty-nine-year-old Mussolini, who controlled only one-seventh of the seats in Parliament, prime minister of Italy. But coronation by royal decree did not suit Mussolini's revolutionary image. So he organized his supporters to "March on Rome" fully twenty-four hours *after* he had been handed power. In this way, Mussolini created the myth that he had been installed by a popular insurrection ignited to counter a Socialist revolution. Italians, demoralized by government incompetence and weeks of anarchy, acquiesced.

In power, Mussolini was like the dog who had chased the automobile, and now that he had caught it, had to decide what to do. His answer was to export his reputation for violence and unpredictability to the international stage. It is tempting to dismiss Mussolini as a buffoon because such a huge gulf yawned between his pretensions and the paucity of Italy's military and industrial power. But braggadocio was incorporated into his style. It was calculated to deceive his enemies and allies as well as to import drama into the lives of ordinary Italians otherwise deprived of excitement. Mussolini required *coups de théâtre* to lend an appearance of forward momentum to a regime that was otherwise ideologically challenged. He delighted in the international consternation that his initiatives evoked. Even in failure, as when forced to back down over Corfu in 1923, he remained the Mad Dog of the Med, the Jack-in-the-Box of European diplomacy, the Monarch of International Mayhem. Italians reveled in Mussolini's theatrics, his pompous uniforms and bombastic speeches, confusing, like their leader, charlatanism, hypocrisy, and histrionics with international prestige and respect. As Italians appeared to crave a burlesque, Mussolini cynically offered them a star turn.[1]

But braggadocio also served to mask the fact that Mussolini exerted an imperfect control over Italy. By totalitarian standards, Italian fascism was both inefficient and timid. Compared to bell cows of state terrorism like Hitler and Stalin, Mussolini was a mere greenhorn. After the outcry caused by the 1924 execution of Socialist Giacomo Matteotti by Fascist hooligans, Mussolini's "Special Tribunal for the Defense of the State" was content to execute only nine political opponents before the war and twenty-two, mostly Slavs, during the conflict. Fewer than 150 Italian soldiers were condemned to death between June 1940 and September 1943, compared with 4,000 during the 1915–18 war. Even Franco, whose power base was also insecure, shot and garroted his foes with an abandon that placed in the shade his Italian counterpart, content in the main to exile his dissidents to small towns in the Mezzogiorno. Mussolini dared not declare general mobilization for fear of exciting the wrath of Italians. Large segments of the educated elite, including university students, were permitted to evade military service, part of the estimated one million Italian males who escaped the uniform. Some 600,000 soldiers were furloughed on the eve of the invasion of Greece in the autumn of 1940 to assuage popular discontent, with disastrous results. Even under German prodding, Mussolini refused to oblige the Italian workforce to adopt wartime discipline or to militarize the inefficient Italian and North African ports. Rationing was slowly and unevenly introduced. Above all, the armed forces and the throne were two institutions with which he dared not interfere.[2]

Historians agree that Mussolini was an opportunist. They disagree over the lengths to which he was willing to carry his opportunism. Some argue that the fact that his words and deeds often attained a celestial level of contradiction indicate a willingness to make common cause with Britain and France if those two countries had permitted him to further his Mediterranean ambitions. Others suggest that Mussolini's political oscillations were a psychological trait, the indication of a lack of self-confidence and courage, a reflection of his lack of political control at home rather than the absence of fundamental direction. Mussolini was certainly a man hollowed of ideals or morals, an egomaniac with an inferiority complex. But Mussolini's vocation was permanently to affront the status quo. As a consequence, Britain and France were always going to be obstacles to his objectives. Even in the spring of 1940, when the Allies offered him a place at the peace table and concessions in Africa to keep him neutral, he ignored them.[3] The trajectory of Mussolini's cooperation with Germany was continuous: the 1936 treaty that formed the Rome-Berlin Axis, the Anti-Comintern Pact of November 1936, his cooperation with Hitler during the Spanish Civil War, his abandonment of the defense of Austrian independence in 1938, and finally the May 1939 "Pact of Steel." Periodic hints of friction in the Axis, as during the South Tyrolean crisis in the autumn of 1939 and the Russo-Finnish War (30 November 1939–12 March 1940), were merely diplomatic teases calculated to give Mussolini an aura of independence that he did not possess. Conflicts of interest between the Allies and Mussolini were so profound that the Duce had no other place to scuttle, given his ambitions and his character, than to Hitler.[4]

There is a consistency in Mussolini's Mediterranean vision that is hard to deny. Even before the Great War's conclusion, he began to insist that the Mediterranean constrained Italy's ambitions. Virtually the only constant theme of a man who consistently refused to be pinned down by ideology or diplomatic options was that the Mediterranean "remains a jail that stifles our life force." Corsica, Tunisia, Malta, and Cyprus constituted its bars, he told the Fascist Grand Council in February 1939, Gibraltar and Suez the guards.[5] This set him on a collision course with Britain and France, who were his major rivals in that sea. He just awaited his moment. "The victory of Hitler is our victory," Mussolini had declared in 1933. Seven years later, he sought to cash in on his prophecy in the best traditions of Mediterranean self-interest.

When Mussolini declared war on 10 June 1940, little did he appear to anticipate the risk he was running. All he wanted was a tiny war, or better still, no war at all. He calculated that the conflict in Europe had entered its concluding phase. France was whipped and Britain was on the ropes. His goal was to secure a chair at the peace table, to reap high political gains from minimal military investment, not to superintend the nativity of a major battleground. He had no strategic plan and refused to coordinate one with Berlin. He lacked reserves of coal, oil, cash, and food, and British control of Suez and Gibraltar would ensure that, if replenishment came, little would arrive by sea. Furthermore, he failed to keep his merchant marine informed of his intentions, so that a third of Italian ships were interned in foreign harbors before fighting had even started.[6] But the Italian dictator had made two devastating miscalculations. First, he had thrown himself across the sea lane of an enemy that was shaken but determined to fight to maintain its vital link with its empire. Second, he had bound over Italy as the handmaiden of a man whose savage capacity for evil made Mussolini's absence of morals and cheap theatrics appear dilettantish by comparison.

Adolf Hitler was convinced of two things: the righteousness of his vision and the infallibility of his judgment. For a man of such monstrous passions to drive the world beyond the extremity of catastrophe required a German people befuddled and disoriented by a Great War experience in which battles won equaled military defeat, economic uncertainty, and political collapse. Even with almost three-quarters of a century of hindsight, that such an ancient and civilized people could surrender to Hitler's spell can be explained more easily than it can be understood.

Contemporary photos of Hitler seem calculated to provoke a public relations disaster. Ill-fitting suits, a homburg which pressed down on his ears, a smile which made him look unsure of himself, practically idiotic, hardly matched the image of a German *Feldherr*. Even photos calculated to show leadership—clenched fists on hips, dark eyes glowering in a scowl of Teutonic determination, the quaint Bavarian costume stretched over a diminutive, middle-aged frame, and a mustache of preposterous dimensions, too narrow to be flamboyant, too high to be elegant—made him look like Kaiser Wilhelm's pantry butler on holiday. Mussolini, a connoisseur in these matters, criticized Hitler's sartorial standards as beneath those required of a serious dictator. In fact, Hitler's photos were so obviously contrived, so blatantly insipid, that abroad Hitler impersonations became standard fare on mess nights and in fraternity follies. Indeed, the resemblance between the German dictator and Charlie Chaplin was so striking that Hollywood cashed in on the opportunity to cast the comedian in *The Great Dictator*.

But Hitler held the Germans spellbound as he spewed a cocktail of venom and malice from torch-lit reviewing stands across Germany—hatred of the Allies, hatred of Versailles, hatred of Jews. Close up, Hitler exuded a somber, if eccentric, banality. In retrospect, Albert Speer, Hitler's architect who rose to become his minister of armaments, wondered how "night after night" Hitler's charmed circle continued to be amused by "endless tirades on the Catholic Church, diet recipes, Greek temples, and police dogs."[7] The attraction of power offers the most obvious explanation. Nevertheless, Hitler's charisma must have been magnetic, for his court, composed of cranks, criminals, and sycophants, endured his endless temper tantrums, hypochondria, and bouts of frenetic energy alternating with lethargy. They remained loyal even as the obvious signs of disorientation caused by the collapse of his illusions exposed his ignorance, amateurishness, and inability to manipulate the forces that he had conjured up with such confidence.

Hitler had few illusions either about Italians or about Mussolini. He considered Mussolini's histrionics transparent but amusing. He recognized *Il Duce* for the opportunist he was, who would rally to the Axis only once victory appeared certain.[8] Indeed, in the aftermath of the fall of France, the German press represented their new ally as a circus clown tidying up after the acrobat's performance and accepting the applause as if it were meant for him.[9] However, had he been a more reflective leader, Hitler might have realized that his partner was a liability, not an asset. For the Italians lacked both the industrial and military capacity to sustain a modern war. The main problem of Italian industry was that it was heavily dependent on imports of oil, coal, and scrap iron, much of it arriving via sea routes vulnerable to British interdiction. Some of these shortfalls could be made up by German imports, which had been increased after British economic sanctions on coal and oil imports to Italy had been imposed during the 1935 Abyssinian crisis. However, German aid became increasingly problematic after June 1941, as Barbarossa sucked up German resources. All of this meant that Italy's agricultural and industrial production would actually decline after June 1940 due to supply bottlenecks caused by Allied interdiction.[10] Despite the fact that German generals gave Italy's military capabilities low marks, and insisted that an Italian presence "would yield no substantial advantages," Hitler continued to press for Italian intervention into the war. The Wehrmacht operations staff could devise no common assumptions upon which to base a joint German-Italian strategy. German generals viewed the Axis as a political wedge for Italian demands for German equipment, with which they were loath to part.[11]

The final point that Hitler appeared to overlook was that his ally was, in reality, his rival. Mussolini's goal was not merely to ride German success in Northern Europe to achieve Italian domination of the Mediterranean. Rivalry lay at the core of the Axis. For Mussolini, the Axis was designed to operate as much *against* Hitler as *with* him. The paradox at the heart of the Axis was that, while Mussolini sought to profit from German momentum to advance Italian claims in the Mediterranean, he also struggled to bar Germany from that sea. Mussolini wanted a "parallel war," not a unified struggle that would diminish his prestige and divide the booty he could collect.[12] This made little difference to Hitler, who had scant interest in the Mediterranean. Hitler's goals lay in Eastern Europe. His targets might sometimes overlap with those of his Axis partner, but they did not coincide.[13] For that reason, he was content to allow Mussolini to ride the crest of German victories until Italian incompetence forced him to intervene in the Mediterranean in February 1941. The Axis was an alliance that faced in opposite directions. Hitler toward the east and Mussolini toward the south. And while each ceded to the other his space, this also meant that they could devise no common strategy to defeat Britain in the Mediterranean. It also meant that Hitler had mortgaged Axis success there to a man who was shallow, mercurial, and politically and strategically incompetent.

THE "PARALLEL WAR"

Mussolini greeted the September 1939 Allied declaration of war on Germany with a partial mobilization order. It proved a disaster. The Italian army, deficient in uniforms, weapons, and barracks space, showed itself totally unprepared for even this limited call-up. With a histrionic flourish of anger, Mussolini decapitated the senior staff of the army and named Marshal Rodolfo Graziani as the army's new chief. But this did nothing to solve his problems, which included the obvious lack of preparedness of his armed forces, Italy's dependence on maritime imports vulnerable to the combined naval might of Britain and France, the king's opposition, together with the news, supplied by his prefects, that the Italian people had no stomach for the war.[14] On 1 September, Mussolini reversed course and declared "nonbelligerency." Italians breathed a sigh of relief. Hitler, for his part, was philosophical. Although Mussolini insisted to Hitler that "nonbelligerency" was not a reversal of his commitment to the Axis, the German leader understood that Italy would join the war only when it became evident that Germany stood on the threshold of victory.[15]

The rapid collapse of the Anglo-French front in May–June 1940 brought Mussolini to the point of panic; he wanted to avoid an all-out war, while at the same time ensure that Germany would not monopolize the spoils. He convinced himself that failure to act might bring about the collapse of fascism or even a German invasion of Italy. The nine months since the outbreak of war in Europe passed in a complete neglect of elementary military preparations. He had even failed to discuss war plans with his military chiefs except in extremely vague terms. Indeed, he had never made it clear to them that he intended to fight at all! The obvious power of German forces as they swept into Norway, the Low Countries, and France broke the dam of war opposition in Italy. At the end of May 1940, as Allied forces were being lifted from the beaches of Dunkirk, Mussolini informed his generals that he planned to declare war the following week. On 10 June 1940, Mussolini joined Hitler's war against the Allies.

What was Italy to attack? It was clear that Mussolini had devoted his energies toward propelling his nation into the war rather than considering how it was to fight it. The institutional structure for strategic planning was lacking, and intentionally so. No proper military planning staffs had been created to prepare strategic options. The chief of staff, Marshal Pietro Badoglio, chaired periodic meetings of the service chiefs. But these men were reluctant to express opinions at variance with the aggressive—and eccentric—preferences of the Duce. To undermine the already limited control of the chief of staff on strategic choices, Mussolini had the individual service ministers report directly to him. But had a proper structure for strategic decision making existed, it is unlikely that rational choices would have been put forward by men of such limited intellectual horizons, with their scant understanding of the maritime capacities of Great Britain, the latent industrial power of the United States, and the racist ferocity of their new ally.[16] Otherwise, they might have suggested an attack on Malta followed by an invasion of Egypt from Libya. This should have eliminated Britain's only base in the central Mediterranean, and threatened the Suez Canal as well as Britain's access to Middle Eastern oil. An Axis presence in Cairo might have sparked popular unrest that would have destabilized Britain's position in the region and perhaps have won control of the oil for the Axis. Strategically, not to mention operationally, this was a long shot for the Italians. But given the fact that they had decided to attack the British empire in the first place, Malta offered a logical, and accessible, initial target. So certain was Hitler that Mussolini would pursue this strategic trajectory that he offered Mussolini 250 heavy tanks for North Africa, an offer Mussolini waved away because he wished to fight his own "parallel war."

Malta lay on the altar, bound and delivered for sacrifice. As war approached, the British had done little to bolster the island's defenses. The British Expeditionary Force destined for France and defense of the home island had been given budget priority. Of the three services, only the navy believed Malta defensible, while London concluded that it could not be supplied in the event of Italian hostility. The better strategic option, the argument went, was to contest the central Mediterranean from Toulon, Tunis, and Corsica, not Valetta. The garrison consisted of four regular battalions backed by two regiments of Maltese territorials (reservists), in all 5,500 troops. With obsolete Enfield rifles, sixty Vickers machine guns, some antiquated artillery pieces, fourteen coastal artillery guns positioned around the Grand Harbor, and a dozen mock-up tanks, they guarded thirty miles of coast and three airfields, behind a thin curtain of barbed wire, pillboxes, and antipersonnel mines. Their transport consisted almost exclusively of bicycles. Antiaircraft defenses were composed of sixteen heavy guns with limited ammunition, which were powerless against low-flying aircraft, two dozen searchlights, and a primitive radar set that worked intermittently. While this force might fend off an initial attempt at landing, it could only succumb to sustained pressure. For this reason, the fleet had been shifted to safer harbors and the evacuation of women and children begun in May. The three airfields, only one of which had tarmac runways, were defended by four rugged Gloucester Gladiator biplanes that by mistake had been left behind in packing crates on the island. When designed in the early 1930s with four machine guns, a canopied cockpit, and an 840-horsepower Bristol Mercury engine that pulsed at speeds of 257 miles per hour, the Gladiator was hailed by the British as the ne plus ultra of fighter aircraft. But the Gladiator honed World War I technology rather than presaged a new fighter era. Heavy combat in France during the "Phony War" of September 1939–May 1940 and during the April 1940 invasion of Norway convinced the RAF that the doughty Gladiator was no match for the Messerschmitt. They collected the remaining Gladiators and shipped them to the Mediterranean, calculating that they could still outpace the Regia Aeronautica's large inventory of Fiat CR42 Falco (Hawk) biplane fighters.[17] The four Gladiators that reached Malta were broken out and assembled. One crashed almost immediately. The remaining three, baptized Faith, Hope, and Charity, came to symbolize Malta's determination to resist against daunting odds. Civil defense preparations consisted of thirteen bomb shelters and sandbags around public buildings. Virtually no first-aid kits existed on the island.[18]

The British position in Egypt was equally precarious. Anti-British feeling surged into the open with news of German success in Europe. On 12 June, the Egyptian prime minister Ali Maher Pasha revealed that Egypt would not declare war unless attacked. Pressure from London forced King Farouk on 23 June to replace Ali Maher with Hassan Saby Pasha, a pro-British but weak politician. Without Egyptian troops, the British commander in the Middle East, General Archibald Wavell, counted only 36,000 partially equipped and ill-organized troops in Egypt. The Fourth Indian, Seventh Armoured, and New Zealand Divisions would later become some of the best in the war. But for the moment they were desperately understrength. Palestine contained a further 27,000 soldiers, some of which were still horse-mounted, while the rest were fully occupied in internal security duties. The collapse of France, which controlled Syria, had stimulated unrest in neighboring Iraq, forcing Wavell to import the Fifth Indian Division to protect the oil fields. The RAF counted no modern fighters or long-range bombers. Against this, the Italians had assembled in Libya the Fifth and the Tenth Armies, together consisting of nine metropolitan divisions of 13,000 men each, three Blackshirt divisions, and two native divisions of 8,000 men each, plus auxiliary troops and frontier guards. These troops were poorly trained, lacked transport, and had heterogeneous equipment. However, the Italian air force counted 425 aircraft in Libya and Rhodes, many of them modern, better armed than the British planes, and capable of being reinforced, against only 205 British planes.[19]

June 1940 presented Mussolini with his most promising strategic opportunities, and he utterly failed to seize them. Mussolini's biographer calls the failure to take Malta "one of the strangest facts of all," especially as Mussolini knew that the British were utterly unprepared to defend it. True, the army had no stomach for an attack. The navy was equally reluctant to cooperate with the army to mount an amphibious operation for which they had no training. Both naval chief of staff Admiral Domenico Cavagnari and Pietro Badoglio, chief of the *Stato Maggiore Generale*, exaggerated the strength of Malta's defenses and deliberately undermined the Duce's directives for a thumping Italian debut into the war.[20] But responsibility for this strategic lapse lay with Mussolini, who repeatedly turned down German offers of assistance against both Malta and Egypt. This failure revealed two of his great defects as a war leader—his unwillingness to listen to expert opinion lest it diminish his status as generalissimo, and his inability to prioritize objectives and focus on clear goals.[21] He calculated that he would get territory at the peace table in any case without bothering to fight for it. It proved a desperate mistake. On 11 June, the Italian air force carried out eight bombing raids on Malta, causing little damage to the harbor but forcing the panicked population of Valetta to load up their donkey carts and flee to the countryside. High-altitude bombing, the Italian air force argued in keeping with the theories of Guilhio Douhet, would "sterilize" Malta without the requirement of an invasion.[22]

On 17 June, after France had asked for an armistice, Mussolini ordered his generals to attack French positions on the Alpine border between the two countries. Mussolini calculated that the possession of some French territory would strengthen Italy's hand during the peace talks. The 20 June assault by twenty-two Italian divisions backed by fourteen reserve divisions against six divisions of an army that had already been defeated proved a fiasco. The Italians lost 631 killed, 2,631 wounded, 616 missing, and 2,151 frostbite casualties to a French army that registered a mere 37 killed, 42 wounded, and 150 missing, and that had resolutely failed to surrender ground. Worse, in the armistice negotiations, the Italians failed to demand that the Tunisian ports be turned over to them—an error, as Libyan port capacity was insufficient to support the North African campaign the Axis would subsequently fight there.[23]

The Italian failure to seize Malta and take possession of Tunisian harbors was matched by Axis inability to spark Britain's Arab powder keg. This lapse in strategic foresight had several sources: one was Hitler's contradictory policy of reconciling German and British imperial interests, while conceding to Mussolini his Mediterranean strategic sphere. In the late 1930s Germany had been more interested in casting out its Jewish population than in picking quarrels with Britain over a Zionist enclave in the Eastern Mediterranean. Besides, Berlin regarded the Arabs as "notoriously unreliable," and was reluctant to alienate Turkey, Egypt, and Saudi Arabia by throwing support behind the grand mufti and his extremists. By 1938, the increasing tempo of Jewish expulsions from Germany had transformed the pro-German attitudes of Palestinian nationalists to the point that the German consul general in Jerusalem feared that Germans would soon be hated as much as the British in the Middle East. Germany lacked diplomatic representation in either Iraq or Saudi Arabia, an inattention to this strategically important area of the world that harmed Axis strategic interests. By May 1939, the looming possibility of conflict with Britain piqued the interests of German diplomats in the Persian Gulf. But the outbreak of war in September closed off these initiatives, especially toward Saudi Arabia.[24]

The outbreak of war caused the Germans to tinker with military options in the Middle East. The German high command, the OKW, considered projects—surreal in retrospect—of allying with the Soviet Union to attack India and the Middle East simultaneously. The option of playing the Arab nationalist card was revived by the Allied defeat of May–June 1940. Arabs looked favorably on cooperation with Germany because they believed that Berlin had no Middle Eastern ambitions. Mussolini pressed claims for Tunisia, part of Algeria, and the expansion of Libya as far south as Lake Chad. He also prepared to demand land bridges between Libya and Ethiopia, and from Tunisia to South Morocco. To assure Italian control of the Suez Canal, he wanted the Sinai Peninsula, Aden, and the islands of Perim and Socotra in the Arabian Sea annexed into the Italian empire, which was also to absorb British and French Somaliland. Fortunately for the Axis, the Arabs remained ignorant of the extent of Mussolini's ambitions. But Hitler's deference to Mussolini's ambitions in the Mediterranean meant that the latitude of Arab nationalists, who had no intention of exchanging British for Italian lordship, to manipulate British–Axis rivalry in the Middle East was circumscribed. Rome's opposition forced Berlin to cold-shoulder 1940 attempts by both Iraq and the grand mufti to gain

German support for an Arab uprising in Palestine that would tie down 30,000 to 40,000 British troops, interrupt the transportation of troops from India, and help the Italians in Libya. In 1940, at least, Axis-Arab cooperation to exploit Britain's Middle Eastern vulnerability was stymied by Berlin's deference to Rome in the Mediterranean, and by Arab suspicion of Italian imperial ambitions.[25]

By themselves, Italian forces lacked the will, and the means, to take advantage of Britain's shaky political base in the Middle East. In Libya, Marshal Rudolfo Graziani replaced Marshal Italo Balbo, who had perished when his plane was shot down by his own antiaircraft batteries. Mussolini must have assumed that his most prestigious commander would infuse energy into the heretofore listless performance of the Italian forces in North Africa. The youngest colonel in the Italian army in 1918, hero of the Senussi war, which had ensured Italian control of Cyrenaica in 1931, Graziani had commanded the October 1935 invasion of Abyssinia. Graziani's forte was brutal treatment of subject populations, which earned for him the nickname "Butcher." In Cyrenaica, concentration camps and mass executions had paved the way to conquest of the Senussi opposition. Similar methods applied in Abyssinia provoked a popular insurrection in 1938 that resulted in his recall. In 1939 he succeeded Marshal Pietro Badoglio as army chief of staff. While in Rome, Graziani had told Balbo to collect the most mobile elements of his forces, equip them with tanks, artillery, water, and supplies, and move against the British. Once in Libya, however, Graziani became the very model of procrastination. He complained that his forces were unbalanced and lacked mobility. He overestimated British strength and dispatched long lists of equipment requests, all the while complaining that the terrain and the temperature did not favor an offensive. Rather than single out his most mobile elements, he insisted on massing his army in a World War I–style advance. In short, he wasted time.

After much prodding by Rome, on 13 September 1940, Graziani's force lurched forward toward Sidi Barrani, a desolate outpost fifty-four miles inside Egypt that consisted of about twenty buildings, including two brothels and a small shop. In Europe, Axis leaders expected to plow forward on a bow wave of Arab nationalism. Badoglio boasted to the Germans that Palestine and Syria would fall of their own accord once Graziani reached the Nile Delta. And had the Italians taken up Hitler's offer of mechanized forces, that might well have happened. In September 1940, the British commander Sir Archibald Wavell was desperately weak, able to muster only elements of two divisions, a scattering of half-trained Australian and New Zealand troops, and eighty-five tanks to oppose Graziani. These he concentrated at the Marsa Matruh railhead 150 miles east of the Libyan frontier. The RAF was outmatched by its Italian counterpart and could only harass Italian troop concentrations. Graziani squandered his huge advantages in a pantomime offensive. Following a heavy artillery barrage, his six divisions shuttered eastward in two columns organized as "hedgehogs"— motorcyclists in front and in the rear, followed by light tanks, rows of vehicles, and truck-borne infantry in the center. It was all very orderly and very targetworthy, like "a birthday party in the Long Valley at Aldershot" (the British army training base), remarked one British officer.[26] Even then, part of his force, without maps or guides, became lost, and almost perished from thirst before being located by the Italian air force. The handful of opposing British battalions fought delaying actions against this parade ground Italian advance, filled the wells with salt, and destroyed the road as they fell back toward Marsa Matruh. On 16 September Graziani reported that his "offensive" had halted. He settled in to build a road and a water line to the rear. While both Rome and Berlin assumed that this was only an administrative pause, in fact it was to be the final "victory" of Graziani's career. The sad truth was that he lacked the will to surge forward in North Africa.[27] Wavell was permitted the leisure to build up his forces. Thus, lack of a coordinated strategic vision on the part of the Axis had, for the moment, allowed Britain to cling to Malta and left unchallenged Britain's precarious hold on the Nile Delta and possibly the entire Middle East.

A SHOW NAVY

A second potential British vulnerability that the Axis failed to attack was the British navy. Because the Royal Navy had tradition and leadership on its side, Italy needed to exploit its advantages of the central position and numerical superiority from the outset. Italy's control of the north shore of the Mediterranean gave the Axis significant advantages. They could bring men and matériel to the theater over land much faster than the British could by sea. The Italian air force flying from bases in Italy, Sicily, or Italian-controlled Rhodes held the whip hand in the central and Eastern Mediterranean. Italy controlled the "central lake" of the Mediterranean—the Tyrrhenian Sea, the triangle of water bounded to the west by Sardinia and Corsica, to the north by Elba, to the south by Sicily, and to the east by the Italian mainland. The elimination of France soothed fears of Italian admirals that Italy's central Mediterranean position in fact constituted a weakness because it opened her to attack and blockade. This allowed them to concentrate on the Sicilian Channel, the traditional sea bridge butressed by Malta and Pantelleria that led south to Tunisia and Tripolitania, to block Britain's east–west sea lanes of communication.[28] For the British, desperate to maintain their links with their empire, this was a critical choke point, a windpipe they fought desperately to keep open against an Axis that only intermittently appeared to recognize its strategic value. Indeed, so overwhelming did the British disadvantages seem in June 1940 that some considered abandoning the Eastern Mediterranean altogether and concentrating at Gibraltar, until Churchill squelched the idea.[29]

Of all Italian forces, the navy received the highest rating by foreign experts. Structurally, it reflected the Mahanian concept of a great battle fleet organized around the battleship and the heavy cruiser designed for titanic blue-water clashes with other fleets. In 1940 the Italian navy was ranked fifth in the world, behind the navies of Britain, the United States, Japan, and France, but larger than those of Germany and the Soviet Union. However, it constituted the most formidable single navy in the Mediterranean, including six battleships, around twenty cruisers, seven of them over 10,000 tons, sixty-one destroyers, seventy torpedo boats, and over one hundred submarines. The surface fleet was divided into two squadrons based at Taranto and La Spezia. The Italian submarine fleet, which was particularly worrisome to the British, was the largest in the world, with the possible exception of the USSR's.[30] It was organized into five squadrons in Italy, one at Rhodes and another at Tobruk. In addition, eight submarines were stationed in East Africa. The collapse of France gave the Italian fleet a numerical advantage over the British in the Mediterranean in every category of ship except battleships and carriers. And even here, the *Littorio* and the *Vittorio Veneto*, which entered service in August 1940, were both faster and better armed than anything in Cunningham's battleship inventory. The modernization of two older battleships, the *Duilio* and the *Doria*, was imminent, while *Zara*-class and *Bolzano*-class heavy cruisers were also deeply respected by the British. The British rushed a squadron, called Force H, to Gibraltar, which evened the odds somewhat.[31] But that did not solve the problem of dispersion for the British. Furthermore, Haifa and the Suez Canal were well within air range of Italian bombers operating out of Rhodes.

But the Italian navy, while formidable on paper, failed to live up to its potential for menace. It lagged in practically every category of naval warfare, being technologically backward, operationally off balance and unimaginatively led. The most obvious technical shortcoming was the failure to develop and deploy radar and sonar in the interwar years, oversights that cost Italian sailors dearly. Early versions of radar developed by the naval communications school at Livorno in 1935–36 were rejected as "futuristic" by a command that refused to deploy them until 1942, and only then at German insistence. Without waterproofing, electrical systems and range-finding equipment tended to dysfunction on capital ships designed for fighting in fair weather. Italian battleships might be capable of hurling a shell as far as twenty miles. But without accurate range finding, radar guidance, or aerial spotting, chances of hitting a target were slim. Light cruisers disintegrated when hit while destroyers were easily swamped in heavy seas. As the Italian navy was forced to shift from main-fleet action to convoy duty, the lack of depth charges and antiaircraft protection, not to mention an adequate grasp of antisubmarine tactics, would prove costly.[32]

Italian Admiral Franco Maugeri blamed Mussolini for the creation of "a show navy, a great, glittering toy that lent added prestige and luster to his regime"[33] but which otherwise was operationally unbalanced. While it became fashionable in the postwar years to blame Mussolini for the inadequacies of the Italian fleet, in fact, most Italian naval shortcomings had been picked from a menu that included a lack of vision and imagination, disputes within the Italian high command over the form the navy should assume, and interservice squabbles. One of these altercations was decided by Mussolini in 1923, when the Duce decreed that the Italian air force, favored as a truly Fascist service, would hold a monopoly on air power. That said, the Admiralty had demonstrated no great enthusiasm for carriers in the interwar years. Defeats at Taranto and Matapan persuaded Italian admirals of the carrier's virtues, too late to complete the conversion of the *Roma*, still in the dockyard when Italy surrendered in September 1943. The absence of an air arm beyond a few primitive float planes meant that Italian admirals were unable to develop a good picture of the enemy. Seldom did the Italian navy dare operate beyond the range of land-based air support. Attempts to increase air-naval cooperation in the aftermath of the Spanish Civil War were largely stillborn. The Italians lacked even the primitive torpedo bombers employed so effectively by the British at Taranto. The Italians had also developed a large capital-ship navy without the logistical capacity to support it. The increasing shortage of oil as the war progressed placed severe limitations on the operational range of the fleet and on the ability of the battleships to sortie at all.

The final Italian naval defect—its leadership—was common to all Italian services. By the 1930s the Italians were investing heavily in capital ships. Italy's naval paradox was that the more the fleet increased in power, the less Italian admirals appeared willing to risk it in battle. The prospect of an encounter with the Royal Navy filled them with dread. In part this was because Italy's small industrial base and lack of raw materials meant that any ship losses could not be replaced. The British, on the other hand, while overstretched, could always summon reinforcements from elsewhere. For the Italians, it was to be a come-as-you-are war. Italian fear of losing irreplaceable ships translated into a lack of aggressiveness, which allowed the British to control the strategic pace of the naval war. This attitude began at the top, where Admiral Angelo Iachino remained fleet commander despite repeated failures to close with inferior British forces or intercept convoys. Iachino's failure to cash in his material advantages at this early stage of the war, to instill initiative and deliver morale-boosting victories, allowed feelings of inferiority and inadequacy gradually to penetrate the lower decks. Cunningham's daring 11–12 November 1940 torpedo bomber attack on the Italian fleet at anchor in Taranto, one that presaged the Japanese assault on Pearl Harbor over a year later, knocked the Italian navy off its fragile equilibrium. It never seemed to recover. The diminishing number of ships as the war progressed encouraged the Italian proclivity to remain harborbound, which in turn denied other admirals and captains valuable sea experience. Even aggressive commanders, like Admiral Alberto Da Zara, who successfully attacked a British convoy off Pantelleria in June 1942, found themselves ordered by combat-shy superiors at the *Supermarina* to return to port. The heavy investment in ships left inadequate funds for manpower and training. Italian ships carried about half the numbers of officers as did ships of the Royal Navy. Ships were plagued by constant turnovers of personnel. How this impacted combat performance is difficult to judge. But British accounts of Matapan suggest that, for instance, crew discipline utterly collapsed on the heavy cruiser *Pola* after it was disabled by a British torpedo. The boarding party from the HMS *Jervis* "came back with a story of chaos on board," according to Commander Walter Scott, the destroyer's first lieutenant. "The officers' cabins had been looted by the ship's company of the *Pola*, and empty Chianti bottles lay everywhere. Verification of this came when a number of the prisoners showed unmistakable signs of inebriation."[34] Unwilling to train for night operations, the Italians did not invest in flashless powder, illumination rounds, and night optics, investments that might have paid high dividends at Matapan. Inadequate training translated into poor gun accuracy, while the lack of aggressiveness meant that unlike the British, Italian commanders were too timid to close with the enemy to swap blows.[35]

The tone for the naval war was set in July 1940 when Italian intelligence deciphered a British fleet message from Alexandria alerting them to the approach of a British squadron at Punta Stilo off the coast of Calabria. The Italians tried to lay a coordinated ambush combining powerful capital ships that outgunned the British force and submarine ambushes with a land-based air attack. Though it was conducted almost within sight of their own shores against an inferior British force taken by surprise, the operation was botched by timid tactics and lack of coordination. As soon as one of the battleships received a hit from British guns, the Italian force threw up a smoke screen and scuttled for port. Even though Cunningham pursued to within twenty-five miles of the Italian coastline, the Italian air force failed immediately to intercept him. While Italian planes harassed his return to Alexandria, they caused his ships practically no damage, leading the British admiral to conclude that Italian aviation could not contain his freedom of maneuver.[36] Ten days later off Cape Spada in northern Crete, two Italian cruisers threw away advantages of speed, range, and firepower against an inferior British destroyer force, which resulted in the sinking of one of the Italian cruisers.[37] While Admiral Cunningham was unhappy with the performance of his ships, even before the availability of Ultra intelligence in October 1940, Punta Stilo and Cape Spada convinced him that offensive tactics against the Italians would pay dividends.[38] A ship hit by an Italian bomb at this stage of the war was an unlucky crew indeed. "Time and again [British] ships would be apparently smothered by the tall, black, leaping splashes from the carpet of bombs simultaneously released," writes naval historian Donald Macintyre of Italian high-altitude bomber attacks. "Time and again they emerged unscathed, to give proof which was to be repeated in every theatre of war, that the chances of even accurate high-level bombing hitting a ship free to manoeuvre, if not negligible, were at least unacceptable."[39]

The year 1940 found the Italian navy at the pinnacle of their possibilities, and they positively declined to go on the offensive.[40] The navy's overly centralized command lifted the initiative from fleet commanders, most of whom lacked aggressive instincts in any case. Italian admirals argued that forays into the Eastern Mediterranean would prove barren of strategic benefit. Even Suez, could it be seized, "would gain nothing of decisive importance."[41] Operationally, the lack of carriers, torpedo bombers, and radar meant that Italian ships preferred to play host to Royal Navy forays in the first two years of the war. Taranto in November 1940 offered the most thumping illustration of the hazards of a stationary, passive, "fleet in being" mentality. When they did go on the offensive, often under German pressure, the results were disastrous. The most catastrophic illustration of the operational and tactical ineptitude of the Italian navy occurred on 28 March 1941 off Cape Matapan in southern Greece, where Vice-Admiral Angelo Iachino, under German pressure, sailed the battleship *Vittorio Veneto*, eight cruisers, and seventeen destroyers to attack British convoys ferrying troops and supplies between Greece and Alexandria.[42] Tipped off by Ultra intelligence, which for the first time in the war contributed significantly to a Royal Navy victory,[43] Cunningham diverted his convoys and prepared to intercept the unsuspecting Iachino. So as not to alert Alexandria's numerous spies, the most notorious of whom was the Japanese consul, who observed the British fleet as he played golf, Cunningham spent the afternoon at his club. His battle fleet, consisting of three battleships, a carrier, and nine destroyers, raised steam and departed on the twenty-seventh after nightfall. None of the four Italian submarines stationed at the mouth of Alexandria harbor reported the fleet's departure.

Iachino's plan was to divide his force, with wings turning north and south of Crete, to catch British convoys in a pincer movement. Early on the morning of 27 March, he learned from radio intercepts that the British had spotted one of his cruiser squadrons. When later that morning he learned that the carrier *Formidable* was at sea, he realized that surprise had been lost and considered canceling the operation. In midafternoon, his cryptographers intercepted Cunningham's indecipherable operation order to British naval forces in the Eastern Mediterranean, which alerted them that the British were likely to converge in force on Iachino's fleet. With no convoy at sea to attack, his sortie became pointless. Iachino considered turning for home, but pressure from the Germans combined with his own insistence that the Italian navy actually *do something* kept him on course. He abandoned his planned foray into the Aegean, where he determined that British air power would be too strong, and decided instead to keep his force intact south of Crete. By now, Iachino was receiving numerous indications that the British fleet was at sea and looking for a fight. He steamed east nonetheless.

A little after 0700 on the morning of 28 March, aircraft from the

British carrier *Formidable* spotted the Italian ships about thirty nautical miles south of Crete and ninety miles east of the approaching British fleet. Following some inconclusive exchanges of salvos with the cruiser force that Cunningham had stationed south of Crete, Iachino turned his squadrons to the northwest at around 1400 hours. At this point, an attack by five Albacore biwing torpedo bombers flying off the *Formidable* commenced. The Albacores had come on line in 1940 to replace the aging Swordfish. The Albacore had an all-metal air frame, an enclosed cockpit, and could carry a 1,610-pound torpedo 930 miles, about 400 miles farther than the Swordfish. Nevertheless, cognoscenti considered the Albacore a bare improvement over its aging sister, only slightly faster and less maneuverable. Fleet Albacores joined the *Formidable* in November 1940. Matapan was their first mission, and they succeeded in hitting the *Vittorio Veneto* on its port side and damaging a screw, but failed to slow it enough to allow Cunningham to catch up. British bombers out of Crete attacked the Italian ships but failed to cause any damage. Iachino radioed desperately for air cover. But as he was at the limit of operational distance, only a single flight of Messerschmitt Bf. 110s from Fliegerkorps X arrived and remained on station a bare ten minutes before they turned for base. As dusk fell, British reconnaissance aircraft flying some fifty miles ahead of the British fleet spied the Italian ships organized in five columns around the stricken *Vittorio Veneto* as it limped toward Taranto at twelve knots. As the sun set, a flight of Albacores out of Maleme in Crete managed to fight their way through the dazzling Italian searchlights, antiaircraft fire, and smoke screens to hit the cruiser *Pola* dead center. Her boilers flooded and electrical circuits out, she went dead in the water. Cunningham steamed northeast, eager to close with the Italian fleet before daylight, when the intervention of land-based aircraft would make his position untenable.

While Iachino's battleship limped for home, radar on the HMS *Valiant* revealed a motionless ship about six miles ahead. The British hoped that it was the *Vittorio Veneto*. In fact, it was the *Pola*. As Cunningham's ships closed in on the stricken Italian cruiser at 2230 hours, suddenly the watch spied massive shapes steaming in line about two miles to their front. These were the cruisers *Zara* and *Fiume* together

with a destroyer escort, which Iachino, blinded by the lack of air reconnaissance and absence of radar, and ignorant of Cunningham's position, had dispatched to rescue the *Pola*. Alerted by short-range radio,
the British battle fleet silently swung into line, as the gun control officers rotated their turrets to sight on the dark shapes barely two miles
away. Suddenly, the destroyer *Greyhound*, at the head of the British
line, switched on its searchlight, catching what Cunningham remembered as the "silvery-blue shape" of the *Fiume* smack in its beam. The
firing gongs went off in the *Warspite* and the *Valiant*, signal for a wall
of orange flame to erupt from the two ships. The unfortunate Italians,
sailing obliviously in line with their guns pointed fore and aft, never
knew what hit them. The British could observe their fifteen-inch
shells traveling down the *Greyhound*'s beam of light to ignite the *Fiume* from bow to stern. Star shells further illuminated the *Fiume* as its
after turret toppled into the sea; the ship listed heavily to starboard and
began to sink. The British then trained their guns on the *Zara*, where
they observed columns of panicked sailors scampering over its upper
decks toward their battle stations. Few reached them. In three minutes
the *Zara*, like the *Fiume*, had become a pyre of orange flame as thousands of pounds of steel ripped into the Italian cruiser. The *Zara*'s
boilers erupted, and her forward turret, caught by a British shell,
pirouetted into the sea. British sailors could see Italians leaping over-
board. It was like being a spectator at a one-sided Rugby match, one
remembered, "a strange mixture of elation, triumph and pity."[44] The
blistered hulks of the Italian cruisers melted into the sea and vanished
from the British radar screens.

The *Greyhound*'s searchlights next caught the destroyer *Alfieri*,
which a broadside fired from the *Barham* at barely 3,000 meters
turned into a smoking hulk. The three Italian destroyers at the rear of
the line rotated toward the British. One got off a torpedo, which
forced Cunningham to swing his battleships ninety degrees and order
them out of the battle so that his destroyers could finish off the crip-
ples. Two of the three surviving Italian destroyers managed to flee.
However, the *Carducci* was caught by the *Stuart*. Torpedoed and
shelled, the Italian destroyer's decks were soon awash. Like jackals after wounded prey, the British destroyers prowled toward the inert *Pola*,

which they found at about midnight. The Italian ship wallowed helplessly, without power or lights and unable or unwilling to rotate its guns. The *Havlock* put two shells into the ship, which seemed to the destroyer crew so outsized that it must be a battleship. Two small fires broke out. But otherwise, the *Pola* appeared undamaged. Two other destroyers arrived at 0140. Their searchlight revealed the demoralized crew of the *Pola* crowded on decks littered with debris, "longing to surrender," as one British officer remarked. The destroyer *Jervis* drew alongside the *Pola* and, to the disappointment of the British sailors, some of whom had armed themselves with cutlasses in preparation for boarding, began to take off the 257 Italian sailors, many of them drunk, who remained on board. Two torpedoes finished off the *Pola*. The oily surface was covered with clusters of small boats, rafts, men clinging to debris, and bobbing corpses. The rescue effort was disturbed at dawn by the appearance of German aircraft. Cunningham had no choice but to turn toward Alexandria. Two days later the Italian hospital ship *Gradisca*, alerted by Cunningham, picked up over 150 survivors left in the water. Greek destroyers picked up others. Only two Italian destroyers escaped the Matapan massacre. In a defeat that one author has called Italy's maritime Caparetto,[45] 2,303 Italian sailors perished.

Matapan exposed significant deficiencies in Italian naval operations, among them the lack of radar, which allowed the British to locate the *Pola* and surprise the ships sent to rescue her; inadequate night operational capability; poor intelligence; and a lack of air-naval cooperation. Iachino was found at fault by a board of inquiry for sending the ships back to aid the crippled *Pola* and generally condemned for his failure to grasp the situation. Matapan also added another nail to the coffin of German-Italian relations. The chief of the German naval liaison in Rome concluded that the Italian navy was ruled by incompetents and called on German officers to take over the fleet. His views were echoed by the naval staff in Berlin, who blasted the tactical ineptitude and inadequate training of the Italian navy. Their conclusion, however, was that in future the Germans must not encourage the Italians to undertake ambitious operations that were clearly beyond their competence, for fear that the Germans might get the blame for failure. Italian officers gave as good as they got, blaming the Germans for forcing the operation in the first place and for failure to provide adequate intelligence as well as for faulty air cover. The only explanation for the defeat that found common agreement between Axis partners was that of treachery. Treachery became a popular explanation for the disaster at Matapan, one subsequently extended to explain high Italian losses on North African convoys. The Germans, including Rommel, also found Italian treachery a convenient explanation for the failure to supply North Africa adequately and for Axis defeats there in 1942. Matapan confirmed and deepened the Italian navy's sense of inferiority. Iachino, one of the Italian navy's few fire-eaters, had reaped the rewards of seeking battle at the head of a technically inferior fleet, without air cover, in an operation that had no clear objective. This warning made other Italian officers reluctant to engage British ships, especially at night when the lack of radar, training in night operations, and antiflash powder put them at a severe disadvantage. Above all, Matapan consolidated British naval dominance of the Eastern Mediterranean, which meant that although severely harassed from the air, British evacuation from Greece and Crete would be free of Italian naval interference, which might have transformed an unsuccessful British operation into a disastrous one.[46]

As the Italians were forced by British pressure to turn to convoy protection, their antiquated antisubmarine warfare techniques and woeful antiaircraft capabilities doomed them to failure. Italy's submarines, while numerous, were slow and poorly ventilated, with short periscopes that forced them practically to the surface to take aim with their defective torpedoes, a suicidal maneuver in the clear Mediterranean waters. And while Italian submarine tactics improved in effectiveness, the British continued to catch Italian submarines on the surface in daylight, perhaps because fuel leaks created foul air, forcing Italian submariners to choose between asphyxiation or destruction on the surface. These deficiencies were repaired somewhat by the arrival of German U-boats, which, in November 1941, scored the double success of sinking both the carrier *Ark Royal* and the battleship *Barham*. But the U-boats were never numerous in the Mediterranean, nor were their attacks sustained.[47]

One real strength of the Italian navy lay with its special forces capabilities, although this force was neglected at the outset of the war. The Italian Tenth Light Flotilla combined an array of weapons including midget submarines, explosive motorboats (EMBs), frogmen, and manned torpedoes called "chariots" or more popularly *maiale* ("pigs"). These submersibles were guided to their targets, the explosive head of the pig detached and fixed to the target's keel, and the time fuse set. Attacks on Alexandria in August and September 1940 by midget submarines failed, as did an October attack against Gibraltar. However, explosive speedboats caught the cruiser *York* in March 1941. The most successful Italian operation came against Alexandria in December 1941, when three pigs were released by the submarine *Sciré* a mile from the harbor entrance. By a stroke of good fortune, they managed to secrete themselves in the wakes of British destroyers returning from patrol and penetrate the net defenses into the anchorage. One pig malfunctioned and sank, but was manhandled along the harbor floor by one of its operators to a position beneath the battleship *Valiant* and the fuse set. The two frogmen were captured as they came to the surface, but refused to reveal the purpose of their mission until their craft exploded, and the *Valiant* settled to the bottom. A second team blew the stern off a tanker, in the process damaging a neighboring destroyer. The third pair sank the fleet flagship *Queen Elizabeth*, and then managed to escape into Alexandria. These two Italians might well have reached the Italian submarine dispatched to retrieve them off Rosetta had not their Italian-supplied British currency, not legal tender in Egypt, led to their arrest. This spectacular raid, revenge for Cunningham's November 1940 attack on Taranto, was particularly devastating to the British coming only a few days after the 10 December 1941 sinking by the Japanese of the *Prince of Wales* and the battle cruiser *Repulse*, which announced the diversion of Britain's increasingly stretched naval assets to the Far East.[48] But while the success of these stealth attacks was on occasion spectacular, they did not tip the strategic balance in the Mediterranean. The effect of special operations was more psychological than attritional.[49]

The failure of Mussolini to warn his merchant navy that he was to declare war resulted in the loss of 254 of Italy's 786 oceangoing cargo vessels in June 1940, or a third of the Italian merchant marine. This was compensated for in part by the fact that fifty-four German freighters abroad in the Mediterranean found sanctuary in Italian ports. But for a nation not only required to supply overseas theaters, but also relying heavily on coastal shipping even in peacetime, Mussolini's negligence constituted a significant own-goal even before hostilities began. As the war progressed, Italy had to shift to smaller and smaller ships to carry the freight, which lowered efficiency.[50] Nor was the maritime struggle to support North Africa helped by the fact that Italian longshoremen regularly looted cargoes.[51]

The Axis partners were no more able to coordinate their strategy at sea than on land. Neither dictator was comfortable commanding over water. Hitler rejected the pre–World War I slogan "Our future lies on the water" as criminally misguided.[52] They shared no common naval doctrine. While the German navy was built around a "hit-and-run" *guerre de course* strategy against enemy commerce, Italian sailors embraced the Mahanian philosophy of the "fleet in being"—that is, the mere existence of the fleet fixes the enemy fleet and prevents him from doing mischief. The German liaison caustically remarked that "fleet-in-being" translated into Italian as "strive for the greatest possible security."[53] In short, Italy's was a stay-home fleet whose main objective, as the Germans noted, was to survive the war, even if Italy lost it.[54]

FELIX

Failure to sever British access to the Western Mediterranean must count as the third missed opportunity for the Axis, along with the failure to seize Malta and Egypt and to take advantage of the temporary weakness of the Royal Navy. Like other Axis miscalculations, this wound was entirely self-inflicted, and sprang from the inability of the Axis to formulate clear strategic objectives in the Mediterranean where the interests of Berlin, Rome, Madrid, and Vichy conflicted. As German attempts to subdue Britain sputtered in the late summer of 1940, Hitler began casting around for other options. The Mediterranean appeared to offer the German leader scope for action. Hitler wanted to coordinate an attack on Britain with a simultaneous thrust at Egypt and Gibraltar. The British hold on Gibraltar seemed to hang by the thread of Franco's whim. Operation Felix was drawn up in August, a three-phase plan that involved a surprise Luftwaffe attack on Gibraltar followed by a systematic shelling of the harbor defenses. A ground assault would subdue the British garrison, as a prelude to hurling two German divisions into Morocco. Raeder persuaded Hitler that Gibraltar must be secured before the United States entered the war. The seizure of the base would also force the British to sail around Africa to reinforce the Eastern Mediterranean, which would put great strain on their shipping resources. Gibraltar would give the German navy a base out of range of British-based aircraft, and allow Raeder to threaten the Central Atlantic with his U-boats.[55] Felix was scheduled to kick off on 10 January 1941. Hitler's task was to gain Franco's approval for the plan.[56]

In October 1940, Hitler traveled to Hendaye on Spain's border with France to convince Franco of the plan's soundness. The meeting was a disaster. The fact that the Spanish leader kept the Führer cooling his heels in the railway station got the interview off on the wrong foot. When Franco finally arrived, the result was instant antipathy. The small, swarthy, overweight Franco failed to match Hitler's vision of a fascist *Übermensch*. On the contrary, Franco looked like a study for a Nazi portrait of Jewish manhood! Nor did Franco endear himself to the Führer by adopting his usual air of self-satisfaction to lecture Hitler in his high-pitched, parade ground voice, in the process predicting that Britain would absorb the best that Germany could throw at it and survive. Franco's final insult was to refuse to sign the protocol that Hitler thrust upon him. Hitler reciprocated by failing to hide both his impatience and his disdain for a beggar country that behaved as if it still commanded the world from Lima to Rome. Hitler subsequently insisted that he would rather spend hours in a dentist's chair than endure another encounter with the Caudillo.

The Hitler-Franco meeting at Hendaye introduced the German dictator to Mediterranean political complexities, and he disliked what he saw. Franco failed to demonstrate sufficient gratitude for Germany's significant role in his 1939 victory. In return for the offer of aid to recover Gibraltar after almost 250 years of foreign rule, the Spanish leader made surprisingly bold demands as a condition for Spain's entry into the war on the Axis side. Reequipment of the antiquated Spanish armed forces and transfer of the French sector of Morocco together with Oran province in eastern Algeria, which contained large numbers of Spanish immigrants, came at the top of his list. When Hitler requested one of the Canary Islands for use as a German naval base, Franco categorically refused. In private, Hitler denounced Franco's demands as "Judaic mercantilism," and suggested that a man so cantankerous, ungrateful, and mercenary must spring from Jewish ancestry. The simple fact was that Franco placed Hitler in the same conundrum in Morocco and Oran as did Mussolini with his demands for Nice, Corsica, and Tunis. Gains for Hitler's Mediterranean allies must come at French expense. Hitler had made a soft peace with France in 1940 precisely because he wanted to neutralize the French empire, and with it the French fleet. Mers el-Kébir and the Anglo-Gaullist attack on Dakar strengthened the view, especially in the Kriegsmarine, that Vichy France's capacity to resist must be strengthened. To give in to Franco's demands in Morocco and Algeria would virtually guarantee the defection of imperial France to the Allied camp and mean that Hitler must divert troops to police duties in France.

The Germans continued to plan for Felix, but the Spaniards refused to commit. Events in the Balkans and plans for the invasion of the Soviet Union began to compete with Felix for resources and attention. Finally, on 8 December 1940, Franco refused to allow Felix to proceed, citing Spanish economic weakness. Mussolini's subsequent attempt in February 1941 to persuade the Spaniard to join the Axis was also rebuffed. In one respect, however, Franco's refusal conferred a strategic blessing, for it allowed Hitler greater latitude to deal with the French.[57]

While the Axis contemplated how best to capitalize on Britain's overstretched Mediterranean defenses, London struggled desperately to cope with the sudden reversal of strategic fortune caused by France's collapse. On one hand, France's surrender was a huge setback for Britain. It meant that, unlike in World War I, Britain and the United States would have to fight their way back onto the Continent. France's collapse was also the event that precipitated Mussolini's entrance into the war, presenting Britain with another enemy to overcome and another theater to contest. The prickly attitude of the Vichy regime, eager to maintain its independence but inevitably driven to compromise with its occupier, further scrambled the strategic equation in a theater of already dazzling complexity. The Royal Navy was locked out of Oran, Algiers, Philippeville, Bizerte, and Sfax, not to mention Ajaccio, Bastia, Toulon, and Marseilles, as well as Dakar in French West Africa. With Malta as the sole British base in the central Mediterranean, the strategic odds there were heavily tilted in Italy's favor. Finally, at a moment when Britain faced the prospect of invasion, an Axis annexation of the French navy conceivably might cost Britain the war. And although French authorities were categorical in their assurances that they would scuttle their fleet rather than allow it to be taken over, what guarantee did London have that this promise could, or would, be respected? Indeed, the Royal Navy had been forced to chase the battleship *Richelieu* back to Dakar when it attempted to sail to Brest. Was it going to spend the entire war keeping a wary eye on French, as well as Axis, ships?

On the other hand, in retrospect, France's defeat offered Britain an opportunity as well as a challenge. Had France not fallen, Mussolini would not have entered the war, at least not in June 1940. Without a Mediterranean theater, the fighting would probably have remained in Northern Europe, where, as in World War I, the Germans would have proven very difficult to defeat. And while the Mediterranean held great risks for Britain, in the long run it pointed to a way back into the war for London and, eventually, even for France. It offered a place where Axis friction and mismanagement could be showcased and exploited. Britain could demonstrate its resolve to fight on, notch up victories, and hone and harden its forces for a Continental invasion. Although the abundance and complexity of strategic choice in the Mediterranean bewildered Allies and Axis alike, French neutrality hurt Hitler more than Churchill in the Mediterranean. Indeed, Hitler may have wondered if he had been wise to defeat France at all. Suddenly he had acquired an Italian ally of dubious value. He was forced to look south to a theater in which he had no interest. He must spread his forces more thinly. Finally, the requirement to keep France neutral severely restricted Germany's strategic options in the Mediterranean.

At first sight, the Royal Navy's attack on its erstwhile ally at Mers el-Kébir, the port of Oran, on 3 July 1940, was a happy development from an Axis perspective. Relations between the Allies rapidly deteriorated once France initiated armistice negotiations with Germany. In Bordeaux, where the French government first sought refuge, Anglophobia reached heights unknown since the Fashoda incident of 1898. In London, muttering about defeatist "Frogs" had reached epidemic proportions—First Sea Lord Admiral Sir Dudley Pound demanded that his French counterparts return all ciphers, plans of minefields, and secret information. Mistrust ran full tilt. The armistice signed between France and Hitler in June 1940 left the war cabinet deeply disturbed about the disposition of the French naval forces. The Germans, and later the Italians, foreswore any intention of seizing the French ships. On 27 June, Admiral Jean-François Darlan informed London, "I repeat that the fleet will remain French or will not exist."[58] The French leaders were no doubt sincere in their insistence that they would scuttle rather than switch sides. But what value did that guarantee carry? Article 8 of the armistice document allowed for Axis "*contrôle*" of French ships. What exactly did that mean? The British took it to mean "control," whereas, in fact, it meant something closer to "administrative verification." Even Britain's own naval experts suggested that the Germans and Italians could never adequately man the French ships even if they seized them.

Nevertheless, Churchill could not risk Britain's survival on the semantics of an armistice negotiation undertaken under duress with powers that had heretofore demonstrated no inclination to keep their word. Furthermore, in negotiating an armistice, the French breached one of the key components of the Anglo-French *entente*. In short, Paris was deserting, breaking their contract. Even Neville Chamberlain, a man notoriously willing to give foreign leaders of dubious character the benefit of the doubt, thought the French had "behaved abominably." Churchill chose to take action. The risks of doing nothing were high. Furthermore, strong action against the French met the prior approval of both the U.S. government, which shared the prime minister's fears for the naval balance, and British public opinion.[59]

On 27 June 1940, Churchill ordered that French ships should be prevented from returning to their home ports. A source of special concern was the disposition of Force X under Admiral René-Emile Godfroy at Alexandria, and the flotilla of two modern battle cruisers, two battleships, a seaplane carrier, and six destroyers at Mers el-Kébir under Admiral Marcel Bruno Gensoul. At Alexandria, the two fleets were anchored side by side. Cunningham, therefore, had no desire to provoke a battle that would decommission his main base in the Eastern Mediterranean for the foreseeable future. He also wished to avoid disagreeable relations with the French, who counted a significant community in Egypt that included the engineers who operated the Suez Canal. British captains visited their opposite numbers on French ships, while large blackboards with signs in French expressing a desire not to fight were paraded around French ships. After some confusion, the French basically agreed to demilitarize their ships and intern themselves, at British expense, for the duration of the conflict in Alexandria.

Things went less smoothly at the military harbor of Mers el-Kébir, which lay about three miles west of Oran. On the morning of 3 July, Gibraltar's Force H, under Admiral Sir James Somerville, appeared outside Mers el-Kébir. It included the carrier *Ark Royal* with thirty torpedo aircraft and twenty-four fighters; the battleships *Hood*, *Valiant*, and *Resolution*, all with fifteen-inch guns; two light cruisers; and eleven destroyers. The French battle cruisers *Dunkerque* and *Strasbourg*, two battleships *Bretagne* and *Provence*, and the seaplane carrier *Commandant Teste*, were aligned in a row, sterns against the breakwater, watched over by the French fort atop the Santon hill, which towered one thousand feet above the sea. In addition, six destroyers and a motley of submarines, torpedo boats, sloops, patrol boats, and minesweepers also crowded the harbor. The British mission, according to Churchill, was "one of the most disagreeable and difficult tasks that a British Admiral has ever been faced with." Admiral Somerville signaled to the French that he had proposals that "will enable you and the valiant and glorious French to be on our side." The destroyer *Foxhound* anchored just outside the harbor defenses at 0805. On it was Captain Cedric Holland, a fifty-one-year-old ex–naval attaché to Paris, who requested permission to meet with Admiral Gensoul, whom he knew personally. Gensoul sent his barge to the *Foxhound* to inform Holland that he was too busy to see him. He then informed Somerville that his proposals "merit no further examination," and ordered them away. Not to be dissuaded, Holland jumped into the *Foxhound*'s launch and sailed toward the *Dunkerque*, Gensoul's flagship, only to be intercepted by the admiral's barge. Holland handed an envelope to Flag Lieutenant Bernard Dufay, and told him he would await Gensoul's reply. When Admiral Gensoul opened the envelope around 0935, he found that the contents offered him four options: fight on from a British harbor; steam to a British port from which his crews would be repatriated to France; sail to a French port in the West Indies such as Martinique, where they would be demilitarized and entrusted to U.S. jurisdiction for the duration of the war; or scuttle.

Somerville's ultimatum caught French sailors at a low moment, when their ability to think through their alternatives was confused by the chaos of defeat, the humiliation of the armistice, and debates in the French camp about whether to fight on or stack arms. There was also a subtext in the French navy's deep resentment of its British ally and rival, a force under whose shadow they had always labored. Within thirty minutes, Holland had Gensoul's reply, which was that French ships would not be turned over to the Germans, and that he was prepared to "meet force by force." In the meantime, Gensoul signaled his superiors that he had been given six hours to scuttle his ships, without mentioning the other alternatives. The chief of staff to French navy commander Admiral Jean-François Darlan, Admiral Maurice Le Luc, replied that Gensoul must prepare for battle. Gensoul ordered his ships to get up steam to depart, a process that took about six hours. At around 1330 hours, when British reconnaissance aircraft reported that the French were preparing to slip anchor, Somerville ordered his planes to drop five magnetic mines at the mouth of the harbor. This "belligerent act" both stiffened French resentment and failed to seal off the harbor entrance. Meanwhile, Gensoul, who was playing for time until his ships were ready, offered to meet Holland for an "honourable discussion." Holland was piped on board the *Dunkerque* at 1615, in the process noting that the French ships were manned, guns pointed seaward, with tugs ready at the stern of each battleship. He probably realized as well that Gensoul had used the time to have his submarines arm their torpedoes while coastal batteries and aircraft prepared for battle. The stifling heat of the admiral's cabin contrasted with the frigid formality with which Gensoul received Holland. The Frenchman rejected Holland's fears that the French ships would fall into Axis hands with indignation and anger. He stubbornly rejected the British captain's argument that to sail to the United States would fulfill the spirit of Admiral Darlan's orders of 24 June. At this point, Gensoul stepped out of his cabin to receive a signal from Darlan that all French ships in the Western Mediterranean had been ordered to converge on Mers el-Kébir. When he returned, Gensoul told Holland that he was prepared to disarm his ships in place. This was flashed to Somerville. Holland prepared to leave the *Dunkerque* at 1725, when a message from Somerville told Gensoul that he would open fire at 1730. The British had intercepted the French message to Gensoul that reinforcements were on the way. Gensoul bade Holland adieu in a way that struck the Englishman as surprisingly friendly, given the tensions of the afternoon and the fact that the two fleets were about to do battle.

As Holland reached the *Foxhound*, the first shells began to fall on the French ships. The battleship *Bretagne* exploded and capsized with its crew of over one thousand sailors. The French could neither maneuver nor bring their guns fully against the British, who fired from a maximum visibility of 15,000 yards guided by airborne artillery spotters. French return fire ceased within less than thirty minutes. Gensoul's flagship *Dunkerque* was disabled while the *Provence* ran aground. The destroyer *Mogador*, its stern blown off, managed to anchor in shallow water. At 1810, Somerville ceased fire to give the French an opportunity to abandon ship and to move beyond range of the shore batteries or any submarines that might have set course for his ships. Miraculously, the *Strasbourg*, preceded by five destroyers, hidden in the confusion of smoke, hugged the shoreline to avoid the magnetic mines dropped by the British, and escaped. Alerted by planes from the *Ark Royal*, Somerville gave chase, but the *Strasbourg* had a twenty-five-mile head start. The next day it reached Toulon, with seven destroyers and the *Commandant Teste*. Six cruisers from Algiers also took the opportunity to regain Toulon. The following morning, three waves of torpedo bombers from the *Ark Royal* returned to send a torpedo into the side of the *Dunkerque*. The operation cost Somerville five planes. At Dakar in French West Africa, planes off the carrier *Hermes* caused enough damage to the battleship *Richelieu* to put it out of commission for a year. Around two hundred French warships, most small or obsolete, were seized in British ports in an operation that vindicated Churchill's fears of how easily Germans might have taken over French vessels. About 3,000 of the 12,000 interned French sailors elected to join the Free French navy. The rest were repatriated. Further attacks on French ships were halted for fear of French retaliation.[60]

The French, of course, were furious at what they saw as yet more evidence of Perfidious Albion's betrayal. The British had used their allied status as camouflage to approach the French port and then treacherously massacre almost 1,300 sailors. In London, Charles de Gaulle choked with rage. The Free French movement almost folded its tent, and recruitment plummeted. The Germans were delighted, denouncing the "cowardly British attack" as "piracy," and insisting that no further proof was required that "the English will fight to the last Frenchman." The British were fortunate that, in Vichy, cooler heads prevailed over Darlan's calls for revenge. "Let us at least allow ourselves time to think," Marshal Pétain, in charge of the French government, informed his colleagues. "The attack on our fleet is one thing, war is another."[61] France's significant air force in North Africa could have made life even more difficult for Malta than it was otherwise to become, while French bases around Africa might have caused the sail around the Cape to become a more perilous enterprise than it already was. Syria might have become a base to unhinge Britain's po-

sition in the Middle East. The hostility of the large French community in Egypt might have become a serious embarrassment. Even
though Vichy contented itself with protests and a perfunctory air attack on Gibraltar, the British would pay the price for Mers el-Kébir at
Dakar in September 1940, in Syria in the summer of 1941, and in the
November 1942 invasion of North Africa. The "martyrs" of Mers el-
Kébir remained valuable arguments in Vichy's arsenal of anti-British
propaganda, pictures of the cemetery with almost 1,300 crosses shown
frequently on French cinema screens.

While most treatments of the Anglo-French naval clash view it as
a tragic misunderstanding, in fact, overall, Mers el-Kébir paid significant dividends for the British. The attack, though in many respects ineffective, virtually eliminated the threat, however remote, that French
warships would fall into hostile hands, at least in the short run. More
important, however, Mers el-Kébir kicked off Churchill's plan to use
the Mediterranean to showcase British resolve to fight to the knife
against the Axis. What the *Times* described as a "melancholy victory"
united the British people. The British Parliament sat silently as Churchill described the action. It then erupted into cheers as Churchill
concluded that Mers el-Kébir "should be, in itself, sufficient to dispose
once and for all the lies and rumors . . . that we have the slightest intention of entering into negotiations . . . with the German and Italian
governments. We shall, on the contrary, prosecute the war with the utmost vigour and by all the means that are open to us until the right-
eous purposes for which we entered upon it have been fulfilled."
Abroad, the news was equally electrifying, at a moment when many
fully expected London to conclude an armistice. Greece, Turkey, and
Yugoslavia took Mers el-Kébir as the first indication that Britain had
every intention of winning the war, and therefore became less inclined to slip into line behind the Axis. In the United States, the
British attack acted as an antidote to appeasers in the State Department like Ambassador Joseph Kennedy, who argued that Britain was
finished. Indeed, Harry Hopkins, President Roosevelt's confidant, insisted that Mers el-Kébir had convinced the American president that
British resistance was serious.[62] U.S. opinion began to view Britain
as a beleaguered David battling an Axis Goliath, an impression re-

inforced by the air battles over Britain in the late summer.[63] Mers el-Kébir was also a first step in making the Free French a tougher, more resilient organization. It was the beginning of the end of the illusion among Frenchmen that somehow their differences were only temporary misunderstandings among colleagues. Increasingly, Vichy treated the followers of Charles de Gaulle as men with a price on their heads, traitors who assisted the British plot to take advantage of France's defeat to steal her colonies.

Finally, Mers el-Kébir stunned Hitler, who thought that the British had gone mad. In the short term, it provoked an "uneasy interest" in the Mediterranean—uneasy because it forced his attention on the need for sea power and operations across water, with which he was never comfortable. Also, the more Hitler studied his strategic options in that sea, the more the complexity of the trade-offs there disheartened him. Mers el-Kébir sparked Hitler's first known interest in Crete, and he urged the Italians to seize it, as well as Cyprus. Mussolini, however, was fixated on Greece and the Ionian Islands.[64] Mers el-Kébir helped to persuade Hitler that the French, of whom he was not overly fond, would defend themselves against the British. The Armistice Commission meeting at Wiesbaden decided that, under the circumstances, it would not insist on the disarmament of French ships. In effect it suspended Article 8, which had been used to justify the British attack.[65] Therefore, Hitler decided to maintain the French empire intact rather than parcel it out between Franco and Mussolini. This complicated his relations with these two dictators, and therefore limited his strategic choices in the Mediterranean. However, Britain's resolve to fight on was a setback for Hitler, who had hoped to reach some sort of compromise whereby Britain would tolerate German hegemony on the Continent in return for Germany's allowing Britain to maintain its empire. If Britain refused to compromise, the reason must be that London counted on the eventual entry into the war of the USSR. Therefore, Hitler chose to ignore those advisers who suggested that the Mediterranean was the place where Germany might best pressure Britain into a compromise peace. The impediments to doing this were, in fact, immense, not the least because neither Franco nor Mussolini would give him access to that theater for the time being. Mers el-Kébir and the complexity helped to convince Hitler that he must attack Russia to strike "the last Continental dagger" from Churchill's hand. Continental warfare and race war, at least, Hitler could understand. The Mediterranean bored and exasperated him.[66]

CHAPTER TWO

"The Norway of the Mediterranean"

F RANCE'S BREATHTAKING defeat in May–June 1940, far from
simplifying Hitler's task, left him to deal with the unfinished business of Britain's continued defiance. On 10 July 1940, the Luftwaffe
launched the *Kanalkampf*, the first of a series of phased attacks on
Britain's air defenses backed by the threat of a seaborne invasion.
Hitler's goal was to persuade Britain to concede defeat and acquiesce
in German domination of the European continent in return for the
freedom to rule its maritime empire. The skies of Britain in that exceptionally fine summer and early autumn of 1940 were etched into
patterns of vapor trails as Messerschmitt Bf. 109s battled RAF Hurricanes and Spitfires to clear away opposition to German bombers—
Dornier 17s, Heinkel 111s, and Junker 88s and 87s. Hitler failed utterly.
Churchill remained determined to resist, the Luftwaffe's attacks
were poorly coordinated and without clear objectives, and the Royal
Air Force slashed debilitating chunks out of the waves of German
bombers and their fighter escorts. London's anxious anticipation of a
German *coup de grâce* against the British Isles in early summer had
evolved by mid-September into cautious optimism that the Führer
had granted a stay of execution. By late summer, small indications that
Hitler planned to attack the Soviet Union in the spring of 1941 had begun to emerge. Once past mid-September, Whitehall concluded that
the Wehrmacht's timetable had become too tight both to invade
Britain, then to swivel east to attack the USSR.[1]

The Battle of Britain officially ended on 30 October 1940, and the air war over Britain settled into a succession of night bombings of British cities that was dubbed "the Blitz." There was every indication of Washington's growing association of its interests with those of Britain's survival, especially now that it was clear that Britain had every intention of fighting on. "Our confident and resolute bearing was admired by our friends," Churchill wrote, "but its foundations were deemed unsure . . . It is odd that, while at the time everyone concerned was quite calm and cheerful, writing about it afterwards makes one shiver." At least the German failure in the Battle of Britain eased Churchill's strategic dilemma of how to defend the Mediterranean without "robbing" the defense of the British Isles.[2]

Balked on the Channel, Hitler turned toward the Mediterranean, where his strategic options appeared more complex and the benefits less obvious, especially in the light of his desire to attack the USSR sooner rather than later. He needed to appease Vichy lest the French fleet and empire tilt toward the British camp. This meant that the menu of inducements offered Franco was too meager to tempt the Spaniard out of neutrality. Franco dithered over plans to cooperate with Hitler to take Gibraltar, demanding a price that Hitler was unwilling and unable to pay.

Hitler's ally, Mussolini, had entered the war with the spectacular but uncontrolled trajectory of a bottle rocket. He had waved away all German offers of assistance to reap an unimpressive dividend of Sidi Barrani fifty miles inside Egypt and had undertaken a couple of inconclusive engagements with the Royal Navy. Hitler's immediate goal was to terminate British resistance. But he did not want to achieve a British defeat in such a way that the collapse of the British empire would benefit nations other than Germany. His staff offered him only operational solutions to strategic dilemmas. In short, Hitler was "an opportunist who had run out of opportunities," which merely confirmed his inclination to attack the Soviet Union.[3]

As Hitler mulled his options in the Mediterranean, Mussolini, too, wished to advance the war in that theater beyond stalemate. Unfortunately for the Italian dictator, his commander in Egypt, Rodolfo Graziani, responded to repeated requests to seize Marsa Matruh with demands for more equipment and more time. What Graziani failed to understand was that his boss required a thumping military success both to nourish a starving Fascist propaganda machine and to convince Hitler that German troops would constitute a superfluous addition to the Mediterranean theater. Mussolini also suffered from strategic attention deficit disorder. Unable to advance his cause in Egypt, he shifted his attentions to the Balkans. In August, he moved troops to the borders of both Yugoslavia and Greece. However, Hitler's insistence that he wanted no conflict in the Balkans, and the requirement to appease civilian discontent with the demobilization of almost one-half of the Italian army—600,000 of 1,100,000 soldiers—in October 1940 ostensibly to help with the harvest, appeared temporarily to deflate Mussolini's belligerency. But this was to underestimate the unpredictability of *Il Duce's* mercurial temperament. Mussolini's decision to attack Greece had several sources. First, it offered a way to circumvent the refusal of his military commanders, led by Graziani, to go on the offensive. Indeed, Badoglio acquiesced in the October demobilization of 600,000 men precisely because he believed that it would rule out an offensive against Yugoslavia and Greece.[4] But when his commanders checked him by a flourish of lethargy on one front, Mussolini simply shifted his focus to another. Second, Mussolini believed that snap decisions taken on the basis of the most minimal evidence of fact demonstrated decisive leadership and a lively strategic mind, especially when they required spectacular reversals of course. His final motive was supplied, at least in his own mind, by Hitler. Given the fact that, for Mussolini, the Axis had the negative objective of excluding Germany from the Mediterranean, he believed he recognized German recommendations of caution for what they were—jealous Teutonic attempts to preempt Italian success.[5]

Mussolini's decision to invade Greece was triggered by news in mid-October that Germany had established a strong military and economic presence in Bucharest at the request of the new Romanian prime minister, General Ion Antonescu. The Italian dictator saw this as one more of Hitler's unilateral acts, like the seizure of Prague in March 1939, taken without consultation. Romania was a country where Italy had significant economic interests and political aspirations. "Hitler keeps confronting me with a *fait accompli*," Mussolini shouted. "This time I shall pay him back in his own coin; he will learn from the newspapers that I have occupied Greece. The equilibrium will be restored."[6]

Mussolini's desire to extract payback from his ally was encouraged by his foreign minister and son-in-law, Count Galeazzo Ciano. Indeed, because of Ciano's impassioned advocacy, the Italian invasion of Greece became known as "Ciano's war," and did little to increase the popularity of a man with a reputation for unctuous ambition. From a prosperous Leghorn family, the son of one of the leading figures of the early Fascist party, the young Ciano, fresh from his legal studies, had frequented what passed in Rome for smart cafe society. In 1925 he surrendered his aspirations to become a journalist and playwright to join the diplomatic corps. Considered witty, gifted, and suave in a superficial sort of way, Ciano spent the next five years in Brazil and China. In 1929 he returned to Rome, where his sister introduced him to Edda, Mussolini's daughter. Marrying into the Fascist firm accelerated a career that had already shown meteoric promise. In 1933 Mussolini named Ciano to head the Foreign Ministry press office. Two years later he was minister of press and propaganda, where he specialized in translating his father-in-law's thoughts for the press. So taken was the dictator by Ciano's rhetorical abilities and by his willingness to volunteer to serve in the Abyssinian invasion of 1935 that he promoted him to foreign minister in 1936, at the age of thirty-three. The Fascist old guard considered Ciano an *arriviste* who had not paid his dues, as had they, by a slow ascension through party ranks. Churchill believed the young Italian foreign minister's character to be weak rather than villainous, so that he was tempted by the allure of "affluence and office" into "wrong courses."[7] Ciano's conceit, his condescension toward subordinates and others whom he considered his social or intellectual inferiors, earned him many enemies. Admiral Franco Maugeri discovered that by 1941, the once-dashing bomber pilot and handsome young prodigy of the diplomatic corps had become so bloated by soft living that he resembled an emperor of the late Roman period. His dark eyes still flashed with a lively intelligence, and he could still muster a "honeyed, sticky charm" for the benefit of those from whom he wished a favor. But his oiled hair and swarthy "night-club complexion" made him look more like a professional gigolo than foreign minister of a major European power.[8]

Ciano's impact on Italian foreign policy was constrained by Mussolini's whimsical disposition and by an almost total absence of moral responsibility. Ciano saw more clearly than did his father-in-law that tying Italian fortunes to those of Germany risked disaster. However, he lacked the influence or the moral fiber to derail either the May 1939 "Pact of Steel" or Italy's declaration of war in June 1940, both of which he opposed. Instead, Ciano encouraged Mussolini to seek compensation for each of Hitler's surprises. In this way, he played midwife to some of Mussolini's more destructive strategic decisions. In April 1939, Ciano had contrived the Italian invasion of Albania in response to Hitler's March 1939 takeover of Prague. Possession of Albania, Ciano argued, would counter the *Anschluss* (the 1938 annexation of Austria), compensate for the Czech takeover, solidify Italian control of the Adriatic, and provide a platform for further expansion against Yugoslavia and Greece. Besides, military occupation would merely formalize a de facto Italian sphere of influence over Albania that had existed since 1918. Albania was occupied at the cost of twelve Italian dead, caused mainly by equipment failures rather than Albanian resistance. However, just as the German absorption of Prague had triggered Anglo-French guarantees to Poland, so the Italian assault on Albania produced similar assurances to Greece.[9]

A year and a half later, Ciano prepared an Italian response to Hitler's appropriation of Romania into the German sphere of influence. Like Mussolini, Ciano had been incensed by Hitler's surprise occupation of Romania. The two men had envisaged Italy as Bucharest's "protecting power."[10] With Ciano's encouragement, Greece was selected as Mussolini's designated victim. The Italian dictator had no long-term strategic goals there. His attack on Greece was directed as much, perhaps more, at Germany than at his Mediterranean neighbor. Greece became a hapless casualty of Mussolini's delusional competition with Hitler, a *fait accompli* that would demonstrate Italy's command of the strategic initiative in the Mediterranean. In the process, Mussolini would also unhinge Hitler's strategy of creating a

Balkan bloc of nations tied to Berlin.[11] An attack on Greece would divert attention from Graziani's failure to take Marsa Matruh. Mussolini denounced Greece as a de facto British ally, a platform for British naval and air power, the "Norway of the Mediterranean."[12] Finally, Greece was selected because neither Mussolini nor Ciano considered Athens capable of serious resistance.

And in truth, in 1940 Greece appeared to be a nation on life support. Pressure to join the Allies in World War I had led Greece to the very brink of civil war, and it never seemed to leave it. British threats to bombard Athens in 1917 resolved the quarrel between pro-Allied Prime Minister Eleuthérios Venizélos and pro-German King Constantine I in favor of the former. Constantine trotted into exile. The outcome of the Great War made Greece's decision to join the Allies appear a happy one. The defeat of Greece's traditional enemy Turkey allowed Greek soldiers to invade Anatolia and to occupy Bursa and Edirne (Adrianople). The Treaty of Sèvres of August 1920 confirmed the Greek takeover of most of Turkey's European territory, as well as the islands of Imbros and Tenedos. Greek administrative authority was recognized around the heavily Greek enclave of Smyrna (Izmir). After five years, the inhabitants would vote on whether to join Greece. Sèvres also awarded the Dodecanese, centered on the island of Rhodes, to Italy.

The Greeks appeared poised to realize many of their irredentist goals against Turkey, a country that contained a two-million-strong Greek minority. But Athens had failed to take Turkish resistance into account. The Turkish parliament refused to ratify Sèvres. In December 1920, Greeks voted for a return of the pro-German Constantine. The British and French, annoyed by this anti-Allied gesture and fearful that the Greeks sought to stir up trouble in the Aegean, cut off war loans to Athens. The French sent direct military assistance to the Turks, while London remained content to lift the naval blockade against Turkey and halt weapons deliveries to Greece. Greek royalists, the wind in their sails following their 1920 electoral victory and the return of Constantine, and eager to preempt Venizélos's expansionist agenda, attacked Turkey in March 1921. At first successful, the Greek offensive came to a baleful denouement when Turkish forces under

Great War hero Mustafa Kemal Pasa smashed the Greek army in Anatolia the following year. "The Greek state and the entire Greek Nation are descending now to a Hell from which no power will be able to raise them up and save them," predicted the archbishop of Smyrna. He was correct. Smyrna and countless Greek villages were reduced to smoldering ruins, Greek Orthodox clergy were murdered by knife-wielding Moslem mobs, and 1,500,000 Greek refugees fled, bringing to an end two thousand years of Hellenic presence in Asia Minor. "The problem of the minorities is here solved for all time," wrote the correspondent of the *Chicago Daily News* as British, French, American, and Italian warships embarked terrorized Greek refugees from Smyrna's burning quays.[13] The Treaty of Lausanne wiped out Greek gains at Sèvres. Mussolini attempted to capitalize on Greece's misfortune to occupy Corfu in 1923, but was forced by international pressure to back down after a few weeks. The defeat rebounded badly on Greek royalists—the monarchy was again cast into exile and a Greek republic was proclaimed under Venizélos in 1924.

"The Disaster" haunted Greece's interwar years. Outcasts from Anatolia joined Greeks who had fled Bulgaria and the Soviet Union to increase Greece's population by 28 percent—in short, almost one Greek in three was a refugee. The Greek economy was simply too undeveloped to absorb this expatriate invasion. Denied the traditional outlet of emigration to the United States, the new arrivals crowded into cities, competing for scarce jobs and annoying their neighbors with their "Turkish" habits and music. As the immigrants overwhelmingly supported Venizélos and the republicans, "old" Greeks in Attica, the Peloponnese, and Crete gravitated toward the monarchists. Venizélos championed a sweeping land reform that turned Greece into a nation of peasant smallholders, and tried to encourage foreign investment, much of it German. But the Depression brought the collapse of the drachma, stimulated social unrest, and returned the royalists to power in March 1933. To reduce the money supply and tax the population, the government resorted to the sophisticated financial expedient of calling in all banknotes, slicing them in half, and returning half to the original owners. In 1935, Venizélos overplayed his hand, attempting a putsch against the royalists. Failure forced him into exile, terminated the republic, and resulted in the recall of George II, Constantine's eldest son, to the throne on the basis of a blatantly rigged plebiscite. The army was purged of republicans; retribution and even assassinations that had begun in the republican period continued. Republicans quarreled among themselves. Some of the more disaffected drifted to the Communists. In the midst of this economic chaos and political confusion, George II appointed sixty-five-year-old General Ioannis Metaxas as prime minister on 3 August 1936.

To the uninitiated, Greece in the years before the war appeared to be a mongrel regime, one in economic vassalage to Germany, with the ideological trappings of a fascist state but with a pro-British foreign policy. This bizarre hybrid was crafted by Metaxas, both in response to his vision of Greek political stability and in an attempt to elude war. In civilian clothes, Metaxas looked more like a doctor or a senior civil servant than a military man. His receding hairline, glasses, and mustache framed a face that looked benign, almost avuncular. Yet this icon of benevolent vigilance belied a career of more than ordinary turbulence and lack of scruple, even by the Olympian standards of interwar Greece. Chief of staff of the Greek army in 1917 and an avowed royalist, Metaxas had opposed Greece's entry into World War I, and paid the price when he followed Constantine into exile. He returned in 1920 to found the Liberal Monarchist Party, and demonstrated his sagacity in April 1921 when he explained to the Greek cabinet that the Turks "mean to fight for their freedom and independence . . . They realize that Asia Minor is their country and that we are invaders. For them, for their national feelings, the historical rights on which we base our claims have no influence. Whether they are right or wrong is another question. What matters is how they feel."[14] An ability to see the other fellow's point of view, or to be correct, did not immediately cause Greeks to clasp Metaxas to their bosoms—he was forced to flee abroad again three years later in the wake of a failed royalist coup that he had engineered. The resurrection of the monarchy found Metaxas in charge first of the Ministry of the Interior, followed by that of the army. He persecuted political opponents, and did not shy away from ordering police and troops to fire on striking workers. Greece was on the verge of revolution, Metaxas assured a wavering George II, who reluctantly named him prime minister.

The king's decision proved a disaster for Greek democracy. Barely twenty-four hours into office, Metaxas sent Parliament packing, suspended the constitution, and decreed a dictatorship. Metaxas's "Regime of Four August" appeared to the casual observer as a poor man's Third Reich, minus the racism. The prime minister proclaimed the advent of the "Third Hellenic Civilization." What he left unexplained, however, was how a country of 7.5 million people, beset by serious economic problems, riven by internal discord, and stalked by external enemies, could expect to replicate the dazzling achievements of fifth century B.C. Athens or Byzantium under Constantine. Military parades and youth rallies that featured push-ups and jogging in place were combined with police terror, censorship, book burnings (including Sophocles and Thucydides!), and an estimated 50,000 deportations, executed under the stern oversight of the trinity of Metaxas "The First Peasant," Metaxas "The First Worker," and Metaxas "The National Father." But the Greek dictator lacked Hitler's rabid charisma or Mussolini's theatrical flair. The Greek people observed, acquiesced for want of a viable alternative, but remained agnostic. In foreign affairs, Metaxas advanced Greek claims to Macedonia, Cyprus, the Dodecanese, and, on a good day, Constantinople. For the moment, however, he was forced to play defense.[15]

Metaxas's problem was that Mussolini and Ciano wanted to fight him. Even though their generals reminded them in October 1940 that half the Italian army had departed on extended furlough, while Graziani immobilized most of the other half in the Egyptian desert, Greece appeared little able to defend itself. Mussolini had spent a fortune bribing Greek politicians and generals,[16] a fact of which Metaxas's political police must have been aware. From Rome's perspective, Greece appeared to be low-hanging fruit. The Greek army counted fourteen infantry divisions and one of cavalry. Although efforts had been made to upgrade Greek forces in the mid-1930s, its weaponry was obsolete, it had almost no tanks and few antitank guns, and was deficient in artillery. The Italians reasoned that terrain, the remoteness of the chosen battlefield along the Albanian border, and the lack of roads and transport meant that northern Greece, although hazardous to attack, would also prove difficult to defend. Furthermore, Bulgaria, on the losing side in 1918, was believed eager to recoup territory in Thrace and Macedonia that it had surrendered to Greece. The close links between Bulgaria's King Boris III and Nazi Germany meant that, in the event of conflict, Athens must divert scarce forces to guard its frontier with Bulgaria. The Greek navy was hardly more than a coast guard, and 180 of the 300 planes in the Greek air force inventory were museum pieces. Metaxas also faced the dilemma that he needed to mobilize his scattered population early if he wanted to ensure a sufficient number of troops on line. At the same time, he did not want to offer Mussolini the excuse of a "provocation." Therefore, he prepared strong defensive positions along the Albanian border and prayed they would resist long enough for him fully to mobilize his army. Once the Italians attacked, he hoped that a counteroffensive northward along the coast with the goal of seizing Santa Quaranta and Valona would force the Italians to supply through Durazzo, almost 150 miles north of the Greek-Albanian border as the crow flies.[17]

THIS "WRETCHED SOLDIERY"

The greatest disconnect in Mussolini's aggressive foreign policy was how to fight his "parallel war" in the Mediterranean at the expense of Britain and France, while avoiding German intervention there, with an Italian army that was inferior to that of its Allied enemies and Axis partner. The classic explanation of the Italian army's poor performance is that lack of enthusiasm for the war among the Italian people found its way into the rank and file. And while it is certainly true that by 1943, the accumulation of defeats dampened morale among both civilians and soldiers, this cannot provide the full explanation for a lackluster Italian military performance.[18] British intelligence officer Sir David Hunt argued that on the contrary, based on POW interrogations and captured letters, Italian morale was high in 1940. "For the first five months of the war, at least, all the prisoners we and the Greeks took spoke with great confidence of a successful outcome and boasted of the future greatness of Italy, victorious at the side of Italy."[19]

Eric Newby noted that the unity of the Italian people behind the regime made the escape of British POWs in Italy, of which he was one, a hopeless enterprise until the collapse of the regime in September 1943, because "there were no members of the Resistance or railway employees of the Left, as there were in France, to help escaping prisoners out of the country along an organized route."[20] An Italian major and lawyer in civilian life captured at Derna in January 1941 explained to British war correspondent Alan Moorehead that "there are many like me who have got nothing out of Fascism, but we don't dislike it enough to rebel against it. Even if we hated it, what could we do about it?" Mussolini's regime would topple from exhaustion, not indignation. "They could surrender to us," Moorehead concluded. "But never to themselves."[21]

Mussolini's problem was not lack of popular support. Rather, there was a yawning gap between Mussolini's ambitious foreign policy objectives and a traditional lack of interest, not to say disdain, for military affairs in Italy.[22] Mussolini's problem was that Italy's military institutions were incapable of delivering the "parallel war" independent of German interference and control that he sought. Given the dulled edge of his military instrument, the agitated insouciance with which Mussolini prepared to attack Greece constituted grand scale criminal negligence. The high command, if not the creature of the Fascist system, was certainly one that valued compliance over competence. To strengthen his control over the military, Mussolini reduced the power of the *Capo di Stato Maggiore Generale* (chief of the general staff), General Pietro Badoglio, to purely advisory functions. This correspondingly enhanced the power of the service chiefs and of their individual ministries. The best that can be said about the Italian service chiefs, as British historian of the Italian military MacGregor Knox notes, is that, left to themselves, most Italian generals would not have fought at all. But by resisting Mussolini with a concerted show of inactivity, Italian generals permitted their boss to fill a strategic vacuum with projects of his own. The result was an absence of coordination between foreign and military policy. Italian initiatives were incremental and ad hoc, while the services failed to produce coherent, coordinated war plans to achieve the objectives. And why should they?

Mussolini insisted on keeping the strings of power in his hands through direct contact with field commanders and by reserving even the most trifling decision making to himself. This invited chaos and made a mockery of the *Commando Supremo*, organized in May 1941 by Marshal Ugo Cavallero to replicate the Wehrmacht high command (OKW). In the minds of Italian generals, Mussolini's command "system" virtually relieved them of all responsibility for the initiation and conduct of operations.[23]

In some respects, this was probably just as well, because, with a few exceptions,[24] Italian senior commanders seldom demonstrated even a rudimentary grasp of the requirements of modern warfare. Lower down, professional Italian officers flocked to desk jobs in the many staffs which the army's proliferation of infantry divisions created, leaving the actual field leadership to poorly prepared reserve officers or aging World War I veterans. The average Italian infantry battalion in North Africa had one, or at most two, regular officers. In a country without a developed military culture or traditions, the army did not enjoy a prestige high enough to attract the more dynamic elements of the middle classes. One lesson Italian military planners had taken away from World War I was that the conscription of too many skilled workers had damaged the war effort. By 1940, therefore, generous exemptions from military service combined with "genteel evasion" by the cultured classes to deny the army much potential leadership. Italian officers developed a caste mentality that caused them to look upon their soldiers with condescension. They insisted on superior rations and privileges as befitting their rank, and lived apart from their men. The NCO corps was too diminutive for the numbers of infantry soldiers in the ranks and lacked initiative. Poorly trained, without solid cadres, Italian soldiers often surrendered when vigorously attacked.

The burden of military service fell heavily on the peasantry, which made up fully half of Italy's population in 1940. Largely illiterate, raised on the threshold of desperation, as impervious to modernization as they were distrustful of authority, these men made poor material from which to fashion a modern army. Carlo Levi, exiled to a small village in the southern Italian province of Lucania in 1935 because of his opposition to the Ethiopian War, discovered a world of "decay and spiritual poverty" governed by a pervasive despair. Peasants were pawns in local power struggles, bullied by the marshal of the *carabinieri*, the priest, or the landowner whose possession of a few more acres of scorched soil than his neighbors gave him squire status—men whose "self-hate," according to Levi, made them "spiteful, bitter . . . capable indeed of any evil." The Fascist invasion of Abyssinia was perceived, even in these scarred valleys, as a reckless enterprise, a "last card." But they accepted it, as they accepted Mussolini, as one of life's tribulations, like hail and failed harvests. "Even if it ended badly, what did it matter?"[25]

The soldiers squeezed out by this brutish system were capable of enduring great hardship, which was just as well, as they were forced to live in filthy barracks, consume substandard rations, and fight with poor equipment. Conditions were especially bad in Libya, where soldiers lacked firewood and water, so they often ate their food cold and, as a consequence of poor diet and living conditions, fell ill in droves. The Italian *Intendenza* (supply corps) was quite inadequate to feed the large numbers—eventually 3.5 million soldiers—incorporated into the forces. It was not clear whether this was a problem of distribution or of hoarding. George Greenfield, a lieutenant in the Buffs, contrasted the multitude of ragged, thirsty, hungry Italians, many of whom were barefoot, who lined the roads begging to be taken prisoner after El Alamein, with the opulent stores overrun in rear areas, a disparity noted by Alan Moorehead two years earlier.[26] One result was that Italian units preferred to stick close to the depots of the overly centralized *Intendenza* for fear that even the most modest displacement would disrupt the supply chain and cause them to starve to death.[27] Field ovens consisted of wood-burning stoves remaindered from the turn of the century that were totally useless in the desert. Rommel complained that Italian soldiers regularly begged food and drink from German troops because they had no field kitchens of their own in North Africa.[28] French colonists described the Italian soldiers who descended on Tunisia in November 1942 as so "revoltingly poor" that they devoured onions unearthed from gardens and even stole from desperately impoverished Arabs just "to get a few *sous*. They are a people without shame."[29] Eric Newby noted that British POWs universally felt humiliated at having been captured by enemies who were so obviously second-rate. "The wretched [Italian] soldiery . . . with their miserable uniforms, ersatz boots, unmilitary behavior and stupid bugle calls . . . What boobs they were . . . like souls in limbo or a lot of untouchables in Hindu India, lost in the low-lying ground which no one ever visited, somewhere between the railway workshops and the cantonment."[30]

Italian soldiers, especially in the more elite units like the Ariete, the Alpine troops, and the Folgore parachute division, might fight tenaciously, especially if coupled with German units as in North Africa. On occasion, even soldiers of less exalted units, if placed in defensible positions where the dangers of flight exceeded those of fighting on, might rise to a heroic gesture, the "valor of despair" born of an anarchic desire to break with conformity, according to Knox. But initiative, teamwork, precision were qualities seldom encountered in the Italian army.[31] Churchill noted that although the British on the Egyptian-Libyan frontier were heavily outnumbered by their Italian enemies in the summer of 1940, they quickly gained moral ascendancy over Italians reluctant to venture outside their fortified camps and quick to surrender. British forces "soon conceived themselves to be masters of the desert . . . they could go where they liked, collecting trophies from sharp encounters."[32] An American historian of the Italian army, Brian Sullivan, argues that the Italians made a measured recovery after the debacle of Greece and Operation Compass in early 1941. This was in part because Badoglio's dismissal opened the way for Ugo Cavallero's superior management and because the Italians were stiffened by the arrival of Rommel and the Afrika Korps. But even this modest invigoration was limited because the Italian army in Russia was given priority in matériel, because of the lack of motorization of Italian forces, and, according to Rommel, because of the propensity of Italian troops to desert in large numbers. The celebrated German commander complained that going into battle with the Italians was like trying to bake cookies with a three-year-old. "The Italians are a millstone around my neck," Rommel grumbled on the eve of the Battle of El Alamein in August 1942. "They're useless except for defense, and even then they're useless if the British infantry attacks with fixed bayonets."[33] Indeed, because Rommel was forced to intersperse his German and Italian forces at El Alamein to stiffen the latter, he was unable to put together a mobile reserve of hard-hitting German armored units to stanch Montgomery's breakthrough in that battle. When, in July 1943, U.S. Civil Affairs Lieutenant William Lessa asked a group of ill-guarded Bersaglieri in Algeria why they did not attempt to escape, "They responded with loud guffaws—imagine wanting to escape after all the trouble they had gone to get captured. Their officers had shot those who wouldn't fight. And before being captured they had not eaten for 5 days because they didn't want to go back for their rations, fearing the Americans would arrive in their absence and not capture them."[34]

The Italian army's social backwardness was matched by its technological and organizational retardation. Despite the fact that Fascist propaganda trumpeted the virtues of Blitzkrieg warfare, Italian Chief of Staff Pietro Badoglio showed scant interest in tanks, other than light and thinly armored models armed with machine guns and flamethrowers. Although on paper the Italian army possessed an armored corps and two motorized infantry divisions in June 1940, these were a pale reflection of their Northern European counterparts, being adequate only for mountain and imperial warfare. This stood to reason, for, in Badoglio's view, his most likely theater of operations would be the Alps, and numbers, not mobility, would prove decisive. And who was in a position to contradict him? In October 1940, the only hints that the Italians might be headed for military disaster were the disappointing but limited results of the June 1940 attack on France and Graziani's timid advance to Sidi Barrani. The Italians had done well enough in Abyssinia and in Spain. Complacency, combined with a dearth of the merest glimmer of professional curiosity in the Italian military, meant that Italy fielded a primarily foot-mobile infantry army organized around a World War I faith in massed formations, frontal attacks, and static defense. It was an army incapable of inflicting surprise, but eminently suited to being taken unawares. The essential difference was that in 1915, the Italian army had been relatively better equipped and more numerous than it was in 1940.

Italy increased the size of its army from 71 divisions in 1940 to 91 by 1943. But this simply bloated an already overstretched infrastructure short on technical upgrades. The Italian army was undergunned, underarmored, poorly trained, and lacked antiaircraft protection. Its ratio of vehicles to men stood at 1 : 20, compared to 1 : 3.6 in the German forces. This made it difficult for Rommel to coordinate operations in the desert between allies of such radically different capabilities. The relative immobility of Italian forces helps to explain why so many Italian soldiers were overrun and captured in the desert during the winter of 1940–41. In the aftermath of El Alamein in October–November 1942, foot-mobile Italians were unable to follow Rommel's epic retreat from Egypt to Tunisia, and surrendered in droves. In the autumn of 1940, only nineteen Italian divisions were regarded as fully equipped, and even these were two-brigade "binary" divisions, less than half the size of their British counterparts.[35]

Much of the army's most modern equipment had been expended in Abyssinia and Spain, and most of what remained was outdated. Italian industry lacked the resources to equip a modern army. Based on 1939 production figures, the Italian army would not be equipped for war until 1949! The bureaucratic nightmare of the arms procurement process joined industrial inefficiency and shortages of raw materials to delay replacement of modern equipment. Italy was almost entirely dependent on Germany for much of its raw materials and oil, as well as communications, transport, and, ultimately, senior leadership. When British forces overran the Italians at Sidi Barrani in December 1940, they were impressed by the proliferation of field telephones, wireless, and signaling equipment. However, they found that Italian vehicles lacked robustness, and the wafer-armored flamethrowers and machine guns on wheels (two-man L3/35 tanks modeled on the Bren machine-gun carrier) that passed for tanks in the Italian army appeared to be death traps. The only true tank in the Italian inventory, the M11/39, was poorly designed and carried only a 37 mm gun. Its riveted armor and high silhouette made it a sitting duck for antitank guns. An M13/40 with a 47 mm gun appeared in 1941. Underpowered and temperamental, these were often abandoned by Italian crews in the Western Desert, where they were overhauled and used by the British.[36] The artillery was the best arm overall in the army, because it attracted a better class of officer and NCO. Nevertheless, its inventory consisted of refurbished World War I guns, many of which had been captured from Austria-Hungary, that were light (65 and 75 mm), horse-drawn, and were far outdistanced by more modern British pieces.[37] The gun sight on the 47 mm antitank gun was so inaccurate at long distances that the operators had to risk suicide to get close enough to British tanks to make their shots count. No system of ground panels and radios existed to coordinate close air support.

Italian military intelligence had its strengths, notably in ciphers and deception. Italian theft of U.S. diplomatic black code from the Rome embassy in September 1941 provided Rommel with access to the dispatches of Colonel Bonner Fellers, the American attaché in Cairo, who reported in great detail on British dispositions and intentions in early 1942. But even this success underscored the weaknesses of the Italian services—the pursuit of the intelligence coup over the systematic collection and analysis of information as the basis for planning.[38] The chief defect of Italian secret services, according to Alan Moorehead, "was an interior rottenness . . . that grew naturally out of the national weakness for exaggeration."[39] Indeed, Moorehead believed that the Italian army's Servizio Informazioni Militari (SIM), like the Italian press, spewed an endless stream of misinformation, leaving the end user unable to distinguish fact from fiction. POW Eric Newby found Italian intelligence interrogations so amateurish that "we learned far more from our interrogators than they did from us."[40] Italian intelligence was a patchwork of competing and overlapping service, colonial, police, and Fascist party agencies whose focus was on espionage and police work. The SIM was distrusted as an agency that supplied information to bolster Ciano's policies. Otherwise, its reports on enemy strength were both vague and exaggerated, sometimes ludicrously so, a situation that probably pleased Italian commanders eager for intelligence-supplied alibis as an excuse to avoid action. It did them no good, however, because Mussolini relied on intuition rather than intelligence, especially unfavorable intelligence, when making his decisions. Nor did Italian commanders factor intelligence assessments into operational planning. Their communications security was so weak that Cairo regularly read the lower-grade ciphers and much of the higher-level material. This allowed British General Richard O'Connor to cut off Graziani's Tenth Army at Beda Fomm in February 1941.[41]

In assessing the Italian air force, it is important to keep in mind that most air forces experienced difficult adjustments at the beginning of the war, not least of all the RAF in the Mediterranean. However, shortcomings in the Italian air force were particularly endemic and exaggerated. Like the other Italian services, Italian flyers never managed to find their rhythm. The Regia Aeronautica had enjoyed the honor of being regarded as the quintessentially Fascist service since its founding in 1923. Air power was viewed by Mussolini as a technical means to break out of Italy's strategic and economic confinement. He also showcased the latest aircraft of the "wings of fascism" to promote the technical achievements of the regime. This brought prestige and patronage to the Italian air force, but little else. Like the other services, the air force ignored or misapplied technology. Many Italian planes were beautifully designed, like pieces of sculpture, but they often ignored fundamental aerodynamic requirements, like lift and acceleration. For instance, the Piaggio P-108, Italy's only four-engine bomber, which entered service in June 1942, was nicknamed "the flying feebleness." The Savoia-Marchetti SM-79 trimotor was first sent to Spain and remained the workhorse of the Regia Aeronautica, although far surpassed by the air forces of other nations. SM-79 pilots did notch some successes against British convoys to Malta in 1941–42, including the sinking of the battleship *Nelson* on 27 September. Italian air force doctrine had developed little beyond a lingering faith in Giulio Douhet's strategic bombing principles, which were advanced as "guidelines" but seldom analyzed or debated. Italian high-altitude bombing proved remarkably ineffective over Malta and North Africa. But beyond the strategic and operational miscalculations of the effects of strategic bombing common to all air forces, the Italian effort failed in part because bombsights were rudimentary, there was no radio contact between the pilot and bombardier, and navigational aids were almost nonexistent. Indeed, the absence of navigational aids and blind-flying instruments caused the crashes of seventy-five Italian planes in flight to Belgium in September 1940 to participate in the

Battle of Britain. Italian bombs, ranging from 100 to 500 pounds, were too light to cause much damage. The incendiary bombs the Italians carried over Malta in 1940 showed an unfortunate tendency to detonate on release.

The outbreak of war revealed that the Regia Aeronautica had ignored the problem of attacking ships, a major oversight, as their rationale in resisting the navy's attempts to include carriers in their inventory was that land-based air force planes offered a better alternative. However, the Italian air force had demonstrated no interest in cooperating with the navy on designing a torpedo bomber. Italian dive-bombers were so dangerous that they appeared to have been designed to hit the ground at the same time as the bombs they released. Italy finally resorted to the purchase of Ju87 Stukas from Germany, but they lacked armor-piercing bombs effective against the British fleet. Fighter pilots resisted the monoplane in the 1930s because the biplane allowed them better to showcase their aerobatic virtuosity. Lightness and maneuverability, they argued, was more important in a dogfight than speed, sturdiness, and firepower. Nothing in their experience in Abyssinia or the Spanish Civil War could shake that conviction. The result was a bloated inventory of open-cockpit Fiat CR 42 Falco (Hawk) biplane fighters that saw extensive service in North Africa. The only redeeming quality of the Falco was that in the early stage of the Mediterranean war, they were pitted against Britain's stock of obsolete planes like the Gladiators sent in 1940 to defend Malta. But as Hurricanes and Spitfires began to appear in the Mediterranean, the Falco became hardly more than a flying coffin, although it continued to see service down to Italy's 1943 surrender in escort, reconnaissance, ground attack, and night fighter roles.[42] Fighter pilots, taking their cue from celebrated World War I German fighter ace Manfred von Richtofen, insist that the man behind the controls determines success, not the configuration of the "box."[43] Some of the Regia Aeronautica's "young eagles" proved to be quite *sportifs*, especially when flying Italy's best mass-produced fighter, the relatively fast (372 miles per hour) but undergunned Macchi 202 Folgore (Thunderbolt) equipped with German Daimler-Benz engines, which appeared in the second half of 1941. Speed and altitude give the pilot the option of declining combat and of initiating it in favorable conditions—that is, from above—hence increasing the probability of survival and success. Unfortunately, the Italians never came up with a competitive monoplane fighter that inclined Allied airmen to flee rather than fight. Performance was also circumscribed by the absence of high-octane fuel, which caused the Italians to resort to castor oil. Italian fighters lacked the range to escort bombers. Nor did they train enough pilots, or train them well enough, to compensate for their high attrition rate. The Italian air force allowed itself repeatedly to be caught on the ground by British attacks, largely because it had no integrated system of air defense radar, fighters, and antiaircraft artillery.[44]

Concentration on the sharp end of aerial combat caused the Italians to neglect maintenance and logistics, which made it difficult, once war began, to maintain a high operational tempo. As many as one-third of Italian bombers were often *hors de combat* due to maintenance problems. The absence of sand filters in North Africa produced an epidemic of engine and machine-gun breakdowns. The combination of inadequate operational tempo and an initial inability to hit ships proved a handicap when trying to prevent the arrival of British convoys to Malta. There was a disconnect between a strategic vision for the Italian air force and the technical capabilities of the planes it purchased. Prototypes were seldom engineered for mass production, and Italian production capacity remained derisory in the context of World War II. For instance, between January 1939 and September 1943, when it surrendered to the Allies, Italy produced 13,253 planes, compared to 72,030 for the Germans, 92,034 for the British, and 163,049 for the Americans. In short, the British were producing almost as many planes in a month as the Italians produced in a year.[45] As in Germany, Italian engineers suffered the handicap of having to take orders from bureaucrats who knew even less about designing and producing aircraft than did they. The result was a proliferation of types, many of which seemed to correspond to no tactical or operational requirement.[46]

Refined strategic calculations and net assessments were not Mussolini's strong suit. He had resorted to his usual tactics of bullying and intimidation throughout the summer, which included the torpedoing of the Greek cruiser *Helle* by an "unidentified" submarine in August. News of German troops in Belgrade, together with erroneous spy reports that the Greek army was about to disband,[47] caused him, on 13 October 1940, to order an invasion of Greece for 26 October. Generals assumed that he meant a limited occupation of Epirus, the Greek province opposite Albania, and of Corfu, for which they had a plan. When *Il Duce* confirmed that he wanted to occupy the entire country, they told him it would take twenty divisions and three months to prepare. Badoglio begged him to coordinate his assault with that of Graziani on Marsa Matruh, so as to preclude any British assistance for Greece. But waiting for Graziani to move was like waiting for Godot. Once Badoglio realized that Mussolini was serious, rather than protest, resign, or contemplate suicide as any honorable commander in his position might have done, he upped the ante, urging that the Italians go all the way to Crete. When Mussolini and Ciano met with their army chiefs and Albanian proconsuls on 15 October to discuss an operation that was to be launched on the twenty-sixth—that is, in eleven days!—they became as giddy as boarding school inmates contemplating their summer holiday. On 19 October, Hitler learned from his foreign minister Ribbentrop, who had been tipped off by Ciano's serial indiscretions, that the Italians intended to attack Greece on 26 or 27 October. At first, he was inclined to disbelieve the news. It was simply impossible to prepare such a significant military operation at such short notice. When he learned that it was true, he exploded with rage, less because he opposed the attack in principle than because he knew the Italians would make a pig's breakfast of it. He also concluded that an Italian attack would give the British an excuse to station planes in Greece that could bomb the Ploesti oil fields in Romania.

But that was in the future. The men in the room decided that Greece was to be devoured in two mouthfuls. The first attack out of Albania would assure Italian control of Salonika with one division, while the remaining eight would push down the Ionian coast, incorporating on the way the islands of Corfu, Cephalonia, and Zante. As more troops were fed into the battle, the remainder of Greece would be overrun. Reckless optimism was the order of the day, as Ciano confidently predicted that the Greeks were so indifferent to their government of royalist toadies that they would not lift a finger to defend it. Those who attempted to introduce a note of cautious realism into the discussions—such as suggesting that the Pindus Mountains, whose peaks reach over 2,500 meters in height, was a formidable barrier to attack so late in the season—were reminded of Hannibal's crossing of the Alps. But the analogy was flawed, as the Carthaginian had attacked Romans, not Greeks. Understanding that farce, not logistics, was the order of the day, and that their careers were on the line, soldiers who had prospered under fascism settled into the euphoria of the moment. Only later, as the planning for the operation proceeded at a chaotic pace, did they attempt, without success, to have Mussolini's demobilization order rescinded.[48] But the Duce could not do this without both appearing foolish and risking popular ire.[49]

At 3 a.m. on the morning of 28 October, Metaxas shuffled to the door of his unpretentious villa in the Athens suburb of Kifisia, summoned by a guard who had mistaken the Italian tricolor that adorned the official car parked outside for that of France. Dressed in his nightgown and ravaged by the cancer that would soon claim him, Metaxas looked tired. Nevertheless, he managed a sly smile as he greeted the Italian minister, Emanuele Grazzi, in French with a semblance of false bonhomie. The two men continued to converse in that language as they walked to the parlor. For a royalist and chief of state, Metaxas led an astonishingly bourgeois lifestyle. The two men settled into a pair of inexpensive armchairs where, surrounded by middle-class mementos of Metaxas's soon-to-be-extinguished life, the Italian ambassador handed the Greek an ultimatum crafted with Cianoesque cynicism. The preamble spoke of "violations of neutrality" and "provocations," such as allowing the British secret service to operate from Greek soil, and other such twaddle. It then demanded that Italian forces be allowed to occupy unspecified strategic points in the country as guarantees that Greece would return to the path of neutrality. Otherwise, Italian troops would attack at 6 a.m. The Italian ambassador, obviously ill at ease, was unable to specify what "strategic points" his government wished to occupy. *"Alors, c'est la guerre,"* Metaxas is alleged to have replied.[50]

Jumping the gun by thirty minutes, Italian forces surged into Epirus and secured a bridgehead across the Kalamas River, while the Third Alpine Division marched toward the Metsovon Pass in the Pindus Mountains. That was the limit of the Italian advance. Appalling weather complicated the disadvantages of an absence of adequate roads, distant, low-capacity ports at Durazzo and Valona, and a lack of vehicles to support forces at the front. Italian morale dropped as Greek tenacity transformed the anticipated walkover into a bitter struggle for survival on the bare Greek mountainsides. By 8 November, the Italian offensive had ground to a halt and had even begun to retreat in the face of local Greek counterattacks. The raw recruits and elderly reservists whom Mussolini had called up to replace the more experienced soldiers and NCOs he had demobilized froze in their trenches. Some even begged to be shot to abbreviate their misery. On 14 November, Greek commander General Alexandros Papagos directed his 232,000 troops backed by 556 guns and 100,000 animals to attack all along the front. The Italian air force made no effort to dislocate Greek troop concentrations. Rather than risk costly head-on attacks unsupported by tanks and antitank guns, the Greeks infiltrated overextended Italian units to attack the enemy from the flanks and rear. In bitter fighting, the Greeks threw the Italians back across the Kalamas and captured Leskovik and Koritsa (Korcë) inside Albania, despite constant harassment by the Italian air force, which made a belated appearance. Because Graziani showed no signs of life at Sidi Barrani, the British took over the occupation of Crete, freeing up more Greek troops for the front, while RAF bombers operating out of both Greece and Malta blasted Durazzo and Valona in Albania and Bari and Brindisi in Italy. Boris III of Bulgaria decided to await events, allowing the Greeks, who were steadily mobilizing, to shift fresh troops from Macedonia. By mid-December, the Greeks had secured their front well inside Albania. Pogradez and Lake Okhrida anchored their northern line, which stretched from the Yugoslav border to the Adriatic coast well north of Santa Quaranta. Mussolini briefly contemplated asking Hitler to mediate an armistice with Metaxas, but was talked out of it by Ciano.[51] Because Mussolini's insane demobilization order was rescinded only on 26 November when he ordered a general mobilization, by January 1941 the Greeks had massed thirteen three-regiment divisions against fifteen Italian two-regimen *divisione binaria*. The RAF continued to substitute for the Greek air force, immobilized for lack of spare parts. Greek submarines inflicted respectable levels of loss on Italian transports plying between Italy and Albania.

TARANTO

As Mussolini's army was thrashed on the Adriatic, the Italian dictator received news that Admiral Cunningham had delivered a devastating blow to the Italian fleet. The timing was pure chance. Originally, Cunningham's timetable was dictated by a desire to celebrate Trafalgar Day (21 October) with a convincing demonstration of the Royal Navy's moral ascendancy over its Italian adversary, and in the process take a step toward evening the naval odds in the Mediterranean. Cunningham's plan was to use Swordfish biplanes off the carrier *Illustrious*, which joined the Mediterranean fleet in September, to attack the Italian ships in their home port of Taranto. Taranto was the Pearl Harbor of the Med, the anchorage at the inside apex of the heel of the Italian boot, from which the Italians extended their maritime reach into the central Mediterranean. The plan was fairly audacious, if only because his primary weapon, the Swordfish, was already obsolete when the war broke out. Armed with a torpedo, the ungainly, three-seat, open-cockpit plane, flying at a relatively slow 138 miles per hour, offered a stress-free target for more modern fighters—virtually every plane in the Axis inventory—and was even fair game for antiaircraft artillery. But before it was phased out of service in early 1942, the Swordfish had the distinction of crippling the *Bismarck* so that it could be finished off by surface vessels, and seriously depleting the Italian fleet at Taranto. Moreover, the demands of the Greek campaign and delays in training the pilots in night flying postponed the operation until November 1940.

Cunningham's plan was to arrange his twenty-one Swordfish into two waves. In each wave, two high-flying planes would illuminate the ships with flares and attract the attention of the searchlights and anti-aircraft batteries while the remainder would skim the water, dodging barrage balloons to launch their torpedoes at the anchored ships.

Early aerial reconnaissance carried by Malta-based aircraft revealed that the fleet had sheltered in the inner harbor, the Mar Piccolo. However, by 11 November, they had shifted to the circular outer harbor, the Mar Grande, whose breakwaters were attached to the small outer islands of San Pietro and San Paulo, between Cape Rondinella and Cape San Vito. The attackers, therefore, knew the position of each Italian ship.

At 2100 on the evening of 11 November, the first wave of twelve planes left the *Illustrious*, stationed about 170 miles southeast of Taranto and about 40 miles off the Greek island of Cephalonia. The moon was three-quarters full when they approached the target two hours later. Alas, the barrage of antiaircraft batteries revealed that they had failed to achieve surprise. Nevertheless, the flare droppers left the formation, while two groups of three planes each skimmed thirty feet above the water in the teeth of intense fire from both shore and ship. The group leader launched his torpedo at the battleship *Cavour*, perfectly silhouetted by the slowly descending flares. The *Cavour*'s forecastle erupted in flames. A minute later two torpedoes found the *Littorio*. Two hours later, all but one aircraft—that which had struck the *Cavour*—had safely returned to the *Illustrious*. At midnight the second wave appeared, hitting the *Duilio* and further damaging the *Littorio*, for the sacrifice of one Swordfish. Cunningham meant to repeat the attack on the following night, but poor weather and a desperate, if unsuccessful, Italian effort to locate the *Illustrious* caused him to turn over the task to Wellington bombers out of Malta. Meanwhile, a British squadron sailed up the Strait of Otranto to sink four Italian freighters bound for Albania.

In retrospect, it is easy to minimize the impact of the attack on Taranto. The *Cavour* was eventually raised, although it never again went to sea. Damage to the *Duilio* and the *Littorio*, though severe, was repaired within six months. But that was in the future. For the moment, Churchill celebrated the news that half the Italian battle fleet had been put out of commission at the price of eleven torpedoes and two Swordfish,[52] especially as Taranto coincided with the Regia Aeronautica's first, and final, air attack on Britain as part of the Luftwaffe offensive. "They might have found better employment defending their fleet at Taranto," he gibed.[53] Cunningham crowed that he had inflicted more damage on the Italian fleet in an hour than Admiral Jellico had done on the German high seas fleet at the Battle of Jutland in 1916.[54] In fact, Taranto changed the naval balance of power in the Mediterranean but imperceptibly. The Italian fleet continued to shun battle, while the Royal Navy was still discouraged from taking the risk of operating too far from the cover of land-based aircraft. Nevertheless, at the time, Taranto sent shockwaves through the world. Although air power enthusiasts had insisted since the 1920s that capital ships were vulnerable to air attack, Cunningham had actually proved this to be so, and in a protected harbor no less! Naval historian Donald Macintyre calls Taranto "the end of the battleship era in naval warfare."[55] Unfortunately for the Allies, the nation that took that lesson to heart was Japan, which applied it at Pearl Harbor and against the *Repulse* and the *Prince of Wales* off Singapore in December 1941. Taranto also infuriated Hitler, for whom, together with Greece and North Africa, it offered yet one more example of Italian incompetence. He began seriously to contemplate intervention in the Mediterranean.

In Rome, the public humiliation of unanticipated defeats at the hands of "Levantines" and British induced a mood that bordered on panic. Ciano called 12 November a "black day" and complained that Mussolini had failed to grasp its significance.[56] The fleet was pulled from Taranto and sailed to more secure anchorages on Italy's Tyrrhenian coast. This removed the threat of an amphibious landing in Greece,[57] and allowed the British to run convoys unimpeded to Malta and Greece. Mussolini blamed everyone but himself for the debacles at Taranto and in Greece. But everyone knew that *Il Duce* had dogmatically denied the value of carrier-based aircraft. As usual when he encountered a setback, Mussolini organized another round of administrative upheaval. Mussolini blamed Ciano, who in turn pointed the finger at Badoglio. Badoglio resigned before he could be sacked, but not before telling Mussolini that his bumbling amateurishness was leading Italy to catastrophe. Badoglio was replaced by Marshal Ugo Cavallero, whose steadier hand at the top of *Commando Supremo*, together with German intervention in the Mediterranean, helped temporarily to decelerate the sharp decline of Italian fortunes. Commanders in Albania were replaced, and ministers and top Fascist party officials, including Ciano, were ordered to "volunteer" for a stint at the front. What the military and the administration lost in efficiency, the Duce reasoned, the Italian people would gain in the morale boost caused by seeing even Italy's most exalted officials obliged to make sacrifices. It also sent the message to the Italian people, or so he believed, that their omniscient leader could run the country without benefit of bureaucrats. But the absurd spectacle of ministers' dealing with routine paperwork in the most primitive conditions of the Albanian front perplexed rather than lifted the national spirit. In the meantime, deprived of his closest advisers, Mussolini issued contradictory orders that transformed a confused situation into a chaotic one.[58] According to Mussolini's biographer, the Italian dictator's refusal publicly to reveal the extent of the damage inflicted at Taranto marks the point when Italians began to rely on the BBC for news, and hence to immunize themselves against Fascist propaganda.[59]

The Greeks had every reason to feel that their stubborn resistance had made evident both their courage and the moral and political bankruptcy of their adversaries. But as 1941 dawned, Greek survival appeared to hang by a thread. Blizzards and cold descended on the mountains, bringing misery and frostbite to the troops. The combination of poor weather and dispersed airfields located too far behind the lines limited RAF effectiveness. This allowed the Regia Aeronautica on clear days to dominate the skies over the front. London made a concerted effort to keep the Greeks supplied. But the British, too, were short of practically everything, including shipping, which was severely stretched to keep convoys moving through the Aegean. Once ashore, the supply chain stretched for hundreds of miles over appalling roads. The problem of even finding ammunition for a Greek army equipped with vintage French and German weapons was a supply officer's nightmare. The Greek army needed to be completely reequipped with modern weapons, but that was simply out of the question in the midst of a campaign.

More ominous still were indications by January 1941 that Hitler's hands-off policy in the Mediterranean was coming to an end. Mussolini had made one too many blunders. His attempt to trump the German occupation of Romania and preempt British presence in Greece as a way to demonstrate his equality with and independence from Hitler boomeranged in Berlin. Italian forces were clearly incapable of realizing Mussolini's Mediterranean ambitions. Worse still, Mussolini's attack on Greece had given the British an Aegean base from which their forces could threaten the southern flank of Barbarossa. Greece must be purged of the British presence before Barbarossa was launched. Because Mussolini could not do it, Hitler must step in, damn the consequences for *Il Duce's* pride.

And those consequences were severe. With the failure of Mussolini's Greek adventure, relations between the Axis dictators entered a new phase. Mussolini, his self-esteem injured, began to resent, even dislike, his German counterpart even as he became dependent on him. He mocked Hitler's rouged cheeks and allegedly deviant sexual proclivities. Mussolini remained mystified, or so he claimed, how this jumped-up corporal whose rumpled khaki costume would make an Italian bus conductor blush, could mesmerize the German people. The man lacked panache. He was a disgrace to dictators![60] Unlike Mussolini, however, Hitler had so far won his wars. On 9 December 1940, Hitler ordered a German Air Transport Group to Italy to help with supply between Foggia and Albania. Further troop reinforcements were suspended after it was decided that Romania and Bulgaria offered a more promising route of advance into Greece than did Albania. Athens and London began to receive ominous reports of German activity in the eastern Balkans. General Papagos wanted to take Valona before a renewed threat on the Bulgarian frontier forced him to shift troops eastward. The RAF moved every available Hurricane fighter and Blenheim medium bomber as far forward as possible to provide support for the attacking Greeks. A Greek offensive was launched on 13 February 1941. But poor weather and evidence that the Italians were preparing their own offensive forced him to call a halt well short of his goal.[61] Greek momentum had been lost. By April, the Italians had deployed twenty-nine divisions in Albania, where they joined 12,000 Albanians in Italian uniform. But Mussolini's Greek gamble had failed ignominiously, at a price of 38,832 dead and missing, 50,874 wounded, and 52,108 ill. Fully 12,368 soldiers had been put out of action by frost-bite.[62] Meanwhile, Graziani malingered at Sidi Barrani.

COMPASS

Mussolini drove the strategic pace of the Mediterranean war in 1940, advancing, or attempting to advance, on three fronts: Egypt, Ethiopia, and Greece. At the same time he kept up a steady pressure on Malta. But because the initiatives of the Italian dictator were unpredictable, the overstretched British had trouble reacting to his strategic thrusts. During the summer of 1940, Italian forces commanded by the Duke of Aosta seized border posts in the Sudan and Kenya. In August he moved against British Somaliland. Little thought had been given to this colony's defense, in great part because it had been assumed that the combination of forces in British and French Somaliland would be sufficient to deter an Italian attack. However, the fall of France compromised the security of the Horn of Africa, as it had of the Mediterranean. On 3 August, Aosta attacked from Ethiopia in a well-organized and -executed three-pronged advance on the Somaliland capital of Berbera. Somaliland's defense lay in the hands of two battalions of African rifles, two of Punjabis, one of the Black Watch, a lightly armed and locally raised Somali camel corps, and a battery of light 3.7-inch howitzers. This was simply not enough to hold off a strong Italian force backed by bombers and heavy artillery. The choice was to evacuate or die in place. The British commander, Major General A. R. Godwin-Austin, elected to fight again another day. The garrison fell back on Berbera, where 7,000 troops and civilians were taken off by the Royal Navy.[63]

Aosta's expropriation of a moonscape of a place that most British probably could not locate on a map hardly constituted a reversal of strategic magnitude. Nevertheless, Churchill was disheartened by Middle East commander General Sir Archibald Wavell's apparent equanimity as a British colony was forfeited after the merest pretense of defense. In the prime minister's view, the "tactical conduct of this affair" seemed to confirm the British army's casual—practically languid—approach to the war. When joined with Narvik in Norway in

May 1940 and Dunkirk the following month, the evacuation of Somaliland suggested that British generals strove above all to perfect the
art of amphibious withdrawal. The impact of yet another retreat on
Britons, who had been nourished on a steady diet of military reverses
since September 1939, and who in August 1940 were a month or so
into the Battle of Britain, might be significant. Pride was also a factor.
"Our only defeat at the hands of the Italians," rankled Churchill.
Worse, it weakened Britain's already precarious position in Egypt,
where "so much depended on our prestige."[64]

Nor did the situation improve over the autumn. The Italian invasion of Egypt in September, though timorous, left the British army in
apprehensive vigilance at the railhead and sometime beach resort of
Marsa Matruh, a collection of low white buildings interspersed with
wilted palm trees arranged along a heat-blasted high street. Meanwhile, the RAF gallantly defended the home island and Malta, and
Cunningham inflicted serious damage on the Italian navy at Taranto.
In October and November, the Greeks absorbed the best Mussolini
could throw at them, and in December counterattacked. "People
pointed to the Greeks and said, 'They can beat the Italians. Why can't
we do something,' " recorded Alan Moorehead. "There was a feeling
of despondency about the army" and in particular about "Headquarters Muddle East," which became the butt of popular humor. Cairo
continued to bask in a "false and easy optimism," as if the war were a
distant preoccupation, something whose progress one followed on the
wireless. Soldiers disembarking from ration-gray Britain continued to
be startled by Cairo's ramshackle opulence. The occasional bout of
"grumpy tummy" seemed a modest down payment on a luxuriant supply of hot baths and cold beer. Officers crowded into the Turf Club,
sweated through polo matches in the baking afternoon heat, or
watched belly dancers at Madame Badia's near the Kasr el Nil bridge.
Gray staff cars nudged cautious paths through shrill throngs of *fella-
heen*, steering toward offices where no one worked between noon and
6 p.m., the hours when the city suffocated under a blanket of dusty
heat. Over everything lingered the aroma of coffee, Turkish tobacco,
and donkey dung.[65]

The evacuation of Berbera sent relations between Wavell and

Churchill down an irreversible path. There was no inherent reason why their association should have so quickly settled into one of fragile antipathy. Both were men of aristocratic lineage. Each was a veteran of the Boer War and of World War I, in which Wavell had lost an eye. Each was an author and historian, who prided himself on his prodigious memory and command of detail. Both realized that they were fighting a world conflict, one that required difficult strategic choices. Each had a powerful mind, with a proclivity for unorthodox solutions tempered by common sense. In part, the absence of an entente between the two men was just bad luck and bad timing. Churchill liked winners, and it was Wavell's fate throughout the war to be hurled into situations where the initiative lay with the enemy. That said, Wavell's detractors argue that his errors of strategic judgment—in particular his acquiescence in the decision to abandon Operation Compass in February 1941 to go to Greece—virtually guaranteed that his World War II career would be one of meager accomplishment.[66] He is also faulted for underestimating Rommel, and then increasing the confusion of the British response to the first German offensive into Cyrenaica in April 1941 by attempting to micromanage his commanders on the spot.[67]

But circumstance does not fully explain why these were two minds seldom operating in unison. No chemistry existed between them, no spark of warmth or fervor animated their common task. Brigadier Bernard Fergusson, Wavell's private secretary, wrote of the "clash of character" between the two men.[68] This may have been in part because Wavell, though regarded as one of the British army's premier trainers of men, was too cerebral, too taciturn, for Churchill's taste. The prime minister required an enthusiasm from his field commanders that bordered on zealotry. He was drawn inexorably to risk takers, men who led from the front, who burned to come to grips with the enemy. Wavell approached his duties with the detachment of an undersecretary in the Foreign Office. He was, above all, a meticulous planner with a talent for administrative detail. As such, Wavell was more attuned to the complexities of an operation than to its visionary possibilities. The British strategist and writer Sir Basil Liddell Hart believed Wavell past his peak, the dynamism he had observed in his close friend in the mid-1930s aged into "hesitancy and conservatism" by 1941. Wavell's disposition was tinged with a touch of fatalism, a quality that allowed him to acquiesce stoically to Churchill's constantly shifting priorities. But observers, including Churchill, often confused Wavell's passive acceptance of circumstance as predestined with exhaustion or absence of mental vigor. In their view, Wavell was too quick to lose heart, to conclude that Victory had defected to the enemy.[69]

Wavell's problem was that he never seemed unconditionally committed to a profession chosen for him by his father, a major general in the British army. Wavell's headmaster at Winchester, probably Britain's most intellectual public school, thought him far too intelligent for a military career. And in truth, Wavell was an academic *manqué*. His education in the ancient classics combined with the terrors of World War I trench warfare to confer a serene outlook on life. Wavell lacked the ruthless disposition that Bernard Montgomery believed the bedrock of effective generalship.[70] He never lost his interest in poetry and history, and used his two periods on half pay in the interwar years to publish books in each field. "My trouble," Wavell once confessed to Lieutenant General Sir Henry Pownall, "is that I am not really interested in war."[71] So respected was Wavell for his intellectual powers that he was invited to deliver the prestigious Lees Knowles lectures at Cambridge University in 1939 on the subject of "Generals and Generalship." He might well have occupied the prestigious Chichele Chair of the History of War at Oxford had Hitler not prolonged his military career. Furthermore, he had an academic's personality, one that thrived on contemplation and privacy. Wavell's wit had a spare, high-table quality, and revealed itself only to those with the capacity to prize it.

Wavell's detachment made him a difficult man to fathom. In public, he carried an air of perpetual melancholy. Alan Moorehead, who greatly admired Wavell's soldierly qualities, conceded that the general was "an island in a sea of garrulousness," a man with no small talk whose deeply lined and tanned face invariably remained "as expressionless as a statue," whatever the occasion.[72] Even when Wavell smiled, which was seldom, the corners of his mouth sagged, and his eyes squinted more in sadness than in mirth, as if he had just been handed another piece of bad news. Reticence to the point of aloofness was the reverse side of Wavell's intellectual brilliance; British historian Ian Beckett describes it as Wavell's "tireless self-sufficiency," an "impenetrable mask" that awed subordinates and exasperated politicians like Churchill to the point of hostility.[73] British historian Percival Spear noted that Wavell "often lost by his silences what he had gained by his initiatives."[74] The incident that cemented what Churchill diplomatically called the "misunderstanding" between the two men was Wavell's decision to keep his plan to attack Graziani in the autumn of 1940 secret from the prime minister.[75] This was done in part for security reasons, as Egypt was an intelligence sieve. But Wavell's real object was to avoid Churchill's meddling, as was his wont, in Wavell's operational dispositions. After this Churchill never fully trusted his Middle East commander.

In fact, it was "Archie" Wavell's personality—or rather lack of it— that helps to explain why the first August 1940 meeting between the prime minister and his freshly appointed fifty-seven-year-old Middle East commander proved such a disaster. Churchill was a whirlwind of activity in August 1940. Directives from Downing Street fell with a frequency that rivaled that of German bombs on London. Churchill's memoirs for this period are filled with directives sent to Wavell, laying out from three thousand miles' distance, in often excruciating detail, the tactical and operational dispositions his commander should adopt. Churchill's micromanagement exasperated rather than energized his subordinates. The elaborate war-directing machinery of the Imperial General Staff that eventually was to cushion commanders from the full brunt of Churchill's mulish enthusiasms as yet existed only in embryo. Visitors to Churchill in those days discerned an atmosphere nourished by both challenge and fear. And no wonder, for it directly reflected Britain's plight.

When Churchill succeeded Neville Chamberlain as prime minister on 10 May 1940, German troops were already careening into the Low Countries. In early July, Soviet ambassador Maisky called on him to ask what his strategy was to be now that France had fallen. "To last out the next three months," Churchill growled. For the new prime minister, Britain's adversity offered redemption for the burned-out promise of his youth. His early career had been nothing short of brilliant: first lord of the Admiralty from 1911 to 1915, minister of munitions in 1917, secretary of state for war and air in 1919, for the colonies the following year, and chancellor of the Exchequer in 1924. But when he resigned his portfolio in 1929, Churchill's moment seemed to have passed. He was a man of Victorian excesses, temperamentally unsuited to timid times, a political buccaneer whose ambitions were too majestic to be contained in the bantam world of post–Great War Westminster. Churchill's moment came in 1940. He confessed to his wife that he thrived in conditions of "catastrophe and collapse . . . Is it not horrible to be built like this?" Unlike Hitler, who encased himself in a Teutonic fantasy, or Mussolini, who evoked the Roman Empire like a circus backdrop, Churchill commanded from the bridge of history. Like his great ancestor the Duke of Marlborough, he had been tapped by Providence to add new episodes to the glorious saga of his small island's resolution and ultimate triumph. Churchill's confidence in the irreversible destiny of his nation, and the role he now was to play in it, energized and sustained him. The history of Britain as Churchill filtered and interpreted it was a declaration of faith in ultimate victory. He had been ordained to deliver it.

Despite the lionization accorded Churchill in the popular mind, postwar literature, including the memoirs of generals and admirals who worked most closely with him, has tended to be critical—when not vitriolic—about Churchill's wartime leadership.[76] Nevertheless, it is difficult to escape the conclusion that the British prime minister stands out as *the* great political leader of the war. From the moment he assumed the premiership, he conveyed his sense of the drama of the historical moment. His rhetoric during the Battle of Britain mobilized the press and public opinion in his own country and sent a strong message to the United States that Britain was fighting a total war.

Churchill's career as a soldier and war correspondent, his governmental experience in managing vast military bureaucracies, and the perspective given him by his studies of military history did not make him popular with the forces. On the contrary, many of Churchill's subordinates argued that the prime minister's experience in military affairs was a disadvantage for at least two reasons. First, it encouraged Churchill's notorious tendency to bully his military commanders and meddle in spheres of activity more properly the preserve of the military chiefs.[77] In his diary, Churchill's chief of the Imperial General Staff from December 1941, General Sir Alan Brooke, blasted his "peevish temperamental prima donna of a Prime Minister, suspicious to the very limits of imagination, always fearing a military combination of effort against political dominance."[78] A second consequence of Churchill's familiarity with military affairs was that it encouraged his conceit that he was a brilliant strategist. As a result, Churchill's strategic decisions were often viewed as eccentric by his senior commanders, who complained that their boss had no concept of the constraints that operational limitations imposed on his choices. Of no theater was this more true than in the Mediterranean, which boasted a selection of options rich enough to befuddle the most discerning strategist. When Admiral Cunningham became first sea lord in 1943, he discovered that Churchill was "a bad strategist but doesn't know it, and nobody has the courage to stand up to him."[79] Likewise, Australia's Prime Minister Robert Menzies, who saw Australian divisions sacrificed to Churchill's decision to defend Greece and Crete in the spring of 1941, thought it fortunate that the British leader's "magnificent and courageous leadership" was able to compensate in part "for his deplorable strategic sense."[80]

American political scientist Eliot Cohen argues convincingly that Churchill's critics have misunderstood both the motivation for his alleged "meddling" in and micromanagement of military affairs, as well as his fundamental strengths as a strategist. Brooke was correct in his observation that his boss "always fear[ed] a military combination of effort against political dominance." Not because he was on the qui vive against a coup d'état. But study and experience taught the prime minister to respect Clemenceau's dictum that "war is too important to be left to the generals." World War I had exposed the limitations of military leaders and the exorbitant penalties paid when politicians defer uncritically to their "expertise." Military organizations were shaped by a "whole habit of mind . . . based on subordination of opinion."[81] Generals were like emperors coddled by staff officer courtiers who flattered their egos and certified their opinions. When Churchill was complimented in November 1943 on the brilliant organization of his chiefs of staff system, he lashed out: "Not at all. It leads to weak and faltering decisions—or rather indecisions. Why, you may take the most gallant sailor, the most intrepid airman, or the most audacious soldier, put them at a table together—what do you get? *The sum total of their fears!*"[82] Churchill's military chiefs treated his tenders of camaraderie with reserve, and answered his enthusiasm with requests for more men and equipment. He attributed to a fear of failure and absence of imagination their reluctance to launch an operation until reinforcements were in place, troops were thoroughly trained, equipment was adapted to theater conditions, and the battlefield was perfectly prepared. He drove his generals toward action, and then questioned, prodded, interfered, and second-guessed their decisions, often on the basis of a cursory and imperfect reading of Ultra intercepts. They, in turn, resented his energy, complained about his ignorance of military affairs, and stonewalled his projects. Churchill's messages and queries, "covering so wide a range of subjects, was like the beam of a searchlight ceaselessly swinging round and penetrating into the remote recesses of the administration," according to Norman Brook, a member of the wartime cabinet secretariat. The result of the prime minister's ceaseless prodding, Brook believed, was to create a sense of purpose and urgency, as well as to communicate the message that "a firm hand was on the wheel."[83] "Churchill viewed one of his most important responsibilities being the goading of his commanders into action," concludes Cohen. "[He held] their calculations and assertions up to the standards of a massive common sense, informed by wide reading and experience of war."[84]

The warlord on a quest for the perpetual offensive, the commander in chief at the epicenter of vast armies and navies, found his generals unimaginative and reluctant to grasp what to Churchill seemed obvious strategic opportunities. In response, Churchill's military chiefs were driven to the point of exasperation by a prime minister who, in the face of the wealth of strategic targets offered by the Mediterranean, behaved "like a puppy in a fire-hydrant factory."[85] His obsessions with the pursuit of operations in Norway and the Eastern Mediterranean have found few postwar supporters. Nevertheless, his fundamental strategic approach was robust and capable of withstanding miscalculations. He instinctively grasped the strategic benefits of fighting in the Mediterranean when many of his service chiefs wanted to husband assets in Britain against the distant possibility of a German invasion. Churchill immediately understood that Barbarossa was a huge miscalculation on Hitler's part at a time when many service chiefs were slow to grasp the fact that it gave Britain its first faint hope of victory. He also employed the Mediterranean to leverage Britain's influence with the United States far beyond what should have been its natural lifetime. Churchill's problem in alliance management was that he tried to direct the war from a subordinate position, which eventually exacted its toll on his relations with Roosevelt.[86]

Churchill, the amateur painter, liked to compare strategy formulation with composing a canvas, in which "few or numberless parts are commanded by a single unity of conception."[87] But rather than an artist at work, many of Churchill's subordinates saw a self-absorbed, insensitive man unable to recognize redemptive qualities in those whose self-restraint he interpreted as an absence of imagination or enthusiasm. His vast military experience and his lifelong fascination for military affairs, combined with the fact that he refused to surround himself with yes-men, made his relations with soldiers frequently stormy. He was quick to judge, often on the basis of pique or prejudice; and once one was judged harshly, it was difficult to appeal the verdict. His long-suffering chiefs of staff—Brooke, Portal, and Cunningham—served him out of loyalty and duty rather than affection.[88] Brooke's task was to curb his boss's impetuosity and try to make him understand the whole strategic picture. "His gaze always settles on some definite part of the canvas and the rest of the picture is lost," Brooke lamented in his diary in 1943. "It is difficult to make him realize the influence of one theater on another . . . He is quite the most difficult man to work with that I have ever struck, but I should not have missed the chance of working with him for anything on earth."[89]

No British general was more exasperated in these early months of the war by the prime minister's inability to set strategic priorities than Wavell. The introductory meetings between Churchill and his new commander in the Middle East lasted between 8 and 15 August 1940. Each man had a problem. Churchill's was one of the lack of success. He was desperate for a victory, anything that could lift British spirits after a summer of catastrophe and build U.S. confidence in Britain. It was one of Churchill's great strengths as a strategist that he saw the Middle East, in particular Egypt, as a place where Britain might confront the Axis at a relative advantage. He also recognized that the loss of Suez would constitute a catastrophe beyond contemplation, "second only to a successful invasion and final conquest [of the United Kingdom].[90] Therefore, he was prepared to invest Britain's limited military resources there in the hope of producing incremental success, at a time when received wisdom called for hoarding assets in Britain against an expected German invasion. Success in the Med would sustain his population by holding out hope of ultimate victory, intimidate potential adversaries like Franco, and persuade the United States that Britain was a worthy ally. Churchill required a general who grasped the prime ministerial vision of war as "a contest of wills," aggressive enough to squeeze strategic advantage from the military assets sent to Egypt by dint of huge effort. And in truth, Wavell was not that man. The responsibility for a command that covered over three million square miles from Cyprus to British Somaliland, from Iraq to Egypt, with barely 90,000 men to garrison it, overwhelmed him. The Italians, in contrast, numbered 250,000 in Libya and 290,000 in Italian East Africa. Furthermore, the Axis retained the strategic initiative. The British were in a reactive mode, and shifting British troops to meet a German attack on Greece would leave Wavell seriously embarrassed in Egypt. Wavell's comparative silence in the face of the prime ministerial monologue about the need for offensive action, his exasperating habit of replying "I see" to every request or observation in a high-pitched, nasal voice that seemed incongruous in a man so large, left Churchill with the distinct impression that Wavell lacked ideas. The prime minister told his secretary of state for war and future foreign minister Anthony Eden to find him another commander. However, as

Eden was both Wavell's friend and his political mentor, no suitable replacement was found.[91] Therefore, Wavell departed London for the Middle East.

Hardly had Wavell's plane touched down in Cairo, however, than news of a new Dunkirk in British Somaliland reached London. Churchill was livid, and demanded that Wavell sack Godwin-Austen. Wavell not only refused to fire his subordinate. He actually reminded the prime minister that "a heavy butcher's bill" that would inevitably have resulted from the defense of Somaliland was "not necessarily evidence of good tactics." Churchill swallowed his considerable anger for the moment, contenting himself with the dispatch of a long directive that laid out Wavell's tasks and the deployment of his forces in minute detail. Wavell later confessed that he "disregarded a good deal of it." In October 1940, Churchill dispatched Anthony Eden to discover the source of Wavell's inactivity. Eden's news that Churchill was contemplating diverting troops to Greece, to follow the RAF contingents already sent there, caused Wavell to reveal his preparations, initiated in September, for Compass—an offensive against Graziani. Nevertheless, Wavell refused to be pinned down to a date, and cautioned his superiors not to "encourage optimism." Churchill was fast becoming exasperated with his Middle East commander. In November, an impatient signal from London offered Taranto and Italian setbacks in Greece as evidence of Italian lack of preparedness and low morale, and urged speedy preparation for an offensive. Wavell replied that it was not possible to launch Compass in November.[92]

Until the Battle of El Alamein in October 1942, the British looked back on Compass as a sort of golden age of Mediterranean combat, when British resolve and improvisation triumphed over a demoralized and poorly led enemy. The British dilemma was that the better they performed against the Italians, the more they advanced the likelihood of Hitler's riding to Mussolini's rescue. For the British, it was never a question of *if* Hitler would intervene, but *when*. The British problem in this period was to establish a firm foundation upon which the future war in the Mediterranean could be conducted. And while the winter of 1940–41 is often viewed as a period of squandered opportunity for London, in fact the ingredients that made Compass such a success pointed the way to future victory in North Africa in particular and in the war in general.

The first element that made Compass a success was an effective British command team. How to pull this together was not obvious in the autumn of 1940. The disappointing performance of the British Expeditionary Force (BEF) in France in May–June 1940 had cast doubt on the competence of many senior army leaders. A few, like Alan Brooke, Alexander, and Montgomery, had distinguished themselves by their steadfastness in the retreat. The chief recommendation of those who remained was that they had yet to be afforded the opportunity to demonstrate their incompetence beyond the shadow of a doubt. The rapid transformation in the war's fortunes in the summer of 1940 suddenly shifted attention from France to the Eastern Mediterranean, an area hitherto regarded as a military backwater. At a time when Labour Party leaders resurrected images of the British officer corps as an aristocratic club more concerned with social standing than competence, the Middle East command was a government press agent's nightmare. Wavell had been dispatched as general officer commanding (GOC) the Middle East in July 1939. To Churchill, Wavell appeared to be tentative, reserved, and at fifty-seven too old for the job. In fact, the reticence that Churchill interpreted as an absence of imagination, Wavell's subordinate commanders viewed as an endearing humility and modesty, and it bound them all the more closely to him.

Wavell's commander in Egypt was the fifty-nine-year-old Henry Maitland Wilson. An old Etonian and infantryman with a watermelon face, mustache, and eyes of penetrating firmness, Wilson gave outsiders the impression that he was Colonel Blimp's understudy, if not his model. A great mountain of a man whose vast bulk earned him the inevitable nickname of Jumbo, Wilson had spent most of World War I directing operations from the safety of châteaux scattered about the French countryside, where he acquired the reputation as a competent staff officer. His interwar years had been spent in India and teaching at the staff college. His commanding officers valued his firmness, authority, and ability to get things done. But, as with Wavell, the suspicion lingered that Wilson's unshakable calm masked a fundamental absence of ideas. Because he was almost a decade older than his cohort, he was regarded as an Edwardian relic in the era of Blitzkrieg warfare. He had reached the rank of major general in 1935, and was promptly placed on half pay. Although recalled in 1937 to command the Second Division, Wilson had remained in England when his division departed for France in 1939. Egypt was thought a more fitting command for a man of his years. And in many respects it was. Wilson provided stable senior leadership at a period when the British army's grip on modern warfare seemed fragile, a survivor in a senior command churned by turmoil. Wilson also proved remarkably adept at navigating the treacherous shoals of Egyptian politics. And although he never acquired a reputation as an able fighting general, he understood the value of offensive operations, and the requirement to base them on sound planning and solid intelligence. Above all, he stood ready to back subordinates capable of taking the fight to the enemy.

That subordinate in the autumn of 1940 was Major General Richard O'Connor. Many remarked on the stark contrast between the elephantine Wilson with his deep voice and deliberate, practically operatic gestures, and the diminutive O'Connor, whose speech was a rapid-fire succession of high-pitched squeaks. Indeed, at first sight O'Connor often struck observers like an overgrown schoolboy. There was nothing adolescent about O'Connor's professionalism, however. He had emerged from World War I with a chestful of medals, earned on the Western Front and in the Italian theater, where he gained experience commanding both infantry and artillery units. Indeed, in the interwar years he had been singled out among the British army's rising stars. He commanded a brigade on the Northwest Frontier of India, a division in Palestine alongside that of Bernard Montgomery, and served as the military governor of Jerusalem at the height of the troubles there, where his evenhandedness earned him the enmity of both Arab and Jew. Indeed, had he not been captured by Rommel in 1941, O'Connor might have finished the war a household name.

A second element in British success was a solid infrastructure to anchor the campaign in the Middle East. From August 1940, convoys from Britain, the Commonwealth, and the empire funneled 126,000 men into Egypt over seventeen weeks, together with ample stores and equipment. And while this demonstrated the benefits of Britain's maritime reach, the trip around the Cape of Good Hope especially placed enormous strains on British shipping, which could only be alleviated by the addition of the U.S. merchant marine and the opening of the Mediterranean.[93] Moreover, once the British were in theater, the Egyptian infrastructure was barely adequate to cope with this influx of men and equipment.[94] For his part, Churchill never fully comprehended that his decision to fight in the desert required the British to create a huge logistical infrastructure. On 7 January 1941, he wired Wavell to ask why fully 350,000 men were stationed in the Middle East command, but only two divisions were fighting the Italians in Cyrenaica? So began the first of the prime minister's many complaints to his commanders in the Middle East about what he saw as the imbalance between "ration strength" and "fighting strength."[95]

A third element in British success was air superiority.[96] This was achieved only slowly in the Mediterranean for three reasons: priority in the most modern aircraft went to the British Isles, which were being "blitzed" nightly; getting aircraft into the theater occasioned huge logistical difficulties; and finally, the RAF had yet to perfect the tactics of effective close air support. Because aircraft took up valuable shipping space that might be allocated to other equipment, London began to search for ways to send planes under their own power to Egypt. Bombers could fly via Gibraltar and Malta to Egypt, although they always ran the risk of being intercepted by Italian and, from 1941, German fighters operating out of Sicily and Libya. There was also the problem of keeping Malta supplied with enough fuel to send the bombers on their way. The favored path, therefore, became the Takoradi air route, ordered into existence on 20 June 1940, as soon as it became obvious that it would no longer be possible to overfly France. Planes were shipped to Takoradi in the Gold Coast (present-day Ghana), where they were assembled, and then flown 3,700 miles along the old Imperial Airways route via Lagos and Khartoum to Egypt. This too required a significant infrastructure investment.[97] The vulnerable link in the route was the portion that passed over Chad. Fortunately for London, Free French forces guaranteed that this French colony did not fall into Italian hands. The first contingent of British airmen and mechanics reached Takoradi on 21 August. The first crated planes followed on 5 September. One Blenheim bomber and six Hurricane fighters departed for Egypt fifteen days later. By October 1943, on the eve of the Allied invasion of North Africa (Torch), which made Takoradi unnecessary, 5,000 British planes had reached the Middle East by this route, as well as a number of American aircraft flown by the American Ferry Service. The task had been an arduous one, however. The support staff shivered with malaria as they endured debilitating tropical heat. The trip over barren wastes was hard on the engines and reduced the fighting life of aircraft. Nevertheless, Churchill credited the Takoradi lifeline with making the difference between survival and annihilation of British forces in Egypt in the dark days of 1941.[98]

Once in theater, the British organized the RAF to better support ground combat. Only gradually did Hurricane fighters arrive to replace the slow and vulnerable Lysanders and Gladiators in British Mediterranean squadrons. The Hurricane became the RAF's first monoplane fighter in 1937, flying a respectable 320 miles per hour with a good rate of climb. Sturdy and reliable rather than exciting, the Hurricane bore the brunt of the Luftwaffe's assault on Britain in the summer of 1940 until production of the RAF's fighter of choice, the more glamorous and better-performing Spitfire, could kick in. The RAF tactic in the Battle of Britain was to send the Spitfires to distract the German fighters while the Hurricanes ambushed the bombers. In the Mediterranean, the Hurricane became a jack-of-all-tasks — interceptor, night fighter, and, armed with a 500-pound bomb load, two machine guns, and four 20 mm cannons, an excellent tank killer. Carrier-borne Hurricanes protected convoys to Malta in the summer of 1942, and, armed with rocket launchers, attacked Axis shipping.

High losses in the Battle of Britain and a shortage of aircrews also retarded the arrival of bombers. Blenheim and Wellington bombers constituted Britain's North African inventory on the eve of Compass. The twin-engine Blenheim medium bomber was a military knockoff of a personal six-seat passenger plane designed in 1934 for Lord Rothermere, owner of the *Daily Mail*. The Blenheim Mark IV, which appeared in 1939, could deliver a 1,000-pound bomb load almost 1,500 miles at 200 miles per hour. Until the appearance of true heavy bombers like the Stirling and Lancaster, the twin-engine Wellington constituted the heaviest of RAF's bombers, capable of carrying a 4,000-pound bomb load 1,200 miles at 160 miles per hour. Although it had a canvas skin, the Wellington could absorb punishment and remained popular in the RAF, which produced over 11,000 of the aircraft. Even after Bomber Command phased out the Wellington over Northern Europe in 1943, it continued in the Mediterranean and elsewhere as a bomber and transport aircraft.

Indeed, one reason why Compass was so slow in getting off the mark was that the RAF had been stripped of many of its aircraft for Greece, leaving only 48 fighters and 116 bombers to support the operation.[99] The Italians were reckoned to have about 500 planes in Libya, evenly split between fighters and bombers. And although this proved to be an overestimate, the Italians could always reinforce rapidly from Sicily. To compensate for numerical inferiority, the RAF planned preemptive bomber strikes on forward Italian air bases. For instance, at El Adem airfield just south of Tobruk, Moorehead counted fully eighty-seven Italian aircraft damaged by British bombing and subsequently torched by the Italians.[100] Also, the first steps were taken in the creation of what later became known as the Desert Air Force (DAF), to ensure the greatest coordination between air power and land operations. Squadrons now mixed fighter and reconnaissance aircraft so as better to cooperate in tactical and artillery reconnaissance, and to give troops protection from fighter harassment.[101]

Superior intelligence and deception made up a fourth element of British success. To further guarantee that the Italians did not catch wind of the operation, the RAF was flown ragged to keep the Regia Aeronautica from investigating the front areas. O'Connor was especially keen that the enemy not detect the two forward dumps of matériel that he was obliged to create fifty miles west of the railhead at Marsa Matruh to economize on his meager transport. Dummy tanks were scattered in strategically insignificant areas of the desert to distract the attention of Italian airmen. Italian Tenth Army intelligence reports subsequently captured during Compass showed that, throughout October and November, agents reported an inordinate amount of British activity. The overall effect, however, when combined with raids of the Long Range Desert Group (LRDG) in southern Libya and the proclivity of Italian intelligence to inflate enemy estimates, was to reinforce the Italian inclination to believe that the British were stronger than was, in fact, the case. Italian air reconnaissance did note an inordinate amount of movement to their front, but attributed it to normal rotation, or to British fears of an Italian attack. Graziani was allegedly warned by his intelligence on 6 December that a British attack was imminent. But he chose to ignore these warnings, either because he was distracted by his own preparations for an attack or because he found other, contrary information more plausible.[102]

While the British denied intelligence to the Italians, they took steps to collect it for themselves. British code breakers had been especially successful in deciphering the Italian air force high-grade cipher. And although British code breaking was blinded for much of January 1941 after the Italians changed their codes, by the end of the month 80 percent of the Italian cipher was being read. This allowed the British to keep track of the deployment of the Italian air force and assess the effectiveness of British bombing raids. At the end of November 1940, British intelligence intercepted the entire Italian air force order of battle in Greece. Much of the operational information of both the Italian and German air forces was transmitted in low-grade ciphers or even in clear. Signals intelligence (Sigint) was also the chief source of information about the Italian army in Libya. By October 1940, Cairo was reading all Italian army ciphers down to brigade level, until the loss of Italian codebooks at Bardia in December caused Rome to change its codes on 4 January. The ability to read the Luftwaffe codes also allowed the British to watch for evidence of German intervention in Libya. The headquarters of O'Connor's Western Desert Force had attached a field Sigint organization that provided a steady supply of decrypted intercepts. This revealed the Italian situation at both Bardia and Tobruk prior to the attacks on those two Italian positions, as well as details of the Italian withdrawal from Benghazi. Sigint was backed up by air reconnaissance and ground patrols. The greatest weakness of British intelligence, one that remained throughout the war, was that they devised no successful method to estimate numbers and equipment.[103]

Wavell also sought to distract the enemy from his real intentions through the Long Range Desert Group, later famous as the "Desert Rats." In the interwar years, the French, Italians, and British had all experimented with motorized desert patrols. Ironically, it had been Graziani and the Italians who had taken the concept to its highest level during the Senussi war. In 1930, Graziani's Auto-Saharan company, which combined Fiat armored cars, camel-mounted infantry, and aircraft, seized the Senussi desert stronghold of Kufra, which he transformed into a base for Italian mobile desert units. The British had to play catch-up to this Italian effort. In the 1930s, Royal Engineers Major Ralph Bagnold made a name for himself experimenting with desert navigation, devices to free vehicles from sand, radiator condensers, low-pressure tires, and other techniques to give expeditions off-road mobility. The publication in 1935 of *Libyan Sands: Travels in a Dead World* was eclipsed by T. E. Lawrence's death in the same year. But *Libyan Sands* made Bagnold something of a cult figure among cognoscenti of desert travel. His experiments led to the creation of "light car patrols" in the late 1930s. However, on Bagnold's retirement, the LCPs were assigned to the Egyptian Frontiers Administration, which used them to combat frontier smuggling. British officers were also stripped out of these groups by the Egyptians in 1938 after LCPs were employed in Palestine against anti-Zionist rioters. The idea of using LCPs in an intelligence and combat, as opposed to a police role, seemed to have expired in the British army by the outbreak of the war.

Their revival owed much to Bagnold's fortuitous appearance in Suez in the early weeks of the war. Recalled to active duty in 1939, Bagnold was on his way to Kenya when a newspaper article alerted Wavell to his passage through the canal. The two men hit it off immediately. Wavell's experience on General Allenby's staff during Britain's World War I conquest of Palestine had made him aware of the potential of irregular forces. Besides, special forces and guerrilla warfare were in the air. Churchill's promise to "set Europe ablaze" with resistance movements combined with British weakness in conventional forces to put military leaders in an experimental mood. There was something about special operations that appealed to the schoolboy spirit that permeated the British officer corps. Churchill was in the process of reviving the commandos. The desert also seemed to Wavell to offer scope for special operations. However, the British commander in the Middle East resisted schemes to finance a Senussi revolt in Cyrenaica, because both Graziani and the British in Iraq had proved that air power and motorization had blocked the indigenous, camel-mounted guerrilla from being able to mount hit-and-run raids. What he wanted was a force that could spy on and distract the Italians while he prepared Compass. Together, Wavell and Bagnold conceived of the Long Range Desert Patrols as units of thirty men with twelve vehicles. Veteran desert explorers were collected. When the Australians proved reluctant to participate, several New Zealanders were persuaded to join. In August 1940, the first party set out to establish a watch post north of Koufra.

This inaugural expedition was a vast success. Not content simply to watch the Italians and set up secret supply dumps in the desert, the LRDPs began to plant mines, attack convoys, and blow up Italian fuel depots and planes on the runways. Soon, British decoders were intercepting Italian signals demanding more troops to protect remote desert outposts and convoys. Delighted with this first experiment, Wavell expanded Bagnold's LRDPs by 60 percent, and set it the mission to carry out a huge raid on Murzuk in the Fezzan, which destroyed three Caproni bombers on the ground as well as a hangar and fuel dump. Bagnold fled into Chad, a Free French–controlled colony, where he made the acquaintance of Colonel Philippe Leclerc. Together, the French and British returned to Italian territory to seize Koufra in March 1941. The fall of Koufra brought Wavell's "huge bluff" program to an end, elevated the LRDPs into the pantheon of British elite units, and caused Bagnold to be acclaimed as the "new Lawrence." However, while the LRDPs continued to carry out raids, their greatest usefulness would be to serve as a forward reconnaissance group.[104]

Other elements in the success of Compass included superior matériel, especially the twenty-five-pounder (102 mm) guns, superior to the Italian 75 mm guns, and forty-eight heavily armored "I" (for Infantry) or "Matilda" tanks, against which the Italians had no defense. Armed with a 40 mm gun, the thick armor of the Matilda made it popular with the British until the arrival of Rommel's panzers, and especially the 88 mm antitank gun, rendered it obsolete. Attempts to upgrade the gun failed because the turret proved too small to accommodate a higher caliber. The armor-casting process also made it difficult to mass-produce. However, the Matilda, fitted with a flail, found its niche as a Scorpion mine clearer. Indeed, Montgomery's advance through Rommel's minefields at El Alamein on 23 October 1942 was preceded by thirty-two Matilda II Scorpions. Compass also witnessed a thorough preparation of a standard not again achieved until El Alamein. In this, Brigadier, later Field Marshal, A. R. Harding played a leading role, as he would in the Italian campaign in 1943–45. The planners took the general operational concept worked out by Wavell, Wilson, and O'Connor and transformed it into a precise plan. Troops were rehearsed in the operation on 25 and 26 November against a replica of Italian positions created near Matruh. Secrecy also worked to the advantage of the British, as Compass relied on surprise for success. Egypt pulsated with agents working out of the Italian legation and local Arabs eager to retail military information. Wavell admitted few men into the secret of Compass. Most of the instructions were given orally, little committed to paper, and nothing put out over radio where it might be intercepted by Italian cryptanalysts.

The Wavell-Wilson-O'Connor plan was ambitious, even foolhardy. After Graziani had settled into Sidi Barrani in August, he began to construct a chain of a half dozen rectangular fortresses running south for about forty miles into the desert. Inexplicably, the Italians had constructed them in two clusters with a fifteen-mile gap between Nibeiwa, the southernmost camp in the northern cluster, and Sofafi in the south. A special patrol of the Second Rifle Brigade verified the gaps in the minefields covering the Nibeiwa camp. Air reconnaissance revealed that the otherwise thick minefields had been left open at the rear of the camps, to allow supply convoys through. Voilà, the route of attack.[105]

The British plan called on the Fourth Indian Division supported by the Matildas to penetrate this gap and attack Nibeiwa from the rear as a prelude to rolling up the two northern camps of Tummar East and West all the way to Sidi Barrani. Meanwhile, the Seventh Armoured Division would prevent reinforcements from the southern camps from intervening. A small 1,800-man force out of Matruh supported by naval artillery would pressure the coastal garrisons to prevent Italian reinforcements from arriving from the north. While deceptively simple, this plan relied on secrecy and surprise to succeed, especially as the two British divisions would be assaulting nine Italian ones. The logistical challenges were also significant. Many units would have to traverse as much as seventy-five miles of desert, the last stretch at night, to be in position for a dawn attack. O'Connor also had only eighty trucks, together with fifty borrowed from Palestine, to carry his infantry into their attack positions and then keep his troops supplied. The RAF was to launch heavy raids on Italian airfields to keep the numerically superior Italian air force from intervening. The camps were also to be bombed all night to mask the noise of the Matildas penetrating the gap and getting into position for a dawn attack. Meanwhile, the Royal Navy would bombard Sidi Barrani from the sea. Wavell had limited ambitions for Compass. He envisaged it only as a great raid, especially as he had received information that the elite Fourth Indian Division was to be withdrawn for Ethiopia, to be replaced by the newly arrived Sixth Australian Division.

On 7 December, the RAF began its attacks on Italian airfields at Tripoli, Benghazi, Tobruk, El Adem, and Gambut. At Tripoli, twenty-nine Italian aircraft were destroyed on the ground by eleven Wellingtons out of Malta. Wellingtons and Blenheims destroyed another ten at Benghazi. Hurricane fighters patrolled the battlefield to keep Italian reconnaissance planes at arm's length. O'Connor began to move his troops forward on 8 December to within fifteen miles of the Rabia-Nibeiwa gap. The Italian air force, remarkably passive, failed to attack the British troop concentrations. During the bitterly cold night, the Fourth Indian Division with forty-eight Matildas and seventy-two guns slipped through the gap to set up attacking positions behind Nibeiwa. This roused the Italians, who sent up flares and fired random shots at the British. The British artillery began to register targets at 0700. Fifteen minutes later, seventy-two British guns smothered the Italian camp in shrapnel and high-explosive shells. The Matildas clattered

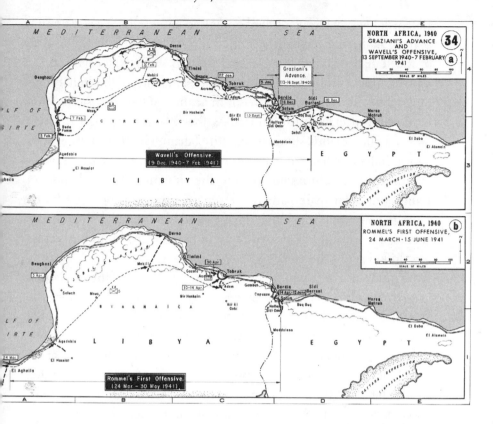

past twenty Italian light tanks on the perimeter and broke into the fortress. Highland and Indian troops, some riding Bren gun carriers—open-topped, tracked vehicles with a mounted machine gun, capable of traveling at speeds of 30 miles per hour—followed the Matildas in, guns blazing. The Italian artillery did not open fire until the British were inside their camp. Italian infantry were caught in their bunkers. A few threw grenades at the advancing Matildas. Those who could bolted for the open desert. Only the artillery attempted to twist their guns toward the east, but they quickly discovered that their shells simply bounced off the Matildas' armor. British artillery was brought forward to fire point-blank into the pockets of resistance. By 1040, Nibeiwa and 2,000 Italian POWs were in British hands at the cost of fifty-six casualties. Alan Moorehead, who arrived in the wake of the British attack, found the flies already swarming over the bodies of dead

Italian soldiers. Mules and donkeys nosed among the debris of battle, braying pathetically as they searched for fodder and water. The body of the Italian commander, General Maletti, lay spread-eagled in his tent, his medals still pinned to his tunic. The guns of the Italian light tanks pointed in every direction, an indication of the confusion caused by the unexpected British attack. As the correspondent sat down to dine on the copious stores of captured hams, bottled cherries, and wines, Indian soldiers trotted past, clutching pieces of heavily braided Italian uniform. British soldiers were already cannibalizing abandoned Italian trucks for spare parts, while engineers commandeered Italian tanks to convert to British use. The ground was littered with grenades, cartridge belts, and rifles tossed away in flight. Pages of unfinished letters drifted across the sand.[106]

The British tanks then turned north to roll up the remaining camps along lines picked out by air reconnaissance as a sandstorm began to kick up. Tummar West put up more of a fight than had Nibeiwa. But the arrival of New Zealand infantry in trucks driven through artillery and machine-gun fire to the very perimeter of the camps put an end to resistance by 1600. The First Libyan Division fled before the small British force advancing down the coast road to make good its escape into Sidi Barrani, a desolate cluster of modest houses now thoroughly shelled by the Royal Navy. On 10 December the British cleaned up Tummar East and isolated the remaining forces at Sidi Barrani. By 11 December a small Italian rear guard held on at Sollum on the Egyptian-Libyan border. Otherwise, the garrison at Sidi Barrani, thinking the British far away, had been surprised and captured almost without a fight, part of the 38,000 Italian troops, 237 guns, 73 tanks, and over 1,000 vehicles fallen into British hands. Long crocodiles of dispirited Italian soldiers dressed in dusty, gray-green uniforms trudged toward Cairo. Hundreds jostled at water points or waited patiently for British guards to hand them cheese and tinned beef from captured Italian stores; "their fear of the waterless desert overmastered any wild idea they may have had for gaining freedom," Moorehead recorded.[107] The British had lost 624 killed, wounded, and missing, together with six Blenheim bombers and six fighters.

"CORN RIPE FOR THE SICKLE"

The victory at Sidi Barrani, coming on the heels of the successful November Greek offensive that pushed the Italians back into Albania and concurrently with British advances in Eritrea and Abyssinia, pumped up British morale. It also helped Roosevelt to force Lend-Lease through Congress in March 1941. But local successes could not alter the fundamental desperation of Britain's strategic situation. The knowledge that German intervention in the Mediterranean was imminent cast a pall of apprehension over the British camp. In November 1940, Hungary, Romania, and Slovakia, sensing that momentum was flowing to Hitler, joined the Tripartite Pact. On 10 December, Hitler ordered Luftwaffe units to the Mediterranean. Churchill confessed that, for all the prewar attention given to air power, no one had foreseen its "violent impact . . . upon our control of the Mediterranean."[108] On 13 December the Führer ordered preparations for Operation Marita, the invasion of Greece and the Balkans, and five days later gave the formal directive for the invasion of the Soviet Union. Churchill told his generals that the Italians were "corn ripe for the sickle," and urged them to invade Cyrenaica. And in fact the three British commanders in Egypt were eager to press their temporary advantage against the Italians before the British troops might be dispersed to deal with other threats. Yet they faced two problems, one strategic and the other operational. Strategically, it was not clear what gains would follow from the pursuit of the retreating Italians into Cyrenaica. On the plus side, the occupation of Cyrenaica would drive the Axis from the North African shore and allow for the creation of more air bases that could attack Sicily and Italy and make it easier to defend Malta from the air. A victory in Cyrenaica would also deliver a severe blow to Italian morale. It would help the Royal Navy toward its goal of opening the Mediterranean. Leopold Amery, a member of the Middle East Committee, argued that possession of the North African shore held "the key to any future operations on a serious scale against Sicily, Sardinia or in the Balkans. It might be the Open Sesame of the whole war."[109]

The debit side of the ledger was heavy with risks, however, especially given the many demands placed on slender British resources. The first was how to attack this great shoulder of land that rises out of the North African coast like a wave breaking toward the west. The obvious route of advance followed the Litoranea, the coast road completed in 1937 that ran from Egypt to Tunis. It linked the four cheerless port settlements of Bardia, Tobruk, Derna, and Benghazi. Along it, neat townships of Italian farmers added splashes of green to an otherwise khaki landscape. And while this invasion route in theory could be supported from the sea by the Royal Navy, it was long, circuitous, and easily blocked by a resolute defender. Much of the terrain was unsuitable for tanks. An inland line of pursuit seemed out of the question. Behind the coast, the virtually impassable boulder-strewn ridge of the Jebel Akhdar, or Gree Mountains, rises to 2,500 feet. South of the Jebel Akhdar, the desert stretches, trackless, toward the Fezzan and Chad. If launched, where was the offensive to stop? At the border that separates Cyrenaica and Tripolitania? Or should the Italians be pursued to Tripoli, with the objective of driving them out of North Africa altogether? If the British committed the manpower and re-sources to this objective—assuming that they had them—what would be the trade-offs in East Africa and Greece? How might Germany react?

Wavell's operational problem was how to exploit Italian disarray at a moment when the British were hampered by their lack of transport and required to feed and evacuate an unexpectedly large number of Italian POWs. Wavell also had to substitute the experienced Fourth Indian Division with the well-trained but so far unblooded Sixth Australian Division. Eighty captured Italian trucks, as well as fifty more from Palestine, were incorporated into the Western Desert Force, which, on 1 January 1941, became the Twenty-third Corps. But the wear and tear on the vehicles, not to mention the drivers, from the great distances over rough desert tracks meant that fully 40 percent of British vehicles were out of service at any one time. The RAF strug-gled to improvise landing fields that put them in range of forward op-erations. On 16 December, Graziani abandoned Sollum and retreated with his four divisions to Bardia, a crinkle in the coastal ridge occu-pied by a scattering of low white buildings. He was closely shadowed by the Seventh Armoured Division. The Australians were moved up 350 miles from the Nile Delta to invest Bardia as the navy worked to get Sollum into shape so that the Australians could be supplied by sea. O'Connor hoped that Bardia could be taken on the bounce, his optimism encouraged by British intelligence reports that generously underestimated the size of the Bardia garrison by about one-half.[110] On the other hand, had his intelligence been more accurate, one might well ask if O'Connor would have risked an advance. His plan was to pressure the garrison with an attack from the east and south, hoping to force an evacuation into the open desert where the fleeing Italians could be caught against the coast. Unfortunately, the garrison commander, General Annibale Bergonzoli, known affectionately as "Electric Whiskers," felt confident that his 45,000 troops and 400 guns huddled behind recently completed defensive works and deep minefields could hold out indefinitely. Early probes by the Australians gave every indication that Italian morale was unshaken. O'Connor would have to assault Bardia head on.

Although the Italian army had so far failed to cover itself with glory, O'Connor was also playing a weak hand. Some of the Australians had been in theater for over a year. But the insistence of their government that they go into battle as a division or not at all delayed their introduction to combat. Gaunt, revolvers stuffed into their belts, their faces grinning gray masks of dirt beneath steel helmets, the Australians were the very picture of toughness. But they had yet to face the test of combat. The Sixth Division had only two field artillery regiments instead of three, and many of their guns were obsolete, so that British artillery units were assigned to support them. Also, given the strong defense and the absence of surprise, the Matildas would follow the infantry after it cleared a gap in the defenses, unlike at Nibeiwa, where the infantry trotted in the wake of the tanks. The attack, launched on 3 January 1941, was reminiscent of a sandy Somme. Australians bent forward under the weight of their equipment moved forward behind a thunder of guns from both land and sea. Sappers cut the wire, lifted mines, rammed Bangalore torpedoes into the slits of pillboxes, and slung bridges over the antitank trench. Matildas followed through the breaches made in the defenses and fanned out into the core of the Italian position. Some Italian positions fought bravely. Others surrendered quickly once they realized that shells fired by Italian tanks and antitank guns bounced harmlessly off the Matildas' impermeable armor. Three battleships and seven destroyers ripped Italian defenses from the sea, while the RAF ruled the sky. By 0800, the familiar crocodiles of Italian POWs were trudging into the desert. By 1500 on 4 January, the final attack by crouching Australians screaming their war cries surged down the burning main street of the town and past the town hall in the wake of the Bren carriers and Matildas, which spurted shells from every gun. They kicked open the doors of the houses and fired bursts into the interiors. An Italian machine gun sputtered near the church, then fell silent. Bardia became an Australian possession. Forty thousand stony-faced Italian POWs crawled out of cellars and caves in the cliffs by the seaside and mingled with the attackers. It soon became impossible to distinguish friend from foe within this mob of seemingly directionless soldiers. Finally, the victors sorted out the vanquished and marched them into barbed-wire pens like dejected football fans whose side has just lost a big match. Each time a British vehicle drove by, however, the Italians broke ranks to clamor for food, water, and cigarettes. Spotter planes from the carrier *Illustrious* droned overhead in search of Italian batteries, which continued to spit shells from the extreme limits of the camp. Down by the harbor, several Italian ships had settled into the blue-green water. The costs to the attackers had been 456 Australian casualties. Electric Whiskers took advantage of the confusion to escape on foot toward Tobruk.[111]

Like every silver cloud at this stage of the war, this one had a dark lining. On 11 January, Hitler ordered that a "Special Blocking Detachment" intervene in North Africa to help the Italians resist superior British armor. The code name for the dispatch of this force, originally designated as the Fifth Light Division, was *Sonnenblume*, or "Sunflower." Fliegerkorps X, in the process of arriving in Sicily, was told to extend its operations to aid the Italians in the desert. Furthermore, relations between Wavell and Churchill were sinking to a new nadir. To the prime minister's consternation, Wavell declined an offer by the South African premier, Jan Smuts, of a division for East Africa, pressing instead for more replacement and support units. He was being told by London to prepare to dispatch troops to Greece, which he resisted, provoking Churchill's anger. Even before Bardia had fallen, O'Connor had put the Seventh Armoured Division on the road toward Tobruk, the only suitable port west of Alexandria, whose capture was vital to support his armies so far forward. The town, which was to occupy such a symbolic place in the desert war, was protected much like Bardia by a half-moon of defenses anchored between eight and nine miles out on the sea. Unlike Bardia's, however, Tobruk's perimeter was reinforced by booby traps worked by trip wires. The Italian air force was practically invisible as the British forces pushed west along the coast. At least 58 Italian planes had been shot down, others had been destroyed on the ground—Moorehead counted 87 broken and burned Italian planes at El Adem just south of Tobruk[112]—and a further 91 had been abandoned and captured intact as the Italians retreated to Maraua, 170 miles west of Tobruk.[113] But the RAF was also redeploying three squadrons from North Africa to Greece. Fortunately for Wavell, on 13 January 1941 the Greek government formally rejected an offer of British troops, so he was given a green light to push on to Benghazi. However, the British were operating at the extreme limits of their logistical support, a situation alleviated somewhat by pressing captured Italian trucks into service. River gunboats from the China station, as well as Egyptian lighters, transported gasoline and water forward along the coast.

The Australian assault on Tobruk on 21 January replicated that on Bardia. Infantry led the way, with the Matildas following. Sandstorms hindered air support. As usual, the Italian artillery proved the most resolute arm, but their courage was compromised by antiquated guns and dud shells. On the first day the Australians broke into the defenses and by nightfall had occupied about half of Tobruk's perimeter. During the night, the Italians began blowing up their installations. The Italian commander surrendered at 1545 on 22 January with his 25,000 troops, 208 guns, 87 tanks, and 200 vehicles. The hulks of a dozen ships, including a passenger ship, lay sunken in the harbor. Fortunately, the Italians had not destroyed the dock cranes, and as usual the warehouses along the docks were gorged with ample stores. As the wounded were taken toward the shore to be loaded aboard ships for evacuation, the Australian brigadier who took the surrender of the town from the immaculately uniformed Italian admiral threatened to shoot an Italian for every Australian injured by one of the numerous mines and booby traps strewn about the defenses. The Italians rushed to show the British sappers where these were. The town was burning and wrecked. Furniture, children's toys, and clothes lay strewn about the streets. Stray cats were everywhere. An Australian soldier fried an egg on the mahogany counter of the National Bank. The attackers had taken 400 casualties.[114]

Sigint revealed that the Italians had decided to abandon Benghazi. O'Connor was keen to capture the important port and complete the conquest of Cyrenaica before Churchill's wild schemes could deprive his advance of momentum. Already the prime minister was ordering the creation of a strategic reserve of four divisions to support Greece and Turkey, an expedition to capture Rhodes, and, in an exercise of complete self-delusion, preparations for the occupation of Sicily! Italian moves in Ethiopia also had to be watched, all of which made it difficult for Wavell to allocate his troops according to a clear set of strategic priorities.[115] However, fighting along the coast road proved to be slow going. A fierce wind swept up clouds of red dust, hail, and rain. Italian resistance had begun to stiffen, and the terrain toward Derna, a coastal oasis of standardized squat, colonial-model bleached houses surrounded by lush banana plantations, pomegranate groves, and vegetable gardens, was broken and unsuitable for tanks. On 29 January, the Italians quit Derna after British batteries had slowly mastered the stubborn Italian artillery, while Australian raiding parties located and eliminated the forward observers. Resigned Italian soldiers prepared their kits for detention as Arabs looted the town, smashing more than they took. Italian settlers begged the Australian soldiers to stay to protect them and their women from the Arabs. Posters of Mussolini, torn and defaced, flapped on the walls. On 1 February, Graziani informed Mussolini that he intended to abandon Cyrenaica. The next day the RAF reported that the Italians were streaming west toward Barce and Benghazi over hills turned velvet by the winter rains, leaving a wake of debris and abandoned equipment.

News of the Italian retreat in conditions of unmistakable rout encouraged O'Connor to risk an advance across the desert south of the

Jebel Akhdar. Air reconnaissance of the proposed route pronounced it "difficult but possible." Sigint also revealed that the Italians had considered that the British might take this route, but discarded the idea as unworkable.[116] O'Connor decided, therefore, to send the Seventh Armoured Division south of the Jebel Akhdar across 150 miles of uncharted desert to cut the coast road south of Benghazi, while the Australians chased Graziani around the Cyrenaican hump. The British plan was as strategically inventive as it was logistically precarious. The Australians had fought two hard sieges at Bardia and Tobruk, while the tanks of the Seventh Armoured Division, already worn out, might not be up to the challenge of a cross-desert race. On the morning of 4 February, the Seventh Armoured Division set out across the desert, armored cars in the vanguard, followed by medium tanks, the Support Group, with the remaining heavier tanks bringing up the rear. Early going was dreadful. The column picked its way slowly forward across wadis and through boulders, as a sandstorm raged around it. Officers stood on the seats of their vehicles like helmsmen at the bar, gripping compasses and peering into the opaque gloom. After fifty miles, however, the boulders gave way to open sand, enabling the armored cars to race ahead.

At noon on 5 February, the advanced guard of British armored cars reached the coastal road south of the small settlement of Beda Fomm just in time to cut off the retreat of the Italian column heading south from Benghazi toward Tripolitania. The head of the Italian column was halted by British mines hastily planted across the road. British artillery fire crashed into the immobile vehicles while British tanks ranged up and down the column on the inland side slashing at their enemies. On the morning of 6 February, the Italians tried to muscle their way through the British blockade, ranging one hundred tanks against twenty-nine medium British Cruisers. The Mark III Cruiser, developed in 1938, was known for its speed (almost 50 miles per hour) rather than its power. Given its light 2-pounder (40 mm) gun, probably the only tanks it could successfully swap blows with were Italian varieties. Fortunately for the British, Italian confusion and demoralization was such that they utterly failed to coordinate their attacks. Italian tanks appeared in small packets, stuck to the road, and made no attempt to maneuver. After an artillery barrage smothered an attempted breakthrough by thirty Italian tanks on the morning of 7 February, white flags began to appear all along the Italian column. It was in good time, as the British had almost exhausted their ammunition.

One historian has called Compass "one of the most dramatically one-sided military campaigns in modern history."[117] Since Sidi Barrani on 9 December, ten Italian divisions had succumbed to an attack by two understrength British divisions. Some 130,000 Italian soldiers had been taken prisoner, along with hundreds of tanks, vehicles, and guns, at a cost of 500 British dead, 1,373 wounded, and 55 missing. O'Connor signaled to Wavell, "Fox killed in the open." Graziani sent exculpatory telegrams to Rome, complaining that he had been forced by Mussolini into a premature advance in Egypt. "Here is another man with whom I cannot get angry," Mussolini replied, "because I despise him." For his part, Churchill had every reason to feel content. "We were alive," he remembered, a bet that many would have been reluctant to place six months earlier. Britain's factories hummed and her army was slowly regenerating both its strength and its reputation. "Victory sparkled in the Libyan Desert," Churchill added, "and across the Atlantic the Great Republic drew ever nearer to her duty and our aid."[118] However, growing evidence of Hitler's intention to intervene in the Mediterranean, as well as increased Japanese aggressiveness in the Far East, made Churchill all the more eager to liquidate the situation in Italian East Africa. Above all, the Red Sea must be cleared for U.S. shipping in preparation for a German offensive in the Balkans.

THE EAST AFRICAN CAMPAIGN

The Italian debacle in North Africa sealed the fate of Italy's other great overseas enclave, Italian East Africa. What Mussolini liked to call the "pearl of the Fascist regime" was a vast trinity of territories that hooked east into the Indian Ocean. Mussolini's 1935 decision to annex Ethiopia, thereby joining it to Eritrea and Italian Somaliland, had begun the downward spiral of his relations with Britain and France. In 1939, Prince Amedeo of Savoy, Duke of Aosta, a forty-one-year-old cousin of the Italian king, had added the title of commander-in-chief of Italian forces in East Africa to those of governor-general of the territory and viceroy of Ethiopia, which he had held since Graziani's departure in 1937. Tall, elegant, cultivated, the duke utterly lacked the touch of low cunning and ruthlessness that might have made him a Mussolini favorite. On the contrary, Aosta's stylish demeanor and excellent English, considered a sign of cultivation in a Continental, made him very popular with the British, who were rumored after his surrender in 1941 to be grooming him to replace Vittorio Emanuele as king of Italy. Unfortunately, the duke died in captivity in Nairobi in 1942. However, if his military abilities offered an indicator of political sagacity, it is unlikely that the postwar House of Savoy would have prospered under Aosta's direction any more than it did under Vittorio Emanuele.[119]

Mussolini's rash decision to go to war in June 1940 had caught Aosta practically unprepared. As war loomed, the duke had traveled to Rome in April successfully to extract a promise of reinforcements. But an early trickle of men and supplies had been promptly stanched by the Royal Navy in June. Nevertheless, Italian East Africa was a significant strategic asset at this point in the war. It lay on the flank of Britain's vital sea routes to Suez from the Cape of Good Hope and from India. Of particular concern to the British was an Italian naval force of nine destroyers, eight submarines, and other assorted vessels based at Massawa in Eritrea. The threat that these posed to the flow of supplies was such that the United States had declared that no American ship might enter the "combat zone" of the Red Sea. This American decision pushed Britain's critical shipping shortage toward crisis and jeopardized the success of British operations in the Eastern Mediterranean. On paper, at least, Italian East African forces appeared formidable in 1940—around 250,000 troops, 323 aircraft, 60 tanks, and 100 armored cars, against British-raised forces that numbered barely 40,000, backed by only 100 aircraft scattered around the borders of the Sudan, Kenya, and British Somaliland. Because the Italian army had changed its high-grade cipher in late summer, British intelligence could offer its commanders only minimal guidance about the Italian order of battle, their state of readiness, and their intentions. Therefore, well into the autumn, the British continued to fear an Italian offensive into the Sudan or Kenya.[120]

Nevertheless, on closer inspection, the Italian advantages evaporated. Seventy percent of Italian forces were locally raised and organized into irregular *bande* under the command of Italian officers and NCOs. Armed mainly with barbed spears and long knives, *bande* were scattered around the territories to keep the usually restive tribes in check. Some, like the Fourth Eritrean "Toselli" Battalion, which was virtually annihilated at Keren, might on occasion fight well. But generally they were as much of a threat to their own officers as to the enemy. The Duke of Aosta counted only one regular Italian division, the Savoia, and a second raised among Italian immigrants, as well as 27,000 Blackshirts, or Fascist militia, organized into battalions. Many of his aircraft were in need of repair and were poorly served by ground staffs, and the pilots had little experience in cooperating with ground operations other than police duties. The Italian strength, as in North Africa, lay in ten artillery groups. Although the duke had built up about seven months of supplies, there were shortages of practically everything, but especially fuel, tires, aircraft and truck spares, and ammunition of all types.[121]

Cut off from outside aid, Aosta clearly had to act quickly, especially while British forces were weak, or be condemned to wither. But Aosta had no strategic plan. His best hope for survival was to coordinate an offensive toward Khartoum and Egypt with Graziani in Cyrenaica. But Graziani had caught a heavy dose of caution, encouraged by Badoglio, who urged Aosta to remain on the defensive, under the assumption that the war would soon be over. A second option would be a lunge toward Djibouti. This would have given him the best harbor in the Horn of Africa, from which his naval flotilla might have dominated the narrow choke point where the Gulf of Aden meets the Red Sea. It would also have eliminated Djibouti as a potential British reentry point. France's rapid collapse and the subsequent Franco-Italian armistice did not completely remove Djibouti as a threat so long as the governor, Paul Legentilhomme, leaned toward the Free French. But Aosta feared that an attack on Djibouti might force Legentilhomme to summon British help. Third, he might strike south to seize Mombasa, denying Britain a deep harbor to discharge troops and equipment from South Africa. But Aosta dithered, convinced that East Africa's fate would be decided elsewhere. Vacillation, combined with the duke's fear that pulling his *bande* from their distant outposts for a coordinated offensive would offer the signal for restive natives to rebel, virtually paralyzed any initiative. Aosta contented himself in July with occupying three British outposts on the Sudanese border and overrunning a desolate stretch of desert in northern Kenya. Acting on the weak assumption that British Somaliland offered a potential base for a British attack, and possibly also in the hope that it might become a bargaining chip in future peace negotiations, he seized that territory in August. But the military effort wasted his scarce resources and distracted him from potentially more lucrative objectives, like Djibouti or Mombasa.

With the Italians rigid in a defensive posture, initiative passed by default to the British. The desire to eliminate the interdiction on American ships traveling to Suez combined with Aosta's geographic isolation to place him squarely in Churchill's crosshairs. The prime minister also hoped that a victory in East Africa might deter Japanese aggression in the Far East, and offer a quick-fix morale boost to the victory-starved British. That said, however, no obvious plan of attack jumped out at strategists sitting in London. Italian East Africa was vast, running two thousand kilometers from east to west and slightly more than that from north to south. But even more daunting than the distances was the terrain. The Ethiopian core of Italian East Africa was a land of lush, savage precipices and profound gorges, surrounded by desert wastes so scorched and corkscrewed by ridges of rock and sand that even veterans of North Africa shuddered at their desolation. Any force aiming for Addis Ababa, a collection of wooden huts graced by white Italian colonial buildings set amid endless groves of eucalyptus at 7,000 feet of altitude, would confront a logistical and tactical nightmare. Although Italian East Africa was wedged in by British territory on three sides and open to an amphibious attack along any of its extensive coasts, no obvious route of invasion beckoned. Both Kenya and the Sudan offered poor logistical bases to support a campaign. Fear of

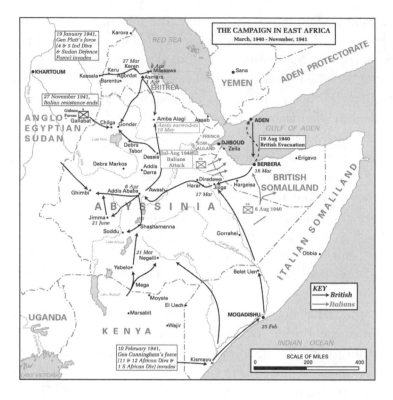

antagonizing the Vichy French removed Djibouti as a possible amphibious entry. The best option, especially given a dearth of British resources, was to foment internal rebellion. Even before war broke out,
Wavell had ordered D. A. Sandford, a former settler in Ethiopia expelled by the Italians, to begin to establish a network of indigenous,
anti-Italian "Patriot" supporters inside the country. On 3 July 1940, the
London-exiled Emperor Haile Selassie was flown to Khartoum on the
promise that Britain would restore Ethiopian independence. Drawing
on a significant community of Ethiopian exiles in the Sudan and
Kenya and contacts inside the country, Sandford led "101 Mission"
into Ethiopia in mid-August.[122]

In the end, the British would advance into Italian East Africa on
three fronts, two from Sudan and one launched from Kenya in the
south. Aosta's defensive plan called for the organization of centers of
resistance in Eritrea, Amhara, and Gojjam, linked by mobile brigades
that would harass the flanks of the British advance. Despite the com-

mand of a vast and inhospitable territory in which to retreat, the duke feared that withdrawal would bring fragile local loyalties crashing down on his head.[123] What Aosta failed to realize, however, was that his every move was an open book to his enemies. In November, Bletchley Park broke the Italian army's high-grade cipher in East Africa, while the Italian air force code was unraveled by Middle East code breakers. Soon, ciphers used by the colonial authorities, the *carabinieri*, and lower military units were regularly read. Aosta's situation report, broadcast daily to Rome, was received by the British as quickly as by Badoglio. In this way the British had daily, sometimes hourly, updates on the Italian supply situation and other weaknesses, as well as details of every Italian move, a vital asset that supplemented the dearth of air reconnaissance. British intercept stations were sited to receive every Italian communication, a task made easier by the fact that the isolation of East Africa meant that the Italians could not make frequent changes to their codes. This ensured a steady flow of detailed information about Italian plans and dispositions, turning the East African campaign into "the perfect [if rather miniature] example of the cryptographers' war."[124]

Intelligence indicated the first British front by revealing Aosta's deteriorating morale from December as Graziani's collapse unfolded in Cyrenaica. The duke requested permission from Rome to withdraw his advanced defenses along the Sudanese frontier, lest he suffer Graziani's fate at Sidi Barrani. Tipped off by his intelligence, Major General William Platt launched an offensive with the Fourth and Fifth Indian Divisions on the heels of the retreating Italians on 19 January 1941, even though his air force and support units were not fully in place. At first, after an entire Italian brigade surrendered to Platt's advancing forces, the British looked for a rerun of Compass. However, General Luigi Frusci at the head of the Savoia Division fought a stubborn retreat that allowed him to fortify the boulder-strewn precipice of the 2,000-foot Asmara Plateau. This, combined with air superiority and Platt's logistical difficulties, worked to Italian advantage. The arrival of South African–piloted Hurricanes as well as help from RAF bases in Aden gradually tilted the air balance in Britain's favor. Platt was able to follow events so closely on the Italian side through signal intercepts that Cairo could claim that no "commander in the field had been better served by his intelligence than the Commander of the forces operating in East Africa."[125] By March, those intercepts revealed Italian strength at Keren to have been reduced by a third, and the Italians were suffering severely from air and artillery bombardment.[126] Still, pressure to shift troops to Greece almost caused Wavell to cancel Platt's Keren operation.[127] On 27 March, after a stubborn battle lasting several days, Indian troops fought their way through the Dongolaas Gorge to seize Keren. This proved the decisive battle of the campaign, breaking open Frusci's front and opening the way to the port of Massawa, which fell to a combined force of Indian and Free French troops on 8 April. Flushed from their lair, four Italian destroyers were sunk by British aircraft while two others were scuttled.

A second axis of British advance would come from the south. By late January 1941, Churchill chaffed that 77,000 African, South African, and Rhodesian forces, gathered through Mombasa, and 9,000 vehicles, mostly trucks driven by Africans 1,500 miles from Broken Hill in Northern Rhodesia to Nairobi to save shipping space, remained "virtually out of action in Kenya."[128] Indeed, Nairobi shimmered like a manicured Surrey garden set in a landscape of endless tea and coffee plantations. Life in the Kenyan capital combined the excesses of the prewar Riviera with the pleasures of colonial Africa. Men golfed at Brackenridge or set out on safari attended by a swarm of beaters and servants. Evening found them in dinner jackets or dress uniform standing before the log fire at the Muthaiga Club in the company of elegant women swathed in baboon pelts and leopard skins. Rationing was a word no one could pronounce, much less spell—tables groaned with game, freshly caught trout, bottles of Rhine wine and champagne. Even beneath this privileged crust, the fact that significant numbers of female drivers and secretaries in khaki had been imported from England and South Africa meant that, unlike Cairo and Alexandria, "every soldier had his girl." Indeed, Alan Moorehead discovered that "the lounge of the New Stanley Hotel was one solid rendezvous." "After the desert I found it all delightful," he confessed, "as though the world were enjoying one long holiday."[129]

Despite Moorehead's contention that the army was eager to move, advances into southern Ethiopia by South African troops over the blistered lava rock of the Chalbi Desert in February met only limited success. However, a strike by two African divisions directed by Lieutenant General A. G. Cunningham, brother of Admiral A. B. Cunningham, into Italian Somaliland in February took him rapidly up the coast to Kismayu and Mogadishu, where the Italians had obligingly abandoned significant stores, including 400,000 gallons of precious gasoline. Distance and the imminent threat of monsoon, rather than the enemy, who put up no systematic opposition, became Cunningham's major enemy. South African engineers moved ahead of the advancing troops to dig wells. The fragile roads rapidly disintegrated under the weight of trucks. The Royal Navy reappeared at Berbera on 16 March. The Italians performed their by now familiar disappearing act, so British Somaliland was quickly returned to its previous proprietor, and Cunningham's supply lines were shortened by 600 miles. Planes based in Aden attacked remaining Italian air bases. Efforts to persuade the Vichy French to open Djibouti so that Cunningham could support his advance west along the rail line through Harrar to Addis Ababa broke up on the escalating animosity between the warring French factions. Nevertheless, after Cunningham handed back a division and a brigade of South African troops and a considerable amount of transport to the Middle East commander, Wavell authorized the advance on Addis Ababa.

As the pursuit entered the mountains, Italians abandoned one strong position after another in the face of Cunningham's advance. A strong air attack on Addis Ababa airfield destroyed thirty aircraft on the ground. On 5 April an Italian officer appeared to beg Cunningham to enter the town as soon as possible to control the native population. The next day, Cunningham's force rode into the Ethiopian capital to set up headquarters in the Duke of Aosta's palace. Almost immediately, British forces were dispatched to outlying communities to retrieve Italian settlers attacked by the restive native population. Italian soldiers, some still in uniform, fought the former *bande,* a situation very confusing to British troops. "Oo the hell are we fighting anyway," Moorehead heard a Cockney soldier ask, "the Wops or them niggers?"[130] The capture of Addis Ababa culminated an eight-week march of 1,700 miles at a cost of 501 British casualties and eight airplanes. In the process, Churchill boasted, 50,000 Italian troops had been killed, captured, or dispersed.

The third axis of advance into Ethiopia was an unconventional one east from the Sudan into Gojjam province by "Patriot" forces, whose goal was to stimulate rebellion and gradually engulf Addis Ababa from the west. Colonel D. A. Sandford, dispatched in August to prepare the ground, faced at least three problems, the first of which was that while the local chieftains had no love for the Italians, they had even less love for each other. A second was the sheer dearth of weapons, and mules to move them, so that the Polish Brigade in Palestine had to be disarmed to provide rifles for the Ethiopians. Sandford's third problem was the man Wavell assigned to work with him — Major Orde Wingate. Diminutive, wearing a full beard and an arrogant scowl beneath a tall, imperial-era pith helmet that looked to have come from either a costume shop or a distant ancestor, Wingate was a pioneer of what was coming to be known as special operations. He had leaped to Wavell's attention as leader of the Special Night Squads, groups of Palestine Jews organized by Wingate to retaliate against the grand mufti's attacks on Jewish settlements and against the Haifa oil pipeline. Wingate was flown into Ethiopia to meet Sandford on 20 November. The plan they worked out with General Platt was to seize a stronghold in Gojjam, install the emperor, and widen the area of revolt, drawing off as many Italian troops as possible. Sandford was made a brigadier and the emperor's personal adviser, while Wingate took over 101 Mission, which he renamed "Gideon Force," with the acting rank of colonel. Mobile attacks on isolated posts and ambushes along the main routes created a deep sense of insecurity in the minds of Italian forces in Gojjam. Success swelled "Patriot" forces, and pressed the Italians ever more into the defensive. As typical in the course of the campaign, the Italian tendency obligingly to abandon stores as they retreated resolved many of Wingate's logistical problems, lessened his dependency on camels, and permitted more daring operations. The presence of the emperor, combined with a special propaganda section complete with loudspeakers created by Wingate, and periodic appearances by the RAF to bomb Italian forts, encouraged *bande* desertion.

With little more than bluff, rapid movement, and sharp attacks, Wingate cajoled and enticed the surrender of over 8,000 Italian troops armed with artillery, with a Gideon Force that numbered no more than 50 officers, 20 British NCOs, 800 trained Sudanese, and 800 partially trained Ethiopians.[131] Wingate received a bar for the DSO he had won in Palestine, and eventually (after recovering from an attempt at suicide) followed his patron Wavell to the Far East and fame as leader of the Chindits in Burma. Haile Selassie entered his capital on 5 May.

The "pearl of the Fascist regime" had endured a mere five years. Italian military performance, if slightly more tenacious than in Cyrenaica, still posted a high POW-to-casualty rate. The fact that native forces had defected en masse was hardly an advertisement for Fascist imperialism. The Italian destroyers and subs at Massawa had demonstrated a stunning lack of energy, failing to inhibit the arrival of British reinforcements at Mombasa or Port Sudan, or oppose the landing at Berbera. Nor had the Italians struck at the etiolated British logistics, but instead had abandoned supplies in their retreat, facilitating the British advance.[132] In February 1941, even before Massawa had surrendered, Churchill grew impatient about scarce resources being funneled into the East Africa campaign. He urged Wavell to clear Eritrea and leave Ethiopia "to rot by itself."[133] The Fourth Indian Division and many of the air squadrons withdrew to Egypt. However, significant forces led by the Duke of Aosta retreated to Amba Alagi, a stronghold at 10,000 feet in the mountains. Between 20 April and 15 May, Aosta stubbornly resisted British and "Patriot" forces, which steadily reduced his perimeter until the duke was obliged to surrender. On 19 May, 5,000 Italian troops marched past a guard of honor to be disarmed. Significant remnants of Italian forces remained in the southwest around Galla-Sidaom and at Gondar, north of Lake Tana. Demoralized, attacked by partisans, and undermined by desertion, they made no attempt at concerted resistance. The main British, Indian, and South African divisions moved to North Africa, leaving mopup operations to African units.[134] The July 1941 surrender of the final resisting Italians to a contingent of Belgians from the Congo, soldiers of a country that Mussolini considered unworthy of the title of nationhood, imposed a special humiliation. As usual, however, the Italian dictator blamed the disgrace on the "deficiency in the Italian race."[135] Churchill's hope that the loss of East Africa, combined with Compass, would induce the implosion of the Italian regime proved an overoptimistic one. Nor did the British victory appear to make much of an impression in Tokyo. However, Britain had achieved at least one of its main objectives in the campaign: on 11 April, Roosevelt lifted the Red Sea and the Gulf of Aden from the list of "combat zones," allowing U.S. ships to proceed to Suez.

CHAPTER THREE

Tactical Triumphs, Strategic Misjudgments

CAUTIOUS OPTIMISM reigned in Cairo in mid-March 1941. London, Bristol, Portsmouth, and South Wales were smothered in the Blitz, while U-boats and the German surface raider *Admiral Hipper* made the Atlantic crossing a perilous one. But Franco resisted Hitler's blandishments to intervene in the war, thereby according Gibraltar a stay of execution. Greece and Cyrenaica were *Italianfrei*. Mussolini's East Africa teetered on the edge of extinction, which would open the Red Sea to U.S. Liberty Ships, whose serial production Roosevelt announced in January. On 1 February, Washington reorganized the U.S. Navy into Atlantic and Pacific fleets. Nine days later, the Royal Navy launched an audacious raid on Genoa, sinking five Italian ships and damaging a further eighteen. The *Regina Navale* never laid a glove on them. The latent volatility of the Middle East remained in abeyance. The spokes of what Alan Moorehead referred to as the "huge wheel [of British dispositions in the Eastern Mediterranean] with Cairo as its hub" stretched south toward Addis Ababa, north to Athens, west to Tobruk and Malta, and east toward Baghdad.[1] Within days, however, Axis offensives in North Africa and Greece, combined with a rebellion in Baghdad assisted by the Vichy French in Damascus, threatened to strike that imperial wheel from its pivot. By the summer of 1941, Britain seemed an Axis thrust away from collapse in the Eastern Mediterranean.

What had gone wrong? Received wisdom holds that British setbacks were the consequence of Churchill's willingness "to scatter and divide forces in a number of separate and disconnected operations."[2] Most criticized is Churchill's dispatch of troops to Greece in late March 1941, which ignored Balkan political realities as it overestimated British military capabilities.[3] Churchill violated the principle of the concentration of force and squandered precious divisions and equipment that Britain amassed by dint of great effort in the Middle East on a doomed enterprise. "Paradoxically," writes British General W.G.F. Jackson, "[British] successes contributed to a cumulative spiral of British strategic misjudgements, which developed concurrently with their tactical triumphs. The impetus of their mistakes gathered momentum with each cycle of decision making until their rush to disaster became irresistible."[4] Churchill's strategic miscalculations were part of a grievous pattern. Like an eighteenth-century physician, the prime minister continued to purge his patient until he practically succumbed. In December 1940, the experienced Fourth Indian Division departed Cyrenaica for an important but sideshow campaign in Italian East Africa, just as Compass metamorphosed from a major raid into a momentum-changing offensive. Constant prime ministerial shifting and scattering of overstretched British forces was not disastrous in the short term only because British generals managed brilliantly to improvise against an Italian enemy that never recovered its equilibrium after Graziani's collapse at Sidi Barrani.

On 11 February 1941, however, four days after the thumping British victory at Beda Fomm, as the road to Tripoli yawned practically defenseless before him, the prime minister halted O'Connor's offensive at the frontier of Tripolitania so that he could redirect troops to the defense of Greece. According to the German official history, at least two things were wrong with this decision. The first is that by halting O'Connor Churchill squandered a strategic opportunity that would not be offered to him again for another two years. Had British forces pushed on to Tripoli, the argument goes, the Germans would never have been able to intervene on the south shore of the Mediterranean, and Egypt would have been secure. "Churchill's decision gave the Germans the opportunity to intervene successfully in North Africa, and two years were to pass before the British, together with the Americans, were able to achieve the final victory there which had been so near in February 1941."[5] Tripoli could have become a bomber base to attack Sicily and hence weaken Mussolini's grip on power. A British advance to the frontiers of French North Africa would have allowed Churchill to charm French North Africa's Vichy proconsuls, presumably after a sincere apology for Mers el-Kébir, back into the war.[6]

The second problem with Churchill's strategic judgment was that by intervening in Greece, the British were tossing good money after bad. British diplomats had failed utterly to construct a Balkan front against a German advance that could serve as a solid foundation for a strategic plan that incorporated all contingencies. The Greeks had batted a good first innings against Mussolini. But Britain's Balkan policy was already in receivership. Greek President Metaxas refused to allow a British deployment to prepare well-sited defensive positions, a logistical infrastructure, and air bases, not to mention a common defense plan, lest this trigger the looming German avalanche. British intelligence was better informed about prospective German movements in the Balkans than it was about the plans of Yugoslavia, Greece, and Turkey to oppose them.[7] In fact, the more British soldiers learned of Greece's military situation, the more desperate it seemed.[8] Absent pure luck or German miscalculation, intervention in Greece could offer little beyond a token gesture of solidarity.[9] Nevertheless, the British reinforced diplomatic failure with the dispatch of four British divisions, of which only one was experienced, to a doomed enterprise in Greece. These formed a barrier against the German invasion so frail that, once the Germans attacked, British forces were obliged to flee for their lives, abandoning their equipment and marooning many soldiers on the beaches. The British move betrayed a serious underestimation of the power of German forces that was all the more surprising given Britain's 1940 experience. From its inception, therefore, British intervention in Greece held the promise of nothing more than another humiliating rerun of Narvik and Dunkirk.[10]

There is much to commend this view. Apart from the shortcomings cataloged above, it demonstrated both indecision and mismanagement in the British camp. Indecision because intervention in Greece continued to be an on-again, off-again strategic proposition vir-

tually up to the disembarkation of British forces in Piraeus. Mismanagement because British troops were distributed among competing
strategic objectives. The forces left to guard Egypt's vulnerable western
flank in Cyrenaica were too enfeebled to carry out the mission. The
experienced forces that had stormed Cyrenaica were replaced there by
the partially trained and equipped Ninth Australian Division and the
understrength and untried Second Armoured Division, on the premise that the Germans could not act in North Africa before May at the
earliest. Meanwhile, Wavell continued to press his campaign in Italian East Africa long after it had ceased to pay any strategic dividends,
in the process tying down two veteran Indian divisions and a South
African division. (Two black divisions in Ethiopia were not considered
suitable for European-style warfare.) "While Churchill misjudged
force levels," General Jackson concludes, "Wavell miscalculated
time."[11]

Still, the problem with the condemnation of Churchill's decision
to aid Greece ignores a central purpose of the Mediterranean commitment. The political and military arguments for defending Athens were
as compelling as the negative consequences of extending Compass to
Tripoli. In London, the failed policy of appeasement was a tough
legacy to live down. British credibility appeared to be at stake in early
1941, a moment when Anglo-French failure to come to Poland's aid
was still fresh in everyone's mind. The strategic penalties for allowing
Greece to fall uncontested to the Axis also appeared, at the time, to be
immense. The cabinet was unable to ascertain Hitler's intentions in
the Eastern Mediterranean. British intelligence traced German troop
movements into the Balkans. But did Hitler intend a seize-and-hold
operation? Or was the Balkan offensive prelude to a plunge into the
Middle East?[12] In the early months of 1941, the cabinet's strategic assessment was that growing evidence of German plans to intervene in
Greece, Yugoslavia, and possibly Turkey indicated ambitious offensive
goals. In its view, Hitler sought to crumble the Balkans, overrun or co-
opt Turkey, and seize Iraq and the Suez Canal from the north. Cairo
disagreed with this assessment, because in their view the Wehrmacht
did not have the logistical capacity for such an enterprise. Nevertheless, the fear persisted in London that Hitler's intention was to attack

Britain's base in the Eastern Mediterranean and force her to divert troops from the defense of the United Kingdom.[13]

Second, the strategic risks of Mediterranean intervention were incurred by Hitler, not Churchill. By choosing to fight in the Mediterranean, Hitler telegraphed the first indications that German strategy was bankrupt. While for some Germans, intervention in the Mediterranean revived venerable ambitions to dominate the Balkans, the Middle East, and part of Africa to secure oil, bread, and strategic position,[14] Hitler had no intention of following through on his Mediterranean thrusts. In the spring of 1941, Hitler's reasons for crashing the Italian-British war were three: bolster his Italian ally, preempt Stalin's intervention in the Balkans, and secure his southern flank in preparation for his June invasion of the Soviet Union. Operation Marita, launched on 6 April 1941, followed by a week Rommel's debut attack in Cyrenaica. These dual offensives, while spectacular, were pulled punches rather than knockout blows. The simple fact was that Hitler saw the Mediterranean as a cul-de-sac. His strategic priorities and ambitions lay elsewhere. So, in the longer term, German intervention in the Mediterranean merely served to showcase Axis weaknesses, among them the dysfunctional nature of the Axis as an alliance and the fact that Hitler had embarked on a world war without the vision of a world power. It possibly impacted the timing of Barbarossa and diverted vital men and materials from the Eastern Front that opened in June 1941. Having conquered Greece and the Balkans, Hitler had to hold them against growing partisan disruption and Allied threat. The troops he dispatched to the southern shore of the Mediterranean were too few to prevail over British, and ultimately Allied, forces. Instead, Marita offered Churchill opportunities for success that ultimately strengthened his cause. In short, it was Hitler, not Churchill, who violated the principle of concentration of force.

Although it was not apparent at the time, the payoff for the British and ultimately the Allies from Hitler's Mediterranean offensive was immense, on the strategic, operational, and tactical levels. Strategically, the Mediterranean offered a dramatic venue where Britain could showcase its refusal to accept German domination of Europe. Britain's Mediterranean operations leveraged U.S. policy and, in the process, extended a European war into a world war. The campaigns in Cyrenaica, Italian East Africa, and Greece, though often considered at best secondary, at worst wasteful, were important building blocks in that process. The first two demonstrated that Britain had the will and capacity for victory, the latter that Britain was willing to accept its responsibilities as a great power, even if the consequences of doing so were (temporary) military setbacks. In April 1939, Britain had given a guarantee to Greece. However, keen not to provoke German intervention, Metaxas had kept the British at arm's length. After Metaxas's death on 29 January 1941, the new Greek prime minister, Alexandros Koryzis, requested on 8 February that the particulars of the British forces earmarked to intervene in Greece be settled. Even though the dangers of intervention were clear, it was hardly the time for Britain to shirk its obligations to an ally. A British refusal to dispatch an expeditionary force to Athens would have had an unfavorable impact on Yugoslavia and Turkey, not to mention Greece. "It was our aim to animate and combine Yugoslavia, Greece and Turkey," Churchill remembered. "Our duty so far as possible was to aid the Greeks."[15] The consequences of a British abandonment of Greece would have struck hard at the morale of the British people, whose memories of the Allied failure to succor Poland were fresh, and for whom the bombardment and anguish of Malta were daily news. The Arab world would have viewed it as a sign of weakness. Above all, it would have diminished support for Britain in the United States. Roosevelt pronounced Britain's defeat in Greece "heroic" and promptly dispatched more matériel. The Mediterranean therefore became the place where the United States could make its power felt, at first incrementally through the introduction of equipment, and finally with her armed forces. From this, it was but a small step to transform the Mediterranean into a bridge that linked the Western democracies with the Soviet Union in an anti-Hitler coalition.[16]

On the operational and tactical levels, Hitler's decision to intervene in a theater where he was endemically weak was a godsend. The requirement to support Axis forces around the Mediterranean enabled the Allies to apply their maritime superiority against Axis weakness. The Italians forfeited their merchant fleet and much of their navy trying to ferry supplies to North Africa. On land, the North African campaign allowed the Allies to experiment with fighting techniques against one of Germany's best field commanders in a place where Rommel was limited to operational and tactical, rather than strategic, successes. Ultimately North Africa helped the Allies to identify their most able commanders, bought time to build up an unstoppable superiority of matériel, and aided a transition to an offensive that took them from Egypt to Tunisia, Sicily, Italy, and, ultimately, into southern France. Therefore, it could be argued that a successful seizure of Tripoli by O'Connor in February 1941, even had it been possible, would have led to stalemate and possibly even put the Allies on the road to defeat. It would have frozen the British, and ultimately the American, learning curve and short-circuited the evolution of a force that could match the Germans in the open field. It would have tempted the Allies to launch an early, and most probably unsuccessful, assault on the Continent in 1943. Churchill had every incentive to entice the Axis into a duel on the Mediterranean's African shore. The strategic consequences for the Allies of factoring the Mediterranean out of World War II would have been uniformly negative.

Finally, one must not ignore that the military arguments for persisting with an offensive toward Tripoli were equally weak in February 1941. Even without a decision to intervene in Greece, a British thrust toward Tripoli was not in the cards in February 1941. O'Connor had reached the end of his logistical tether at Beda Fomm. The Seventh Armoured Division was in serious need of refitting, and the Second Armoured Division that replaced it was undertrained and insufficiently equipped. Rommel and elements of the Fifth Light Division, the force that subsequently would gain fame as the Afrika Korps, had begun to disembark at Tripoli on 14 February to constitute, together with four Italian divisions, a "blocking force" against a British advance. Of course the counterargument is that the forces earmarked for Greece or left to mop up in Italian East Africa could have captured Tripoli. But the difficulty was how to get sufficient forces there and sustain them before Rommel grew strong enough successfully to defend Tripoli. The Royal Navy doubted that it could support an advance to Tripoli and maintain the bases and lines of supply, especially given its shortages in light craft, escorts, local defense vessels, mine sweepers, and shore-based personnel, all while honoring its other commitments.[17] The January 1941 arrival of Fliegerkorps X in the Mediterranean had announced the opening of a new day in the maritime war, when land-based aircraft would begin to challenge Britain's maritime dominance. Stukas seriously damaged the carrier *Illustrious* off Malta and sank the cruiser *Southampton* near Crete. The bombing of Malta intensified, and it was no longer safe to pass convoys through the central Mediterranean. The Cape route was secure, but long and expensive in shipping. The Lend-Lease bill had passed the U.S. House of Representatives on 6 February 1941, and became law on 27 March. In that month, President Roosevelt declared that "the end of compromise with tyranny" had come, and U.S. aid would flow to Britain "until victory." Encouraging words, but in the meantime, the RAF feared that Tripoli would require a large number of planes and antiaircraft artillery to defend, equipment it did not have. From January, too, German planes from Rhodes were sowing the Suez Canal, as well as Sollum and Tobruk, with both magnetic and acoustic mines, which periodically closed down Suez and caused serious logistical backups. Benghazi was regularly bombed. Therefore, it was not at all obvious that the major threat to Egypt came from the west rather than the north, especially given the inconclusive nature of British intelligence appreciation. Nor did anyone at the time, least of all Hitler and the German high command, anticipate that within a month of landing in North Africa Rommel would be capable of dismantling all the British gains in Cyrenaica.

"THE NEW DUNKIRK AT SALONIKA"

Rommel's success in Cyrenaica, combined with news of Rashid Ali's coup in Baghdad, transformed an already tenuous British plan for intervention in Greece into a desperate gamble. Whatever the political and strategic benefits of aiding Greece, it rapidly became clear to those organizing the intervention that British strategy was anchored in wishful thinking. The British understood that only the most battleworthy troops should be sent to confront the Germans. However, of the three divisions and two brigades nominated for the expedition, only the Sixth Australian Division was battle-tested.[18] The navy complained that it lacked shipping to transport and supply men for Greece, and that the combination of the Italian navy and the Luftwaffe would make it difficult to keep the sea lanes of communication to Greece open. It feared that Germans traveling overland could strike well into Greece before British forces were in a position to oppose them. Finally, the British army was unhappy with the Greek plan. In particular, it was upset that the Greeks had not abandoned forward positions in Albania and Macedonia, and fallen back to a position north of Larissa known as the Aliákmon line. Unless this was done, a German thrust through Yugoslavia would split the Greek armies in the east and west and compromise the British intervention.[19] Thus, from the outset, the British accepted a risk of Olympian stature in Greece. When journalists selected to cover the Greek expedition gathered in the Hotel Cecil in Alexandria, a gloomy toast was raised to "the new Dunkirk at Salonika."[20]

One reason the Greeks could not disengage to reconstitute a more coherent defense line farther south was that on 6 March, the Italians launched a twenty-eight-division offensive along a twenty-mile front against the fourteen Greek divisions in Albania. Mussolini, eager to achieve a breakthrough before the Germans could attack, arrived in Albania to supervise operations. A week passed before it became clear that once again, an Italian offensive had sputtered. Mussolini declared—unconvincingly—that the attack was never intended to be anything more than a "reconnaissance in force," and returned to Rome in disgust.[21] Nevertheless, the Italian thrust had caused the Greek army to expend much of its ammunition, which, combined with a winter of unimaginable misery spent in the mountains, had left Greek forces in sad shape. Worse for the British, Greek success against the despised Mussolini had made Greek generals even more reluctant to surrender territory for which so much blood had been shed. Although British troops arriving in what was designated as "W Force" were cheered by the Greek population, official Greece was ambivalent, even hostile, to the British rescue attempt. The fatalism of inevitable defeat permeated the Greek high command, which, having fought doggedly against the Italians, instinctively realized that the

German, Italian, and Hungarian divisions that massed in Bulgaria and around the frontiers of Yugoslavia were beyond their capacities to delay, much less defeat. The Greek government was desperate not to provoke the Germans, to the point that General Maitland "Jumbo" Wilson, W Force's commander-in-chief, arrived in Greece in civilian clothes as "Mr. Watt." Athens had asked for nine British divisions as the minimum credible deterrent. When Wilson appeared with two divisions and an armored brigade, plus some odds and ends of tanks and artillery and a promise of more to come, disappointment in Athens deepened into disillusionment.

Furthermore, the arrival of the first of what would eventually balloon into 58,364 British and Commonwealth troops threw fragile Greek logistics into crisis. No vehicles remained for the newcomers to requisition, while the Greeks were so short of food and supplies that the British had to guard their own supply bases and airfields against the depredations of their own allies. Clearly, this was a "come as you are" intervention that would require a much larger administrative "tail" than Cairo had calculated. The few roads supporting the designated British defensive line running from the mouth of the Aliákmon River northwest to the Yugoslav border turned to mud in the inclement spring weather. The success of the British intervention and the defense of Greece depended on the Yugoslavs' putting up a stout resistance, otherwise the armies might easily be split by a bold thrust through the Monastir gap. In this event, it would be extremely difficult to retreat through the traffic-clogged mountain defiles that lined the route if the Luftwaffe dominated the skies, as seemed likely.[22] Nor were British movements in Greece any secret to the Germans— British troops discharging in Piraeus were astonished to find that because Greece had yet to sever diplomatic relations with Germany, the local consul and the military attaché brazenly recorded the disembarkation of British units.[23]

Unfortunately, the British arrival in mainland Greece was ill-timed. Hitler, who feared that Mussolini's defeat would create a Balkan front just at the moment that he planned to attack the Soviet Union, had carefully laid the diplomatic groundwork for Operation Marita, the directive for which he signed on 13 December 1940. The purpose of

Marita was to bind Southeastern Europe to Germany, both economically and politically, to drive Britain from the Continent, and secure his southern flank in preparation for an invasion of the USSR. The Hungarian government had joined the Tripartite Pact on 20 November, giving Hitler a staging area from which to invade Yugoslavia in case, as seemed likely, Yugoslavia refused to acquiesce in a German advance on Greece through its territory. In January 1941, General Ion Antonescu announced that he had abandoned neutrality, and allowed German divisions to install themselves in Romania. King Boris, won over by Hitler's promise of a land link to the Aegean once Greece was defeated, agreed in January to the passage of German troops through Bulgaria, and in February German and Bulgarian military representatives met to work out the details. The Germans bridged the Danube at three points to better permit the passage of troops. At the end of the month, Ribbentrop announced Bulgaria's decision to join the Tripartite Pact. By 28 March, the Germans had massed fourteen divisions in Bulgaria.[24]

To counter Hitler's Balkan initiative, Britain hoped to create a defensive alliance among Turkey, Greece, and Yugoslavia. From the beginning it was destined to fail. In early March, Ankara, petrified of both the USSR and Germany and hostile to Greece in any case, informed London that it would not participate in a war against Germany. The reaction of the Greek government, caught between the threat of a German attack and the realization that British aid would probably be too little to defend their country, was to bend over backward to assure the Germans that they would not allow British troops into their country. Even in late March, with 35,000 British forces already on Greek soil, Athens still sought German mediation to end their war with Mussolini. Greek generals even offered to stop fighting if German troops replaced Italians on their front. But Hitler's desire to protect the Romanian oil fields and to prevent the British from using Greece as a forward base, and his promise of Greek territory to Bulgaria, meant that Greek efforts to dissuade him from an invasion were, from the beginning, destined to fail.

Yugoslavia offered a test case, if another were required, of the difficulties of fighting a world war amid the parochial feuds and volatile loyalties of the Mediterranean. From its inception in December 1918, the Kingdom of Serbs, Croats, and Slovenes was regarded as Versailles's reward for the Serbs' support of the Allies in 1914. Early signs that this confederacy of southern Slav communities, each nursing its own constellation of resentments based on the real or imagined injustices of the past, might achieve a fragile stability all but vanished in 1929, when King Alexander, weary of chaotic and ineffective parliamentary rule, suspended the constitution and "reluctantly" proclaimed his personal dictatorship. "Yugoslavia" became a turbulent and melancholy kingdom where "centralist" Serbs ruthlessly forced a policy of "national oneness" on minority "federalist" communities, especially the separatist Croats eager to cultivate ties with fascist Italy. Exiled Croats in Hungary and Italy formed the Ustaše, shorthand for "Rebels—Croatian Revolutionary Organization," which recruited members throughout Europe and America to carry out a terrorist campaign inside Yugoslavia. This was met with ferocious reprisals by Serb policemen, especially in Lika and western Herzegovina, considered Ustaše strongholds. Croats got their revenge in October 1934 when Alexander was assassinated in Marseilles during a state visit to France. But Ustaše satisfaction was short-lived, because Hitler determined that Yugoslav unity was an essential element in his plan to shatter the Petite Entente and transform Yugoslavia into an economic colony of Germany. Italy was encouraged to abandon its designs on Yugoslavia and focus its ambitions on Africa.[25]

Alexander's successor, the regent Prince Paul, attempted to appease Croat nationalists by granting home rule in August 1939, an act that enraged Serbs. But Axis success encouraged the divisive forces in Yugoslav politics. Montenegrins joined Croats in their hopes that Mussolini would grant them complete independence. Macedonian loyalties lay with Bulgaria, while the Moslems of Bosnia and Herzegovina, together with large Albanian, German, and Hungarian minorities, remained unenthusiastic "Yugoslavs." Belgrade, aware of its economic dependence on Germany, the absorption of Hungary, Romania, Bulgaria, and Albania into the Axis orbit, as well as the inability of the British to aid in its defense, desperately searched for ways to stay out of the war. Attempts at a Yugoslav-Soviet rapprochement died with the Nazi-Soviet Pact of August 1939. Throughout the winter and spring of 1941, Hitler, in an attempt to protect his rear during an attack on Greece, subjected the Yugoslav government to intense pressure, while adding the inducement that Salonika would be handed to Yugoslavia upon a German victory over Greece. On 25 March, the Anglophile Prince Paul buckled and signed the Tripartite Pact. The reaction was immediate—Slovenes and Serbs took to the streets, attacking German property. A bloodless 27 March military coup in Belgrade

THE BALKANS, 1941

INVASION OF YUGOSLAVIA
AND GREECE, APRIL 1941

expelled Prince Paul and placed King Peter on the throne. Both Hitler and Churchill interpreted the coup, and the popular approval it elicited, as evidence of pro-British sentiments in Yugoslavia and that Britain's policy of uniting Yugoslavia and Greece in a common defense pact was on the verge of success.[26] Rather, it was much more an indication of a popular desire to remain out of the war. A furious Hitler ordered his generals to crush Yugoslavia in a spectacular fashion to demonstrate the penalties of defiance. Because his attack on the Soviet Union was scheduled for the summer, Hitler lacked the leisure to negotiate with the new government of a Serbian people whom he detested in any case.[27]

Yugoslavia constituted hardly more than a speed bump against a German advance, and in many respects facilitated it. On Palm Sunday, 6 April, the German minister in Athens called on Prime Minister Alexandros Koryzis to declare war. At the same time waves of Luftwaffe bombers plastered Belgrade, paralyzing the government and high command as well as killing many civilians. Supplied with excellent intelligence on Yugoslav troop deployments, the German Twelfth Army stationed in Bulgaria attacked through Nis toward the capital, while German, Italian, and Hungarian troops poured across Yugoslavia's northern borders. The Yugoslav army, though a million strong, was poorly equipped, poorly trained, and riven by ethnic rivalries—while Serbian units often fought to the limit of their capabilities, Croats and Macedonians were quick to surrender. The German attack caught the Yugoslav army awkwardly split between Belgrade and the southeast of the country. It proved difficult to mobilize and fight simultaneously. Senior generals were divided in their attitudes toward the coup and the new government. With few antiaircraft and antitank weapons, the Yugoslavs were virtually powerless to halt the German advance. The prime minister reminded the Soviets that they were obligated by treaty to assist Yugoslavia. But Moscow merely replied that the spread of war was "extremely regrettable." On 10 April, German troops assisted the birth of an independent Croatia under Ustaše leadership. On 13 April, Belgrade was overrun. Five days later the government threw in the towel.

The dual German offensives in the Balkans and in Cyrenaica

caught the British in the act of shifting troops into position in Greece. They also meant that the Seventh Australian Division and the Polish Brigade slated for Greece were retained by Cairo for the defense of Egypt. The RAF could spare only eighty aircraft for Greece, which meant that British planes would be outnumbered ten to one. One result was that while for the first time British units in Greece had mobile "Y units" to intercept German signals, Sigint was not supplemented by air reconnaissance. The real intelligence advantage enjoyed by the British in Greece was the daily intelligence appreciation based on Luftwaffe Enigma intercepts, which at least allowed British commanders to know the identity and location of German divisions and corps, and a general indication of their movements. But given the chaos and disorganization of the retreat, the weakness of British forces, and the minuscule intelligence staff assigned by Cairo to W Force, intelligence could not be a decisive factor in the campaign. Events moved so quickly in Greece that neither Cairo nor Athens could get an accurate picture of the evolution of the campaign, beyond the fact that it was failing badly. However, it is clear that intelligence helped the British to avoid encirclement and extract as many troops as they did by giving information upon which to base timely withdrawals.[28]

The initial German attack came out of Bulgaria against the Metaxas line in Macedonia. There, Greek resistance against the German Eighteenth Mountain Corps was tenacious, and only slowly did the Greeks retreat. The Second German Armored Division detoured through Yugoslavia to outflank the Metaxas line near Lake Dojran. Heavy Luftwaffe attacks prevented Greek forces from blocking their advance toward Salonika, which fell on 8 April. Politically, it would have been difficult, if not impossible, for the Greeks to abandon Salonika and fall back to the Aliákmon line. But the fact that they did not cut off 60,000 Greek troops in Macedonia, who were forced to surrender. While the loss of Salonika was a psychological blow, the rapid collapse of Yugoslav resistance fatally compromised Anglo-Greek resistance, because it allowed the Germans to split the Aliákmon and Albania defense lines by attacking through the Monastir gap toward Florina, which fell on 10 April. From Florina, a German column cut behind

Greek lines holding the Italians in Albania. Greek generals in Albania hesitated to withdraw. However, Wilson, warned by Ultra that he faced eight German infantry divisions, three motorized divisions, and two panzer formations combining two hundred tanks, coming along routes that military intelligence had deemed impassable by armor, pulled stakes and bolted south.[29] The Greeks in Albania were not so lucky: when they attempted to fall back to the Aliákmon Valley on 12 April, they were cut up and forced to surrender. As retreating British and Greek forces crossed the Thessalian Plain to Larissa, Hitler ordered his generals to prevent the British from evacuating their troops by sea. But with the Greek army disintegrating around him and threatened with encirclement, that was precisely what Wilson intended to do.

On 14 April, Cairo began to prepare for another Dunkirk, this time in Greece. The RAF withdrew its remaining planes to Crete, leaving the retreating armies at the complete mercy of heavy Luftwaffe attacks. "From dawn to dusk there was never a period of more than half an hour when there was not an enemy plane overhead," wrote Robert Crisp, a South African lieutenant in the Royal Tank Regiment. "It was the unrelenting pressure of noise and the threat of destruction in every hour which accentuated the psychological consequences of continuous retreat . . . I had never seen so many men so unashamedly afraid as I saw on the bomb-torn roads of Greece."[30] Disconsolate Greek soldiers tossed their rifles into roadside ditches. Broken-down tanks, abandoned trucks, smashed wagons, and dead animals, bloated and contorted into grotesque poses, littered the roads, but failed to halt the traffic flow toward the south. The advancing Germans were slowed by British demolitions, by lack of fuel and ammunition, and by the occasional obstinate stand, such as the one Australians and New Zealanders made at Thermopylae. But Athens's will to fight on was rapidly cracking—on 16 April, General Papagos urged Wilson to withdraw from Greece to save his country from further devastation. Two days later, Prime Minister Koryzis committed suicide. Leaderless, several ministers began to talk of surrender. On 20 April, General Tsolakoglou on his own initiative requested an armistice from the Germans. On 21 April, sixteen Greek divisions surrendered to the German Twelfth

Army at Yannina, a fact that Wilson confirmed through Ultra, and Italian forces crossed the Greek frontier. The king formed a new government and left for Crete on 23 April.

The next day, 7 cruisers, 20 destroyers, 2 infantry assault ships, and 19 troopships arrived to begin a week-long evacuation. Because the Luftwaffe had no night capabilities, British ships stood offshore during daylight, arrived at 11 p.m., loaded often by ship's boats and motor caiques, always slow business, and departed by 3 a.m. Footprints on the sand were then obliterated so as not to alert German air reconnaissance of departure locations. Most ships would sail rapidly to Suda Bay in Crete, deposit their passengers, and return the next evening. British soldiers spent daylight hours dispersed in woods, houses, and groves, puncturing tires, ramming shells the wrong way into gun barrels, draining oil out of running engines, shooting horses, and blowing up munitions dumps. On 26 April, German paratroopers dropped on the Isthmus of Corinth to cut off British troops still in the north. But this had been anticipated by Wilson, so that by the time they secured the isthmus, most British troops had reached the Peloponnese safely.[31] When, on 30 April, German forces reached the southern tip of the Greek mainland, the British calculated that over 50,000 soldiers, including a number of Greeks and Yugoslavs, had got away. However, the British had suffered at least 12,000 casualties, including a large number of men crammed on three transports sunk at Raphina-Nauplia. Eight thousand trucks were abandoned on the beaches. The most disheartening tragedy was the surrender of 7,000 soldiers, including a large number of Jewish volunteers from Palestine, at Kalamata on the Peloponnese. This had been due to poor defense and the fact that on 28 April an audacious German raid on Kalamata had captured the naval liaison officer, which disrupted communications with the ships offshore. The combination of fighting on shore and confusion caused the naval commanders to conclude that they could not risk their ships, so they sailed away. A dispirited garrison made up principally of administrative troops and 2,000 Cypriots and Palestinian Jews surrendered the next morning.[32] The RAF had lost 153 pilots and 209 planes, while two Royal Navy warships were lost. The only good news was that the damage would have been far greater had the Luftwaffe not been engaged in bombing Malta and supporting Rommel's advance in Cyrenaica. The cost to the Germans of Marita was 250 killed in action.[33]

CRETE — "THE GRAVE OF THE GERMAN PARATROOPER"

The battle for Crete was unique for two reasons. To begin with, it was the first time Ultra intelligence alerted the British to a German plan, and hence, in theory, placed them in a position to defeat it. Second, Crete marked the first use of paratroopers, hitherto employed as a supplement to advances by ground troops, to seize a strategic objective. Neither Ultra nor the paratroopers fulfilled their promise on Crete. But while intelligence based on Enigma intercepts would become an important weapon in Allied arsenals, Crete became the grave of the German paratrooper.

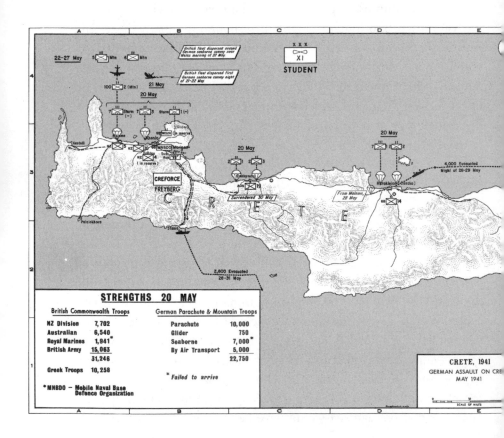

STRENGTHS 20 MAY			
British Commonwealth Troops		**German Parachute & Mountain Troops**	
NZ Division	7,702	Parachute	10,000
Australian	6,540	Glider	750
Royal Marines	1,941*	Seaborne	7,000*
British Army	15,063	By Air Transport	5,000
	31,246		22,750
Greek Troops	10,258		

* Failed to arrive

*MNBDO — Mobile Naval Base Defence Organization

CRETE, 1941
GERMAN ASSAULT ON CRETE
MAY 1941

SCALE OF MILES

Crete had, so far, been the stepchild of the Mediterranean war, both because the belligerents had other preoccupations and because neither side could quite figure out how to fit the island into any sort of strategic plan. The German victory in Greece, however, suddenly placed Crete at the crossroad of the Mediterranean war, the point at which Operation Marita hurling down from the north impacted Cairo's Middle Eastern defense perimeter. One reason why Crete was so difficult to incorporate into any sort of rational calculation was that neither its location nor its configuration lent itself to any obvious purpose. In Allied prewar planning, Crete was viewed as a platform to check Italian operations on Rhodes. As a consequence, a French force out of Syria was designated to occupy Crete should Greek neutrality be violated by Italy. On 1 November 1940, the British had occupied Crete's primary harbor at Suda Bay to liberate Greek troops to fight Italians on the Albanian front. Churchill assured the House of Commons that Suda, a slip of sea that lies on the island's northwest coast about 350 miles from Alexandria, offered the Royal Navy, starved for bases in the Eastern Mediterranean, "a second Scapa." It was an anchorage from which the Royal Navy could shield supply lines running between North Africa and the Aegean, as well as an air base to shepherd convoys sailing between Malta and Alexandria. The problem was that Wavell lacked the troops to garrison Crete properly. A weak brigade group with a few antiaircraft guns occupied Suda, while the RAF constructed three airstrips, the most important at Maleme practically next door to Suda. But with the Italians stalemated in Greece, pressure seemed to be off Crete. This changed as evidence grew early in 1941 of plans for German intervention in Greece. Nevertheless, Cairo, with other, more pressing priorities, had done almost nothing to turn Suda Bay into a citadel, nor Crete into a fortress. Suda could berth little more than two destroyers or two small freighters at one time. Lack of antisubmarine defenses meant that larger ships could only refuel and depart.[34] Suda's vulnerability was brought forcefully home on 26 March, when the cruiser *York* and the tanker *Pegasus*, at anchor in Suda, were holed by Italian special operations driving explosive-pack speedboats.

Crete had first come to Hitler's attentions in July 1940. Following the British attack on the French fleet at Mers el-Kébir, he suggested that the Italians seize Crete and Cyprus to sever British links to Greece through the Aegean. But it is hard to believe that the Führer was serious. Rather it should be seen in the context of what one historian has called "a veritable Crete craze" which infected the German forces, especially the navy, in the summer of 1940. Hitler's was almost a casual comment, one made during what the Führer's staff referred to as his "map traveling" in the interlude before Barbarossa, when Mediterranean speculations and projects burgeoned in both the British and Axis camps.[35] When Italy attacked Greece on 28 October 1940, Hitler offered to take Crete with two paratroop divisions. But Mussolini waved him off, and the German dictator, for the moment, did not insist. However, when British troops disembarked on the island on 1 November, Hitler felt moved to tell Ciano that Italian incompetence was beginning to affect German interests. Specifically, he feared that Ploesti was now vulnerable to air attack.[36]

But the stunning success of Marita caused the Germans once again to focus on Crete. Operation Merkur (Mercury) seemed the logical follow-on plan to Marita, the natural next step that exploited the momentum of the Balkan campaign. But Crete had not been folded into the original operational plan. Only in March 1941 did General Kurt Student, chief of the German airborne forces, draw up a plan for the invasion of Crete, a plan revealed to Hitler on 21 April. There were sound strategic reasons for seizing Crete, especially so the Luftwaffe could attack the Suez Canal, while covering the flank of Rhodes in case the British tried to seize it. But the real attraction of Merkur was that it fitted nicely into Hitler's concept of the Greek campaign as a dike to hold the southern flank for Barbarossa. Yet Merkur had been thrown into question by Rommel's success in Cyrenaica. The army and the navy argued that priority should go to the elimination of Malta. RAF bombers from Malta pounded Tripoli, while ships and submarines slashed at the supply routes between Sicily and North Africa. Hitler, lacking the means to take both Crete and Malta, had to choose. On 21 April,[37] Hitler, correctly suspecting that the arguments for Malta masked a more fundamental objection to Barbarossa, ruled in favor of Crete. "There'll be time for Malta later," he insisted. From

Hitler's perspective, the conquest of Malta would not knock Britain out of the war, while the conquest of Crete would free him to attack the USSR.[38]

Even before the German offensive of 6 April, British intelligence began to receive indications that large airborne forces, part of the newly organized Fliegerkorps XI, were massing troop transports and gliders and training for an operation. At first it was assumed that these troops would be part of the main attack on Greece, much as paratroops had participated in the 1940 invasions of Norway and the Low Countries. On 24 April, an encrypted message revealed that Göring had designated some of them for a special mission, which was revealed two days later when paratroops seized the Corinth Canal. But Enigma continued to transmit indications of further operations. Intelligence from Italian sources suggested that the German paratroops might be dropped into Syria to aid Rashid Ali's 3 April coup in Iraq. Crete was identified as a likely objective. But so was Cyprus, a stepping-stone to Syria. Only on 26 April, the day Hitler approved Merkur, did Luftwaffe Enigma intercepts refer specifically to "operation Crete." Nevertheless, for almost another week, Cairo continued to suspect that Crete was a "feint" for the real objectives of Cyprus and Syria. But Luftwaffe orders on 1 May to cease bombing Maleme and mining Suda Bay, and to prepare a photographic mosaic of the island, left the command in no doubt that Crete was the objective.[39]

British reaction to this news was ambivalent. Cairo pointed out that Britain lacked the resources to adequately defend an island that, from the British perspective, faced in the wrong direction. The north shore of the island rises slowly to a spine of 8,000-foot-high mountains, which drop precipitously to the south shore. Suda and other ports on the north shore are only 200 miles from Athens, but 350 from Alexandria and 200 from the nearest landfall in Cyrenaica, which, thanks to Rommel, was now in Axis hands. Ships sailing to Suda from Egypt had to pass through the Kaso Strait to the east or the Kíthira Channel to the west, where they would be sitting ducks for Axis aircraft. Besides, planning a defense for an island 180 miles long where the few towns were linked by only one inadequate road running parallel to the front would be virtually impossible without mobile defenses, good communications, and heavy weapons. Churchill wavered over whether Crete was worth defending. But, at the end of April, against the advice of his service chiefs, the prime minister ordered that Crete must be held.[40]

The man selected to deal with this crisis was Major General Bernard Freyberg, commander of the New Zealand Division—"the Div," as its members called it. On the surface, Freyberg appeared an excellent choice to organize the defense of the island. Though thrown untested into Greece, his New Zealanders, recruited from a small but intensely patriotic population, rapidly proved to be among the most solid soldiers during what was otherwise an ignominious rout of the British Expeditionary Force. This spoke to Freyberg's strength as a good trainer of troops. That he had been one of the last senior officers to be evacuated from Greece hardly surprised those who knew him, for it spoke to his second strength—his legendary reputation for bravery. Freyberg had been born in London in 1889 but emigrated to New Zealand as a young child. A champion swimmer and dental student when war broke out in 1914, Freyberg traveled to London where, through Churchill's intervention, he was commissioned into the Royal Naval Division. At Gallipoli in 1915 he won a DSO when he swam to the beaches to guide the invasion boats to their objectives. The following year he won the Victoria Cross in Flanders. "The Great Saint Bernard," as Churchill called him, simply knew no fear. During country-house weekends between the wars, after the ladies had withdrawn, Freyberg was frequently prevailed upon to strip and display the scars of his twenty-seven combat wounds. While reviewing troops, he would frequently stop in front of a soldier and ask: "You been in action?" When the reply was affirmative, Freyberg would demand a catalog of campaigns—Greece, Crete, the Desert. "Ever been wounded?" the general would ask. If the reply was "No, sir," Freyberg shot back: "Why the bloody hell not?"[41] The most popular of many legends circulated about Freyberg was that in 1914 he had fought with Pancho Villa against U.S. troops in Mexico (untrue but he never denied it).

By 1941, Freyberg's once-slim six-foot swimmer's frame had broadened to an impressive bulk. In his lemon-squeezer hat, Sam Browne belt, and khaki shorts, he looked like an ill-tempered scoutmaster. Though some senior New Zealand officers found him a trifle too Anglicized for their tastes, the troops appreciated Freyberg's relaxed attitude toward military formalities. For them, he was a real soldier's soldier, one who never shied away from visiting the front lines to ensure that his men had plenty of beer and cigarettes. His concern for the welfare of his men extended to casualties—Freyberg was determined to preside over no New Zealand Passchendaele in the Mediterranean. In February 1944, U.S. Fifth Army commander Mark Clark discovered that limits Freyberg set on the number of casualties he would accept in "the Div" made him a plan buster at Cassino.[42] Freyberg understood that coercion and formality were unnecessary in a unit with strong group loyalty, where men would not dare disgrace themselves through cowardice lest their reputation at home be sullied. British soldiers in particular found his informal, no-nonsense style a refreshing change from the patronizing attitude of their own generals, who might appear in the cool of the evening in freshly starched uniforms and swagger sticks, surrounded by red-tabbed staff officers, to shout "Good show. Carry, on chaps." They would then disappear in a cloud of dust that inevitably invited an artillery and mortar barrage lasting a quarter of an hour. In the meantime, they were well beyond harm's way. Lieutenant General Oliver Leese, corps commander under Montgomery, who eventually rose to command the Eighth Army in Italy, was insulted when a New Zealander leaned out of the back of a lorry to offer him a bottle of Chianti. "Bernard, you really must do something about it," an offended Leese objected. But Bernard had no intention of doing anything to alter the relaxed attitude of his Kiwis.[43]

Despite these strengths, Freyberg was not the ideal commander to lead the defense of Crete. He had retired from the army in 1934, to return five years later when New Zealand sought someone to command the division they were raising for the war. His brilliant record in World War I, the patronage of Churchill, who deeply admired men of action, and the dearth of obvious candidates in the small island nation made Freyberg a lock for command. Political pressure from New Zealand, which, like Australia, became increasingly dissatisfied with British handling of Commonwealth troops in the Eastern Mediterranean, made him politically bulletproof. Freyberg's clout in Wellington and his friendship with Churchill gave him political leverage far beyond his rank. However, those who worked closely with him quickly discovered a man of changeable moods, as capable of easy elation as he was of profound depression.[44] He could also be remarkably stubborn, as he proved in February 1944 when he successfully insisted on the destruction of the abbey at Monte Cassino against the obvious desires of his superiors, who argued that it had no military value and would only hand a propaganda victory to Hitler. World War II found the New Zealander's youthful drive and killer instinct somewhat diminished. Montgomery was to complain in the autumn of 1942 that leisurely pursuit by Freyberg's corps contributed to Rommel's escape after El Alamein. Nor was Freyberg considered the British army's most intellectual general—"a nice old boy, but a bit stupid," was Montgomery's brusque verdict.[45] This was a pity, because Freyberg would be forced to make sense of an operation the likes of which no one had yet encountered—a massive airborne invasion.

If Freyberg was an artifact of an attritional World War I style of combat, the man he faced in Crete was a leading evangelist of the German army's faith in employing innovative operational techniques to achieve dramatic strategic results. Unlike, for instance, the idea of mechanized divisions, with which the old Reichwehr had experimented in the dark days between the Treaty of Versailles and Hitler's decision to rearm in 1935, airborne troops were an idea imported from, of all places, the Soviet Union. The major protagonist for airborne troops in the German army was Kurt Student. Son of an ennobled but impoverished Brandenburg family, Student had surrendered his youthful dreams of medical school *faute d'argent*. Instead, his education consisted of a series of cadet schools that led inexorably to his commission in the Yorkschen Jäger regiment at Ortelsburg in 1911. Two years later, the young infantry lieutenant, who by his own admission had a head for neither numbers nor heights, was sent on a flying course. In the air, Student had discovered his vocation. He fought World War I as a fighter pilot, eventually commanding a fighter squadron (*Jasta*) until wounded in 1917. In the 1920s, Captain Student joined a group of ex-aviators under the direction of the *Fliegercentrale* of the clandestine general staff to organize "gliding clubs," nurseries of the future Luftwaffe. This work took him to the Soviet Union, which, under the 1922 Treaty of Rapallo between Europe's two pariah nations, supplied training bases for Germany's clandestine rearmament. Nevertheless, to qualify for promotion, Student had to return to command an infantry battalion.

From Hitler's accession to power in 1933, German rearmament began to emerge from the shadows of Versailles prohibition. Student became director of the technical training schools for the air arm under Göring's new Ministry of Aviation, whose job was to turn out mechanics for the new air force. In August 1935, as Hitler announced the nativity of the Luftwaffe, Student was promoted to colonel commanding the Test Center for Flying Equipment, where the prototypes of German fighters, bombers, and transports were refined for serial production. So far, Student clearly was regarded by his superiors as an organizer and administrator rather than a fighter and innovator. However, a mass assault of 1,500 airborne troops that Student witnessed during the 1937 Soviet maneuvers became his epiphany. Student returned to Germany an avid apostle of airborne infantry. It was an ideal vocation for an officer with both infantry and air experience. Furthermore, his timing was right—the atmosphere in the German forces was receptive to those with an innovative and experimental mindset. Hitler encouraged technical and operational innovation in his forces as a way to steal a march on his European enemies. Furthermore, the Junker 52, a three-engine passenger plane converted to a bomber in 1935, was being downgraded to a transport plane. Capable of carrying sixteen to eighteen fully equipped soldiers 800 miles at a cruising speed of 132 miles per hour, Ju52s were available in large numbers. A potential training school existed at Stendhal. All that was required was an operational concept for the use of airborne forces. Student, working with an enthusiastic subordinate, Heinrich Trettner, who would remain his chief of staff for much of the war, argued that the mass descent of airborne forces ahead of conventional forces could paralyze enemy command elements and seize communication choke points. Essentially, Student and Trettner offered an updated, airborne version of the storm trooper tactics developed by German forces in World War I. The subsequent disorganization of the enemy command structure would hand German mechanized divisions an inestimable advantage in maneuver warfare.

Student was ordered to form Fliegerdivision 7, which in 1938 was transported in 242 Ju52s as part of the force to occupy the Sudetenland in the wake of the September 1938 Munich conference. The high command decided to keep Fliegerdivision 7 as a parachute division and create a separate glider force, the Twenty-second Division. At Darmstadt, Student oversaw the evolution of the DFS 230 glider, capable of carrying a pilot and nine fully equipped airborne soldiers. Despite what he believed was a spectacular demonstration of paratroop potential during maneuvers at Niedersachsen in the summer of 1939, his troops were kept in reserve during the September invasion of Poland. Nevertheless, he continued to expand his airborne forces, adding 75 mm pack howitzers, 20 mm antitank guns, engineers, and signals and medical support. Student's first problem was that Fliegerdivision 7 was a vagabond force, under the command of the Luftwaffe, which had no use for it, but disowned by the Wehrmacht, which did not list it in its organization. The second problem lay with Student himself. A huge gulf existed between the dynamism and innovation of the concepts he espoused and his unassuming, almost bland character. Despite his legendary personal courage, Student lacked the charisma of a Rommel or a Kesselring. His personality blended the decorum of a pastor with the deliberation of a scientist. His modesty, patience, calm, and insistence on deliberation and precision were interpreted as evidence of mediocrity rather than of cautious tenacity and strength of conviction. Many of his superiors dismissed the infallibly courteous Student as an unassuming, run-of-the-mill officer fit only to manage technical establishments. His high-pitched voice and halting speech, aggravated by a head wound received in the 1940 invasion of Holland, disadvantaged him in debates with the numerous airborne agnostics who peopled the upper echelons of the Wehrmacht. They viewed Student as a visionary guided by intuition rather than rational calculation.

Airborne forces were pulled from obscurity by Hitler, whose enthusiasm for unconventional solutions and unconventional forces grew as he contemplated how to crack the Franco-British front in the autumn of 1939. Student was assigned the task of seizing the Belgian fortress of Eben Emael, north of Liège, which commanded the entry to Belgium from Maastricht in the Netherlands. On 10 May 1940, German airborne troops seized crossings over the Maas River and Albert Canal, while eighty-five glider troops landed on top of Eben Emael and neutralized it with explosive charges. The 1,000-man garrison surrendered the next day to follow-up forces. Student later claimed that the seizure of Eben Emael was the most daring and significant action by a small body of men during the entire war. Student then led his two airborne divisions in an attack on Holland. The descent of paratroops—even rumors of paratroops—struck fear in the enemy population. The idea that German paratroops were bravely defending vital bridges, crossroads, and airfields also gave an extra incentive to regular forces to surge forward and rescue their comrades fighting behind enemy lines. In retrospect, the perception of airborne success exceeded the reality. But it merged with the image of a German Blitzkrieg force that was modern, fast, and tough. It certainly had many in Britain worried that airborne troops offered a means for the Germans to establish a beachhead in Britain as the prelude to an amphibious invasion. In September 1940, Student was promoted to lieutenant general.[46]

After recovering from his head wound, Student took his concept of airborne forces to the next level by forming Fliegerkorps XI under Göring's patronage. The airborne corps contained a paratroop *Sturm-regiment* (shock regiment) commanded by a general, a paratroop division, an airfield-landing division, ten transport plane groups composed of 500 Ju52s, and reconnaissance planes. Rather than being a mere adjunct to land operations, airborne forces could actually be used in a strategic role as a stand-alone force. German paratroops had executed what many British later interpreted as a dry run for Crete by seizing the Corinth Canal on 26 April. A first wave of bombers forced the antiaircraft artillery to open fire, so they could be silenced by a second wave of dive-bombers. Then the Ju52s appeared, flying slowly, wingtip to wingtip, at very low altitudes to disgorge two paratroop battalions on both sides of the canal, followed by weapons drops marked by different-colored chutes. Some paratroops in this operation died because the Ju52s flew too low to give their chutes time to open. Thigh fractures were common. But they did take the few New Zealand troops guarding the canal by surprise. The New Zealanders managed to blow the canal bridge. However, this success essentially did the Germans' work for them, because it cut off the rear guard still north of the canal, forcing them to evacuate via beaches in Attica.[47]

The German verdict was that the paratroop drop on the Corinth Canal had been a success. It had disrupted British communications, sown temporary confusion, and cut off the British line of retreat to the Peloponnese. Nevertheless, the weaknesses of airborne operations were also revealed: the relatively high casualties, the absence of heavy armaments, and the fact that the airborne assault succeeded against a force that was already in retreat. In fact, the Corinth operation was much more reminiscent of the seizure of the Albert Canal bridges the year before—a limited action by a relatively small force to seize a tactical objective ahead of an advancing main force. Nor was the relative German success at Corinth due to the paratroops per se. The New Zealand Division's rear guard moving south from Athens was certainly strong enough to push the paratroops out of the way, but decided to evacuate off the Attica beaches once they realized that the critical bridge had been blown by their own troops. However, Student was uninterested in the limitations of airborne forces. He had bigger plans for Fliegerkorps XI—he convinced Hitler that airborne forces could take Crete.[48]

The prime minister burned to defend Crete because he believed that Ultra intelligence handed him an unbeatable hand, an absolute gold mine of information on the German assault plan. Ultra revealed the movements of German airborne troops, their concentration, and the stages of their assault. The plan went like this: Paratroops would drop on the three airstrips along Crete's north coast at Maleme-Khania, Heraklion, and Rethimnon. As at Corinth, the drop would disorient the few defending troops, allowing the paratroops to secure the airfields as a prelude to the arrival of airborne infantry from the Fifth Mountain Division in Ju52s, as well as dive-bombers and fighters—1,280 aircraft in all. Disorganized, confused, their communications interrupted and without air superiority, the British would be unable to resist the amphibious invasion that would bring in the heavy equipment. For once, however, the Germans seemed to have exceeded the bounds of caution. Merkur bore the amateurish hallmarks of a plan hastily prepared at the Hotel de Grande-Bretagne in Athens. First, it violated the principle of concentration of force by scattering the invasion among three separate objectives that could not be mutually supporting. Second, the command arrangements were chaotic. To place Wehrmacht troops under the general authority of the Luftwaffe offered a recipe for discord from the beginning, because neither understood the other's capabilities, nor were either prepared to listen. Third, the Luftwaffe, with an insufficient number of planes and operating out of primitive airfields in Greece, lacked the resources to support it. The original number of airdrops had to be reduced from seven to four. Takeoff schedules would be determined by the limited capacities of Greek airfields rather than by the tactical situation on the ground in Crete. Fourth, the Germans lacked the sea lift, and sea control, to support an amphibious operation, especially out of Greek ports that the Luftwaffe had thoroughly destroyed during Marita. They pulled together any hulk that would float, a motley of sixty ferries, yachts, fishing boats, and caïques, which made the German invasion of Crete look like a reverse Dunkirk. The Italians agreed to provide escort vessels. Fifth, Merkur was based on the faulty intelligence that many British troops had been pulled off Crete to quell the rebellion that had broken out in Iraq in April 1941. But Student waved away all criticism, insisting that the psychological impact of the descent of airborne forces would erase all objections based on material factors.[49]

The greatest flaw in Student's plan, the one of which he could not be aware, was that the British knew its every detail. It was rare for Enigma to broadcast a plan in such detail. Usually intelligence analysts had painstakingly to piece together a picture of enemy intentions using fragments of information. However, because the operation was contentious, last-minute, and because Fliegerkorps XI was scattered over half of Europe, the plan was broadcast down to its last detail. In Ultra, Churchill clutched a "heaven-sent" opportunity to land a snot knocker on the unsuspecting Germans. Furthermore, Freyberg had plenty of time to prepare his trap. One of the great ironies of air operations in general is that the huge infrastructure air forces require means that they are the least mobile of forces. The Germans required nearly three weeks after the conquest of Greece to collect the troops and resources for the invasion of Crete. The attack was set for 17 May, later postponed to 20 May. The slight flaw was that British military intelligence vastly overestimated the numbers of German airborne troops at 25,000 to 30,000, with 10,000 in the seaborne operation. The true numbers were 15,750 and 7,000 respectively.[50] To offset this, the Germans significantly underestimated the numbers of British troops holding the island. Intelligence would show Freyberg just where to concentrate his troops.

To be fair to Freyberg, what looked to Churchill in London like a golden opportunity was, on closer inspection, fraught with problems. When Freyberg arrived on Crete on 1 May 1941, the regular garrison of 5,000 British and 7,000 Greek soldiers had been swelled to nearly 30,000 men by the arrival of refugees from Greece, dumped there rather than in Egypt so that ships could turn around quickly to pick up more evacuees. Many of these men were "odds and sods"—administrative personnel—while regular units evacuated to Crete had left their equipment in Greece. Lack of time and shipping sabotaged plans to replace this hodgepodge force with well-equipped regular units from Egypt. Only about 2,000 men were brought in to reinforce what was now called Creforce, while 7,000 unessential personnel were evacuated. The Royal Navy ferried in artillery, antiaircraft guns, and a few tanks, but rapidly discovered that German air superiority forced their convoys to come in at night or risk destruction. As during Marita, the RAF could do little to contest German air superiority. The twenty serviceable British planes on Crete were quickly driven away by Luftwaffe attacks. Hurricanes equipped with drop tanks could fly the 350 miles from Egypt to make brief appearances over the battlefield. Their main opponent, the German Messerschmitt Bf. 110 "Jager," a twin-seat, twin-engine "heavy" fighter designed for long-range operations, had made its reputation in the Polish campaign of 1939 and as an executioner of RAF bombers over German skies. However, the Bf. 110 had disappointed during the Battle of Britain, where it proved sluggish and less maneuverable than the agile single-engine Spitfire.

Hurricane pilots discovered that if you locked in on the tail of a Bf. 110, its single rear-facing machine gun could not protect it. When attacked, Bf. 110 squadrons would fly in a circle to protect each other's "six," an effective defensive tactic that, nevertheless, reduced the plane's offensive potential. Its strength, as the Germans discovered, was as a fighter-bomber able to carry a bigger bomb load greater distances than the aging Stuka. Nevertheless, over Crete, the Bf. 110 was still faster than the Hurricane[51] and flew from airfields only 200 miles away. Freyberg concentrated his New Zealand Division, supported by 3,500 Greek troops, to defend the airfield at Maleme. Nearby Canea and Suda Bay were defended by 17,400 British and Australian troops. Around 5,000 Australians and Greeks defended Rethimnon and 8,000 British and Greeks Heraklion, which he thought would be the main objective of the German assault. In addition, 6,000 "odds and sods" were scattered among the defenses. To survive against repeated Luftwaffe assaults, these men were forced to disperse and invent prodigies of camouflage, which confused the Germans about their true strength. On 15 May the Royal Navy stood off to the south and west of Crete, out of immediate air range but ready to intervene against an amphibious attack.

As at Corinth, the bombers droned through the azure skies over Crete at dawn on 20 May. British antiaircraft artillery spit puffs of flak skyward around Maleme and Canea, the signal to Ju87 Stukas to peel earthward from 13,000 feet at 300 miles per hour to inflict the "shock and awe" that had left Blitzkrieg victims from Warsaw to Athens with memories of the plane that seemed to be everywhere at once, and whose wailing siren gave the impression that the pilot had deliberately singled them out for attack. The Stuka's main value was as mobile artillery, an adjunct to land operations. By 1941, however, it was obsolete — its 120 miles per hour climbing speed too dawdling to qualify it for escort by fast fighters like the Messerschmitt Bf. 109, and with an unfortunate tendency to disintegrate when hit by machine-gun bullets from predatory Hurricanes. RAF pilots relished "Stuka parties" as a form of risk-free recreation. Indeed, the grim joke of Stuka crews was that their plane was so sluggish that their survival depended on the British overshooting.[52]

So far, the German attack unfolded like a rerun of the Corinth Canal attack on a grander scale. Unlike Corinth, however, the second wave of between 5,000 and 6,000 men, mostly from the shock regiment of Fliegerkorps XI, were hauled in by glider, followed by paratroops. Seen from the ground, the clouds of attackers, slowly descending like silk mushrooms out of a busy sky, offered a spectacle that was serene, practically peaceful, if one did not consider the deadly brawl that would follow the landing. Creforce exacted a heavy toll on these invaders: "Shoot for the feet," British NCOs barked. Some who were not dead when they landed were probably executed by the British or by Cretan villagers, some as they dangled helplessly in olive trees. Even those who survived often could not reach the containers of heavy weapons dropped for them. Rethimnon and Heraklion remained in British hands. Scattered groups of paratroops mustered for attacks on Canea or Maleme, which succeeded in killing many of their officers but in little else. One of Student's assumptions was that an airborne invasion would disrupt enemy communication. What he had not counted on was that a successful defense, together with inevitable delays at airfields in Greece, would also throw the German

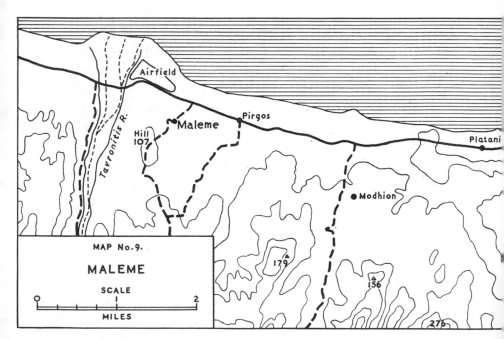

MAP No. 9.

MALEME

SCALE

0 1 2

MILES

plan into turmoil. Fighter and bomber support mingled with para-chute drops. The second wave, ignorant of the fate of the first wave, floated toward a landing zone that seemed alive with smoke and shrap-nel. By the evening of 20 May, over half the attackers had been killed and none of the vital airfields on Crete had been captured.

That night, refugee paras regrouped in the bed of the Tavronitis River to the west of Maleme, or on the heights to the south. At this point, however, things began to go wrong for the defenders. During the night of 20–21 May, the New Zealand troops abandoned the knoll that defended Maleme to the west, allowing the Germans to occupy it as well as part of the airfield on the next morning. On the morning of 21 May, a by now desperate Student ordered more paratroop drops to the west of Maleme to reinforce his troops holding a section of the air-field. He also ordered his Ju52s to land at Maleme even though the airfield was only partially occupied by the paras. The German trans-ports bellied onto a runway on which Freyberg had placed no obsta-cles, dug no pits, spinning and crashing through a gauntlet of British machine-gun and small arms fire. Paratroops flung open the doors and sprinted across the exposed runways for cover. By the evening of 21 May, Maleme was in German hands, the runway littered with the shattered and bullet-ridden carcasses of over eighty transports. The paratroops then began to push east. At this point, Freyberg's failure to lay out the defenses of Maleme to encompass the Tavronitis Valley or the areas south of the base came back to bite him. He also continued to focus on Heraklion, which he continued to believe was the main German objective.[53] Freyberg failed to see that Maleme was the key to the battle, which he must defend at all costs. Instead, he kept many of his troops at Canea and Suda facing seaward to parry the amphibious assault that he expected to be the principal attack.

In fact, two German attempts to reach Crete by sea were thwarted by Royal Navy destroyers that rammed and machine-gunned the crowded caïques, leaving soldiers of the Fifth Mountain Division and the Fliegerkorps XI staff flailing helplessly in the blood-red water, al-though at a cost of two cruisers and a destroyer caught steaming to-ward the Kíthira Channel in daylight by the Luftwaffe. In retrospect, the Germans should have attempted their amphibious invasion in daylight, when they would have been assured of air cover. Even the loss of three ships was a price Cunningham was unwilling to pay, and he recalled his fleet to Alexandria on 23 May. In the early hours of the morning of 22 May, a New Zealand attack came close to retaking Maleme. But daylight brought the intervention of the Luftwaffe and a German counterattack drove the New Zealanders back almost to Canea. This placed Maleme beyond British artillery range and allowed the Germans to fly in fighters. On 27 May, Canea was overrun after a strong Luftwaffe pounding. Suda Bay fell on the following day.

The Battle for Crete was lost. The British concern became to evacuate as many troops from the island as possible. Freyberg, his supplies running low, ordered his soldiers to trek south over the mountains to Sphakia on the south coast, where they could be evacuated. The Germans, slow in realizing the direction of the British retreat, instead headed down the coast road toward Rethimnon and Heraklion. The Royal Navy managed to evacuate about 4,000 troops at Heraklion on the night of 28–29 May. Unfortunately, 800 of them would never see Alexandria, as the Luftwaffe caught the British flotilla at 6 a.m. in the Kaso Strait and executed terrible butchery on the crowded decks.[54] The Germans did little to impede the crocodile of men who filed over the mountain toward Sphakia. But this made the trek over the mountain no easier for the thousands of footsore soldiers, who jettisoned helmets, water bottles, and equipment along the dusty track. By day, many sheltered in caves and gullies to avoid the attentions of the Luftwaffe. At night they queued up on the beaches, patiently waiting their turn for rescue. Most failed to make it. At Sphakia, the Royal Navy was able to evacuate 13,000 troops. But the decision to abandon the evacuation was taken after Ju88s sank the cruiser *Calcutta* on 1 June. The toll on the Royal Navy had been heavy. Ships had to stand off beyond air range during the day and come in at night to evacuate troops from the beaches. This meant that they could not begin embarkation before midnight, so that daylight frequently caught them before they were beyond air range. "The bomb comes down, you try to find cover and cannot, the ship heels over trying to dodge the path, [the bomb] misses and a great spout of water is thrown up only yards from the ship," recounted one veteran of Crete. "If any tells you that in those circumstances he was not frightened I would say he was either a monumental liar or a very brave man." Soldiers who had avoided death on Crete discovered that on a ship there was no place to run. Some beleaguered ships, like the *Orion*, arrived at Alexandria with their decks awash in the blood of 250 dead and over 300 wounded. Undamaged ships would discharge rescued soldiers and then turn around for another run. Sailors under constant air attack for a week began to develop "stukaritis," the naval equivalent of shell shock. Men went white, could not eat, and finally collapsed in nervous breakdown. Resentment against the naval command seethed in crews ordered time and again to risk their lives without adequate air cover, to the point that Cunningham prepared warrants for hanging in case he needed to squelch any mutinies. Finally, on 1 June, Cunningham judged that ship losses and crew morale required that evacuation operations be suspended.[55]

Crete proved a costly operation for both sides. Almost 12,000 British and Commonwealth troops had been abandoned on the beaches along with several thousand Greeks. A total of 1,742 had been killed or were missing, and another 2,225 wounded. In addition, the Royal Navy had lost three cruisers and six destroyers and had four other capital ships severely damaged. Some 2,000 seamen had perished. However, Student had won a Pyrrhic victory, and he knew it. He was enraged by the death in combat of 6,000 paratroopers, including a high percentage of officers, the elite of the German forces. Every surviving paratroop veteran of Crete was awarded an Iron Cross. The only explanation for such high casualties in the mind of many Germans was that the paratroops had been treacherously murdered by Cretan civilians. Göring ordered that the male populations of whole villages be executed in reprisal. For twelve days, German paratroops exacted vengeance on the local population, a sad forerunner of Axis occupation of much of Europe.[56] Fliegerkorps XI had lost so many aircraft that it had ceased to exist as an effective formation. Although Student continued to concoct scenarios for airborne operations, most notably against Malta in 1942, German paratroops were never again used in a strategic role. In future, they would be either used as regular line infantry or dropped as reinforcements to plug gaps in beleaguered Axis defenses, as in Sicily in 1943.

"BACK EVERY FORTNIGHT"

Despite the mauling endured by German airborne forces in Crete, Marita/Merkur appeared to have been an astounding success for Hitler. He had supported his faltering Italian ally, sealed his southern flank against British attack, and secured the supply line from the Black Sea to Italy. Turkey would be intimidated into neutrality. On the debit side, historians debate whether the invasion of Greece and Crete actually delayed Barbarossa. The two offensives were intertwined to the point that it is impossible to separate them. The general weight of opinion is that shortage of equipment and weather meant that Hitler would not have been ready to launch Barbarossa any earlier than June in any case.[57] In the end, the benefits of occupying Yugoslavia, Greece, and Crete were purely defensive. Hitler was forced to disperse forces to occupy the Aegean and Crete, islands that might easily have been supervised from the air from Rhodes. Crete's offensive potential, though immense, was never realized, because for Hitler the Mediterranean could never be more than a peripheral theater. The occupation of Crete failed to alleviate the supply situation to North Africa by forcing the British to abandon Alexandria, as predicted by Mussolini. Perhaps the greatest hidden benefit of the fall of Greece and Crete for the British was that it spared Malta. Italian ships sailing to North Africa still had to run the Malta gauntlet. Nor did Crete ever serve as a stepping-stone to other, potentially more profitable, opportunities in the Middle East via Cyprus, as Mussolini urged.

On an operational level, Student called Crete the "grave of the German paratrooper" because it broke Hitler's faith in the offensive power of airborne forces. This was fortunate for the Allies, for it came at a time when a rebuilt Fliegerkorps XI, in conjunction with an amphibious operation and close air support, would most probably have sealed Malta's fate. In many respects, Marita/Merkur was, for Hitler, the war's flood tide. With Barbarossa in June 1941, Hitler turned his back on strategic possibilities in the Mediterranean. The beleaguered in the Mediterranean would soon cease to be the British and become the Germans, who had committed themselves to fight in a geographically complex theater with inadequate resources, a poorly adapted force structure, and an undependable ally.

But that was in the future. In the short term, however, the manner in which the British had intervened was the subject of close questioning during a secret session of the House of Commons on 5–6 May. Churchill was roasted over the lack of preparation for Crete's defense during the six months that it had been occupied by the British. In private, the prime minister, too, was appalled by the absence of defensive preparations. Göring's boast that Crete proved that there are "no impregnable islands" struck a nervous chord in London, so that the British began to study how to protect their airfields against airborne attack.[58] The governments of Australia and New Zealand, many of whose troops had been abandoned on the beaches and who confronted an increasingly belligerent Japan, began to question Churchill's conduct of the war. Historians have criticized Freyberg's direction of the operation. He made poor use of intelligence that pointed to the airfields' being the primary objective of the German attack and the center of gravity of the island's defense. He inexplicably limited the Maleme defenses to the edge of the runway, and continued to give priority to Heraklion and the threat of an amphibious invasion, even as the Germans threatened to capture the airfield. But in the short run, the Mediterranean as the "grave of British generals" failed to claim him. On the contrary, Freyberg was told by Wellington to consult his government in future if he doubted the propriety of any order,[59] a privilege he began liberally to invoke.

In Britain, the prestige of the army hit a nadir, as it was again obvious that it was woefully unprepared to wage war against the Germans. "BEF," the popular joke ran, stood for "Back Every Fortnight." One of Churchill's goals had been to appeal to American opinion. The fall of Crete coincided with turmoil in Iraq and the spectacular loss of the battleship *Hood* to the *Bismarck* in the Atlantic, making some in Washington wonder "whether we've really got the hang of the thing."[60] Other Americans tended to be more indulgent. Roosevelt praised the British defense of Greece as "heroic."[61] In Cairo, a meeting between American war correspondents and an advance party of U.S. officers agreed "there's no question of the courage of the British. In the face of great odds, they go into battle without hesitation. That is what's so heartbreaking. These boys and men die with such courage."[62]

Churchill rationalized the British ejection from Crete as a case of winning by losing—that the island became a prison of two Axis divisions and freed up a potential British garrison for offensive operations elsewhere. But Crete would have given the British air bases 250 miles closer to the Ploesti oil fields in Romania, posed a threat to Greece that would have forced Hitler to maintain more troops there, and offered another base from which to attack Axis supply lines to North Africa. By making the Germans divide their resources to cover Crete, the British could have taken some pressure off Malta. For the moment, however, Churchill was forced to rationalize yet another defeat.

PARTISAN WARFARE IN THE BALKANS AND GREECE

The tide of Mediterranean war that had swept through Southeastern Europe in the spring of 1941 with Marita soon receded toward North Africa and the Middle East. While Churchill, and eventually the Americans, concentrated on ejecting the Axis from North Africa and overthrowing Mussolini, a vicious partisan war was brewing on the Balkan Peninsula. The defeat of Yugoslavia and Greece combined with a brutal and destructive Axis occupation to break down old power structures, discredit traditional elites, shatter a fragile ethnic and religious balance, and resurrect a folklore of past injustices, separatist dreams, and revolutionary aspirations. The result was complex, multi-sided civil wars in which resistance movements emerged to combat the victimization of occupied populations, and, above all, to position themselves to seize power. While leaders at the time, and postwar historiography since, defined the Balkan struggles as between collaborationists and resisters, in effect the Balkan situation, made complex by family, clan, village, ethnic, regional, and religious allegiances, defies tidy categorization. At one time or another the main Communist and non-Communist resistance groups sought accommodation with the Axis occupiers.[63] The fact that the most dynamic resisters were Communists became a concern for all Allied governments. London in particular feared that the European shore of the Mediterranean east of the Pyrenees might end the war under Communist control.

YUGOSLAVIA—"THE GALE OF THE WORLD"

No sooner had he occupied Yugoslavia than Hitler began to reorganize it and lash its economy to that of the Reich, which was dependent on Balkan raw materials.[64] Industrialized northern Slovenia was incorporated into Germany, while Italy took the rest, including Ljubljana. The Croats and Moslems in Croatia were accorded "Aryan" status and given the hinterland of Slavonia, Bosnia, and Herzegovina to become the Independent State of Croatia (Nezavisna Drzava Hrvatska or NDH), under Italian tutelage. Some Adriatic islands, Dalmatia, and a chunk of Istria were reserved for the Italians, who also embraced Montenegro as a protectorate. Albania, an Italian client state, was allowed to annex Kosovo. The Germans of the Banat to the northeast of Belgrade were allowed self-government. Hungary and Bulgaria carved slices off the Yugoslav carcass as reward for enlisting in the Axis. Administration of both Yugoslav and Greek portions of Macedonia was assigned to Bulgaria, as was much of western Thrace, although the Germans retained control of Salonika. In August 1941 the Serbs

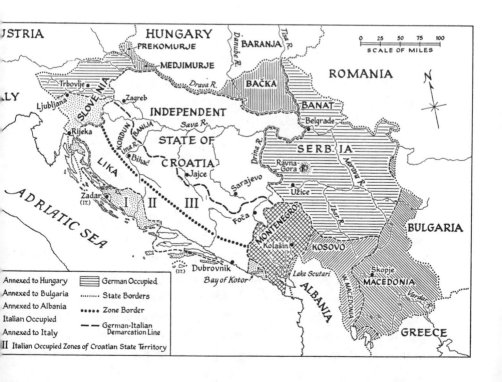

were granted a "Quisling" government under General Milan Nedić underpinned by the Serbian fascist movement, the Zbor (the Yugoslav Patriotic Unity Movement), in the hope that it would take some responsibility for quelling resistance to German rule.

Like every German occupation, especially in the East, the Balkan asylum was organized on a system of racist repression and economic plunder that offered its inmates the narrow choice between decimation and rebellion. In making their calculations for war, German commanders had failed to factor in costs of occupation and repression, instead relying on local collaborators to absorb these tasks. It proved to be a serious error. Not only did the brutal policies of Germany's local allies stimulate rebellion, hence creating a significant vulnerability on Hitler's Balkan flank, but also, German commanders eventually discovered that the outlay for repression was considerable at a time when every soldier was required on more important fronts. Bulgarian police killed thousands of Greeks in Thrace and imported Bulgarian settlers to occupy their lands. In Macedonia, where Bulgarians introduced their education system and established their church, police tortured and hanged Serbs from lampposts. Axis sponsorship deprived the Croat regime of the slightest whiff of legitimacy, but it did serve to induce apathy and compliance in the Croat population. The dynamic element in the NDH was the ultra-nationalist, anti-Semitic Ustaše ("Insurgents"), the common name for the Croatian Revolutionary Organization that grouped as many as 200,000 followers under Ante Pavelić, a fanatical Croat nationalist who returned from Italian exile to rule an expanded Croatia. Hardly had Pavelić been catapulted into power in May 1941 than he set out to solve the "Serbian problem" through a campaign of expulsion, murder, or forced conversion of two million "Oriental" minorities and Communists unfortunate enough to have been incorporated into the bloated borders of the NDH. In the major cities, kangaroo courts tried and executed by the hundreds "traitors" whose only crime was that their Serbian ethnicity threatened the ethnic purity of the NDH. In the countryside, even these cursory legal formalities were ignored.[65] For instance, in July 1941, 250 peasants in the town of Glina, a Serb enclave located on the old military frontier that separated Austria-Hungary from the Ottoman Empire, agreed to convert to Catholicism to save their skins. Ustaše guards led them into the Serbian Orthodox church and told them to lie face down on the floor. The doors were locked and Ustaše thugs appeared to butcher the peasants with spiked clubs.[66]

Yugoslavia was transformed by occupation and civil war into a charnel house. In Sarajevo, Wehrmacht soldiers made common cause with Croat mobs to loot and destroy synagogues by shooting down chandeliers and tossing grenades at the holy scrolls. Ustaše and Germans cooperated to round up, execute, or deport Jews and Gypsies. Some Jews were able to flee to Italian-administered territory, where they were harassed but otherwise kept out of Ustaše clutches by General Mario Roatta, who insisted that to hand them over would stain the honor of the Italian army. Upon the Italian surrender in September 1943, some Jews were able to evacuate out of Split to southern Italy. Most were not so lucky: between half and three-quarters of the 40,000 Jews in the NDH perished. Many got no farther than the notorious Ustaše-run Jasenovac camp on the Sava River about sixty miles southeast of Zagreb. Officially, Jasenovac was a "work camp" where, according to the Croatian state newspaper, even Gypsies were "given a chance at last to work for the good of society—for the first time in their legendary nomadic history."[67] Thousands died there, including most of Croatia's Gypsies, from typhus and starvation. The alternative for the inmates was to be transported across the Sava to the village of Gradina, where the favorite tool of execution was the hammer. Jewish women were sent to Luburić north of Zagreb, where girls as young as fourteen were routinely raped by camp guards. In Serbia the Germans, assisted by ethnic Germans and Serb fascists, carried out a comprehensive extermination campaign in July–August 1941 whereby Jews in the Banat were taken out and shot in groups of fifty into mass graves. Next came the turn of Belgrade Jews, despite appeals from German civilian officials that the executions had merely succeeded in transforming the Banat's Mačva Valley into a hotbed of partisan resistance. By early 1942, the "delousing truck" which fed exhaust back into the compartment that contained the victims made its appearance in Serbia. By the summer of 1942 Berlin boasted that Serbia was *Judenfrei*.[68]

In conditions of Ustaše mayhem, with persecuted Serbs in the NDH fleeing into Serbia, Montenegro, and disputed sections of Bosnia, large areas of which remained unoccupied by Axis garrisons, resistance sprang up rapidly and found no shortage of recruits. Resisters were also able to take advantage of the fact that German frontline troops were redeployed for Barbarossa, leaving a light occupation force to guard the Belgrade–Bulgaria highway. Forty-eight-year-old Colonel Draža Mihailović collected refugee Serb soldiers brushed aside by Marita in the mountains of Bosnia, Montenegro, and Serbia into a movement called the Chetniks (from *četa*, "company," a reference to the nineteenth-century guerrilla bands that had opposed the Turks), with an operational headquarters in the Ravna Gora mountains about seventy-five miles south of Belgrade. Mihailović was a classically trained soldier and decorated Serbian hero of the Balkan Wars of 1912–13 and of World War I. In the interwar years he had served as military attaché in Sofia and Prague and on the general staff. But his intense pro-Serbian sentiments continually set him at odds publicly with politicians and superiors alike, a habit that had won him a court martial and a brief imprisonment after he clashed with General Nedić. He had also become a tireless advocate of the reorganization of the Yugoslav army along ethnic lines, much like the old Austro-Hungarian army. The strengths of his movement lay in the military, police, or bureaucratic origins of many of his followers and in the support of the peasantry in central Serbia, where the Chetniks, whose beards distinguished them from the clean-shaven Communist partisans, were able to tap into a folklore of rebellion against Turkish occupation ingrained in the national consciousness. Mihailović's legitimacy came from his affiliation with King Peter's government-in-exile in London, which promptly promoted Mihailović to general and eventually to the rank of government minister to enhance his status with the British. London, keen to promote a successful resistance movement, favored him with military assistance until 1943, glorified meager Chetnik success against the Axis, and turned a blind eye to Chetnik violence against Croats and Moslems.[69]

By the end of 1942, however, the Chetniks had become more a liability than an asset to the Allied cause. Mihailović's followers were little more than a confederacy of political factions, a rump of dissident—and defeated—military officers who rejected Nedić and the Zbor, but who refused to bury their prewar quarrels and divisions in the interests of a unified resistance. Tito's lieutenant Milovan Djilas dismissed the Chetniks as "a conglomeration of Serbian liberal nationalists, terrified peasant masses, Serb chauvinists, and fascists." The only consistent element in their political program, rooted in "national and religious myths," was intolerance. "The Chetniks were so disorganized and undisciplined that even bandits could join them," according to Djilas, admittedly not an impartial observer.[70] Their dispersion and the fact that each Chetnik unit remained rooted in its region, even its village, answerable to a *vojvoda* or leader who often refused to acknowledge central direction, made it difficult for Mihailović to coordinate a national military strategy. The local ties of Chetnik bands and their peasant recruits, combined with the fact that Mihailović's goals included the "biological survival" of the Serbian people, made Chetnik *vojvodas* reluctant to carry out attacks that would bring down reprisals on the local population. Indeed, many Yugoslav military men understood the power of the Wehrmacht and were reluctant to take them on. Therefore, intermittent Chetnik cooperation with the Germans became an early characteristic of a movement that directed its principal aggression toward Moslems, Croats, and Communists.[71] According to Churchill, this happened because the Germans blackmailed many Chetnik leaders by seizing their families in Belgrade and elsewhere as hostages against attack. Others, however, collaborated out of conviction or hostility to Tito's Communists.[72] Ironically, although both the political resolve and the military effectiveness of the Chetniks were limited, their genesis in the Yugoslav army caused Axis commanders to overestimate their military potential and hence concentrate disproportionate resources against them until 1943.[73]

Chetnik association with King Peter's government-in-exile, although it gave them a veneer of legality, also proved a handicap in the long run. The restoration of the Serbian monarchy in an ethnically cleansed Greater Serbia failed to kindle the enthusiasm of Yugoslavia's non-Serb minorities. "The spirited boy king"[74] and his government, initially greeted as valiant exiles when they debarked in London in

June 1941, rapidly proved themselves a collection of inept ministers and scheming courtiers under the leadership of a headstrong adolescent monarch. They bickered over responsibility for the April 1941 collapse, split on how to address Ustaše massacres of Serbs, and quarreled over whether or not the king should be allowed to marry. The only thing that united them was a fear of Communism. But beyond that, they were never able to articulate a vision for postwar Yugoslavia.[75] In the first half of 1942, Yugoslav forces evacuated by the British from Greece in 1941 and assembled in Egypt mutinied against their Yugoslav commander. Exquisitely timed to coincide with Rommel's June 1942 offensive into Egypt and the fall of Tobruk, this rebellion served further to discredit King Peter's government in London. In August 1942, the Soviets denounced Mihailović for trying to cut a live-and-let-live deal with the Italians, a sin they would later overlook when Tito tried unsuccessfully to reach a similar accommodation with the Germans. In May 1943, thirty-one-year-old Captain F. W. "Bill" Deakin, a slight, soft-spoken Oxford don and personal friend of Churchill's, was parachuted by Cairo into Yugoslavia with the job of establishing a British military mission with the resistance. His conclusion, reported by the British chiefs of staff in June 1943, was that "it has been the well-organized partisans rather than the Chetniks who have been holding down the Axis forces."[76]

In contrast to the Chetniks, the partisans of the Yugoslav Communist Party (KPJ) constructed a truly national organization around a prewar core of roughly 8,000 party members. They welcomed all Yugoslav ethnicities including Jews. Their proletarian provenance meant that brutal Axis reprisals against "notables and persons of substance," which induced caution in Mihailović, left partisans unmoved.[77] Unlike the locally recruited Chetniks, the multiethnic partisans were generally insensitive to local concerns and deliberately calculated their attacks to provoke maximum retaliation, which would instill hatred, radicalize the population, help them overcome the deep ethnic and clan loyalties endemic among the South Slavs, and generate a wellspring of recruits. They also had a political organization whose method of gaining and retaining the loyalty of the civilian population was unequaled by the Chetniks.[78] The result, complained Dr. Harald

Turner, chief of the occupation administration, was that the partisans attracted recruits who "in the past, would never have dreamed of co-operation with them. Some go so far as to prefer Bolshevism to the occupation of our troops—and these are the people on whose cooperation we were counting. My impression is that even the news of the capitulation of the Soviet Union would not cause these bandits to capitulate . . . They are tougher than anything you can imagine. What is more their organization is excellent. It might serve as an example of the perfect secret organization."[79]

The singular strength of the partisans, and a major reason why the Yugoslav resistance, unique among European resistance movements, rose to postwar power, lay with the capabilities of their charismatic leader Josip Broz, who adopted the revolutionary pseudonym Tito. A Croat whose adolescence was passed in apprenticeship to a locksmith, Tito had acquired his education, such as it was, in the early 1930s either in prison under the tutelage of learned revolutionaries or through the rote learning of Moscow cadre academies, where he had absorbed the Marxist classics. Despite his impeccable revolutionary credentials, Tito made an unorthodox insurgent. A man of action bored by the endless theoretical arguments beloved of the revolutionary intelligentsia, he demonstrated a bourgeois affinity for dandified dress, ballroom dancing, and upward social mobility—he always described himself as an "engineer" in his forged papers. As partisan leader, he wore a specially made Soviet pilot's cap with an enameled red star with a hammer and sickle on it, superior to the old Yugoslav royal army garrison caps with stitched-on cloth stars issued to his troops. Even before the Germans surrendered in May 1945, Tito presided in liberated Belgrade in uniforms so laden with gold braid that they appeared to have been specially tailored for the *caudillo* of a Latin American junta rather than the leader of a people's revolutionary movement. Stanford-educated OSS major Franklin Lindsay, sent to work with the partisans in 1944, complained that Tito's sartorial fantasies proved contagious in a partisan officer corps eager to distance themselves socially from the proletariat: "These junior officers take advantage of their authority to get for themselves the best of the meager supplies available," he noted. "Nearly all officers had 'Tito' jackets tailored from British and American greatcoats supplied in our air-drops, then took second greatcoats to wear over the jackets. Meanwhile, the troops shivered in ragged remnants of civilian clothes and German uniforms."[80] Before the war, Tito had acquired a small property with party funds where he built a villa and produced wine of which he was exceedingly proud. By the war years, the dark face and deep-sunk eyes of the youthful revolutionary had swollen into the portly frame and outwardly jovial manner of a Croat bourgeois.

Tito's military preparation was limited to service as a sergeant in the Austro-Hungarian army in World War I. Captured by the Russians and sent as a POW to Siberia, he converted to Communism following the 1917 Russian Revolution. One of Tito's closest wartime collaborators, Milovan Djilas, considered him a better politician and strategist than field commander. Djilas found Tito nervous and indecisive in action, too overwhelmed by the chaos of battle to keep a clear head and issue timely orders. Ingenuity, resourcefulness, and sangfroid in the face of the enemy were not his strong suits. Lindsay complained that Tito's addiction to large staffs, concentrated logistics, and targetworthy "liberated" areas actually made the partisans less efficient and more vulnerable to German counteroffensives.[81] Rather, Tito looked to inflict as many casualties as possible on the enemy and, when pressed, move on to "liberate" a new area with the core of his force and so preserve the revolution. He always left a cadre of partisans behind to engage in sabotage actions. This meant that his followers had to endure several grueling "long marches" during the war as they fought their way out of contested areas to settle in those that were lightly policed. Victories came despite his poor generalship, often on the basis of initiatives by subordinate commanders, a fact that Tito's vanity made him loath to acknowledge. Nevertheless, "Tito was not petty as a commander, nor did he stifle the initiative of his officers," Djilas concluded.[82]

Tito understood that the war would be long and arduous, and that the partisans must begin slowly.[83] In 1941 he entered into cautious collaboration with the Chetniks, although the divergent goals of the two organizations, and the fact that Germans could blackmail Chetniks into divulging intelligence on partisans, rapidly set them at odds. The result, Churchill wrote, was "a tragedy within a tragedy."[84] Tito's first "capital," at Užice in western Serbia, only twenty-five miles distant from that of Mihailović, became the fragile center of a revolutionary empire. Despite a functioning postal system, railway, newspaper, weapons factory, bank, schools, dance hall, and cinema, all calculated to bolster partisan morale, Djilas complained that the "Republic of Užice" exuded a shabby "air of impermanence," induced in part by peasant suspicion of the partisans.[85] By mid-1942 Tito had abandoned his initial strategy of trying to control large swaths of Yugoslav territory to give credibility to his movement, because this gave his German and Ustaše opponents a target against which to concentrate. He also learned that it was easier to attack Italians and Chetniks to seize their arms and supplies and to leave the Germans alone.[86] And while in theory this gave Tito ample opportunity to develop his skills as a field commander, his main contribution was to master a factious and argumentative party capable of acting with unforgiving brutality and to impose his iron will on the partisan movement. Indeed, one of Djilas's main tasks in 1941–42 was to halt Communist-led reigns of terror in Montenegro following that province's revolt against Italian attempts to create an independent monarchy there. Djilas failed.

Unlike the secretive, reclusive Stalin, Tito was a gregarious man, eager to give impromptu speeches, deeply attached to the party and to his troops, whose sufferings moved him as much as their victories left him elated. The weakness of the partisans reflected Tito's weaknesses. His conceit that he was a brilliant military commander was overlooked by his followers, mainly because they admired the cunning and political acumen with which he built a movement, and by his grasp of the fact that the resistance offered a new form of political power, one that he possessed the driving ambition to harness.[87] But the fact that the "Marshal" seemed more interested in eliminating "class enemies" and sparking a popular revolution as a prelude to the establishment of a Soviet-style republic than in rallying Yugoslavs of all persuasions around the task of defeating Germans caused conflict with Stalin, who admonished Tito for allowing his partisans to wear red stars on their caps. The Soviet dictator argued that a unified "patriotic front" would be more militarily effective and divert German divisions from the

Eastern Front. He also feared stoking Allied fears that resistance movements would initiate Communist power grabs in liberated countries.
In Tito's defense, his priority was to install a Communist regime in Yugoslavia, and only secondarily to assist the USSR, which, after all, gave
him less aid than did the British. The "Marshal" also understood that
a beguiling vision of socialist revolution constituted the only inclusive
ideology capable of melding Yugoslavia's multiple ethnic groups into a
truly Yugoslav movement. Therefore, social revolution became insep-
arable from resistance in Yugoslavia, and the partisans' main unifying
ideology.[88] This did not make the partisans popular, as most Yugoslavs
wanted neither to return to the past nor a revolution.[89] But it guaranteed that the most dynamic, forward-looking elements of the population would rally to them. The rest must follow—repression by the Axis
and their local allies gave them no choice!

Aggressive partisan tactics forced Chetniks to follow suit or lose
credibility. But intramural competition also incited members of each
group to launch imprudent attacks that caused needless casualties and
brought down cruel reprisals on the hapless civilian population. In the
long run, however, Axis reprisals strengthened the partisans, because it
radicalized the population while making the Chetniks less willing to
take risks. Even Djilas confessed that early partisan actions in Montenegro demonstrated more enthusiasm than expertise, and succeeded
only because the Italians had no stomach for a fight and usually surrendered as soon as it became apparent that the partisans would prevail. The Italians seldom ventured beyond the towns, which made it
easier for the resistance to organize the countryside.[90] The Germans,
on the other hand, set the gold standard for mayhem when, in the
middle of October 1941, in response to an increase in acts of sabotage,
they massacred an estimated 1,700 inhabitants of the town of Kraljevo
after the German garrison there was attacked by a joint partisan-
Chetnik force. Massacres in other towns followed. Soon a routine was
established, with German troops moving into a village, carefully regis-
tering males over the age of fourteen, and then shooting fifty of them
for each German casualty inflicted by the resistance. While the ferocity of German reprisals induced caution, even collaboration, with the
Zbor and Chetniks,[91] partisans countered by burning tax and other

civil records to undermine Axis efforts to administer the country and take a census of potential victims.[92] The scale of German reprisals and the arrival of the first British Special Operations Executive (SOE) mission to Mihailović's headquarters in October 1941 increased the inherent suspicion between the two resistance groups, which actually came to blows in November 1941. A major Wehrmacht offensive in December 1941 drove the 2,000 surviving partisans from Užice and Montenegro toward Italian-occupied southeastern Bosnia, and then again toward western Bosnia, where Croat repression had produced a raging civil war. The Germans spurned Mihailović's November 1941 offer to collaborate with them to flush out the partisans, and instead drove the Chetniks out of Ravna Gora into eastern Bosnia, where Mihailović exacted revenge on Croats and Moslems in retaliation for Ustaše atrocities against Serbs.

Despite apparently devastating success in the winter offensives of 1941–42, with thousands of resisters killed in action or executed as POWs in line with German high command directives, the insurgency refused to succumb. In western Bosnia, Tito reorganized his partisans into "proletarian brigades" for the long war against the occupying forces. These "brigades" eventually became "divisions," and then, on 1 November 1942, the People's Liberation Army of Yugoslavia. Tito also laid the foundations for an intelligence service that, Djilas believed, was one of the keys to partisan survival.[93] Lindsay thought the intelligence situation largely a wash: both sides were deeply penetrated by "collaborators," and the Germans were able to track and attack partisan movements by following Allied airdrops of supplies to partisan units, which "stirred up a hornet's nest," and monitor radio transmissions between OSS and SOE operatives and their base in Brindisi. The greatest partisan advantages in Lindsay's estimation were popular support, which meant that they were tipped off in advance of an Axis offensive; and mobility, which allowed small partisan bands to stay one step ahead of their pursuers. However, the advantage of civilian support was forfeited when German pressure drove the partisan army from safe areas and put them "on the road," where restricted routes of escape made them vulnerable to ambushes.[94] In June 1942, Tito marched the core of his force of around 3,000, followed by herds, pack animals, and wounded, into the remote mountainous region of the NDH astride Bosnia and "inner" Croatia. This devastated land proved a fertile ground for recruitment among bands of Serb refugees who led a precarious fight against Ustaše violence, and even among Croats and Moslems alienated from the collaborationist NDH. He could also evade pursuit by shifting between Italian- and German-occupied areas. Tito was bolstered by Soviet propaganda that portrayed the partisans as the only truly "Yugoslav" resistance, a People's Liberation Army whose units contained all ethnic minorities. This impression was reinforced and the partisans were legitimized by the organization of the multiethnic Anti-Fascist Council for the National Liberation of Yugoslavia in Bihac in November 1942. By late 1942, Hitler understood that he had a serious rebellion on his hands in the Balkans.

GREECE: "A COMPLICATED AND DISAGREEABLE SITUATION"[95]

Resistance in Greece was slower to organize than in Yugoslavia, and ultimately less successful, for several reasons. First, the military, which provided the foot soldiers of the resistance in both countries, had been more thoroughly defeated and disorganized in Greece than had its Yugoslav counterpart. Second, Greece was a culturally and ethnically homogeneous country where national unity was an established fact and not a bone of contention. There was no equivalent of the Ustaše to jumpstart resistance by victimizing the majority population. Third, the Greek Communist Party—the KKE—proved less effective in overcoming the divisions of Greek politics to build a national resistance than did the Yugoslav Communists. This occurred in part because, unlike in Yugoslavia, a call for revolutionary change offered no fundamental appeal as a unifying ideology for the mass of Greek peasants who filled the ranks of the resistance. Stalin left Greek Communists largely without direction in formulating policy and strategy, and no Greek Tito emerged to fill the leadership vacuum. Finally, while it can be argued that British and American meddling in the internal politics of the Greek resistance actually helped to create the conditions that led to the outbreak of civil war in 1946, British armed intervention in Greece in October 1944 prevented the insurgency from taking over Athens, and gave anti-Communist opposition a sanctuary and the time to organize, unlike in Yugoslavia, where the intervention of the Red Army delivered the strategically important capital to Tito. Greek Communists lost the momentum that the liberation would have given them. Instead, they were drawn into negotiations, disarmed, and out-maneuvered. Diehards took to the hills, where they were isolated and eventually defeated. Atrocities carried out by Communists against hostages tarnished their resistance record, and caused the forfeiture of much of the moral high ground that their wartime resistance had gained for them in the Greek population.[96]

Unlike in Yugoslavia, where armed and scattered soldiers quickly came together almost immediately to form resistance groups, many of the Greek soldiers who might have formed the core of a resistance had been evacuated by the British to Crete and eventually Egypt. Some military refugees from the debacle wandered the hills of northern Greece, subsisting as bandits. Officers left behind went home, where they stayed out of trouble until mid-1942, when the Italians suddenly concluded that they posed a security threat and tried to round them up. Rather than face internment in Italy, many fled into the arms of the National Republican Greek League (EDES), formed in the autumn of 1941 by a bearded, obese officer of dubious character named Napoleon Zervas. Insofar as EDES was united by any binding ideology, Zervas represented the Venizélist republican strain of Greek politics. But EDES, like the EKKA of Colonel Demetrios Psarros, active in Roumeli, was essentially a military organization, unaffiliated to any political party, and so had no program that could serve as a basis of a wider popular mobilization or supply a vision for postwar Greece, beyond a desire to push national borders north into the irredenta of Albania, Yugoslavia, and Bulgaria.[97] Under pressure from Churchill and the Foreign Office, which feared a Communist takeover of Greece, Zervas sent a message of loyalty to the exiled King George on 9 March 1943 in return for a significant increase of weapons and cash from London.[98] It was a step toward healing the "National Schism" that had riven Greek politics since World War I, insofar as it began to push the "bourgeois" parties into a reluctant coalition against the Communists.

But it also served to make the resistance in Greece much more complex than a straightforward struggle between "resistance" and "collaborationists." The parliamentary political parties had been discredited by their acquiescence before the war to the Metaxas dictatorship, and by their inability to respond to the desperate famine that struck Greece in the first winter of the occupation.[99] And while EDES gained a foothold in Epirus in Ionian Greece mainly through networks of personal and family contacts, and by capitalizing on the ethnic friction between Greeks and Albanian Moslems in the region, it was dismissed by the British SOE as a "collection of useless officers" notable for its administrative anarchy. Many EDES officers had links to the govern-

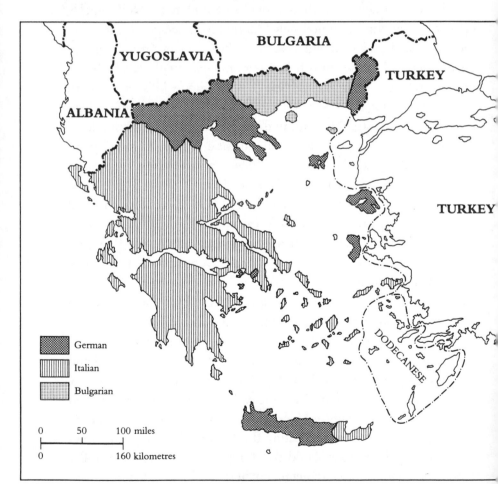

German

Italian

Bulgarian

0   50   100 miles

0   160 kilometres

ment of General Georgios Tsolakoglou, commander of the Third Corps in western Macedonia, who had surrendered to the Germans. Like the Chetniks, EDES had no desire to make a bad occupation worse by attacking the Axis.[100]

Greece was far less susceptible to disintegration and hence revolution than was Yugoslavia, a second cause of the relatively slow start of the Greek resistance. National independence, achieved in the struggles of 1821–29, was a long-established fact that no party sought to overturn. The generally apathetic tone of prewar Greek politics lingered into the opening months of the war. Traditional politicians, convinced that they need only await liberation by Britain, were careful not to adopt attitudes that might jeopardize their positions, pensions, or families.[101] Ethnic minorities composed but a fraction of the Greek population: pockets of Moslem Albanians—called Chams—some of whom worked in militias assigned to Wehrmacht operations, lived around Filiates in the northeast. Vlach, in the remote mountains of Thessaly, and Macedonian separatists were courted by the Bulgarians. Otherwise, Greece was a culturally and linguistically homogeneous nation. The Bulgarians drove as many as 200,000 Greeks out of central Macedonia when they occupied it in 1943. The Italians also armed the Vlach minority in 1943, who then set about terrorizing Greeks. Fewer than 10,000 of Greece's estimated 80,000 Jews escaped deportation and death at the hands of the Nazis.[102]

The country was divided between German, Italian, and Bulgarian occupiers, who immediately set about stripping it of assets, seizing food and transport. Factories closed down for lack of raw materials or because their machinery had been sent north, throwing many out of work. The Tsolakoglou government, saddled with the costs of the occupation, which in 1942 gobbled up 90 percent of the Greek budget, recklessly printed money, causing inflation to soar, a problem that worsened as SOE began to flood the country with gold sovereigns meant to underwrite resistance activity. With the harvest reduced by as much as a third because of the spring 1941 mobilization, farmers hesitated to sell in markets where they risked seizure or payment in worthless drachmas. Areas hoarded food rather than send it to starving cities. The result was a desperate famine by late autumn of 1941. The lethargic response of Greece's leadership class to the crisis, combined with the fact that most Greeks were utterly preoccupied with survival in the starvation winter of 1941–42, postponed the transition from latent hostility to the Axis to open resistance. When Greeks did begin to resort to resistance, it was the Communists who were best placed to organize it.

Formed in 1918, the Kommounistikon Komma Ellados (KKE) in the interwar years had been barely a blip on the Greek radar screen. The absence of a large Greek working class and traditional Communist disdain for peasant grievances deprived it of a significant natural constituency. The Comintern's support of the cession of Macedonia and western Thrace to Bulgaria left the party bitterly divided between its pro-Moscow wing—known as the *hadjis* because of their strength among refugee activists from Asia Minor—and nationalists who bridled at calls for party discipline. By following a Popular Front strategy and remaining silent on the issue of Macedonian cession, the KKE captured fifteen National Assembly seats and just under 10 percent of the vote in the 1936 elections. This relative ascendancy proved short-lived, however, as the Metaxas dictatorship dissolved Parliament in August and launched a campaign of repression that reduced the KKE to a handful of hunted faithful. The collapse of Greek resistance in the spring of 1941, followed by Barbarosa, opened new vistas for the KKE. A leadership vacuum was created by the fact that the royal government-in-exile was cut off from Greece, the traditional politicians who remained responded inadequately to the crisis, and the Axis occupiers continued to squeeze the country mercilessly. The Communists' familiarity with a clandestine, secretive existence, their political agenda, and their techniques of mass mobilization allowed them to fill it. The National Liberation Front (EAM) was founded under Communist auspices in September 1941, followed by the National Popular Liberation Army (ELAS) in April 1942. By the liberation in 1944, EAM/ELAS claimed to have organized one-third of Greece's six million people. EAM's political appeal lay in its rejection of the Metaxas dictatorship and the king, and as a popular, patriotic, democratic expression of a desire for decentralization and local autonomy within Greece. Internationally, the EAM advocated the removal of Greece from the game of power politics.[103] Unlike Zervas's EDES, which was utterly dependent on London and the SOE, EAM/ELAS actively opposed British attempts to manipulate the political outcome in Greece.[104]

Although EAM/ELAS emerged as the strongest Greek resistance group by far, they remained fragmented geographically and politically. They were closed out of traditionally royalist areas in the south, whose population had no folk memory of resistance to Turks or Slavs and no Communist loyalties. The heavily garrisoned islands and eastern Macedonia and Thrace, where Bulgarians proved effective against resistance activity, also proved to be barren ground for the resistance. Crete early on established its own resistance organization with British aid independent of EAM. Villages were often divided in their loyalties, some understandably apprehensive that an EAM/ELAS presence invited reprisals from the Germans or collaborationist Greek Security Battalions.[105] No Greek Tito emerged to unify the scattered resisters into an ideologically and militarily coherent movement—the pro-Comintern general secretary Nikos Zachariades and many of his lieutenants had been arrested by Metaxas and subsequently deported by the Germans. Zachariades's replacement was his "nationalist" rival Giorges Siantos, a genial, self-effacing ex–tobacco sorter and army sergeant from Thessaly known affectionately in the KKE as "the old man." Siantos applied a "patriotic front" strategy to broaden the base of EAM/ELAS. Nevertheless, Siantos maintained a deep, some claimed even "obsessive," distrust of "bourgeois" politicians as well as Communist dissidents, whom he regularly denounced as "scum" and "enemies of the people."[106] The recruitment of socialists and republicans into a Communist-run front organization complicated already serious problems of control over a dispersed organization whose local leaders, many of whom were not Communists, insisted on charting their own course. It also created distrust between Communist leaders like Siantos and his rank and file, as well as sabotaged cooperation among resistance groups.[107]

Greek Communists discovered that liberation, not revolution, was the goal of most Greeks. While EAM appeals to social justice, gender equality, and democratic institutions certainly attracted many to its ranks, revolution offered only limited appeal as a unifying ideology in a country where national unity was already an accomplished fact, unlike in ethnically splintered Yugoslavia. It also complicated the EAM/ELAS "national front" strategy as well as cooperation with the British.[108] The spirit of Communist internationalism was deliberately underplayed in a movement that feared alienating the peasantry by using Communist slogans or putting red stars on the caps of the *andartes*—Greek guerrillas whose name deliberately recalled the bands that had fought the Turks in the independence war. Greek Communists found even less support in Moscow than did Tito, because Stalin was keenly aware of Greece's strategic value to Britain. Out of touch with the Comintern since 1939 and without instructions from Stalin before the summer of 1944, EAM/ELAS was denied a clear direction and an international context in which to make its decisions. Stalin's summer 1944 directive to the KKE to cooperate with the British placed them in the dilemma of having to stand up for Greek interests against the British to shore up their national base on one hand, while supporting the international movement by carrying out Stalin's policy on the other. Their attempts to satisfy both masters made EAM appear obstructionist and eventually caused them to be outmaneuvered, fragmented, and politically isolated by the prime minister in the government-in-exile, Georg Papandreou.

In its organizational aspects, the Greek Communist resistance came to resemble Chetniks more than the Yugoslav partisans. ELAS's military chief Aris Velouchiotis was unable to exercise absolute authority over Greek Communist *kapetans* and their peasant followers, most of whom were not Communists. These men were more likely to behave like Chetnik *vojvodas*, highly territorial petty despots whose "bands," numbering between thirty and one hundred persons, gained control of the population and hence the food supply in an area, and then fought off other resistance groups who tried to invade their territory. In fact, in terms of brutality, some EAM/ELAS *kapetans* could see the Security Battalions and SS-sponsored "death squads" home any day of the week. In March 1943, ELAS captured regular army Colonel Stephanos Saraphris in a fight with a rival resistance organization, and persuaded him to take over military command of ELAS.

Saraphris organized a headquarters and staff to coordinate operations among "battalions," "regiments," and "divisions." He introduced a rank structure, formal military discipline, training, and a coherent administrative system. Velouchiotis became *kapetanios* in charge of recruitment, supply, propaganda, and administration. A political commissar, Andreas Tzimas, was named to make certain that the EAM/KKE political line was applied throughout ELAS. But the reluctance of the British to arm Communists, which limited recruitment; the absence of radios that would allow coordination of the bands dispersed across the mountains of northern Greece; the inadequacy of the food supply, which kept village-dependent bands small and scattered; and the presence of the Wehrmacht, which made any large-scale operation a suicidal undertaking, meant that most of Saraphris's reforms remained cosmetic ones. In any case, the more ELAS came to resemble a formal military organization with an inadequate support structure under Saraphris's leadership, the less flexible and effective it became as a guerrilla army.[109]

Precursors to resistance took the form of a general breakdown of order in the cities, as people began to steal food and gasoline to survive, and to carry out minor acts of sabotage against Axis troops. "People's committees" organized by trade unions and professional organizations formed spontaneously in the first winter of the occupation to pressure local authorities to do something about the famine. The KKE realized that they must work with these "bourgeois" groups to exploit popular disgust with the ineptness of the Tsolakoglou government and to expand their base by appealing to a general desire for social activism. Nowhere was this discontent more pronounced than in the countryside, where farmers were fined, thrown into prison, and had their crops confiscated. Some joined groups of soldiers marooned by the war who lived chiefly by brigandage and sheep rustling in the mountains of Roumeli, Thessaly, and Macedonia. By the summer of 1942, as these ex-soldiers joined with peasants to resist crop requisition expeditions sent out from the towns, to raid government warehouses, and to burn tax and land records, references to *andartes* first began to appear in government reports. By the autumn of 1942, dispersed and poorly armed bands had begun to form in the mountains.[110]

CHAPTER FOUR

Rommel's War: A Perfect Battlefield

F OR MANY, the battle fought in the Western Desert became the sine qua non of World War II in the Mediterranean for at least two reasons. First, combat there, while frequently bloody, remained almost chivalrous, free of the barbarism and massacres that characterized fighting on other fronts—"A knight's tournament in empty space," in the view of Australian journalist Alan Moorehead.[1] Desert combat was detached, impersonal, in part because the ground over which the armies campaigned possessed, in itself, no value. "Up the Blue," in Eighth Army jargon, the 1,500 sparsely populated miles between Tunis and Cairo, was sacred soil to none of the soldiers who fought to dominate it. In this respect, the massive tank battles fought over the great sand wastes appeared to parallel and replicate in essential respects the naval struggle in the Mediterranean more than any other land encounter in the theater. The desert resembled a stretch of sea that offered strategic advantage to the side that could control it. Vast tank armadas maneuvered like cruisers between islands of infantry scattered across wastes of rock, gray salt bush, and yellow grit. Captain Robert Crisp, a South African serving with the Royal Tank Regiment, compared dust-covered German convoys to the nautical counterparts, "the grim panzers sliding along the flanks like destroyers round a fleet of merchant ships."[2] "In some indefinable way," wrote the British historian Ronald Lewin, "the purity of the desert purified the desert war."[3] The opposing commanders faced each other like rival admirals, competitive but without rancor, masters of mechanized and tactical systems, each maneuvering to scupper his opponent. In short, the desert offered a perfect battlefield for a "war without hate," "to be judged from a purely operational point of view."[4]

A second reason that the desert war is remembered practically with nostalgia, especially in the British camp, can be attributed to the character of the man whose name is indelibly associated with that struggle—Field Marshal Erwin Rommel. Rommel's presence in North Africa from February 1941 until his departure two years later made the North African war both dramatic and principled. Rommel was the quintessential fighting soldier, a risk taker who, having mastered the principles of mobile warfare in France, reenacted in the desert the audacity of Hannibal, Napoleon, and Robert E. Lee. As commander of the weaker army, he had to stay on the offensive to survive. In his quest for the decisive battle through bold, unorthodox maneuver, Rommel elicited the awe and respect of his opponents even as he humiliated them. In his memoirs, the British prime minister pays tribute to a general who forfeited his life in the failed conspiracy against Hitler in July 1944. "In the somber wars of modern democracy chivalry finds no place," formed Churchill's epitaph for Rommel.[5] Under a less principled, less honorable commander, the German Afrika Korps might easily have descended to a level of thuggery displayed by too many Wehrmacht units on the Eastern Front and elsewhere. But Rommel's high standards of personal behavior, his refusal to countenance commands from Berlin that contravened the rules of civilized combat, like those ordering the execution of commandos and members of the Jewish brigade, "created for the Afrika Korps an essentially wholesome climate of opinion." In short, Rommel was a German officer of the old school, a gentleman "who might lose his temper, but never his honor."[6]

On the other hand, Rommel was as popular neither in the German army nor among German historians as he continues to be in the "Anglo-Saxon" world. And this is not because ultimately he failed in the desert. After all, short of miracles of Allied miscalculation, it is difficult to see how he could have prevailed there. Rommel unquestionably possessed the instincts and operational virtuosity of a great field commander. However, overweening ambition combined with an inability, or unwillingness, to acknowledge his strategic limitations compromised these undisputed gifts. Far from being a relic of an earlier, more chivalrous era, Rommel was in fact the poster boy for a German army that made a devil's bargain with Hitler. Rommel's gambling instincts stretched to politics as well as to operations, and he lashed his fortunes to those of the Nazi juggernaut. Rommel was the wrong man for the job in North Africa. His ambition and lack of diplomacy jeopardized both Berlin's relationship with its Italian ally and Germany's longer-term strategic goals in the Mediterranean. As Hitler was unprepared to commit the resources to the Mediterranean that would take him to Suez and the Persian Gulf, Berlin would have been better served by a less ambitious, less flamboyant, more defensive-minded general to stabilize Italian failure in North Africa in February 1941. Given Hitler's obsession with the defeat of the Soviet Union, his reluctance to venture into the Mediterranean, the weakness of their Italian ally, and the inability to carry out joint and combined operations in a maritime environment, the Wehrmacht never had a chance seriously to threaten Britain's position in the Middle East. But Rommel's decision to take the offensive in North Africa dramatized the War in the Desert and helped to transform the Mediterranean from a strategic backwater to the pivotal theater of the European conflict.[7]

Germany's Mediterranean goals, limited to preserving Mussolini in power and confining the war on the Mediterranean's North African shore, required only stalemate, not victory. Seize Malta, adopt a defensive posture in Tripolitania to shorten the supply line across the Mediterranean and in North Africa, and transform the Western Desert into another "forgotten front," the Burma of the European theater. The last thing in Axis interest was to select a battleground where oil, sea power, and a practically unassailable base in the Nile Delta forfeited every inherent strategic advantage to the British. Rommel offered an amateurish British army an operationally gifted opponent against whom the home team could sharpen its skills. Nor was it in Berlin's interest to dispatch a general who would dramatize the struggle for Suez, and hence allow Churchill to showcase North Africa as a vital test of British resolve and of London's worthiness as a U.S. ally.

Therefore, when the German military attaché in Rome, General Enno von Rintelen, complained that "Rommel was just not a great strategist," he was not merely voicing general-staff resentment against an upstart outsider.[8] For it was clear from the beginning that Rommel's primary goal in North Africa was to embellish his own renown. He was unwilling to be constrained by Berlin's limited strategic ambitions there, and so played Churchill's game. The chief of the German general staff, Franz Halder, understood that the Germans would be fighting at a severe disadvantage south of the Mediterranean. Therefore, the goals should be to stabilize the Libyan front and postpone the inevitable defeat of the Italians in North Africa until the war could be won in other theaters.[9] Operational success that stopped short of "the enemy's unloading ports" hardly amounted to more than a series of monster raids that placed Berlin in the worst possible strategic posture in the Mediterranean, for they combined, in the words of a prescient 1941 German high command report, "the worst imaginable conditions for defense, with the most difficult rear communications."[10]

In the long run, Rommel's passage through the Mediterranean proved to be a great boon to the Allied cause. He offered his opponents a high standard against which to measure their effectiveness and to hone their tactical and operational skills. Rommel's victories came against armies that were disoriented, poorly trained, and that had yet to comprehend, much less counter, the superior German tactical and operational system. His victories almost single-handedly forced the Anglo-American alliance closer together, imparted a sense of urgency to it, and confirmed Roosevelt's decision to commit American troops to the Mediterranean in 1942. "The Champ" as *Time* magazine called him in 1943, put a face on the enemy, thereby personalizing Allied objectives. Rommel's defeat at El Alamein in the autumn of 1942 offered both an operational coming of age in the Western Alliance and a huge tonic to British morale. Once Montgomery took over the Eighth Army, Rommel was never again able to defeat it. Furthermore, through his own impetuosity, Rommel had thoroughly discredited himself with his superiors at the very moment from late 1942 that he began to display a modicum of strategic sanity.

"A SPLENDID MILITARY GAMBLER"

Despite his image as the quintessential German officer, Rommel was neither a Prussian nor an aristocrat. Son of a school headmaster, Rommel joined the 124th Infantry Regiment of the Württemberg army on graduation from secondary school in July 1910, having been previously rejected by both the artillery and the engineers. His commanding officer at the cadet school was unimpressed by the soldierly potential of a lad who seemed both sickly and overly serious for his age, refusing to smoke or drink, practically reclusive. He damned Rommel with faint praise as a "useful soldier." Commissioned a lieutenant in 1912, Rommel spent the next two years training recruits at his regiment's depot near Stuttgart. However, 1914 seemed to bring him alive. What his superiors had interpreted as a self-absorbed aloofness was transformed in combat into a fanatical eagerness to volunteer for the most dangerous missions. He spent the next two years in the trenches of France, twice wounded, awarded the Iron Cross second and first class. Transferred to Romania, he was again twice wounded. On leave in 1916, he married Lucie Mollin, whom he had met in Danzig before the war.

September 1917 found Rommel on the Italian front as part of General Otto von Below's Fourteenth Army, dispatched to bolster the flagging Austrians. The following month he won a *Pour le Mérite* for actions at Monte Mataiur and Longarone, part of the Caporetto offensive, after he complained formally that this highest of German decorations had been awarded to another officer by mistake. After the war, he prevailed upon the official historian to correct the record to reflect what he believed to be his vital role in the breakthrough. Henceforth Rommel was seldom without the blue, gold-trimmed, enameled Maltese cross that dangled from a black-and-silver ribbon around his neck. While his success showed both courage and initiative, it was achieved against an Italian opposition that was in disarray and in full retreat— during the entire ten-day battle leading to the surrender at Longarone, Rommel's battalion took only fourteen casualties. Nevertheless, the experience instilled in him the belief that audacity bought success. Nor was he modest about his exploit: throughout the interwar years, young officers or hostesses naive or foolish enough to call attention to his decoration triggered a two-hour recitation of his conquest of Monte Mataiur and Longarone.[11]

At the war's end, twenty-seven-year-old Captain Rommel battled red revolutionaries in Westphalia. He spent the 1920s as the commander of a rifle company and an instructor of tactics in Dresden before being given his own battalion in 1933. Although Rommel met Hitler briefly in 1935, Rommel's biographer, David Irving, claims that he was "virtually non-political."[12] But political neutrality was a meaningless term in 1930s Germany. Rommel, like his fellow officers, supported the expansion and transformation of the Weimar Reichwehr into the Wehrmacht. Nor was expansion per se enough for these officers. It was an article of faith among veterans of the Great War that they had been stabbed in the back in 1918 by German civilians eager for peace while their courageous army still fought on foreign soil. Because Rommel found German youth soft, unprepared for sacrifices, "against authority, against their parents, against the church and against us too,"[13] the Nazi program that promised to militarize the German people appealed to him. He embraced, some believed with an excess of zeal, the Wehrmacht's decision to become, together with the Nazi Party, the "second pillar" of the Führer state. From 1933, Germany's military leaders forged a "special relationship" with Hitler. According to German historian Jürgen Förster, this was "based on the common idea of a new community of blood and destiny, capable of enduring the most difficult circumstances and thus preventing another national collapse" like that of November 1918.[14] Furthermore, Rommel came to admire Hitler's "incisive" leadership, especially his murder of SA leader Ernst Röhm and the taming of Röhm's loathsome organization, which Rommel interpreted as evidence of the Führer's "genius."[15]

Rommel was drawn to the Nazis as a fast ticket for an ambitious officer who was neither Prussian, Junker, nor a member of the prestigious general staff, the nursery of German generals. On the contrary, he made no secret of the fact that he despised these men, "smooth, cold, black at heart," an attitude of contempt hardly calculated to win him the good will of his superiors.[16] In 1936, while an instructor at the Potsdam *Kriegsschule*, he was put in charge of Hitler's escort for a

Nuremberg rally. The next year, his *Infanterie Greift an*—"The Infantry Attacks"—was published to great acclaim and became a best-seller. Nevertheless, he remained, like his French counterpart Charles de Gaulle, an outsider—decorated, published, but absent from the Wehrmacht's list of future army commanders. However, once Rommel determined that he could advance through political, not military, connections, he began actively to cultivate prominent Nazi figures like Baldur von Schirach, leader of the Hitler Youth, volunteering to speak at length to youth rallies about—what else?—Monte Mataiur and Longarone. For his part, von Schirach came to resent what he saw as Rommel's attempt to "transform my Hitler Youth into some sort of junior Wehrmacht." Rommel's break came in 1938 when he was put in charge of Hitler's military escort to Czechoslovakia. He met Himmler, attended Nazi indoctrination seminars for Wehrmacht officers made compulsory from 1938,[17] and began to sign off his correspondence with "Heil Hitler!" The German dictator, an outsider himself, took a liking to an officer who broke the Junker staff officer mold of the Wehrmacht's upper echelons. In any case, Hitler intended to replace the fragmented, segregated officer corps with a single Führerkorps loyal to the party.[18] In 1939, Rommel escorted Hitler to Prague and Memel, and commanded Hitler's mobile headquarters during the Polish invasion of September. Hitler rewarded him by promoting him to general and placing him in charge of the victory parade through Warsaw. Rommel skewered the Wehrmacht's lukewarm support for National Socialist ideals, and savored the tongue-lashing Hitler delivered to his senior generals on 23 November 1939 over their reluctance to attack France. Rommel asked Hitler for, and was given, command of the Seventh Panzer Division in February 1940, over the protests of the personnel section, which noted, correctly but in vain, that infantryman Rommel had no experience with tanks.[19] The panzer divisions, designated as a special arm in 1938, enjoyed a status denied the infantry, which did not even have its own inspector general. Rommel ached for panzer prestige.

With an eye on his political future, Rommel invited rising Nazi stars like Karl-August Hanke, one of Propaganda Minister Joseph Goebbels's senior aides, and Karl Holtz, editor of *Der Stürmer*, an anti-

Semitic newspaper, to join his division staff. Both of these future Gauleiters (party regional leaders) whispered Rommel's name in the highest Nazi circles and guaranteed him an elephantine share of media attention. Nor did he neglect his military duties. He fired officers whom he determined were not up to scratch, demanded high standards of physical fitness from those who remained, and maneuvered his units of Panzer IIIs and IVs and Czech 38T tanks across the German countryside in preparation for the invasion of France.

On 10 May 1940, the Seventh Panzer surged into northern Luxembourg and Belgium as part of Hans von Kluge's Fourth Army. Riding in the vanguard of his division in a specially adapted Panzer III command vehicle, Rommel ignored threats to his flanks and rear, calculating correctly, as at Monte Mataiur and Longarone, that the enemy was simply too dazed and disoriented to react. On 13 May his troops forced a crossing over the Meuse, but took heavy casualties. Oblivious to personal danger, Rommel supervised the construction of a pontoon bridge over the Meuse behind a smoke screen of burning houses, pushed his tanks across, and drove forward. His technique was to advance by fire, guns blazing away at forests and villages that might contain enemy defenders. This was costly in munitions, but kept the enemy off balance. On occasion he bluffed French troops into surrendering prepared positions by having his tankers ride toward them waving white handkerchiefs. Confused, the French failed to open fire until the Germans were upon them. Soon, Rommel's panzers were raging in the French rear, sowing further confusion among men who were already bewildered and largely leaderless. French troops began to surrender in vast numbers. At Avesnes, a convoy of French reinforcements meekly allowed themselves to be directed to a car park where they were disarmed. Rommel drove the vanguard of his division relentlessly forward, outrunning both his logistics and much of the rest of his division, which simply did not know where he was. On 19 May his troops took Cambrai. Two days later, he faced a crisis when heavily armored British Matildas, invulnerable to the 37 mm guns of his panzers, counterattacked at Arras. Only by pressing his 88 mm antiaircraft guns into action did Rommel stanch the British attack. The halt at Arras also allowed Rommel's logistical tail to catch up.

On the twenty-seventh, Hanke appeared to bestow the Knight's Cross on Rommel, by Hitler's order, the first divisional commander in France to receive the decoration. This sign of Rommel's favor with the party hardly increased his popularity with his fellow commanders. Oblivious, he lapped up the honors of victory. He drove his division through the night to beat the competition to Lille. This, he explained to his wife, was so no one else might claim credit for his success, as in 1917. On 2 June, Hitler made a great fuss over the only division commander invited to attend a conference of his generals at Charleville in the Ardennes. From 5 June, Rommel formed his division into a square and steamrollered forward. Living on captured British and French rations, they reached the Seine at Sotteville, then turned north toward Dieppe and Saint-Valéry-en-Caux, where troops of the French Ninth Corps and the Fifty-first Highland Division surrendered to him. He then turned south, crossed the Seine at Rouen, and by 18 June was at Cherbourg. In barely five weeks the Seventh Division had bagged almost 100,000 POWs at the cost of forty-two tanks.[20]

Rommel became the toast of Germany, praised for his audacity. However, he also became the center of controversy in the army when he published his memoir of the campaign, entitled *The Ghost Division*, a nickname allegedly bestowed upon the Seventh Panzer by the bewildered French. Von Kluge, Rommel's commanding officer, noted that Rommel had intentionally falsified diagrams to reflect credit on himself, while ignoring the contributions of others, especially the Luftwaffe. He also complained that Rommel's decisions were impulsive rather than well thought out. The general commanding the Fifth Panzer, Rommel's brother division in the Fifteenth Corps, was stung by Rommel's criticism of the Fifth's slowness, especially as Rommel repeatedly snatched the Corps's bridging equipment and heavy tanks for himself, thereby stalling the Fifth's advance. Others pointed out that the Seventh Panzer had notched up the highest casualties of any division in the campaign, a preview of his attitude in the desert when some subordinates complained that Rommel demanded senseless sacrifices of his troops, especially during the sieges of Tobruk.[21] They were also scandalized when Rommel recommended Hanke for the Knight's Cross, although Goebbels's protégé had clearly failed in combat. Rommel then compounded his error when, in a fit of pique, he rescinded his recommendation after Hanke suggested that his civil service grade in the Ministry of Propaganda meant that technically he outranked Rommel.[22]

For better or worse, the campaign for France confirmed what would become the salient characteristics of Rommel's command style, beginning with his preference to lead from the front. This certainly kept his division moving relentlessly forward and was a great morale boost for the troops. However, it also contributed to confusion because his headquarters staff received few orders and often had no idea where he was. Second, France in 1940 now joined Italy in 1917 to stunt Rommel's maturation as a commander, for each confirmed in his mind the value of speed and even bluff in securing victory. Rommel had discovered a formula for success, which he sought to apply in all circumstances. The fact that his achievement had come against the French Ninth Army, composed of "B" infantry divisions of older reservists and lightly mechanized cavalry, who, without air support, were hopelessly outclassed by Rommel's panzers backed by mechanized infantry and Stuka dive-bombers, was immaterial to Rommel. In the same way, his early victories against anemic and poorly led British forces in the desert in the spring of 1941 nourished his growing self-confidence, not to say narcissism, and steeled him against self-analysis, reflection, introspection, and, above all, doubt.

Rommel's shortcomings proved to be symptomatic of the Wehrmacht's institutional mindset. Facile success against a respected French army that had stopped them cold in World War I inspired the conviction in the German military that tactical and operational success led inexorably to strategic victory. Churchill called Rommel "a splendid military gambler."[23] But the entire German Blitzkrieg system was a wager based on narrow calculations. The tendency to underestimate the enemy, to discount factors like industrial capacity, and the failure to take into consideration the larger strategic picture—these were hereditary failures in the German army—raged like a communicable disease among German generals in the wake of France's collapse. And why not? German soldiers were supermen, energized by victory, contemptuous of their enemies, impelled forward by arrogance to new conquests. The Wehrmacht's doctrine and training had stood the most severe tests. That constituted the "lessons learned" from the fall of France! An offensive mentality, a *toujours en avant!* command style settled upon the German officer corps. Rommel was simply one of its most flamboyant practitioners. It occurred to few of them that one day their opponents would be capable of paying them back in their own coin, and with interest.[24] From a command perspective, Rommel, like the Wehrmacht high command in general, remained a psychological adolescent until his defeat at El Alamein triggered the realization that Germany was going to lose the war. By early 1943, Rommel had matured as a strategist. But by then it was too late. "You can only understand Rommel by taking his storming of Mount Mataiur into account," one of his fellow instructors at Dresden commented years later. "Basically he always remained that lieutenant, making snap decisions and acting on the spur of the moment."[25]

Rommel's cavalier attitude toward logistics constituted his third weakness. Again, this was not merely a personal imperfection—logistical difficulties seldom discouraged the most ambitious operational planning in the Wehrmacht.[26] He had repeatedly outdistanced his logistical base in France, but managed to survive by borrowing from other units and pillaging captured Allied stocks, all the while criticizing his staff for their failure to keep up with their elusive commander. But a logistical deficit that had been a mere inconvenience in France would become a nightmare as the Wehrmacht ventured into the vast, roadless spaces of Russia and North Africa. When in March 1941 Rommel was asked by General Franz Halder how he planned to supply the two panzer corps he was requesting for North Africa, he replied: "That's quite immaterial to me. That's your pigeon."[27] Rommel seemed unconcerned by the fact that his great aim of conquering the Nile Delta and beyond was utterly divorced from any realistic appreciation of the means at his disposal.[28]

This lack of capacity for introspection and self-criticism predisposed Rommel to his fourth defect—he was a whiner. While he ached to bask in the popular adulation spun by success, his narcissism rendered him incapable of accepting responsibility for failure. In his mind, setbacks could never be attributed to his lack of self-restraint.

Instead, he blamed setbacks on others—his subordinates, his men, his Italian allies, or poor logistics. Finally, in France Rommel discovered that publicity counted for as much as deeds in advancing his career. His image was largely contrived, first by the Nazis and subsequently by the British, who magnified his skills and qualities as alibis for their own incapacity. The manner of his death at the hands of a vengeful Hitler also encouraged myth making. Posterity preferred to revere Rommel as a patriotic martyr, the embodiment of all that was best in German military traditions—character, chivalry, modesty, and professionalism.[29] Nazi propaganda marketed Rommel like a film idol in the wake of the fall of France. They had their work cut out for them. By 1940, the thin, intense youth of Longarone had eased into stocky middle age. Although his admirers claimed to detect cunning in the suspicion of a smile that occasionally spread over his face, and character in his angular jaw line, his features were otherwise unremarkable, even nondescript. The down-turned corners of his mouth conveyed no hint of humor. In his civilian overcoat and fedora, he looked like a Soviet dignitary about to take the salute from atop Lenin's tomb. Adding a touch of theater were his high-peaked military cap, the Perspex sand goggles captured from the British at Mechili in April 1941, and the Zeiss binoculars, especially when he was filmed peering into the desert in search of his quarry. With his hands invariably clasped behind his back, leaning slightly forward to fix his object with the piercing gaze of his steel-blue eyes, Rommel conveyed the impression of a man in communion with his destiny—cool, detached, severe. In the summer of 1940, Rommel's public appeal was unmistakable. Young German officers set out on pilgrimages to sit at the feet of the commander of the Seventh Panzer Division's "horsemen of the Apocalypse," the leader of the "Ghost Fleet" whose "tanks carve long, bloodstained trails across the map of Europe like the scalpel of a surgeon." His cunning and his character were praised. Rommel, the infantryman, appeared everywhere in jodhpurs, riding boots, and crop. He spent much of August 1940 reenacting events for *Victory in the West*, a German propaganda film about the fall of France. French Senegalese troops, furloughed from their POW camp, were coached by Rommel on the proper way to surrender for the cameras. This media adulation merely whetted Rommel's appetite for medals and promotion.[30]

The simple truth was that Rommel was a much greater boon for British propaganda than for the Germans. The goal of Churchill from the beginning was to entice the United States into the war. Rommel's reputation as the great genius of armored warfare at a stroke gave London a credible alibi for its failures in the desert. Churchill's concern that the British must score victories to be seen as a worthy partner for the United States was misplaced. In fact, both Hitler and Roosevelt were drawn into the Mediterranean by the weakness of their allies. It was Britain's beleaguered helplessness that evoked most sympathy in Washington and helped to prepare the American people psychologically to intervene in the war. The Battle of Britain encouraged the passage of the destroyers-for-bases bill, as the fall of Greece eased Lend-Lease legislation through Congress. But Rommel offered the *pièce de résistance*. He personified the Mediterranean war, gave it a human face, breathed panache into a remote, uncomfortable, and hitherto dreary battlefield. He restored drama to a Mediterranean war that otherwise offered only a succession of disjointed clashes in far-away, sand-blown spots that most people could not locate on a map. As the British had so far failed to manufacture a larger-than-life general to publicize their struggle, a character to capture the imagination *outre Atlantique*, then it must embrace one from the other side. When, in January 1942, before the House of Commons, Churchill paid tribute to "a very daring and skilful opponent . . . and, may I say across the havoc of war, a great general," he scored a brilliant propaganda coup. Unlike the "dull butcheries on a gigantic scale"[31] that passed for warfare on the Eastern Front, the battles in the desert were dramatic contests of tanks, fought by bronzed and hardened armies led by flamboyant generals—Rommel, Montgomery, Patton, Bradley. This was no rerun of the slogging matches of World War I, of Flanders and the Somme. Desert outposts were taken and forfeited, kilometers seized and surrendered. How boring would the Mediterranean have been, how irrelevant might it have become, had Wavell pushed on to Tripoli in February 1941!

AFRIKA KORPS

The success of Operation Compass lent urgency to German preparations, which dated from the summer of 1940, to intervene in the Mediterranean. On 3 February 1941, Hitler justified to representatives of the Wehrmacht and Luftwaffe high commands his decision, taken in early January, to send an armored blocking force to Tripoli. Libya was militarily insignificant, he told them. But its loss might jeopardize Mussolini's hold on power and free up British forces to make mischief in southern France or the Balkans. The Luftwaffe was to intervene immediately, attacking Malta to allow the passage of the Fifth Light Motorized Division to Tripoli with the task of stabilizing the crumbling Italian front. The Fifth Light, under forty-nine-year-old General Johannes Streich, had been pieced together from elements of the Third Panzer Division. Despite its lack of desert experience, it proved to be a formidable and hard-hitting force.[32] A panzer division was to follow. Hitler cast around for a commander-in-chief for his two-division force. His first choice, Erich von Manstein, was jettisoned in favor of Rommel, who "knows how to inspire his troops."[33] On 3 February, Rommel was summoned to Berlin from France, where he had been training his division for the invasion of England, and informed that he was to become "Commander-in-Chief, German Troops in Libya." On 6 February he left Berlin for Rome and Tripoli with explicit instructions that German troops "will not be committed to pointless battle." His orders were to establish a defensive front near Buyarat on the Gulf of Sirte and use his mobile forces to repel any British attempt to outflank it. Tactically, Rommel would be subordinate to the Italian command in North Africa. On 19 February the new force was baptized the *Deutsches Afrika-Korps*.[34]

The 13,000 German soldiers of the Fifth Light Motorized Division that had disembarked at Tripoli by 10 March 1941 were soon to be joined by 18,000 men of the Fifteenth Armored Division and another 10,500 from the Luftwaffe. This force formed only a minuscule portion of the 6,387,000 men under arms in the Wehrmacht at the turn of the year, but it was fairly typical of the strengths and weaknesses demonstrated by German forces early in the war. Tactically and operationally, the Germans were light-years ahead of their opponents in 1941. German officers emerged from a solid tradition of professionalism that stretched back to the great Helmut von Moltke, Bismarck's chief of staff in the 1860s and 1870s, and beyond. Unwittingly, the Allied victors had reinforced and deepened this tradition when, at the Versailles Conference of 1919, they had forced the consolidation and distillation of the four armies of imperial Germany into a 100,000-man Reichswehr, which would become the embryo of German military expansion from 1933. During the interwar years, the German army was obsessed with how to deal with a two-front war. As a consequence, they developed a doctrine that relied on mobile forces able to shift rapidly from front to front to counterattack advancing French and/or Polish troops. From 1933, the German military combined modern armament with Hitler's offensive political goals to transform a defensive doctrine based on counterattack into an offensive force designed for conquest. The German operational and tactical system was based on the tight coordination of armor, infantry, and air forces to stun and then overwhelm the enemy in a series of unrelenting, rapid offensives. The core of the offensive system was the panzer group, consisting of two to four panzer and motorized corps.

In 1941, panzer divisions were equipped with four main battle tanks: PzKw (*Panzerkampfwagen*) I, II, III, and IV. The redeeming quality of German tanks was that unlike several of their British counterparts, they were mechanically reliable. The PzKw I and II were light tanks, armed with machine guns and, on the PzKw II, a 20 mm gun. As these tanks became outclassed and reduced to reconnaissance roles, the PzKw II was transformed in 1943 into a platform for flamethrowers, mobile artillery pieces, and a 105 mm antitank gun, and employed as a turretless supply carrier. The PzKw III medium tank, produced from 1937, was the "warhorse" of the Afrika Korps. Agile, armed with a 37 mm gun whose armor-piercing "arrowhead" was particularly effective against British Matilda infantry support tanks, the PzKw III carried a crew of five at almost 25 miles per hour. Later versions were given thicker armor and up-gunned to 50 and even 75 mm. But by 1944, many PzKw IIIs, now outclassed on the battlefield by heavier tanks, were converted to tank recovery vehicles. The PzKw IV, the backbone of the panzer division, was the most respected tank in the German inventory in this period. The British especially feared the armor-piercing shells of its short 75 mm gun, which could "crock" a British tank from a distance while remaining impervious to British anti-tank guns. But as the PzKw IIIs became obsolete, there were never enough PzKw IVs to fill the gap. Mobile recovery-and-repair vehicles that could return damaged tanks quickly into battle—while the British often had to abandon their disabled but reparable tanks—constituted another German advantage in this period.[35] Spearheaded by these tanks, panzer divisions would rip open the enemy front and surge into the rear areas to disorganize the command-and-control system. Meanwhile, infantry armies would slice through to crush encircled enemy forces and seize strategic objectives. The Luftwaffe assigned an air reconnaissance squadron to each panzer division and detachments of fighters and Stuka dive-bombers to front areas to support mobile operations. These tactics were perfected in Poland in 1939 and in France the following year. The emphasis was on "mission-type orders," rapid decisions made by small staffs, and flexibility anchored in a well-understood doctrine and training along uniform lines that allowed mixing and matching of units to meet different tactical situations. Even fairly junior commanders could be allowed great latitude to take initiatives because all officers were trained within the framework of a single, coherent doctrine.

This operational system was underpinned by the tenacious fighting qualities of the German soldier. Why German soldiers fought so well, even in the face of defeat, is a question that has agitated historians. One school contends that the German system of training recruits built up a strong system of "primary-group" loyalty that was carried into the units. This view holds that German soldiers were essentially apolitical, indifferent, even hostile, to Nazi propaganda. Their best chance to survive, which was their primary concern, was to stick together as a group.[36] A contrary school contends that primary-group loyalty could not possibly explain German combat motivation, as the huge casualties absorbed by German forces, especially from June 1941 on the Eastern Front, meant that the primary group seldom survived for long. Rather, German combat tenacity can be attributed to the successful amalgamation of traditional "soldierly qualities," conditions on the front that discouraged desertion and fraternization with the enemy, and the association of the army with Nazi values and race war both in the officer corps and among the rank-and-file soldiers.

Despite a carefully nurtured post–World War II image of an apolitical German army cast unwillingly into a criminal enterprise by a fanatical leader, in fact the Wehrmacht was Hitler's willing victim and collaborator. The armed services had been highly politicized by World War I and its aftermath, and were deeply hostile to the Weimar Republic. German military leaders cooperated with Hitler before the outbreak of war to rearm Germany far beyond the needs of self-defense precisely because they rejected the verdict of Versailles. The execution by Hitler of Ernst Röhm and his Brownshirt followers in 1934 sealed the bargain between the Führer and a military convinced that they would retain their monopoly on armed force. Some opposed the 1936 remilitarization of the Rhineland, the occupation of Austria, and the dismemberment of Czechoslovakia in 1938. But this was because they feared a vigorous Allied reaction, not because they opposed Hitler's goals of a powerful Germany in possession of territory forfeited in 1918. Nor did the high command resist the increasing Nazification of the armed forces, because, like Hitler, they believed the army and Germany had been "stabbed in the back" in 1918 by a soft, war-weary population. Hitler won the support of the generals precisely because he promised to militarize the population, which he did with a vengeance.[37] Forty-five percent of Wehrmacht officer candidates between 1939 and 1942 were party members.[38] Most of the younger recruits arrived in barracks with ideological baggage acquired in school and the Hitler Youth that emphasized discipline, respect for authority, racism, anti-Bolshevism, national expansion, and a quasi-religious faith in the Führer. This indoctrination continued in the army, beginning with the personal oath of loyalty that all pledged to Hitler. Everyone was taught both to have an absolute faith in Hitler's judgment and to view the enemy, especially on the Eastern Front, as barbarians. Allied victory, they all came to believe, would result in the destruction of Germany.[39] Officers of the German navy, led from 1928 to 1943 by commander-in-chief Erich Raeder, were extremely hostile to the Weimar Republic and rejoiced at the Nazi victory of 1933. They threw themselves with enthusiasm into the development of "an inner attitude . . . that naturally resulted in truly national socialist views." Both the Nazis and the navy took great pride in the fact that no naval officer was implicated in the July 1944 assassination attempt on Hitler. Indeed, the poor relationship that eventually developed between German and Italian military leaders in North Africa and the Mediterranean stemmed in part from German disappointment at how resistant their Italian colleagues seemed to be to fascist ideology.[40]

How far the ideological commitment of the German forces survived Axis military reverses beginning in the autumn of 1942 is an open question, however. "The Hitler myth," the popular belief in the Führer's wisdom and infallibility that held the Third Reich together, was on the decline from the winter of 1942–43, and Germans began to take their distance from the Nazi party even before Allied armies crossed their borders. Defeat revived popular skepticism, suspended in 1939, that war would only bring misery upon Germany. Judging by Kesselring's warnings to his command about complaints against the leadership as the war progressed, the same disillusion with the Nazi regime that infected the civilian population tainted the army as well. Everyone continued to do their duty, more out of a backs-to-the-wall sense of survival than any desire to realize the racist ambitions of the National Socialist state. However, they probably took grim counsel from the graffiti artist who, in March 1945, decorated a Berlin wall with the recommendation: "Enjoy the war—the peace is going to be terrible."[41]

The weaknesses of the German forces were the reverse of their strengths. The German army in World War II, as in World War I, was a blunt instrument, expert at winning marginal victories against obliging opponents. After the fall of France, however, it never managed to translate operational success into strategic victory. Its operational and tactical edge also began to erode, although imperceptibly at first. The small staffs, good C3I, and emphasis on "battle drills"—that is, rehearsals of operational and tactical situations—which facilitated rapid decisions against weak and disorganized enemies, proved totally inadequate against large, increasingly expert, and well-supplied Allied forces. German intelligence was inadequate, stripping German commanders of the ability to assess enemy intentions, a critical flaw, especially as German forces were thrown on the defensive. Logistics did not figure prominently in operational planning.[42] The increasing emphasis on ideology and belief in the Führer as the cornerstone of military cohesion discouraged criticism and self-analysis. The warnings of General Wilhelm Ritter von Thoma, who was to surrender the remnants of the Afrika Korps to Montgomery after El Alamein, that the brilliant success of the panzer groups in Poland and France might prove ephemeral against an enemy with air superiority and solid defensive positions, fell on deaf ears.[43] The stunning achievements of the opening offensives also discouraged consideration of matching ends to means in a longer war of attrition. In part, this was the consequence of the German army's traditional emphasis on tactical and operational dominance, which discouraged considerations of strategic consequences. It was also the intention of Hitler, who, having politically emasculated his high command, assumed personal command of the army on 19 December 1941. He divided power among his underlings, forcing them to come to him to resolve conflicts. In the armed forces, this command system led to division and competition rather than rational strategic planning. The individual services charted and fought their wars in discrete compartments. The army set up separate commands for the Eastern Front and all other fronts, including the Mediterranean. Göring ran the Luftwaffe as his private air force.[44] Grand Admiral Erich Raeder remained focused on Mediterranean conquests, although this was clearly of only secondary concern to Hitler.[45]

The unwieldy nature of the German command structure, its focus on operational and tactical success at the expense of strategy, and Hitler's micromanagement of operations deprived Germany of the central-planning agencies, interservice staffs, and interallied mechanisms for coordinating that characterized the Western democracies. A Council of Ministers for Reich Defense created in 1939 lasted only three months. Attempts by armaments minister Albert Speer to revive it in 1942 failed. The war economy depended on pillaging occupied territories so as not to place undue hardship on a German population that Hitler believed capable of regressing to its back-stabbing mentality of 1918. Only after the obvious failure of Barbarossa were frantic attempts made to centralize planning and production. The OKW controlled the armaments factories, while the remainder of production fell under the Plenipotentiary for the Economy. The Allied strategic bombing campaign forced German industries to disperse. This lowered productivity per unit, led to production bottlenecks, and further strained the German communication and transportation systems. The military and industry competed for manpower, which left the Wehrmacht short of reserves to fill the huge losses it began to absorb in Russia. This required German industry to resort increasingly to forced labor as the war progressed.[46]

The Germans began the war with significant advantages. But as German forces were progressively attrited, the panzer armies lost their offensive punch. Panzer divisions that began the war with an average of 328 tanks were down to 73 by 1943. By 1942, it was apparent that German industry lacked the ability to maintain the Wehrmacht's technological edge. The slow development of mass-production techniques, the dispersal of German forces over widely scattered fronts poorly served by roads and railways, and the lack of equipment standardization as the Germans pillaged and appropriated the armories of defeated European armies, demonstrated how little prepared Berlin was to fight a long war. Furthermore, the Germans, banking on quick victories, had neglected their logistical infrastructure in favor of strengthening the sharp end of their forces. In the first year and a half of the desert war, the Germans managed to stay one step ahead of the British in the tank race by adding additional armor, a more powerful gun, or a better mix of high explosive and armor-piercing shell.[47] Once it became apparent by the autumn of 1942 that the Panzer III and IV tanks and the T-38 Czech tanks were outclassed by U.S. Shermans and Soviet T-34s, the Germans had desperately to play catch-up.[48] The "Panther" and "Tiger" tanks that began to come on line in the summer of 1942 packed a wallop. The PzKw V "Panther" incorporated the sloped armor of the T-34, and combined a powerful 75 mm gun, a wide track, and the relative speed of 34 miles per hour to make it what some consider the best battle tank of World War II.[49] The PzKw VI "Tiger" was the heaviest tank of the war. It incorporated the redoubtable 88 mm gun, while its thick frontal armor defied all but the most powerful Allied antitank guns. But they were difficult to produce and could be transported long distances only by rail, a severe drawback in North Africa. In the Mediterranean they were considered lethargic, unwieldy beasts that maneuvered badly over broken ground, were susceptible to breakdown, and were vulnerable to shots from the side or rear. Nor were there ever enough of them. The lack of heavy repair equipment and adequate stocks of spare parts meant that damaged tanks could not easily be patched up in forward areas. As a result, these monsters were increasingly used as static artillery pieces to anchor fixed defensive positions. As the war progressed, German soldiers were forced to fight with fewer tanks and artillery pieces, and dwindling supplies of fuel and ammunition. Because the Wehrmacht invested little in transport, relying instead on horses to carry their logistics, they were severely disadvantaged in Russia and North Africa, and forced to depend largely on a steady supply of captured vehicles, obligingly provided by the British. (The odds were equaled somewhat in the Italian mountains, where mules became the beast of choice for both sides.)

The Luftwaffe faced a similar decline in quality as losses mounted on widely dispersed fronts. Production stagnated between 1939 and 1942, both because of poor management by Göring and because, with the exception of the Focke-Wulf 190 fighter, prototypes proved to be technological failures. Therefore, as the Allies began to put more high-performing planes into the skies, the Luftwaffe, unable to evolve new prototypes, continued to rely on obsolete ones. The Stukas, so terrifying in 1940 against no-show air opposition in Poland and France and obsolete British planes in the Mediterranean, began to outlive their usefulness; Hurricanes and Spitfires began to shoot them from the skies and force them to approach on flat-trajectory runs where their bombing was ineffective. The main German fighter, the Messerschmitt Bf. 109, was considered the best and fastest fighter in the world when it first appeared in 1937. It had first won its spurs in Spain and had continued to be upgraded throughout the war. The robust Bf. 109 was superior to the Hurricane and even exceeded the Spitfire in its angle and rate of climb. Its fuel-injection Daimler-Benz DB 605, 1,650-horsepower engine could move at 342 miles per hour. Nor, unlike the

Spitfire's Merlin float-carburetor engine, would it cut out when movement into a dive created negative g (excessive upward force). The Bf. 109 could swoop on its unsuspecting prey from 30,000 feet in a fast dive to kill it in one pass. But the Bf. 109 was also a "man-eater"—its torque, narrow undercarriage, and cramped cockpit made it unstable and difficult for beginners to handle, especially on takeoff and landing. At high speeds, the controls became very heavy and required a pilot of considerable strength to maneuver the joystick. It was far less agile than the Spitfire in pulling out of a climb, and had a more limited turning radius, which gave the British plane a leg up in a dogfight. The Spitfire was also faster at low altitude, which, when combined with poor rearward visibility for the German pilot, practically reclined in his cockpit, made it vulnerable to surprise from behind.[50] Improvements to the Bf. 109 little impacted the Mediterranean theater as, from 1943, the Germans were forced to withdraw most of their remaining aircraft for homeland defense.[51] But even before this redeployment, the lack of aviation fuel made it difficult for new pilots to train adequately, and they were progressively outclassed by Allied pilots. The Germans sacrificed most of their crews used to train bomber pilots when they conscripted them to fly the transports to the relief of Tunis and Stalingrad in 1942–43. But the German army continued to fight on because, despite these difficulties, they were imbued with the belief that character, based on the Nazification of the forces, could overcome operational difficulties.[52]

But this was in the future. In the opening months of 1941, the Germans stood at the pinnacle of their powers. The passage of the Afrika Korps to Tripoli was achieved without incident, largely because Fliegerkorps X, ordered to the Mediterranean in December and boosted to a strength of 510 planes, had begun a massive bombing campaign against Malta in January. This forced the RAF to transfer its Wellington bombers to Egypt. German planes damaged the carrier *Illustrious* so badly that, after a precarious visit to Valetta harbor for repairs, it sailed for the United States. German planes also sank the cruiser *Southampton* and began to mine the Suez Canal and Tobruk harbor.[53] British convoys were no longer safe in the Mediterranean, and Malta was locked in siege. German air superiority had, for the moment, trumped sea power, forcing the British onto the defensive in the central Mediterranean. But Fliegerkorps X, though a formidable force, was unable adequately to perform all missions—protect Axis convoys to Tripoli, suppress Malta, attack Suez, provide close air support in North Africa, and harass British convoys out of Alexandria and Gibraltar—over the Central and Eastern Mediterranean, especially as the Italian air force did little heavy lifting.[54]

But this was a "logistical" problem that troubled Rommel little. Hardly had he arrived in Tripoli than Hitler's general began to agitate for more troops. German intelligence estimated that the British had fifteen divisions in North Africa, while he had only two German divisions and two Italian divisions that Gariboldi allowed him to take to the Mugtaa Defile, 435 miles east of Tripoli and only 25 miles from British-occupied El Agheila. Still, the understanding was that the Italians controlled the war. Rommel's command extended only to the Fifth Light Division and, when it arrived, the Fifteenth Panzer Division, which were to provide a mobile reserve behind the Italian-held front.

Rommel was immediately plagued by the supply problems that would haunt the Afrika Korps for the next two years. Not only was the sea route between Italy and Tripoli subject to interdiction by British submarines, surface ships, and planes, but also, Tripoli harbor had berthing capacity for only four ships. Because the harbor was under constant threat of bombardment, the requirement to discharge ships as quickly as possible and distribute their contents to depots around the city gobbled up most of the available transport of the supply companies. Supplies then had to be dispatched to the units that Rommel had sent to the Tripolitania-Cyrenaica border, where he wanted to build a large supply depot to support mobile operations into Cyrenaica. A limited amount of shipping was available to shift some stores up the coast. But most had to be trucked up the Via Balbia by both Italians and Germans. Italian gasoline did not suit German vehicles, and Italian food did not suit German troops, who began to report sick in increasing numbers. Soldiers, including officers and NCOs, were expected to toil in the desert heat on a daily water ration of two pints per man for "all purposes." German equipment was not designed to withstand the rigors of the climate—just the trip between Tripoli and the front required an overhaul for the German tanks. But then British equipment, too, was plagued by mechanical problems. And, of course, the all-pervasive sand was a constant fact of life in the desert for both sides.

> When men stripped, they found the sand had blown up inside their shorts and was caked in small ridges against the hair on their thighs [wrote Captain George Greenfield]. It had worked inside the woolen hose-tops, had rimmed their eyes and ears and matted the short hair on their necks. No breech-cover could protect a rifle from the insidious sand that clogged the bolt and jammed the magazine. The sand could never be kept in place because it had no permanent place. It spread in a thin film on paper, on tents and on food. It had no properties of its own. It took in the heat of the sun so that at midday bare flesh could not stand its painful contact. The cold night air chilled it, the winds moulded it into heaps . . . Sometimes the *khamsin* blew, a hot fierce wind that plucked up the sand in a mad dance so that the whirling dust obscured the sun and blotted out the day. Nothing could stand against the onrush of sand that choked everything in its way, whipping under tents and blankets and, when it subsided, leaving every object covered inches deep.

When, at El Alamein, Greenfield's British troops overran an Italian position and discovered a large supply of condoms kept for the clients of the Italian army's mobile brothels, the men promptly fitted them over their rifle barrels to keep out the sand.[55] Sand reduced the life of a motor by one-half, largely because the standard German filters were inadequate to cope with it. The sand that jammed the turrets of Rommel's tanks, obliging him to stop in mid-desert to dismantle and clean them, offered precious time to the retreating British to escape Rommel's early offensive into Cyrenaica in April 1941.[56]

THE SECOND "BENGHAZI HANDICAP"

Apparently unaware that the British were thinning out North African forces for Greece, Rommel was surprised and emboldened by his easy advance to the Cyrenaica border. Already, his ambitious imagination conjured up visions of seizing the Suez Canal.[57] On 19 March, Rommel flew to Germany in an unsuccessful attempt to persuade Hitler to allow him to carry out an offensive into Cyrenaica. But Hitler was firm that Rommel was to restrict himself to limited offensives required to protect Tripolitania. To be fair to Rommel, a defensive strategy based on fixed positions manned by infantry backed by artillery would have surrendered the initiative in North Africa and put time on the side of the British. Best to advance, employing to the full German superiority in mobile warfare. If Rommel could reach the Nile Delta, he might snatch a considerable advantage. At the very least, an offensive would succeed in keeping the British off balance.[58] Rommel's advance into Cyrenaica developed in rather the same manner that O'Connor's had against Graziani in December 1940.

From 18 March 1941, German air reconnaissance and "Arab agents" began to report that the British were withdrawing forces from El Agheila, and had left only a rear guard at the Mersa Brega defile. German attempts to confirm this with Italian military intelligence failed because, whatever the Italians knew, they proved reluctant to share it with their Axis ally.[59] The Fifth Light pushed to El Agheila, which fell with barely any resistance. General Streich then advanced to Mersa Brega, which to him seemed lightly held. Rommel cognoscenti debated whether his lunge toward Egypt was a premeditated move, or whether his decision to slip the leash was a spur-of-the-moment impulse based on his growing realization that there were practically no British troops in front of him. Rommel justified himself with the claim that he had merely wanted to seize Mersa Brega and Agedabia before the British could fortify it.[60] Mersa Brega fell to Streich on 31 March, the day after Wavell had signaled that he did not believe Rommel capable of attacking for another month.[61] Rommel dispatched every available truck to fetch gasoline from the forward supply dump near El Agheila. The Fifth Light then lunged forward on the heels of the retreating British and took Agedabia on 2 April. Rommel's quandary now was that he had only one panzer regiment in his inventory. The Fifteenth Panzer Division was in the process of disembarking in Tripoli and Gariboldi refused to release the motorized sections of the

Brescia Division. In fact, the two men quarreled violently when Gariboldi, citing the insecure supply situation and directives from both Rome and Berlin, ordered him to break off his advance. However, Rommel seized on an ambiguous 4 April message from Hitler to inform Gariboldi that he had been given a free hand to do as he pleased. At a stroke, Rommel gave himself the green light to advance while simultaneously carrying out a coup against Italian control of the war in North Africa. Rommel had appointed himself de facto commander of all units on the fighting front.[62]

Rommel's advance at the head of the Fifth Light Division and the Italian Ariete and Brescia Divisions placed the British in a particularly delicate posture. The thrashing the Italians had received at Beda Fomm on 7 February, which included the loss of most of their equipment, convinced Wavell and the Defence Committee in London that the Axis would be in no state to challenge British control of Cyrenaica before May at the earliest.[63] Churchill became concerned as Enigma traffic, based mainly on Luftwaffe intercepts, charted the buildup of German forces in Tripoli and their deployment forward. But it gave no indication of the intentions of a commander who, at this stage of the war, was an unknown quantity to the British.[64] Therefore, in March, Wavell had dismantled the Thirteenth Corps, composed of the seasoned Seventh Armoured and Sixth Australian Divisions. The Seventh Armoured needed a complete overhaul after eight months in action. The Sixth Australian Division was dispatched to Greece together with the Seventh Australian Division, the New Zealand Division, and an armored brigade group. Two newly arrived, inexperienced divisions—the Ninth Australian and the Second Armoured Division—joined the Third Indian Motor Brigade in Cyrenaica under the command of Lieutenant General Philip Neame. The Second Armoured disembarked from Britain to inherit a heterogeneous collection of captured Italian M. 13 tanks and worn-out British ones, only half of which were "runners." The Ninth Australian had so little transport that they had to abandon a brigade in Tobruk. The remainder could not reach El Agheila before it fell to Streich. Neame complained that he had one-fifth of the force required to defend Cyrenaica, as well as inadequate staff and signaling equipment to coordinate combat operations over vast distances. But Wavell informed him that he "had nothing left in the bag" to give him. The Royal Navy was occupied transporting troops to Greece.[65] In effect, Rommel's attack caught the British before they could man and harden their forward defenses at Agheila, while the lack of adequate staff, communications, intelligence, logistics, and tanks made it difficult to organize an "elastic" defense.

British weakness meant that, despite the bantam size of his forces, Rommel's advance was like kicking in an open door. As he moved toward Benghazi, Wavell had little intelligence that would dispel wishful thinking and the best-case operational scenarios on which the decision to go to Greece was based. Enigma traffic reported Rommel's "stay put" orders from Berlin. Unlike the Germans who aggressively patrolled forward on ground and in the air and monitored British movements through Sigint, the British army was too weak to gather accurate tactical intelligence through its own patrols and complained of the lack of RAF air reconnaissance. British Sigint units that earlier had performed well against Italians were now stymied by tighter Italian codes. Without training in German codes, they were unable to predict German moves because the Italians seldom mentioned movements of German units. At this stage of the war, the British were unable to read the Wehrmacht Enigma traffic, and probably would have paid little attention to it if they had. Even so, until August 1941, Enigma-based intelligence went only to Cairo and was seldom disseminated to the field. In any case, the British collapse in Cyrenaica was so rapid that troops would have been hard pressed to operationalize good intelligence even had they been given it.[66]

Rommel's thrust into Cyrenaica triggered what the British referred to as the "Second Benghazi Handicap." Wavell flew in from Cairo to Barce, north of Benghazi, on 2 April to confer with Neame and Gambier-Parry. He decided to fire Neame, whose tactical dispositions and conduct of the battle he found to be "deplorable,"[67] and bring in O'Connor, who arrived from Cairo on 3 April. O'Connor pointed out that he knew neither the units nor the situation, and persuaded Wavell to retain Neame in command with O'Connor to "advise" him. Wavell's untimely intervention and his imposition of a divided command made the British reactions tentative, unsure, above all tardy.

Still, it probably did not make the difference between victory and defeat.[68] He instructed Gambier-Parry to defend Benghazi, then decided it was impractical and ordered gasoline and ammunition stocks to be exploded, followed by a withdrawal. As a result, many British tanks ran short of gasoline and had to be abandoned. Wavell believed, mistakenly, that Benghazi would mark the limit of Rommel's advance based on a back-of-an-envelope calculation that Rommel simply could not sustain a large number of troops 674 miles from Tripoli.[69] Rommel plowed into the confusion of British troops who were receiving contradictory orders from commanders who had no idea where the enemy was. He built wood-and-canvas tank chassis mounted on Volkswagens to deceive British air reconnaissance that his force was heavy in armor. He pressed every available truck into a supply chain back to Arco dei Fileni ("Marble Arch"), his advance supply depot in Tripolitania, to collect fuel and supplies. Taking advantage of German operational flexibility, he divided his troops into four columns, three of which cut overland through the hump of Cyrenaica to converge on Mechili, while a fourth, made up of the Brescia Division, pursued retreating British troops along the coastal road.

Rommel planned to rally his dispersed forces at Mechili and then break toward the coast between Derna and Tobruk to cut off British troops retreating along the Via Balbia. Rommel directed, coordinated, and berated the commanders of his independent columns from a Storch light aircraft as they toiled across Cyrenaica. Lack of gasoline, navigation errors, thermos mines, engine overheatings in the 120-degree temperatures, and the incredibly rough country scattered Rommel's forces and delayed the advance. As his soldiers spread over the desert, it became difficult for the Luftwaffe to support them or to protect them from sporadic RAF attacks.[70] On 8 April, one of his columns cut the Via Balbia from the south at Derna, but was too late to block retreating Australians who fled into the concrete-and-barbed-wire sanctuary of Tobruk. In fact, the ability of the retreating British forces to reach Tobruk was the only high spot in the campaign for Wavell. But the British commanding officers, Neame and O'Connor, were not so lucky: having become lost in the desert, they drove into a German battalion and were captured. The British also forfeited General Gambier-Perry, commander of the Second Armoured Division, 60 officers, 1,700 men, and much equipment when they were surrounded and captured as they attempted to break out of Mechili. At Derna, Rommel found both water and gasoline to continue his advance. Demonstrating German adaptability and genius for improvisation, Rommel again re-formed his forces into a new battle group that combined newly arrived elements of the Fifteenth Panzer and the Fifth Light and pointed them toward Tobruk, which, his intelligence told him, was lightly defended. The presence of numerous British ships in the harbor was an indication that the garrison was being evacuated.[71] He decided to rush it, a tactic that had brought him such great success in the past.

Unfortunately for Rommel, the ships in Tobruk harbor were actually delivering reinforcements that included tanks, artillery, and antitank and antiaircraft guns. Rommel's lightning reconquest of Cyrenaica, which in scarcely more than a week had bagged two of the three most senior enemy generals and a division commander, had thrown the British into confusion. Churchill demanded that Tobruk be held, as did Admiral Cunningham, keen to protect Alexandria.[72] Enigma erroneously told Wavell that, although Rommel had exceeded his orders, he was not planning to take Egypt. Rather, his attack had been hastily improvised, although the extent of his logistical difficulties was not revealed.[73] Therefore, the British commander-in-chief in the Middle East began to redirect reinforcements scheduled for Greece toward Tobruk. The defenses there were hastily put in order by the commander of the Ninth Australian Division, Major General L. J. Morshead, a veteran of Gallipoli, as his troops streamed into the fortress from the west. A mobile group based on the Second Armoured Division was formed at El Adem, about thirty miles south of Tobruk, to harass the German siege, but later withdrew toward Egypt because it was too small to survive. A Western Desert Force, the kernel of the future Eighth Army, was cobbled together from two incomplete divisions and a Guards brigade to hold the Egyptian frontier. Simultaneously, Wavell was trying to manage the fighting in Ethiopia, Eritrea, and Greece, while monitoring an emerging rebellion in Iraq.

But if Wavell was finding it difficult to stay focused, Rommel's stunning advance convinced the German commander that he was reliving the fall of France. His intelligence served him incompletely— his maps were rudimentary and inaccurate, the Italians offered no indications of the fortifications and minefields they had abandoned in January, and his air reconnaissance could give him only an imperfect picture of British intentions. But it probably made little difference. Rommel, a man with a chronic case of victory fever, was determined that the British would not escape from Tobruk as they had at Dunkirk. He failed to perceive the stiffening British resistance, nor was he prepared to tolerate excuses from his subordinates. Instead, he berated and insulted those who asked for ammunition, fuel, or time to repair their vehicles and rest their exhausted soldiers. He needed Tobruk because it blocked the Littoranea, the coastal road popularly called the Via Balbia, his route to the Nile, which his troops had already rechristened the Rommelbahn. Possession of Tobruk harbor was also vital to sustain the momentum of his advance. Above all, he needed Tobruk to nourish his ego. He set up his headquarters in an Italian trailer situated in a deep gully, relatively immune from air attack, and toured the battlefield in a captured British ACV, a windowless box on giant balloon wheels, which he called his *Mammut* (mammoth).

Rommel's decision to seize Tobruk, although perfectly in keeping with his seat-of-the-pants conduct of the Cyrenaica campaign, was not illogical. As during the campaign for France, he counted on the disorganization of the defenders to carry the day. Morshead's garrison numbered about 36,000 people, of whom about two-thirds were combat troops and the rest "odds and sods"—an assortment of refugees, base troops, and POWs. His breathless soldiers barely had time to familiarize themselves with the thirty-mile defense perimeter along which infantry battalions were assigned five miles of front to hold.[74] But while the British confusion was great, it was matched by disarray on the Axis side. Rommel ordered General Heinrich von Prittwitz und Graffon, newly arrived commander of the Fifteenth Panzer Division, to break into the town. But von Prittwitz's hurriedly organized advance was halted by the Royal Artillery. In the process, the general's armored car took a direct round from an antitank gun, leaving a vacancy at the top of the Fifteenth Panzer. Undeterred, convinced that the British were in a state of panic and collapse, Rommel ordered lightly armed elements of the Fifth Light and the Brescia Division to storm Tobruk backed by twenty tanks, all he had in his arsenal, on the afternoon of 11 April. As the attackers from the machine-gun regiment moved forward, they discovered a large tank trench, backed by an impassable wall of barbed wire. Rifle fire from the Australian infantry drove them to ground. The low rumble of engines announced the tank assault. Low steel silhouettes appeared out of the dust and smoke, but came to a halt before the antitank ditch. Tank commanders standing in the open hatches of their turrets and speaking to their drivers through their Tannoy earphones ordered their vehicles to turn east, moving parallel to the Australian lines as they searched for a way to cross the ditch. Engaged by British cruisers and artillery, the Germans lost a PzKw III, two Italian tanks, and an armored car before they withdrew, leaving the infantry pinned down and desperately scraping shallow shelters in the rock-hard ground. Hurricanes appeared overhead to strafe the German position, dismal work unpopular with pilots, which cost the British three planes. Vigorous Australian patrolling discouraged attempts by German engineers to mine the defenses under cover of darkness.

Rommel had, in effect, carried out a reconnaissance in force. Undeterred, he ordered a renewed attack on 13 April. British air reconnaissance detected the Germans massing for the attack, so that when engineers went forward to blow up the antitank obstacles, while German infantry positioned themselves 500 yards away to rush through the breech, Morshead was not surprised. Rommel's attack, which kicked off at 1700 hours, succeeded in breaking Tobruk's outer skin after bloody bayonet and grenade skirmishes at close quarters. At 0500 on 14 April, panzers, transporting infantry on their turrets, rumbled through the breach. Australian infantry let them through, then closed the gap to the supporting infantry, leaving the panzers isolated. Having penetrated half a mile into the fortress, the tanks inexplicably stopped. Morshead massed his artillery and antitank guns and positioned them to the flank and rear of the panzers. At first light, the panzers fired their engines and rumbled forward, only to be met by the sting of British 25 pdr guns firing over open sights. The turret of the lead tank was knocked off its chassis. The tanks belched 75 mm shells back at the antitank guns, which continued to shift their positions. But without accompanying infantry, there was no way the panzers alone could deal with the antitank guns. The lead tanks tried to withdraw, but ran into the following panzers, causing a confused melee that eventually sorted itself out as the tanks lurched eastward to try to outflank the British antitank guns. But British cruisers firing hull-down and antitank guns pounded them from all directions, while machine-gun fire killed most of the crews of the German 88 mm antitank guns. Transmissions and brakes began to fail. Panzer crews, some of them on fire, leaped from their tanks and called for medics. At 0700 Streich called off the assault, to Rommel's fury, demanding that it be properly prepared with reconnaissance and air and artillery support. But the survivors of the Fifth Light's machine-gun battalion were still pinned down within the fortress from the failed attack on the eleventh. By 20 April all of these had been killed or taken prisoner, as they had exhausted their water and ammunition. Rommel had lost 280 men dead or captured, including a general, the commander of the machine-gun battalion, and 17 of 38 tanks committed to the attack.[75] This was the first setback of Rommel's career. He raged at Streich, whom he blamed for sabotaging the attacks through slow compliance to orders and outright "disobedience." He quarreled with his chief of staff and fired his operations officer, who suggested that Rommel's dalliance at Mechili had allowed the British time to escape to Tobruk. He became desperate to take the fortress, especially as the Nazi propaganda machine, aroused by his stunning advance into Cyrenaica, now closely reported his every move. Rommel continued to insist that the defenders were weak, that they were evacuating, that he would be in Cairo in a week.[76]

On 16 and 17 April he hurled the newly arrived Ariete Armored Division at the defenses, with predictable lack of success—the British repelled this attack as well, in the process taking twenty-six officers and almost eight hundred POWs. Afterward, Rommel ungraciously claimed not to have been surprised by the Italian failure, given the inferiority of Italian equipment and lack of training. Nevertheless, he had so weakened his forces that the British might well have been able to counterattack successfully, had they not continued to overestimate German strength. The grumbles of German commanders at Tobruk over Rommel's hasty and ill-prepared attacks soon found an echo in Berlin, especially as Rommel's demands for reinforcements fell on an OKW that was massing all its resources for the invasion of the Soviet Union. The Italians, too, rejected Rommel's requests for more soldiers. He was told that the farther he advanced toward Egypt, the more precarious his logistics would become, while the resistance of the British would harden. Bardia, eighty miles east of Tobruk, had fallen to the advancing Germans on 12 April. Weak units of the Fifth Light and and Fifteenth Panzer reached Sollum on the frontier and, after a brief skirmish, occupied the Halfaya Pass. Rommel's messages to Berlin evidenced a touch of panic. He called for U-boats and more planes. Halder, who suspected that Rommel had gone "stark raving mad," sent Lieutenant General Friedrich von Paulus to North Africa to take stock of the situation and to explain to Rommel that Berlin had no more troops to give him.[77]

Even so, Halder managed to scrape together five infantry, one engineer, and two coastal artillery battalions for North Africa. The problem of getting them there proved to be more difficult, however. Guided by Ultra intercepts, British submarines based in Malta managed to pick off several Italian freighters and the cruiser *Armando Diaz*. On 16 April, Royal Navy destroyers guided by reconnaissance aircraft out of Malta surprised an Italian convoy off Tunisia, sinking five freighters and two Italian destroyers. On the morning of 21 April, Cunningham bombarded Tripoli harbor for an hour. Lack of fighter escorts also delayed the arrival of air-transported troops. Only the requirement to use all available ships to evacuate Greece, combined with the laying of a mine barrage outside Tripoli harbor, temporarily relieved Royal Navy pressure on the supply lines to North Africa. Nevertheless, the naval staff complained that between 8 February and 1 May 1941, the British had managed to sink twelve of the twenty-nine ships on the Naples-to-Tripoli run, and put five others out of commission. On 24 May, the Italian liner *Conte Rosso* was sunk with 1,500 Italian troops on board. In a sign of deteriorating relations within the

Axis, the Germans blamed the high losses on Italian incompetence. Nor was the situation likely to improve as the Luftwaffe, in the process of gearing up for the Balkan campaign, began to shift its forces toward the Eastern Mediterranean, leaving the Regia Aeronautica responsible for air cover over the central Mediterranean. With few aircraft to spare, the Luftwaffe did manage to send a group of Bf. 109 fighters and another of Stukas to North Africa to compensate for Rommel's lack of artillery. These managed to drive the RAF out of the Tobruk airfields and began to attack ships coming into Tobruk harbor.[78]

Despite the fact that he was over a thousand miles from his supply base at Tripoli and many of his men were sick with dysentery, Rommel persisted in what the Italians considered his unwholesome obsession with Tobruk. He set another attack on the fortress for 30 April. Belatedly, the Italians had produced plans of Tobruk. But rather than reassuring him, the revelation of a thirty-mile perimeter, nine miles deep, of 128 interconnected strong points, tank trenches, barbed wire, and concealed machine-gun and antitank bunkers with overlapping fields of fire should have given him pause. The defenders had taken steps to strengthen the defenses even further by adding deep minefields. A dozen Matildas had been ferried in, as well as 5,000 tons of supplies. In contrast, many of Rommel's troops were newly arrived. Nevertheless, he threw them into combat without proper preparation—he even forbade reconnaissance so as not to alert the enemy. A combined night assault by the Fifteenth Panzer (fighting on foot, as its tanks had not yet arrived), the Ariete Division, and the Fifth Light advancing behind a wave of Stukas and artillery would, he hoped, manage to penetrate Tobruk's defenses. Engineers succeeded in opening a breach, through which poured the foot soldiers. It was a classic German infiltration attack—infantry followed closely behind a creeping artillery barrage, avoiding posts and strong points as they moved toward the fortress's interior. The artillery barrage also destroyed British telephone lines, disorganizing the defense's response. But follow-up forces armed with mortars, flamethrowers, and machine guns were stopped cold by Australian strong points, each held by a dozen or so men, which refused to succumb. In the confusion, made greater by night and a rising sandstorm, German commanders lost control of the battle. Morshead sent artillery spotters forward to call in bombardments on supporting tanks.

Daylight on 1 May brought only an opaque gloom as dust thrown up by bombardments combined with morning mist to produce a battlefield where the antagonists were practically invisible to each other. British air reconnaissance reported sixty Axis tanks within the perimeter with more approaching. Rommel opened his attack at 0800. Unless gunners waited until they could peer into the slits of German tanks, British antitank shells simply bounced off the armada of advancing panzers. Tobruk appeared doomed when, suddenly, the lead tank halted, black smoke belching from its belly. Explosions began to occur among the lead vehicles, separating treads from sprockets, smashing tracks, sending tanks sideways. Seventeen panzers lay disabled in a minefield. The British wisely withheld artillery fire to preserve the mine barrier. The panzers retreated back through the breach.[79]

Fighting continued until the morning of 4 May. Von Paulus, who had given Rommel permission to carry out the assault, agreed that exhausted ammunition stocks and 1,200 casualties were reason enough to call a halt. He forbade Rommel to renew an attack until more reinforcements and supplies arrived, an order confirmed by Berlin on the next day. "The crux of the problem in North Africa," von Paulus reported to the army high command, "is not Tobruk or Sollum, but the organization of supplies." The Italians refused to ship supplies by sea to Benghazi because of Royal Navy interference. This left only the 1,100-mile "Rommelbahn," and the Axis lacked the transport to make it an effective supply artery. The two-division Afrika Korps required 24,000 tons of supplies a month just to survive, and another 20,000 to undertake an offensive. The Luftwaffe needed 9,000 tons and the Italians needed 63,000 tons. Of this 116,000 tons, Tripoli could only handle 45,000 tons a month in the best possible conditions.[80] Halder concluded that, through his impetuous advance, Rommel had got himself into a situation in which he could neither advance nor withdraw. For his part, Rommel lashed out at his subordinates, his troops, and the Italians, all of whom he blamed for his failure. He fired

Streich, commander of the Fifth Light, whom he accused of coddling his men.[81]

The British held at Tobruk, where intense Stuka attacks in May gradually subsided into desultory artillery bombardment. Lord Haw Haw ridiculed the "rats of Tobruk" as "self-supporting prisoners."[82] But the fact remained that they survived, a monument to Rommel's, and Germany's, failure. The morale, and the health, of the German besiegers began to deteriorate on a poor diet of tinned sardines, olive oil, soft cheese, and a meat supplied by the Italians stamped "A.M.," which the German soldiers called "*Alter Mann*" (Old Man).[83] The British defeat in Greece combined with the collapse of the Cyrenaica front stung Churchill. Ultra intelligence had relayed von Paulus's appreciation of the situation to the prime minister, as well as news of the exhaustion of German forces.[84] Understanding that Rommel's attack had shot its bolt, he was keen to regain the initiative in North Africa before the Fifteenth Panzer could be brought up to full strength. Throwing caution to the wind, he ordered the "Tiger" convoy of six fast transports escorted by the battleship *Queen Elizabeth* to steam across the Mediterranean for Egypt between 6 and 12 May with around three hundred tanks, some of which were new-model Crusaders—undergunned (57 mm) and mechanically unreliable, but at 27 miles per hour faster than other cruiser tanks—and fifty-three Hurricane fighters. One of the transports was sunk when it hit a mine, carrying with it fifty-seven tanks and eleven fighters.

But before the "Tiger" convoy could arrive, Brigadier W.H.E. Gott was ordered to relieve Tobruk. Despite the fact that it took the Germans by surprise,[85] Operation Brevity, launched on 15 May against 6,000 German and Italian frontier troops commanded by Colonel Max von Herff, proved a complete failure. The British were thrown back to their side of the frontier in less than twenty-four hours. In the process, they revealed a misunderstanding of German tactical doctrine that would require months to clear up. This stemmed from an apparent reluctance of German tanks to engage British armor. They failed to understand that German doctrine required antitank units, especially those armed with the redoubtable 88 mm guns, to fight enemy tanks. British intelligence also failed to detect the German antitank guns on the Halfaya Pass, or the fact that Rommel had shifted much of his armor from Tobruk to the front. Because the distribution system had yet to be worked out, much Enigma information generated by Bletchley Park was out of date by the time it reached the field. All of these intelligence failures were repeated during Operation Battle-axe a month later.[86] Finally, the British attack demonstrated to Rommel the fragility of his defenses on the Halfaya Pass, which he took steps to reinforce.[87] The only benefit the British reaped from Brevity was that news of the British attack rattled Rommel, who fired off frantic messages to Berlin. This momentary panic earned him a rocket from Wehrmacht commander-in-chief Field Marshal Walther von Brauchitsch, who demanded more "sober" appraisals in future. There was clearly a widening gulf between the high command's skeptical opinion of Rommel's abilities and his burgeoning media image as the "people's general," carefully nurtured by Lieutenant Alfred-Ingemar Berndt, a senior official in the Propaganda Ministry whom Rommel had assigned to his staff.[88]

Churchill, exasperated with the apparent inability of his generals to deliver victory, urged Wavell to use the new tanks as soon as possible to drive the Germans out of the Halfaya Pass and Sollum and to relieve Tobruk. Wavell assembled the Fourth and Eleventh Indian Divisions, recuperated from Ethiopia, the Twenty-second Guards Brigade, and two armored brigades, one of which had Matilda "I" (for infantry) tanks and the other a mix of Cruisers and the new Crusaders. This force, of around 29,000 men, was placed under General Noel Beresford-Peirse. Wavell complained that with a maximum speed of 24 miles per hour the Matildas were too slow for desert warfare (although their heavy armor frightened the Germans), their radius of action was too limited, and their 2 pdr (40 mm) gun lacked punch. The medium Cruiser tanks, while fast, were outclassed by German models and "only two jumps ahead of the workshops."[89] Indeed, all British tanks were liable to breakdown. Only in the summer of 1942 did the British fit some of their powerful 3.7-inch antiaircraft guns with antitank sights to fight the Battle of Gazala.[90] British armored cars were far inferior to the eight-wheeled German versions, and were vulnerable to air attack, which made reconnaissance difficult. Wavell also noted that once again his armored forces had been weakened to support operations against Syria. Realizing that Tobruk was beyond his range, he instead sought to secure frontier positions and gain enough ground to establish an airfield west of Sollum so as better to support Malta. The fact that the bulk of German tanks were believed to be tied down before Tobruk, while the frontier was guarded by only seven German and nine Italian battalions, augured well for the operation.[91]

Operation Battleaxe, launched on 15 June, was predicted by German intelligence, based on traffic analysis of British radio intercepts and aerial photographs of the buildup.[92] Despite initial British superiority of armor and aircraft, after three days of largely inconclusive fighting which saw the capture of Sollum, the British called off their attack. Once again they had been unable to overcome the German 88 mm guns dug in on the Halfaya Pass, which could destroy a British tank at 2,000 yards. The Germans initiated the use of their tanks and antitank guns in combination, a technique they developed with great skill. Because the British lacked recovery equipment, they could not recuperate damaged but reparable tanks. British tank crews were poorly prepared, and division training to teach infantry–armor cooperation was, on the whole, inadequate. British units still had too few vehicles to support mobile operations against a more experienced German foe. Lack of radios continued to impede coordination of operations. The British still failed to comprehend that tanks were to be used against "soft" vehicles, leaving enemy tanks to antitank guns. The sprawl and confusion of desert battlefields, often obscured by smoke and sandstorms, made it difficult for aircraft to identify front lines and so support offensive operations.[93]

For his part, Rommel was furious at the performance of his troops. Although they had successfully repelled the British attack and inflicted many more tank and aircraft casualties than they had absorbed, largely with 88s dug in on the Halfaya—which British troops now called "Hellfire"—Pass, they had failed to take advantage of British overextension to turn a defensive victory into a battle of annihilation. German intelligence had built up a good picture of the British order of battle and tipped off the German commanders in good time about British moves.[94] But the British had won by not losing. The RAF had spotted, attacked, and slowed German encircling movements, giving the British time to withdraw. Rommel had also attempted to control the battle from Tobruk rather than devolve command to a general on the spot. This did not stop the Reich propaganda machine from trumpeting Rommel's great victory at Sollum. Hitler proposed that Rommel be promoted to full general, a suggestion opposed by Halder, who complained of Rommel's "pathological ambition."[95]

Battleaxe brought to a conclusion the first phase of the Anglo-German confrontation in the desert. Both sides pushed significant changes in their organization. Sollum led to Rommel's virtual emancipation from the control of the Berlin general staff. Franz Halder, chief of the army general staff, attempted to organize a combined German-Italian army in North Africa under Field Marshal Wilhelm List, the victor of Greece. In preparation for this, a large liaison staff under Lieutenant General Alfred Gause arrived to coordinate operations with the Italians in North Africa. Halder's idea was to create a structure that would control Rommel. But Rommel turned the table on Halder by promptly absorbing Gause and his staff, which he used to bring the six Italian divisions in Cyrenaica under his control, giving him eight divisions in all. In the event, an army was not authorized, but a compromise sub-army force called a *Panzergruppe*—Armored Group—was created. The Italians complained, and, for once, Berlin sympathized with them. But Rommel's subordinate commanders dared not voice opposition lest they be fired. Knowledge among Rommel's superiors that the "Desert Fox" enjoyed Hitler's favor, and did not hesitate to go over their heads to appeal directly to the Führer, made OKW reluctant to challenge him. In fact, Hitler was much pleased with his protégé, who had pushed the British out of Cyrenaica and thus secured the Libyan flank on the eve of Barbarossa. As a consequence, rather than be controlled, the forty-nine-year-old Rommel was promoted to full general and made commander of Armored Group Africa, with Gause as his chief of staff, while Lieutenant General Ludwig Crüwell replaced him as commanding general of the Afrika Korps. Gariboldi, who had fought so hard against Rommel, was replaced by General Bastico. But, although Rommel's political position was secure, the war in North Africa was now completely overshadowed by the Russian campaign. Rommel's strategic dilemma—unable to retreat but incapable of advance—appeared unchanged.[96]

For Churchill, the waste of tanks sent at such great peril through the Mediterranean was "a most bitter blow."[97] He had never shown great confidence in Wavell, a man of few words who failed to convey either energy or resolve. When, at the end of April, Churchill learned that Wavell had prepared "Mongoose Plan," a scenario for the abandonment of Egypt, he sputtered with rage at the "defeatism" of a command general who could contemplate retreat. In response, he issued a "backs to the wall" order that "the Army of the Nile is to fight with no thought of retreat or withdrawal."[98] For his part, the laconic Wavell was seldom able to articulate his viewpoint when badgered by the prime minister. Instead, he saw Churchill's constant messages as irritating, hurtful, signs of lack of confidence in his foresight and determination. He countered by attempting to keep Churchill in the dark about his operational plans, which only stimulated further distrust. Wavell had lost Greece and Crete. He lacked the imagination to put himself in the mind of his adversary, instead calculating Rommel's intentions based on his logistical limitations. It galled Churchill that Wavell had surrendered Benghazi without a fight, which the Germans immediately transformed into an important supply base.[99] Rommel's ability to take advantage of Wavell's miscalculations in Cyrenaica had shattered the general's morale. Battleaxe was a failure, despite the great hopes the prime minister had placed in it. And although this was not entirely Wavell's fault, even the small successes the British had enjoyed in Iraq and Syria had been accomplished over Wavell's protests and threats to resign. "Wavell was a tired man," Churchill conceded. "It might well be said that we had ridden the willing horse to a standstill."[100] He dispatched Wavell to serve as commander-in-chief in India, and replaced him with General Sir Claude Auchinleck. Air Chief Marshal Longmore was recalled and replaced with Air Marshal Tedder. Wavell had complained of the constant burden of having to refer political decisions to London. Therefore, a minister of state for the Middle East was appointed with direct access to the war cabinet to handle political questions that had so burdened Wavell. An intendant-general was created to handle logistical matters and supervise the growing infrastructure the British were creating to support the North African campaign.

AUCHINLECK

In at least two respects, General Claude Auchinleck appeared to be a worthy successor to Wavell. First, the two men seemed similar in both career and character. Like Wavell, Auchinleck arrived at Britain's top fighting command with few qualifications other than the fact that, so far in the war, he had failed to put a foot wrong. In May 1940, Auchinleck had annoyed Churchill, then first lord of the Admiralty, by his rather lukewarm support for the Narvik expedition, an invasion of Norway in which Churchill placed great faith before the Allied collapse in France aborted the operation. However, Auchinleck had subsequently revived the prime minister's favor when, as commander of Southern Command, his strong presence and high character had struck Churchill. Auchinleck was tall, distinguished, with reddish hair and clear blue eyes. His face had the texture of a wrinkled chamois, testimony to a career spent mainly in India. Alan Moorehead, who met Auchinleck in Cairo in July 1941, described him as "strikingly handsome," with an easy charm and an intensely curious mind.[101] Churchill's admiration of Auchinleck's vigor grew when, as commander-in-chief in India, Auchinleck was quick to send soldiers to suppress the revolt in Iraq.[102] Second, Auchinleck had made a reputation in the interwar years as one of a small number of armor enthusiasts in the British army, an advocacy that had brought his name to Churchill's attention.[103] In a country at once mesmerized and intimidated by Rommel, a man who appeared to be in the forefront of thinking about armored warfare seemed just the ticket to elevate the British army in North Africa into the age of mechanized combat. But the truth was that as of July 1941, Auchinleck had yet in his career to crack a tough nut.

His shortcomings as commander would become more obvious as his tenure lengthened. While Churchill wanted "a new eye and a new hand in this theater," in some essential ways Auchinleck could have been Wavell's double. At first glance, the new commander's gregarious charm and easy humor seemed a refreshing change from Wavell's wall of donnish reserve. But it soon became apparent that Auchinleck was happiest in his own company, a loner deficient in the ability to animate his command. He loathed public speeches or broadcasts, and shunned all but the most obligatory social engagements. Even Auchinleck's partisans concede that he was a minimalist where comfort was concerned. His official residence in Cairo resembled a mournful, empty mausoleum.[104] Churchill described his desert head-quarters on the Ruweisat Ridge in August 1942 as "a wire-netted cube, full of flies and important military personages."[105] As soon as he took over command of the Eighth Army in August 1942, Montgomery nick-named it "the meat locker" and promptly closed it down.

Unlike Wavell, Auchinleck had spent World War I almost exclusively fighting Turks in Iraq. At the same time, one had the impression that, like Wavell, Auchinleck might have prospered in another profession, the Indian Civil Service in particular. However, the death of his officer father when he was only eight years old obliged Auchinleck's cash-strapped widowed mother to accept army scholarships for him to Wellington and Sandhurst. Like many impecunious but well-connected young officers, Auchinleck had joined the Indian army out of cadet training and never left it. Many young officers selected India before 1914 because it offered inexpensive living, plenty of sports, and the possibility of seeing some action. Although he performed honor-ably on the Northwest Frontier and in World War I, nothing distin-guished him early on as an officer of promise. Auchinleck's talents for organization, compromise, and committee work began to emerge in the interwar years when he demonstrated the great qualities of hu-mility, humanity, and integrity that elicited such devotion from his subordinates. He needed all the tact he could muster, for the "Indianization" of the interwar army that accelerated as war ap-proached lowered its appeal among British officers, who argued— somewhat ironically—that the cohesion of the officer corps, not to mention military discipline, was being jeopardized by men whose first loyalty was to their caste.[106]

Unfortunately, the subcontinent hardly offered serious officers a stimulating environment for professional development. The prewar Indian army was, in the words of American historian Stephen Cohen, "a 'primitive' military organization; a caste-like association isolated from a hostile world, which regarded itself as self-sufficient and unique."[107] The interwar years in India witnessed the "Poona Colonel" bestowing professional recognition upon officers with the highest polo handicaps or the best racing record. A distinct sense of inferiority permeated the Indian army, a feeling that it ranked beneath the British army as a social and professional organization, but that its primary purpose—to keep India from falling into chaos—gave it a special and important political mission. Much of the army's time was spent in "aid to the civil," performing police duties and suppressing communal disorder, or quelling tribal mayhem on the frontiers. As World War II approached, however, the "Indianization" of the army combined with the awareness that it lacked the capability to cope successfully with a major opponent to rattle the army's sense of self-sufficiency.[108] The 1938 Auchinleck Report decried the screw-gun and mule corps condition of the Indian army and called for a significant arms upgrade. That upgrade, however, would eventually come from the Americans, not the British. As commander-in-chief in India, Auchinleck ended the segregation of Indian and British officers in separate battalions, equalized pay, and also established links between the army and the Congress Party. This was a first step in the transition of the army's basis of discipline from that of personal honor to patriotism. Units whose recruitment was once segregated by caste, religion, or ethnicity were mixed with no apparent loss in combat efficiency. One result of Auchinleck's efforts was that, despite political troubles and a deeply ambivalent attitude to Allied success among the Indian elite, the Indian army expanded from an armed constabulary of 175,000 men in 1939 to a modern force of almost two million, including 15,740 Indian officers, who fought with great valor in the various theaters. Indeed, the Fourth and the Seventh Indian Divisions were considered among the best troops fielded by any army in the war. Congress Party ambivalence toward the war effort contributed to the fact that Moslems were disproportionately represented in army ranks, making up roughly a third of the Indian soldiers. Despite these successes, Auchinleck's most fervent admirers conceded that he was more respected than loved in the Indian army.[109]

Unfortunately, humanity was not part of the job description in the

Western Desert in 1941. Auchinleck, like Wavell, was a gentleman pitted against a ruthless commander of daring and skill. Apologists for both Wavell and Auchinleck blame their failure on inferior equipment and Churchill's unrealistic and premature expectations of victory over Rommel. Montgomery, the argument goes, simply arrived in August 1942 to take advantage of the infrastructure and even the battle plans prepared by Auchinleck.[110] There is some truth to this accusation. The British had lost much equipment in France and Greece. The result was that, into early 1942, they continued to produce obsolete weapons just to arm their troops until U.S. production could kick in and a new plant could be set up in Great Britain.[111] It is equally true that Churchill, armed with Ultra intercepts that showed Rommel was operating on the thinnest of margins, was impatient for success.[112]

But a dispassionate analysis suggests that fault lay less with the quality of weaponry than with the way Wavell and Auchinleck employed them. Both generals perpetuated a defective British command style that destined them to join the deposed nobility of Britain's Middle East leadership. Before any commander could win the battle, he had first to grip the Eighth Army, in much the same way as Rommel used his formidable personality, lead-from-the-front command style, and the Prussian staff system to dominate his Afrika Korps. This was difficult for Wavell and Auchinleck, château generals content to appoint subordinates to run the desert battle while they preoccupied themselves with paperwork in Cairo. This proved disastrous in the Eighth Army, which, at this stage of the war, was a heterogeneous collection of imperial and home forces, embellished with a drizzle of exotic émigré formations. Even divisions were ad hoc aggregations of miscellaneous units that seldom trained together. As a consequence, corps, division, and brigade leaders, divided into factions arranged around service, regimental, or personal affiliations—even social standing—were often at odds and generally displayed staggering deficiencies in team spirit. Operational orders were often arrived at by consensus among senior officers who had scant preparation for high command and who, unlike their counterparts in the German army, were not served by a retinue of trained staff officers capable of formulating clear, direct orders based on the commander's intentions. The vagueness and inevitable lack of clarity that ensued telegraphed the distinct impression to subordinate commanders that no one was in charge higher up.[113] Auchinleck ran the Eighth Army from a distance, much like a reclusive headmaster presiding over a collection of divided and competitive boarding school "houses." The subsequent vacuum of authority was filled by a consortium of "OK people,"[114] drawn principally from the Guards, the Greenjackets, and the cavalry, who dominated the Eighth Army much as the Pop ruled Eton. The British official history points out that the British commander maintained a curiously inverted relationship with his subordinates, approaching them like a chief of staff with suggestions rather than grasping control with a firm hand. "He continued to think more as a staff officer than a commander."[115]

Leaving subordinate commanders extreme latitude to run their own show with the merest "suggestions" from higher up constituted a command style that, later on, would cause confusion and some ill feelings between British and U.S. commanders in the Mediterranean. At this stage of the war it might have been less catastrophic had the choice of subordinates been inspired. Alas, such was not Auchinleck's case. The mediocre caliber of Auchinleck's underlings was universally seen as a troubling sign of his inferior judgment and further evidence of what Moorehead believed was Auchinleck's "chip on his shoulder" about appointing "good generals from England."[116] Montgomery agreed that Auchinleck's Sepoy general background had left him with a (well-deserved) "inferiority complex."[117] The fact that Auchinleck had spent his career in India may have meant that he simply had not met many "good generals from England." But the real problem was that there were few "good generals in England" full stop. This was in part because the British army in the interwar years had done little to prepare middle-ranking officers to take over division and corps commands and senior staff positions. There was also a dearth of officers in the British army with armor experience. One of the debilitating legacies of facile triumphs over Italians was that British armored units were slow to understand that inter-arm cooperation of tanks, infantry, and artillery, rather than tank-on-tank engagements, offered the key to victory.[118] Despite his advocacy of armored warfare, Auchinleck understood Rommel's methods no better than had Wavell—"he has no idea how to fight Germans," Montgomery insisted of his predecessor. "He has a good brain, but cannot harness it to the job at hand."[119] Indeed, Montgomery insisted that Auchinleck had no consistent doctrine on which to base the training of his troops, that he did not understand how to integrate armor into battlefield operations, and that his infatuation with tanks, far from demonstrating an avant-garde approach to modern war, was instead a throwback to the romanticism of cavalry.[120] In Montgomery's view, Auchinleck lacked both the knowledge and the inner toughness to whip Rommel.[121]

In fact, Auchinleck inherited a strategic situation in July 1941 far more favorable than that of his predecessor. Greece, Crete, and East Africa had been eliminated as theaters, and the dissension in Iraq and Syria resolved. In September, Roosevelt asked Congress for an additional $6 billion for Lend-Lease, while the first of six U-boats entered the Mediterranean through the Strait of Gibraltar. Tojo became prime minister of Japan on 16 October. The bulk of the German army was engaged against the Soviet Union. By October, German troops reached the Sea of Azov and took Yalta, severed the rail link to Leningrad, and launched Operation Typhoon, the offensive against Moscow. Although a residual fear persisted that, should Russia fall, then the Germans might sweep down on the Middle East through Turkey or the Caucasus, this constituted a remote contingency. For the moment, the British army was able to concentrate its resources and attentions against Rommel in Cyrenaica. The opening of the Red Sea to American shipping in July released a gush of supplies that included 770 tanks, 34,000 trucks, 600 field guns, as well as mortars, antiaircraft artillery, and antitank guns.[122] At the same time, severe supply and manpower problems for the Axis in North Africa condemned the impatient Rommel to inactivity and allowed Auchinleck to get the jump on him. The British continued to reinforce Malta, which the Italians appeared powerless to prevent. Allied interdiction efforts were guided by Sigint, air reconnaissance, and Luftwaffe Enigma traffic, with an occasional assist from broken Italian army and air force ciphers. From June 1941, the breaking of Italian naval ciphers, which gave the British precise fleet and convoy sailing times and routes, became routine.[123] Between January and August 1941, 51 Axis ships were lost and another 38 damaged on the Naples–to–North Africa route. During the summer, 190 fighters were flown into Malta from carriers that approached as close as they dared from the west before launching their planes. In October the British constituted K Force at Valetta, which consisted of two light cruisers and two destroyers. Guided by operational intelligence, these successfully sank all seven ships of an Italian convoy on 7 November, reducing Rommel's supplies to their lowest level yet. These attacks forced the Luftwaffe into convoy protection, took pressure off the British shipping to Tobruk, and allowed the RAF to bomb and mine Axis harbors.[124] So desperate was the Axis situation that in the autumn of 1941, Hitler, over the protests of his admirals and generals, ordered U-boats from the Atlantic and planes from the Eastern Front to the Mediterranean to protect the convoys. The Italians turned destroyers into tankers and troop carriers to reach Benghazi and submarines into delivery systems for munitions to Derna and Bardia.[125]

Each side had reorganized its forces. On paper, Rommel's Panzergruppe Afrika, which came into existence on 31 July, appeared impressive: the Italian Twenty-first Corps had three partially motorized infantry divisions opposite Tobruk. The Afrika Korps under Crüwell had grown to four divisions—Fifteenth and Twenty-first (formerly the Fifth Light) Armored Divisions, the Ninetieth Light, and the Italian Savona Division. An Italian motorized corps of three divisions, not part of Panzergruppe Afrika but operating with it, rounded off the Axis force of ten divisions.[126] The Germans had began to add plates of face-hardened steel to their PzKw IIIs and IVs that made them more resistant to British antitank fire. A long-barreled 5 cm gun was added to both tanks, which proved very effective against British tanks.[127] Rommel's Sigint organization was reading British coded signals traffic down to division level. Rommel was also greatly aided by sloppy British radio security which allowed him both to construct an order of battle for the British and to divine their intentions during the course of Crusader.[128] Nevertheless, Rommel's troops were camped down on two fronts, before Tobruk and along a defense line running from the sea inland for about thirty miles in front of Sollum. Also, Rommel was short of tanks and artillery, while the men were so undernourished and plagued by malaria that fully 22 percent of the nearly 50,000 German troops were reporting sick. The Luftwaffe in Cyrenaica counted only seventy-six planes ready for action, although they could call on reinforcements from Greece and from the Italians.[129]

For his part, Auchinleck named Lieutenant General Alan Cunningham, brother of the admiral who had successfully directed the British conquest of Italian East Africa, to head the newly created Eighth Army, consisting of two corps.[130] The ruddy-faced Cunningham reminded Moorehead more of a businessman than a soldier— soft-voiced with an easy smile and an air of efficiency. Those who served under Cunningham, however, found him to be a distant, short-tempered leader economical with words of encouragement.[131] There could be no doubt, however, that Auchinleck and Cunningham were in the process of assembling a massive army. The road from Cairo to the Libyan frontier was a vast traffic jam, "a wonderfully encouraging thing to see," of "tanks, heavy lorries and 25 pounder guns, craft guns, travelling workshops, water wagons, ammunition trucks and still more tanks," Moorehead wrote. "It went on for many miles . . . That little piratical force Wavell had sent to Benghazi had become a great army."[132] Unlike Rommel, however, who burned for action, Auchinleck, despite Churchill's carping about his four months of inactivity, appeared perfectly content to allow his forces the leisure to reequip and train. Auchinleck's reluctance to give battle occurred in great part because his tank force, the core of the Eighth Army that was to take on Rommel's panzers, was simply inferior to its opponent. The new American-built Stuarts—called "Honeys" by the British—were fast (36 miles per hour) and highly maneuverable. But they carried only a 37 mm gun, a sponson machine gun, were lightly armored, and had only a seventy-mile range. The lack of a gyro-stabilizer in the early models to keep the gun steady as the tank moved over undulating ground meant that the Stuart had to stop to fire. Outclassed by their heavier German opponents, the Stuarts were soon confined to reconnaissance and observation tasks. Robert Crisp, who commanded a squad of "Honeys," claimed that the PzKw IIIs and IVs "had to be dealt with by subterfuge and the grace of God," because the "peashooter" 37 mm gun on his Stuart had an effective range of only 600 yards. The medium Crusader tanks, rushed into production to replace the slow Matilda "I" tanks, were immensely unpopular in the Eighth Army because they were undergunned, mechanically unreliable, and vulnerable to German antitank guns. These were gradually replaced by the Valentine, which still carried only a 40 mm gun, later upgraded to a 57 mm, and the slow but popular American-built Grant tank, armed with a 75 mm gun mounted on a sponson and a 37 mm high-velocity antitank gun in its turret. The greatest British advantage was that the Eighth Army was now fully motorized.[133]

For once the Eighth Army would have air superiority, a second advantage. In the wake of Battleaxe, Air Chief Marshal Sir Arthur Tedder had recognized the need to assure better support for ground operations. In October 1941 he formed the Desert Air Force under the command of Air Marshal Sir Arthur Coningham. A New Zealander and World War I fighter ace, "Mary" (a corruption of "Maori") Coningham pioneered methods of air-ground cooperation that were later adopted by the USAAF.[134] The early days of the DAF were inauspicious ones, however. The bulk of his pilots for the nine fighter squadrons, six medium bomber squadrons, and one tactical reconnaissance squadron were South Africans flying aircraft that were no match for the Messerschmitt Bf. 109s. For this reason, assignment to the DAF was virtually a death sentence for pilots for the first six months of its existence. By the late autumn of 1941, however, the Luftwaffe was scattered over several fronts and so weak in North Africa that prospects for effective air support appeared good. British commanders came to rely on the DAF to supplement their relative lack of artillery. Because the scattered nature of fighting in the desert made it difficult for pilots to distinguish friend from foe, the DAF preferred to fly interdiction missions behind Axis lines rather than offer close air support that risked friendly-fire accidents.

The British had also laid the foundation for what would eventually become a formidable intelligence machine. Luftwaffe Enigma traffic combined with an Army/Air Photographic Interpretation Unit, set up in Cairo, gave Auchinleck excellent knowledge of the whereabouts of Rommel's units, their supply dumps, and their minefields. It set the number of German tanks at 385, remarkably close to the real number of 390. Army Sigint, known as the Y Service, had broken both the tactical Luftwaffe codes, which gave them target lists, and also the Wehrmacht's medium-grade cipher. Cairo was able to reconstruct networks, frequencies, and call signs of German units in Libya. The persistent British blind spot was that they remained largely ignorant of the power of the 88 mm guns, which had caused so much mischief during Battleaxe.[135]

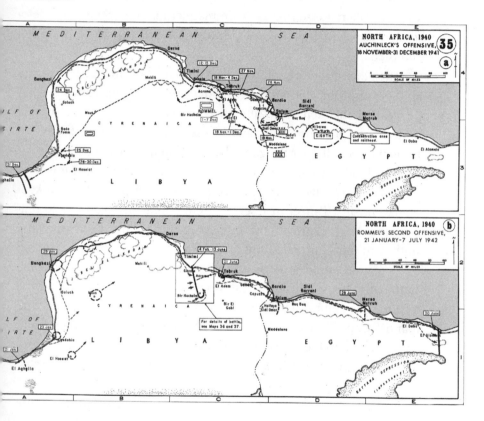

CRUSADER

London judged that Rommel's next assault on Tobruk was imminent and an immediate offensive was required to prevent the fall of the fortress.[136] Axis intelligence was aware that the British were pushing the railway forward from Marsa Matruh, constructing pipelines, and stocking materials. They had also built up a fairly accurate picture of the British order of battle. An attempt on 14 September 1941 by the Twenty-first Panzer Division to disrupt these preparations on the Sollum front with a "reconnaissance in force" designed to overrun British supply depots caught the British by surprise.[137] But it faltered when the German tanks, stalled for lack of gasoline, were savaged by the RAF. Axis shipping losses in the Mediterranean remained a high 23 percent in September. Worried by the lack of coordination in the Axis war effort in the Mediterranean, Hitler named Luftwaffe Field Marshal Albert Kesselring as "Commander-in-Chief South" in October and dispatched planes and U-boats from other theaters to support Rommel.

After this flutter of activity, the Germans became fairly complacent—British preparations for Crusader were camouflaged by desperate weather that kept Luftwaffe air reconnaissance grounded, by the radio silence of British units, and by the fact that Rommel, fixated on his plan to assault Tobruk, ignored the British mobilization. Even after the British offensive kicked off, he persisted in believing that it was no more than a spectacular raid. Nevertheless, as a precaution he kept the Twenty-first Panzer in reserve.[138] Cunningham's plan was to outflank the Axis defensive positions along the Sollum front from the south with the Thirtieth Corps, which held the main British armored forces. These would drive as if they were to relieve Tobruk from the southeast. This would draw out Rommel's armor, which could be destroyed at Gabr Saleh. Once Rommel's armor was engaged, the infantry-heavy Thirteenth Corps would swing around the Sollum front, advance north to the sea, and then turn west to link up with a sortie by the Tobruk garrison. In effect, Rommel's forces would be encircled and surrounded.

There were at least three things wrong with the plan. First, the British, while enjoying a quantitative superiority in matériel and logistics, were numerically equal to Rommel's force. Moreover, the Germans would be fighting the battle close to their supply depots, while the British would have to resupply from Egypt.[139] Given the vast distances in a battlefield that would cover hundreds of miles, with no fixed fronts and etiolated logistical lines, the very idea of surrounding

Rommel with an army of equal size was ambitious. Moorehead reckoned "it was like penning a savage bull in a hencoop."[140] A second problem was that the British violated the principle of concentration of force, on both a strategic and a tactical level. While on paper the British intended to assemble their forces at Gabr Saleh, in practice, by sending his armored brigades on a peripheral sweep and setting them different tasks, Cunningham invited dispersion, allowing Rommel, with the advantage of the central position, to attack them piecemeal.[141] This operational advantage would accentuate the British tactical defect of attempting to fight tanks with tanks, rather than letting antitank guns take care of tanks and sending their tanks after "thin-skinned" vehicles.[142] Finally, in seeking an encounter battle, Auchinleck and Cunningham were playing to German strengths in maneuver and tactical virtuosity, especially their ability to combine armor and artillery attacks.[143] Even were the British to prevail through sheer muscle, they would likely be so weakened that strategic success would elude them.

Crusader, or the "winter battle," was a confused melee that reflected poorly on both commanders. After several postponements that infuriated Churchill, the British attack opened on 18 November with the Thirtieth Corps moving ninety miles behind the Sollum front, past groups of nomads, "always a chimerical vision," remembered South African Robert Crisp, "a glimpse of a world that had no part in ours."[144] With Rommel still fixated on attacking Tobruk, initiative on the German side fell to the commander of the Afrika Korps, Johannes Crüwell. Son of a wealthy Dortmund family, Crüwell was considered by many to be Rommel's intellectual superior. Perhaps realizing this, Rommel allowed Crüwell a degree of latitude that included direct disobedience. The unhealthy command relationship between these two men led to a disjoined German effort that ultimately forfeited the battle.[145]

On 19 November, Crüwell counterattacked with his panzers, forcing the British armor to retreat. From the twentieth, Crüwell tried to attack east to cut off the advancing British forces, but was hampered by lack of gasoline and ammunition. Cunningham ordered a breakout from Tobruk on 21 November. At 0300, Polish infantry began a diversionary sortie on the west side of the perimeter. The main attack came three hours later just south of the Bardia road. British infantry jogging behind Matildas tore through the barbed wire and got into the Axis gun pits, but at the cost of one hundred casualties. The Black Watch took up the charge. But the tanks and armored cars stalled in a hastily laid minefield. Engineers came forward and, under intense fire, began to clear a path through the minefield. Bagpipes played "Highland Laddie" as the Black Watch moved forward through the smoke. Matildas crushed the machine-gun nests as infantry swept up the crews of antitank guns. The first of what were to be almost a thousand sullen German POWs streamed toward Tobruk. Cruiser tanks moved forward, while tank recovery vehicles towed disabled hulks in for repair. The British had registered an impressive four-mile advance on a two-mile front on the first day. Attacks continued for another two weeks, gradually widening a salient in the German siege lines. But this simply made the Tobruk breakout vulnerable to counterattack.[146] Cunningham, unaware of the scale of his tank losses and encouraged by widely optimistic reports of German tank losses,[147] renewed his attack on 22 November, but failed to take the airfield at Sidi Rezegh. In confused fighting the Fifteenth Panzer overran the headquarters of the British Fourth Armoured Brigade. Meanwhile, the New Zealand Division and the Indians penetrated German defenses on the Sollum front and advanced toward Tobruk, in the process seizing the airfield at Gambut. By the morning of 23 November, Cunningham realized that his tank losses had been catastrophic, and he began to demonstrate the hesitation that would cost him his job. But the news for the British during the day got worse, not better. For Crüwell, tossing aside Rommel's orders, massed the Ariete and the Eighth and Fifth Panzer Regiments to overrun and annihilate the Fifth South African Brigade, one of the two brigades of the Thirtieth Corps's only infantry division. However, the frontal assault, while glorious, cost Crüwell 72 of 162 tanks and many of his best officers.

Both Auchinleck and Rommel were determined to go for broke. The British commander, calculating, on the basis of intelligence reports of German fuel shortages, that Rommel "is fully stretched and desperate," and that the British could reinforce while Rommel could not, ordered Cunningham to attack "even to the last tank."[148] For his part, Rommel, bolstered by Crüwell's crushing of the Fifth South African Brigade and his superiority in tanks, decided to disrupt British communications and relieve his garrisons at Bardia and Sollum/ Halfaya with a bold thrust by his two panzer divisions southeast toward the Egyptian frontier. Crüwell protested that Rommel should first con- solidate his gains before tearing off for the enemy rear. He also noted that the British were far stronger and less disorganized than Rommel imagined. Crüwell's case might have been strengthened had he known that the British had been made aware of Rommel's intention through Luftwaffe intercepts. In any event, it did not save Cunning- ham. In typical Rommel lead-from-the-front style, he set out toward the Egyptian frontier, leaving command responsibilities in the hands of his operations officer, a young lieutenant colonel.

All battles seem like chaos to the participants. But Crusader falls into the Oscar category. As the Twenty-first Panzer charged toward Egypt with Rommel at the head, panic spread among British forces. Moorehead witnessed a line of German armored cars "driving in front of them, like stampeding cattle, hundreds of British lorries, ambu- lances and supply wagons." He joined the stampede: everyone hastily threw their belongings into trucks and took off. "All day for nine hours we ran. It was a contagion of bewilderment and fear and ignorance . . . It was a crestfallen and humiliated little group of men that finally felt its way towards the frontier wire fence as dusk fell."[149] Such was the chaos that even British intelligence was unable to establish a clear pic- ture of what was happening.[150] When Rommel reached the wire de- noting the border, he sent von Ravenstein with his Twenty-first Panzer Division north toward Halfaya Pass while he waited for the Fifteenth Division to catch up. At dusk, he wandered across into Egypt with his chief of staff and a driver, became lost, his vehicle broke down, and he and his chief of staff spent the night of 24–25 November on the Egyp- tian side of the frontier. He was rescued by Crüwell, who just hap- pened to be passing by, otherwise he might easily have been captured in an area swarming with British soldiers. Cunningham was not so lucky: on the evening of 25 November, Auchinleck replaced him with Major General Niel Ritchie, after Cunningham, fearing that Rommel might eliminate his armored forces, asked permission to retreat to Egypt to regroup.[151] "This was a shock, but not really a surprise," wrote Crisp. "Even right down at the bottom of the ladder it was impossible not to be aware of the absence of firm direction and purpose from above. Everyone welcomed the change as the beginning of an era of greater decisiveness. Nobody had ever heard of Ritchie."[152]

Ritchie came by his anonymity quite naturally. A Scot who had served on the staffs of Wavell and Auchinleck, Ritchie was tapped by Auchinleck as a temporary commander to fight the battle with the commander-in-chief Middle East looking over his shoulder. Ritchie remained in charge of the Eighth Army because he won the battle and because no obvious candidate emerged to replace him. But Ritchie proved to be a very tentative commanding officer, with a proclivity for interminable and inconclusive staff conferences. He imparted no sense of urgency to his subordinates, who concluded that he was merely a front for Cairo, which continued to call all the shots long distance. Because Ritchie failed to assign specific tasks to his subordinate commanders, Rommel wiggled off the hook.[153]

For the next three days, both generals lost control of the action. "Apparently nobody, not even the enemy, knew what the hell was going on anywhere," Crisp believed. In part this was because, like Rommel, British generals were also "tearing round the desert looking for brigades and regiments; telling each group separately what they had to do; trying to make something cohesive out of that utter confusion." The frenetic activity by commanders on both sides almost made one nostalgic for châteaux generalship. Crisp wondered laconically if "we wouldn't all have been better off if the Generals had stayed at their posts."[154] Infantry held or attacked positions while armored forces wandered the extensive battlefield with little direction, bumping into each other. Moorehead recalled the chaotic scene:

Lost groups of men roamed about, passing and repassing through enemy lines. Convoys of vehicles were scattered over 100 miles of desert, not knowing where to go. Batteries of guns and groups of tanks were left stranded in empty desert. Men who believed they were holding the end of a continuous salient suddenly found the enemy behind them . . . Then the enemy in turn would seek to carry off his booty and prisoners only to find that his own base had vanished and that he was in the midst of strong British formations.

Germans continued their practice of pressing captured British vehicles into service, which made for surprise encounters in the desert. Crisp was astonished when two obviously lost German tanks, "turret closed, jinking about a bit," raced right through the Fifth South African Brigade's supply echelon. Soldiers on both sides had been made POWs and then were recaptured by their own troops as many as four times.[155] Major General Johannes von Ravenstein, commander of the Twenty-first Panzer Division, was not so lucky—the New Zealanders ambushed his Mercedes on his return from a conference with Crüwell on 28 November and made him prisoner. Field hospitals took in casualties of all sides, while doctors continued to operate no matter which army occupied their surgeries. At night, as the desert grew quiet and cold, and moonlight transformed the desert landscape into strange collages of shadows and shapes, British forces would settle into protective leaguers. It was a prudent but ultimately self-defeating tactic because on occasion it allowed hard-pressed German units to escape. It also conceded the battlefield to German recovery units, able to recuperate broken-down or damaged tanks in their tracked and wheeled tank transporters unopposed.

Rommel's giant raid toward Egypt scattered his forces, exhausted his meager fuel stocks, and diminished the power of his attack. It allowed the New Zealanders to advance along the coast toward Tobruk and seize his airfield at Sidi Rezegh. Deprived of air cover, Axis troops were pounded by the RAF. With Rommel either completely out of touch or issuing orders that bore little relationship to the actual situation, German commanders referred to Panzergruppe or Afrika Korps headquarters for instructions. According to Crisp, although Rommel's race to "the wire" on the Egyptian frontier caused panic in the Eighth Army's rear echelons, at that moment the British understood that they had won the battle. "We just assumed that the German commander had made one hell of a blunder and in due course would get it in the neck . . . In my own mind I had not the slightest doubt that if the Afrika Korps and its two panzer divisions had stayed in command [of the airfield at Sidi Rezegh], they could have fought the Eighth Army to a standstill."[156] On 26 November the New Zealand Division driving in from the east made contact with the Tobruk garrison. Their seizure of the airfield at Gambut gave the RAF a forward base from which they could pound the scattered German forces. This forced Rommel to abandon his expensive thrust toward Egypt on 27 November and return to Tobruk to take on the New Zealand Division.[157] In what his biographer calls nothing short of an "astonishing success" based on Rommel's determination and the inability of the British to concentrate their armor, by 1 December the Panzergruppe had forced the New Zealanders to retreat back toward the frontier.

Rommel's success had left him with 17 light PzKw II tanks useful mainly for reconnaissance, 31 PzKw IIIs, the warhorse of the Panzergruppe, and only 9 PzKw IVs. Undeterred, Rommel ordered yet another attack east in an attempt to link up with the Sollum front. This was repelled with heavy losses, in part because Rommel was desperately short of tanks. But also, the British had reconstructed their intelligence picture of the enemy, using captured documents that allowed Sigint to break German codes, maps, and POW debriefs, including that of von Ravenstein, which identified German troop positions and minefields.[158] In effect, this meant that if Ritchie pressed his attack, Rommel was done for. And that is precisely what Ritchie did. Realizing that he was locked in a battle of attrition, he ferried in additional reinforcements from Britain, Syria, and Egypt and hurled them at Rommel. Commanders stood in the turrets of their tanks until their legs ached, bouncing over the desert, maneuvering to ambush an opponent, shouting orders to drivers and gunners who labored in their metal compartments that stank of sweat, gasoline, and gunpowder. On 4 December, Rommel, pressed around Tobruk, decided to relinquish all ground east of Tobruk, a tardy decision that cost him much of his remaining supplies and many German and Italian soldiers who became POWs. Abandoned German camps, complete with their elaborate tank repair shops, littered the desert like sailing ships without crews.

By 7 December, after emissaries from Rome and Berlin informed him that he could expect neither supplies nor reinforcements, it was gradually dawning on Rommel that he had lost the battle. In fact, in the month of November, 62 percent of the supplies sent from Italy to North Africa failed to arrive, forcing the Axis to reduce shipments in the following months.[159] Rommel ordered a withdrawal to Ain el Gazala, about fifty miles west of Tobruk. There, Rommel vented his anger on General Bastico, his titular superior, threatening to withdraw to Tunisia and have himself interned with his German divisions. (The idea of the great Erwin Rommel surrendering his pistol to a baffled Vichy French admiral must have left Bastico paralyzed with laughter.) Axis forces stranded at the Halfaya Pass and at Bardia by Rommel's retreat surrendered in late December and early January. Meanwhile, as the British attacked his defenses at Gazala on 15 December, Rommel organized a withdrawal to Tripolitania. British pursuit was hindered by supply problems and occasional counterattacks by Crüwell, who had been reinforced by forty-five tanks arriving at Benghazi and Tripoli. Bad weather kept the RAF grounded.

On the surface, Crusader appeared to be a great victory for the British. This was the first-ever defeat of the Wehrmacht. "Here then we reached a moment of relief, and indeed of rejoicing, about the Desert war," Churchill intoned.[160] With a force about equal in numbers to that of the Axis, the British had driven Rommel from the gates of Egypt and relieved Tobruk, in the process inflicting losses of 340 tanks, 332 planes, 2,300 killed, 6,000 wounded, and 30,000 missing or captured. One of Rommel's corps commanders had been bagged and two others killed. Crusader was retribution for exceeding his orders and invading Cyrenaica. He had underestimated the British, and lunged forward even though he lacked the power both to lay siege to Tobruk and to advance into Egypt. When the inevitable counterattack came, he had at first ignored it and then attempted to defeat it with bold maneuvers that were beyond his force's capabilities. He had failed to husband his resources and consolidate his success, instead squandering the tactical superiority of his troops by sending them piecemeal against often tenacious British defense. And even when they succeeded, the costs of tactical victory meant strategic defeat.

But the British victory was tempered by the realization that this time there had been no Beda Fomm. Rommel had escaped. More-over, the punishment inflicted on the British demonstrated that on the tactical level, they had been outfought by the Germans. Commanders had been unable to keep tabs on their troops, who, dispersed to avoid air attack, might never find their units again. The British refusal to paint distinguishing marks on their vehicles meant that "a number of Eighth Army v. Eighth Army encounters took place," Crisp wrote.[161] Communications had failed, as both sides underestimated the difficul-ties of controlling troops over vast tracts of desert. Shortage of radios and cipher staffs meant that orders arrived late or not at all. Whereas the Germans committed their forces in a sound tactical manner, British assets were too often dispersed and attacks ordered with too lit-tle artillery or air support.

For instance, because the British failed to understand that the antitank gun was the proper counter to tanks, they dispersed their tanks to provide protection to nonarmored units. British Cruisers had proved unreliable and the Stuart too light, unlike more robust and more powerful German vehicles. Antitank guns lacked punch. The Germans reported that British generals, in their attempt to micro-manage the battle, had left their subordinate commanders too little initiative. The British were courageous, but "a certain shyness of inde-pendent action existed."[162] Losses of around three hundred planes to a heavily outnumbered Luftwaffe convinced the British that they needed to upgrade to the Spitfire to match the Bf. 109. But the good news was that a basis had been established for air-ground cooperation in the Eighth Army.[163]

In the final analysis, the British owed their victory to Rommel's mistakes, the weight of their matériel, and superior logistics. Moore-head believed that the impact of Rommel's setback on the British and American publics had been squandered by overly optimistic projec-tions of success during the three-week-long battle.[164] Overextended supply lines, combined with tank losses that far exceeded those of Rommel, removed any hope that Auchinleck could pursue to Tripoli. The farther west the Eighth Army progressed, the worse its supply sit-uation became—an old story in the desert! Fuel ran low, and men were reduced to a diet of bully beef, biscuits, and tea. Tanks broke down, and no spares arrived to repair them. Worse, just as the British were advancing on land in the Mediterranean, they were retreating on the sea. Hitler ordered an entire air corps transferred from the Russian front to Italy and North Africa, to regain control over the sea route to Tripoli. Benghazi was bombed and mined, its quays reduced to a chaos of fractured concrete, and the harbor entrance choked with sunken ships, making it difficult for the British to use it as a forward supply base. Malta was subject to renewed pounding. Meanwhile, U-boats transferred from the Atlantic sank the carrier *Ark Royal* and the battleship *Barham* in November. Force K was seriously compromised in December when two of its ships were sunk and two damaged when they encountered a minefield off Tripoli. "Thus was extinguished the light of 'Force K,'" Churchill lamented.[165] Also on the night of 18–19 December, the battleships *Queen Elizabeth* and *Valiant* were sunk by Italian human-torpedo crews in Alexandria harbor, despite intelligence warnings that the Italians might do something desperate to prevent the fleet from intervening against convoys from Italy. The tempo of Italian convoys picked up, so that on 5 January 1942 a six-ship convoy escorted by four Italian battleships reached Tripoli with 54 tanks, 19 armored cars, 147 vehicles, and 2,000 tons of aviation fuel, enough to equip four panzer companies.[166]

The only really good news for London was that the United States had entered the war on 7 December. But even these joyous tidings were tempered by news that the Japanese had begun the conquest of the Philippines and had sunk the *Prince of Wales* and the *Repulse* in the Pacific on 10 December. In the same month Japanese troops took Hong Kong and began an advance on Singapore. This was bad news for Cairo, because forces earmarked for the Mediterranean were diverted to the Far East. The Eastern Mediterranean fleet, the glue that bound the British effort in the Mediterranean, now had neither carriers, battleships, nor heavy cruisers. Therefore, the fleet was in no position to protect the flank and supply an Eighth Army advance to Tripoli, even had Auchinleck been inclined to go there. Nor could it be in a position seriously to interdict the Italian convoys to North Africa. Auchinleck, Gott, and Norrie seemed to Moorehead to be wrapped in the gloom of an awareness of the fact that it would be only a matter of time before Rommel would again be in a position to seize the initiative.[167]

ROMMEL'S RECONQUEST OF CYRENAICA

They were correct. Despite the pessimistic outlook recorded by Moorehead, Auchinleck fell into the Wavell trap of underestimating Rommel's ability to counterattack based on his allegedly "acute" logistical difficulties. British intelligence optimistically estimated that two-thirds of Rommel's forces had been casualties during Operation Crusader. Auchinleck and Ritchie were also distracted by Malta's desperate situation, mopping up Axis garrisons at Derna, Bardia, and the Halfaya Pass, planning for an advance into Tripolitania, and catching up on routine business neglected during the winter battle.[168] Despite the fact that the British army was debilitated by its victory and was experiencing severe logistical problems, Auchinleck rejected the idea of holding at Benghazi while he built up his forces. Instead, he pushed to the Tripolitania border.

Rommel called Auchinleck's bluff.[169] Resupplied from Tripoli with tanks and fuel and tipped off by the intercepts of the American military attaché in Cairo, Colonel Bonner Fellers, who radioed to Washington of the weakening of the RAF, the punishment Malta was receiving, and Auchinleck's supply problems, Rommel struck on the morning of 21 January 1942.[170] Preparations for his attack were masked by bad weather, radio silence, Rommel's failure to inform his superiors of his intentions, and the British conviction that the commander of Panzergruppe Afrika was on the ropes. Italian commanders who were to participate were informed by word of mouth at the last minute. Both Auchinleck and Ritchie were away from the front. Even after the attack was launched, British intelligence continued to insist that it was merely a reconnaissance in force carried out with Italian units, which Rommel had too few supplies to sustain.[171] An encircling movement captured a thousand British POWs and over two hundred vehicles. But, to Rommel's disappointment, the bulk of British forces scuttled away along the coast. Rommel then feinted toward Mechili, as if he were going to take the well-worn southern route across Cyrenaica, but then chose to pursue the retreating British around the hump of Cyrenaica, aided by intelligence that revealed confusion and dissension in the British ranks. It began to look as if the Wavell debacle of a year earlier was about to be repeated. This worried Berlin, eager not to replicate the overextension caused by Rommel's earlier advance on Egypt, as much as it did the British. Kesselring and Cavallero were dispatched to rein in Rommel. But Rommel, his Panzergruppe raised to the status of a Panzerarmee Afrika on 22 January, waved away his nominal superiors with the warning that only Hitler could order him to stop. On 29 January, Benghazi fell, and with it quantities of POWs, 1,300 trucks, ammunition, and food. The capture of Benghazi shortened Rommel's supply line. But fuel shortages forced him to hold back the heavier Afrika Korps units, leaving the pursuit to light reconnaissance forces with practically no air support. By mid-February, Rommel had set a new record, advancing 610 kilometers across Cyrenaica in fifteen days. Despite these impressive gains, Axis casualties during the winter fighting had been considerably higher than those of the British.[172] Nevertheless, the precipitous British retreat combined with high British losses in tanks and vehicles convinced Rommel that the enemy was ripe for defeat. Delighted, Hitler promoted Rommel to colonel general. Churchill explained to an exasperated Parliament that, in Rommel, the British faced "a great general." Auchinleck ordered Ritchie to stop forty miles west of Tobruk and dig in on a north–south line running from Gazala on the coast to Bir Hacheim, a small Italian desert outpost about fifty miles from the sea.[173]

CHAPTER FIVE

"The Great Kingdom of Terror"

T HE LATE WINTER and spring of 1942 were not happy times for
the British. Rommel's second desert offensive had kicked off in
late January, as Nazi leaders, led by Heydrich, met at Wannsee outside
Berlin to prepare the "Final Solution." In February, massive lifts of
Jews to concentration camps began. The German battleship *Tirpitz*
was shifted to Norwegian waters, and the first Arctic convoy was attacked by U-boats. On 11 February, the battle cruisers *Scharnhorst* and
Gneisenau together with the heavy cruiser *Prinz Eugen,* which had devoured British merchant shipping before seeking refuge at Brest, escaped through the Channel in broad daylight and headed for Kiel.
And this despite repeated warnings from the French resistance, Ultra,
and photo reconnaissance that an escape was imminent.[1] The capitulation of Singapore to the Japanese on 15 February, after only desultory
British resistance, completed a hat trick of winter disasters. If British
public opinion was made "depressed and querulous" by the news, Australian attitudes, already sensitized by World War I experiences at Gallipoli, reinforced by Greece and Crete, teetered on outrage after yet
another of their divisions under British leadership was delivered into
captivity. Although the fall of the Philippines struck U.S. morale hard,
at least the forlorn American garrison on Bataan held out for three
months, and Corregidor for a fourth. American confidence in Britain's
value as an ally was shaken. Meanwhile, Auchinleck whined about the
inferior quality of British tanks and the lack of training of his troops,

and insisted that Rommel's three German and half-dozen ill-equipped Italian divisions were too strong to assault. Meanwhile, the Russians launched a series of offensives all along their front. Churchill, by now programmed to protest the "mismanagement" of his generals,[2] summoned Auchinleck to London for a rendering of accounts. But his commander-in-chief Middle East ducked the invitation, pleading pressure of business, thereby confirming Churchill's pessimism about the army's "lack of vigor," atrophied fighting qualities, and second-rate generalship.[3] On 5 March, Churchill named General Sir Alan Brooke to the chair of the British Chiefs of Staff Committee.

Churchill's pressure on Auchinleck to take the offensive in Cyrenaica was prompted by fears that Malta would soon join Dunkirk, Greece, Crete, and Singapore on the requiem list of British catastrophes. By April 1942, Malta had already endured a twenty-two-month blockade that had begun with the first Italian bombing raid of 11 June 1940. After an initial panic, the population had adjusted to Italian bombing with a stoicism characteristic of an island race bred to endure sieges. During the first six months of the war, the Italian bombardments had been of such a desultory nature, and caused so little damage, that they became nightly entertainment for the families who gathered on the roofs of Valetta to observe the nearly innocuous pyrotechnics. The latest films could be flown in; gaps in the barbed wire and an absence of mines permitted visits to the beach; sweets and sodas were still available in cafes. The 11 November 1940 attack on the Italian fleet at Taranto, followed by the collapse of the Italian army in Cyrenaica, lifted the fear of imminent invasion that hovered over the Maltese population. When Admiral Cunningham visited Malta in the *Warspite* on 20 December 1940, 20,000 Maltese lined the shores of Valetta harbor to cheer him. However, Cunningham was far from pleased by the lack of defensive preparations and public shelters on Malta, for which he blamed the governor-general, Major General William Dobbie.

Dobbie had been called out of retirement to preside over an island that, initially, few in London expected to salvage. The general was neither a gifted administrator nor a soldier of vision. But as a symbol of indomitable will and a spirit of stern self-sacrifice, Dobbie suffered no equal. A member of the Plymouth Brethren, the six foot, four inch tall soldier remained persuaded that he enjoyed direct communication with the Almighty. In normal times, Dobbie's Scripture-laced pronouncements delivered from the governor's mansion with the deep, resonant voice of an Edwardian vicar might have evoked popular skepticism, not to say derision, on the part of the deeply Catholic Maltese. But Dobbie worked like a sedative on strained island nerves. His integrity was beyond reproach, while, beneath a stern, humorless demeanor, he was guided by a Cromwellian desire to "do the right thing." He demonstrated a genuine concern for the well-being of his flock, martyred for Britain's salvation. When a particularly fierce air raid struck during a Council of Government meeting in early 1942, the nervous participants quivered beneath tinkling chandeliers, impatient for the sign from the governor-general to bolt for the air raid shelters. Dobbie merely repaired to a balcony, dropped to his knees, and prayed. He then returned to the room to announce in Delphic tones, "God has spoken, and so shall it be." The meeting continued. The pious Maltese admired his mysticism and stuck close to him during air raids because they believed that he enjoyed divine protection. Dobbie was the reincarnation of Saint Paul, another holy man brought by God to Malta from beyond the sea. "When the proper time came," they told each other, "God would fall in line with the governor."[4]

In January 1941 it looked like the "proper time" had, at last, arrived in the form of Fliegerkorps X. At a stroke, the shallow "Italian-proof" bomb shelters scraped out of the yellow limestone cliffs seemed poor protection against the fury of the Luftwaffe. The streets of Valetta, the "Three Cities" across the Grand Harbor, and Sliema opposite Valetta across the Marsamuscetto, became choked with rubble and body parts during the 116 raids inflicted by the Germans over the next four months. The British tried to defend with the "box barrage," adopted from London's defense against the Blitz, and by flying in a few dozen Hurricanes from carriers. But these offered scant defense against the waves of Ju88s, Heinkel 111s, and Stukas, which, arriving in groups of forty, dropped heavy and medium bombs and seeded the harbor with mines, the opening performance in a tightly choreographed air show that was invariably followed by the appearance of dozens of strafing

Messerschmitt Bf. 109s and 110s. People fled to the countryside or spent the night standing up in a fetid, urine-soaked, abandoned railway tunnel on the outskirts of Valetta that did duty for a public shelter, listening to an oratorio of screeching rats crazed by the bombing.

Malta's Calvary eased somewhat in May 1941 as Fliegerkorps X departed for Greece and Barbarossa. A few fast merchantmen dashed to Malta with supplies, while the "magic carpet service" of submarines from Alexandria brought in aviation fuel, spare airplane parts, medicines, seed potatoes, and dried milk. An Italian special forces raid in July with explosive motorboats and human torpedoes called "pigs," designed to sink a six-ship convoy at anchor in Grand Harbor, was detected by radar and foiled. (Italian special forces would have better luck with their "pigs" at Alexandria in December 1941.) However, Malta realized that it had merely been given a stay of execution, not a parole. Thirty miles of runways were added to Malta's three airfields, along with primitive aircraft pens made from empty two-gallon petrol tins filled with crushed stone, to accommodate the island's sixty bombers and over a hundred Hurricanes. Machine shops were moved underground. An attempt to create submarine pens foundered on the lack of laborers to build them. Life in Valetta gradually returned to something close to normal: the curfew was relaxed, the Yacht Club resumed competitions in the mine-infested waters, dinner-dances revived at the exclusive Sliema Club, and cultural evenings at the British Institute opened to packed houses. Children poked the rubble in search of rats, for which they were paid a penny each. Meat was a rarity, but tomatoes, potatoes, and onions made for a nutritious, if monotonous, diet.

The arrival of the surface raiders of Force K in October 1941, combined with revivified bombing campaigns against North Africa and Italy by Malta-based bombers, ratcheted up Malta's nuisance value to the Axis. It also ushered in what the Maltese called the Black Winter of 1941–42. The series of disastrous blows to the Royal Navy in December 1941 revived the fear of an invasion of the island. On 2 December 1941, Kesselring was appointed commander-in-chief South and tasked with "the suppression of Malta." Luftflotte II was coordinated with a naval blockade in a strategy calculated to strangle the island by denying it to British convoys. Rommel's January 1942 counterattack, which took Benghazi and carried him to the Gazala line, removed the air cover for convoys from Alexandria. The Italian plans for an invasion, in the works since October 1941, were resuscitated. They stepped up their bombing of the island, while Hitler ordered every available plane that could be spared from the Eastern Front to "neutralize" Malta. By day, large groups of German bombers protected by Messerschmitt Bf. 109s pounded the airfields, the harbor, and finally the town. At night, the Italians took up the relay. Every twenty-four hours, Valetta was saturation-bombed with the intensity of Coventry in 1940. The record sixteen raids on 7 February 1942 kept the Maltese in their fetid shelters for thirteen hours. Fleas, lice, and scabies were so common that the Maltese joked that scratching had become their preferred leisure activity. In late March a shelter was hit by a 500-pound bomb, killing 122 people. Near the principal airbase at Luqa, many of the occupants of a shelter drowned when it was flooded by a nearby reservoir damaged by a bomb. The attackers began to drop delayed-action bombs, timed to go off at meal times, and pocket-sized bombs disguised as thermos bottles, fountain pens, and jackknives. By the end of March, the RAF had lost 126 planes destroyed on the ground and a further 20 shot down in the air. This was music to the ears of Rommel, who received 150,000 tons of supplies.

Grand Harbor became a graveyard of ships. The once virid waters were covered with a film of oil that threatened to catch fire, and with decomposed corpses that periodically rose to the surface from the destroyer *Jersey*, sunk in the harbor with all hands when it hit a cucumber mine. The government shifted to an outlying village. In January 1942, a small convoy arrived in Valetta, the first since September. An attempt to convoy in supplies in February was aborted, while the two surviving ships of a heavily escorted four-ship convoy that arrived in March were gutted before they could off-load more than 5,000 tons of cargo. Dobbie put the island on siege rations. One officer remembered a meal that consisted of three spoonfuls of lentils and a sardine, the allocated ration for a fighting soldier. Civilians queued for hours for a ladle of unappetizing watery stew composed of dirty, poorly cooked vegetables flavored with goat or horse meat and prepared by ill-tempered staffs in "Victory Kitchens," which usually meant in the street. Pasta ran out in April, and the winter crop of Cyprus potatoes proved disappointing. Electricity was scarce, and no kerosene was left for cooking, light, or heat. The menu for a gala meal at the Residency consisted of radishes and dry bread. On 15 April 1942, King George awarded the George Cross, given for bravery, to Malta, the only instance of its being bestowed on an entire people. This merely produced graffiti that read *Hobz, mux George Cross* ("Bread, not George Cross"). One Maltese noted that his island had been reduced to "the great kingdom of terror."[5]

Attempts to fight back against the 400 Axis planes based on Sicily so ships at Valetta could be discharged were unsuccessful. Churchill feared that the island would succumb by mid-June at the latest, even without an invasion. Although the density of antiaircraft guns sited around Grand Harbor was practically unequaled, Axis planes seemed immune to their fire.[6] Sixty Hurricanes and twin-engine Beaufighter torpedo bombers, a robust fighter-bomber armed with four 20 mm cannons that resembled the Bf. 110, remained to defend Malta. Their pilots were considered "dead men on holiday," powerless against the Bf. 109s that escorted enemy bombers. Kesselring staggered his raids to catch British planes refueling on the runways, a laborious process that had to be carried out with five-gallon drums because there was no electricity to run fuel pumps. Malta-based submarines had to sink to the harbor floor during the day to avoid being bombed. Malta's supreme value, even during the period of intensive bombardment, was as a night refueling stop for bombers flying from Gibraltar to Egypt. In April, to bolster Malta's capacity to defend itself, Churchill asked Roosevelt for the loan of the *Wasp*, which carried more planes than did the older British carriers. On 20 April, two days after sixteen stripped-down B-25s under Jimmy Doolittle flew off the *Hornet* 650 miles east of Tokyo, the *Wasp* launched forty-seven Spitfires from a point 600 miles west of Malta. Only one failed to reach the island. Unfortunately, thirty planes were destroyed on the tarmac while refueling.

Opinion in Britain was split over whether the stepped-up air campaign against the island and the massing of forces in southern Italy pointed to an Axis invasion. But as winter turned to spring, increasing indications of invasion preparations were being given by Luftwaffe Enigma intercepts.[7] Meanwhile, Dobbie reduced the already meager bread ration to ten and a half ounces a day in a desperate attempt to eke out stocks until July. By May, a frantic Churchill concluded that Malta faced either invasion or surrender, or a combination of both, while Auchinleck devoted his energies to inventing excuses for inaction.[8] On 7 May, the day after General Wainright surrendered 15,000 American and Filipino troops on Corregidor and as the Battle of the Coral Sea raged, Dobbie was suddenly replaced with the ex-chief of the Imperial General Staff, General Lord Gort. Dobbie's administration had been faulted for its many inefficiencies and general lackadaisical approach to the island's defenses. But the rumor was that Dobbie had become so distressed about the island's suffering that he was about to turn it over to the Axis.[9] On 10 May, Churchill directed Auchinleck to prepare a North African offensive for early June at the latest, or resign.[10]

That the British disagreed on German plans for Malta is hardly surprising given the fact that a debate raged on the German side over Malta's fate. Kesselring understood that the air dominance over Malta offered only a temporary solution—Luftflotte II's planes were needed elsewhere. During an angry interview in February 1942, Kesselring exacted a worthless promise from Hitler to invade the island. Hitler opposed taking Malta for a variety of reasons—he was preoccupied with the Russian front, Crete had made him shy of paratroop operations, and he was unenthusiastic about mounting a joint operation with Italians. In March, Rommel agreed that Malta should be seized, a trifling concession because he thought that he would be unable to resume his offensive at Gazala before the summer. However, the success of the air campaign against Malta meant that the Axis lost only 9 percent of supplies sent to North Africa in February and March. By April 1942, it was an unlucky Axis ship indeed that perished on the North African route. The inflow of supplies positively bloated Rommel's Panzerarmee. He also feared that time was working in favor of Auchinleck. The longer he waited, the stronger the Eighth Army became.

Despite the fact that neither Hitler nor Rommel was particularly keen to seize Malta, the invasion plan—Herkules—was firmed up at a meeting between Hitler and Mussolini at Berchtesgaden on 1 May. The plan called for Rommel to attack the Gazala line in late May or early June to push the British back to the Egyptian frontier and seize Tobruk. When this was done, an attack on Malta would be unleashed in mid-July. Kesselring argued that Axis priorities were backward, but contented himself with a spurious commitment to take Malta. What he failed to realize was that "once Rommel had got his propaganda machine going," it became difficult to override him.[11] An airborne corps of German and Italian paratroops were to drop on Malta's three airfields, followed by an amphibious landing of five Italian divisions delivered by the Italian navy and protected by U-boats on Malta's south coast. The Luftwaffe and the Regia Aeronautica would transport the paratroops and provide air cover.[12]

By the time these plans were confirmed, however, Malta's salvation was assured. On 28 April, the air offensive against Malta was curtailed. Kesselring could no longer hold back planes required on the Eastern Front and to support Rommel's advance on Tobruk while the Italians dithered over plans to invade in July or August, and Hitler and Jodl opposed committing even token German forces to an Italian-led enterprise.[13] On 9 May the *Wasp* returned with another delivery of sixty Spitfires. This time they survived, because of Kesselring's withdrawal of Luftwaffe assets and because the airfields on Malta were better prepared to receive them.

THE BATTLE OF GAZALA

As early as 30 April, Cairo began to receive intelligence warnings of Rommel's offensive preparations. By the end of April, air assaults on Malta trailed off as planes were shifted back to Russia to support the German offensive west of the Donets and to North Africa. Ultra warned that Rommel's attack could come at any time after 22 May.[14] Auchinleck was not complacent. He merely believed that a defensive battle against Rommel offered more advantages than a preemptive spoiling attack. The commander-in-chief Middle East had rejected Churchill's suggestion that he take direct command of the coming battle. Instead, he allowed General Niel Ritchie to arrange the Eighth Army into seven defensive "boxes" echeloned for forty-five miles south from the

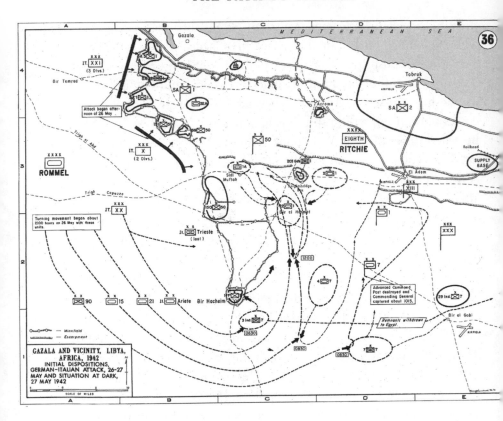

Gulf of Bunbah, along a limestone step that rose in places to an altitude of 600 feet to Bir Hacheim, an inauspicious collection of moles, pillboxes, and minefields on the site of an abandoned Italian desert camp that stood beside a dry well at the confluence of several desert tracks. Each "box" was surrounded by deep minefields, a few tanks, and guns that fired in all directions, and was supplied with enough food, water, and ammunition to last through a week's fighting. Behind this forward wall were smaller defensive positions placed across the obvious routes of advance reaching northward to Tobruk. The result was that the British position formed an interlocking "system" that resembled an inverted triangle with the apex at Bir Hacheim. Gaps between the defensive positions were patrolled by 849 tanks, 316 of which were new Grant tanks. The Grant was designed by the Americans with British input, and rushed into production after the fall of France to match the speed and power of the German panzers. The winning feature of the Grant was its 75 mm gun capable of penetrating 2.36-inch armor at 500 yards. Beyond firepower, the Grant had drawbacks, chief among them the fact that no turret large enough to handle the 75 mm gun yet existed, so that the gun was mounted on a sponson. Therefore, to traverse the gun, the tank had to turn. The Grant also had a high, targetworthy profile and a riveted construction, which caused bolts to fly about inside when the tank was struck. Nevertheless, the Grant was thought able to meet 340 German and 225 Italian tanks on a more than equal footing.[15] Wavell declared the Gazala line to be "just about the natural balance in the desert," in the dead center of Cyrenaica. "Whatever army crossed this point was looking for trouble."[16]

Despite the formidable appearance of the Gazala "system" with its two-corps-strong garrison, Rommel concluded that he had no choice but to attack. He realized, and he claimed that his men also understood, that the summer of 1942 offered a final window of opportunity to achieve decisive victory in North Africa before the global balance of forces shifted against Germany.[17] Ritchie's dispositions on the Gazala line were shot through with vulnerabilities that Rommel hoped to exploit. First, although the "boxes" were individually strong, they were sited too far apart, especially in the southern part of the line, to be mutually supporting. Ritchie had hoped to compensate for this by stringing deep minefields between the boxes. But a minefield not covered by fire can be breached at leisure. Second, Ritchie held his mobile force too far to the rear, so that it could not quickly concentrate to crush Rommel's penetration of the position, upon which the success of his defense depended. In fact, the British Court of Enquiry convened in June 1942 to investigate the Battle of Gazala and the fall of Tobruk concluded that British generals remained firmly gripped by a mentality of château generalship. Ritchie at Gambut and Auchinleck at Cairo remained too distant to stay abreast of developments in the battle.[18]

A third weakness of Ritchie's plan was that it failed to anticipate that the line could be bypassed in the south, as Cunningham had done to Rommel's defenses at Sollum. At Gazala, Rommel decided to return the compliment. Ritchie's armored forces, concentrated too far north, were unable to counter an outflanking move in the south.[19] Fourth, Rommel understood that the British had a poor command of inter-arm cooperation. Indeed, even British troops from the same arm failed to cooperate. This stemmed in part from poor preparation of senior officers and the absence of trained staff personnel in the British army. However, poor cooperation was aggravated by personality clashes, which meant that the British command under the distant and nominal supervision of Auchinleck ensconced in Cairo too often behaved like schoolboys squabbling in the absence of the housemaster.[20] Fifth, Rommel knew that, unit for unit, his three divisions of German troops could outfight the British. (The capabilities of his eight Italian divisions were questionable.) His British enemy spent so little time training that they had yet to master new weapons, like the 6 pdr (57 mm) antitank gun they received before Gazala, and integrate them into an operational system, much less rehearse their battle plan.[21] Sixth, the Germans enjoyed significant air superiority, massing 400 operational aircraft against 190 RAF planes.[22] Finally, while British intelligence told of the preparations for Rommel's attack, British commanders were divided on its timing and its direction. They also both seriously underestimated Rommel's strength and completely misdiagnosed his plan, despite POW interrogations and copious German radio traffic, practically an open book for the British Y services, that pointed to a thrust against the southern part of the line.[23]

The Battle of Gazala opened on 26 May as almost the mirror image of Crusader. As a torrid *khamsin* from the south whipped up billows of sand that reduced visibility to as little as ten yards, Rommel used his Italian divisions to attack the British defenses head on while he swung 10,000 vehicles of the Fifteenth and Twenty-first Panzer Divisions and the Ninetieth Light, organized on a thirty-five-mile front, around the southernmost "box" at Bir Hacheim, which the Ariete Division was set to capture. Luftwaffe flares and incendiary bombs were dropped on Bir Hacheim to guide the advance of what was called "the great march" through a bright, moonlit night. Meanwhile, the Trieste Division was ordered to penetrate the gap between the Free French Brigade Group at Bir Hacheim and the 150th Brigade Group's box thirteen miles to the north. Success would open a direct line of communication to the German troops in "the great march" as they swung around Bir Hacheim and lunged at the east leg of the inverted British triangle. But the Italians became bogged down in minefields in the south of the Gazala line, where they were machine-gunned by South African infantry and savaged by British tanks. After two days, Rommel's divisions had bypassed the British boxes and, "spread out like the fingers of a man's hand,"[24] had penetrated into the heart of the British defensive triangle, in the process badly smashing up three British brigades and capturing the commander of the Seventh Armoured Division. The Luftwaffe attacked British fighter bases with unaccustomed fury. British troops locked themselves into their boxes and fired in all directions. "It was a brilliant opening," Moorehead remembered, "as if a gang of thugs had invaded a house and were prowling through the passageways, while the inmates had locked themselves in their rooms."[25]

So far, the British had witnessed a typical Rommel offensive—innovative, noisy, calculated to produce maximum confusion and intimidation. But Rommel's intelligence had failed accurately to pinpoint British defensive positions, especially armored concentrations. As a result, when Ritchie unleashed his new Grants with their 75 mm guns and six-pounder antitank artillery, Rommel watched about a third of his tanks go up in smoke. The shells of the PzKw IVs merely ricocheted off the impermeable Grant armor, leaving "a dent like a hoof print."[26] Axis units, driven forward by Rommel, became intermingled, scattered, low on fuel and ammunition. Ambulances careened about the battlefield, while huge recovery vehicles lumbered through the chaos in search of repairable tanks and guns, a "bloodstream of armor" that their crews hoisted onto trailers and trucked to mobile workshops in the rear. Rommel directed the fury of his attacks at a box baptized Knightsbridge by the British. Debris from explosions and dust thrown up by vehicles were churned into a sandstorm by a scorching south wind. The landscape darkened into an opaque blue dusk. It was like fighting a battle inside a bag of unmixed cement. It became impossible to see, much less to eat, because any food exposed for more than a second became covered by a thick film of sand. Each vehicle that nosed through the tempest was preceded by a walking soldier who tried to indicate a direction and pick out obstacles. Most soldiers, their heads swathed in towels, cursed the short trousers that exposed their knees to a sand blasting. They focused their energies on breathing, and dreamed of a steaming cup of sand-free tea. But the Guards units at Knightsbridge withstood every assault. The effectiveness of Luftwaffe intervention had been reduced in great part because of the lack of visibility, and because Rommel was so keen to lead from the front that he neglected to coordinate the battle. British resistance had been stiff. Both Rommel's chief of staff and his operations officer were wounded and had to be evacuated by air, while Afrika Korps commander Crüwell was captured when his Storch observation plane was shot down. German units, deep inside the British positions, were virtually encircled and thrown into deep confusion. Rommel's plan had assumed that the two southernmost boxes would fall easily to Ital-

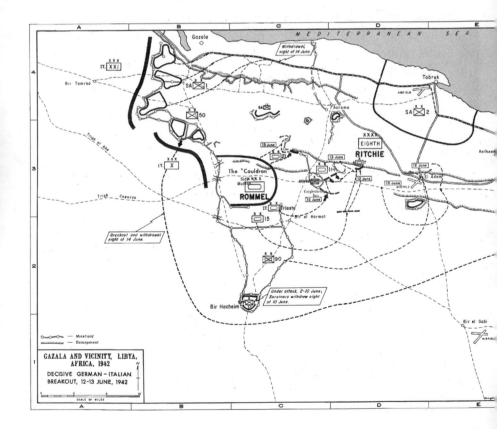

GAZALA AND VICINITY, LIBYA, AFRICA, 1942

DECISIVE GERMAN – ITALIAN BREAKOUT, 12-13 JUNE, 1942

ian attacks. In fact, the Free French garrison at Bir Hacheim remained a thorn in his side—the requirement to detour around the southern apex of the triangle lengthened Rommel's logistical tail, which was vulnerable to slashing raids run out of Bir Hacheim by French Brigadier Pierre Koenig.

By 28 May, Ritchie and Auchinleck had concluded that Rommel's attack had run out of steam. From Cairo, a congratulatory "Well done, Eighth Army" message arrived from Auchinleck. Ritchie's headquarters at Gambut trembled with optimism, persuaded that the moment had arrived to extinguish their opponent's hitherto spectacular career. All that was needed was to send in the infantry to mop up the battlefield.

But the British stuck to their boxes, an inexplicable demonstration of inactivity that permitted Rommel to showcase his infallible ability to snatch victory from the most barren of circumstances. He concentrated his forces in an area called the Cauldron—the Germans called it the *Wurstkessel* (sausage boiler)—a depression set in the midst of the British positions, and, on 29 May, personally led a supply convoy to it. A second piece of luck materialized in the person of Field Marshal Albert Kesselring. The relationship between the fifty-six-year-old commander-in-chief South and Rommel was potentially a tense one. In part, this was because the command boundary between the Luftwaffe field marshal and the Wehrmacht panzer army commander was ill-defined. Kesselring had also made common cause with the Italians in criticizing Rommel's overly ambitious North African offensives and in supporting Herkules. Kesselring's irrepressible optimism and avuncular manner contrasted with Rommel's humorless intensity and honed ambition. Prepared for a row, Rommel was amazed when Kesselring offered to substitute for the captured Crüwell as head of the Afrika Korps, hence placing himself under Rommel's orders. However, the experience failed to increase Kesselring's admiration for Rommel's command style: "I then learnt the difficulties of a commander whose hands are tied by subordination to a headquarters that issues no orders and cannot be reached," Kesselring complained.[27] Rommel hunkered down, his antitank guns in position, and awaited the British attack that came on the thirtieth, the same day as Bomber

Command's thousand-bomber raid that "dehoused" 45,000 people in Cologne. Neither side gave much ground as they traded tanks. But it was clear to Rommel that unless he could break out of his near encirclement, he would be in serious trouble.

Had Ritchie concentrated his force against Rommel and moved rapidly to attack him, he might have netted a dead Desert Fox. Instead, he allowed Rommel a free hand to assault the 150th Infantry Brigade box to his east, which fell on 1 June. This opened up a direct supply route to the east, and convoys poured through for the supply-starved Axis forces. Ritchie's belated attempt to attack the Cauldron on the night of 1 June is described by the British official history as a "fiasco." At a stroke, the French position at Bir Hacheim was transformed into an Allied island awash in an advancing tide of Axis ironmongery. The taciturn and sallow-faced French General Pierre Koenig rejected three summonses to surrender. Rommel repaid Koenig's Gallic obstinacy with a hail of steel and by launching three separate assaults on the French position backed by waves of Stukas, all of which were repulsed. A 10 June attack by the Ninetieth Light and the Trieste Divisions, led in person by Rommel, convinced Koenig that his position had become untenable. With water supplies low, artillery shells virtually exhausted, and accurate German counter-battery fire limiting the ability of French guns to defend the perimeter, Ritchie ordered Koenig to bolt for British lines eight miles to the rear. After nightfall on 10 June, a line of Free French vehicles, Bren guns blazing, burst through the Axis encirclement. Flares lit up the night sky, vehicles exploded into funeral pyres as they drove over mines, and the breakout dissolved into a series of blind firefights. Although the actual siege had proven remarkably low in casualties, the escape cost the brigade nearly a thousand men and most of their equipment. German Lieutenant Kämpf described the 25 officers and 820 men captured at Bir Hacheim as "Red Spaniards, Swiss, Czechs, Poles, and Negroes—riff-raff of the worst kind." Only 10 percent were French. Hitler ordered that any German political refugees—that is, Jews—captured at Bir Hacheim were to be executed. To his everlasting credit, Rommel incinerated the order and refused to comply.[28]

While Rommel concentrated on eliminating the Free French,

ABOVE: Italian troops attack Greek positions in Albania in 1940. Note that the lead infantryman has just been hit.
BELOW: Hitler and Franco meet on the Franco-Spanish border, 23 October 1940.

ABOVE: Italian soldiers in North Africa follow a New Zealand armored car into captivity. BELOW: Advance elements of what would become the *Deutsches Afrika-Korps* disembark in Tripoli in February 1941.

TOP: A German column in Greece takes cover during a British artillery barrage in April 1941. CENTER: General George Tsolakoglu, Commander of the First Greek Army on the Albanian front, surrenders to General Jodl (left) in April 1941. BOTTOM: The Duke of Aosta, Viceroy of Italian East Africa, surrenders to the British at Amba Alagi on 20 May 1941.

Erwin Rommel

ABOVE LEFT: The under-gunned, thinly armored M13/40 was the best tank in the Italian invent
ABOVE RIGHT: The crippled tanker *Ohio*, lashed between two destroyers, is towed into Malta
Grand Harbour on 13 August 1942.

Hitler and Muss
in Florence

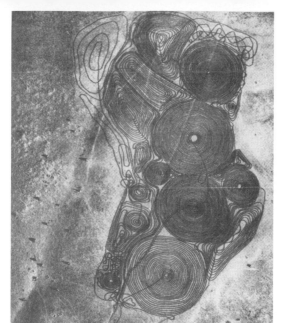

An Axis airfield in Tripolitania, ploughed over by retreating Germans

Eisenhower and Mark Clark confer with French Admiral Jean François Darlan in Algiers, 13 November 1942.

U.S. troops reoccupy Kasserine Pass on 26 February 1943.

General Juergen von Arnim

CENTER: The sixty-ton "Tiger" tank with its high-velocity 88-mm gun
BOTTOM: British First Army commander General Kenneth Anderson with Omar Bradley in Tunis

TOP: An American soldier examines a German "Bouncing Betty" S-Mine.
CENTER: A Siebel Ferry in Tunisia
RIGHT: Montgomery interviews Italian General Messe, as Freyberg looks on.

American Sherman tanks enter Palermo, 22 July 1943.

ABOVE LEFT: Montgomery and Patton in Sicily
ABOVE RIGHT: Kesselring, von Rintelen, and the Prince Di Savoia

Ritchie threw an Indian infantry brigade and a tank brigade into the Cauldron on 5 June. As in previous British actions, this uncoordinated attack exposed the mottled menu of command ideas among British generals as well as an absence of doctrine that required tanks, infantry, and artillery to work together.[29] Fifty-eight of seventy British tanks were lost to antitank guns and mines. Rommel counterattacked, overrunning the headquarters of both brigades, seizing 4,000 POWs and much artillery. In the confusion, Desert Air Force found it impossible to establish a bomb line, and so shifted their attacks to Rommel's supply lines. Rommel, who had seemed on the ropes after the first three days of battle, had turned the tables on a sluggish and unresponsive British command that lacked the ability to seize the flow of the battle.

The main value of the tenacious French defense of Bir Hacheim was that it had given Ritchie time to recover from his pounding in the Cauldron. His position was far from hopeless—although he had lost two boxes, the main British defenses were still intact and gaps had been filled in with five new battalion-sized strong points. On paper, his armor remained formidable, while Rommel had forfeited many tanks and about one-third of his infantry were casualties. When Rommel attacked north on 12 and 13 June, the Fifteenth and Twenty-first Panzer Divisions badly cut up the Second and Fourth Armoured Brigades, which lost about 140 tanks. Once more, the British tanks operating on their own without artillery support or infantry to silence antitank guns simply offered themselves up to sacrifice. By the evening of 13 June, Ritchie realized that the 50 Cruisers and 20 Matildas left to him were inadequate to protect his southern flank. On the morning of 14 June, he ordered the Gazala line to be evacuated, and his forces to fall back to Egypt to regroup. German troops attacking from the south came in sight of the sea as night fell on 14 June. "The battle has been won, and the enemy is breaking up," Rommel noted laconically on 15 June.[30] In the meantime, the Japanese lost four carriers at Midway, the Wehrmacht knocked at the gates of Sebastopol, and the Czechoslovak village of Lidice was destroyed, 198 men shot and 184 women sent to Ravensbrück in retaliation for the assassination in Prague of Reichsprotektor Reinhard Heydrich. Thirty-two more Spitfires reached Malta.

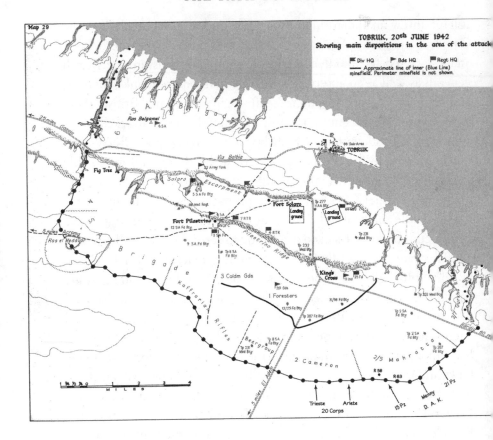

Map 29

TOBRUK, 20th JUNE 1942
Showing main dispositions in the area of the attack

Div HQ   Bde HQ   Regt HQ
—— Approximate line of inner (Blue Line)
minefield. Perimeter minefield is not shown.

DEFEAT AND DISGRACE

Ritchie's retreat order left open the question of Tobruk's fate. Auchinleck's preference was the somewhat equivocal one that Tobruk was to be held only if Rommel did not invest it,[31] an improbable prospect now that the Gazala line had been abandoned. Well aware of the logistical and strategic strains of the 1941 siege, Auchinleck was keen to avoid a reenactment of the earlier investment. Nevertheless, Tobruk blazed as a symbol of British resolve, a fortress, Churchill reminded his Middle East commander, that Cairo could not forfeit without severe political and psychological consequence. Therefore, on 16 June, Auchinleck instructed Ritchie to make Tobruk siegeproof. Unfortunately, the defenses of the fortress had deteriorated during the winter, leaving what Moorehead described as a "hideous," sulfur-colored collection of crumbling, bomb-damaged houses aligned beneath a rocky promontory. Tommy graffiti—"Score—100 not out!" and "Free Beer Tomorrow!"—decorated the crumbling walls. Sections of the perimeter minefields had been lifted and few antiaircraft guns remained to defend the harbor, which in any case was choked with the half-submerged carcasses of bombed-out ships. "It was difficult to see any tradition in this squalor, or feel the sense of history and heroic deeds," Moorehead wrote. "War had made this place accursed."[32] The garrison that had withstood months of siege warfare had been replaced by a hastily mobilized assortment of British and Indian infantry battalions and an understrength South African infantry division commanded by General Hendrik Klopper, a newly promoted staff officer with little operational experience. Furthermore, Ritchie rather burnished Klopper's serious predicament during a visit to the garrison on 16 June. The bald truth, however, was that Tobruk contained no antitank regiment, while a single motorized battalion of Coldstream Guards constituted its mobile defense. Furthermore, the rapid advance of the Afrika Korps had overrun the British airfields and forced the Desert Air Force back into Egypt, where it could offer little support. Auchinleck and Ritchie were distracted by multiple tasks—defend Tobruk, prepare defenses on the Egyptian frontier, and extricate the Eighth Army from the Gazala line before it could be cut off by Rommel's advance.

In any case, it could be no secret to the garrison that the Eighth Army was fleeing pell-mell toward the Egyptian frontier. Command pessimism and panic trickled down to the rank and file. Moorehead detected a "strange sort of atmosphere" that prevailed over the doomed garrison, "a kind of apathy and ugliness one could not describe but felt very strongly. The very earth looked exhausted." The heroism that had sustained Tobruk in previous sieges was spent. Tobruk's new defenders "had come as tenants into a strange house,"[33] disoriented, confused, out of place. Rommel, capitalizing on his momentum and British disorganization—units were mixed up, demoralized by the rapid collapse, without orders and equipment—prevailed upon Kesselring to call up every available bomber in North Africa and some from as far away as Greece and Crete and concentrate them against the fortress. Klopper, on Ritchie's instructions, had positioned his forces to the west and south of the fortress in the direction of the

Gazala line, from which Rommel was expected to emerge. Instead, Rommel revived a plan dating from October 1941 to approach Tobruk from the southeast. On 17 June, Axis troops took Gambut, occupying the airfield, driving back the Seventh Armoured Division, and giving the impression that they were aiming for Egypt. In the process, he also captured large stocks of petrol. On the next two days he moved his troops toward Tobruk. Finally, at 8:30 on the morning of 20 June, Rommel's attack kicked off with Stukas, their air-activated sirens blaring as they swooped on the Eleventh Indian Infantry Brigade, slashing gaping holes in the barbed wire and minefields. German and Italian artillery concentrated a carpet of steel along a two-kilometer wedge, a fanfare for the two German armored divisions that rolled through the gray smoke screen and over the tank ditch on prefabricated bridges laid by German engineers. British resistance stiffened, but Klopper, who had very little grasp of the seriousness of his situation, failed to send enough reinforcements and press counterattacks. Around noon, Rommel redoubled the rabid Stuka attacks to aid the advance of his panzers. Two hours later, few British guns and tanks remained to oppose the German advance. By evening the Afrika Korps had overcome tenacious resistance to take Tobruk down, lobbing shells at British ships that fled to sea behind a protective smoke screen. Klopper, thinking his headquarters was about to be overrun, ordered his phones and radios destroyed, taking away his ability to coordinate the scattered defenders. The British troops who held out in the western portion of the fortress were attacked at 5:30 on the morning of 21 June. Klopper sent his last message to Eighth Army, and at 9:40 he surrendered. Tobruk, with its 2,000 vehicles, 5,000 tons of supplies, 1,400 tons of fuel, and 33,000 defenders, including five generals, belonged to Rommel, at a cost of 2,490 casualties.[34] "It was a defeat as complete as may be," concluded Moorehead.[35]

News of the sudden collapse of a citadel that since the spring of 1941 had become a symbol of British resistance in the Mediterranean fell like a thunderclap. In Berlin, Rommel was proclaimed one of history's great warriors and promoted to field marshal. London's mood was somber. Greece, Crete, Singapore, and now Tobruk joined Gallipoli in 1915 as prototypical examples of Commonwealth courage squandered by poor British planning and indifferent leadership. This was particularly destabilizing in South Africa, whose government of English-speakers had gone out on a limb to support the Allied cause against the opposition of its pro-German Afrikaner population. Now, fully one-third of South Africa's field force languished in Axis POW camps. British newspapers compared Tobruk's demise to the fall of France and speculated on the forthcoming loss of Suez and Rommel's surge toward the oil wells of the Middle East.

The fall of Tobruk diminished what little confidence Churchill still retained in Auchinleck. Plans for a retreat to Palestine were discussed in British army circles and lists of demolitions drawn up. And while Auchinleck's defenders vehemently rejected the notion that he planned to vacate the delta,[36] a *fin de régime* atmosphere had clearly gripped Egypt. The fleet departed Alexandria, where demolition squads prepared to blow up the docks and bunkering stations. Alexandria seemed a ghost town—defenses abandoned, shops shuttered; the bar at the Cecil Hotel on the waterfront, normally jammed with women and naval officers, was now half empty. Cairo edged toward panic—the British embassy and GHQ Middle East began to burn secret documents, and Air HQ left for Ismailia, followed by the naval operations staff and the U.S. military headquarters. Banks were besieged, the shares of the Suez Canal Company plunged 16 percent, as German planes flew overhead to scatter facsimiles of Bank of England script with the message in Arabic proclaiming that sterling was now worthless. Trains and roads leading east toward Palestine were jammed.[37] "Guns of all sorts, RAF wagons, recovery vehicles, armoured cars and countless lorries crammed with exhausted and sleeping men, were pouring up the desert road into Cairo," Moorehead recorded, "an immense lizard over a hundred miles in length . . . We asked ourselves, 'Is the whole army in retreat?' "[38] For Egyptian nationalists, humiliated by the February 1942 crisis, during which the British had offered King Farouk the choice between the appointment of a pro-British prime minister or abdication, Rommel's approach was hailed as if it were Mohammed's second coming. Cries of "Long Live Rommel!" could be heard among the *fellahin*, who convinced themselves that the conquering Axis would introduce land reform. Rumors circulated that a suite had been reserved for the German field marshal at Shepheard's Hotel. Friction between locals and British servicemen increased. Berlin made desperate efforts to contact Farouk and the "Free Officers" movement to prepare an uprising. Egypt's pro-British prime minister interned Axis sympathizers, including an ex–prime minister, and padlocked the Royal Automobile Club, a center of pro-Axis intrigue.[39]

Churchill, who received news of Tobruk's fall in the White House in Washington, where he was trying to convince FDR to sign on to a British strategic plan for winning the war, remembered it as "one of the heaviest blows I can recall during the war . . . a bitter moment." As at Singapore, the fall of the Tobruk garrison to an attacking force half its size assumed a symbolic value that far outweighed its military significance. The rapid collapse of a fortress that had been heroically defended for so long appeared to offer a devastating commentary on the quality of British arms, the morale of British soldiers, the capacities of British generalship, and the logic of British strategic decision making.[40] Ironically, however, this setback proved for Churchill to be a blessing in disguise for at least three reasons. In the first place, Tobruk's fall did not alter the strategic balance in the desert. Operationally, the fortress had been a military liability, vacuuming up men, ships, and matériel that the desperately overstretched British urgently required elsewhere. One reason the garrison succumbed so rapidly in June 1942 was that Auchinleck had resolved to cut loose from the burden of defending it, and so had garrisoned its neglected fortifications with his least seasoned troops. To have become embroiled in yet another siege at a time when the Royal Navy in the Eastern Mediterranean was severely weakened would have strained British resources intolerably. Now it was Rommel's turn to discover what the British had long realized—that Tobruk was practically unutilizable as a forward supply base because its harbor was too small and too vulnerable to air attack.[41]

The second adverse consequence of Tobruk's collapse for the Axis was that it signaled to Washington Britain's, and more specifically Churchill's, apparent weakness, which resulted in what Roosevelt historian Kenneth S. Davis calls "a defining moment" in the Anglo-

American alliance. In the summer of 1942, Churchill insisted that he was "politically at my weakest and without a gleam of military success."[42] But the historian of British civil-military relations, Hew Strachan, has pointed out that in fact Churchill was no more vulnerable in the summer of 1942 to parliamentary overthrow than was Egypt to Rommel's panzers. There was no viable alternative candidate for prime minister. The Mediterranean was only one of the theaters in which the British were fighting, so that setbacks in a remote North African battlefield could be politically contained. While the army leadership might attempt to lay responsibility for their repeated failure to defeat Rommel on the prime minister's desk, they would find no support in the other services. Churchill's strong backing of the strategic bombing of Germany, and of the Royal Navy in the Battle of the Atlantic, meant that these services would not make common cause with the army in a quiet campaign to oust the prime minister, as they had done to Prime Minister Asquith in 1915. "Churchill's political survival rested on his being the public embodiment of the will to win," Strachan writes. "This, for the soldiers, elevated him to the point where professional frustration gave way to political respect."[43]

But from Washington's perspective, it was precisely Britain's military weakness and the possibility of Churchill's political vulnerability revealed by the fall of Tobruk that began the process through which Roosevelt committed to a Mediterranean strategy, against the advice of his secretary of war and his military advisers. The fact that the news arrived as Churchill and Roosevelt conferred in the Oval Office deepened the personal bonds between the two leaders. Under the initial shock of the news, Roosevelt asked quietly, "What can we do to help?" Churchill immediately requested, and was given, 300 Sherman tanks and 100 self-propelled 105 mm antitank guns, which were stripped from U.S. armored divisions and put on fast ships to Suez. Six groups of American heavy and medium bombers and fighters were also dispatched to Egypt to join the group of B-24 bombers that had been there since May 1942. These were to play a significant role in the British victory at El Alamein in October 1942.

More important, Tobruk indicated to Roosevelt the apparent vulnerability of Churchill's political position. The heavy defeat, on 25 June, of the government's candidate in the Maldon by-election was taken as a gauge of British anger over the fall of Tobruk, and an indication of growing public frustration over Churchill's war leadership. There was great relief in Washington when the prime minister survived a 2 July no-confidence vote in the House of Commons over his "catastrophic bungling" of the war. The fact that only 25 of 500 British MPs voted against him indicates the solidity of Churchill's position. Nevertheless, Roosevelt instinctively understood that a public rebuff of Churchill's Mediterranean strategy by a U.S. refusal to support it, essentially an alliance vote of no confidence by Washington, would humiliate the prime minister and weaken his position, even if it failed to precipitate his downfall. Churchill was the pivotal figure of the alliance, whose defiant rhetoric had inspired the free world in Europe's darkest hours. His bulldog "will to win," whatever the costs, was a requirement for victory. Any Churchill successor would probably be less supportive of the USSR, more inclined to make peace, especially if the Soviet Union collapsed, less willing to meld Britain's war-making machinery with that of the United States.

Roosevelt understood as well that any perception of faint resolve in London would cast U.S. strategy into disarray, as his "America First" enemies reemerged with the argument that Europe's perpetual quarrels were not America's business, especially as Hitler appeared invincible. The pressure to negotiate a peace with Berlin and hurl American forces at Japan would increase. Worse, the very fabric of democratic societies throughout the world, including in America, might be at stake.[44] Roosevelt began to craft plans for Operation Torch, over the objections of his secretary of war, Henry Stimson, and his chief of staff, General George Marshall. Dwight Eisenhower was appointed to command U.S. forces in Europe on 25 June. U.S. troops were to prepare to land in French North Africa not later than 30 October 1942. Therefore, the fall of Tobruk, by emphasizing Britain's apparently enfeebled position in the Eastern Mediterranean and Churchill's political vulnerability at home, triggered the U.S. commitment to a Mediterranean strategy. In this way, Washington, like Berlin, was enticed into a peripheral theater by a faltering ally. Unlike Hitler, however, Roosevelt had far more to gain, and far less to lose, by a strategic investment in the Mediterranean.

The third curse of Tobruk for Axis prospects was that once again, Rommel's operational triumph stimulated Hitler's victory fever. Just at the moment that the strategy of the Western Allies found a solid footing, Axis strategy was catapulted into disarray. "News of the swift capture of a fortress that had been so fiercely contested the previous year sent Hitler and Mussolini into such raptures that they forgot all their existing plans," concludes the official German history.[45] As has been seen, the Axis strategy ostensibly called for Rommel to advance to the Egyptian frontier and then halt while Herkules overwhelmed Malta, thus liberating his supply routes from British air and sea attack. The main proponents of this strategy were Admiral Raeder, Kesselring, who wished to free up the Luftwaffe for other tasks, and Cavallero. Rommel and Hitler, reluctant converts to Herkules, welcomed the fall of Tobruk as an opportunity to surge into Egypt with no intervening Maltese phase.

Rommel's problem was that he lived permanently on the wrong side of what Clausewitz called "the culminating point of victory" — in short, such was Rommel's appetite for victory that he became oblivious to his own overextension. His dilemma lay not between an attack on Malta or Suez, but rather between an advance that at least held out the hope of victory and a defensive posture that would lead to certain defeat. Rommel believed that his very weakness required him to press forward rather than exhibit the patience to build a foundation for success. His philosophy of victory was founded on bluff and inducing confusion in the minds of the enemy. Forward motion also sustained his momentum through the capture of supplies that Axis logistics were able to deliver only erratically. He argued that stores seized at Tobruk and Matruh allowed him the logistical stretch to reach Cairo or Alexandria by the end of June without having to depend on the vagaries of seaborne supplies. He was also reluctant to afford the winded Eighth Army any respite while Kesselring withdrew air assets for a speculative invasion of Malta. The very weakness of his army required him to deploy his superior weaponry, good intelligence, able subordinate commanders, and psychological edge over British forces to retain the strategic initiative. To transition to the defensive, as the Italian *Commando Supremo* and even his own chief of staff Fritz Bayerlein urged him to do, was to invite a British counterattack that ultimately must result in defeat.[46]

Rommel was also drawn forward by intelligence based on Fellers decrypts that spoke of plummeting British morale and the massive destruction of tanks. This forward posture was endorsed by Hitler, skeptical of the success of an Italian-led invasion of Malta, and, since the victories at Gazala and Tobruk, fantasizing about the collapse of Britain's Middle East position in a gust of Arab insurrection. Keen to eliminate North Africa as a potential landing area for U.S. forces, Hitler also ignored Cavallero's argument that an advance into Egypt would make an Allied landing in French North Africa more, not less, likely. In the mind of the Führer, Rommel's argument that the Eighth Army was on the ropes and must not be allowed to catch a second breath was persuasive. He canceled Herkules and presented the Italians with a *fait accompli*. Mussolini, as usual on the prowl for cheap success, crossed to North Africa to prepare a triumphant entry into Cairo. On 23 June, Rommel was given permission to advance on Egypt.[47]

In the meantime, despite the easing of the air offensive against Malta caused by the transfer of planes to Russia and North Africa, the island seemed on the point of asphyxiation. Antiaircraft guns were practically out of ammunition, and the RAF was low on fuel and spare parts. The garrison seemed psychologically prepared to "go into the bag." Food became an obsession for everyone, and mass starvation was only temporarily averted by a bumper crop of tomatoes. Everyone, including Governor-general Lord Gort, was emaciated. Tuberculosis, pneumonia, pellagra, dysentery, and a stomach complaint popularly baptized "Malta Dog" were rampant. Infants and the elderly began to die in ever larger numbers. In a desperate effort to keep the island from surrender, Churchill organized a fourteen-ship convoy around the fast tanker *Ohio*, loaned by the United States. The "Pedestal" convoy, guarded by two battleships, four carriers, seven cruisers, thirty-three destroyers, and twenty-four submarines and minesweepers, as well as more than two hundred planes, cleared Gibraltar on 10 August. For the next four days it endured a massive sea and air assault by forces alerted to the convoy's approach by Axis intelligence. The carrier *Eagle* was sunk. On 13 August three battered freighters arrived at Valetta to be greeted by a population that sobbed with joy. The next morning, the *Ohio*, its decks awash and littered with the scattered carcass of a German bomber, arrived, under tow and lashed between two destroyers to keep her from sinking. Pedestal saved Malta, and allowed offensive operations to resume against Rommel's supply lines at the very moment that Rommel prepared for his first confrontation with Montgomery.[48]

Historians disagree over whether the Axis decision to spare Malta in the summer of 1942 really marked a turning point in the Mediterranean war. Surprisingly, perhaps, given its proclivity to dissent from many German strategic decisions taken during the war, the German official history sides with Hitler and Rommel, and concludes that the Axis lacked the power to seize the island in the summer of 1942. Rommel's only option was a *fuite en avant*.[49] Israeli historian Martin van Creveld goes even further, insisting that the British defense of Malta between 1940 and 1943 was so much wasted effort, because the Axis capture of Malta would not have alleviated Rommel's logistical difficulties. Lack of fuel for ships and escorts and Italian reluctance to risk ships on a dangerous route meant that supplies piled up in Italian ports that were never sent. Once supplies reached North Africa, limited port capacity there, the shortage of trucks and coastal shipping, mechanical wear and tear on trucks and drivers forced to traverse the huge distances between the ports and the front lines along the Via Balbia, not to mention the fuel consumption of motorized convoys, all contributed far more to Rommel's defeat than did Malta-based air and sea interdiction. The convoy battles fought out in the central Mediterranean did not decide Rommel's fate.[50] In fact, the overwhelming majority of maritime shipments sent from Italy actually reached North Africa.[51] British historians have tended to dissent from this view, pointing out that on several occasions Rommel's offensives were delayed, postponed, or failed because vital cargoes, especially fuel, were simply not able to penetrate the screen of Malta-based attacks. Therefore,

Malta denied Rommel the logistical margin, especially of fuel, necessary to allow him successfully to carry out maneuvers.[52]

In many respects, this is an artificial debate. Rommel's logistical problems arose both from convoy interdiction and from distribution difficulties once supplies reached North Africa. Malta was simply one vital piece in an elaborate British campaign against Rommel's supply lines. Ship sinkings rose in the late summer and autumn of 1942, the critical period when Rommel hammered on Egypt's door, in great part because the British put Ultra into the business of locating Italian convoys, sent submarines back to Malta, and stepped up RAF attacks on convoys identified by Ultra, especially those traversing the vital choke point of the Corinth Canal. The success of the British interdiction campaign was an important, though not decisive influence on the different outcomes at Gazala and at Alam Halfa and El Alamein.[53] For these reasons, Rommel failed to build up strategic stockpiles of fuel and ammunition to sustain his offensives. Therefore, he became dependent on "just in time" delivery to carry out operations. Even slight fluctuations in ship arrivals impacted his operational capability, as the Battle of Alam Halfa would demonstrate. Nor could Rommel's campaign of North African conquest be sustained indefinitely by the expedient of living off captured British supplies. The long-term effects of the attrition of naval and air assets on Axis ability to maintain a foothold in North Africa were also debilitating. World War II in the Mediterranean was a war of attrition. The Axis began the war in the Mediterranean with a shortage of cargo space. This problem only increased as ships and fuel expended in the attempt to supply Rommel in 1941 and 1942 were assets lost in the winter of 1942–43, when the retreat to Tunisia, with its superior port capacity, railways, and shorter supply lines should have eased his logistical problems while greatly complicating those of the Allies.[54] Malta remained an important base of attack against Axis lines of communication until the Axis surrender in Tunis in May 1943.

Strategically, the advantages offered by Malta to the British were those of the Mediterranean in microcosm. Malta was a place where the Royal Navy and the RAF could attack German strength residing in the Wehrmacht. The requirement to "neutralize" Malta distracted significant Luftwaffe assets and played a role in the shifting balance of power between the Luftwaffe and the RAF, as well as between Eighth Army and Panzerarmee Afrika, in the summer of 1942. Kesselring informed Rommel that he lacked the assets both to suppress Malta and to support Egypt. He pressed over five hundred planes into the supply effort to Egypt, Crete, and Greece. In August, as Rommel was preparing his attack against Montgomery's positions on Alam Halfa, fully 784 Axis aircraft were detached in a vain attempt to stop the Pedestal convoy from reaching Malta with its valuable supply of food and fuel. Much of the strategic reconnaissance of North African ports and air bases was carried out from Malta. Malta provided a stopover for bombers on the way from Gibraltar to Egypt. Finally, Malta was "one tiny bright flame in the darkness," as Roosevelt called it, whose loss would have dealt a serious blow to British morale.[55]

THE "FIRST ALAMEIN"[56]

The collapse of the Gazala line and the surrender of Tobruk came as close to humiliation as anything the Eighth Army had yet experienced in the desert. Having lost about half his troops and most of his armor, Auchinleck cast about for a place to make a stand. His first inclination was to set up a defensive screen on the Egyptian frontier, while he reorganized his shattered forces at Matruh. However, Rommel whipped his exhausted army forward, determined to allow the disorganized British army no respite. Therefore, Auchinleck dropped back to a place where the passage to Cairo narrows to a thirty-eight-mile strip that runs from a small railway station called El Alamein on the Mediterranean coast south to the Qattara Depression, a vast stretch of salt marshes and sand dunes impassable to tanks. The land in between offered a lunarlike landscape of sand flats, low hills, and razorback ridges, the most prominent of which were Ruweisat and Alam Halfa. Inside this unflankable thirty-eight-mile funnel, Auchinleck organized three principal strong points on low hills about fifteen miles apart. His plan was to canalize Rommel's advance between these fortresses with static elements, allowing British mobile forces organized into "artillery battle-groups" to slash at Rommel's flanks and rear. On 25 June, Auchinleck belatedly fired Ritchie and assumed direct command of the Eighth Army.

Rommel crossed the Egyptian frontier on 23 June, closely behind a British force that frantically detonated defensive positions, supply depots, and water points as it retreated. Although he boasted that his men were in an "aggressive and confident" mood,[57] early signs that Rommel's momentum had slowed were obvious. For starters, the RAF, not the Luftwaffe, ruled Egyptian skies. His attack, in the absence of adequate intelligence, on the British garrison at Matruh on 26–27 June, succeeded through sheer blind luck and the fighting qualities of his troops. Over eight thousand British POWs were taken, along with significant supplies. But Bernard Freyberg's Second New Zealand Division fought to the knife, sparing neither medical staff nor wounded in their largely successful efforts to break out. A more methodical resistance on Auchinleck's part against a force that numbered only fifty-two tanks, whose howitzers had spent their ammunition, in which water was strictly rationed, and that had outdistanced its air cover might have acutely embarrassed Rommel's advance. But the German commander took strength, rather than counsel, from his "brilliant victory" at Matruh. When, on 30 June, after an advance of 350 miles in ten days, Rommel reached the rudimentary British defenses at El Alamein less than one hundred miles from Alexandria, he resolved to attack.

Unable to outflank the British position, Rommel planned to charge Auchinleck head on in the hope of a breakthrough. But his intelligence imparted an imperfect idea of the strength and location of British units,[58] while his men were on the edge of exhaustion. But the British, too, were desperately short of armor and guns, their hastily laid-out positions offered inviting gaps between defensive "boxes," and their combat groups were frantically scraped together from rear-echelon personnel.[59] Rommel's opening attack, launched in suffocating heat and in the teeth of a sandstorm on the late afternoon of 30 June, collided on the following day with a tenacious resistance put up by Indian and New Zealand forces, backed by virtually unimpeded RAF bombing. Rommel settled into the very slogging match that his opening attack had been designed to preclude. Lack of Luftwaffe support robbed him of reconnaissance and air cover. The enemy had overrun Rommel's radio-intercept service and captured his valuable codebooks. The intelligence windfall revealed to the British the eye-popping consequences of their lax radio procedures, and the damage done by the Fellers decrypts. The American attaché was packed off home, silencing a most fruitful source of intelligence on the state of British preparations and intentions. The forfeit of his Sigint and limited air reconnaissance condemned Rommel to fight blind, thrusts that Auchinleck, armed with Ultra and Y Service intercepts as well as air reconnaissance photos, was able to anticipate and to parry.[60] The Italians and Germans frantically flew in reinforcements, including paratroop units scheduled to attack Malta. But these troops came without vehicles and taxed German mobility still further. The booty captured at Tobruk took time to redistribute and did not fill all needs. Rommel had no spare parts for the captured British vehicles on which he depended for mobility and logistical support. He demanded a reinforced air umbrella to counter the heavy RAF day and night bombing of his rear areas. But Kesselring reminded him that because half of the Axis bombers in North Africa had been withdrawn to attack Malta once Rommel and Hitler decided not to invade, not enough planes were left adequately to support the Panzerarmee, much less bomb the enticing sprawl of British logistical complexes.[61] He also pointed out to Rommel that he could not continue to tolerate "a two-sided threat to our supply lines—from Malta and Alexandria."[62] Some of Rommel's divisions were reduced to an effective strength of 1,500 men, while his two armored divisions had slipped to twenty and six tanks respectively by 3 July. British bombing made supply difficult, even at night, and exacted a heavy psychological toll on his men. Rommel finally called off his attack on 3 July after the Ariete (armored) Division scattered under a New Zealand assault, abandoning most of its artillery.

The third of July 1942 marked the turning point of the North African campaign.[63] Although Rommel would try to resume his role as pursuer, the simple fact was that the British were no longer on the run. It was Rommel who now transitioned from hunter to prey. The shift in momentum in the Mediterranean was temporarily veiled by the surrender of 90,000 Soviet troops at Sebastopol and the savaging of Arctic convoy PQ 17. On 4 July, USAAF bombers joined the campaign in Western Europe.

During the next days, Rommel attempted to consolidate and extend his position to the Qattara Depression, while fending off British counterattacks. On 10 July, the Italian Sabratha Division melted into captivity under an attack of the newly arrived Ninth Australian Division—the "Rats of Tobruk" of the 1941 siege—who also terminated the distinguished career of the 621st Long-Range Reconnaissance Company, a vital component of Rommel's fast-shrinking intelligence capability. A renewal of the Australian attack on the following day (11 July) overran Bersaglieri and Trieste Division positions. Rommel moved to redistribute his German divisions as "corset bones" to stiffen the Italians, whose positions, betrayed by Ultra, were singled out for British assault. New Zealand and Indian units virtually destroyed the Brescia and Pavia Divisions on 15 July, as thirty-one more Spitfires flew into Malta from the carrier *Eagle*. But the New Zealanders in particular paid a heavy price when the Fifteenth Panzer Division rode to the rescue. On 17 July the Trieste Division was again savaged by the Australians. British success continued to be curtailed by their serial inability to coordinate all arms operations and the absence of a unified command concept among British planners.[64] By the time fighting came to an exhausted and inconclusive end on 27 July, the day Rostov fell to Army Group B, neither side had managed a breakthrough, although both had sustained significant casualties, none more so than the New Zealanders.[65]

By tossing in every available Axis unit to plug the gap, Rommel had succeeded in stanching the British advance. But Rommel's gamble on sustaining his forward momentum in the hope of reaching the Nile Delta had failed, and left him in a difficult situation. After three weeks of waiting in Libya to make his triumphal entry into Cairo, Mussolini boarded the plane for the return flight in a sour mood. On 3 August, Churchill arrived in Cairo on an American Liberator aircraft. He did not like what he saw. Auchinleck had taken advantage of Rommel's overextension to halt his advance. But he had produced only stalemate, not victory. Given the British commander's inherent faith in mobility, belief in the decentralization of command, and propensity to organize his army into ad hoc "battle groups," Churchill concluded that victory was unlikely to occur on Auchinleck's watch. The prime minister found Auchinleck's briefing uninspired. When Auchinleck's "uniquely stupid" chief of staff, General T. Corbett, informed Churchill that he was to take over command of the Eighth Army, Churchill was appalled. His tours of Eighth Army units revealed a "baffled and somewhat unhinged organization." Clearly, the British commander in the Middle East had failed to infuse a sense of purpose and direction into his command. Auchinleck's refusal to commit to an offensive in Egypt to help Operation Torch was the last straw.[66] After experimenting with some combinations, Churchill finally settled on General Harold Alexander, Eisenhower's deputy for the projected North Africa landings, to replace Auchinleck as the Commander-in-Chief Middle East. At Imperial General Staff Chief Alan Brooke's suggestion, Lieutenant General Bernard Montgomery, head of South-Eastern Command, was named to lead the Eighth Army after General Sir William Gott, Churchill's first choice, was killed on 7 August when his plane was shot down. American marines landed on Guadalcanal, and Eisenhower was chosen to lead Torch. Auchinleck became commander-in-chief in India as Wavell was elevated to viceroy. As he departed for Moscow on 10 August, Churchill informed Alexander that "your primary and main duty will be to take and destroy at the earliest opportunity the German-Italian Army commanded by Field Marshal Rommel together with all its supplies and establishments in Egypt and Libya . . . [This] must be considered paramount in His Majesty's interests."[67]

CHAPTER SIX

Monty's War: El Alamein—
The Unnecessary Battle?

THE AUTUMN OF 1942 marked the turning point of the war. The German summer advance to the gates of Egypt, the Volga, and the Caucasus Mountains was halted, then reversed, first at El Alamein and then at Stalingrad. It is certainly possible to argue that a German victory in either battle might have sent the war off on another trajectory. Britain's leaders feared that a Soviet collapse could open the Middle East to an invasion from the north. This, in turn, might put France, Spain, and Turkey firmly into the Axis camp. The success of Torch and the fate of Malta seemed to be on the table at El Alamein. British failure to deliver victory could have jeopardized the U.S. commitment to Churchill's Mediterranean strategy, led to a premature invasion of the European continent in 1943 that probably would have failed, and caused a shift of U.S. assets to the Pacific.[1] The nightmare scenario for the Allies was an unfavorable outcome in the Mediterranean, combined with the loss of Stalingrad followed by a Soviet peace overture to Hitler, with the consequence that the Axis would win the war.

On the other hand, although the outcome of neither battle was a foregone conclusion, it is difficult to conjure up a convincing scenario for a German victory so long as the Allies kept their nerve. Churchill seemed at a low ebb politically in the summer of 1942. The disastrous

Dieppe raid of 19 August and heavy shipping losses in the Atlantic combined with the defeat at Gazala and the fall of Tobruk to revive charges of strategic mismanagement and failure to find a general capable of delivering victory. But his burgeoning strategic partnership with Franklin Roosevelt and the fact that Churchill had no serious rival for the premiership made him politically bulletproof. Churchill's handy defeat of the no-confidence vote in the Commons on 1 July shattered Hitler's illusion that appeasers in Britain would force Churchill out of office and sue for peace. "Area bombing" from the spring of 1942 brought the war to the doorstep of the German people. At the very moment that Rommel had run out of steam in Egypt, Hitler speculated that sluggish progress on the Eastern Front might accelerate with an assist from the Mediterranean.[2] But as usual, the Führer's vision outran reality. For all his operational brilliance, Rommel could deliver only stalemate in North Africa, and stalemate did not put time on the side of the Axis. Rommel's inability twice to break through to Egypt drove him to the edge of psychological and moral collapse because it offered irrefutable evidence that the Axis had run out the line on their operational capabilities in North Africa.[3]

The vast American juggernaut was rumbling into play by the summer of 1942. American production was kicking into high gear, with new equipment arriving daily in North Africa. Torch, planned for the autumn, would bring U.S. ground forces into direct contact with Axis troops in the Mediterranean, sealing an American commitment to that theater that promised to balloon. The landing of Allied troops in French North Africa would strike Rommel in the rear. Churchill argued that Torch "would be greatly helped by a battle won in the Western Desert,"[4] because a British victory would influence the attitude of the French. But the French seemed oblivious to a battle fought two thousand miles from Algiers. Indeed, French attitudes were influenced more by the strength of Anglo-American forces in Algeria and Morocco than by the fate of Rommel in Egypt. But win or lose at El Alamein, an Allied menace from the west would sooner or later suck Panzerarmee Afrika out of Egypt to defend its lines of communication with Tripoli. Even factoring in the successful Axis invasion and defense of Tunisia in December 1942, at the very least it was logistically impossible for the Axis to defend two North African fronts situated almost 1,500 miles apart. Torch would force Rommel to retreat. Therefore, from a strategic perspective, El Alamein was a battle that need not have been fought.

But if the Battle of El Alamein lacked a strategic rationale, for Churchill its political purpose was transparent. El Alamein offered Britain its last solo performance of World War II. From November 1942, the hitherto dramatic Afrika Korps–Eighth Army duel in the desert would be subsumed into the larger Allied enterprise. It would shed its comparatively chivalric qualities and join in character, if not in scale, the industrial war being fought on the Eastern Front. El Alamein offered a final opportunity for the British army to prove that it had—at long last—mastered the techniques of modern warfare. It would wipe away memories of British debacles in France in 1940, Greece, Crete, Singapore, Gazala, and Tobruk, and demonstrate to the world that British soldiers could fight. For Churchill, this would vindicate his commitment to the Mediterranean, and dull parliamentary criticism of his strategic missteps there. Victory at El Alamein would prove that it was not Churchill's strategic judgment that was at fault. Culpability, rather, lay with his generals' inability to operationalize his strategy. Victory at El Alamein would demonstrate to Roosevelt that Britain was a worthy ally, and assert Britain's credibility and weight in the Western Alliance. The elements of British success had been assembled in North Africa. Churchill required a commander able to translate the quantitative edge that the Eighth Army had enjoyed over Rommel for a year into a qualitative superiority.

Bernard Law Montgomery was not Churchill's first choice to lead the Eighth Army. Indeed, Montgomery might well have finished a rancorous and unpopular major general had it not been for the patronage of the chief of the Imperial General Staff, Alan Brooke. A corps commander in France in 1940, Brooke had picked out Montgomery, a small, intensely competitive man with an angular, almost ratlike face, as one of the few capable division commanders in the British Expeditionary Force. Evacuated at Dunkirk, Montgomery spent the next two years in corps commands, eventually rising to lead South-Eastern Command, where he distinguished himself as a trainer of troops. However, Montgomery's competitive character and outspoken views expressed with undiplomatic candor made him such a controversial figure that neither Wavell nor Auchinleck reached down to pluck him for important jobs in the Middle East or Burma. Montgomery had been quietly warned after Dunkirk to contain his public criticism of his superiors. He took no notice. If anything, promotion, victory, and his growing reputation combined to shrink what little restraint remained. "In defeat, indomitable; in victory, insufferable," should have been Montgomery's motto, according to desert wits. He treated his superior Harold Alexander with barely disguised contempt and belittled the fighting abilities of American soldiers and the capabilities of U.S. and Canadian generals, as he shamelessly promoted the exploits of *his* Eighth Army. British First Army commander General Kenneth Anderson was declared by Monty to be "completely unfit to command an Army; he must be far above his ceiling and I should say Divisional Command is probably his level."[5] The fact that Montgomery was correct failed to endear him to his critics. Even his patron Brooke shied away from offering him an important combat role for fear that Monty would "do something silly."[6] "God's not feeling well," Saint Peter said to the psychiatrist. "Thinks he's Monty," ran a favorite anti-Montgomery joke. But the dearth of winning generals in the British army meant that Montgomery's chance was fast approaching, *faute de mieux.* His slow shuffle to the head of the queue had made him the commander designate of the British First Army for Torch. But Montgomery seems to have been barely a blip on Churchill's radar screen until Brooke and even Auchinleck, who had borne the brunt of Montgomery's scathing disparagement, recommended him to command the Eighth Army in August 1942. Churchill preferred General Sir William "Strafer" Gott, a young and dynamic corps commander in the Eighth Army. But he acquiesced in Montgomery's appointment after Gott was killed on the way to take up his command when his plane was shot down.

At first glance, Montgomery possessed just those qualities of caution, deliberation, and an insistence on matériel superiority before he would act that Churchill had deplored in both Wavell and Auchinleck. A childhood starved of affection and a Tasmanian upbringing combined with a career spent in unfashionable infantry regiments and colonial postings to make Montgomery a true outsider in the upper echelons of the British army. Worse, it left him a psychological and social cripple. The rough humor and bullying that had characterized Monty's passage through the schoolyard matured into tactless conceit as he rose in rank and reputation. Montgomery's professional self-confidence slithered over into vanity after his victory at El Alamein. Monty knew all the answers, which he delivered with the bold certitude of a Vatican encyclical. "He has an exceptionally small head," U.S. General George Patton observed. "That may explain things."[7] Although Monty's multitude of critics considered him a conceited, unimaginative plodder, his opinions were founded on both experience and mature reflection. World War I had taught him the futility of lavishing casualties on poorly conceived and ill-planned operations. In the interwar years, he remained the heretic of the cult of panzer worship that gripped the imagination of theorists of armored warfare and "tank armies" like Sir Basil Liddell Hart and his army acolytes. He was acutely conscious from the end of 1942 that matériel must be used unsparingly to economize on Britain's rapidly diminishing manpower pool and bolster the fragile morale of his conscript army.

In many respects, the Sahara offered the perfect competitive arena for two highly individualistic outsiders. With Rommel, Montgomery shared egotism, vanity, and a burning desire to prove himself within a military establishment that regarded him as something less than a gentleman. Each man sought to induce an appropriately ascetic frame of mind to fight in the wastes of North Africa—Monty renounced both tobacco and alcohol so as better to focus his energies on the war. Rommel, "virtually a non-drinker and a non-smoker" in any case, ate so little on campaign that a special cook was procured for him and fresh fruits and vegetables were flown to North Africa to alleviate his chronic illnesses.[8] But otherwise, the two men were professional opposites. Surprise, improvisation, and *coup d'oeil* were not Montgomery's strong suits. He remained the pope of infantry, the impresario of the Queen of Battle, an agnostic of any operational theory that relied for success on extemporization, delegation of unsupervised command responsibility, and the disorganization and demoralization of the enemy.

The British general's style was calculated, deliberate, attritional. He left little to chance, but was a stickler for training and "battle drills" on the German model, to ensure that the discrete parts of his army worked to a common objective. Alan Moorehead noted Montgomery's "messianic desire to make converts and to prove his doctrines were the right ones."[9] The Eighth Army's intelligence chief was amazed that, unlike Auchinleck, Montgomery actually paid attention to intelligence, because it gave him an insight into Rommel's mind.[10] Monty was no château general like Wavell and Auchinleck. He commanded from the forward edge of the battlefield, from a mobile field headquarters, and insisted that his subordinate commanders do so as well. But neither was he a Rommel-style leader who surveyed the front lines from a Storch aircraft, landing long enough to improvise battle groups, redirect attacks, and exhort troops to greater efforts in the hope of achieving a knockout blow. On the contrary, Montgomery minutely planned his attacks in advance, and then he spent most battles reading or writing letters. He disliked being awakened except in the most dire emergencies. A battle was a work of art. But fighting was not like throwing paint at a canvas. Monty designed his battles in a classical style, as things to be carefully composed, nurtured, modified, and adjusted.

Montgomery's ruthlessness and narcissism should not be confused with callousness. He cared about his soldiers. He was very conscious of the fact that his command was an army of civilians, whose purpose was to defend a democracy and restore the status quo in Europe. Montgomery is hailed (or damned) as the British general who stopped trying to imitate Rommel and instead applied an operational and tactical style adapted to his civilian force. The stunning metamorphosis of the Eighth Army under Montgomery from the "army that couldn't shoot straight" to the gravediggers of the Afrika Korps laid waste to the lame stab-in-the-back alibis advanced by his less successful predecessors, who blamed their lack of success on inadequate matériel, Churchill's interference, or the failure of British soldiers' fighting spirit. Old desert sweats at first dismissed Monty as just another London-imposed "Ingleezi." But he quickly smashed their "desert trade unions" run by the Guards, the Greenjackets, and the cavalry.

Unlike Rommel, however, Monty's vanity never led him to sacrifice men for his own glory and self-aggrandizement. His often clumsy and ill-conceived showmanship was dismissed in Guards regiments and the Cavalry Club as Monty's contrivance of "playing to the prols," further evidence that the Eighth Army commander was not the "right sort." But it was calculated to win the affections of his men, to animate and imprint his personality on his command. For this reason, Montgomery was known to his staff as "Master" or "the Oracle."[11] Montgomery adapted to, and molded, the bohemian style of the Desert Army inspired mainly by Anzacs eager to distinguish themselves from more pukka British units. Dressed in a black beret, corduroy trousers, and gray sweater, he projected a casual disregard for formal military custom that helped to amalgamate a mongrel force cobbled together from the farthest ends of the British empire. "Montgomery had given the men a tremendous eagerness and there was always a stir along the road when the general drove past, a black beret on his head, his lean ascetic face looking always intent and preoccupied," Moorehead recorded. The Desert Army that rode into Tunisia after their epic 1,500-mile march from El Alamein in their odd assortment of British, German, and Italian vehicles all painted desert yellow, looked as if it had been equipped in a Cairo rummage sale. The men, "too gaunt and lean to be handsome, too hard and sinewy to be graceful, too youthful and physical to be complete," had nevertheless developed the arrogant swagger of conquerors. They had even acquired their own slang, a sort of bastardized Arabic so incomprehensible that Tunisian Arabs, who quickly adopted some of the expressions, assumed they were speaking English.[12]

Montgomery's immediate senior as commander-in-chief in the Middle East was General Harold Alexander. In some respects, the two offered a balanced command team, as Alexander compensated for some of Montgomery's more public shortcomings. A strikingly handsome aristocrat educated at Harrow and Sandhurst before being commissioned in the Irish Guards in 1910, Alexander was celebrated in the army for both his courage and his charm. Harold Macmillan found Alexander to be an understated personality, "with a quiet and whimsical humor."[13] He emerged from the trenches of the Western Front and

a two-year campaign fighting Communists in Latvia as a highly decorated thirty-one-year-old lieutenant colonel and one of the British
army's coming men. However, Alexander demonstrated in full measure the British gentry's respect for martial valor over intellect, at least
in the eyes of two of his Staff College instructors in 1926, Alan Brooke
and Bernard Montgomery. "[We] concluded that he had no brains—
and we were right!" Montgomery insisted with characteristic diplomacy. But intellect counted as a dubious asset in an army that prized
family connections, the right schools, fashionable regiments, and
an affable disposition. Conspicuous, if not brilliant, service on India's
Northwest Frontier caused Alexander to be regarded as a competent
regimental soldier with a sound grasp of tactics. Dunkirk in 1940 was
his finest hour. By extricating his division from almost certain capture,
he confirmed his reputation in Churchill's eyes and assured his promotion to corps command. But Brooke remained skeptical of Alexander's mastery of armored forces. Nor did Alexander's brief command
in Burma in 1942, where he presided over a thousand-mile retreat in
the face of inferior Japanese forces, burnish his reputation in the
CIGS's eyes.

Officially, Alexander ranks as one of World War II's great soldiers.
No one else besides Eisenhower secured the surrender of two army
groups, one in Tunisia, the second in Italy. Alexander's strengths were
his diplomacy, his sense of duty, and his reputation as a fighting soldier. Setbacks failed to agitate his Olympian calm. He worked well
with Eisenhower and had the "adulation of his American subordinates," according to Omar Bradley,[14] a vast asset when orchestrating a
frequently factious multinational coalition. His diplomacy helped to
contain the fallout from some of Montgomery's more outrageous
proclamations. At the same time, he understood that the self-centered
Montgomery was, at this stage of the war, the only general among the
Western Allies capable of delivering success. So he gave Montgomery
his head despite Monty's practically serial insubordination.

Alexander's "diplomatic" personality qualified him to suffer the
tantrums of prima donna generals that the Mediterranean seemed to
manufacture on an almost industrial scale. While his admirers, like
Harold Macmillan, believed his technique of leading by "auto-

suggestion" remarkably effective, others ascribed it to an absence of character. Montgomery interpreted Alexander's unflappable charm as evidence of intellectual vacuity and a screen that masked a fundamental indecisiveness. Fighting generals in the Mediterranean—Montgomery, Patton, Mark Clark, Oliver Leese—regarded Alexander as a "straw man," an empty tunic suited to the ambassadorial requirements of coalition warfare. They felt that they "carried" him with their victories, over which he presided but to which he contributed practically nothing. They took advantage of his reluctance to act forcefully and paid scant attention to his "suggestions." Indeed, Montgomery treated Alexander with an unvarnished contempt that shocked even the blunt Patton. Monty's advice to Mark Clark was to "just tell [Alex] to go to hell" if he received orders he did not care to execute.[15] Alexander's reserve little influenced the course of the war so long as he had to deal only with Montgomery. But as the Americans became ever more important players and the war moved to the north shores of the Mediterranean, friction inevitably developed between highly competitive generals that Alexander lacked the intellectual stature and force of character to mediate. He proved too diffident, too shy of exerting his authority, too "constitutionally lazy," to force his factious subordinates to cooperate. He abhorred staff work, and found it difficult to grasp the context of a battle. He lacked the temperament required for higher command. For these reasons, he was usually content to let events take their course rather than set policy, plan ahead, take the initiative, and "grip" the campaign. Brooke believed Alexander out of his depth as a strategist, and in Italy sent General Sir John Harding to create a staff machine and to provide him with some ideas. Unfortunately, Harding's ideas espoused through Alexander were uniformly bad ones—oppose the invasion of southern France (Anvil) and attack Germany through the Ljubljana Gap—especially because they brought out the worst in Churchill's romantic imagination.[16]

The army that Montgomery and Alexander inherited in August 1942 was, in Churchill's words, "oppressed by a sense of bafflement and uncertainty."[17] This was not merely a prime ministerial justification of the leadership surgery he had been obliged to perform. One of Auchinleck's senior staff officers wrote that his command was "in a rather bewildered state . . . They have just lost a big battle, which they felt they ought to have won." The Eighth Army had taken 102,000 battle casualties since November 1941 and had nothing to show for it.[18] Some blamed setbacks on inferior equipment. Others sought generational explanations, laying the blame for shortcomings in British military performance on the fact that the World War II generation was simply inferior to their World War I fathers. Wavell, noting that British troops were too quick to surrender rather than fight their way out of tight situations, concluded that "for the time being we have lost a good deal of our hardness and fighting spirit."[19] The director of military operations believed that "[the British] are undoubtedly softer, as a nation, than any of our enemies, except the Italians."[20] Cairo was full of "free Britishers," deserters who paid native thieves to "knock us blokes about and pinch our pay books."[21] British desertion rates were so high in Egypt in 1942 that Auchinleck asked the war cabinet to reinstate the death penalty for desertion.[22] The problem was that the British, like the Americans, were a conscript force raised by a democratic society that could not be disciplined and ordered to fight as if they were men with a military vocation. They had to be handled sensitively by leaders who understood their limitations. Montgomery was always careful to tailor his battle plan to the capabilities of his soldiers. Once his troops achieved victory, their confidence and pride in themselves grew, and one could place greater demands on them.

Most agreed, however, that for a year and a half the Eighth Army had been outfought and outgeneraled by Rommel. Auchinleck and Ritchie had failed to meld the Eighth Army into a coherent force. The British generals had been too clever by half, shattering units and then reassembling them into "brigade groups" and "battle groups," all in the name of "flexibility." An army "broken into a thousand fragments" had forfeited the ability to focus its superior power, and was instead overwhelmed brigade by brigade while the rest of the army looked on like spectators, or arrived too late to help. Infantry, armor, and the RAF were not cooperating, and the superiority of British artillery was forfeited because there was no central control of the guns. Attacks that should have succeeded in July when the Italians were at the end of their tether and the Germans were hard pressed to carry the entire burden faltered because, Montgomery believed, of "gross mismanagement, faulty command, and bad staff work." Repeated failure and loss of confidence in the high command had denied the heterogeneous collection of nationalities and units that composed the Eighth Army any faith in themselves. Without a sense of victory as an entitlement, there was nothing to bind the Eighth Army together, give it purpose, strengthen its discipline, or stop too many of its soldiers from surrendering when hard fighting would bring salvation.[23]

According to his biographer, Montgomery arrived in Cairo on 12 August 1942 "with a vengeance." "The troops had their tails right down," the Eighth Army's new commander noted. He made a quick tour of the front, moved Auchinleck's Spartan and flyblown headquarters on the Ruweisat Ridge close to the sea and out of German artillery range, and told his new chief of staff, Brigadier Freddie de Guingand, to issue an order announcing that the Eighth Army would fight on its existing positions on the El Alamein line "alive or dead." "Brigade groups" and "battle groups" were as passé as Auchinleck's "mobility and fluidity" fighting style. The Eighth Army would now fight in divisions. His one concession to Teutonic military organization was to create what he called a *corps de chasse* of three armored divisions and one infantry division equipped with the American Sherman tanks donated by Roosevelt. This *corps de chasse*, which he designated as his Tenth Corps under the command of Herbert Lumsden, later replaced by Brian Horrocks, was obviously inspired by the Afrika Korps, though heavier in armor.[24] Monty had begun to infuse the Eighth Army with a sense of purpose and self-confidence. One officer remembered Monty's addresses to the troops as "straight out of school speech-day," but he gave the impression that at last someone had "got a grip."[25] Churchill noted "a complete change of atmosphere" on his return to Cairo from Moscow on 19 August.[26] The morale boost was due in no small part to the influx of equipment, especially three hundred new Sherman tanks. But these could not arrive in time to stave off a German buildup of tanks, artillery, and antitank guns that presaged Rommel's imminent offensive.

Oddly, Montgomery's new command found their general remarkably poised as he prepared to confront the scourge of the Eighth Army.

Montgomery was already absorbed by preparations for his own autumn offensive against Rommel, and regarded the imminent Axis assault as merely a holding action. He divined that Rommel's attack would be a repeat of that on the Gazala line: a night start would break through the British desert flank at El Himeimat and race for thirty miles over open desert. At dawn it would turn north to roll up the British position from the south. Ultra forwarded Rommel's 15 August situation report which told of his concentration in front of the southern portion of the Alamein line for a breakthrough, a concentration confirmed by air reconnaissance. As a consequence, Axis formations there became the target of round-the-clock bombing from 21 August. This time Rommel would not succeed, however, for at least four reasons. First, there was no surprise. Montgomery had integrated an "Ultra intelligence team" into his staff, so as better to process information forwarded from Bletchley Park, the "Government Code and Cypher School" located north of London. Ultra intelligence, backed by Y Service decrypts and air reconnaissance, gave advanced warning of the attack.[27] Second, the Qattara Depression constricted Rommel's room to maneuver. Unlike the Gazala line, which had been vulnerable to an outflanking maneuver, the narrow front offered by the Alamein position turned his attack into a frontal assault.[28] Third, Montgomery had no intention of replicating Auchinleck's system of "boxes" that could be isolated and conquered piecemeal. He planned to have an interlocking front line solidly anchored on the Ruweisat and Alam Halfa Ridges, which he would not abandon because they were the keys to the coming battle. Fourth, rather than commit his tanks to an encounter battle where they could be impaled on Rommel's 88s, Montgomery dug them in on the Alam Halfa ridge, and forced Rommel to come onto his antitank guns or shun battle. "Lure the Germans on," he said. "Everything dug in. And let Rommel come on . . . down the side of the ridge . . . And then when the moment comes, we come in at his soft stuff . . . It's a case of dog eat rabbit."[29]

For his part, Rommel understood that he must attack the Eighth Army in a last bid to take the Nile Delta before growing British strength based on U.S. assistance put that objective beyond reach. In any case, he had no choice because Hitler and Mussolini had made it clear that they wanted Egypt.[30] The announcement of Montgomery's appointment barely registered with the Axis commander. He continued to count on British command ineptitude and their habit of trying to "hunt" his panzers with their pathetic "battle groups." Nor was Rommel well served by his intelligence. The capture of 621 Radio Intercept Company on 10 July had revealed the Fellers leaks while at the same time destroying his radio intercept service, which he was able to reconstruct only on the eve of the battle in late August. This meant that the German picture of British strength was incomplete.[31] Rommel's force counted almost 40,000 German troops and 30,000 Italians, many of whom were sick, as was their commander, and all of whom were battle-weary. More ominous for the British was the gathering of at least 230 German tanks, over 170 of which were "specials" with hardened front armor and 50 mm guns, together with 26 PzKw IV Specials armed with a 75 mm gun. Against this, the British could only muster 71 Grants and a motley assortment of 400 obsolete, lightly gunned Valentines, Matildas, Stuarts, and Crusaders. Nor did the Allied antitank gun possess much of a punch. According to American General Lloyd Fredendall, "the only way to hurt a kraut with a 37mm. anti-tank gun is to catch him and give him an enema with it."[32]

But Rommel had considerable problems nevertheless. While Hitler insisted that the Panzerarmee be kept fully equipped, he refused to authorize the staff and support troops Rommel required to manage his operations. Rommel's summer losses had not been made good, in part because the decision to bypass Malta, combined with the British mustering of Ultra intercepts to pinpoint supply shipments from Italy to North Africa,[33] meant that cargo deliveries to North Africa were down by 43.5 percent. And while ammunition and rations were adequate, his shortage of petrol was a constant source of worry that caused him to postpone his offensive until the end of the month and to consider limiting his objective to the destruction of the Eighth Army (rather than a push to Suez).[34] His relations with the Italians had hit a nadir since July, when he had fired a screed to Berlin complaining of lax discipline, low morale, and the lapses of Italian troops in battle. Rommel's stinging rebuke of Italian performance forced the Duce on 22 July to offer a humiliating apology to Hitler. Rommel also won the right to report directly to *Commando Supremo* in Rome, rather than to General Bastico in Tripoli. Rommel even attributed his supply shortages to Italian malfeasance.[35] The Luftwaffe numbered 450 serviceable planes to 400 in the Desert Air Force. But the British counted another 140 medium and 25 heavy bombers that could fly in from Palestine, as well as a small force of U.S. Army Air Force planes. The USAAF inventory included B-25 two-engine "Mitchell" medium bombers, named for Billy Mitchell, a pioneer of American air power. Jimmy Doolittle had led sixteen specially modified B-25s to Tokyo in April 1942. Later versions of the B-25 were fitted with a 75 mm–caliber M4 cannon in the nose, fourteen machine guns, and eight rocket racks under the wings. This formidable armament, together with its normal 2,000-pound bomb load, made the B-25 an impressive ground support weapon. The USAAF fighter component consisted of Curtis P-40 Kittyhawk IIs. The P-40, designed in 1937, was the most conspicuous U.S. fighter in the first two years of the war, and, like the Mitchell B-25, also saw service with the RAF. Armed with six 50-caliber machine guns and capable of a respectable 367 miles per hour, the Kittyhawk was considered superior to the Hawker Hurricane but was outperformed by the Spitfire and Bf. 109. Therefore it was usually assigned to ground support, rather than interceptor, tasks. The Axis planes were often grounded for lack of fuel, or were distracted by attacks on Alexandria and against the Pedestal convoy fighting its way through to Malta.

"THE SIX-DAY RACE"

Rommel's attack kicked off at 10 p.m. on 30 August with enough fuel for four and one-half days of operation.[36] It hit disaster almost immediately when it snagged on minefields between Alam Nayil and El Himeimat that were deeper and more complete than expected. This was a predictable consequence of inadequate reconnaissance of the southern portion of the line through which his attack was to pass for fear of alerting the British. Throughout the night, as sappers worked feverishly to clear a path through the mines, British artillery and the Desert Air Force, guided by flares, pummeled the exposed and inert Panzerarmee Afrika. The able commander of the Twenty-first Panzer

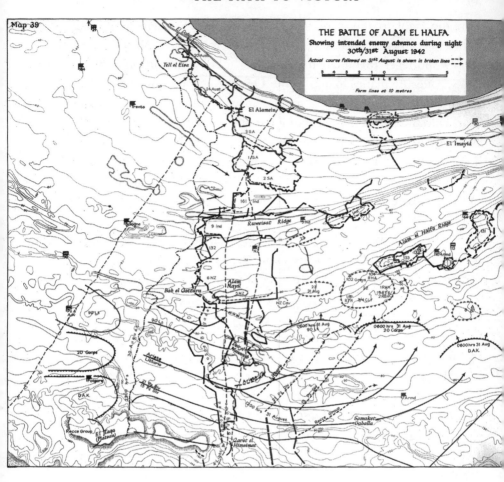

Division, Major General Georg von Bismarck, was killed, while General Walter Nehring, leader of the Afrika Korps, was badly wounded. By 8:30 on the morning of 31 August, Rommel's panzers had broken clear of the minefield. But the Italians, without mine detectors, were still entangled in it, badly dislocating the timetable of an army that, by now, should have been slashing into British positions thirty miles to the east. The instinct of a commander who counted on speed and surprise to carry the day was to cancel the attack and consolidate, using the British minefields as defensive cover. Rommel dithered for two hours before he finally elected to forge ahead to recoup his sunk costs in casualties. His tanks struck out eastward over the open desert under the merciful cover of a sandstorm, moving parallel to the Alam Halfa ridge to their left, the key to the British position. A combination of the lack of fuel and fear of leaving British tanks on his flanks forced him to turn north "earlier than we had intended."[37]

This was precisely what Montgomery had calculated that Rommel must do if he lacked fuel, if he had been delayed by the minefield, or if the Desert Air Force had punished him severely. In this expectation, Montgomery had prepared a lethal killing ground. As the German tanks became bogged down in soft sand (forcing them to consume yet more precious fuel), the dog began to eat the rabbit. British tanks, artillery, and antitank guns dug in on a solid defense line running from the New Zealand position on Alam Nayil to the west to Alam Halfa on the east began to hammer Rommel's static forces. Rommel waited in vain for the British mobile "battle groups" to sally forth, as in the days of Auchinleck and Ritchie, to be dismantled by 88s. At dusk, the Desert Air Force reappeared. All night long under a flare-lit sky and into the next morning, the RAF slashed at the Axis forces with an intensity not yet seen in the desert, "as if on a practice run," complained a German battle diary.[38] Hot shards of shrapnel sang through the German positions, their lethal effects multiplied by rock splinters. Burning vehicles and a pall of smoke cast an eerie light over the battlefield. As daylight broke, British tanks and artillery took up the relay. The Fifteenth Panzer Division tried to swing around the east flank of the Twenty-second Armoured Brigade to attack the ridge head on. The Twenty-first Panzer Division could not support it for lack of fuel. British fighters denied Stuka dive-bombers their plunging, high-altitude attacks, the high wail of their sirens announcing to troops below the arrival of their lethal ordnance. Instead, the planes that had pummeled Warsaw in 1939, terrorized the Western Front in May–June 1940, and laid waste to Valetta, were corralled into stealthy, flat, silent, and inaccurate bombing runs. By noon on 1 September, British tanks had sealed off Rommel's advance to the north and east, while the impassable Qattara Depression blocked movement to the south. His men were exhausted and their nerves shot from two nights without sleep under a perpetual bombardment. The final blow came with the news that the tanker *Abruzzi* with 611 tons of fuel had been disabled by British air attacks off Benghazi.[39] Rommel, whose attack counted for success on this "just in time" fuel delivery, had no choice but to retrace his steps beneath a punishing RAF bombardment to his original start line. His retreat began on the next day, accompanied by exhortations to the Luftwaffe to defend their Panzerarmee comrades.

Even in victory, Montgomery was faulted for failing to "settle accounts with the Axis spearhead" and "[finish] the North African Campaign at one stroke." Rommel was desperately overextended, vulnerable to an annihilating counterstroke that would sever him from his base and smash him with artillery. This wasted opportunity, critics complained, defined Montgomery's style, and hence the character of his command. The Eighth Army "would eschew the battle of manoeuvre and, with the finest equipment, bring the enemy down to its own pace just as one has often seen a slow polo team put the brake on the harder riding side," wrote British General Sir Francis Tuker.[40] But Montgomery saw Alam Halfa simply as stage one, realizing his initial goal, of a two-stage battle. Why risk the armor he needed for his autumn offensive, or sacrifice infantry not yet trained to the standards he intended, before he launched an offensive against an opponent as formidable as Rommel? To underline this point, Montgomery needed only to indicate the fate of Freyberg's crack New Zealanders, who took almost 700 casualties when they attacked Rommel's retreating forces on the night of 3–4 September. Monty's defensive victory had raised the morale of his army and instilled faith in their commander, restored confidence in ultimate Allied success, and given him an important psychological edge over his vaunted opponent. And while his lack of aggressiveness appears to have allowed the Axis to retrieve most of their disabled armor, British intelligence estimated damage to guns and "soft" transport to have been significant.[41]

The failure at Alam Halfa left the Axis camp firmly in the clutches of denial. They had triumphed so many times over the Eighth Army that they refused to believe that, had Rommel kept his nerve, they would have been free of the cursed desert and washing their feet in the Nile. Rommel had made three decisions that cost him the victory.

He had hesitated for two hours once the minefield had been cleared, allegedly forfeiting surprise. His head-on attack against British positions anchored on the Alam Halfa ridge, when he might easily have circumvented them, was puzzling. Finally, having decided to attack, he had failed to push it through. The German command believed that "we had the British on the run," and that the "old" Rommel would have finished them off at Alam Halfa.[42] The standard Axis alibi for the defeat became the failure of Rommel's will. By August 1942, Rommel was both sick and mentally exhausted. Hitler concluded that his favorite general had been kept too long in the desert, and recalled him for a much-needed rest.[43]

But a more dispassionate analysis can only conclude that Rommel did not lose the Battle of Alam Halfa; rather, Montgomery and the British won it. Stout defense, tight battle management, air superiority, and sea control that denied Rommel supplies had exposed—at last—the myth of the independent power of German armor.[44] What the Germans failed to realize, as Montgomery's biographer insists, is that the Desert Fox had, at last, been outfoxed.[45] At no time did Rommel forfeit surprise, because Montgomery understood his intentions, as well as the fact that his lack of fuel restricted his options. Rommel insisted that the real blow that lost the battle for the Axis even before it was engaged was the remarkable success of British attacks on Axis supply lines in the second half of August 1942, an effort greatly assisted by Ultra intelligence.[46] Rommel's German detractors argue that the lack of fuel was merely an unconvincing excuse. Kesselring insisted that if Rommel had the fuel to retreat for thirty miles back to his start line, and to fight until 6 September, he had had enough to forge ahead.

But the truth was that Rommel's plan at Alam Halfa had been based on wildly optimistic assumptions that went unchallenged because of poor intelligence and because Axis success had hitherto relied on British mistakes and on ineffective interdiction of supply lines. Even assuming that Rommel could have seized the Alam Halfa ridge, and perhaps a British supply dump or two, he still would have lacked the fuel to reach Alexandria and the delta. He would have sacrificed many of his tanks, which he could replace only with difficulty. His casualties had been limited to 536 men killed and 52 tanks disabled (of which 40 were reparable). The British lost more tanks, many of them victims of the 75 mm guns on the "specials," and had taken 1,750 casualties, almost half in the failed New Zealand attack of 3–4 September after the battle had already been won. The Axis nemesis, as Montgomery had predicted, was the "soft stuff": the 400 trucks destroyed mainly by night air bombardment deprived Rommel of the very mobility on which he had built his success.[47] Rommel was indeed psychologically exhausted and in need of a rest. But his real "problem" was that he acknowledged, at last, that the Germans had reached their apogee. The entire Blitzkrieg system had been based on bluff. At last Rommel had met a British commander with air superiority who knew how to raise the ante. Rommel matured as a strategist because of this realization. But it was too late—Alam Halfa was the first step toward Rommel's state-assisted suicide two years later. Hitler continued to live in his own strategic fantasyland. The Führer increasingly displayed zero tolerance for generals whose pessimistic prognoses and wary advice reminded him that the Allies had begun to "close the ring."

For the British, Alam Halfa was a tremendous morale boost. The Eighth Army, at last, had been given a task within its capabilities. They had observed Panzerarmee Afrika being hammered for two days. Staff officers at last served a commander with a focus and a sense of purpose. Although El Alamein is celebrated as Montgomery's crowning achievement, the Battle of Alam Halfa was the turning point of the North Africa campaign. Kesselring realized its immense strategic significance. The British had fought their first successful defensive land battle of World War II. Malta had been saved. British control of the Middle East was secure. The RAF was growing progressively stronger. The USAAF's first appearance in the campaign was merely the appetizer that announced a full menu of strategic and tactical contributions that would lead to total Allied air dominance. Not only would the accretion of Allied air power squeeze the Axis supply bottleneck south of the Mediterranean, but also, air superiority would allow the Eighth Army greater freedom of maneuver. This was especially worrying as Montgomery had broken the code on the German tactical system.[48] A second Allied landing in North Africa, Kesselring believed, was only a matter of time. This would force the Axis to fight on two land fronts as well as struggle to keep the sea lanes of communication open. In hindsight, the best course open to Rommel would have been to retreat to somewhere like the Halfaya Pass, where he could have shortened his supply lines. But Rommel "believed in the strength of the Alamein Line," Kesselring remembered. For his part, Montgomery asked London to tone down the significance of the victory so as not to hasten Rommel's withdrawal. He, too, was eager to fight on the Alamein line.[49]

"BATTLE WITHOUT HOPE"

The advantages for each commander of fighting on a line that stretched forty miles from the sea to the impassable Qattara Depression were apparent. For Rommel, now condemned to the defensive, it offered a fearful barrier that the British could not circumvent, but would be obliged to tackle head on. He understood that he was forfeiting Axis superiority in mobile operations. But a static defense offered a way to minimize British control of the air—"we could no longer rest our defense on the motorized forces used in a mobile role, since these forces were too vulnerable to air attack."[50] Therefore, the customary pattern of desert battles hitherto initiated with a feint along the coast followed by a southerly hook through the desert to pin the opponent against the sea and force him to withdraw in confusion and disarray would not be repeated at El Alamein. Rommel's design for his position, guarded by roughly 100,000 troops,[51] was World War I intensified. He placed a light screen of infantry outposts with guard dogs to warn of a British approach in front of a forty-mile-long belt of half a million antitank and antipersonnel mines and booby traps that varied between 2.5 and 4.5 miles in depth, nicknamed the Devil's Garden. Inside this explosive girdle were mine-free "hollow areas" which would invite attacking troops to move left or right, thus dissipating the forward momentum of the attack. Behind this belt he set the main infantry defenses on the "corset-bone" principle of interspersed German and Italian battalions, backed by artillery and one hundred 88s and a further hundred 76.2 mm antitank guns.

A British raid on Tobruk to destroy the harbor installations on the night of 13–14 September ended disastrously with the loss of two destroyers and a cruiser and over 700 casualties.[52] Commando raids against Benghazi and Al Marj were equally unsuccessful. The only beneficial result from the British perspective was that Rommel placed the Pavia Division at Matruh and the Ninetieth Light Division on the coast fifteen miles west of El Alamein to guard against an amphibious landing. British intelligence kept a watchful eye on this division, for its commitment to the line eventually would determine the trajectory of the British thrust. Should the British threaten a breakthrough, a reserve of German panzers and Italian mobile forces dispersed to the rear beyond artillery range would rush forward to plug any breach in the line.[53]

The Axis position at El Alamein had weaknesses, the major one being its distance from its supply bases at Tobruk and Benghazi. But in Rommel's view, no better position east of Tobruk existed to make a stand. While on paper the Axis army appeared formidable, increasingly effective attacks against Axis supply lines out of a revived Malta had left units short of replacements and equipment. His troops had been on half-rations and many were sick with jaundice. Battalion strong points were assigned 3,000 meters of front. The minefields, though deep, lacked antipersonnel mines and barbed-wire obstacles, especially in the northern sector, where the breakthrough would occur. Nor were many of the mines fitted with antilifting devices, as would later be the case. Italian guns, in particular, lacked the range to deal with British counter-battery fire, and so had to be deployed dangerously far forward to be effective. One of his greatest weaknesses remained lack of fuel for his panzers, which would also be outnumbered two to one by British tanks.[54] Luftwaffe strength was diverted for convoy escort and to launch a major air offensive against Malta between 10 and 19 October aimed at suppressing Maltese-based attacks on Axis supply ships. The air offensive failed with considerable losses, because of beefed-up Maltese air defenses and the arrival on the island of modern Spitfires, which now outnumbered German attackers. Ultra revealed that Kesselring's major airfields in theater were flooded and his operational strength was down. This gave the British command of the air and denied the Germans vital reconnaissance that would have identified the British buildup to his front.[55] Indeed, the death of the most celebrated Axis fighter ace in Africa, Captain Hans-Joachim Marseille, on 30 September 1942, cast a pall of apprehension over the Luftwaffe, which took it as emblematic of the declining fortunes of German air power.[56]

Rommel's decision to intersperse German and Italian battalions invited confusion because each was dependent on its own supply system. The placement of two German and two Italian armored divisions in an elongated defense in depth behind his line constituted one of the most significant defects in his defenses. Rommel claimed subsequently that he had to do this to bolster Italian resolve, because he lacked gasoline to move large formations longer distances, and because more compact armored formations would be vulnerable to air attack. But this prepositioning would condemn him to commit his tanks piecemeal against threatened British breakthroughs.[57] Finally, Rommel himself would not be in command in the early stages of the battle: on 23 September he departed on furlough to Austria, turning over command of Panzerarmee Afrika to General Georg Stumme, a man with no experience of Africa. Stumme was concerned about the supply situation he inherited.[58] Nevertheless, for public consumption, at least, he professed confidence in at least two things: that the British would not be ready for an attack before November, and that when that attack came, "we're going to wipe the floor with the British."[59]

Rommel subsequently complained that British superiority in matériel preordained an Axis defeat.[60] Allied reinforcements, mechanically reliable Sherman tanks armed with a 75 mm gun, as well as 849 of the new 6 pdr antitank guns and 900 field and medium artillery pieces including the American 105 mm self-propelled howitzer—the "Priest"—rumbled westward, raising clouds of dust, toward the Alamein line. Montgomery calculated his advantages in numbers, material superiority, and proximity to his supply base. So far, the Eighth Army had failed to demonstrate much aptitude for open desert fighting. However, the fixed front and attritional character of the coming battle suited the temperament of an army less adept at maneuver but with an overwhelming advantage in tanks, artillery, and air power. By mid-1942 the Eighth Army at last had enough radios to allow the rapid transmission of orders, so as better to control the battle, concentrate forces, and rapidly coordinate artillery barrages in the face of evolving tactical situations. Intelligence, especially photo-reconnaissance and Y Service intercepts, gave the British a precise picture of Rommel's dispositions, while the RAF denied the Luftwaffe an opportunity to sniff out British preparations.[61] But British advantages in numbers and matériel, while significant, were no guarantee of success. The British had enjoyed relatively greater matériel superiority before Crusader in November 1941 and Gazala in May 1942. At Alamein, Montgomery's numerical superiority was significant, but it was debatable that it matched the two-to-one superiority in manpower that World War I generals believed necessary for offensive success.[62] Despite the confidence-boosting victory at Alam Halfa, a sense of foreboding persisted in an army where relations between infantry and armor were strained by two years of mismanagement and lack of a clear delineation of tasks. Montgomery's newly organized *corps de chasse* would need to prove itself capable of pursuit once the breakthrough occurred. Furthermore, Churchill harassed him to the point of resignation. Rommel must be put to flight, the prime minister insisted, well before the Allied landings in French North Africa—Torch—occurred in November, so as to tip French support to the Allies. Rommel's defenses set a formidable task for Montgomery. Overall, the coming battle was shaping up to reenact a Somme in the sand.

Montgomery's supreme disadvantage was that his troops, many of them newly arrived in the desert, needed time to train to his plan. Tommies were rotated out of line to fire new 6 pdr antitank guns at panzer silhouettes pulled along tracks at six new ranges set up along the coast. Engineer battalions were prepared at Monty's new school of mine clearing. Infantry and tanks rehearsed coordinated attacks on hills that resembled those at El Alamein. To deceive Rommel, a hoax assemblage of wood-and-canvas artillery pieces, a phony pipeline, empty jerrycans, imitation supply dumps, every detail of an assaulting force down to latrines with mannequins crouched over them, was set up near the southern part of the line. Meanwhile, the real assault force in the north was concealed by netting and underground petrol dumps. Crusaders and Shermans rumbled under canvas covers mas-

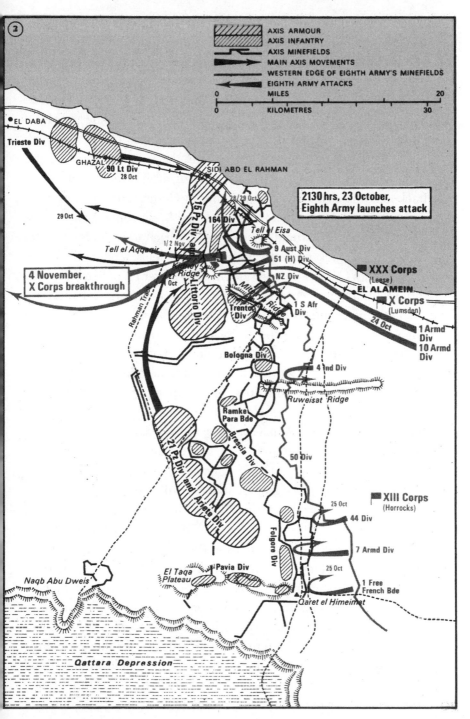

AXIS ARMOUR
AXIS INFANTRY
AXIS MINEFIELDS
MAIN AXIS MOVEMENTS
WESTERN EDGE OF EIGHTH ARMY'S MINEFIELDS
EIGHTH ARMY ATTACKS

MILES 0 — 20
KILOMETRES 0 — 30

EL DABA
Trieste Div
GHAZAL
90 Lt Div
28 Oct
29 Oct
SIDI ABD EL RAHMAN
28/29 Oct
15 Pz Div and
164 Div
Tell el Eisa
9 Aust Div
51 (H) Div
Tell el Aqqacir
1/2 Nov
Ridge
Oct
Littorio Div
Rahman Track
NZ Div

**2130 hrs, 23 October,
Eighth Army launches attack**

**4 November,
X Corps breakthrough**

Miteiriya Ridge
Trento Div
1 S Afr Div

■ **XXX Corps**
(Leese)
EL ALAMEIN
→ **X Corps**
(Lumsden)
24 Oct
1 Armd Div
10 Armd Div

Bologna Div
4 Ind Div
Ruweisat Ridge
Ramke Para Bde
Brescia Div
50 Div

■ **XIII Corps**
(Horrocks)
25 Oct
44 Div
7 Armd Div
25 Oct
1 Free French Bde

21 Pz Div and Ariete Div
Folgore Div

Naqb Abu Dweis
El Taqa Plateau
Pavia Div
Qaret el Himeimat

Qattara Depression

querading as trucks, while, in replacement motor pools to the rear, bogus tanks substituted for the real articles moved forward in the night.

Montgomery's plan, code-named Lightfoot, was to attack with three corps on two axes simultaneously. The southern part of Rommel's line would be assaulted by the Thirteenth Corps under Lieutenant General Brian Horrocks, who had been a mere battalion commander in Montgomery's Third Division during the fall of France. This diversionary attack, Montgomery calculated, would fix the German troops in the south, and prevent them from concentrating against the breakthrough attack near the coast. There, the Thirtieth Corps under the newly arrived Guards General Oliver Leese, backed by air support and a massive artillery barrage, would smash open a breach in the German line. Once they had broken into the German minefields, tanks of the newly created Tenth Corps—the *corps de chasse*—under Lieutenant General Herbert Lumsden, would growl forward to shield the infantry and mine-clearing engineers as they "crumbled" the sides of the breach to widen it. This would force the German armor to commit to support its defending infantry, where they would be taken apart by the Shermans and new 6 pdr antitank guns. The guts would be ripped from the German defenses. "If every tank crew, and every 6-pdr A. Tk. gun team, will hit and disable one enemy tank, then we must win," Montgomery told the Eighth Army.[63] A massive air campaign against Axis rear areas and air bases by five hundred RAF fighters and bombers began on 19 October.

The twenty-third of October marked full moon. Two thousand white-gloved MPs directed traffic forward through a luminous desert night: tanks, water carts to keep down the dust, and refrigerated trucks, vampire bats painted on their sides, full of plasma and other medical supplies. In the distance, German guard dogs, alerted by the low rumble of activity to their front, barked. Montgomery retired to bed. Around 2130, the low moan of bombers could be heard overhead. Ten minutes later, Montgomery's "killing match" stabbed with "a barrage of immense weight," Rommel complained, "over the whole line, eventually concentrating on the northern sector. Such drum-fire had never before been seen on the African front, and it was to continue throughout the whole of the Alamein battle."[64] Looking east from the

German positions, the horizon seemed suddenly aglow with fire. Seconds later, fountains of rock and sand began to erupt among the Axis strong points. British engineers armed with long-handled mine detectors connected to earphones that pinged when they detected metal, or prodding the ground with bayonets, cleared twenty-four-foot—two tank widths—paths through the minefields, gaps they marked with white tape and orange and green pin lamps. Antitank mines were "deloused" by removing the igniter. Small soup-can-shaped, shrapnel-rich S-mines had to be disarmed by jamming a nail into the hole to engage the safety pin. At some points, the Germans had even rigged aerial bombs as mines. The engineers, advancing at two hundred yards an hour at best, were trailed by helmeted infantry, their bayonets gleaming in the moonlight, white crosses etched on their fifty-pound packs to avoid friendly fire, who dodged forward on a 7,000-yard front behind guide officers with compasses toward Rommel's smoke-shrouded line. Tense and deadly work, it was also slow. By morning, the British armor was lined up, motors running, as in a parking lot at rush hour.

The sustained thunderclap from nine hundred heavy guns and bombers surprised and confused Stumme. His intelligence had given him a fairly accurate picture of the British order of battle, but divided on whether Montgomery's attack was imminent or would not come before November, when the phony pipeline that reached toward Quarel el Himeimat in the south would be completed. Lack of Luftwaffe air reconnaissance combined with British camouflage of their preparations also confused him about the main British axis of attack.[65] Now that the attack had begun, Stumme had no idea against which of the two main thrusts and myriad minor raids to concentrate, so that his artillery interdiction was intermittent and ineffective. His outposts and forward bunkers had fallen silent, imploded by shells, their occupants either dismembered or toppled by concussions that left their bodies unmarked but lifeless. Some of the Italians, terrified by the intensity of the bombardment, streamed toward the rear. Those who remained in the line fought with rifles, as many of their heavy weapons had been mangled by high explosives. Within eight hours, the Thirtieth Corps had breached the minefield and occupied the Miteiriya Ridge. Royal Navy demonstrations along the coast kept the Axis alert to the possibility of an amphibious end run. Thick smoke screens, telephone lines cut by artillery bombardments, and Desert Air Force bombing and jamming of Axis radio frequencies by Wellington bombers flying over the battlefield made it difficult for Stumme to gain a clear picture of the battle. So, in the best Afrika Korps tradition, he set out at first light to see for himself what was happening at the forward edge of the battlefield. His staff car blundered into an Australian machine-gun nest. As the driver attempted furiously to reverse, Stumme turned gray, clutched at his chest, staggered from the car and collapsed in the sand, dead of a heart attack. Hitler ordered Rommel to return to Egypt. Until his arrival, however, leadership of the battle devolved onto Afrika Korps commander Ritter von Thoma.

Having broken into the Axis position, Monty was ready for the second, "crumbling" phase of the operation to begin, with his troops attacking north and south to widen the breach. This required Lumsden's Tenth Corps armor to move out in front of the infantry to destroy the panzers that would inevitably counterattack. But stiff Axis resistance made the British advance a suicidal endeavor. Fires within the columns of jammed-together vehicles proved contagious. Montgomery had difficulty prodding Lumsden forward. And no wonder—88s turned advancing tanks into roman candles. The night of 24–25 October became, for Montgomery, the crisis of the battle, as Lumsden begged him to call off the attack. Rommel's Storch aircraft landed at his headquarters on the evening of 25 October to find von Thoma in a sullen mood. Petrol and munitions were in short supply, while the Eighth Army was camped out in the middle of his defensive positions. If the Tenth Corps was losing tanks, counterattacks by the Fifteenth Panzer had led to "frightful losses" to British artillery "firing five hundred rounds to every one of ours"[66] and to RAF bombs, losses that he could ill afford. Temporarily stymied, on 26 October Montgomery untangled the confusion of tanks and withdrew Tenth Corps to the rear. Lumsden was ordered to ready a *corps de chasse* to pursue after the breakthrough.[67] Monty had decided to fight his battle as an infantry-artillery encounter. In the south, the methodical advance of Horrocks's Thirteenth Corps had stalled. Nevertheless, Rommel's defenses in the north had been severely mauled and his troop strength there reduced by as much as one-half in some units. Only 31 of 119 tanks remained serviceable in the Fifteenth Panzer Division.[68] A 26 October counterattack by the Fifteenth Panzer and the Littorio Division against the Thirtieth Corps salient on "Hill 28" (which the British called "Point 29") was shattered by the Desert Air Force amid what Rommel described as "rivers of blood." He complained that he lacked the artillery shells to drive the British out of their newly won position. An attempt by the Luftwaffe and the Italian air force to strike at the British positions was thwarted by the intervention of over sixty Desert Air Force fighters and a density of antiaircraft fire the likes of which Rommel had never seen. The Italians jettisoned their bombs over their own lines and scuttled for base. The dangerous British penetration north of Miteiriya Ridge caused him to commit the Ninetieth Light Division on 26 October, followed by his mobile reserve of the Twenty-first Panzer Division and much of the artillery from the southern part of the line, an irretrievable decision, as he would lack the petrol to send them south again. He wanted to bring the Ariete as well, but kept them in place to deal with Horrocks's southern thrust, which was already through the first belt of minefields. He then ordered his troops to hold all positions "to the utmost."

Strong Axis counterattacks in the late afternoon of 27 October were smashed by the Desert Air Force, heavy artillery fire, and the stout defense of the Rifle Brigade backed by 6 pdr antitank guns. A further counterattack ordered by Rommel for the next day, 28 October, was foiled by air assault even as it was concentrating, with high casualties. This turned the tide of battle. Rommel, the initiative now out of his hands, complained that the incessant air attacks exhausted and demoralized the defenders and inflicted heavy casualties. Even when German attacks got rolling, they met a line of antitank guns and hull-down tanks ensconced in well-defended positions as at Alam Halfa. Rommel calculated that Montgomery had put only half his force into the attack. "It was obvious that from now on the British would destroy us bit by bit."[69] Montgomery, too, was absorbing high losses, but these were losses that he could afford, while Rommel could not. Rommel considered falling back to give battle at Fuka sixty miles to his rear, out of range of the Desert Air Force. But he lacked the gasoline, while the armies were so tightly interlocked that he could not figure out a way to disengage. By the night of 28–29 October, as he contemplated a withdrawal, Rommel wrote a melodramatic letter to his wife preparing her for his death. He transferred more units from the south to put against the threatened breakthrough in the north. His fuel running short, he received the further devastating news that the Ultra-guided attack on his supply lines was biting hard—on 26 October, the tanker *Proserpina* had been set afire and her sister ship the *Tergesta*, which carried both fuel and ammunition, had evaporated under air attack. Three days later, Rommel got the "shattering" news that the tanker *Luisiano* had been torpedoed off Greece. The *Luisiano* was joined at the bottom of the Mediterranean within seventy-two hours by the *Tripolino* and the *Ostia* laden with gasoline and ammunition, which were sunk almost within sight of Tobruk. The dribble of fuel ferried in by the Luftwaffe failed to satisfy even minimal requirements.[70]

Montgomery was increasingly badgered by a nervous Churchill, eager to make his breakthrough before Torch, scheduled for 8 November, reached North African beaches, and afraid that Monty was allowing the battle "to peter out." He need not have worried. Ultra revealed that Rommel had shifted the Ninetieth Light to the extreme north of the line to counter the Australian advance along the coast, and that the Axis was desperately short of fuel; Montgomery began to shift troops from the southern part of the line for the final breakthrough just south of Point 29. At the same time, he kept up the attacks by the Ninth Australian Division, regarded by the Germans as the best in the Eighth Army, in the extreme north of the Alamein line to give the impression that the breakthrough would come along the coast. Operation Supercharger, launched under a ferocious artillery barrage on the night of 1–2 November, aimed to smash through Italian units directly to the west of the Thirtieth Corps salient, rather than along the coast as the British supposed that Rommel anticipated.[71] The New Zealand Division, supported by obsolete Valentine tanks, advanced on a 4,000-yard front behind a creeping barrage so dense that Kiwis collapsed from the fumes, as they cleared mines to allow the First Armoured Division of Tenth Corps to penetrate Rommel's screen of antitank guns before daybreak. By the morning of 2 November, von Thoma informed Rommel that he had lost two-thirds of his 88s and was down to thirty-five serviceable German tanks. His 5 cm antitank guns were unable to stop Shermans, tanks superior even to the redoubtable PzKw IV, which were overwhelming his forces. His communications jammed or shot to pieces, Rommel's picture of the battle was obscured and distorted. But he could see British armored cars already squirting through the minefield and ranging about in the open in search of "soft stuff" and headquarters positions. At eleven o'clock in the morning, news reached him that British tanks had broken through. Units of the Littorio and Trieste Divisions were already breaking line and heading west. Rommel ordered the Twenty-first Panzer Division to counterattack. Although Y Service alerted Montgomery, many British tanks perished in the assault. But Montgomery simply kept coming on.

By the morning of 3 November, Rommel's infantry and artillery were down to one-third of their opening battle strength, and only thirty tanks remained operational. Realizing that he had expended his reserves and that his line was about to break, Rommel had already resolved on the afternoon of 2 November to order a retreat, and radioed this to Berlin, a message intercepted by British code breakers at Bletchley Park.[72] When Hitler learned of Rommel's plans for a retreat, he hit the ceiling, and immediately issued an order to stand fast till "Victory or Death!" A "dumbfounded" Rommel tried to stop the flight, but without conviction. In any case, it was too late—by noon on 3 November, the RAF reported that Italian units were leaving the line. But Rommel's vacillation suspended the retreat of German units for most of 4 November. At noon on 4 November, Rommel asked Hitler for permission to retreat. By evening, even Rommel, with Kesselring's connivance, had given up on making his men fight in place. Without waiting for a reply, at 1730 he ordered a flight that soon transformed the Via Balbia into a vast traffic jam. That night, Hitler blessed a retreat that was already a *fait accompli*. For his part, von Thoma denounced Hitler's "stand fast" order as sheer "lunacy." Rommel's biographer alleges that von Thoma, in an act of defiant treachery, put on all his medals, packed a bag, and rode toward the British lines, an account disputed by other historians.[73]

El Alamein is interpreted as a pivotal battle because strategically it marked a turning point in the war, while operationally and tactically it announced the coming of age of British forces under a commander who had, at last, found the measure of the Germans. Hitler's "stand fast" order at El Alamein triggered the estrangement between Hitler and Rommel, who now understood that Germany had lost the war.[74] Not surprisingly for the victory-starved British, El Alamein summoned up ancestral memories of the triumphs of Trafalgar and Waterloo. In London, Churchill wept with joy when he received the victory telegram from Alexander. Churchill boasted that El Alamein "marked the turning of 'the Hinge of Fate.' It may almost be said, 'Before Alamein we never had a victory. After Alamein we never had a defeat.' "[75] El Alamein appeared to have removed the threat to the Middle East and saved Malta. But the strategic importance of El Alamein is overstated. Rommel's limited strength denied him the ability to capture Suez, especially so long as Malta remained in British possession. And once Anglo-American forces landed in his rear in French North Africa, the Axis lacked the capability to sustain a front in Egypt, or even to hold out in North Africa, as Rommel realized.[76] Therefore, Torch, not El Alamein, marked the turning point of the war in North Africa. Win or lose at El Alamein, the game was up for Rommel in the Western Desert. From now on, the Axis would be playing defense. And it was impossible to win on the defense.

The importance of El Alamein was political and psychological rather than strategic. Indeed, one is driven toward the inescapable conclusion that Churchill pushed Montgomery for a battle *before* Torch precisely because he required a victory that vindicated his Mediterranean strategy, strengthened British confidence in his war leadership, and affirmed to the Americans Britain's weight in the alliance. Above all, El Alamein destroyed the stab-in-the-back myth advanced by Auchinleck as an alibi for his repeated failure. The question resolved by El Alamein was, Can British soldiers really fight? El Alamein had been a victory of morale, one that hinged on the ability of British forces to sustain a grueling twelve-day battle. At a stroke, the Eighth Army had reversed the verdict of Dunkirk, Greece, Crete, Tobruk, and Singapore.[77] Moreover, they had been prepared to absorb significant casualties to do it— 4,600 men dead or missing, almost 9,000 wounded, 500 tanks and 111 guns lost. But many of the tanks were reparable, while Rommel was left with only a handful of German tanks out of his original 249. Three Italian divisions had virtually ceased to exist. The British held 30,000 Axis POWs, including nine German generals.[78] The professionalism of German arms that had for so long taunted and humiliated the British had been equaled and surpassed. After El Alamein, the acronym BEF (British Expeditionary Force) stood for something other than "Back Every Fortnight." The Germans would now live the same indignities of retreat, strafing, and defensive stands that they had inflicted on the British since 1940. El Alamein marked the debut of Montgomery and his Eighth Army as the gold standard against which all other Allied generals and armies would be measured until 1944. This could but reflect glory on Churchill, prolong his influence in the alliance beyond what would have been its normal lifetime, and possibly save his government. No wonder he wept at the news of victory.

Hardly had the smoke of battle cleared than Montgomery's reputation as a brilliant general who created a force and devised a battle plan that at last put the Allies on the offensive was in dispute. Rommel sniveled that his defeat was the result of the superiority of British matériel and his lack of gasoline.[79] Some historians have adopted Rommel's alibi as historical explanation, interpreting Montgomery's success at El Alamein as a "ponderous *Materialschlacht*," a World War I–style slogging match during which Montgomery powered to an inevitable victory through superiority of matériel. Montgomery's conduct of the battle was merely "academic" because ultimately Rommel "succumbed to the logic of sheer attrition."[80] Indeed, even Churchill drew the analogy between El Alamein and "many of the battles of 1918."[81] There is something to be said for this view. El Alamein was certainly a tough battle, and Montgomery's superiority of matériel was an essential factor in his victory. El Alamein also demonstrated that infantry attacking at night with plenty of artillery support could seize their objectives without tank support, a revival of the techniques of 1918 applied by the British for the remainder of the war.[82] Yet the British had enjoyed matériel superiority over the Germans in North

Africa for at least a year before El Alamein. This had failed, nevertheless, to translate into victory on the Gazala line, or at the "First Alamein" fought by Auchinleck. Therefore, the training of the army, its ability to perform coordinated inter-arm operations, and generalship could not have been entirely unrelated to the outcome. El Alamein cannot be dismissed merely as a crossover point when Allied matériel superiority made victory inevitable.

While superiority in matériel was a necessary condition for the British victory, it was not a sufficient one. The British, at last, had outfought the Panzerarmee Afrika. Rommel had underestimated his opponents, failed to form a mobile reserve, and instead frittered away his armor in piecemeal counterattacks, much as the British had done in early desert battles. Nor had he trained his infantry to attack at night with artillery and tank support. But Rommel had not merely lost the battle. Montgomery had won it through the use of tactical surprise to seize forward positions, and then shifting temporarily to the defensive to allow Rommel to batter away in futile daylight counterattacks that could be shattered by the Desert Air Force. On the other hand, Montgomery's tactic of breaching the enemy line on a narrow front had succeeded in part because Rommel lacked the artillery to concentrate on the British breakthrough point. This tactic, employed by Montgomery in March 1943 against the Mareth line in Tunisia, was abandoned in that offensive after barely a day because Axis artillery fire caused too many casualties. Nor was it to prove successful at Monte Cassino in the opening months of 1944.

Montgomery's reputation as a commander was also diminished from the beginning by the fact that Rommel escaped to Tunisia with what was left of his mobile forces, where he continued to cause considerable headaches for the Allies. Liddell Hart faulted Montgomery for missing a "magnificent opportunity" to cut off and destroy Rommel's tank-depleted forces. Even Montgomery's chief of staff, Freddy de Guingand, "thought he ought to have rounded up the enemy."[83] "Here, surely was an army for the taking," had Montgomery been inclined to take it, concluded British historian John Ellis.[84] As El Alamein came to be seen as an incomplete victory, so Montgomery's generalship came under microscopic scrutiny. He was accused by

Rommel of exhibiting "astonishing hesitancy and caution" during the battle. Montgomery was a plodder in the World War I style, a general who relied for success on a rigid plan anchored in a deliberate infantry advance behind a wall of massive firepower.[85] Despite the fact that during Rommel's post-Alamein retreat Montgomery was given excellent intelligence, not only on the anemic state of Rommel's forces, but also on his intentions to flee west as fast as possible,[86] Rommel repeatedly danced away from what should have been assured destruction. His escape adds credibility to charges that Montgomery was too cautious and insufficiently resourceful to trap a nimble foe. Even the British official history calls Rommel's retreat at the head of almost 70,000 beaten troops "remarkable," especially as Hitler's meddling delayed Rommel's departure from the Alamein line by almost a full day. It attributes Rommel's successful exit in part to the German's fearsome reputation and Montgomery's anxiety that a counterattack might deprive him of his gains.[87]

Montgomery's biographer insists that Montgomery had every intention of trapping Rommel, and initially showed no signs of the excessive caution that his detractors folded into the Monty legend. Nigel Hamilton attributes Rommel's escape to "a mixture of lethargy, confusion, caution, lack of communication and administrative chaos." To pursue, he required a level of personal initiative on the part of his subordinate commanders for which they showed scant flair. His armored commanders were not cooperating with each other, much less with the other arms.[88] The Eighth Army, disorganized at the conclusion of the battle, was in any case insufficiently trained, still too much the "amateur army," to apply a bold scheme of pursuit. The euphoria of victory, the requirement to round up tens of thousands of POWs, many in a pitiable state, supply problems made more acute as the British moved farther from their base, and heavy rains that confined the Eighth Army to the road slowed Montgomery's advance. To the surprise of the British, their thirsty Shermans, so formidable on the battlefield, proved almost a liability in pursuit, as they moved only three miles on a gallon of gasoline and had constantly to be refueled. The Desert Air Force was slow to deploy forward because it lacked airfields. In any case, poor strafing techniques, the wrong kind of bombs, an absence of adequate ground control methods, and fear of flak undermined their ability to support the advancing ground forces.[89] As the Eighth Army moved west, its advance was split among the competing objectives of trapping Rommel, seizing and creating airfields to support the advance, and taking Derna so that Malta could be relieved. The Ninetieth Light sowed minefields in Rommel's wake and fought tough rear-guard actions that kept the pursuers at bay. Finally, bad habits left over from the Auchinleck days when mobile groups went into defensive laagers for the night "like Biblical caravans" slowed the pursuit.[90]

In Montgomery's defense, although entrapping German armies became the Holy Grail of Allied operations, retreating German armies, even when severely mauled, proved practically impossible to trap, for several reasons. Even when surrounded, German commanders failed to panic. They had grown used to fighting their way out of encirclements in Russia, unlike Soviet forces after Barbarossa that tended to surrender when encircled. German units knew how to move fast and fight hard even when surrounded—especially when surrounded. Apart from hopeless circumstances caused by Hitler's direct intervention, as at Stalingrad or Tunis, any blocking force that could be thrown across their path was usually too weak to stop them. This meant that Rommel's escape after El Alamein was no fluke, but part of a pattern repeated by the Wehrmacht in North Africa, Sicily, Italy, Normandy, in their retreat up the Rhône in 1944 in the forefront of Anvil, and numerous times in Russia.

Nor would the entrapment of the remnants of Rommel's Panzerarmee after El Alamein have made much of a difference to the course of the North African campaign. Rommel's capture would have given the British the brief satisfaction of bagging a leader whose repeated and often improbable victories had made him a sort of *Übergeneral*. But one can argue that Rommel's escape was actually beneficial for the Allies, because the need to rescue him was the primary rationale for the Axis rush into Tunisia in December 1942, where they would fight at a disadvantage. Rommel's escape kept in the field a general against whom the Allies could continue to hone their tactical and operational skills. His presence in Tunisia offered fledgling U.S. forces in particular an inkling of what they were up against, discredited inferior U.S. generals, and allowed Generals Patton and Bradley to come to the fore. The poor relationship between Rommel and von Arnim in Tunisia compromised German operational effectiveness there. Nor, in faulting Montgomery, must one overlook the fact that Rommel was so demoralized by defeat, so keen to get away, that he, too, passed up opportunities to counterattack overextended British forces or make stands on strong positions. Attempts by Rome and Berlin to make Rommel stand and fight rather than bolt across North Africa received exasperated replies that the enemy was too strong, while Axis troops were disorganized and had forfeited most of their equipment, which led Axis leaders to conclude that Rommel had lost his nerve. Hitler tried to divert attention from the flight of his erstwhile favorite general at the head of his whipped army across North Africa by claiming that German forces had captured Stalingrad.[91] For his part, Rommel had matured as a commander. But maturity was a positive disadvantage in an enterprise that sustained itself by bluff and desperate operational improvisation. Rommel's realization that henceforth Hitler would micromanage his operations, and that his Führer was willing "to subordinate military interests to those of propaganda," loosened the bond between the field marshal and his hitherto enthusiastic patron.[92] At El Alamein, Rommel was defeated psychologically as much as, even more than, he was beaten militarily. Once its commander had relinquished his mental edge over the British, the Afrika Korps never regained its capacity to wound, mesmerize, and intimidate the Eighth Army.

CHAPTER SEVEN

"FDR's Secret Baby"

S INCE THE FALL of France in June 1940, each side had desired the huge shoulder of French Africa that muscled into the seas from Dakar on the Atlantic coast to Tunis on the central Mediterranean. Hitler's flirtation with strategic projects in the Western Mediterranean and South Atlantic in the year between the fall of France and Barbarossa foundered on Franco's refusal to cooperate, his desire to keep Vichy France neutral, and the primacy of his goals in Eastern Europe. Churchill coveted the strategic position of the French enclaves but, after the abortive attack on Dakar in September 1940, his forces and ships had been stripped and stretched for other ambitious enterprises barely within British means. London nurtured the hope that, one day, their former French ally would reenlist in the anti-Axis coalition. Operation Crusader had been launched in the autumn of 1941 on the strategic speculation that the ejection of the Axis from Libya would bring British forces to the frontier of French North Africa, where they might contact the anti-German ex-chief of the French general staff and Vichy *délégué général* in Africa General Maxime Weygand, a first step toward enticing the French back into the war. But British planning for this contingency under the code name Gymnast ceased in April 1942, largely due to the opposition of the American chief of staff, General George Marshall. America's military chiefs displayed little patience with what they saw as Churchill's Mediterranean dawdle. In their view, the Germans could be beaten only in Northern Europe.

They pressed for Sledgehammer, the invasion of northern France in 1942 (which became Roundup in 1943 and finally Overlord in 1944). However, the strategic pendulum in the Mediterranean swung back toward French North Africa in the summer of 1942. The battle on the Gazala line, which climaxed in the 20 June fall of Tobruk, followed by the desperate defense of Egypt in July, revived the moribund Operation Gymnast, which, in any case, had never been far from the prime minister's thoughts. Its new name was Torch.

The decision to associate the United States with Britain's Mediterranean campaign, in the process forcing the Allies to begin to define a Mediterranean strategy, became the central moment of Franklin Roosevelt's tenure as commander-in-chief. That Roosevelt would, for once, fail to defer to the opinions of his military advisers was somewhat surprising, for at least three reasons. First, unlike the prime minister, the American president did not pride himself on his mastery of military strategy. To go against the unanimous advice of the American military elite as well as his own secretary of war, Henry Stimson, who did everything short of resigning to sabotage an enterprise that he dismissed as "FDR's secret baby,"[1] was, if not daring, at least utterly out of character. A second cause for surprise was that, like Marshall and the American people generally, Roosevelt tended to be suspicious of British motives. In the summer of 1942, polls revealed that at least a quarter of Americans believed that Lend-Lease had been wasted on a country that was not fighting hard enough and whose leaders were "bunglers." Rather than seeing Churchill as the inspiring leader of a heroic ally, many Americans believed him a schemer who enticed America into the war and then contrived to make U.S. troops bear the brunt of the fighting. True, much of this anti-British sentiment was confined to American isolationists, well represented in America's German and Irish communities, and Roosevelt's political opponents. But Anglophobia also ran rampant among U.S. service chiefs and in the State Department. The columnist Walter Lippmann acknowledged to his friend, the British economist John Maynard Keynes, that the war "has revived the profound anti-imperialism of the American tradition," with its "inherent anti-British sentiment." Roosevelt's dilemma, then, was how to manage this "remarkably close but particularly strained" alliance,[2] to support the British in the Mediterranean without appearing subservient to London's agenda. Despite the view put forth by Churchill in his memoirs that he, the Old World realist, had to guide and instruct a naive American president unschooled in geopolitical issues,[3] Roosevelt was firm in his direction of U.S. policy. In the president's mind, America's interests did not stretch to the rescue and resuscitation of the British empire. Instead, he sought to calibrate America's strategic choices so that, by the war's end, Washington could defend its world interests outside of the traditional power politics framework dominated by Great Britain and the Soviet Union.[4]

Roosevelt's Mediterranean intervention was also something of a surprise given that the American president's suspicions of Churchill's motives were magnified by their ambiguous personal relationship. The accepted view, promoted especially by Churchill, was that few world leaders in history have established such a "special relationship." Churchill assiduously courted Roosevelt: "No lover ever studied every whim of his mistress as I did those of President Roosevelt," the prime minister confessed.[5] The result was a rapport unmatched among alliance chiefs, an "easy intimacy" between "two men in the same line of business—politico-military leadership on a global scale."[6] This "rare sense of comradeship" both steeled and facilitated the Anglo-American partnership.[7] This interpretation of the Roosevelt-Churchill relationship rests on a solid foundation of evidence. After all, one of Roosevelt's primary motives in opting for Torch was to solidify the Anglo-American alliance. Torch marked "a turning-point in the whole war," Roosevelt wrote to Churchill. "We are now on our way shoulder to shoulder."[8]

However, one of Roosevelt's biographers has suggested that the president disliked Churchill. The relationship between the two men had got off on the wrong foot when Churchill snubbed Roosevelt, then assistant secretary of the navy, during a 1918 visit to London. Roosevelt nursed his bruised pride over this incident for twenty-three years; when the two men next met at the Atlantic Conference in August 1941, the American president complained to his close associates about what a "stinker" Churchill had been, "lording it over us." And though the two men evolved a close and to all outward appearances amicable working relationship, it is difficult to know how much Roosevelt's legendary charm and acting ability masked a personal distrust of what he saw as the prime minister's antiquated "Victorian" views.[9] Harold Macmillan, too, perceived that Roosevelt's "outward show of friendship" toward the prime minister cloaked "a feeling of hostility—perhaps even of jealousy."[10] Roosevelt fully expected that his "special relationship" with the United Kingdom was not destined to survive the war.[11] But in the summer of 1942, Churchill's survival as prime minister, and in the president's view, the stability of American politics, hinged on salvaging Britain's position in the Mediterranean.

Not only did Roosevelt opt for Torch, but also the firmness with which he imposed his decision on a skeptical cabinet and practically mutinous high command seemed completely out of character. Despite his public reputation for decisiveness, Roosevelt was a natural procrastinator. His detractors charged that his indecision stemmed from the fact that he lacked any logical or moral framework to order the facts that cluttered his brain. The truth was probably more prosaic. Roosevelt avoided resolving issues with dispatch because resolution deprived him of options and removed his ability to cajole, to manipulate personalities and factions, to arrange compromises, which was his preferred modus operandi. But the war telescoped Roosevelt's options, compressed his decision cycle, forced him to set goals and select a strategy for achieving them. Procrastination, especially on the strategic level, was a luxury the war denied him, especially in the summer of 1942.[12]

Roosevelt's decision for Torch marked the defining moment of America's entry into World War II, and of World War II *tout court*. No other operation surpassed Torch in "complexity, in daring—and the prominence of hazard involved—or in the degree of strategic surprise achieved," concludes one official history. "The most important attribute of Torch, however, is the most obvious. It was the *first* fruit of the combined strategy. Once it had been undertaken, other great operations followed as its corollaries . . . In short, the Torch operation, and the lessons learned in Africa, imposed a pattern on the war."[13] One of Roosevelt's biographers claims that Torch was also vital for the future of American democracy and marked a turning point in "the course of world history."[14] In retrospect, however, why Torch seemed so daring or surprising is difficult to fathom. The U.S. juggernaut had been gaining momentum since 1940. Roosevelt was under pressure to launch a "second front." The rival plan, Sledgehammer, was a nonstarter, not least because Great Britain opposed it. Among Churchill's more persuasive arguments against Sledgehammer was that failure was guaranteed, a point driven home by the bloody repulse of the Dieppe raid in August 1942. A cross-Channel invasion that carried unblooded U.S. troops on insufficient numbers of amphibious landing craft, backed by inadequate stocks and reserves in Great Britain, across an insecure sea, to pitch them, with tentative air cover, into the teeth of one of history's most formidable military forces, was an invitation to a massacre. The ensuing battle, assuming that it lasted more than twenty-four hours, would make Rommel's shoot-up of the Eighth Army at Gazala and Tobruk look like a Boy Scout outing. (Indeed, the death or capture by 1600 hours of two-thirds of the troops that landed on the Dieppe beach on 19 August 1942 carried a high level of predictability for the larger enterprise.) Churchill and his chiefs of staff knew that Britain, which would bear the brunt of Sledgehammer, and even of its successor Roundup, would have one crack at a Continental invasion. Failure would terminate Britain's contribution to the alliance as much more than an aircraft carrier moored off the coast of Europe. In the long run, Roosevelt was less interested in preserving British forces than of buying time so that the cross-Channel invasion, when it came, would be an American-dominated enterprise. In the short run, Britain's refusal to consent to Sledgehammer at this stage of the war was reason enough for Roosevelt to support Torch. He had no intention of risking Allied unity to prop up the impeccably flawed logic, strategic naïveté, and operational optimism of the American service chiefs.[15] Time would work for an American domination of the alliance, and time was what the Mediterranean option offered in abundance.

Unlike Chief of Staff George Marshall, who favored Sledgehammer as a way to divert German forces away from the Eastern Front even though he expected it to fail,[16] Roosevelt was keenly aware of the political and strategic risks of a premature Continental invasion. Despite the contention of the "brute force" school that Allied victory in World War II was an unrelenting march toward an inevitable conclusion, it is not difficult to imagine that different strategic choices would have produced different outcomes. The argument of this book has been that the Mediterranean was the pivotal theater of World War II for the Allies. It provided incremental success, in the process buying time for the Allies, who might otherwise have rushed into poor strategic decisions that might have fragmented the alliance and ultimately cost them the war, no matter how strong their material base. The failure of a cross-Channel invasion might have put a stake through the heart of Churchill's political career. It certainly would have emboldened Roosevelt's enemies. At least one historian has suggested that the substitution of Halifax or Lord Beaverbrook for Churchill or Wendell Willkie for Roosevelt might not have significantly altered the Allied relationship or the strategic direction or outcome of the war.[17] Nevertheless, it requires a great leap of faith to imagine two other leaders of stature rising to the challenges of that conflict with the same capacity to inspire and direct as the Roosevelt-Churchill team. Internal dissension over strategic choices within the two democracies would certainly have increased, tensions that would have been communicated to the alliance. Failure of a cross-Channel invasion in 1942 or 1943 would have increased pressure on the United States to redirect military assets to the Pacific. Japan could not have escaped destruction. But what of the European Axis? Mussolini would have survived, and Stalin would have been stripped of much U.S. aid, as well as the prospect of a "Second Front." Might the Soviet dictator then have negotiated a separate peace with Hitler? With the USSR out of the war, could the Anglo-Americans have hoped for a successful invasion of the Continent? Might the atomic bombs have been dropped on Berlin and Rome rather than on Japanese cities? While it is difficult to answer these questions with any degree of certainty, it is not difficult to imagine World War II in Europe with an entirely different script, and possibly an entirely different ending.

The important thing was that whatever his personal feelings toward Churchill, the American president could not imagine operating the alliance with any leader other than the prime minister. Roosevelt was keen to place U.S. ground and sea forces against Germany in 1942 as a way to shore up Churchill's position in Britain and prevent the collapse of British army morale. In a year of important Congressional elections, Torch would give a first taste of victory to an American public that, so far, had witnessed an almost unrelieved series of setbacks and defeats. In the process, Roosevelt could justify his "Europe First" policy, silencing in part the demands from the navy and the Pacific lobby for resources. West Africa would be seized, thus depriving U-boats of potential bases from which to strike at Allied shipping and threaten the Western Hemisphere.[18] The pressure of a major operational commitment would kick-start U.S. war production. The opening of the Mediterranean offered the shortest route to deliver U.S. aid to the USSR via Persia (Iran). At the Casablanca Conference of January 1943, even the U.S. Navy conceded that control of the Mediterranean would save shipping and supplement the suspension of the Arctic convoys during the winter months. The air force spotted infinite possibilities for new bases from which to attack Europe.[19] Torch was a first step in the revival of France as a fighting ally and as a player in the postwar world. It offered a vehicle to attack the Axis by taking out its weakest member. North Africa might not provide a "Second Front" to satisfy Stalin in the short run. But if Stalin was patient, the Second Front, when it came, would be an American-dominated enterprise. The Soviet dictator apparently recognized this and, despite some grumbling, concluded that he could hang on.[20] World War II was a war of attrition. Germany must be worn down, bled, exhausted before it could be overwhelmed. Torch offered the first step in asserting American predominance over the Western Alliance and of making sure that, at the peace, U.S. influence would predominate. Although Torch could not be a uniquely American enterprise, its U.S. component would be far greater than in Sledgehammer. An American general, Dwight D. Eisenhower, would command it. Unlike World War I, where the Allies had to learn to fight in the teeth of German strength, in the Mediterranean, American troops would experience their combat initiation in a region where the Axis was relatively weak.

American Chief of Staff George Marshall proved a formidable adversary of Torch, even for a politician as experienced as Roosevelt. A man universally admired for his integrity and his work ethic, the sixty-two-year-old Marshall joined "Ike" Eisenhower in the popular mind as a quintessentially democratic soldier. Marshall's soft eyes, straight mouth, and gray hair divided by a high part telegraphed the impression of a man of businesslike disposition focused on the organization of war. The press praised Marshall's "civilian mind," and felt none of the *frissons* of discomfort in Marshall's presence as when confronted with the praetorian posturing of a Douglas MacArthur or the straight-backed histrionic militarism of George Patton. During the 1930s, Marshall's "talent spotting" of mid-ranking officers like Eisenhower whom he deemed competent to hold high command became legendary. In the wake of Pearl Harbor, Marshall had streamlined the ramshackle War Department into an organization capable of conducting a world conflict. From Roosevelt's perspective, Marshall's one drawback was that he seemed inoculated against the president's voluble charm. This was quite intentional: Marshall, who prided himself on his self-control and logical approach to problem solving, did not want his opinions swayed by unjustified feelings of personal loyalty or emotion. Marshall's British opposite, General Sir Alan Brooke, found the American chief of staff ponderous and self-satisfied. To outsiders like Brooke, Marshall appeared to combine all the limitations of a staff general who approached war as an organizational problem rather than as an impassioned crusade. "Marshall's thoughts revolve round the creation of forces and not their employment," Brooke concluded.[21]

While Marshall's strengths undoubtedly lay in the planning, organization, and execution of war, rather than in the devising of strategy, he was hardly a soldier insulated from the political and social reality of wartime America. A Pennsylvanian and 1901 graduate of the Virginia Military Institute, Marshall was derided by his enemies as a "New Deal general" because in the 1930s he had served with the Illinois National Guard and as a supervisor for Civilian Conservation Corps camps in the South. Marshall treated these normally career-terminating assignments for ambitious officers as an opportunity to explore the realities and the challenges of Depression-era America. It led him to grasp the symbiosis between Roosevelt's governmental activism, social regeneration, and military readiness. But it also left him with an aversion to wasted effort. For Roosevelt, the uncertainty of war meant that, as in politics, one must always be ready to improvise and adjust. For Marshall, however, the achievement of incremental victories in remote theaters against the enemy's weakest ally so as to buy time with an impatient public was an alien, un-Clausewitzian concept. The chief of staff had a history of loyal opposition to some of FDR's more enlightened military decisions before Pearl Harbor—the decision to share aircraft production equally with Britain, to send surplus U.S. destroyers to the Royal Navy in exchange for a takeover of British bases in the Caribbean, Lend-Lease, the occupation of Iceland, the transfer of the fleet to Pearl Harbor, and the reinforcement of the U.S. garrison in the Philippines.[22]

For all his reputation as a man of rationality and restraint, Marshall was nevertheless an impatient, even impetuous, personality. The Mediterranean seemed to promise an inconclusive recess on the margins of world conflict in a theater where the United States had no strategic interests. He burned to come to grips with the Wehrmacht, *mano a mano*, on the beaches of northern France. Torch as part of Roosevelt's strategy to buy time to ensure U.S. predominance in the alliance and in the postwar world was a political dimension lost on Marshall. To the American general, it smacked of more presidential procrastination, Roosevelt's legendary inability to make clear-cut decisions, even of a transparent strategy to grab a cheap victory to influence Congressional elections in November 1942. "The leader in a democracy has to keep the people entertained" was one of Marshall's more cynical remarks.[23] From his purely military perspective, Marshall believed that the Mediterranean offered no prize worth the bones of a Mississippi National Guardsman. His operational mind grasped that the inevitable outcome of Torch would be to suck resources into the Mediterranean in such vast quantities as to make Roundup (the 1943 successor to Sledgehammer) an impossibility. Second, he suspected correctly that Churchill's strategic goal in Torch was to bolster Britain's imperial ambitions and postpone the final showdown with Germany. But Marshall's problem was that no viable alternative existed beyond a half-baked invasion of France, which even he conceded would probably fail. So when, on 25 July 1942, Roosevelt ordered his chief of staff to move "full speed ahead" on the planning for Torch, Marshall complied with the president's orders like an obedient subordinate.

But just because the American military was obliged by their commander-in-chief to join Torch did not mean that the Allies shared common goals for the expedition. For the British, the primary purposes of a North African campaign were to prove the worth of their troops and to expel Rommel. Allied control of the North African shore would open possibilities for expeditions and campaigns in the Mediterranean limited only by Churchill's fertile strategic imagination. Risk-averse American planners, influenced no doubt by Marshall's skepticism on the utility of the Mediterranean theater, were inclined to see the difficulties rather than the opportunities in Torch. The invasion of North Africa was for them a huge gamble—on the surf, on the combat performance of untested and undertrained troops, on the political attitudes of North African Frenchmen, on the Axis reaction. Keen to ensure against the least likely contingencies, they were equally aware that they had no strategic reserve to ensure against failure.[24] The inability of the Allies to agree on the goals of the North African invasion, or on the dimensions of its perils, was to compromise its effectiveness and set a pattern for subsequent Allied operations in the Mediterranean.

Torch posed problems on the strategic, operational, and tactical levels. The major strategic fear was that Franco might combine with the Germans to occupy Gibraltar, isolate any forces that had sailed through the strait, and turn his roughly 130,000 troops in Spanish Morocco against the invasion. At the very least, he might make air bases available to the Luftwaffe. The French reaction to an invasion posed a second strategic conundrum. The 1940 fall of France had rendered the normally complex pattern of French political life totally incomprehensible to "Anglo-Saxons." The collapse of the French army in barely six weeks in the face of a foe that they had resisted successfully for four years in World War I had stunned the world and set confused and humiliated French leaders stalking for scapegoats. The government under Marshal Philippe Pétain, established in the spa town of Vichy in the "free" or unoccupied zone of southern France, had no problem dipping into the recent French past to round up the usual defeatist suspects. Jews, Freemasons, socialists, Communists, foreigners, the English—just about anyone else who failed to fit into their conservative, Catholic schema—were denounced as having undermined the will of the French nation to defend itself. Both U.S. and British policy had sought to appease Vichy in the hope that eventually it would return to the Allied fold. But appeasement was too often sacrificed to the requirements of war. The list of French grievances against the British was extensive, beginning with the evacuation at Dunkirk and running through Mers el-Kébir, the internment of the French squadron at Alexandria, attacks on Dakar, Syria, and Madagascar, the seizure of French warships in British ports, and Churchill's support for the Free French under Charles de Gaulle.

The French army in North Africa, nominally set by the Franco-German armistice of 1940 at 100,000 men, had been starved of replacements by the Axis so that it numbered only 74,763 under-equipped and relatively demoralized officers and men by November 1942. And while French leaders in North Africa worried about an Allied invasion, they did not think it likely before 1943. Instead, they kept the bulk of their forces and their most modern equipment in Morocco deployed against the possibility of invasion from Franco's troops through the Spanish Rif. The political attitudes of this garrison were difficult to gauge. While there was widespread sympathy for the Allied cause, the military leadership understood that the war hung in the balance in the autumn of 1942 in the Western Desert and at Stalingrad. Any premature declaration for the Allies would invariably precipitate an Axis occupation of the "free zone" and of French North Africa, which would strip Vichy of its nominal independence. The German Control Commission based in Wiesbaden, which monitored French military activity in North Africa, had concluded in May 1942 that the armistice army had "only a limited capability" to defend North Africa from a seaborne invasion and would "stand fast for only a very short time." In fact, the 5 May 1942 British landing on Madagascar might be taken as an anticipation of the politically calculated nature of a Vichy response. At first the French resisted, but failed to counterattack the relatively small British force. Diégo-Suarez fell in three days. The governor-general retreated to the south of the island with his remaining forces and refused to sign an armistice until 6 November, only two days before Torch. In this way, the Germans had been satisfied that Vichy was vigorously defending its remaining imperial outposts from Allied encroachment. At the same time, French resistance had been so listless that the British counted only 107 casualties for the entire seven-month campaign.[25]

Operationally, Torch offered the first experience of joint Anglo-American planning. On 6 June, fifty-two-year-old Lieutenant General Dwight Eisenhower, commander of the U.S. Army in the European theater, was appointed "Commander-in-Chief, Allied Expeditionary Force." At first glance, Eisenhower would appear to fall into the category of leaders who have greatness thrust upon them, for little in his upbringing prepared him for a task so monumental that men far better equipped to assume the burden might have shirked it. A mechanic's son raised on the wrong side of the tracks in Abilene, Kansas, Eisenhower defied his parents' Mennonite pacifism and profound antipathy to the military to accept a 1910 appointment to West Point, from which he graduated with no great distinction. Marooned Stateside during World War I, he helped to organize America's first tank corps. But the interwar army with its slow promotion and dull duties was no place for a man churned by ambition. His rise to prominence was facilitated by his technique of finding "the strongest and ablest man. I forget my own ideas and do anything in my power to promote what *he* says is right." The "strongest and ablest man" in the 1930s was Douglas MacArthur, whom Eisenhower served during MacArthur's tenure as chief of staff from 1930, and subsequently in the Philippines where he was military commander. During his nine years with MacArthur, Eisenhower gained a reputation as a cautious but courageous and temperamental officer willing to disagree, sometimes volubly, with his imperious boss. But in MacArthur's service, Eisenhower honed "his ability to find common ground between competing priorities and people," his greatest asset, in Carlo D'Este's estimation.[26]

In 1939, his friend Mark Wayne Clark organized Lieutenant Colonel Eisenhower's assignment to Washington, where a robust "old boy network" anchored in West Point and the Command and Staff

College at Fort Leavenworth, Kansas, combined with Marshall's patronage, catapulted him up the career ladder and kept him there through the severe criticism of his handling of the North African campaign. Eisenhower, Mark Clark, and Patton emerged as the stars of the series of 1941 maneuvers held in Louisiana, Tennessee, and South Carolina.[27] News of Pearl Harbor caused Marshall to call Brigadier General Eisenhower to Washington to become deputy chief of the War Plans Division. Marshall's reorganization of the War Department advanced him to major general, and by June 1942 he was assigned by Marshall to head the Observer Group in London, with Mark Clark as his deputy. Marshall was concerned that there was no understanding in London of the future U.S. role in the war, and he wanted Eisenhower to explain his point of view. When Roosevelt ordered Torch, Marshall decided that Eisenhower, the man on the spot, would command it.[28]

Eisenhower's open, friendly demeanor and ready smile "as broad as a Kansas prairie" radiated the sincerity and optimism of the American Midwest. Second Lieutenant Paul Fussell writes that Eisenhower was "the only general my troops and I respected—for his kindness, his understanding of the soldier's needs and fears, his distance from the vainglory and love of violence manifested by General Patton." Even for a skeptic like Fussell, Eisenhower represented "memorable counterbalancing evidence of human decency," even nobility, in a U.S. Army otherwise characterized by "cruelties and fatuities."[29] But the positive spin given Eisenhower by the press was not always shared by those closest to him. He was a remarkably insecure man, who craved recognition, especially from his old boss MacArthur. He was also extraordinarily thin-skinned when it came to criticism, and frequently lashed subordinates with his volatile temper. Eisenhower's latest biographer rejects the accusation that Eisenhower had a wartime affair with Kay Somersby, if for no other reason than the Allied commander's Versailles-like existence left him no private moments to think through strategic problems, much less carry out illicit assignations with his driver. Nevertheless, Somersby offered Eisenhower much-needed emotional support, although her presence at Ike's side on unit tours and in high-level meetings invited gossip and further strained his already tense marriage.[30]

The British found Eisenhower too emotional, too easily distracted by political events, or too immersed in campaign minutiae to be a great commander.[31] With his typical sense of diplomacy, Montgomery complained of Eisenhower's "high-pitched accent and loud talking," his excitability, and his tendency to micromanage operations from afar by telegrams, lightning visits to the front, and conferences. "He knows practically nothing about how to make war, and definitely nothing about how to fight battles." Montgomery explained Eisenhower's promotion, like that of Alexander, as the product of coalition warfare in which "the weak and charming prospered" in the upper reaches of command while the battles were won by men of more ruthless disposition.[32] Many Britons felt that Eisenhower was carried by his chief of staff, Bedell Smith.[33] George Patton, who agreed with Montgomery on little else, ungratefully complained that Eisenhower, who repeatedly intervened to salvage his career from his serial indiscretions, was "just a staff officer, not a soldier." He referred to Ike as "Divine Destiny," and called him a "straw man" highly placed precisely to do Britain's bidding.[34] Patton was at least half right. Eisenhower did owe his appointment to lead Torch at least in part to Brooke, who saw it as a way to get the American out of London and place him "on a pedestal"[35] supported by British command experience. In this way, Brooke calculated that he could "restore the necessary drive and coordination which had been so seriously lacking" in Eisenhower's command,[36] and better ensure British control of Mediterranean operations. But Brooke's maneuver also served to place Eisenhower in the middle of the action, and gave him what Stephen Ambrose calls a "remarkable grant of power" to arbitrate the three most important strategic decisions of 1943: how to resolve the French imbroglio, whether to invade Italy, and how to govern that country.

Eisenhower was inexperienced and lacked ruthlessness. Patton and Omar Bradley, who chafed at Eisenhower's practically born-again commitment to evenhandedness in the Anglo-American alliance, learned in Sicily to ignore his orders if they went against their purpose.[37] But Ike's diplomatic skills were invaluable. And even those who criticized him most harshly, like Montgomery and Patton, instinctively liked him in spite of themselves. Harold Macmillan praised Eisenhower as a "jewel of broad-mindedness and wisdom," a leader willing to give all sides a fair hearing before reaching a decision.[38] Eisenhower's main accomplishment, according to Carlo D'Este, was "to weld and hold together the machinery of war."[39] "General Eisenhower has worked a miracle," one Foreign Office official confessed in January 1944, "the full wonder of which is not perhaps appreciated; and I doubt whether it would have been possible under a British chief on such a scale and in circumstances of such publicity."[40]

Allied Force Headquarters (AFHQ), which Eisenhower took over on 14 August 1942, reflected its new commander's strengths and weaknesses. Its success lay in the fact that it reflected Eisenhower's quasi-spiritual devotion to the alliance, and Marshall's philosophy that a divided command invited calamity. Eisenhower's desire to forge a combined staff with an absolute prohibition on favoritism continued the policy fostered by Churchill of building a truly integrated Anglo-American effort. Churchill's strategy was not a disinterested one, however. Eisenhower sought to lash the United States to the British war effort, but to integrate the staff to make sure that the acceleration of U.S. power did not leave Britain in its wake.[41] This had begun in 1942 with the creation of the Combined Chiefs of Staff (CCOS), as well as committees that pooled British and American transport and munitions production, and the combined intelligence operation at Bletchley Park. Whenever possible, British commanders were given American deputies and vice versa. But bridging these national divides by demanding loyalty to the alliance rather than to one's own country was counterintuitive for officers whose every sinew of allegiance was to the nation-state. The problem became more acute after AFHQ moved to Algiers in the wake of Torch. Eisenhower's headquarters was seldom free of the tensions and competition that characterized the Anglo-American alliance. The lackluster British performance through July 1942 prior to Montgomery's arrival had the Americans complaining in the summer of 1942 that "the British are absolutely incapable of exercising command or using equipment." Some in official Washington felt the need to "put an end to their tendency to cave in and look to us to save the situation," and were extremely critical of Roosevelt's commitment to a Mediterranean strategy.[42] On the other hand, the inauspicious debut of U.S. troops in Tunisia caused the British to fear that "our Italians" were not up to the task of fighting Germans. When, in an attempt to nip these tensions in the bud, Eisenhower shipped back to the States an American officer who had denounced one of his colleagues as "a British son-of-a-bitch," his compatriots grumbled that Ike was too ready to sacrifice American interests on the altar of Allied unity.[43] Patton called AFHQ "a British headquarters commanded by an American."[44] On the other hand, the British felt that AFHQ was definitely an "American empire" in which they were assigned inferior but essential tasks, much "as the Greek slaves ran the operations of the Emperor Claudius."[45] As AFHQ was increasingly called upon to make important political decisions in North Africa and Italy, the Americans appointed the American consul in Algiers, a self-assured, thirty-eight-year-old stoop-shouldered diplomat from Milwaukee named Robert Murphy, "U.S. Diplomatic Minister at AFHQ." To counter the influence of Murphy, whom the British considered a second-rate Anglophobe, London named Harold Macmillan "British Minister Resident at AFHQ." But overall, AFHQ was taken as evidence of Eisenhower's success as a coalition builder, his ability to find compromises and work with difficult personalities. This reputation helped him to avoid the sack at the Casablanca Conference of January 1943.[46]

Ike's weaknesses were also displayed at AFHQ, directed by the "intense, tempestuous, and harassed" Walter Bedell Smith.[47] The British complained that the organization of AFHQ was at once unwieldy and undignified, and reflected the U.S. Army's amateurish approach to war. AFHQ's morale was made brittle by the emotional peaks and valleys of its chain-smoking boss. The 1,000 officers and 5,000 enlisted personnel, shoehorned into the once-elegant St. George Hotel on a palm-covered hill overlooking the port of Algiers, were ruled by a sense of drift and "restless confusion."[48] The requirement to preside over the "aimless bustle" of AFHQ, to receive the constant horde of visitors, allowed Eisenhower to distance himself from the front four hundred miles away in Tunisia, relieving him of the requirement to make hard decisions face-to-face with ground commanders. Instead, he sat in Algiers "writing endless letters," according to Omar Bradley, dispatched from Washington in February 1943 to take command of the Second Corps in the aftermath of the Kasserine debacle.[49] "I have known a number of G.H.Q.s," wrote Alan Moorehead. "But never one as congested as this. Admirals were working in sculleries, and as like as not you would find a general or two weaving their plans in back bathrooms and pantries."[50] Montgomery dubbed AFHQ "a dreadful party," made worse by Eisenhower's passivity and indecision, his reluctance to delegate, his fear of taking risks, and by the intrigues of Eisenhower's ambitious deputy General Mark Clark, who short-circuited normal channels of command in ways that the British believed unfavorable to them.[51] U.S. correspondent A. J. Liebling found that the energies of the British, American, and French Allies at AFHQ were absorbed in a keen competition to requisition Algiers's most sumptuous villas.[52] For Moorehead, AFHQ reverberated with the intrigue, suspicion, and quarrelsome atmosphere of Algiers, "a mean and petty betrayal of men at the front who were fighting for something quite different."[53]

The operational challenges faced by Eisenhower's planners were significant: How to invade a mountainous region 1,200 miles long from Morocco to Tunis, defended by around 75,000 French troops, with a largely untried Allied force dispatched from bases in the United States and Great Britain at the beginning of the stormy season? The solution favored the more conservative operational approach of the Americans, which compromised the bolder British strategic goals. The British argued that the intervention forces must land as far east as possible, in Bône and possibly Philippeville, so as to reach Tunis quickly before Axis troops could establish a bridgehead there. The Americans, reluctant to stick their heads in the Mediterranean "bag,"[54] and arguing that lack of carriers made it difficult to protect troops landed in eastern Algeria against Axis air attacks launched from Sardinia and Sicily, preferred to shift the center of gravity of the attack to the west. By ensuring against an uncertain Spanish reaction at the expense of a highly probable Axis invasion of Tunisia, Marshall guaranteed an unequal race for Tunisia with no better than a 50 percent chance of success for the Allies. In the final version of Torch, 65,000 troops divided into three "Assault Forces" would sail from the United States and the United Kingdom in 370 merchant ships escorted by 300 warships. The Royal Navy would bring the Eastern Assault Force, composed of 20,000 U.S. and British forces from Great Britain, to seize Algiers. As soon as they set foot ashore, the troops in Algiers would become the First (British) Army under Lieutenant General Kenneth A. N. Anderson. Anderson was to move east to preempt the inevitable Axis advance on Tunisia. The Central Assault Force of 19,000 U.S. troops under Major General Lloyd Fredendall also left from Britain to storm Oran. The Western Task Force of 25,000 U.S. troops under Major General George Patton sailed from the East Coast of the United States to land on the Atlantic coast of Morocco. The American troops in Oran and Morocco would become the Fifth (U.S.) Army.

The more conservative American version of the plan failed to eliminate operational risks altogether. The approach of huge convoys of ships and the buildup of aircraft at Gibraltar telegraphed the possibility of a huge operation. The numbers of amphibious craft were limited, and in any case the haste with which Torch had been cobbled together had cut rehearsal time to the bone. The high surf on the Atlantic coast of Morocco threatened to swamp the invasion craft. Even when safely on shore, the inadequacy of and distance between the French ports would make it difficult to concentrate large numbers of troops rapidly. The U.S. Navy was proving uncooperative about shipping. Contemplating these difficulties threw Eisenhower into a funk so profound that he considered petitioning FDR to cancel the operation.[55] The only rays of hope seemed to be Robert Murphy's very optimistic assessment that the French would not oppose the landing so long as it was U.S.-led.[56] Still, Eisenhower took steps to place fortune on his side. In mid-October, Mark Clark was secretly ferried by submarine to Algiers, where he learned from Major General Charles Mast, chief of staff of the French Nineteenth Corps, that with four days' notice he could neutralize virtually all army resistance. Murphy assiduously cultivated the commander of the French troops in North Africa, General Alphonse Juin, who made no secret of his pro-Allied attitude.[57] On 6 November, French General Henri Giraud, a tall, elegant cavalryman who had been captured in 1940 and subsequently sprung from a German POW camp, was flown to Gibraltar to broadcast an appeal to his countrymen to rally to the Allies. Roosevelt placed Torch off-limits to Charles de Gaulle's Free French forces, both because he believed that de Gaulle's organization was an intelligence sieve and because their presence would guarantee an adverse reaction from the staunchly pro-Vichy North African garrison.

By far the biggest imponderable of the operation for Eisenhower was how the untested American troops might perform in their first major operation. In North Africa, the United States would pose the same agonizing "Can we fight?" question that had tortured the British until El Alamein. The "American way of war" relied on a small cadre of professional officers, many of them West Point–educated,[58] who would provide the training, leadership, and general direction for the mass of volunteers and conscripts mobilized for a conflict. This system had served the United States well enough at least since the Mexican War of 1846–48. And it would continue to serve the country well in World War II, especially in the upper ranks. Although the war produced egregious failures like Fredendall at Kasserine and Lucas at Anzio, and ultimately successful but controversial generals like George Patton, Mark Clark, and even Eisenhower, overall the United States was spared the agonizing quest for quality leadership in the upper ranks of the army that hampered the British in the war's early years. A primary reason for this can be traced to the intolerance of American society overall, and of FDR in particular, for attitudes of martial self-importance in American generals. Exceptions existed, of course, like George Patton and Douglas MacArthur, men who believed their heritage and destiny set them apart, and above, the social and political conventions of the democracy they served. Roosevelt, however, laid out the parameters of his expectations in April 1939 when he reached down to number thirty-four on the army's seniority list to pluck George Marshall to serve as chief of staff. Intimate experience of Depression hardships, and perhaps his experience as a VMI cadet, reinforced Marshall's aversion to military narcissism and self-importance and steeled his determination to fill the upper ranks of the American army with men able to harness the nation's energies efficiently to the business of winning the war. "American high military leadership in the 1940s is still impressive for its matching of individual to task, for its sloughing off of militaristic vainglory, for its coordinating of one and all with the purposes to which the President gave voice," writes American historian Eric Larrabee.[59]

Marshall provided the link. One of his first acts as chief of staff was to persuade Congress to create a board to identify unfit officers and allow the secretary of war to "reassign" them. This allowed him to reach far down seniority lists to promote diligent and conscientious officers, men of common outlook and tradition who, like Dwight Eisenhower, were quite junior. These men, a West Point and Leavenworth mafia, were thrust into high positions of responsibility. The effect trickled down from the Pentagon to the battlefield. The combat leaders the United States Army identified in North Africa continued to prove their value in Sicily. Patton, Bradley, Clark, Terry Allen of the First Division, Lucian Truscott of the Third Division, Troy Middleton of the Forty-fifth Division, Hugh Gaffey of the Second Armored, and Matthew Ridgway of the Eighty-second Airborne would provide a solid core of leadership in Italy and Normandy.

The problem with the "American way of war" was that it took time to bite, as conscription was introduced, industrial production kicked in, troops were war-hardened, and the best field commanders were identified. World War II proved no exception. The lightning buildup of American forces that had begun with the 1941 "Victory Program," which increased military spending from $5 billion to $20 billion, exploded on the outbreak of war, eventually reaching $82 billion annually by 1944. But it proved difficult to translate this cornucopia of cash immediately into offensive military power. Eventually, the combination of 205-ton, four-wheel-drive trucks, amphibious DUKWs, which gave over-the-beach supply capabilities, and self-propelled artillery meant that, by the Sicily campaign of July–August 1943, the U.S. Army would outstrip its British ally in speed, maneuverability, and firepower. But in the short run, the requirement to equip and train so many men in such a short time meant that the ongoing development of quality weapons took a back seat to the immediate requirement to equip a mass of soldiery.

Some 16.1 million Americans eventually served in the World War II military. An army that numbered 200,000 men in 1939, ranking seventeenth in the world just behind that of Romania, expanded to 8.3 million by 1944. These had to be conscripted and trained. The pressure of rapid expansion forced the military to adopt qualitatively inferior weapons systems.[60] Ships had to be found to transfer men and equipment to distant theaters. The U.S. Army's shortcomings became apparent almost immediately in North Africa. These stemmed from at least three causes.

First, the army lost out in the battle for quality manpower against the Roosevelt-favored navy and army air force, which argued that they required better-educated personnel to perform more skilled tasks. The navy and AAF also recruited in excess of their needs, parking men in noncombatant—even nonmilitary—roles and hence depriving the army of a potentially valuable source of officers and specialists for intelligence, photo reconnaissance, radio listening, POW interrogation, and so on.[61] Within the army ground forces the lowest-quality recruits were reserved for the infantry. While men of higher social status undoubtedly found their way into the infantry, the rifle custodians were drawn overwhelmingly from the ranks of "hicks, Micks, and spics." America's disfavored were acutely conscious of the fact that they clung to the bottom rung of the U.S. military caste system and nurtured a deep resentment of the exploitation of GIs—"Goddamned Infantry." In short, Tom Brokaw's "greatest generation" was represented on the front lines by its least favored members. From the end of 1943, the dearth of replacements caused Marshall to intervene to give priority to the infantry, so that toward the end of the war that arm was—at last—receiving quality recruits, while America's allies and opponents were scraping the bottom of the barrel.[62]

Second, the requirement for four support troops for every combatant, combined with the fact that 70 percent of U.S. casualties from 1943 were in the infantry, shrank the pool of reserves available to ground forces. Army units were perpetually understrength and lacked the training, reserves, and numerical superiority required for successful offensive operations. This problem became more acute as the increased tempo of operations from 1943 gave ground units little time to

integrate replacements and recover from the high losses of junior officers and NCOs. After watching American troops in training at Fort
Jackson, South Carolina, in the summer of 1942, British General Is-
may speculated that it would be "murder" to place them against German soldiers.[63] He was not far off the mark. Montgomery complained
that American soldiers "haven't got the light of battle in their eyes,"
and blamed it on the poor quality of American generals, who did not
know how to inspire their subordinates. Alexander, observing American troops in 1943, called them "soft, green, and quite untrained . . .
They have no hatred of Germans and show no eagerness to get in and
kill them."[64] "Wasn't the ground war, for the United States, an unin-
tended form of eugenics," Paul Fussell, who himself served in the infantry, comments cynically, "clearing the population of the dumbest,
the least skilled, the least promising of all young American males?"[65]

A third reason for a relatively lackluster performance was a failure
of inter-arm and interservice cooperation. As in the British army, artillery, naval support and air power became essential prerequisites
for the success of U.S. ground troops. In this respect, U.S. forces
counted the advantage of being able to follow the lead blazed by the
RAF and the Royal Navy in air support and amphibious operations.
Allied air superiority increased with the introduction in 1942 of the
twin-tailed, twin-engine P-38 "Lightning," the first U.S. fighter to exceed 400 miles per hour and that could climb close to 40,000 feet. So
favored was the P-38 by American aces that German pilots called
it "the devil with the twin tail." This was followed by the P-51
"Mustang," which began life in 1942 as a reconnaissance plane before
transitioning in 1943 into the best fighter of the war. The P-51H, introduced in 1944, was armed with six machine guns, could fly a brisk
486 miles per hour, and earned its spurs accompanying long-range
bombers over Germany. By 1944, U.S. pilots dominated the skies and
enjoyed a three-to-one kill ratio. The absence of Luftwaffe predators
eventually allowed "horsefly" artillery spotters in light Cessna aircraft
to take to the air in Italy. The ability to support amphibious operations
was increased by the development of the Landing Ship Tank (LST)
and larger Landing Craft Infantry (LCI), as well as close-support naval
craft. Much U.S. air power was siphoned off for strategic bombing,

however, and the broken terrain of the Mediterranean theater reduced artillery effectiveness. This, combined with poor training, ruled out complicated schemes of maneuver and complex fire plans. Infantry attacks often became murderous undertakings, which induced caution in subsequent operations. American forces demonstrated some of the same deficiencies as the Eighth Army: poor infantry–armor cooperation; American tanks reverting to their cavalry heritage to charge off unsupported on their own; and an "operational caution" that made commanders reluctant to seize battlefield opportunities. This prudence was reinforced by the feeling that many U.S. weapons were inferior to those of the Germans and that tactical intelligence was lacking.[66]

In retrospect, it seems hardly possible that Torch took anyone by surprise, because Eisenhower had to guarantee that the operation packed such a wallop that Vichy resistance would crumble instantaneously. Rumors of an imminent Allied invasion of North Africa had rattled around Axis staffs and European capitals at least since June 1942, rumors that accelerated in early November.[67] Three hundred fifty aircraft, many of them Hurricanes and Spitfires brought by sea, uncrated and assembled on the runway, were crammed wingtip-to-wingtip on Gibraltar's airstrip, while Algeciras Bay, carefully observed by the Italians, was crowded with auxiliary ships. Allied planners feared that should the Germans get wind of the expedition, between 50 and 75 U-boats could be concentrated against the convoys as they steered for the strait. Fortunately for the Allies, the autumn of 1942 caught German naval commander Grand Admiral Erich Raeder and U-boat chief Karl Dönitz locked in a bitter dispute over how best to position Germany's submarine fleet. Dönitz's 17 November decision to shift twenty U-boats from the Atlantic to the Mediterranean was a case of too little too late.[68] As a result, even the slowest of the Allied ships carrying much of the expedition's equipment, at sea for over a month, arrived unmolested off the North African coast. The faster ships departed the United States and the Clyde between 22 and 26 October, preceded by an eye-popping prodigality of air reconnaissance and naval escorts. Between the night of 5 November and morning of 7 November, 340 ships passed through the Strait of Gibraltar.

Fortunately for the Allies, the Vichy French and the Axis fell victim to self-deception. U-boats lurking between Cape Verde and the Azores were diverted to Madeira to attack a convoy returning to Britain from Freetown. British intelligence disoriented its German counterpart by inundating it with rumors that played on German fears of an invasion of Norway, Sicily, the Aegean, and southern France. Therefore, for German intelligence, North Africa was crowded off the radar screen of potential invasion destinations. In Algiers, French Admiral Jean-François Darlan refused to believe the Americans capable of putting three hundred ships on the Atlantic, much less of invading North Africa, before 1944.[69] The most obvious explanation for the immense naval activity was that the ships were a repeat of the Pedestal relief convoy to Malta, combined with an attempt to muscle through the Mediterranean with supplies for Montgomery. The British perpetuated this deception by replicating the course and employing wireless

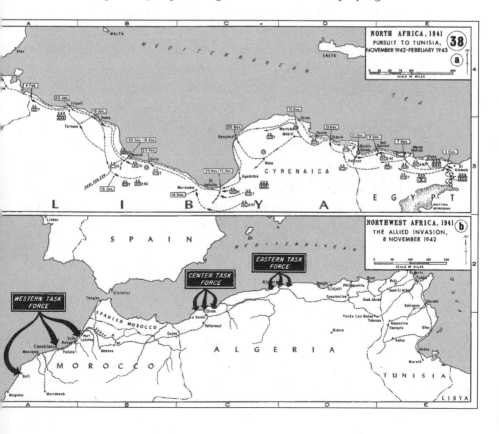

behavior characteristic of previous Malta convoys among the ships bound for Algiers and Oran.[70] The southern convoy was thought to have Dakar as a target, a replication of the failed 1940 attack on the West African port.[71] The success of Allied deception was boosted by the fact that the Germans rejected any intelligence that might rattle their relations with the Vichy French. Hitler remained convinced that the French would defend North Africa if attacked, and turned a cold shoulder to Italian demands for a preemptive occupation of Tunisia.[72]

Ironically, the invaders chose the same beach near Algiers that the French had used in their 1830 invasion of North Africa. Roosevelt broadcast a message of friendship to *"la France éternelle,"* while General Giraud echoed FDR's call to his countrymen in North Africa to rally to the Allies. The American Psychological Warfare Bureau blanketed North Africa with radio messages and 30 million leaflets entitled *Souvenez-vous?* ("Do You Remember?"), extolling the memories of Franco-American cooperation in World War I and emphasizing the U.S, rather than Allied, nature of the operation.[73] Young men loyal to General Mast and the Free French seized most of Algiers's communications centers, including the central post office, which controlled the telephone and telegraph lines, and placed General Juin and Admiral Darlan under house arrest. The destroyer *Broke* landed 250 men of the 135th Infantry right in Algiers harbor to seize the oil installations and power station and prevent ships from being scuttled to block the harbor. The airfield at Maison Blanche southeast of the city was occupied by American troops, and Spitfires and Hurricanes from Gibraltar began to land by 10 a.m. General Mast persuaded French sailors manning the fort at Sidi Ferruch west of Algiers to surrender to American troops, who could then roll onto the broad beach unopposed. Planes from British carriers off the coast landed on Blida airfield without incident.

The Algerian landings unfolded like a slow pantomime. Troops were settled on the wrong beaches. Officers raced up and down unfamiliar roads in requisitioned black Citroëns searching for their scattered commands. Bullets from snipers and isolated machine-gun nests kicked masonry out of walls and felled unsuspecting GIs. Elsewhere,

French *pieds noirs*, many dressed for Sunday mass, gawked and enterprising merchants opened their shops in the hope of attracting the khaki-clad customers. Moslems, attired in dirty djellabas and sandals, squatted in doorways or strolled through the sniping with casual nonchalance. Only the children seemed energized enough to gouge sweets or cigarettes out of the invaders. Gradually the Americans collected their forces and moved toward the Casbah of Algiers, its square white houses layered like the kernels of a pinecone against the side of the hill, above a blue bay.

The relatively slow advance of the Allies into Algiers allowed Juin and Darlan to turn the tables on their captors. Darlan radioed Vichy to ask for German air support against the invasion, a communication that was intercepted by Allied code breakers. On the afternoon of 8 November, Darlan authorized Juin to conclude a cease-fire in Algiers. U.S. troops entered the city at 1900, just as Vichy severed diplomatic relations with the United States. The off-loading of troops moved from the beaches to Algiers harbor. Landings to the east and west of Oran went unopposed. An attempt at Oran to replicate the Algiers landing of troops right on the jetties of the town's crescent-shaped harbor, however, was repulsed with heavy casualties by several French destroyers, two of which were sunk as they attempted to sail out past the breakwater to attack the landing fleet. Hurricanes from two escort carriers destroyed seventy French planes on the ground at the La Senia airfield. A planned airborne assault on Oran's two airfields by U.S. paratroops flown in from Cornwall failed when the formation became dispersed in a storm over Spain. The U.S. First Infantry Division landed behind smoke screens on the beach at Arzeu east of Oran. The advance toward the town was delayed by a few shore batteries until they were silenced by British naval gunfire. Fierce French resistance in some of the small suburbs was bypassed. Units of the French Foreign Legion (the only troops the Americans feared, because Hollywood had endowed them with a fearsome reputation) racing north from their celebrated headquarters at Sidi bel-Abbès were attacked by American-piloted Spitfires operating out of the captured airfield at Tafaraoui. Tanks of "the Big Red One" rolled into Oran on the morning of 10 November to a rapturous popular welcome.

On the Moroccan coast, heavy surf caused the loss of many landing craft. Nevertheless, Safi, 140 miles north of Casablanca, surrendered, and the Americans began disembarking Sherman tanks to advance on Casablanca, where Resident General Auguste Nouguès had easily foiled a pro-Allied attempt to arrest him and had ordered the troops to resist. Port Lyautey fell to Lucian Truscott's troops after a stiff three-day fight. At Casablanca, the most murderous action was naval, but it was fairly one-sided. French warships sallied out of Casablanca harbor to attack the U.S. armada. Four French submarines and six French destroyers were sunk or driven ashore by naval gunfire and by planes off the carrier *Ranger*. The heavy cruiser *Primauguet*, launched out of Casablanca at 21 knots like a missile directed at the invasion fleet, was holed below the waterline by shells from the *Massachusetts* and strafed by U.S. planes. Its engine room flooded, the captain and half its crew dead, the French cruiser limped for shore, ran aground, and burned. The battleship *Jean Bart* barely had time to fire seven shells before it settled into the mud of Casablanca harbor, her guns silenced and her keel perforated by shells from the *Massachusetts*. Ten merchant ships tethered to the docks were blasted to the bottom. Patton's landing north of Casablanca was, if anything, more confused than in Algeria. His 20,000 troops, scattered over miles of beach, milled about with a lack of direction or urgency that infuriated Patton. Fortunately, the defending French, neither numerous nor well organized, were demoralized by the bombardment from the U.S. ships standing off shore. The American move from the small harbor at Fedala south toward Casablanca was slowed by logistical difficulties. As General Patton's forces massed to take the city on the eleventh, news of the French capitulation in North Africa arrived. The price in casualties paid by the Allies for French North Africa was a fairly light 1,225 for the Americans and 662 for the British.[74] The French counted 1,346 casualties, mostly in Oran and Morocco.[75] American General Lucian Truscott believed that the landing "would have spelled disaster against a well-armed enemy intent on resistance."[76]

On the morning of 9 November, Lieutenant General Kenneth Anderson, at the head of his newly christened British First Army,

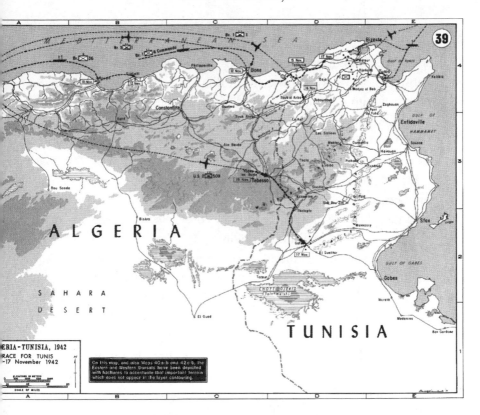

which at this stage of the war was hardly more than a scratch force of 12,000 men, began to move toward Tunisia, which, it was hoped, could be seized before the Axis was able to build up a bridgehead there. He was destined to be disappointed. Despite the urging of some of his military chiefs that the time had come to abandon North Africa, Hitler understood that the southern shore of the Mediterranean constituted a base from which Southern Europe, and in particular his Italian ally, could be assaulted.[77] Anderson's first targets were the ports of Bougie and Bône. His forces were shadowed by a naval supply convoy and the British Seventy-eighth Division, which moved slowly along the coast. Eisenhower contemplated sending this floating reserve directly to Tunis, but instead dropped it at Bougie, only one hundred miles east of Algiers, which was entered without resistance on 11 November. Eisenhower's caution forfeited the only opportunity to pre-empt the Axis seizure of Tunisia. Eisenhower also rejected suggestions that follow-up floating reserves be sent to seize Sardinia, which could have become an important base for attacking Tunisia and Sicily.[78] But British troops and ships came under increasing attack by Axis aircraft. British paratroops were dropped on Bône the next day in an attack co-ordinated with a commando landing to seize the harbor and airfield. By 14 November, Spitfires had occupied the Bône airfield, but had to defend it vigorously against Axis air attacks out of Sardinia and Sicily. Meanwhile, U-boats and Italian submarines converged on the coasts of Morocco and Algeria and began to sink supply ships in ever greater numbers, although they, too, paid a high price. The Italian navy, plead-ing a fuel shortage and the lack of air cover, elected to stay in harbor, thereby preserving their fleet-in-being.

On 14 November, Anderson ordered his forces to move eastward along hairpin roads and high mountain passes dominated by pine forests, hoping to reach Tunis in about a week. The countryside was spectacular, but progress was slow. " 'Attention! Rallientair!' [sic] signs appeared frequently," wrote gunner Spike Milligan. ". . . Camel trains all laden with goods followed tracks two or three hundred feet above us, moving slowly with dignity no civilization had managed to speed up. At sundown the Arabs turned towards Mecca to carry out their de-votions, a religious people, more than I could say for our lot, the only time *they* knelt was to pick up money."[79] On the next day, Anderson made contact with French General Georges Barré, commander of the 10,000 French troops in Tunisia, who had slowly withdrawn toward Al-geria as Axis troops settled into Tunis on the invitation of the Vichy government and with the assistance of the French navy.

Although without any contingency plan, the Germans reacted quickly to news of Torch. Hitler, determined to transform Tunisia into the "cornerstone" of Axis defense of North Africa, ordered his generals to transfer strong armored forces there.[80] By 9 November they had seized El Aouina airfield at Tunis and rapidly began to ferry in troops and supplies in numerous transport aircraft. By the end of the month, 15,000 German troops were on the ground, including both paratroop and panzer battalions. Bits and pieces of Italian units also drifted in by sea. General Walther Nehring, who commanded this hodgepodge of Axis forces, calculated that the Allies must attempt to seize Tunis and

Bizerte. He set screens of troops to delay the Allied advance from the west. The preliminary clashes occurred from 17 November as British soldiers advanced toward Mateur, a town about twenty miles south of Bizerte, across a parched, dun-colored countryside. Two days later German troops drove the French out of Medjez el Bab, hardly breaking a sweat. But at least this opening skirmish gave an indication that the French, though poorly armed, would henceforth fight on the Allied side.

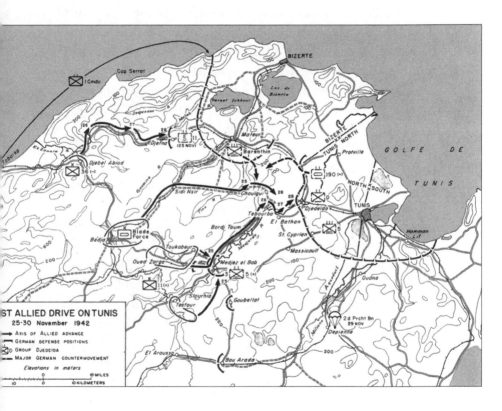

Having met opposition, Anderson was more eager than ever to move his forces forward in strength before he launched his drive toward Tunis. However, his advance was hampered by congestion in the port of Algiers, North Africa's rudimentary transportation system, and a lack of vehicles, sacrificed in favor of troops on U.S. transports. Anderson moved west in two prongs, a southern thrust aimed at Tunis, while a northern push reached for Bizerte. A British attempt to recapture Medjez, which stood across the road to Tunis, was repulsed on the twenty-fourth when a battalion of Lancashire Fusiliers was savaged by German paratroops firing 88s and machine guns. On the same day, elements of the First (U.S.) Armored Regiment reached Djedeida, about ten miles west of Tunis, where Stuart tanks rampaged down a hill onto an unsuspecting German airfield. Stukas and Bf. 109s being refueled and rearmed were exploded, pilots and ground crew scattered by the 37 mm guns of the Stuarts. The American tanks departed at nightfall, leaving behind the wreckage of twenty German planes. The American raid rattled Nehring, whose nerve had to be restored by Kesselring, who flew in from Italy to oversee operations. By the twenty-seventh, the First Army appeared to be closing in on Tunis. The Germans abandoned Medjez and tightened their defensive ring around the Tunisian capital, while omnipresent Luftwaffe fighters popped from behind hills and ridgelines to bomb and strafe Allied units. On 27 November, British troops took Téboura. From the hills above the town, the roofs and minarets of Tunis beckoned only four miles distant. But by 29–30 November, the momentum had been sucked from the First Army advance. Too many things weren't working—not enough artillery, too little Anglo-American cooperation, too little combat experience, too little air support. Bône offered only a dirt strip 135 miles from Tunis for a handful of P-38s, while the Germans flew an estimated 850 fighters off all-weather airfields in Tunis and Bizerte. "We were more oriented toward fighters and bombers than we were toward ground support," confessed USAAF General James H. Doolittle, who admitted that logistical problems and poor communications formed the principal obstacles to air force efficiency.[81] He might also have mentioned a lack of planes and airfields to park them on. German defenders also knew a thing or two about defending, as the Argyll and Sutherland Highlanders discovered when they tripped a well-crafted German ambush on Highway 7 near Jefna on the way to Bizerte. The subsequent slaughter as the British struggled to wrest the hills above the road from the Germans made Anderson temporarily suspend his drive toward the two Tunisian cities.

On 1 December, the Germans counterattacked British troops outside of Djedeida from three directions with their newly formed Tenth

Panzer Division, commanded by Russian front veteran General Wolfgang Fischer. In three days of fighting, the British and their American reinforcements gave ground as German tanks rolled right off the docks and into combat. It was classic Blitzkrieg, 1940 vintage. Sixty-ton monster PzKw VI "Tiger" tanks sporting an 88 mm gun also made their first crushing battlefield appearance in North Africa, as German forces chaperoned by screaming Stukas pressed inexorably toward Tébourba. Inexperienced American tankers in undergunned Stuart and high-silhouette Lee tanks, which the British called Grants, were skewered by 88s as they maneuvered inexpertly sans artillery and infantry support. A few Allied soldiers cut their way out of flaming Tébourba. But over one thousand became POWs. Anderson apologized to Eisenhower for the debacle, a premature gesture, it turned out, as the list of things to apologize for lengthened as the German attack rolled through Tébourba and made for Medjez. Poor discipline, inexpert leadership, and confused orders had temporarily reduced the American Combat Command B to a phantom force. British forces seemed to be reliving the confusion and error that characterized the Eighth Army's early days in the Western Desert. A second, late-December Allied push toward Tunis snagged on a ridge that the British nicknamed Longstop Hill. What the Coldstream Guards captured at some cost on the night of 22–23 December was forfeited, to British disgust, later that day by the Big Red One. The Coldstreams retook the hill on Christmas Eve at the cost of 500 casualties, only to surrender it on the next morning to the Germans, who christened it Christmas Hill. Torrential rain poured on Tunisia. Depression gripped AFHQ at Algiers. On 8 December, Colonel General Jürgen von Arnim arrived from the Russian front to command Axis troops in Tunisia, now known as the Fifth Panzer Army.

THE DARLAN DEAL

Operation Torch laid bare for the Americans something that Hitler and the British had grasped from the war's beginning: the political complexities of operating in the Mediterranean at least equaled, and often surpassed, the daunting operational challenges of that theater. Traditionally, soldiers prefer to win wars and leave the political battles to the politicians and diplomats. But Eisenhower rapidly discovered that politics fashioned operations in the Mediterranean. His political baptism occurred in mid-October, when his deputy Mark Clark returned from a secret, if slightly comic, visit to a remote coastal farmhouse near Algiers to coordinate cooperation with pro-Allied Frenchmen led by General Charles Mast, deputy commander of Vichy's army in Algeria. Clark speculated that the French would offer little resistance. Discussions with tall, mustachioed, cane-toting General Henri Giraud at Gibraltar on the eve of the invasion revealed to the American commander that he was about to wade into a quagmire of pent-up Gallic resentment and vitriol: with a combination of "arrogance and independence" that characterized Giraud's stiff-necked style, the French general insisted that his price for cooperation was nothing less than command of the Anglo-American invasion of North Africa![82]

The Allied invasion further scrambled an already bewildering French situation. It offered a direct challenge to the legitimacy of the Vichy regime and the authority of the commander-in-chief of its forces, Admiral Jean-François Darlan. Keeping French North Africa and the French fleet out of the war was Vichy's raison d'être. Neutrality provided Marshal Philippe Pétain's only leverage with Hitler. The Führer had paid a high price to keep Vichy neutral, which included vetoing Mussolini's demand for Corsica and Tunisia, and Franco's desire for Morocco and Oran. With Algiers in Allied hands, the Germans no longer had any need to appease Pétain. Instead, they occupied the so-called free zone on 11 November and attempted to seize the French fleet at Toulon, which promptly scuttled itself rather than be seized by the Axis, or defect to the Allies. Italian forces landed in Corsica and joined the Germans in the invasion of long-coveted Tunisia.

The Axis occupation of southern France, Corsica, and Tunisia, and the scuttling of the French fleet at Toulon, should automatically have thrown French loyalties to the Allies. But to assume rational behavior on the part of the French was naively to discount Darlan's capacity for intrigue. It was further bad luck for Eisenhower that Torch surprised Darlan in Algiers, to which he had come to visit his son, suddenly stricken with polio. Darlan was not completely lost to the Allied cause. Son of a center-left politician from the French southwest, politically Darlan stood apart from the usual cast of French ideological reactionaries, a technocrat legacy of the defunct Third Republic rather than a priest of Vichy's "National Revolution." A short, moon-faced, charisma-challenged chief of staff of the French navy in 1940, Darlan had assumed the role of naval minister in Pétain's June 1940 government, rising to the post of deputy prime minister from December. Britain's "betrayal" at Mers el-Kébir had incensed Darlan, who twice met with Hitler to offer him tight French collaboration—the use of airfields in Syria and French North African ports, the exchange of naval intelligence, and a combined Franco-German aircraft deal. Darlan was widely viewed as Pétain's *dauphin* until, in April 1942, he was passed over for prime minister, at Berlin's insistence, in favor of Pierre Laval, a chain-smoking former socialist turned reactionary whose swarthy complexion and trademark white tie had earned him the nickname "the Jamaican." The admiral continued to serve as commander-in-chief of the French armed forces and high commissioner in North Africa, nevertheless. Darlan's unexpected arrival in Algiers on 4 November threw Allied calculations into chaos because the admiral's presence trumped the ability of local commanders like Juin and Mast to seize the initiative.

Contemporaries and historians have tended to view Darlan as a shallow opportunist,[83] which he undoubtedly was. But it was difficult even for opportunists, especially Vichy opportunists, to know which way to jump in November 1942. These were men who regarded themselves as realists, but who had been significantly disoriented by a war in which, in their view, it was difficult to reconcile French interests with the goals of either side. Vichy's strategy was to opt out of the war, cut the best deal they could with Hitler, and use the interlude to rejuvenate French character, whose shortcomings they blamed for the debacle of 1940. But Vichy credibility was steadily eroded as the German occupation tightened, French standards of living plummeted, and the resistance movement grew. Nor had the correlation of forces as yet obviously come to favor one side or the other in the war. El Alamein had been fought only days earlier. American and Japanese forces contested Guadalcanal. On 4 September 1942, the Luftwaffe launched a 1,000-

plane offensive over Stalingrad, where German and Soviet forces remained locked in a deadly battle. The fledgling USAAF had begun to bomb targets in France. The British took Tananarive, the capital of Madagascar, in September. U-boats ravaged Allied shipping in the Atlantic. Although as a Vichy minister Darlan had actively pursued collaboration with the Germans, there is some evidence that he had attempted to make contact with the Americans in September 1942 as rumors of an impending Allied invasion of North Africa swirled in diplomatic and military circles.[84]

The invasion utterly unsettled Darlan, torn between his desire to avoid a fight with the Anglo-Americans that he knew he could not win, yet fearful of showing a willingness to cooperate with the invaders that would precipitate an Axis invasion of the "free zone" and possibly of North Africa itself. Darlan ordered desultory resistance mainly to demonstrate to Vichy and Hitler that he had not completely rolled over. At the same time, he continued tiresome negotiations with the Allies characterized by Darlan's equivocation and much table pounding by a frustrated and irate Mark Clark. Darlan's initial fear was that Torch was merely a Dieppe-scale raid that would trigger an Axis counterinvasion. With inadequate intelligence, he played for time until he could grasp the scale of the Allied presence. "Hypnotized by the dread consequences of an Allied commando raid in the Empire, conditioned to neutrality in a stalemate war, schooled like all officers to fire back when fired upon, the officers fought back," American historian Robert Paxton writes of the Vichy response to Torch. "At precisely the moment when their timetable was being made obsolete at Stalingrad, they observed it to the letter."[85] The French admiral finally ordered a cease-fire on the morning of 10 November. In Tunis, Vichy's resident general, sixty-two-year-old Admiral Jean-Pierre Estéva, longing for retirement and careful to supply the Germans no pretext for reprisals against the "free zone," took his orders from Laval, who told him at 1:15 on the morning of 9 November to make Tunisian airfields available to incoming Axis forces. By evening, ninety German planes had touched down at El Aouina airfield outside of Tunis. On the tenth, Tunisian ports were flung open to the Axis.[86] In Algiers, the price of a cease-fire required to save Allied lives and secure Algeria and Morocco was that Darlan would continue to exercise authority in North Africa "in the name of the Marshal," that is, Pétain. "The present senior officers retain their commands, and the political and administrative organizations remain in force."[87]

Eisenhower arrived in Algiers on 13 November to ratify the agreement with Darlan, to persuade the French admiral to order the French fleet to sail from Toulon, and to stiffen French resistance to the arrival of Axis troops in Tunisia. Like most Americans, Eisenhower lacked the capacity to fathom the mindset of a "Frog" leadership that resisted Allied troops in the name of "honor," but who welcomed Germans into Tunisia with open arms. If Ike was not a Francophobe before November 1942, he was fast becoming one. He possessed neither the understanding nor the patience to deal with a people he considered "selfish, conceited worms."[88] Stephen Ambrose argues that Ike could justifiably have reneged on the Darlan agreement as U.S. troops were safely ashore and in charge, because he had evidence of Darlan's double-dealing and because Darlan was definitely damaged goods. But Eisenhower "probably never even considered dumping Darlan,"[89] because he feared that French factiousness might erupt into civil war, which would compromise further Mediterranean operations.[90] Nor did he want to be saddled with the task of governing and supplying French North Africa, even though limited Allied intervention in the economic direction and support of French North Africa was required.[91]

Roosevelt accepted that there would be a heavy political price to pay for Ike's military expediency, although he and Churchill had only themselves to blame for giving carte blanche to a pair of neophyte generals to negotiate a highly visible political agreement that risked the demoralization of an Allied public.[92] Omar Bradley, soon to join Eisenhower in North Africa, argued that Ike failed to anticipate the strength of the adverse public reaction to an arrangement that neither secured the French fleet nor prevented the Germans from occupying Tunisia, and that left the collaborationist Vichy regime with its discriminatory civil legislation intact in North Africa.[93] When, on 14 November, news of the "Darlan deal" reached Britain and the United States, popular opinion exploded with rage. The columnist Walter Lippmann led a chorus of press denunciations of the agreement with a "Quisling government" in a land allegedly "liberated" by Allied armies. "Are we fighting Nazis or sleeping with them?" highly respected CBS newsman Edward R. Murrow intoned from London. Eisenhower was portrayed as a naive soldier completely taken in by the wily French-man. Officers of the U.S. Army Psychological Warfare Bureau were so incensed by what they saw as Eisenhower's betrayal of democratic principles that, on their own, they began to gather evidence against Vichy "atrocities," an act of political defiance that landed them in hot water.[94] FDR tried to defuse the anger by pressing Darlan to relax discriminatory legislation against Jews, and by inviting de Gaulle to visit him in Washington in December.[95] Although his chiefs of staff supported Eisenhower, Churchill came under strong pressure from his own foreign minister Anthony Eden and from Parliament to repudiate Eisenhower's action. The moral supremacy of the Western Alliance within the framework of the Atlantic Charter was at stake. *New Yorker* writer A. J. Liebling suggested that if Torch needed an electoral slogan, it should be: "Keep the rascals in."[96] The British Foreign Office notified its U.S. counterpart that "we are fighting for international decency and Darlan is the antithesis of this." Some British diplomats suspected that Darlan's retention was a U.S. missile directed at British support for de Gaulle.[97] There was even a fear that Stalin might view the Darlan arrangement as evidence that FDR and Churchill might eventually strike a separate and cynical peace with a German version of the French admiral.[98]

Eisenhower defended his arrangement with Darlan in the name of military expediency—"We are being realistic," Clark told an incredulous press corps.[99] Marshall insisted that the deal had spared precisely 16,200 American casualties, an arithmetical sleight of hand arrived at by subtracting the 1,800 actual U.S. casualties from the worst-case planning estimate of 18,000. The American chief of staff took the unprecedented step of imploring the press to defer criticism that could only help the British oust Eisenhower in favor of Alexander.[100] Roosevelt's chief Republican opponent, Wendell Willkie, prepared to denounce the Darlan deal on national radio as "an outrageous betrayal." Only the energetic intervention of Republican Secretary of War Henry L. Stimson dissuaded him. The British minister of information,

Brendan Bracken, called Darlan a "Quisling Sailor" and a "Judas [who] will not hang himself."[101] Under pressure from Marshall, Stimson, and close presidential adviser Harry Hopkins, Roosevelt released a statement claiming that the arrangement with Darlan was "temporary," and did not constitute a recognition of Vichy's continued governmental writ in North Africa. He promised to open North African prisons and abrogate Vichy's anti-Semitic legislation. This provided Eisenhower with the political cover he needed. But French North African authorities, who had issued a campaign medal for resisting Allied forces, applied Roosevelt's promises with glacial speed.[102]

"Darlan alone possessed the authority which almost all could recognize with a sense of legitimate relief," concludes the British official history. "Without him, internal conflict might easily have produced widespread chaos. His fortuitous presence in Algeria, far from being the calamity it appeared, turned out to be for the Allies the best thing that could have happened." According to this view, Darlan continued to serve the Allied cause honorably until his death six weeks later.[103] One of Roosevelt's biographers, Robert Dallek, agrees that the admiral "brought a quick halt to French resistance, saved lives, and put Dakar under Allied control."[104] Those who complained that Darlan was hardly a democrat failed to appreciate that the application of American idealism made for poor policy in the complex and ambiguous political environment of the Mediterranean.[105]

It is difficult to agree with these conclusions, however. Even at the time, reporters noted that the deal had saved no Allied lives, for resistance to the Allied advance had already ceased in Algiers and Oran. Only in Casablanca had the fighting continued. But even there, the resident general of Morocco, General Auguste Noguès, had already decided to cease resistance even before news of the cease-fire reached him. French professional soldiers, having carried out their *"barroud d'honneur,"* were prepared to rally to the Allies, not least because their pay would continue and their tatterdemalion forces would be modernized. The alternative for them, after all, was a POW cage. Darlan's power was bestowed on him by Clark and Eisenhower. It did not spring from his link to Vichy "legitimacy." As for Eisenhower's aversion, one embedded deep in the psyche of the U.S. armed forces, to being saddled with the running of French North Africa, plenty of capable Frenchmen loyal to the Allies were ready to assume that burden had Roosevelt followed a more enlightened policy toward the Free French. The Darlan deal further poisoned relations with de Gaulle and with the French resistance, which began to wonder what a U.S.-led "liberation" would mean, and kept the French situation in turmoil until the end of the war and beyond.[106] It "bruised" relations between the British and the Americans over French policy, and rattled British confidence in Eisenhower's ability to operate in the Mediterranean's complex political environment.[107] It jeopardized the moral underpinnings of, and hence popular support for, the Allied cause in France and Europe. The biggest risk of the Darlan deal was that it threatened the solidity of the alliance by suggesting to Stalin that the Western Allies were mere opportunists. In fact, it demonstrated a political opportunism to match what George Marshall saw as the strategic opportunism that informed Churchill's war management. The price the Western Allies would pay to smooth over that impression was huge. At the Casablanca Conference of January 1943, Roosevelt and Churchill were forced to repair the possible misconceptions in the minds of Stalin as well as of their own peoples introduced by the Darlan deal with a declaration that they would fight on until the "unconditional surrender" of the Axis.

The Darlan deal underlined the ambiguities of strategic decision making in a peripheral theater where political attitudes were anchored in expediency rather than in ideology or fast loyalties, where military outcomes were incremental rather than decisive. When Eisenhower opted for operational expediency over political principle, he was simply "going native" by responding to Mediterranean political realities. Darlan was a decidedly unattractive character, but he was hardly Goebbels. Roosevelt was no keener than Eisenhower to launch a project of social engineering in French North Africa. All the American president required was a few cosmetic reforms that would remove the issue of Jewish persecution from the newspapers. Roosevelt's anti-Gaullist policy had severely restricted Eisenhower's options. However, in the final analysis, Ike's "expediency" argument was rejected by those who saw the war as a unified whole, and who refused to countenance the view that a peripheral theater permitted the application of a separate standard of moral and strategic flexibility. Oliver Harvey, Anthony Eden's private secretary, called Eisenhower's justification of the Darlan deal "Munich reasoning."[108] It also underlined the requirement to give thoughtful guidance to the political repercussions of any allegedly "operational" decision by inexperienced American diplomats and officers.[109] Unfortunately, Eisenhower was to confront a similar dilemma in Italy less than a year later.

And lest the Allies believe that they had won over an important and "honorable" French convert, Darlan's subsequent behavior lifted any illusions about his sincerity. In Clark's presence, Darlan ordered French troops in Tunisia to resist Axis forces, which began to arrive from 9 November in ever larger numbers. As soon as Clark left, Darlan revoked his order. Allied calls for Admiral Estéva to resist the influx of German and Italian troops into Tunis fell on deaf ears. Darlan merely "invited" the French fleet to sail from Toulon to North Africa, which it never did. On 27 November, as German troops assaulted the naval base at Toulon, the French opened the sea cocks and blew up the boilers of their Mediterranean fleet. Sixty-one ships settled to the bottom of Toulon harbor. And while this was a blow to the Allies, it was an even greater blow to Admiral Raeder, who had counted on the cooperation of the French fleet to help him regain naval superiority in the Mediterranean.[110] The Darlan deal prolonged the spirit of Vichy in North Africa. "There was a constant procession of people back and forth to Vichy by way of Spain," Moorehead recorded. "From the hoardings and placards in every street and in every public place the unhappy features of Marshal Pétain gazed down on this unparalleled political mess." Only gradually were the Vichy *Travail, Patrie, Famille* ("Work, Fatherland, Family") slogans replaced with Giraud's *Un Seul But—La Victoire* ("A Single Goal—Victory").[111] Darlan made no move to honor Roosevelt's requests to lift anti-Jewish laws and decrees, while Allied supporters were (temporarily) stripped of their military rank and even their French nationality. Murphy turned a blind eye to the 9,000 Jews and other pro-Allied political prisoners incarcerated in North African concentration camps, a fact recorded by the Allied press. The American diplomat continued to help Darlan block Free

French attempts to gain political influence, while AFHQ together with Patton and Fredendall increasingly appeared to be working hand in glove with the most reactionary rump of the ex-Vichy regime. In private, the president denounced the French admiral as a "skunk." For his part, Ike had come to North Africa to fight a war, not "to improve the condition of the Arabs, or relieve the persecution of the Jews." He considered French North Africa "a boiling kettle" and had no desire to meddle in local affairs.[112] In December, Eisenhower, stung by press criticism of the Darlan deal and its aftermath, imposed censorship on all political news from the theater. But censorship boomeranged because it only increased complaints about AFHQ's "cowardly and mendacious" policies and Murphy's muddled judgment from Lippmann and Willkie. Censorship increased support for de Gaulle and helped to undermine Roosevelt's backing of Giraud.[113]

The brouhaha abated only temporarily when a young royalist assassin, Fernand Bonnier de la Chapelle, strolled into Darlan's study and gunned down the admiral on Christmas Eve 1942, "an act of providence," according to Clark, that "lanced . . . a troublesome boil."[114] The admiral was replaced by Giraud.[115] But Clark's sigh of relief was premature. Unfortunately, the intellect of the immaculately groomed Giraud, who always "appeared to have emerged directly from the barber's shop,"[116] failed to match his impressive bearing. He and his new governor-general in Algeria, the corpulent and repugnant Marcel Peyrouton, who as Vichy's minister of the interior had helped to shape Pétain's anti-Semitic laws, continued to incarcerate Gaullists, whom they held ultimately responsible for Darlan's assassination,[117] to the chagrin of U.S. public opinion. Eisenhower succinctly summarized Giraud's shortcomings: "reactionary, old-fashioned, and cannot be persuaded to modernize . . . He has no, repeat no, political acumen whatsoever." But Roosevelt persisted in obstinate opposition to de Gaulle, who in the president's mind resembled a power-hungry Latin American general.[118]

"A STRATEGIC FAILURE"

Anglo-American leaders gathered in sumptuous requisitioned villas in Casablanca's upscale seaside suburb of Anfa in January 1943 to discuss the future. Roosevelt arrived via a circuitous route that had taken him through Miami, Trinidad, Brazil, and Gambia before his plane touched down in Casablanca. The bomber that brought Churchill had flown a more prosaic route straight from Britain. Casablanca teemed with Patton's soldiers. The air was fragrant with lemon and mimosa. But the future was clouded by the present. For American planners in particular, Torch had come to symbolize "the *ad hoc*, opportunistic nature of Allied planning in the Mediterranean," a "periphery pecking" strategy that selected targets because they were considered soft options rather than because they advanced Allied strategic goals.[119] American historian Stephen Ambrose calls Torch "a strategic failure."[120] Dispersed and unbalanced Allied forces had been landed too far west to guard against an imaginary German thrust through Spain and Gibraltar to North Africa. Patton in Morocco had monopolized armored forces that should have gone to Anderson's First Army. The Axis had rushed an army into Tunisia, prolonging a campaign that should have been concluded by Christmas. The invasion of Europe was postponed. Rommel, who should have been smothered in a defensive pocket at Tripoli, was alive, reinforced, and as dangerous as ever. The Darlan deal kept the "kettle" of French politics boiling, sowed dissension among the Allies, and rattled confidence in Eisenhower's political judgment and military leadership. Ike's future as Allied commander was thrown into doubt.[121]

Yet no obvious alternatives to Torch existed in 1942. Even the fiercest opponents of the Mediterranean strategy, like Marshall, were made aware that adversaries less divided and better equipped than the Vichy French would have turned the invasion into a bloodbath. An assault on Northwestern Europe would not be practical before the spring of 1944. Nor was Torch devoid of strategic gain for the Allies. It had outflanked Rommel in Egypt, thus guaranteeing his withdrawal and eventual retreat. It led to the resignation of Admiral Erich Raeder. A battleship admiral who had dreamed of resurrecting Germany's World War I high seas fleet, Raeder had been one of the few senior German commanders willing to plead the strategic value of the Mediterranean to Hitler. The loss of the French Mediterranean fleet had placed Raeder's dream beyond reach. Raeder's January 1943 replacement, Grand Admiral Karl Dönitz, was a submariner, a *guerre de course* warrior whose primary trait was loyalty to Hitler. Dönitz resisted committing U-boats to the Mediterranean, especially after he lost fourteen German and Italian submarines in the Mediterranean, at the very moment that Axis land and air resources poured into the Tunis bridgehead.[122] The Axis continued to fight a seaborne campaign with a dwindling stock of maritime assets, in the process vindicating Churchill's Mediterranean strategy and his war leadership. The British prime minister had drawn his American ally into the Mediterranean, the only place where, practically, the Allies could fight a ground war against the Germans and Italians in 1942 and 1943. Roosevelt had pursued his "Europe First" policy and dampened down demands for a strategic shift to the Pacific. Eisenhower had not proven particularly adept at dealing with the French. But he had been saddled with Roosevelt's prohibition on dealing with de Gaulle and the Free French. At least the French had been brought back into the Allied fold. The Anfa agreement of January 1943 would begin the process of France's rearmament and its reentry into the war, an important prerequisite to the invasion of France, to France's contribution to the defeat of Germany, to the future stability of post-liberation France, and to its role in the postwar world.

While the conservatism of Torch had kept Anglo-American forces from preempting the German move into Tunisia, and some hard fighting lay ahead, strategically they held the upper hand in North Africa. For the Axis, the twin Allied surge into North Africa from east and west meant, at the very least, an intensification of the war. According to Montgomery's biographer, the Mediterranean went from being a campaign subsidiary to the Eastern Front, to its counterpart. "Overnight the strategy, tactics and morale of the war in the West overturned," Hamilton writes. "In Allied eyes, the future suddenly seemed miraculously hopeful."[123] The fact that the strategic situation had shifted to the Allied advantage resurrected barely latent tensions between Rome and Berlin. Ciano urged Mussolini to strike an armistice with the Allies while there was still time. But the Italian dictator, increasingly showing the physical ravages of illness and worry, ordered Libya to be held to the last man. In private, however, he admitted that the game was as good as up in North Africa.[124] He dismissed Cavallero, whose disillusionment had increasingly found an outlet in criticism of *Il Duce*.[125] Nor did the deteriorating situation in the Mediterranean cause a fundamental reevaluation of strategy in Berlin. As the war "reached a phase of strategic hopelessness," Hitler's wishful thinking took over.[126] In a curious inversion of analogies, Hitler had declared that Tunisia would become "the Verdun of the Mediterranean,"[127] a salient in the Allied line that would defy all attempts to pound it into submission. But by committing to the southern shore of the Mediterranean at the end of a precarious supply line between two advancing Allied pincers, Hitler had, in effect, stuck his head "in a bag," offering the Allies the opportunity to achieve a stunning strategic coup. Germany's days of victory were now behind it. Its years of anguish had begun.

CHAPTER EIGHT

Tunisia: "The Verdun of the Mediterranean"

T HE INITIAL AXIS dash into Tunisia from 9 November was a momentary reaction to the news of Torch, without forethought or planning. Axis intervention had been calculated to deny Tunisian ports and airfields to the Allies, slow down their eastward advance, and save Rommel's German-Italian army. Strategic justification to support the decision was mustered after the fact. So long as the battle was confined to North Africa, Hitler considered the Mediterranean a peripheral theater that little threatened his Continental empire. But he was like a gambler egged on by a profligate comrade. Good money followed bad. Hitler's commitment to defend North Africa set the seal on the German-Italian Axis,[1] much as the Mediterranean commitment and Casablanca had solidified the Western Allies. Mussolini, his defensive perimeter imploding, chirped that Tunisia was "the front line of Europe."[2] The Duce had not been present at Casablanca, but it was not difficult to divine the trajectory of an enemy advance from Allied-occupied Tunisia to Sicily. Like Kesselring, he feared that Italy would be hammered from the Axis.[3] Hitler was preoccupied with the deteriorating situation on the Russian front, where, on 10 January 1943, seven corps-sized Soviet armies launched a massive offensive against the two German armies at Stalingrad. Two days later, the Hungarian Second Army cracked in front of Kharkov. Manstein's Army Group Don struggled to keep Rostov under German control and protect the German pocket in the Caucasus. With calamity threatening in the

East, Hitler declared that Tunisia would be "decisive," "the corner-stone of our conduct of the war on the southern flank of Europe."[4] The Allies would have difficulty fighting there, he reasoned, because they would be forced to utilize most of their shipping to supply the campaign from both ends of the Mediterranean. Tunisia must be held until autumn, Fifth Panzer Army commander Colonel General Jürgen von Arnim was told, to steal the summer months favorable to an Allied invasion of Italy.[5]

The Axis decision to occupy Tunisia made little sense, however. North Africa had been squeezed dry of strategic value by 1943. For two years, Rommel had bought time, kept the British on the defensive, and protected the rump of Mussolini's North African empire. But the Axis could no longer make time work for them in North Africa. The beginning of 1943 was clearly the moment to cut and run, not to re-inforce failure. The Germans were desperately overstretched on the Eastern Front and on the verge of losing an army at Stalingrad. They were beginning to reap the lean harvests of their emphasis on tactics and operations over the mundane details of the development and production of matériel and logistics. The inability of the Axis war machine to sustain Panzerarmee Afrika had contributed directly to Rommel's defeat at El Alamein. And while Rommel's capacity to evade entrapment after El Alamein provided further evidence of his tactical skills, the fact remained that he was in precipitous retreat and no amount of cajoling from Berlin and Rome could force him to turn and fight. Hitler and Mussolini might have extricated Rommel's beaten but valiant force, gained a Dunkirk-like propaganda victory, preserved their dwindling resources, and consolidated their defenses on Europe's southern shore. But neither Axis leader was psychologically prepared to confront the reality of impending defeat in the Mediterranean. Both began to speak, and think, in clichés.

Torch, coupled with El Alamein and the virtual destruction in January of the Italian Eighth Army in Russia, drove Mussolini deeper into his strategic fantasies. As always, he refused to take responsibility for the consequences of his decisions. On one hand, he continued to insist that he had foreseen the Allied invasion of North Africa. There was nothing to worry about because Torch had overextended the Allies and made an Axis victory "mathematically certain." He turned a deaf ear to General Giovanni Messe, who urged him to repatriate his army from Tunisia before it was too late. Nor did he follow up his son-in-law Count Ciano's counsel to open negotiations with the Allies. At the same time, he blamed everyone but himself for Italian reversals—the Jews, the Vatican, the Italian people, the Germans, his own generals. As usual when he sought to deflect blame for disasters of his own making, he ordered a bureaucratic reshuffle both as a way to demonstrate that he was in charge and to penalize those allegedly responsible for the latest setback. A Fascist thug named Carlo Scorza was named the new party secretary, with the mission to revivify the flagging fighting spirit of the Italian people. The sycophants in his cabinet were treated to another round of ministerial musical chairs. When the music stopped, it was discovered that one new minister had been snatched from a mental institution to serve. Chief of the Italian high command General Ugo Cavallero, considered too pro-German, was relieved by Army chief of staff General Vittorio Ambrosio, a move that alarmed the Germans. Ambrosio initially refused the job, but was ordered by Mussolini to accept it. When he was asked what he intended to do, Ambrosio replied, to Mussolini's great chagrin, that his first priority was to extricate the Italian army from Tunisia. Mussolini's most loyal associates could but be aware that *Il Duce* was ill, distracted, merely stumbling through the motions of leadership; they plotted to replace him. All it wanted was for the king to make a move.[6] Even the ever optimistic Kesselring complained that "the Italians went into action with even less enthusiasm than before."[7]

The Axis counted several short-term advantages in Tunisia in logistics, in air support, and in their command team. By seizing Tunis ahead of the Allies, the Axis commanded the central position, which the Anglo-Americans would have to attack, and supply, from opposite directions. Axis forces would be operating close to their base. Bizerte and Tunis were only 120 sea miles from Sicily, 300 from Naples, along a route hedged by a mine barrier to discourage British surface and submarine attack and ringed by Axis airfields in Sardinia, Sicily, Pantelleria, and in Tunis itself. Auxiliary ports at Sousse, Sfax, and Gabès could supply Rommel's forces once they fell back to southern Tunisia. The front was never far from the ports, minimizing the land transport problems experienced by Rommel in the Western Desert.

The problem for the Axis was that even though their lines of communication were substantially shortened, they operated on increasingly narrow logistical margins. By mid-February 1943, "Dieter" von Arnim's force numbered 110,000 troops, including 20,000 Luftwaffe personnel and 33,000 Italians, organized into the Tenth Panzer Division, the Italian Superga Division with subsidiary units, the 334th Division, the Hermann Göring Division, and numerous smaller units. The Germans counted around two hundred tanks, including the new PzKw V (Panther), eleven PzKw VIs (Tigers), and the *Nebelwerfer*— literally "smoke thrower"—a wheeled launcher that fired a volley of six 5.9-inch rockets that so terrified American troops at Kasserine.[8] The forty-five-ton Panther had been developed to counter the formidable Soviet T-34, and incorporated many of its features, including sloped armor, a 75 mm gun, wide tracks, and a powerful V-12 engine. But production difficulties, further complicated by Allied bombing, meant that no more than 6,000 of these versatile vehicles were produced. Hitler assured Kesselring that the sixty-ton Tiger armed with its 88 mm gun would be "decisive" in Tunisia. Unfortunately for the Germans, the "furniture van," as its crews nicknamed it, was mechanically unreliable and guzzled precious petrol at the rate of just under a gallon a mile, which classified the Sherman as environmentally friendly by comparison.[9] Such was its weight that the Tiger chewed up tarmac and collapsed bridges, which further reduced its mobility. Allied gunners, now armed with 6 pdr antitank guns, quickly learned that the lethargic Tiger was too thin-skinned to deflect armor-piercing shells.[10] The arrival of Rommel's forces in Tunisia at the end of January 1943 virtually doubled the number of tanks.

German transport planes, while a formidable logistical asset, could not take in the slack in both the Tunisian and the Stalingrad pockets. The Ju52s and six-engine Me323s were difficult to combine in the same air armada because they flew at different speeds. The air convoys shuttling between Italy and Tunis became a straggling tributary of aircraft, difficult for Axis fighters to defend from increasingly bold Allied pilots.

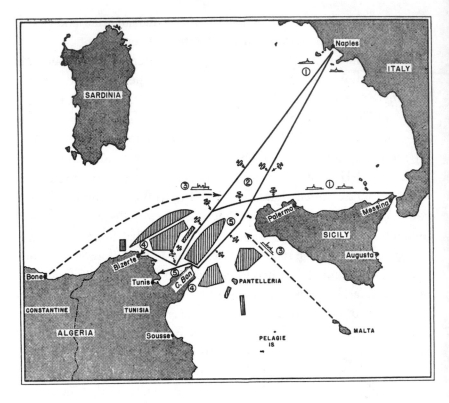

French merchant ships confiscated when German forces occupied southern France in November 1942 failed to replace a decimated Italian merchant marine that had already lost three-quarters of its tonnage by January 1943. The attritional war guided by Ultra and waged from Malta against Rommel's supply lines since early 1941 was extended to Tunisia. British submarines operating out of Algiers and Valetta sank seventy-two Axis ships adding up to 221,000 tons in the first five months of 1943.[11] Chaotic Italian ports often required a month to load a ship, while damaged vessels laid up unrepaired in Italian shipyards. Many Axis tanks, guns, vehicles, and eventually soldiers were transported on fragile, shallow-draft Siebel ferries. These easy-to-load craft resembled two barges lashed together, each propelled by its own engine. Their shallow drafts made them less vulnerable to mines and torpedoes, while low-level air attacks were discouraged by an abundance of antiaircraft artillery. But the carrying capacity of these craft was severely limited, so that they depended for efficiency on a rapid turnaround, which exhausted crews and lessened the odds of survival with each trip. This was especially the case because the trip across the Sicilian narrows could not be completed at night even by ships laying up at Palermo or Trapani in Sicily. Dawn made surface craft vulnerable to attack by Malta-based aircraft. Once the ships arrived in Tunisia, French stevedores and railway workers refused to unload, so that arriving Axis troops had to discharge their own ships. The result was that despite shortened supply lines, the Axis would be no better off in Tunisia than in Egypt, able to supply barely half of the logistical requirements of its forces. Indeed, German General Walter Warlimont noted on his return to Berlin from a February visit to von Arnim that the Axis position in Tunisia was a logistical "house of cards."[12]

As usual, Kesselring glossed over Axis weaknesses by pointing out Allied difficulties in assaulting Tunisia across the wild mountains of eastern Algeria and through the Libyan Desert.[13] And in truth, the Allies faced a logistical nightmare. Algiers, the major port to supply the First Army, lay five hundred miles as the crow flies from Tunis, supplemented by smaller harbors at Bougie and Philippeville. A narrow-gauge French train ran along the coast, but lacked coal and was inadequate in any case for military use. It became quickly apparent that the Allies must rely on the rudimentary harbors and road system of eastern Algeria. Five thousand trucks were hurriedly shipped from the United States in late January to support the distant front. Unfortunately, many of these, together with their cargoes of rations and munitions, were signed over to Arab drivers, never to be seen again.[14] Indeed, pilferage and theft remained a constant problem for the Allies in North Africa, as it was to be in Italy. Once supplies reached the front, mules remained the favored method of transport in Tunisia's hilly terrain.[15] Tripoli, seized by Montgomery on 20 January 1943, became the Eighth Army's main supply base. But it would take almost six weeks to restore Tripoli harbor, wrecked by Allied bombing and Axis demolitions, to working order. And even then, supplies had to be delivered around the Cape of Good Hope and through the Suez

Canal before they could travel the nine hundred or so miles from Alexandria to the front.

Nevertheless, the momentum of Allied logistics was slowly building, and with it a superiority in matériel that the Axis would be increasingly hard pressed to offset with deft maneuver. The Churchill infantry tanks began to arrive in large numbers, as did the Shermans, to replace the obsolete Valentines and Crusaders of British armored divisions. In mid-January, the 17-pounder antitank gun appeared on the First Army front, as did 7.2-inch howitzers, another step in Allied ascendancy in artillery. For Alan Moorehead, a veteran of the early fighting in Egypt and Libya, the transition from "the dusty and dilapidated-looking Eighth Army" to the well-supplied luxury of the First Army in its palm-fringed, Côte d' Azur–like setting in Algeria came as a shock.[16] U.S. Second Corps commander Omar Bradley also noted that by the spring of 1943, "our ragged, uncertain supply lines had been shaped into a well-oiled machine, delivering more than adequate stocks."[17]

The air situation also favored the Axis in the short run. The Germans had reinforced the Luftwaffe in the Mediterranean from October in response to the Allied buildup at Gibraltar and Rommel's situation in the Western Desert, so that by 10 November Fliegerkorps II counted 445 combat and a whopping 673 transport aircraft.[18] Thus German fighters included the formidable Focke Wulf Fw. 190s, a lethal killing machine that first appeared in 1941. At 389 miles per hour, the Fw. 190 was considered both faster and more versatile than either the Spitfire or the Bf. 109. Later versions were pepped up to fly at 425 miles per hour, and had two of their four machine guns replaced by 20 mm cannons. German pilots, operating from all-weather airfields close to the front, were adept at close air support of ground troops, and therefore could reestablish the air umbrella that had been lacking in Egypt, as well as ease the Axis supply burden in Tunisia. The Axis problem was that their defense had no legs. Rome was down to only four hundred modern fighters, and the Italian aircraft industry struggled to replace lost planes. The Germans also discovered that they lacked the aircraft to fight in the Mediterranean, support the Eastern Front, and defend Germany against the Allied bombing campaign. In the Mediterranean the Luftwaffe was poorly configured and trained to provide tactical support, air supply, long-range bombing, and convoy interdiction. The Luftwaffe lacked these all-around skills largely because Hitler and Göring believed that air power should support a Continental war, not a maritime one.[19] Indeed, much of the air reinforcement of the Mediterranean came at the expense of interdiction efforts against the Arctic convoys to Archangel and Murmansk.

At the turn of the years 1942–43, however, Allied air forces were still improvising and thus poorly placed to challenge the Luftwaffe. Unlike Axis planes, which operated from established airfields in the central position, Allied aircraft flew out of hastily constructed airstrips at Tebessa and Thelepte on the Algerian-Tunisian border and near Constantine in Algeria, fields that turned to soup in the Tunisian winter. The nearest all-weather base was at Bône, 120 miles from the front. Allied bombers flew from as far away as Cyrenaica and Malta. But Allied air strength increased only gradually, so that not until March 1943 did the Allies count enough planes both to attack Axis shipping and to support the land campaign. Initially, also, Allied air operations and target selection were not well coordinated between the RAF and the USAAF.[20] Nor had the newly introduced Allied air forces in the West yet acquired the Desert Air Force's expertise in close air support.[21] Allied air operations were initially directed against Axis air bases around Tunis. Ground troops, miserably bivouacked in cold, muddy olive groves and slit trenches a quarter deep in liquid, endured the attentions of Stukas and other Luftwaffe predators while cursing their own absentee pilots.[22]

A final Axis advantage, at least on paper, was that they brought together an experienced command team of Kesselring, Rommel, von Arnim, and eventually Messe at the head of tough, battle-experienced troops. In contrast, the Allied effort, especially on Tunisia's western front, remained very much a work in progress divided among a coalition of inexperienced generals. The newest Axis commander in North Africa was the fifty-three-year-old scion of a family put on earth to breed generals for the Fatherland. A tall, severe Prussian Guards officer and highly decorated veteran of both the Eastern and Western Fronts in World War I, von Arnim was on a trajectory toward general-

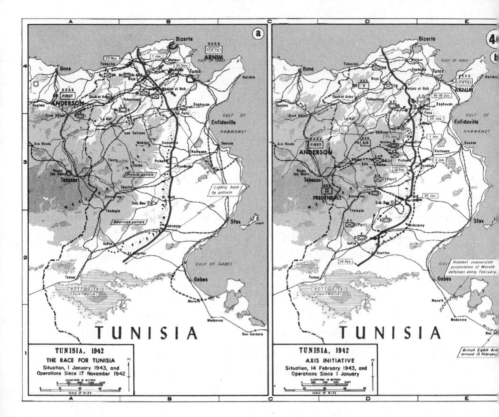

ship that had barely dipped during the interwar years. His birthright as a member of Prussia's military elite, solidified by marriage to the daughter of a high-ranking staff officer, smoothed the way to several high-profile general-staff positions. Major General von Arnim's newly created Fifty-second Infantry Division was in the process of organizing during the Polish campaign, and was assigned only a walk-on part in the campaign against France the following year. Nevertheless, in the autumn of 1940, Lieutenant General von Arnim, the infantry general, was given command of the Seventeenth Panzer, a division he led into Russia as part of Heinz Guderian's Second Panzer Group in June 1941. Barely four days into the campaign, the Seventeenth Panzer was turned over to Wilhelm von Thoma after von Arnim was seriously wounded. He returned in October, however, to lead his old command to seize an intact bridge over the Desna that made it possible to capture the important railway junction at Byransk, in the process round-ing up over 30,000 Soviet POWs. For this feat von Arnim was promoted and given the command of the Thirty-ninth Panzer Corps. In November 1942, after a tough winter campaign and a summer offensive that saw his corps break through to relieve the German garrison encircled at Kholm, von Arnim was promoted to colonel general and named to lead the Fifth Panzer Army in Tunisia.

Von Arnim's debut in North Africa was a promising one. He rapidly organized what was in effect a pickup force to solidify and enlarge a tenuous Axis bridgehead around Tunis. He drove American units off Longstop Hill, which set off an explosion of discontent among British Guards units that had taken it at such great cost, and hence gained domination of the Medjerda Valley and the route to Tunis. Operation Eilbote (Express Messenger), launched on 18 January 1943, pushed three understrength French divisions and the British Sixth Armoured Division off the Eastern Dorsal and, at the end of the month, captured the Faid Pass. Von Arnim designed operations in early February that embarrassed both French and U.S. units. Indeed, so confident was he of the powers of his Fifth Panzer Army that he believed that with reinforcements he could advance out of his Tunis bridgehead and, with the aid of an Arab insurrection, reach Algiers and even Oran.[23]

The arrival of Rommel's force in southern Tunisia at the end of January, however, altered the chemistry of the Axis command. It is certainly possible to interpret the subsequent clash of the two German commanders as one between the far-seeing Rommel, who believed that a decisive defeat must be inflicted on Anderson's First Army before Montgomery arrived, and von Arnim, the competent if cautious tactician, content to win local success.[24] But there were no "decisive victories" to be won by Axis forces in North Africa, certainly not in 1943. Tunisia could be no more than a holding operation, something that von Arnim internalized with a spirit of sacrifice inherent in the psychology of his caste. His job was simply to preserve his forces and delay the inevitable for as long as possible.

The conflict between the two men was a personal one arising from their different origins and conflicting personalities. Von Arnim was the quintessential general-staff insider—diligent, competent, professional—who contemplated Germany's Nazi rulers with Junker contempt. Lacking von Arnim's Prussian and general-staff connections, the Swabian Rommel was continually forced to play for broke, snuggling up to Hitler, chancing life and career in risky exhibitions calculated to attract publicity. Rommel's dislike of von Arnim, nursed since the two men were captains, exploded to the surface in Tunisia. He complained that von Arnim was not a team player, that he withheld troops for "small private show[s] of his own," and that he lacked the experience to fight "our western enemies."[25] The constant pressure to perform in stressful battlefield conditions had exacted its toll. Kesselring noted of Rommel that "since El Alamein, he had not been fighting back with the uncompromising vigor I have been accustomed to expect."[26] Rommel both outranked and detested the stiff Silesian aristocrat with his pinched face and brush mustache, and determined to cooperate with him as little as possible. This personality clash at the top of the German command, one that Kesselring, sitting in Rome, was unable to resolve, would disturb Axis command relations beyond the usual catalog of German-Italian disputes.

At the end of January 1943, Hitler told Kesselring that, as commander-in-chief South, he was to coordinate the operations of von Arnim's Fifth Panzer Army and Rommel's German-Italian Panzer Army, which on 30 January 1943 was renamed the First Italian Army. After a marathon chase from Egypt, Rommel crossed into Tunisia and settled into the Mareth line, a Maginot-like defense system constructed in the interwar years to repel an Italian attack from Libya and considerably upgraded by Axis engineers.[27] At Mussolini's insistence, the Führer also acquiesced in the appointment of Giovanni Messe to replace Rommel. But Rommel defied all intrigues to oust him from Tunisia until 9 March. When he finally took over the First Army, Messe discovered that all the German troops in his command were directly answerable to the German commander-in-chief through his legacy chief of staff, Colonel Fritz Bayerlein. Meanwhile, neither von Arnim, who took over Army Group Africa, nor Kesselring paid the slightest attention to their nominal superiors at *Commando Supremo*. In fact, Kesselring had installed his entire operations staff at *Commando*

Supremo headquarters, which added to German-Italian misunderstanding.[28]

The Allied command pooled many ingredients of failure: incompatible British and American strategic objectives, contrasting command styles, conflicting personalities that accentuated the problems of interalliance rivalry, and inexperience. The first problem had been temporarily resolved by Roosevelt's intervention to force Marshall to cooperate with the British in the Mediterranean, and by the fact that, in 1942–43, there was really no alternative to a Mediterranean strategy. The strong personalities at the top of the Allied command sometimes conflicted. But overall, their service professionalism provided a common outlook and a framework for compromise in their strategic debates.[29] Ultimately, all must cooperate to win, and it was Eisenhower's ability "to find common ground between competing priorities and people," according to his biographer Carlo D'Este, which eased that spirit of cooperation.[30] But different levels of experience at this stage of the war produced frustrations in both camps that made Anglo-American differences appear worse than they were. What appeared to Brooke to have been a mishandling of Torch and the initial advance into Tunisia caused the British Chief of the Imperial General Staff to consider Eisenhower a bantam commander totally out of his depth. Therefore, he contrived to promote Ike "into the stratosphere and rarefied atmosphere of a Supreme Commander" while the day-to-day running of operations would be in the hands of a British troika of Alexander, Cunningham, and Tedder. However, what Eisenhower initially took to be a cooperative arrangement soon unveiled itself as a Brooke stratagem to run the Mediterranean war through a London-based committee backed by his commanders on the ground. Indeed, Churchill envisaged Eisenhower as a sort of "constitutional monarch" imported to reign over a bickering assembly of British soldiery.[31] Marshall supported his subordinate by having him promoted to full general so he would at least equal his nominal subordinates in rank. But American attempts to have their voice heard in Tunisia were undermined by the poor combat performance of inexperienced U.S. troops.[32]

Eisenhower's efforts to impose unity on the battlefront were sabotaged by national rivalries and by his natural reluctance to make hard decisions. He hesitated to impose himself on British and French commanders, while a camaraderie with old West Point classmates, especially if they were Marshall protégés, perpetuated a lack of coordination. Eisenhower complained that the stiff-necked Giraud, qualified on a good day to be an average "divisional commander," was infected with megalomania and tightly monitored Juin and Barré, who seemed otherwise well disposed to cooperate with the Allies.[33] After tiresome negotiations, the French finally agreed to place their troops under the nominal command of Anderson's First Army, which in turn answered to AFHQ in Algiers. But Eisenhower was too far from the front and too distracted by *l'affair Darlan* and its aftermath to exercise effective control.

This put the war in Tunisia into the hands of fifty-two-year-old Lieutenant General Kenneth Anderson. Tall, thin-lipped, with a receding hairline and a gaze of benevolent indulgence, out of uniform Anderson might easily be taken for a vicar on holiday or a bank manager in a middle-sized town. Badly wounded on the Western Front, Anderson had finished World War I in the Middle East. The interwar years sent him through the obligatory India postings, and concluded with a division command at Dunkirk in 1940. Experienced Anderson watchers calculated that a division just about matched his organizational skills. His deep religious faith, rather than stirring his resolve and bolstering his confidence, put him in a taciturn, pessimistic frame of mind. He seemed simultaneously eager to succeed but resigned to disappointment. Oliver Leese found Anderson's attitude toward Eighth Army success to be a cocktail of "jealously and inferiority complex. It gave me no feeling of confidence. In fact only contempt." According to Leese, Anderson had little notion of how to employ armored forces, and appeared totally baffled by the opportunities offered by the drop of paratroops in advance of his thrust toward Tunis to seize airfields.[34] Montgomery believed Anderson to be "neither skilled or gifted," judging him "a good plain cook" incapable of imaginative or complicated operations.[35] After watching Anderson operate in Tunisia, Monty was unwilling to concede even minimal culinary skills to the

First Army commander. Patton, who otherwise agreed with few of Montgomery's assessments, for once concurred that Anderson "seems earnest but dumb."[36] Anderson's shortcomings were magnified by the inexperience and detachment of Eisenhower.[37] Americans, already adjusting with difficulty to the air of aloof superiority and patronizing exasperation adopted by British officers toward their U.S. counterparts, found Anderson blunt to the point of rudeness, a characteristic that Anderson's apologists attributed to his cheerless Scots disposition. For his part, Anderson ascribed his brusque manner to the fact that he was fundamentally a shy person.[38] He nevertheless succeeded in casting a pall of scrupulous melancholy over this vast amalgamation of forces from his distant headquarters at Laverdure, south of Bône, in Algeria.[39]

Anderson's caustic personality unsettled relations with the commander of Second Corps, Major General Lloyd Fredendall, who narrowly edged out George Patton as the U.S. Army's leading Anglophobe. A native of Wyoming, where his father had been sheriff of Laramie, the fifty-nine-year-old Fredendall was a "Marshall man" who inherited Second Corps when Mark Clark ducked the job. It proved an uninspired choice. Like Anderson, Fredendall boycotted the front, preferring to shuffle papers and disparage "Jews, Negroes and the British" from his concrete-encased bunker well to the rear.[40] Patton complained that Fredendall's poor performance in maneuvers meant that he should never have been sent overseas. In combat, the commander of the U.S. Second Armored Division, Major General Ernest Harmon, condemned Fredendall as "a physical and moral coward."[41] The Americans, stuck at the extreme southern end of the line in Tunisia, whose troops were periodically attached to the British First Army or the French Nineteenth Corps, complained that command arrangements were so confused that no one was quite sure who commanded whom.[42] As a consequence, Allied forces were scattered along an attenuated front that stretched 250 miles from the Mediterranean in the north along the Eastern Dorsal range of mountains, which stood sentinel over the plains of central Tunisia. The front was manned by undertrained and underequipped troops, supported by an inadequate road network and an uncertain chain of command. For an experi-

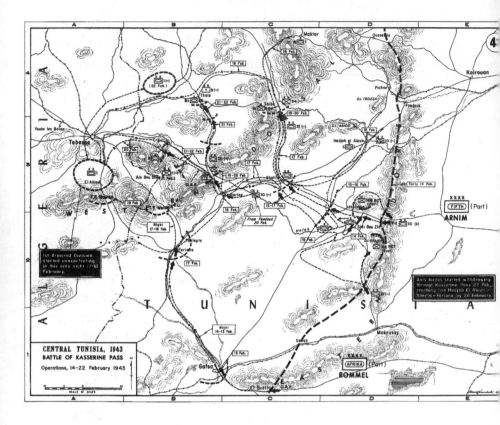

enced German leadership with a practiced eye for opportunity, the faulty Allied disposition in western Tunisia simply screamed out for assault.

KASSERINE

Limited German operations in January 1943 had demoralized the French, who, though courageous, looked as if they had been equipped in a Moroccan flea market. George Patton, who generally regarded non-Americans as inferior, potentially subversive, or both simultaneously, conceded that "one had to respect [the French] for fighting so well with such junk."[43] On 30 January, the Twenty-first Panzer Division, on loan to von Arnim from Rommel, seized the Faid Pass, a narrow gap in the Eastern Dorsal that controlled access to the central Tunisian coastal plain, from the French, and defied attempts by the U.S. First Armored Division and British Guards and paratroops to retake it.[44] Fredendall's 2 February attack on Maknassy failed ignominiously when GIs bolted for the rear in the face of Stuka attacks. Fredendall had performed poorly, failing to support the French at Faid Pass and feeding troops piecemeal into combat. GIs had shown themselves undertrained and underdisciplined. Anderson began to retire badly mauled French units to rearm them and await reinforcements. Gaps in the line were plugged with U.S. troops taken from Fredendall's Second Corps, which reduced American forces at the southern end of his line to a single combat command, roughly half an armored division. On 12 February, Rommel celebrated the two-year anniversary of his arrival in Africa with an impromptu band concert outside his campaign trailer. "We must do our utmost to beat off the mortal dangers which beset us," he wrote to his wife.[45] He recognized that in these etiolated Allied defensive dispositions lay an opportunity to inflict a blow against the Americans whose strategic implications might exceed its modest tactical achievements. A rapid offensive could break the weak crust of the U.S. defenses in Tunisia and allow him to rampage through eastern Algeria and ravish and demoralize the virgin U.S. Army much as the Germans had confused and disorganized that of France in 1940.[46] Buy time, buy time.

At 0630 hours on St. Valentine's Day, the Twenty-first Panzer Division with eighty-five tanks and twenty-one 88s flared out of the Maizila Pass. At the same time the Tenth Panzer headed east out of the Faid Pass. Both under von Arnim's orders, their target was Combat Command A of the U.S. First Armored Division and the 168th Regimental Combat Team of the Thirty-fourth Infantry, a National Guard division, at Sidi Bou Zid in the Eastern Dorsal. Huge gaps in intelligence meant that Allied commanders were caught completely by surprise. Sources noted that the Twenty-first Panzer was on the move and that von Arnim's forces were concentrating around the Faid Pass, which seemed to indicate a local, spoiling attack to deepen the Axis bridgehead, knock the Allies off balance, and delay Anderson's offensive. But Ultra decrypts gave no inkling of Rommel's desire to turn the Allied southern flank in Tunisia by a daring offensive, and the Allies were getting precious little other information. Besides, the Axis supply difficulties were also documented, so that the possibilities of a stunning swing around the Allied southern flank *à la* Gazala seemed fanciful, as proved to be the case. Nor were provisions for lower-grade intelligence in place in the First Army. Panzers rampaged through awakening U.S. bivouacs, sowing the usual panic and destruction. Tanks flamed like torches and artillery positions were overrun. At 0730 the ubiquitous Stukas added their bombs to the mayhem. By evening, Sidi Bou Zid was in German hands. Germans, led by Arabs, combed the battlefield for GI survivors. Even after U.S. forces at the Faid Pass lost over 54 tanks, 59 half-tracks, and 26 guns, both Anderson and Eisenhower agreed that a potentially reinforcing Combat Command B should be retained farther north against an attack they considered likely in that sector. As the German offensive developed, a disorganized Allied intelligence found it difficult to grasp German intentions.[47]

A gallant but naively suicidal U.S. counterattacking force, the Second Battalion of the First Armored Regiment, set out for Sidi Bou Zid in the early afternoon of 15 February. Sherman tanks and infantry mounted on half-tracks made dust trails as they rolled east across an open plain cut by wadis. The enemy was ominously silent. A little before 1500, a flare arched in the sky, signal for the hillsides to erupt in muzzle flashes from concealed 88s of the Tenth and Twenty-first Panzer Divisions. German shells dislocated turrets, ignited vehicles, and scattered infantry, who found few hiding places in the grudging folds of the flat terrain. By nightfall, the desert had sprouted a bumper crop of black smoke plumes. Throughout the night, refugees from the battle who had escaped capture or death stumbled home, dirty, confused, angry. The Americans had forfeited another 54 tanks, 27 half-tracks, 29 guns, and several hundred casualties. Von Arnim seemed out to beat Sitting Bull's record.

Rommel, who had been overseeing defensive arrangements against Montgomery's advancing Eighth Army at the Mareth line on the frontier with Libya during 14–15 February, appeared on the battlefield on the morning of the sixteenth. The sight of Axis troops advancing through shoals of shattered American equipment and prowling Arabs energized him. Memories of Gazala and Tobruk translated into visions of collapsing the Allied position in Tunisia and eastern Algeria.

Gafsa, where retreating American troops had blown up their ammunition dump before decamping, thus destroying the center of the town, was an open invitation for Arabs to misbehave. Any building left intact was swarming with looters, who looked up from their work long enough to shout "Hitler" and "Rommel" as he passed. U.S. forces were in disarray and American commanders "jittery" and, according to Rommel, "showing the lack of decision typical of men commanding for the first time in a difficult situation."[48]

On 17 February, Rommel overran the main Allied air base in the southern sector at Thelepte, where retreating troops had destroyed fuel dumps and thirty aircraft they could not evacuate. He then moved north toward Kasserine, where he hoped to link up with von Arnim's forces coming from the east across the dry valley that separated the Eastern and Western Dorsals. However, at Kasserine, Rommel discovered that von Arnim had taken his two panzer divisions through Sbeïtla, which fell in the evening of the seventeenth after a stout American defense. He then turned north toward Thala on the road to Le Kef instead of west toward Tebessa. "I was convinced that a thrust beyond Tebessa by the combined armored and motorized forces of the two armies would force the British and Americans to pull back the bulk of their forces to Algeria, thus greatly delaying their offensive preparations," Rommel wrote. Against experienced commanders, this would be a risky move. But the Americans were "beginners" who would "lack the nerve" to take advantage of his overextension.[49] Besides, the southern flank of the Allied line had dissolved into a flood of beaten men, panicked beyond the control of their officers. At Rommel's request, Kesselring agreed that the Tenth and Twenty-first Panzer Divisions should be sent toward Kasserine to be reunited with the Afrika Korps. With this strengthened command of three panzer divisions, Rommel would blow away the American defenses at the Kasserine Pass and storm westward and turn north to Le Kef and Algeria and beyond. The Twenty-first Panzer was to follow a parallel road toward Le Kef through Sbeïtla, an ancient Roman settlement, and Sbiba.

On the morning of 19 February 1943, it looked as if a repetition of Gazala was in the offing as the 26 panzers and 23 obsolete Italian tanks of the *Kampfgruppe Deutsches Afrika Korps* pushed toward the Kasserine Pass, a mile-wide breach through the Grand Dorsal range. The pass, flanked by two high peaks and bisected by a highway that leads to the Algerian border thirty miles to the west, was defended by roughly two thousand half-trained U.S. infantry combat engineers backed by a battery of French 75 mm guns strung out along a three-mile front. Despite appallingly sited defenses and ill-laid minefields, Rommel's motley collection of Bersaglieri and Panzer Grenadier troops, veterans of his earlier desert battles, made only slow progress. Poor weather kept both air forces away. The French guns kept his tanks at bay. Most of the day and into the evening German infantry infiltrated the high ground on either side of the pass as Axis artillery ranged on the shallow American defenses. Von Arnim had been slow to release the Tenth Panzer, which crept westward across the valley that separated the Eastern and Western Dorsal. Rommel arrived at Kasserine village midmorning on 20 February and berated his commanders for their slow progress. This jumpstarted the Axis attack. By evening, Italian tanks were five miles beyond Kasserine. Americans who had not been killed or captured were on the run, trying to avoid capture by Axis soldiers or death at the hands of well-armed gangs of Arab bandits. The battlefield looked as if it had hosted a demolition derby. The ground was littered with almost two hundred destroyed U.S. tanks, as many guns, and jeeps and trucks too numerous to inventory. Dead bodies had already been stripped by the marauding Arabs while some of the four thousand American POWs were gathered into groups and marched toward the rear by their exultant captors.

But at the very moment of victory, when the Allies seemed to be in utter confusion, Rommel called off his offensive, thus depriving his ultimate virtuoso operational performance of any strategic gain.[50] Might Rommel have transformed Operation Frühlingswind, the fight at Sidi Bou Zid and Kasserine, into anything more than a local tactical success? Kesselring argued that Rommel's heart had never been in the operation from the beginning, so he made the mistake of acquiescing in the northward turn toward Thala and Le Kef, rather than moving westward toward Tebessa to outflank the Allied position.[51] Rommel's biographer believes that he did not persist because he was demoralized, and that he had in any case achieved his goal of humiliating the Americans and was eager to return to the Mareth line to deal with Montgomery's advance from Libya.[52] For his part, Rommel claims in his memoirs that he had thrown Allied plans to attack Axis forces in Tunisia off balance, delivered a victory that would bolster Mussolini's position, and instilled "from the outset an inferiority complex of no mean order" on the Americans.[53] Others suggest that the offensive collapsed under accumulated attrition exacerbated by punishing Allied air and artillery attacks from 22 February, which exacted a high toll on irreplaceable German equipment. Rommel's advance had opened his flanks to counterattack, and he was suffering from a severe shortage of ammunition and fuel. Von Arnim, who had diverted his attack northward toward Thala and Le Kef and held back a portion of the Tenth Panzer Division during a critical phase of Rommel's attack at Kasserine, was refusing to cooperate.[54] At Thala, the Tenth Panzer had been held in check by a hastily improvised British-French-U.S. force under Brigadier Cameron Nicholson, deputy commander of the British Sixth Armoured Division. Allied reinforcements were rushing in. Rommel's culminating point of victory had crested. The Axis flood in Tunisia began slowly to recede. Kesselring's usual optimism gradually deflated as Allied resistance stiffened beyond Kasserine.[55] Besides, it is unlikely that even in the best circumstances Rommel could have afforded to send three divisions rampaging into eastern Algeria with the Eighth Army fast approaching from the east. By 23 February, Rommel was in full retreat, destroying bridges and sowing a wake of mines. No amount of prodding by Eisenhower could persuade Fredendall to counterattack him as he withdrew through the Kasserine bottleneck.[56]

Kasserine roiled the Allied camp, but the nature of the coalition, the fact that the Allies lacked a deep bench of proven commanders, and the fact that the system of selection and training of combat troops was difficult to modify at short notice limited their ability immediately to rectify the problems. On 20 February, Eisenhower named Alexander deputy commander-in-chief of Allied forces in French North Africa and commander of the Eighteenth Army Group to coordinate the operations of the First and Eighth Armies in Tunisia. While Alexander was particularly disturbed by "the poor fighting quality of the Americans" and Fredendall's "dithery" command style,[57] there was plenty of blame to share. The new deputy commander wondered if Anderson was "big enough for the job," a complaint repeated by the Americans, who pointed out that the First Army commander was remote, was focused on British troops in the north, and had been oblivious to the situation at the southern extremity of his line. He had scattered Second Corps piecemeal along the broad front. Anderson would probably have been sacked by Alexander had Montgomery agreed to release his Thirtieth Corps commander Oliver Leese to take over the First Army. But Montgomery refused, and without any other obvious candidate, Anderson kept his job.[58]

But personalities aside, the Allies' real problems, Alexander believed, began at AFHQ level, where no overall policy or plan of campaign had been devised for either the ground or the air war in North Africa. This was a barely veiled criticism of Eisenhower, who failed to define a strategy and instead allowed his staff to evolve plans that he "brokered into policy."[59] Eisenhower had condoned—by failure to correct it—the jumble of French, U.S., and British units sited along poor defensive positions. The theater commander had lacked the knowledge or the energy to ensure that the techniques of close air-ground coordination worked out by the Desert Air Force in the Western Desert were integrated into Torch from the beginning.[60] Eisenhower had been aware of a poor command climate in Second Corps, of feuds between the profane, mulish fifty-eight-year-old Fredendall and his subordinates before the battle, but could not decide who had the better argument. U.S. commanders had shown a complete inability to use terrain and to trade space for time. Ike had also fretted about the poor training, discipline, and endurance of GIs in Tunisia, but had failed to correct casual American attitudes toward war.[61] Fredendall, who had slept in his command bunker at Djebel Kouif, fifteen miles north of Tebessa, while his troops were being slaughtered sixty miles away, was awarded a third star, then sacked by Eisenhower. Ike's intelligence chief, British Brigadier Eric Mockler-Ferryman, returned to Britain accused of allowing the Allies to be surprised. Other, lesser, heads also rolled. But Fredendall was not the only commander remote from the battlefield, and the problems of intelligence were mainly systemic, not the result of the appreciation of one officer. Even an Eisenhower admirer like Omar Bradley admitted that the humiliation at Kasserine coming on top of the Darlan deal and the failure to beat the Germans to Tunis in December meant that the supreme commander was lucky not to have been fired. "Ike led an extraordinarily charmed life," Bradley concluded.[62] This time the Mediterranean "graveyard of generals" failed to claim an obvious candidate.

The disappointing combat debut of American troops would cast a long shadow over Allied relations. Surprisingly, Rommel, whose two years as Italian partner and British adversary had made him a connoisseur of dysfunctional armies, was less disparaging about U.S. shortcomings than were the British. He found much to admire in the skill and tenacity of the American defense beyond Kasserine, the standardization of U.S. equipment, and the "flexibility and accuracy of the American artillery." While American troops obviously lacked experience, he believed the U.S. command had reacted fairly quickly to mass their reserves at the key passes to deny the Axis a chance to exploit their tactical gains.[63] But Rommel's opinion was not shared by other Axis commanders, who jammed the airwaves with scornful comments about the U.S. performance, messages intercepted, interpreted by Bletchley, and forwarded to AFHQ, where they catapulted Bedell Smith, Eisenhower's chief of staff, into spasms of rage.

For two years in the Eastern Mediterranean, the British had lost battle upon battle, in the process taking casualties they could little afford, auditioned a gaggle of failed commanders, and been forced to repudiate a number of tactical and operational methods. Indeed, before Montgomery delivered victory at El Alamein, the British army had been laying the groundwork for a stab-in-the-back explanation of their losses that amalgamated the excuses of poor equipment, Churchill's meddling, and the fact that British soldiers were simply not made of the same mettle as their fathers in World War I. For this reason, one might have expected noble statements of condolence and encouragement for their new American teammates to pour forth from British headquarters.[64] El Alamein, however, had given the British a huge superiority complex. Alexander complained to Brooke that the American soldier was "soft and fat . . . they simply do not know their job as soldiers . . . unless we can do something about it, the American Army . . . will be quite useless and play no useful part whatsoever."[65]

And in truth, senior American officers agreed that the debut performance of U.S. troops had been embarrassing. At Kasserine, the "greatest generation" failed to exhibit any innate distinction. Mark Clark, who was to command the Fifth Army in Italy, believed the lack of fighting spirit exhibited by some American forces in Tunisia came from inexperienced junior officers who had no idea how to enforce discipline. When Clark remonstrated with a drunk American sergeant slouched on a street corner in Oudjda in Algeria while holding a dog on a leash, the sergeant merely replied, "Don't bite the general, doggie."[66] According to Churchill, Kasserine confirmed earlier prejudices among some "silly people—and there were many," that the United States was "soft . . . They would fool around at a distance. They would never come to grips. They would never stand blood-letting. Their democracy and system of recurrent elections would paralyze their war effort. They would be just a vague blur on the horizon to friend or foe. Now we should see the weakness of this numerous but remote, wealthy and talkative people."[67] Even for those free of such preconceived prejudices, the embarrassment of a brash American ally whose latent and soon-to-be-manifest power would dwarf the British effort and hence shrink London's influence in the coalition stimulated a supercilious, if temporary, satisfaction. These were men who, in more lucid moments, knew full well how steep the learning curve could be when confronting German forces. In such conditions, the Mediterranean proved its value as the nursery of alliance solidarity and U.S. combat efficiency, without which the American generals and their Republican allies in Congress, too, might have conspired to conjure up a stab-in-the-back explanation for the failure of Sledgehammer.

The arrival in Tunisia of the self-consciously tatterdemalion Eighth Army in their assortment of German, Italian, and British vehicles painted desert yellow created a hierarchy of conceit in the Allied camp. The tanned, weather-beaten conquerors of Rommel viewed the First Army as parade ground soldiers, "neat and regimental . . . pale and earnest."[68] "I think we were rather hard on First Army," remembered one Eighth Army veteran. "We'd forgotten what we'd been like when we were green troops. And by then our tails were up, you see, we were a frightfully arrogant lot really. We'd had these successes and—'there were these silly chaps making a balls of it' sort of attitude."[69] Moorehead attributed Eighth Army swagger to the feeling of invincibility they had acquired under Montgomery, and the fact that they were a heavily colonial army composed of ANZAC, South African, and Indian troops with an inborn disdain for Poms.[70] In the spring of 1943, Mark Clark admired the Eighth Army as a "real fighting outfit. They showed a cocky confidence in their own abilities that was impressive." Nevertheless, Clark found much to criticize in a force that resembled a Gypsy caravan rather than an army, beginning with "careless dress" and indifferent discipline. The Eighth Army's tendency to pack their vehicles bumper to bumper on the road suggested little more than a nodding acquaintance with the Luftwaffe. "They would have been duck soup for an enemy air attack."[71]

The First Army in turn contrived to look down upon the Americans of Second Corps as novice warriors, made soft by inadequate training, lack of battle experience, and an indecently comfortable standard of living. Most seemed addicted to Italian and German radio, not because they were susceptible to the message of Axis Sally (expatriate American citizen Mildred Gillers), but because the Axis stations played the latest jazz hits with an absolute minimum of propaganda.[72] The British both envied and mocked the brash independence and indefatigable optimism of the GI, his monthly fifty-dollar paycheck, and comparatively appetizing C-rations, each with gum, cigarettes, and enough toilet paper to keep a British platoon supplied for a week. Indeed, GIs adventurous enough to dine on a British "compo" meal of mutton stew and kidney pie made every attempt to avoid a repeat encounter.[73] Nevertheless, at this stage of the war, especially after the sobering events of Kasserine, GIs tended to be rather overawed by Eighth Army, which seemed tough, experienced, disciplined, and confident—in short, possessed of every military virtue seemingly in short supply in the American army. Within months, however, battle-experienced GIs had begun to complain that the British adopted an altogether too leisurely approach to the war, and were too concerned with brewing up a pot of tea when they should be pushing to "get the show on the road." The realization began to seep in that the British army was a brittle force bled white in North Africa, a placeholder that filled a gap until the mammoth legions of Soviet and American forces would close in on their Axis quarry.[74]

If Tommies and GIs shared little else at this stage of the war, they were unanimous in their contempt for the "Frogs." Memories of the heroic French soldiers of the Great War had already been shattered by France's ignominious collapse in 1940, an event that resurrected un-flattering clichés about the French as an effeminate, excitable, and quarrelsome people infected with a "Maginot mentality." The am-biguous attitudes of French forces during Torch, Darlan's equivoca-tion, and the generally sullen reception given Anglo-American troops, who expected to be welcomed as liberators by French civilians in Al-geria, planted the impression that the French were untrustworthy. Indeed, even the least educated foot soldiers rapidly detected that French North Africa was a desperately dysfunctional society—a su-preme but insecure French settler population that imposed itself on an undifferentiated mass of Moslems living in conditions more squalid than those of Negroes in the American South. But they rapidly discov-ered that the first word they were required to master to discourage swarms of beggars that besieged every Allied vehicle and camp was *allez*. The apparent indifference with which the population of Algeria, both French and Moslem, regarded the Anglo-Americans, barely dis-guised a mood of hostility and latent violence that lurked just beneath the surface. Although superficially beautiful, French North Africa exuded an indefinable odor of excrement and putrefaction, and the soldiers hated it.

Anglo-American distrust of the French rapidly turned to astonish-ment as they eased into line next to a comic-opera, tatterdemalion motley of Moslem troops, North African *pieds noirs* of European de-scent, refugees from German-occupied France, and semi-Westernized Sephardim. The Arabs displayed *haute couture* creativity, turning GI-issued mattress covers into burnooses. Clothed in bits and pieces of British, American, and targetworthy French colonial uniforms, supple-mented with civilian clothing, the French were like chattering pirates of Penzance rather than a regular army. Armed with museum-quality weapons, diminutive and ill-nourished French soldiers trotted to battle behind mustachioed officers mounted on horseback, followed by swarms of braying mules and rebellious camels swaying under ill-balanced loads. French rations and pay were derisory, even by British standards. Tobacco, the universal currency of the Anglo-American troops, was hoarded as a rare and precious commodity by the French.

Although the French eventually contributed nearly ten divisions to the Allied effort, in the process taking 23,500 dead and 95,000 wounded between the Tunisian campaign of 1943 and the surrender of Germany in May 1945, they languished in a chasm of Allied contempt for the remainder of the war.[75] Insults among Allies, real and imagined, too numerous to chronicle, were to characterize the remainder of the campaign and pursue the three Western allies into Italy.[76] Eisenhower's way of dealing with incidents of inter-Allied friction was to force miscreants to apologize, while allowing Alexander to relegate U.S. forces to demeaning auxiliary tasks. This so incensed Marshall that he intervened to force Eisenhower to allocate Second Corps a greater role in the final conquest of Tunisia.

The problem could only be solved once Eisenhower convinced the Americans in his command that "this is not a child's game." Alexander's well-meaning but patronizing attempts to establish "battle schools" where British officers trained U.S. units, to assign British liaison officers to American command posts, and to send detailed instructions to U.S. units about how to conduct operations were deeply resented by the Americans.[77] Clearly, the United States Army would have to get its act together on its own. General Leonard Gerow, training infantry replacements in Scotland, was told by his longtime friend Eisenhower to "ruthlessly weed out" inadequate officers. Eisenhower's most dramatic gesture was temporarily to transfer General George Patton from organizing the Seventh Army in Morocco "long enough to kick II Corps in the butt and lead it into its initial battles as a corps."[78]

"Kicking butt" was the activity of choice for the autocratic, flamboyant, frequently coarse, pistol-packing Patton. Son of a California lawyer, Patton was a paradoxical mélange of humility and megalomania, geniality and rage, heroics and lunacy. From the moment he matriculated at West Point in 1904, Patton had distinguished himself as an ambitious martinet who excelled on the drill field, not in the classroom—indeed, the joke at West Point is that Patton's statue faces away from the library. Upon graduation, he selected a wife who could assist an ambition considered gargantuan even in Washington, where Second Lieutenant Patton cultivated important generals and politicians such as John J. Pershing, Army chief Leonard Wood, and Secretary of War Stimson. A severe wound acquired while fighting in the Saint-Mihiel salient in 1918, followed by the award of a Distinguished Service Cross, failed to atone for Patton's outspoken political views, hard drinking, and reckless polo playing in the interwar army. Under the influence of his wife's family of wealthy Massachusetts industrialists, Patton jettisoned his father's Wilsonian principles, as well as the senior Patton's advice that the "club wit" who strives to dominate conversations was seldom a social success. Prejudice defined Patton's outlook and his conduct. In 1932 he enthusiastically joined then–chief of staff Douglas MacArthur to flush "Communist" Bonus Army marchers from the capital, in the process unceremoniously ejecting from the marchers' encampment the ex-sergeant who had saved his life in France. As chief of army intelligence on Hawaii in 1936, he drew up lists of prominent Japanese-Americans to be seized as "hostages" on the outbreak of war. His anti-Semitism exceeded by a considerable margin the polite golf club standards of America between the wars. General Joseph Stilwell called Patton a "braggart," while George Marshall's wife publicly admonished Patton that his profanity and "outrageous" statements little became a man who aspired to general rank.

Despite his World War II reputation as the U.S. Army's primary practitioner of armored warfare *à la* Rommel, Patton was in fact an eleventh-hour convert to tanks, preaching right up to the 1939 fall of Poland the virtues of the horse and the benefits of arming cavalrymen with a straight saber of his own design. He owed his promotion to his cultivation of influential generals like Pershing and cavalry chief General John Herr, and politicians, especially Secretary of War Henry Stimson, who personally intervened to place Patton on the major general list in the spring of 1941. Marshall also dropped his reservations about Patton's suitability for command after his vigorous performance at the head of a mechanized corps in the 1941 South Carolina maneuvers.[79] Omar Bradley, who both served under and commanded Patton, described him as "the most fiercely ambitious man and the strangest duck I have ever known." He alternated social grace and personal warmth with a degree of vulgarity and a predisposition to demean and humiliate his subordinates that even GIs found disturbing. His celebrated and controversial speeches to the troops, delivered in a high-pitched, squeaky voice, were practically "comical . . . altogether lacking in command authority," Bradley remembered.[80] But even his detractors had to admit that the tall, slightly balding Patton, with a solid chin, thin lips, and penetrating eyes that stared from beneath white eyebrows, had charisma. He also had an inimitable style. Patton's wardrobe of eccentric uniforms of his own design earned him GI nicknames that included "Flash Gordon," the "Green Hornet."

While Patton counted his fierce devotees, many believed him more respected than loved by the GIs. His tendency to humiliate subordinates and thunder when encountering even minor setbacks caused some to conclude that he was highly neurotic, if not downright insane. The British, to whom Patton became a source of unrelieved amusement as well as frustration, invented unimaginative nicknames for him that included "Chewing Gum" and "Cowboy." "I had heard of him, but I must confess that his swash-buckling personality exceeded my expectation," Alan Brooke noted in January 1943. "I did not form any high opinion of him, nor had I any reason to alter this view at any later date. A dashing, courageous, wild and unbalanced leader, good for operations requiring thrust and push but at a loss in any operation requiring skill and judgment."[81] Patton retained a mystical belief that he was repeatedly reincarnated as a valorous soldier who died a horrible death in combat. According to one of his biographers, this faith in reincarnation became a mechanism to control his fear of death. It also sent him into an uncontrollable rage in the presence of soldiers who, in his view, had shirked their duty, because he felt that they failed to realize that death in combat was their destiny.[82]

Ike's instructions to Patton were to "be perfectly cold-blooded" about firing anyone not up to the task.[83] This was not an easy task, as Patton's problems were similar to those faced by Montgomery when he took over the Eighth Army in August 1942. Three of the four divisions in Second Corps had "an inferiority complex and the other but the valor of ignorance."[84] His division commanders lacked ruthlessness and were, in Patton's view, oversensitive about casualties. He had more or less to make do with Fredendall's staff, in whom he had no confidence, and he lacked the time properly to retrain the 90,000-strong Second Corps before it again went into battle.[85] Therefore, he relied on the performing arts and the imposition of vexatious disciplinary rules to alleviate the inferiority complex under which GIs labored in the shadow of British General Montgomery's celebrated Eighth Army, not to mention Rommel's Panzerarmee Afrika. Patton arrived at Second Corps headquarters at Djebel Kouif standing erect "like a charioteer" in the lead car of a siren-blaring cavalcade of armored vehicles bristling with machine guns. Although the American press quickly latched on to Patton as the U.S. Army's answer to "the Champ," as *Time* magazine called Rommel, theatrics substituted poorly for more solidly grounded military virtues. Patton quickly identified a lack of discipline as one of his command's major problems. He therefore enforced a strict regime of military courtesies and uniform regulations, including the requirement to wear ties, leggings, and helmets on duty—Patton's "beanie campaign"—to remind his troops "that the pre-Kasserine days had ended, and that a tough new era had begun."[86] "If men do not obey orders in small things, they are incapable of being led in battle," Patton recorded in his diary. "I *will* have discipline—to do otherwise is to commit murder." So began the "$25 Derby," named for the fines liberally imposed by "Gorgeous Georgie" on those who were found without helmets, including nurses in hospital wards and men in latrines. Despite some local success, Patton's impact was limited. American troops stood by while Montgomery smashed his way into Tunisia. A humiliated Patton lamented at the end of March that "Our people, especially the 1st Armored Division, don't want to fight. It's disgusting."[87]

Rommel's success at Kasserine was stripped of strategic significance because the Axis was simply too weak to break the iron grip of Allied forces closing in around them. In late February, von Arnim launched Operation Ochsenkopf (Oxhead) on a sixty-mile front against

British troops in the north. Although his forces made some advances over the next two weeks, capturing over 2,500 British troops, he paid a significant price in casualties and lost equipment.[88] These were losses he could ill afford, because Ultra and photo reconnaissance allowed Allied pilots, submarines, and Force K out of Malta and Force Q out of Bône to locate and attack Axis ships at sea. During the opening months of 1943, almost a quarter of Axis supplies shipped from Italy failed to arrive. Aircraft were by far the most productive hunters, followed by submarines, which were nevertheless forced by mines, patrols, and shallow waters to hunt north of Sicily. The ports of Tunis, Bizerte, Sousse, Sfax, and the airfield at Gabès offered profitable targets for Allied bombers, which destroyed quays and cranes, even ships in harbor. Aircraft from Malta laid mines that virtually closed down the smaller ports on Tunisia's eastern coast by the end of February 1943. Considerable success against Axis ships in January was topped by the sinking on 21 February of the tanker *Thorsheimer*. Meanwhile, Malta-based fighters continued to exact a steady toll of slow-flying Ju52s and six-engine Me323 transport planes, made more vulnerable as the Luftwaffe's ability to supply fighter escorts decreased.[89]

The Allied ascendancy in the air took longer to achieve, because American and British air forces continued to follow their own paths until the end of April 1943, and because Anderson and Air Vice Marshal Sir William Welsh, in charge of Torch air operations, did not get along. The Twelfth USAAF under General "Jimmy" Doolittle lacked experience and exhibited an indiscriminate appetite for targets. As a consequence, Allied close-support air operations went through most of the stages in the learning process already experienced in the desert. Doolittle admitted that the Americans had to learn much about logistical support. At the same time, he complained that the army demanded air support for every jeep and wire repair party that went forward.[90] Welsh continued to direct the RAF to attack the Luftwaffe rather than support the ground forces. In any case, air support of ground troops was hampered by poor radio communications, nor was it centralized with fighter control and radar in the forward areas.

Only in February 1943, when Air Marshal Sir Arthur "Mary" Coningham, former commander of the Desert Air Force, took charge of

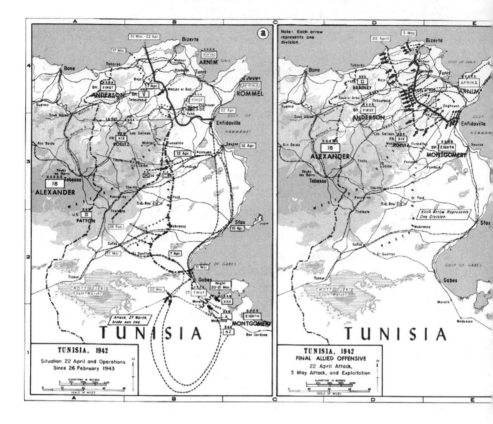

air operations in North Africa, did the situation begin to improve. Coningham had never placed support for ground forces at the top of his agenda, which was one reason why his relations with Montgomery and subsequently Patton remained permanently strained. He was a big-picture commander who argued that air forces had multiple roles. Control of American and British bombers was centralized into the Northwest African Tactical Air Force, and they were taught to fly in formation with fighter escorts. Kesselring, for one, did not welcome Coningham's strategic orientation, noting that high-altitude bomber attacks on Axis harbors in Italy and North Africa "introduced a new phase of the war in the air" which he found difficult to counter.[91] Coningham's replacement as head of the Desert Air Force was Air Vice Marshal Harry Broadhurst, a fighter pilot hero of the Battle of Britain who had served as Coningham's chief of staff. Broadhurst improved the ground support techniques of Desert Air Force so that it became a true artillery on wings.[92] Tanks were ignored as targets in favor of more profitable "thin-skinned" vehicles. Radar and signals communication was expanded and improved. Squadrons were shifted from field to field in response to the tactical situation, rather than nailed to a particular base. Maintenance, supply, and repair shops were centralized and many placed in the hands of French firms.[93]

Once Rommel had failed seriously to unhinge the Allied buildup, then it could only be a matter of time before Axis troops in North Africa succumbed. The problem for the Allies was that the Germans still showed fight, and they had a 30 April deadline, imposed by the January conference at Casablanca, to finish the campaign so that Operation Husky, the invasion of Sicily, could go forward. To accomplish this, Alexander determined that Anderson would put pressure on the Axis from the west, occupying their reserves, so that Montgomery might punch through the Mareth line and surge up the coastal plain from the south. Allied air and naval forces would strangle seaborne reinforcement. Once the Axis perimeter was suitably shrunken and suitably anemic, the First Army would surge forward and seize Tunis and Bizerte. The disadvantage of this plan, from a U.S. perspective, was that Alexander relegated Patton's Second Corps to a diversionary attack toward the Eastern Dorsal with the goal of drawing Germans away from Montgomery's front at Mareth, capturing lost airfields, and securing Gafsa to be used as a future logistical base for the Eighth Army's northerly advance toward Tunis.

Patton's attack kicked off on 16–17 March in a heavy rainstorm. Gafsa had been left undefended, but heavily booby-trapped, by the Axis. Mud, mines, and an occasional appearance by the Luftwaffe, or any plane for that matter, which halted the column and sent the Americans scurrying for cover, slowed the advance toward El Guettar. The attack against the 7,000-strong Italian Centauro Division, entrenched in the boulder-strewn hills that rose abruptly to 600 feet above El Guettar and the Maknassy Pass twenty miles further east, proceeded methodically. But Orlando Ward, commander of the U.S. First Armored Division, hesitated at the mouth of the Maknassy Pass because he lacked air cover and because Patton received orders from Alexander to hold in place so as not to block Montgomery's advance from Mareth up the coastal plain toward Tunis. In doing so, Alexander passed up a golden opportunity to cut off the Italian First Army when little but disorganized Italian units lay between Patton and the sea.[94] First Armored's dithering gave von Arnim time on 22 March to commit the Tenth Panzer to block what he saw as an American attempt against weak Italian opposition to reach the coast and split the Fifth Panzer Army from the Italian First Army. This was precisely the reaction that Alexander had wanted. Unfortunately, the U.S. First Armored Division was severely mauled by von Arnim when it tried to seize the heights north of Maknassy. Patton got a small measure of revenge the following day when, acting on intelligence that predicted a German attack, the First Infantry Division, backed by tank destroyers and artillery whose "time-fired" shells burst over the heads of the enemy, ambushed elements of the Tenth Panzer along the Gabès–Gafsa highway, forcing the Germans to withdraw. But despite enormous matériel superiority combined with Patton's desperate efforts to drive his men forward, Second Corps could manage what Bradley confessed were only "inconclusive operations."[95]

Patton's diversionary attack was planned to coincide with Montgomery's thrust through the Mareth line and the Gabès gap. On 6 March, Montgomery, forewarned by Ultra and by his own intuition that Rommel's withdrawal from Kasserine presaged an attack on the Eighth Army, had parried an assault by three panzer divisions at Medenine, in a brilliant defensive stance that struck many as a rerun of Alam Halfa. Over eight hundred guns blistered the vanguard of panzers, and then shifted register to smother a massed infantry assault. " 'The Marshal' [Rommel] has made a balls of it," Montgomery declared, categorizing Rommel's shallow daylight attack with naked tanks shorn of infantry support against his entrenched antitank guns as "foolish." In fact, Rommel's humiliation had been so exquisite that he began to suspect that his plans had been compromised, although his suspicion inevitably fell on the Italians rather than on Enigma.[96] Three days later, Rommel departed Africa for good and bequeathed his army to Messe.

The contrast between the American embarrassment at Kasserine and Montgomery's "model defensive battle" at Medenine, during

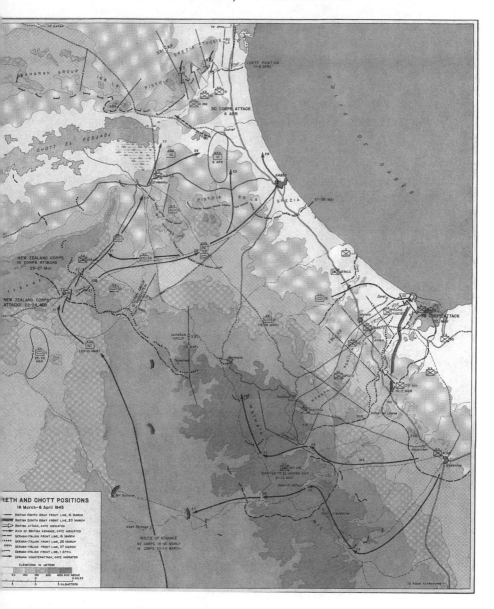

which Tommies recovered much GI chocolate and cigarettes lost at Kasserine, both inflated Montgomery's vanity and deepened his contempt for U.S. troops.[97] In the eyes of his critics, Monty's expanding ego encouraged both his natural propensity for head-on attacks and his fear of taking risks. Some in Alexander's headquarters concluded that by the time he arrived in Tunisia, Monty had become "a little man who has been playing big. He will not risk failure after success — will not co-operate and is thinking of himself alone."[98] The next operation would prove more arduous, however, for Montgomery would have both to penetrate the Mareth line and to seize the Gabès gap between the salt marshes and the coast. The Axis had upgraded the original French version of the Mareth line with the addition of minefields and a forward outpost line to deepen the defenses. Montgomery's plan was to fight a "break-in" battle against the Axis defenses at Mareth with Oliver Leese's Thirtieth Corps. Meanwhile, Freyberg's 27,000-strong New Zealand Corps would swing behind the Matmata hills in a wide left hook and come at Gabès through the Tebega Gap in the rear of the Mareth line from the west. So effortless had been Monty's triumph at Medenine that he fully expected a repetition of El Alamein at Mareth. Instead, Leese's 20 March attack, although supported by thunderous artillery, was carried out on too narrow a front across a rain-soaked Wadi Zigzaou against a heavily mined line held by two German and four Italian infantry divisions, backed by the Fifteenth and Twenty-first Panzer Divisions. The Axis was able to concentrate its artillery and machine guns against the narrow break-in point, so that the attacking infantry, with inadequate armor support, became sitting targets for a counterattack by the Fifteenth Panzer. Bodies of British soldiers and smoldering hulks of Valentine tanks lined the steel-swept Zigzaou. Twenty-four hours and 2,000 casualties later, Montgomery was forced to abandon Leese's attack.[99]

Thereafter, Montgomery's hope shifted to Freyberg's left hook. But it, too, had been discovered on 19 March by Messe as it foundered in an unfamiliar, broken, and rain-soaked countryside. By the time Freyberg reached the Tebega Gap, he met stiff opposition from the Twenty-first Panzer and 164th Light Divisions. The British breakthrough came after nine days' hard fighting during which Montgomery reinforced Freyberg with the Tenth Corps, the Fourth Indian Division, and close tactical bombing by the Desert Air Force that provided an airborne "rolling barrage" ahead of attacking New Zealand infantry.[100] The dead lay so thick that it reminded older veterans of the Western Front. Messe had to split his panzer divisions between the

Second Corps front, the Mareth line, and blocking Freyberg's end run toward Gabès at the Tebega Gap, severely stretching the Axis defenses. The Germans fought a murderous rear-guard action against the New Zealand flank attack that allowed Messe to withdraw from the Mareth line on 28 March to make a stand on the Wadi Akrit, a choke point between the sea and the salt marshes.

Montgomery called for Patton to attack Messe's rear, cutting off his retreat. Patton's troops reoccupied a thoroughly devastated Gafsa. The First Armored Division was to move on Maknassy while the First Infantry Division was sent through El Guettar ten miles south of Gafsa. The Big Red One fought a successful, even brilliant defensive battle at El Guettar on 23 March, American artillery for the first time unveiling an array of maneuver and firing patterns that shattered an advance by the redoubtable Tenth Panzer Division. Further north at Maknassy, however, difficult terrain, inadequate air support, dissension in the leadership, and tactical inexperience stymied the First Armored's advance. Patton, at Alexander's insistence, relieved First Armored commander Orlando Ward, despite the fact that the general had grabbed a rifle and led one attack himself, collecting a wound, a Silver Star, and a Distinguished Service Cross in the process. Ward's command style was too soft, too tentative, Eisenhower explained when the former division commander appeared in Algiers. Alexander informed Montgomery that the role assigned Second Corps had been "too ambitious." The Americans might in any case be attacked in the rear by the Tenth Panzer should they advance toward Wadi Akrit. Alexander then reversed himself on 25 March and ordered Patton forward. But this time, the Big Red One reinforced by the Ninth Infantry Division failed to break through the Tenth Panzer's defenses at El Guettar.[101] The Germans had carved solid defenses in the high ground from which 88s and mortars belched at American tanks advancing across a green field. Far to the rear, Long Tom artillery spattered the German defenses while bombers assaulted them from above. A tank struck by a yellow burst stopped dead and ceased firing. Seconds later, the turrets would erupt into flame. Sometimes figures would spring from the hulk before a jet of black smoke shot skyward from the hatch. Other tanks and infantrymen would sweep around the stricken vehicles and continue forward. The Germans withdrew 5,000 yards, leaving a field littered with burning tanks, toothbrushes, tangled wire, dud shells, and dead bodies, revenge for their earlier defeat at El Guettar.[102] A week of fighting and three thousand casualties produced no breakthrough for the Americans, much to the disgust of Patton.

Before dawn on 26 March, Montgomery stormed the Axis lines with three infantry divisions. The Tenth and Twenty-first Panzer Divisions peeled off from the Second Corps front to reinforce against the Eighth Army, but still Patton failed to move. Nevertheless, Messe was in full retreat by the next day. With the collapse of the "Chott line," in Kesselring's view, the Italian forces became a "broken reed" and "the end of the Tunisian campaign was in sight."[103] But the escape yet again of the remnants of Rommel's force from the Wadi Akrit caused recriminations all around. The British blamed the Americans, while others suggested that Montgomery had lost focus and that the Eighth Army was simply too ponderous to trap the agile Axis forces. Montgomery rubbed in the American humiliation and further disturbed Anglo-American relations by winning a B-17 Flying Fortress with a U.S. crew from Bedell Smith on a bet laid on 2 April as he prepared to attack the Wadi Akrit that he would arrive in Sfax by 10 April.[104]

Time appeared to be running out for Axis forces in Tunisia. Messe retreated 120 miles north to Enfidaville. The First and Eighth Armies locked a stranglehold on the bridgehead backed up to the Gulf of Tunis, which gaped like an open mouth toward Sicily, begging for supplies. Within his hundred-mile perimeter von Arnim counted 250,000 soldiers. But these men were besieged by twenty Allied divisions and, in any case, had little to fight with. The U.S. Second Corps, now under Omar Bradley, was sent north to the Mediterranean coast to threaten Bizerte. The British Fifth and Ninth Corps sat astride the road to Tunis. These abutted the four divisions of the French Nineteenth Corps before Pont du Fahs. Finally, the Tenth Corps of the Eighth Army occupied the southeastern sector at Enfidaville. Since January, Luftwaffe strength had been reduced by half to 178 aircraft, while the Italians could muster only 65 against almost 3,000 Allied planes. The Allied advance had overrun many of their airfields, which made the Axis air effort practically powerless. The massive Allied air buildup now operated from close-in, all-weather runways. "Blessedly!—we no longer had to dive for slit trenches to save our skins from Luftwaffe bombs and machine gun bullets," Bradley remembered.[105]

By the end of April, von Arnim described the Axis supply situation as "catastrophic." The 64,000 tons of supplies per month reaching Tunisia by sea during the winter had dwindled to 43,000 in March, 29,000 in April, and a bare 3,000 in May. The Axis was having to rely on smaller, faster "KT" ships (*Kriegstransporter*, similar to the Allied Landing Ship Medium) to sail without escort. And while these usually got through with cargoes like tanks, the carrying capacity of KT ships—600 tons—was too limited to make a difference. One-third of the Hermann Göring Panzer Division and half of the 999th Afrika Division sent from Italy in March failed to arrive. The Italians simply ceased sending replacements. Palermo, Messina, and Naples were heavily bombed. Two huge ammunition ships blew up within sight of Tunis on 6 April while being attacked by Allied bombers.[106] In all, 230 Axis ships were lost between March and May on what Italian seamen now called the "death route," taking with them almost 42 percent of fuel and cargo dispatched to North Africa. The last merchant ship reached Tunis on 4 May. Fuel was in such short supply that planes could not take off nor repaired tanks be moved from workshops to the front.[107] Nor could air transport make up for ship losses. Operation Flax, launched by Coningham on 5 April, aimed to drive the Luftwaffe from the skies. On what became known as the "Palm Sunday Massacre," P-40s and Spitfires jumped a fleet of Ju52s and their fighter escorts, shooting down between 50 and 70 transports and 16 fighters. Sixteen of the huge six-engine Me323s carrying fuel and reinforcements went down in flames on 22 April, causing Göring to suspend all transport flights.[108] Well-connected senior officers suddenly contracted illnesses that required them to hop one of the diminishing numbers of Axis transport planes returning north after having ferried in last-minute reinforcements. Axis morale sagged as troops began to joke about "Tunisgrad," obliging von Arnim to issue warnings against "rumor-mongering" and "defeatist opinions." Arab merchants did brisk business selling safe-conduct leaflets dropped by the Allied Psychological Warfare Bureau to Italian soldiers, 80 percent of whom presented them like redemption certificates as they entered POW cages in May.[109] Hitler and Mussolini, meeting at Klessheim near Salzburg on 7 April, concocted the fantasy that Tunisia would be held until autumn. Nevertheless, on 20 April, Kesselring, no longer smiling, began to withdraw what remained of his Luftwaffe units.[110]

Operation Vulcan became Alexander's final plan to submerge Axis forces in Tunisia. The Eighth Army was to feint from the south around Enfidaville, while Anderson's First Army provided the main thrust to drive on Tunis from the west. Montgomery observed caustically that Alexander's plan evidenced all the imagination of a "partridge drive," and protested that "Anderson is not fit to command an Army in the field; everyone knows it, including his own army." But he understood that Alexander was trying to "bolster up" Anderson. Alexander's advance was fragmented, poking weak fingers at von Arnim's coiled garrison from too many directions. But Montgomery had lost interest in the campaign and seemed content with the Eighth Army's diversionary role, in part because he was eager to rest and refit units in preparation for the invasion of Sicily.[111]

For his part, Patton returned to Morocco to resume command of the Seventh Army and prepare for the invasion of Sicily. Eisenhower publicly praised Patton so that his departure was not seen as a stain on the performance of Second Corps. But the flamboyant American general went out to poor reviews—his performance had "lacked imagination and vigor." Patton's energies went into acting out before the press and GIs. Otherwise, he demonstrated limited judgment and a poor command of the logistical requirements of modern war, and proved unable to establish a solid working relationship with the air force. "He was a fighter and a good tactician," one of his subordinates said of Patton, "and that's about as far as I could go."[112]

On 16 April, Patton's deputy Omar Bradley, a quiet, undemonstrative infantryman from Missouri who had been Eisenhower's classmate at West Point, took command of Second Corps. Eisenhower considered Bradley "about the best rounded, well balanced senior officer we have," one destined for the highest commands.[113] Bradley's understated efficiency contrasted dramatically with Patton's lead-from-the-front showmanship. Bradley also benefited from a series of feature articles written by popular journalist Ernie Pyle, which depicted him as the quintessential "GI general," efficient, ego-free, and concerned to avoid unnecessary casualties. S.L.A. Marshall, official historian of the European theater, believed Bradley's GI-friendly reputation to be a journalistic contrivance. "The real Omar Bradley was rather narrow-minded and utterly intolerant of failure," writes Carlo D'Este, who also accuses him of being deeply jealous of Patton.[114] But even the soft-spoken Bradley was outraged when he learned that Alexander had written Second Corps out of the final assault on the Axis pocket in Tunisia. This confirmed the suspicions shared by Bradley and Patton that Eisenhower's desire to be conciliatory toward the British had blinded him to the requirement to give U.S. forces a prominent role in the final battle. Bradley flew to Algiers to extract from Eisenhower a portion of front for Second Corps on the Mediterranean coast.[115]

On the night of 19 April, Operation Vulcan kicked off with an attack by four divisions of Brian Horrocks's Tenth Corps against the Italians nestled in the dun-colored hills north of Enfidaville, which Montgomery likened to the "N.W. Frontier of India." And although Horrocks gained little ground and took significant casualties in some of the hardest fighting the Eighth Army had experienced since El Alamein, this forced von Arnim to counterattack unsuccessfully and with high casualties on 21–22 April with the German Ninetieth Light and 164th Divisions and the Fifteenth Panzer.[116] The Eighth Army's modest success was not replicated on the First Army front, however, where Axis troops, entrenched in broken and easily defended terrain behind screens of mines and protected by deadly accurate artillery fire, deployed all their defensive skills against British and American attackers. Nevertheless, Enigma revealed that the Axis supply situation was dire.[117] Von Arnim found it necessary to withdraw his lines five miles to the rear on the night of 24–25 April because his troops were exhausted, and he lacked the reserves to counterattack the pockets of Allied advance. On 23 April, Second Corps launched its attack. Avoiding the valleys that were mined and easily defensible from the hillsides, it advanced along the high ground toward Mateur, keeping supplied by mule. U.S. troops captured and held Hill 609 in a bitter six-day battle, and then on 3 May seized Mateur on the heels of the retreating Germans to cut Axis troops off from Bizerte. Bradley believed that the Thirty-fourth Infantry, severely criticized by the British for lack of élan, and the First Armored Division, undervalued because of lackluster performance in earlier battles, had recovered their honor in these attacks.[118]

Despite the progressive advance of the First Army, by 26 April Montgomery complained that Vulcan had become little more than a "dog's breakfast" of easily parried piecemeal attacks along a broad front. He feared that he would be called on to employ units he had earmarked for Operation Husky if Vulcan continued to limp toward a prolonged and agonizing finale. Montgomery's plan to accelerate Vulcan evolved in the final days of April. He considered, and rejected, a "blitz" up from the south, after the British Fifty-sixth Division, made up of South Londoners newly arrived from Iraq, collapsed under an Axis counterattack and forfeited two important hills north of Enfidaville on 29 April.[119] Montgomery proposed to Alexander to transfer the "Desert Rats" of the Seventh Armoured Division, the Fourth Indian Division, and the 201st Guards Brigade to the First Army for a hard strike through the Axis center to Tunis. "You don't want to attack on the whole front," Montgomery told Alexander. "That suits the Germans fine! They've got no transport, no petrol . . . the thing is to pick the best place and then overwhelm it. And the Air Force'll see they [the Germans] don't move anything—they haven't the petrol to move anything. Then just punch home—you'll be through in 48 hours."

On 30 April, Horrocks was told to take command of the Ninth Corps on the First Army front to organize Operation Strike. The British attack kicked off at 0300 hours on 6 May along the Medjez el Bab–Tunis road behind a barrage of 442 guns and significant support by the Desert Air Force. Von Arnim, who had been alerted by the troop movements from the Eighth Army to the First Army front, was nevertheless surprised by the timing of the attack. There was little he could do to impede it, as he was reduced to seventy-six tanks and had practically exhausted his artillery shells. Indeed, one wonders if Montgomery's "concentration of force" plan would have succeeded had von

Arnim not been forced to spread his troops and his meager matériel thinly around his entire perimeter. By noon, the British infantry had cracked the German line, and Seventh Armour moved toward Tunis with a caution characteristic of the Eighth Army's fighting style. Alan Moorehead, who followed in the wake of the advancing Seventh Armoured Division, recorded that visibility was so limited by thick smoke and dust that the greatest danger came from collision with another British vehicle rather than from German resistance.[120] When British troops reached Tunis in the afternoon of 7 May, the streets filled with delirious crowds. Groups of glum German soldiers stood among the joyous civilians, their rifles slung on their shoulders, watching the British roll by. A few offered feeble resistance, firing shots or tossing a grenade. Italian soldiers traded their uniforms for civilian clothes. Elsewhere, freed British POWs stood about in the rain.[121] Spike Milligan saw two German officers sipping a final cognac on a cafe terrace before going into the bag. A klatch of Italians tried to surrender to his squad, only to be informed that the Tommies, too, were prisoners of the British army.[122]

Von Arnim, who had decided to defend neither Tunis nor Bizerte, which had been taken by Second Corps, ordered a retreat to Cape Bon and to the Enfidaville sector, where he intended to make last-ditch stands. But many of his forces lacked the fuel to move, while his logistical and command system had collapsed. Admiral Cunningham ordered Operation Retribution, patrols of destroyers to ensure that no Axis troops could be evacuated by sea.[123] On 7 and 8 May, Hitler exhorted his troops to fight to the last round. But while knots of Axis soldiers fought on, it was clear that organized resistance had ceased. On the ninth, the remnants of the Fifth Panzer Army, about 40,000 men, surrendered to the U.S. First Armored Division.

No other single incident of the war brought me more satisfaction—indeed, elation—than that long procession of abject Axis POW's [Bradley wrote]. A string of Germans as far as you could see coming down the road in German trucks, walking, Arab wagons and horses, anything they could get, they were riding down the road toward our headquarters at Mateur in northern Tunisia, and you could just see they had been fighting hard for a considerable time, and if you could capture a dozen German prisoners in one day, that was quite an accomplishment, and to suddenly see 40,000 of them![124]

On the twelfth, von Arnim destroyed his communications center, severing contact with both Europe and his remaining troops. He surrendered to the British Fifth Corps. On the same day Mussolini promoted Messe to marshal of Italy and authorized him to surrender. The next day the Italian commander turned himself in to Freyberg. On the night of 12–13 May, the Afrika Korps signaled that its ammunition was exhausted and it could no longer fight. Its chief of staff surrendered to the Fourth Indian Division.[125]

Operation Torch and the conquest of Tunisia are usually considered a series of wasted opportunities for the Allies. Timid planning placed Allied armies well behind the starting line in the "Race for Tunis." Lack of Vichy French resistance, Eisenhower's inability to keep his eye on the ball, and the fact that Anderson was not up to the task allowed the Germans to prolong the campaign for eight months, in the process inflicting over 70,000 casualties on the Allies.[126] If Tunis had been seized before the Germans could establish their bridgehead, Rommel would have been bagged from the rear, the Italian mainland could have been attacked in the early summer of 1943, and Allied armies might have camped in the Po Valley by the first snows.[127] To equate the quarter of a million Axis soldiers captured at "Tunisgrad" with the similar numbers trapped at Stalingrad, according to historian John Ellis, is "extravagant," a claim launched by "particularly unperceptive" propagandists. Twenty *German* divisions were lost at Stalingrad, compared to seven and a half *German* divisions surrendered in Tunisia.[128]

On the other hand, the loss of the Race for Tunis worked to Allied advantage. The Axis decision to reinforce Tunisia had proven disastrous. Between them, Hitler and Mussolini had offered two new Allied armies a place where they could learn to fight at low risk. "In Africa we learned to crawl, to walk—then run," Bradley wrote, relieved in retrospect that U.S. forces had avoided "an unthinkable disaster" if a premature invasion of France had been decided upon.[129] Unsuitable commanders like Fredendall and Anderson were jettisoned and more able men selected. The United States Army, after initial difficulty at Kasserine, began to show its mettle by the final stages of the campaign, initiating the American ascendancy in the Western Alliance. By contrast, the first hints of General Bernard Montgomery's limitations as a commander appeared as the machinelike Eighth Army rolled out of the North African desert to strike unsuccessfully at the hills of the Enfidaville line. The "Verdun of the Mediterranean" became the cauldron of Allied unity. The first joint Allied campaign launched the beginnings of the resurrection of France and announced the rebirth of the French army. The Allies learned to manage the potentially serious divisions and accommodate the diverse political requirements of the alliance. Victory validated Roosevelt's "Europe First" strategy and gave an enormous fillip to victory-starved Allied populations.

Nor were Axis losses in Tunisia negligible when compared with those of Stalingrad—far from it![130] The fact that Hitler's two defeats in North Africa and Russia were practically simultaneous magnified their impact. Unlike the Allied armies in North Africa, which could give ground at no strategic risk, Axis forces, their escape route severed and their backs to the wall, found that defeat spelled annihilation. The Axis had sacrificed well over 230,000 of their best troops,[131] a significant portion of their air forces,[132] much of Italy's merchant marine, and vast quantities of supplies that might have been more profitably expended on the Eastern Front. The tremendous Allied buildup in the Mediterranean forced Hitler to spread his troops to guard against an invasion throughout Southern Europe and denied him the opportunity to amass a strategic reserve.[133] News of the fall of Tunis caused Hitler to dispatch ten new German divisions to the Balkans and seven to Greece,[134] thereby raising the immediate costs of "Tunisgrad" to at least twenty-four German divisions destroyed or parked in dead-end theaters. On 6 June 1944, twenty-four German divisions stood ready in Greece, the Balkans, Bulgaria, and the Dodecanese to repel an Allied invasion of the Eastern Mediterranean.[135] The Allies had cleared the south shore of the Mediterranean, carried the war to Mussolini's back door, and brought Italian fascism, and with it the Axis partnership, to the point of meltdown. Ciano, faced with invasion from the south and aware of Hitler's growing embarrassment on the Eastern Front, intrigued to put together a coalition of Axis satellites including Romania and Hungary to opt out of the war. Ciano's defeatism caused Mussolini to fire him as foreign minister in February 1943, part of a purge of moderate Fascists willing to make a separate peace. The invasion of Tunisia also brought down the pro-German Cavallero, the man who had been responsible for the faint renaissance of Italian military proficiency after the removal of Graziani. After Tunisia, the Germans concluded that the Italian army had been destroyed as an effective force. They began to take notice of plots to oust Mussolini. Hitler prepared Operation Alaric to occupy Italy so as to keep the war as far as possible from the frontiers of Germany.[136]

Nor did the Axis draw the obvious lessons from their defeat. German soldiers who crowded into POW cages in Tunisia consoled themselves that they had lost North Africa because their supply system collapsed, not because they had been outfought. The view that Allied matériel—brute force—rather than combat effectiveness had won North Africa for the Allies became a necessary myth for Axis soldiers. Like every myth, this one contained an element of core truth. The Germans were excellent soldiers and the Allied superiority in matériel was vast and increasing. But Allied matériel superiority became an alibi for men who continued to delude themselves that operational virtuosity could somehow make up for the absence of a balanced force structure and a viable strategy. The lesson that men like Albert Kesselring took away from Tunisia was that he could use the unforgiving terrain of Southern Europe to fight a series of defensive campaigns that would negate the Allied superiority in resources. In this way he could buy time for the Axis. "British army no good!" a German on his way to captivity in the back of a truck shouted at a Tommy. "Who put you in the f——g cattle truck?" came the reply.[137] Kesselring failed to accept that the Axis was headed for the cattle truck in the Mediterranean. But much more hard fighting lay ahead before that could happen.

CHAPTER NINE

Husky: "One Continent Redeemed"

I N MAY 1943, Churchill reviewed the butcher's bills of the North African campaign for the Axis—950,000 troops killed or captured, 2,400,000 gross tons of shipping, 6,200 guns, 2,550 tanks, and 70,000 trucks lost. The Allies had "arrived at this milestone in the war," the prime minister told the American Congress. "We can say, 'One continent redeemed.' "[1] The post-Tunisia follow-on campaign had been resolved at Casablanca, where Brooke argued the strategic advantages of Mediterranean momentum—the Axis's southern flank yawned from Greece, through the Balkans, to southern Italy. Strategic initiative belonged to the Allies, able to coil and strike from the sea faster than the Axis could react over tortuous land routes. The Mediterranean would yield air bases to strike at the heart of the Axis, defeat Italy, and possibly entice Turkey into the war. American Chief of Staff George Marshall grumbled that British strategy was "opportunistic," that the Mediterranean squandered scarce resources on secondary—read "British imperial"—objectives. Nevertheless, he was forced to concede even before he arrived in Morocco that a cross-Channel assault invited disaster until the Atlantic was cleansed of U-boats and enough men and supplies—twelve divisions, according to an optimistic Eisenhower— had been accumulated in Britain to sustain a European campaign. This would mean that Operation Sledgehammer/Roundup could not be carried out before spring 1944. The Allies had accumulated military assets in the Mediterranean. The question became, what to do with them in the meantime?

For a man who prided himself on his logical, step-by-step approach to war, Marshall arrived in Morocco remarkably unprepared to do anything but cast a veto on the alternatives as Brooke defined them. Brooke attributed this to the fact that American planning, torn between the European and Pacific theaters, lacked a consensus and hence a strategic focus.[2] Nor did the Americans possess at this stage of the war a staff system or officers skilled in committee work capable of mustering arguments that could compete with a British vision of how the war should be conducted. One strategic option open to the Allies was to assemble Sardinia and Corsica as steppings-stones to an invasion of southern France. Operation Brimstone would require fewer troops and landing craft, and so could be mounted more rapidly with British ground forces. Indeed, Brimstone has gathered advocates among historians who argue that it might have avoided, or at the very least curtailed, the practically two-year slogging match up the boot of Italy.[3] At Casablanca, Brimstone found an articulate champion in Lord Louis "Dickie" Mountbatten, Queen Victoria's great-grandson and chief of combined operations, who canvassed British planners for support and even began to erode the Chiefs of Staff (COS) endorsement of Sicily as the next target.[4] The CIGS found an unexpected ally in George Marshall, however, who joined in Brooke's opposition to Brimstone: the capacity of air bases, not to mention the ports, on Sardinia was limited. Even the British planners conceded that Sardinia might not fall rapidly if reinforced. Indeed, one drawback of Brimstone was that Hitler and Kesselring actually believed an attack on Sardinia or Greece to be strong possibilities, a fact that Allied planners were able eventually to turn to their advantage with Operation Mincemeat, the "man who never was."[5] Hitler also believed that any Allied attack on Italy would have as its objective the establishment of a springboard for an offensive into the Balkans.[6] The Axis, alerted by an attack on Sardinia, would certainly dispatch a strong garrison to Corsica, which could translate into a hard campaign for a craggy island with an underdeveloped infrastructure and of marginal strategic value. Therefore, a campaign conceived as "minor" could escalate to jeopardize future operations, including a cross-Channel invasion. Roosevelt, having opted for Torch as a first step to assert U.S. preeminence in the alliance, was loath to bless a British-dominated Brimstone. Nor was Churchill about to implement a plan that bypassed, or at the very least postponed, the invasion of Italy. He also believed Brimstone too small in scale to satisfy Stalin that it would suck significant numbers of German forces from the Eastern Front. Brimstone was relegated to the post-Husky agenda, when follow-on operations in the Mediterranean would be decided.[7]

Operation Husky—the invasion of Sicily—became Brooke's preferred option. Not surprisingly, given Britain's maritime perspective, Sicily had been considered a potential target from September 1942, when Brooke had dusted off and upgraded older invasion plans.[8] The major advantage of Husky from Marshall's perspective was that it would reopen the Mediterranean as a direct sea route to the Middle East, Iran, and the Soviet Union, economizing 225 merchant ships in turn-around time from the longer Cape route. In return for supporting Husky, he secured a commitment from the British COS to resume planning for Roundup. Roosevelt and Churchill saw Sicily as a major operation, one that would announce the Allied return to Europe and pay potentially far greater strategic dividends than Brimstone. The scale of the operation would be more likely to mollify Stalin. The fall of the island might topple Mussolini without an invasion of the Italian mainland. An Italian collapse, according to Brooke, would leave the Axis fifty-four divisions and 2,200 aircraft short of the minimum required to hold the balance on the Eastern Front.[9] On 23 January 1943, Eisenhower was tasked with planning an invasion of Sicily "with the target date as the period of the favourable July moon." Ike's deputy, Harold Alexander, would command all Allied land forces in the Sicilian operation.[10]

Translating the Casablanca compromise into an effective invasion plan proved no easy task, however. Husky was to be the largest amphibious operation yet attempted by the Allies—indeed, the largest before Overlord—one that required a great deal of coordination. The designated commanders of the major invasion forces—Alexander, Montgomery, and Patton—were distracted by the Tunisian campaign, as were many of the units they planned to use. Eisenhower remained aloof from the planning of an operation whose inputs came from Washington, London, Algiers, Malta, and Tunisia. Without the commander's overall vision and authority, the operational and administrative planners of Task Force 141 at AFHQ in Algiers, as well as those for the Eighth Army in Cairo and the Seventh Army in Rabat, were rudderless in designing their invasion. When the Allied military leaders at last focused on the task of projecting two armies onto the narrow beaches of a mountainous triangle of an island with an inadequate road network garrisoned by nine Italian and two German divisions, few were satisfied with the results. Montgomery, who was to lead the Eastern Task Force (Eighth Army), complained that the plans presented were driven by the perceived requirement to seize air bases and ports throughout the island. The Allied invaders would settle like starlings over ten scattered coastal invasion points that were not mutually

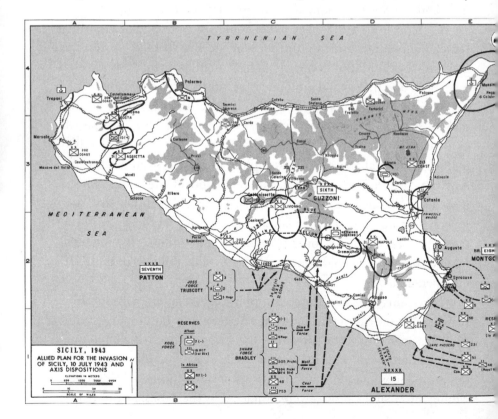

supporting, thus violating the principle of concentration of force and opening themselves to piecemeal defeat. Montgomery spat disgust at a plan that reflected "woolly thinking" and that had "no hope of success." He signaled to Alexander that he had "no intention of doing some of the things they suggest."[11]

Despite Monty's objections, the original plan had much to recommend it. It allowed each army to control its own ports, forced the defenders to split their response to each landing, and permitted each army to advance on their own axes toward Messina, which was essentially how the campaign developed in any case.[12] Monty's alternative plan, presented to Bedell Smith in the lavatory of AFHQ, called for the concentration of the two invading armies against the southeast corner of the island. Its assumption was that the invaders would meet strong resistance, which was unlikely given the poor Italian showing in North Africa, and the fact that the Germans would have only four divisions on the island to oppose eight-plus Allied divisions. The Eighth Army would land four divisions and one independent infantry brigade on beaches between Syracuse and Cape Passero fifty miles to the south. Their immediate task was to seize the port at Syracuse as well as Italian air bases on the Catania plain south of Mount Etna, a 10,740-foot snow-capped volcano whose mass squatted across the path north to Messina. Patton's Western Task Force (Seventh Army) would come ashore west of Scoglitti on the south coast, initially with three infantry divisions, to seize the port at Licata and the airfield at Gela. Perhaps the most daring operational experiment folded into Husky was the plan to land the American Eighty-second Airborne Division and the glider-borne British First Airborne Division ahead of the main force on the night of 9–10 July to capture key strategic targets.

Montgomery's plan was eventually adopted, but not without considerable bloodletting. Nor did the committee structure of Allied decision making, with each member operating out of headquarters hundreds of miles apart, ease coordination, all the more so because the committee was presided over by a supreme commander who behaved more like a CEO in charge of external relations than an operational commander. The most strategically profitable option was to land close to Messina, thus severing Axis troops on the island from the Italian mainland. However, Messina lay beyond the range of fighters operating from North Africa.[13] Marshall pushed without success for a preemptive invasion with a small force before the Axis could strengthen its defenses. Air Marshal Tedder objected that Monty's plan left too many airfields in Axis hands—Montgomery, Tedder complained to Patton, "thinks of himself as Napoleon . . . he is not."[14] Airmen wanted central control of air assets so as better to fight Axis planes, and not parcel them out to support ground and sea operations.[15] This caused Admiral Cunningham to fear for the safety of his ships concentrated at the southeastern tip of the island and vulnerable to air attack. Many questioned the ability to supply two armies across beaches with the impressive but as yet untried DUKW—a six-wheel, 2.5-ton amphibious truck—without the early capture of a major port. Churchill blasted Eisenhower's failure to stiffen operational planning and denounced Ike's pessimism as "pusillanimous and defeatist." Montgomery imperiously demanded control of U.S. troops, which predictably brought Patton to a vigorous boil.[16] After the problems in inter-Allied relations caused by the disposition of Second Corps in Tunisia, one would have thought that Eisenhower and Alexander would have been more sensitive to the need to give Americans a prominent role in the fighting. Instead, under Montgomery's plan, Patton's Western Task Force (Seventh Army) became the Cinderella of Husky, a handmaiden whose duty was to hold Montgomery's flank as he and the Eighth Army battled their way up the island's east coast to snatch the prize of Messina. The tempestuous Patton was unlikely to play second fiddle to the supercilious Montgomery for long, especially as Eisenhower and Alexander failed to assign specific objectives to the ground commanders. For those closest to the action, Eisenhower and Alexander seemed men of straw, devoid of ideas, irresolute, commanders to be bullied, threatened, cajoled, and blackmailed by their irascible subordinates.

Another weakness of Husky was that air, sea, and ground operations were poorly coordinated, largely because, Montgomery believed, Eisenhower had failed to create a combined operations headquarters. Tedder at Tunis and Cunningham at Malta made no plans to interdict the Strait of Messina, a grievous oversight, as it was across this two-mile stretch of turbulent water that the Axis would resupply, and eventually escape. Alexander's limp command style failed to impose a unified operational vision upon his two strong-willed army commanders.

The Allied plan did have considerable strengths, however. Husky reflected Montgomery's concern that the plan fall within Allied capabilities and provide for concentration of force.[17] It caught Italian morale on the downswing. Powerful Axis voices argued that Sicily was the next Allied objective. Indeed, so vulnerable did Sicily seem that in August 1941 Mussolini had ordered all Sicilians working for the government on the island to be transferred to jobs on the mainland. Their patriotism impugned, indignant islanders protested so that the order was never enforced. But Italians were increasingly able to peer through the hypocrisy of government claims that twelve million Italian soldiers stood ready to die for the motherland to realize that the Italian war effort teetered on the brink of collapse.[18]

Things were going badly for the Axis. Throughout the spring, the Soviets had continued to advance on the Eastern Front, where, in early July, two million men and 6,000 tanks mustered before Kursk. RAF and USAAF bombing of Germany, including the "Dambusters Raid" of 16–17 May, intensified. High U-boat losses caused Admiral Dönitz to break off operations against Allied Atlantic convoys in May. The Jewish uprising in the Warsaw Ghetto had been extinguished, but the resistance in France, Greece, and the Balkans gathered momentum. As the Allied juggernaut approached Europe from the south, Axis leadership was divided on the next Allied objective. Enigma revealed in March that Sicily was regarded as the most likely target, although Crete, Sardinia, and Corsica were also believed to be threatened.[19] Hitler's assumption of direct command meant, in the words of the German official history, that "by the end of 1942 the Wehrmacht Operations Staff was no longer a critical corrective but an amplifier of Hitler's wishful thinking."[20] Operation Mincemeat reinforced the Führer's intuition that Sardinia and Greece were the most likely objectives. He was therefore reluctant to reinforce Sicily.[21] Instead, he raised the number of German divisions in the Balkans from eight to eighteen, and those in Greece from one to eight.[22]

Albert Kesselring was equally in the dark about Allied intentions. As a good Luftwaffe general, he speculated that the capture of the "aircraft carriers" of Sardinia and Corsica offered the Allies the options of leaping east to Rome or north to France.[23] Until the fall of Tunis, Kesselring's opinion would have mattered little. A Franconian schoolteacher's son who had served mostly on artillery staffs during the Great War, Kesselring became one of the artillery officers selected to create the Luftwaffe in 1933. He had helped to choreograph both the smashup of Warsaw in 1939 and the Battle of Britain in 1940, before being sent to the Russian front and then in December 1941 to coordinate Axis operations in the Mediterranean. Alas, Kesselring rapidly discovered that his exalted title as *Oberbefehlshaber Süd* (commander-in-chief South) conferred little real power. Command of German troops in the Mediterranean defaulted to the *Commando Supremo*, whose chief of staff, Cavallero, initially had kept Kesselring at arm's length. Hitler was smitten with Rommel, who virtually ignored the more conservative advice of his titular commander, simply doing what he pleased and begging the Führer's post hoc forgiveness. Kesselring bore his discounted status with his signature smile, as he deployed his considerable charm and fluent Italian to win over his allies. Unlike his German counterparts who were driven to distraction by Italian puff and incompetence, Kesselring treated the deficiencies of his Axis partners with a tactful clemency that won their friendship. The result was that the Italians sought Kesselring's counsel and allowed him to disentangle the supply lines to North Africa, the key to which, he insisted, was Malta. At this stage of the war, *Oberbefehlshaber Süd* probably swung more weight in Rome than in Berlin, where Hitler rejected Kesselring's plea, heated to the point of disrespect, to seize Malta in the spring of 1942. Hitler suspected, wrongly, that the Italophile prejudices of his southern commander blinded him to Italian treachery and made him insufficiently vigilant in protecting German interests. But Hitler counted no more loyal servant than Kesselring. Beneath his bright bonhomie and suave diplomacy, "Smiling Albert" remained a

tough, no-nonsense German general. His allegedly pro-Italian sympathies did not blind him to Italian treachery—quite the contrary: he
took the precaution of infiltrating German divisions into the peninsula
in the summer of 1943, insurance against Italian defection. As the Axis
position in the Mediterranean continued to crumble under Hitler's incompetent direction, Kesselring tolerated no grumbling in his command. As a consequence, his subordinates became frustrated beyond
patience with Kesselring's tendency to spin the most desperate circumstances, especially when the commander-in-chief South committed men, including irreplaceable pilots, to hopeless tactical situations.

But in the summer of 1943, as Mediterranean battlegrounds shifted
to Europe's southern flank, Kesselring's stock was on the rise—Rommel had been eclipsed, and Hitler moved inexorably toward annexation of what had hitherto been regarded as Mussolini's bailiwick. Even
as his Luftwaffe succumbed to the crush of Allied air superiority,
Kesselring unveiled his talents as a master of defensive warfare, the
general with an instinctive feel for battle, able to inflict maximum
damage on the enemy before withdrawing to fight another day. Respected historians of the Italian campaign have assessed Kesselring as
"as good a general as emerged from the German Army in the Second
World War and certainly the best on either side in the Italian theater."[24]

However, Smiling Albert's usual optimism was tempered in the
summer of 1943 by the lassitude of the Italian navy, the diminishing
strength of his air forces, the poor state of the "gingerbread" fortifications on Sardinia, Sicily, and Pantelleria, and the hostility of the Italian chief of staff, General Ambrosio. He categorized the state of the
Italian garrison on Sicily as "hopeless," although in public he insisted
that Italian combat performance would turn around once Italians defended their homeland.[25] General Alfredo Guzzoni alerted Rome to
the appalling state of Sicily's coastal defenses and complained that the
200,000-man Italian Sixth Army defending Sicily was undertrained,
underarmed, and unenthusiastic. Hitler therefore relented and reinforced Sicily with two "improvised"[26] German divisions, the 15,500-man
strong Hermann Göring Division and the Fifteenth Panzer Grenadier Division. The Hermann Göring Division, a Luftwaffe unit resus-

citated to replace the original lost in Tunisia, was about a third below strength, while the 16,000 men of the Fifteenth Panzer Grenadier Division had been assembled from Tunisia escapees and the scrapings of German forces in Italy. But the Germans counted plenty of tanks, artillery, and antiaircraft artillery, as well as 30,000 Luftwaffe ground troops used to man antiaircraft defenses.[27] These were to be commanded by General Frido von Senger und Etterlin and his corps commander, a one-armed tank officer named General Hans Hube.[28] Nevertheless, Kesselring complained that Axis forces had no experience in defending against an amphibious invasion. Planes of Luftflotte II and flak units were transferred to the island, bringing to 1,750 the number of Axis aircraft within striking range of Sicily.[29] Fortifications were strengthened and supplies stocked. A ferry service of naval barges, assault boats, and Siebel ferries protected by a hedge of antiaircraft batteries provided the logistical bridge across the Strait of Messina. Kesselring was convinced that, in the two and a half months between the fall of Tunis and the onset of Husky, he had at least ensured Sicily against an Allied *coup de main*.[30] But Allied air reconnaissance that showed Italian women bathing in the surf on a designated invasion beach tipped off commanders that their objectives had not been mined or otherwise fortified.[31]

The Allied assaults on the islands of Lampedusa and Pantelleria, "the Italian Gibraltar," ordered by Eisenhower on 11–12 June 1943, were criticized as a distraction that prevented naval and air forces from concentrating on the forthcoming invasion of Sicily. Corkscrew, code name for the operation, also pointed to Sicily as the likely invasion site, as these islands lay directly on the path of Allied convoys negotiating the ninety miles between North Africa and Sicily.[32] But bad relations between Axis commanders and divisions over potential Allied objectives translated into lethargic preparations to defend Sicily. Possession of Pantelleria, with its significant air base and radio direction-finding (RDF) station, allowed the Allies to intensify air attacks on Sardinia, Sicily, and the Italian mainland. Allied preparatory bombing forced the Luftwaffe to abandon bases on the island to fall back on Calabria and Apulia, while the Italian air force virtually ceased to exist. Although the Luftwaffe did emerge in some strength in August to protect the evacuation of the island, its appearances in July were inter-mittent and largely cosmetic.[33]

Axis intelligence detected the loading and departure of Allied ships from North African ports in the first days of July. General Guz-zoni placed his troops on alert at 1900 on the evening of 9 July.[34] For-tunately for the Allies, whose experience of amphibious warfare had so far been limited to a practically resistance-free Torch, Husky caught Sicily's Axis garrison in an unbalanced defensive posture. Kesselring overruled Guzzoni's desire to concentrate his forces in the southeast-ern corner of the island, which the Italian commander correctly be-lieved to be the most likely point of invasion. The Napoli and the Hermann Göring Divisions were assigned to the southeast quadrant. The best Italian division on Sicily, the Livorno, was placed to guard against an invasion along the south coast around Agrigento and Gela. Finally, the Aosta and Assietta Divisions, together with the Fifteenth Panzer Grenadier, stood guard on the western tip of the island behind Marsala, Trapani, and Palermo. Kesselring also split the German divi-sions into four *Kampfgruppen* to reinforce the Italians, rather than keep them as a mobile reserve to hit the Allied invasion beaches while they were vulnerable. At the same time, he instructed subordinate commanders to react quickly to an Allied invasion without waiting for Italian orders.[35] Kesselring's scattered defense virtually guaranteed that, apart from the American beachhead at Gela, the initial Allied land-ings were practically strolls on the beach.

THE HORSE RACE

The inexperience of the Husky planners, as well as testy relations be-tween air, sea, and ground commanders, who cooperated with bad grace if at all,[36] became apparent when airborne operations began tragically on the night of 9–10 July. Approach routes from Tunisia had not been well defined. A gale pitched up, causing the delicate gliders to yaw and strain against their towropes. Two gliders snapped free of their C-47s and pirouetted into the sea. The pilots of tow planes, inex-perienced in war and disoriented by searchlights, flak, and the billow-ing clouds of smoke and dust that shrouded the Sicilian coast, released many of their Hadrian and Horsa gliders early at low altitude. Headed into a stiff wind, without navigational aids to guide them over a night-black coast, and with insufficient height, over seventy gliders ditched at sea, either drowning their occupants or forcing them to cling to the wreckage to await rescue. Other gliders, tracked by tracer bullets, crash-landed in orchards or vineyards, exploded on impact, or came to earth far off target. A Horsa carrying Bangalore torpedoes was caught by flak and exploded. A mere dozen gliders landed near their designated targets. As U.S. paratroops, packed shoulder to shoulder in C-47s, approached the Sicilian coast, the sky suddenly blazed with searchlights, exploding flak, and tracers. It was bright enough to read a newspaper inside the planes. Shrapnel pattered on the metallic skins of the planes like light rain. As the red jump light flashed in the fuselage, the men stood up, shuffled toward the black door, and, one by one, pitched themselves into space. The gale scattered and twisted the parachutes and slammed the paratroops into the cement-hard ground near Gela. Small groups of men collected themselves and made the best of a bad situation by roaming over the Sicilian countryside cutting telephone lines and ambushing isolated Axis patrols. On 11 June, a follow-up drop by the Eighty-second Airborne was savaged by its own antiaircraft artillery as it flew over the beaches. "Like a covey of quail the formations split as pilots twisted their ships to escape," Omar Bradley remembered as he watched helplessly from the *carabiniere* headquarters at Gela. "Ready lights flashed in the darkened cabins and parachutists tumbled out of the twisting aircraft. Some landed on the division fronts where they were mistaken for German raiders and shot while hanging in harness." Twenty-three aircraft were shot down by friendly fire, earning for Patton a severe, and unmerited, tongue-lashing from an angry Eisenhower for his "bumptious but rather disorganized executive management," the first sign of a crack in the hitherto tight relationship between the two men.[37]

Apart from the unexpected gale, which particularly affected the U.S. Third Infantry Division at Licata, the 2,590-ship armada, preceded by a screen of minesweepers, successfully closed in on the Sicilian shore at dawn. Large LSTs plowed through the surf with the first of Husky's 180,000 troops. The landings were practically unopposed because, according to Kesselring, "the Italian coastal divisions were an utter failure." Many of the Sicilian soldiers of the Napoli Division guarding the southeastern coast fired a burst or two at the invaders, then departed on French leave. At first light, Allied planes swept the skies over the invasion fleet and beaches, drawing bursts of fire from "excitable" Allied antiaircraft gunners.[38] Syracuse and its important port slipped undamaged into Allied hands, while the commander of the Italian fortress at Augusta surrendered even before he was attacked.[39] Allied bombing and poor communications disorganized the Axis defense. The only serious opposition was met by the U.S. First Infantry Division and assorted paratroops at Gela. Regiments of the Italian Livorno Division and elements of the Hermann Göring thrust down the road toward the airfield at Ponte Olivo and Gela beyond. A stubborn defense by U.S. paratroops, who ambushed a column of Panzer Grenadiers at Piano Lupo, a barren fortified hill that dominated a road intersection seven miles north of Gela, took the momentum out of the German attack. The Germans trained an 88 mm gun on Piano Lupo. But when their tanks tried to bypass the American position, two were disabled by bazookas, forcing the rest to withdraw. Guzzoni reassembled his troops for a more concerted attack on the next day, 11 July. Sixty panzers stormed toward Gela in two prongs, submerging a battalion of the Big Red One, placed at a disadvantage because the storm had delayed the arrival of antitank guns and tanks across the beach. In Gela, Patton, who spied the tanks thundering down the road, grabbed a navy ensign with a walkie-talkie and ordered up gunfire from the *Boise* standing offshore. But the tanks kept coming, despite the best efforts of the division artillery, firing at 500 yards, to stop them. The refusal of the U.S. paratroops and infantrymen of the First Division to withdraw separated the panzers from their following infantry. The *Boise's* guns found the range of the panzers, twenty-four of which went up in smoke as the Hermann Göring Division advanced to within 2,000 yards of the beach. At noon, U.S. tanks began to thread through the cleared minefields and move through Gela. By nightfall the beachhead was secure.[40] Bradley, Second Corps commander, blessed Patton's decision to substitute the First Division for the Thirty-sixth. "Only the perverse Big Red One with its no less perverse commander [Terry Allen] was both hard and experienced enough to take that assault in stride," Bradley wrote. "A greener division might easily have panicked and seriously embarrassed the landing."[41]

On 12 July, the day that the Second SS Panzer Corps opened a final, desperate, and unsuccessful offensive in the Battle of Kursk, Kesselring arrived in Sicily by flying boat, as most of his airfields on the island were captured or bombed out of commission. The good news was that an invasion of Calabria, which had particularly concerned him, was no longer a cause for worry. Therefore, he ordered up two regiments of the First Parachute Division and the Twenty-ninth Panzer Grenadier Division from the mainland, together with 232 antiaircraft guns sited with overlapping fire up to 23,000 feet to defend the Messina Strait. But there was plenty of bad news. The German commander, who, with his usual optimism, had been inclined to dismiss the Sicilian invasion as a "Dieppe raid,"[42] discovered that a solid Allied beachhead swaddled the southeastern corner of the island from Licata to the foot of Mount Etna. Air dominance was going to be a problem, because "the transfer of [Allied] fighter pilots to the [captured] airfields was remarkably swift," Kesselring noted.[43] The Italian command was in total disarray, as Ambrosio begged Mussolini to exit the war. Berlin's response to the situation was sluggish, in part because the German high command was divided over the wisdom of defending Sicily. They were also in the midst of Zitadelle, the offensive to retake Kursk launched on 5 July. In fact, Hitler was forced to close down Zitadelle on 13 July to free up resources for Italy, which he saw as the key to the defense of the Balkans.[44]

Allied troops pushing inland toward Enna and Nicosia threatened to cut the east–west route across the center of the island. From Nicosia, it was but a brief fifteen-mile march to San Stefano and the north coast, where the Allies might corner the three Axis divisions deployed on the eastern tip of the island. Guzzoni and von Senger had not hesitated to recall the Fifteenth Panzer Grenadier Division from western Sicily as soon as the scale of the Allied landing in the southeast became apparent. Allied intelligence confirmed on 14 July that Axis forces were bleeding out of western Sicily to reinforce the eastern half of the island.[45] Hitler secretly ordered Kesselring to create the

Fourteenth Panzer Corps to wrest control of the campaign from the vacillating Italians. On 15 July, Kesselring gave Hans Hube the happy news that daylight air support was to become a mere memory for the Wehrmacht. Over the next days, Kesselring struggled to establish a defensive line that could contain the Allied advance for "as long as possible" before he would be forced to evacuate the island. Fortunately for him, his improvised defense was rescued by the mistakes of the Allied command and their unimaginative, "methodical" operational approach.[46]

The Allied invasion of Sicily cracked the political foundations of the Axis. The more Italian fortunes deteriorated, the more the regime attempted to induce the illusion that *Il Duce* was infallible. Italians snapped to attention before radios broadcasting war bulletins and, in cinemas, rose as one when Mussolini strutted, chest out, across the screen. The mere whisper of his name in an Italian schoolroom brought students and professors alike bolt upright. But the invasion of the Italian homeland signaled that these outward displays of fealty were little more than a popular pantomime. The Italian leader looked cadaverous. His intellectual powers were in obvious free fall. He became consumed by a fear of being poisoned. By the spring of 1943, discretion brought on by fear and opportunism had been supplanted by open criticism of Mussolini's judgment even among many hitherto loyal henchmen—Ciano conspired to replace him, and Hitler, alert to the mutiny swelling around his ally, prepared to occupy Italy and supplant Italian garrisons in the Balkans should Rome abandon the Axis. Secret Italian contacts with the British through Lisbon brought demands for total capitulation, which Mussolini rejected because it would finish Italy as a "great power."

If the swift collapse of the "impregnable" Pantelleria delivered a body blow to the regime's morale, the invasion of Sicily was the jaw-breaker. On 16 July, a group of Fascist high officials called for a meeting of the Grand Council, which had not assembled since 1939, to discuss Italy's situation. Their resolve was strengthened when, at a summit with Hitler at Feltre in northern Italy on 19 July, *Il Duce* sat like a scolded puppy through the Führer's tirade about Italy's failed war effort. In the words of U.S. war cartoonist Bill Mauldin, Mussolini "reminds a guy of a dog hit by an automobile because it ran out and tried to bite the tires." He should have stayed on the sidewalk.[47] Mussolini's failure to defend Italian interests at Feltre coincided with the first Allied air raid on Rome, a sign to Italians that their country stood on defeat's doorstep and that the regime's death agony had commenced. King Vittorio Emanuele suggested that Mussolini seize the moment to resign. At the end of a tempestuous ten-hour meeting of the Fascist Grand Council at the Palazzo Venezia on 24–25 July, the members voted 19 to 7 to ask the king to set a new course and to restore the powers that Mussolini had stripped from Parliament, the government, and the Grand Council. On the afternoon of 25 July, Mussolini traveled to the palace for his weekly audience with the king. But the meeting proved far from routine—the diminutive monarch informed the stunned Duce that Pietro Badoglio was now prime minister. As the deposed dictator walked out into the sunlight, he was surrounded by *carabiniere*, thrust into a police van, and driven away. Badoglio shifted his captive around among a series of islands and prisons to prevent the Germans from locating him as the new government laid the groundwork for Italy's war exit.[48]

News of Mussolini's arrest pitched Hitler into a rage: he vowed to " 'mop up' the royal family and Badoglio."[49] The Italian defection, he feared, would prompt Hungary and other satellites to desert. Mussolini's overthrow caught Hitler at a low point. Massive bomber raids on 27–28 July had raised a firestorm in Hamburg that killed 50,000 people. For the first time, "window," strips of metal foil that confused German radar, was used. The Hamburg raid was followed in August by air attacks on Nuremberg, Berlin, ball bearing plants at Schweinfurt and Regensburg, as well as the rocket research station at Peenemünde. In Italy, Turin and Genoa were hit. Milan was bombed four times in August. U-boats and the U-tankers that supplied them were being lost at an alarming rate. Hitler transferred eight divisions to Italy, brought Italian troops in the Dodecanese under German command, and took control of the railways around the Brenner Pass.[50] Hitler told Kesselring to prepare to evacuate his troops from Sicily, but, because he distrusted his southern commander's pro-Italian sentiments, he told him little else.[51] From Berlin's perspective, Kesselring was a dog that

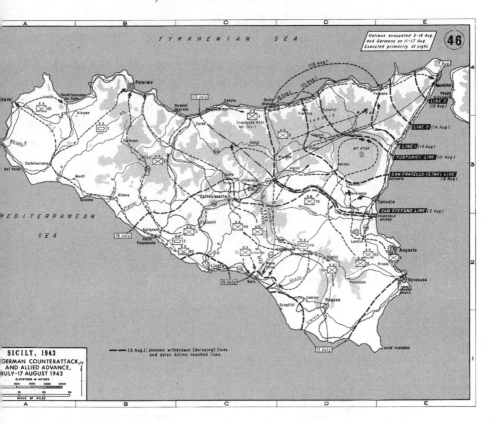

couldn't hunt. Trusting and naive, he had failed to sniff out Italian treachery and so placed German interests in jeopardy.[52]

Unfortunately, Alexander and Montgomery chose this moment of Axis distraction to commit what many historians regard as the crucial mistake of the Sicilian campaign, one that arguably transformed the invasion from a battle of maneuver into an attritional struggle that postponed the campaign's outcome and raised the costs in Allied casualties. On 12 July, Montgomery proposed that the Twenty-third Armoured Brigade, and infantry of the Fifty-first Highland Division and the First Canadian Division, collectively known as "Harpoon Force," should strike west along Route 124 through Vizzini to Caltagirone. His purpose, Montgomery maintained, was to cut behind the Hermann Göring Division, which was attacking the U.S. First Division bridgehead at Gela. He would then turn north through Enna and Leonforte toward Nicosia, thereby giving priority to his "left hook" around

Mount Etna.[53] This was a significant change in the axis of advance that would alter the boundaries between the two Allied armies and seize the road along which the U.S. Seventh Army planned to advance, effectively shouldering the Americans out of any significant contribution to what was expected to be a brief campaign.

Alexander, meeting with Patton on the thirteenth, failed to mention that he planned to shift the boundary between the two Allied armies in Montgomery's favor.[54] The U.S. Forty-fifth Division pushed the Hermann Göring Division northward, thus taking away the opportunity for the British troops advancing from the east to hit it in the flank. In fact, the Forty-fifth Division's northward trajectory would take it into the flank of the Canadian First Division as it advanced west along Route 124. On the evening of the thirteenth, Montgomery told Alexander to expect a huge traffic jam on Route 124 between Vizzini and Caltagirone unless Patton's advance from the south was halted and his troops redirected back to his beachhead at Gela. Alexander instructed Patton to keep his army west of Route 124.[55] At Gela on 14 July, Patton struck a match, lit a large cigar, and began to rethink his options.

Soldiers at the time, and historians since, have been universal in condemning Montgomery's decision as a monumental lapse in judgment, and with good reason. Montgomery's purpose was to repeat the "Mareth maneuver" that had overextended Axis defenses in the open desert. But Sicily was not North Africa. His "left hook" was hemmed in by the broken terrain and stone walls of Sicily, confining his armor to a few narrow and easily obstructed roads. This reduced him to diminutive, brigade-sized attacks. The decision to shunt the Americans sideways both compromised chances for a rapid triumph in Sicily and destabilized the fragile chemistry of the Anglo-American alliance. According to Carlo D'Este, a historian of the Sicilian campaign, the situation created by this decision was nothing short of "ludicrous."[56] In the first place, by occupying Route 124, Montgomery obliged Patton to shift the agreed-upon line of demarcation between his Seventh Army and Montgomery's Eighth Army well to the west. In doing so, the U.S. Forty-fifth Division was forced to let the hard-pressed Hermann Göring Division off the hook and surrender the opportunity for a "break out," according to Omar Bradley. The Americans were much better placed than was the cautious, methodical Montgomery to cut the island in half from south to north, and then pivot behind the German defenses. In Patton, they counted a dynamic cavalry commander impatient to exploit Axis disarray and showcase U.S. superiority over the British in four-wheel-drive trucks, armor, and artillery. "We had reached the main road north," Bradley recorded. "With our superior trucks and self-propelled artillery we could move much faster than the British. The enemy front before us was soft from his withdrawals; he was concentrating in the main before XIII [British] Corps at Catania, not us. We were in the ideal position for a fast run to the north coast—before the enemy could organize his defensive perimeter—and an encircling right turn toward Messina."[57]

Had the Americans been able to seize Enna by 16 July, the Fifteenth Panzer Grenadier Division and the Italian Twelfth Corps might well have been cut off in western Sicily. The Americans could then have swung north of Mount Etna along Route 120, forcing the Germans at Catania to retreat along the coast to Messina. At the same time, Montgomery would have kept his Thirtieth Corps concentrated, rather than dispersing them against the German defenses on the Catania plain.[58] Instead, the Forty-fifth was obliged to return to Gela and then redirect its advance toward the northwest to cover the flank of the U.S. First Infantry Division. In the process, they were forced to use much of the transport that should have been carrying supplies up from the beachhead. Canadian troops of the Eighth Army's Thirtieth Corps advanced along the Vizzini-to-Caltagirone highway largely on foot, under a blistering sun, with inadequate artillery. Even Montgomery's biographer concedes that by splitting his force, Montgomery rendered the Eighth Army too weak to take either Vizzini or Catania. By 17 July, Ultra revealed that slackening British pressure had resolved the crisis in German units defending the foot of Mount Etna.[59] With the Forty-fifth Division ordered back to the south coast, the Hermann Göring Division turned east to face the advancing Canadians without fear of being attacked from two directions. Also, German paratroopers dropped on Catania and dug in to block Montgomery's advance north along the coast road.[60]

The "stolen road" incident constituted "perhaps the deciding moment of the whole Sicilian campaign," according to Nigel Hamilton. "By splitting his army and refusing the help of Bradley's 2 US Corps, Monty had unwittingly passed up the last chance he would have of a speedy conclusion to the campaign."[61] Its origins lay in Montgomery's, and the Eighth Army's, overconfidence and sense of superiority over the Americans, his ignorance of the tactical situation, and the fact that campaign objectives had not been clearly delineated in the planning stage. Finally, it showcased Alexander's inability to "grip" the battle and impose a vision on two highly competitive commanders.[62] Patton and Bradley correctly saw Alexander's order as a vote of no confidence in U.S. abilities and an insult to the U.S. Army, one that sought effectively to sideline the Seventh Army and prevent it from playing any meaningful part in the campaign.[63] Bradley remembered that he was "as hot as Mount Etna" over an order that was "so outrageous, so obviously wrong," because the Seventh Army was poised for a breakout, one that would have facilitated a parallel advance by Montgomery toward Catania. He pleaded in vain to Patton to protest it, and speculated that Patton's uncharacteristic quiescence came from his fear of being relieved by Eisenhower as the result of the paratroop calamity and atrocities carried out by some American troops against Axis POWs, for which the supreme commander, in a fit of rage, blamed Patton.[64] Another of Patton's biographers has suggested that he welcomed the order because it liberated the Seventh Army from acting as flank guard for the Eighth and allowed him to set his own campaign objectives.[65]

With the Seventh Army sidelined, Montgomery's plan to advance toward Catania called for a commando unit to seize the bridge at Lentini, followed by an airborne drop on the Primosole Bridge over the Simeto River, ten miles north of Lentini and seven miles south of Catania, on the night of 13–14 July. At dawn on 14 July, a force composed of the Fiftieth Division reinforced by an armored brigade and a commando unit would drive up Route 114 over the Lentini Bridge, up to Primosole, and then enter Catania on 15 July. The plan went disastrously wrong from the beginning for two predictable reasons. First, it failed to allow for unanticipated Axis countermoves. Second, the plan relied for its success on an experimental operational technique that had already proven its shortcomings—the airborne assault. The unexpected happened on 12 July, as elements of the German First Parachute Division began to arrive at Catania and rushed south to reinforce troops of the Hermann Göring Division at Primosole. This led to what Kesselring called a "fluke success" when they were on hand to oppose the subsequent British drop, the second weakness of the plan.[66] As during two earlier operations, British airborne transports destined for Primosole with a load of 1,800 troops were again shot down, forced to return to base, and dispersed by friendly flak. Paratroops were scattered over the countryside and separated from their equipment. Only 300 British airborne troops eventually found their way to Primosole, which they were surprised to discover was firmly in the hands of tough German paratroops rather than surrender-prone Italians. Nevertheless, the British grabbed the bridge and hunkered down to await rescue by the Fiftieth Division advancing from the south. Unfortunately, the Fiftieth Division encountered stiff German resistance at Lentini, where the British commandos had been ejected from the bridge, and failed to advance. After fighting off German attacks all day, by nightfall on 14 July the British paratroops at Primosole exhausted their ammunition and scattered rather than surrender. The Fiftieth Division tanks appeared that evening after the Germans abandoned the defense of Lentini. But it took them until the morning of 16 July to retake Primosole after bitter fighting that left them too exhausted to advance northward.

The Thirteenth Corps continued to batter toward Catania in an unimaginative assault that employed neither naval gunfire nor close air support effectively. Hube dropped paratroops to shore up weak places in his line. Montgomery toyed with plans of bypassing the German defenses before Catania with an amphibious operation toward Messina, but never carried it out, probably because he lacked landing craft. He also continued to believe, against the evidence, that he was on the brink of victory.[67] Instead, he ordered the Fifty-first Highland Division to march on Paterno to fill the gap between the Thirtieth and Thirteenth Corps. Having now split his forces among three axes of attack, none of which was succeeding, Montgomery was stuck. His hesitation, his decision to split his army leaving neither the Thirteenth nor the Thirtieth Corps strong enough to break through, and his poor coordination of naval and air power allowed the Germans to solidify their defenses at the foot of Mount Etna. Inland, the Canadian division plodded along Route 124 in a suffocating heat through bush and boulder mountains bristling with German strong points. Leonforte and Assoro were captured on 22 July.

As the early promise of a rapid conclusion of the Sicilian campaign metamorphosed into a slogging match across an island "pregnant with hard mountains,"[68] the sense of unease shared by Allied troops in North Africa that the Mediterranean strategy was a wasteful and inconclusive enterprise resurrected itself. Those who saw the leap to Sicily as an escape from Africa, an entry into a European continent rich in strategically lucrative targets, quickly discovered the resemblance between the two Mediterranean shores. As war correspondent Richard Tregaskis stared at the curved harbor of Licata, past a bleached cluster of stucco squares to stark hills beyond, the soldier standing next to him on the deck of the LST muttered, "It looks just like Africa."[69] "*Dopo Roma, c'e'l'Africa*"—After Rome, it's Africa—northern Italians insisted. Allied soldiers found the jabbering crowds that lined dusty roads giving the V sign and shouting "*Cigaretta! Americano!*" or "*Viva Ingleterre!*" appeared more African than European, although Sicilian effusion struck the Anglo-Americans as less genuine and more contrived than Arab taciturnity. Ragged crowds appeared out of nowhere to loot shops and ransack official buildings in newly liberated towns. "Sounds of breaking glass and furniture being upset mingled with the joyful babble of the vultures," wrote war correspondent Richard Tregaskis, who witnessed one such mass looting at Catania. Sicily even smelled like Africa![70] As in Africa, roads lined with the blasted hulks of overturned vehicles twisted through a landscape antique with vineyards and almond and olive groves. As in Tunisia, the tranquillity of the countryside belied the lethality of the battle fought to dominate it. Each gray ridge was fortified, and had to be seized by small parties of infantry preceded by a creeping artillery barrage that drummed like a concert on the mountains, "a rattling, wooden tone" on the lower slopes that transitioned to a metallic rasp as an explosive plume shifted to the higher elevations, like a volcanic eruption in reverse. "The further we went the higher the mountains were," declared the chaplain of the First Infantry Division. "There was no end of them in Sicily."[71]

With time on his hands, Patton became fixated on seizing Palermo as a headline-grabbing exercise to draw attention back to the Seventh Army, and then strike east toward Messina. On 17 July he flew to Tunis to secure Alexander's permission to run Bradley's Second Corps, composed of the First and Forty-fifth Infantry Divisions, to the north coast near Terni. The remainder of the Seventh Army—the Eighty-second Airborne, Third Infantry, and Second Armored Divisions organized as a provisional corps—would tour western Sicily, where only the remnants of Italian units still existed, and capture Palermo in the bargain. Alexander's acquiescence to Patton's request was yet another desperate mistake. Montgomery's biographer argues that an Eighth Army front stiffened by American forces would have caused German defenses around Etna to implode. When, on 19 July, a chastened Montgomery asked Alexander to transfer U.S. troops to his front, it was too late— Patton had bolted north. "Alexander could have won a great victory," Hamilton concludes, had he acted to reinforce Eighth Army's front. Instead, the British Seventy-eighth Division, held in Tunisia for the follow-up invasion of Italy, had to be brought in to shore up the tiring Eighth Army.[72]

Bradley, too, complained that the Seventh Army's thrust into western Sicily was strategically barren. Although Patton confided to his diary that study of his rapid south–north bisection of Sicily would become core curriculum in command and staff colleges, its sole purpose was to allow Patton, followed by a swarm of reporters and cameramen, to showcase the speed of the U.S. advance and the 21 July fall of Palermo to raise the profile of U.S. troops in Sicily. The only dividend was the capture of large numbers of demoralized Italian troops enticed to surrender on the promise of a parole for Sicilian natives.[73] On the minus side, the rapid advance had further scattered and disorganized Patton's headquarters, never a model of efficiency at the best of times. Administrative confusion, combined with the slow resuscitation of Palermo's harbor, blocked by thirty-four sunken ships, would mean that Bradley's Second Corps continued to encounter significant supply problems as it advanced east through the mountains of Sicily's north coast toward Messina. The Germans had strengthened their defenses around Mount Etna. Eisenhower remained unimpressed, and began to shift his preferences for future command toward Omar Bradley—in August, Ike told Marshall that Bradley should command U.S. troops in Britain preparing for Overlord.[74] Nor did Palermo's capture advance the American cause in inter-Allied relations—to the annoyance of an enraged Patton, the BBC continued to emphasize that the Eighth Army carried the brunt of the fighting while "the Seventh Army had been lucky to be in western Sicily eating grapes."[75] Patton, already established in the public mind and in the mind of his soldiers as a strutting braggart, was heading for a fall.

The Allied disposition now arced around German defenses running from Catania on Sicily's east coast, to Adrano at the foot of Mount Etna, and then through the desperate terrain around Nicosia to San Stefano on the north coast. This was not so much a perimeter as a collage of strong points organized by Hube. Advanced posts, sited on spurs or dominating steep ravines that gave clear fields of fire, protected main defensive lines nestled in folds of terrain and reverse slopes to shield them from artillery and air attack. These fortified positions were garrisoned by the Hermann Göring Panzer Division and the Fifteenth and Twenty-ninth Panzer Grenadier Divisions, elements of the paratroop division, and odds and ends of Italian troops. Given a landscape so chaotic that Tunisia looked by comparison like a billiard table, and a deficiency of tarmac that precluded maneuver, the Allies would have to assault each strong point head on. During a 25 July meeting in Syracuse among the three commanders, Montgomery decided to make the best of a bad situation to propose that Patton seize Messina. Second Corps would move east along two axes: Route 120 from Nicosia through Troina to Randazzo, and along Route 113 on the north coast. These two parallel roads, although only fifteen miles apart in places, were separated by the Caronie Mountains, the highest in Sicily after Etna. This meant that the two thrusts could not be mutually supporting. Rather, each division would have to carve its own advance along serpentine roads that surmounted high mountain passes, plunged into gorges, and twisted around ridges and cliffs that offered natural fortresses to the defense. The rugged country, the absence of roads, a lack of pack animals to supply advances in the mountains, and the stifling July heat made Allied operations slow to develop and easy for the German defenders to counter.

That said, however, time was not on the Axis's side. Patton, the glow of Palermo dimmed, became obsessed with winning what he called the "horse race" to Messina ahead of the British. Allied domination of the air, while mitigated by the tumultuous terrain, poor ground-air communications, a proliferation of air headquarters, the difficulty of identifying bombworthy targets, and fear of friendly fire, at least guaranteed that the attackers would not be overly troubled by the Luftwaffe.[76] And while Allied air superiority barely disturbed the ferry traffic across the strait, bombing of rail lines in Calabria had reduced supplies reaching Messina to a trickle by the end of July. Allied bombing also disrupted Axis communications. Mussolini's overthrow on 25 July diminished further the threadbare loyalty of those Italian troops still fighting on—rumors flew through Italian ranks that an armistice was days, if not hours, away. For the Germans, the agonizing logistical asphyxiation of North Africa, the fear of entrapment, the desire to stick close to the port of embarkation, played out again in Sicily. Unlike von Arnim and Messe in Tunisia, however, Hube determined that Messina would be his place of escape, not another giant POW cage. He laid plans from 1 August for a phased retreat and evacuation across the strait.

The U.S. First Division, hampered by supply problems and poorly coordinated air support, ground slowly along Route 120 in the teeth of tenacious and skillful resistance put up by the Fifteenth Panzer Grenadiers. American troops attacking along knifelike ridges and up steep slopes encountered artillery (some of whose shells were time-fused to explode overhead), mortars, and snipers. Nicosia fell on 27 July. The battle for Troina, the highest town in Sicily, lasted almost a week, and was the bloodiest fought by U.S. troops in Sicily. U.S. intelligence underestimated both the strength of the defenses and the obstinacy of the defenders. The First Division had to cross a string of fortified ridges up to a mile high, which channeled their attack down a barren, cup-shaped valley and turned Route 120 into a killing ground. Troina was a typical Sicilian hill town of narrow, twisting streets, standing like a citadel across a pass that the Americans would have to seize if they wanted to advance toward Messina. The approach was sliced by deep, mine-sown gorges shielded with murderous defensive artillery and mortar fire from reverse slope positions that were impossible to observe and hence difficult to counter. A 1 August assault on the town was repelled. Over the next days, U.S. troops slowly captured the ridges that dominated Troina to the north and south. In the forefront of the advance was Patton's friend Colonel Paddy Flint, who, stripped to the waist, a black scarf tied around his neck, rifle in hand, led his Thirty-ninth Infantry Regiment. Ground was seized, then the troops dug in to fight off the inevitable German counterattacks. On 5 August, the First Division, joined by a regiment of the newly arrived Ninth Division with an attached company of French Moroccan *goumiers*, irregular troops used as scouts and skirmishers, began a wide cross-country sweep to the north with the goal of striking behind the town and cutting off the German retreat. On 6 August, the Germans, fearing that their exit roads would be severed, abandoned Troina, leaving 1,600 dead. The retreat from Troina was part of a general withdrawal toward the coast that had begun when the Hermann Göring Division thinned out its lines around Catania and moved north. The battered First Division was relieved by the newly arrived U.S. Ninth Division.[77]

The Forty-fifth Division advanced along the coast road against the Twenty-ninth Panzer Grenadier Division at an agonizing pace, as the Germans demolished sections of the road that ran along precipices over the sea. Attacks that depended on seizing bridges across narrow gorges could be countered by strong concentrations of Axis artillery. Infantrymen had to traverse streams at the bottom of narrow gorges and then scale cliffs 900 feet high as German soldiers rolled hand grenades down at them. The difficulties of calculating distances in the steep terrain meant that friendly artillery shells often exploded in the faces of attacking troops. On 31 July, an exhausted Forty-fifth Division, which had seized the town of Motta and then held it against furious counterattacks, was replaced by the Third Infantry Division. But the Germans fell back to the San Fratello line, a series of trenches, pillboxes, minefields, and gun emplacements that ran perpendicular to the sea along the boulder-strewn San Fratello Ridge over the Furiano River.

Patton frothed with impatience at the slow progress toward Messina. According to Bradley, this was the moment that Patton displayed in full measure his "shallowness" as a commander—his tendency to micromanage operations, his profanity, his "butt-kicking," which demoralized rather than inspired his troops, his reliance on intuition and speed rather than planning and organization for success.[78] His casualties were mounting, and replacements were scarce. A noisy Axis air raid on Palermo had put Patton's nerves on edge. On 3 August, Patton grabbed a handful of Purple Hearts and entered the Fifteenth Evacuation Hospital near Nicosia. He was on a morale-boosting exercise, as much for himself as for the troops, who, he believed, were inspired by his presence. As he strolled among the bandaged patients making small talk, his eye fell on Private Charles Kuhl of Mishawaka, Indiana. When Patton asked Kuhl what ailed him, the private replied, "I guess I can't take it." Patton flew into a rage, slapped Kuhl in the face, called him a "sonuvabitch" and a "yellow-bellied bastard," and ordered him back to the front. Corpsmen rushed to protect Kuhl, who was found to be suffering from combat fatigue, malaria, and chronic dysentery. Six days later, Patton repeated the performance, complete with threats and profane epithets, at the Ninety-third Evacuation Hospital near Sant'Agata di Militello, assisted this time by one of his celebrated pearl-handled pistols. He drew the pistol and waved it in the face of a terrified soldier suffering from severe shell shock, whom Patton accused of malingering. The doctor was forced to intervene after an irate Patton, who had departed, returned to strike the soldier a second time.[79]

Inability to break the San Fratello line caused Patton to order Bradley and Third Division commander Lucian Truscott to carry out an amphibious "end run" to be coordinated with a frontal attack on the German positions. These were made possible by the formation on 27 July of Naval Task Force 88, known as "Patton's Navy."[80] The first of three "end runs," carried out on 8 August, was calculated to outflank the San Fratello line, block escape routes, and force a German withdrawal. They might have been strategically profitable had they been carried out on a regimental scale at points where beaches and roads coincided. But small numbers of LSTs and hasty planning forced by Patton's impatience to reach Messina limited the first operation to a mere battalion insertion at St. Agata, six miles behind the San Fratello line, hardly more than a commando raid. This simply succeeded in placing a small packet of U.S. troops behind German lines with inadequate air support, where they were threatened with extinction by overwhelming force. Although Bradley claimed that the Germans were unsettled by the maneuver and large numbers of prisoners were captured,[81] the official history records that the Axis troops were already pulling out of the San Fratello line because the fall of Troina had exposed their left flank. The large numbers of prisoners were Italians of the Assietta Division who realized that they had been deserted by their Axis allies.[82]

But the German pullout at San Fratello was only a tactical withdrawal, not a retreat, for they were soon reestablished on a line as formidable as San Fratello at the Naso Ridge about twenty miles east of San Fratello. Patton ordered a second landing for 10 August to seize Monte Cipolla, which dominated the coastal highway between the Naso and Brolo Rivers. Truscott and Bradley pointed out to Patton that Third Division troops advancing along the coast had yet to reach the Naso position in force and therefore would not be able to link up with the amphibious operation. When they requested a postponement, Patton exploded with rage. Six hundred fifty U.S. troops were inserted at Brolo beach in the early morning hours of 11 August. The force reached the beach without incident, but were soon detected by the Germans, who swarmed like hornets, lighting up the night with flares. The beleaguered battalion had repeatedly to be saved by naval gunfire, air strikes, and long-range 155 mm artillery. But U.S. fire support was only intermittent, especially after German planes intervened to attack and drive off the American ships. The retreating Germans were able to force their way through the small and lightly armed blocking force.[83] By the time that Patton ordered a third "end run" east of Cape Milazzo, the Germans were retreating so rapidly that the Third Division overran the beachhead and were there to greet the amphibious task force as it hit the beach. The same fate greeted Montgomery's amphibious operation launched on 16 August to bypass minefields north of Taormina.[84] By then, however, the first U.S. patrols had reached Messina.

In the early days of August, Allied intelligence began to report the increasing pace of the German withdrawal. A copy of the evacuation plan was captured on 31 July, and decrypts from 1 August ordered a "practice" evacuation. On 3 August, Alexander informed Tedder and Cunningham that the "full weight of navy and air power" must be brought against the evacuation. "You no doubt have coordinated plans to meet this contingency." On 11 August, Alexander timidly told Tedder that "the general impression, and only an impression, is that the Germans may withdraw across the Straits shortly." Through 13 August, however, AFHQ in Algiers appeared convinced that increased ferry traffic was simply an indication that the Germans were evacuating non-essential personnel and equipment. On 14 August, Alexander signaled Tedder that the evacuation "has really started."[85]

However, a tardy alert probably does not account for the feebleness of Allied reaction, as it must have been apparent from the shrinking Axis perimeter and the increase in ferry traffic across the strait that an evacuation was under way. Rather, the failure of Allied attempts to cut off the Axis retreat can be explained by poor organization, lack of imagination, and inactivity. The wide dispersion of headquarters in Malta, Tunis, and Algiers did not facilitate joint planning. Montgomery had so far proved reluctant to use amphibious operations. An airborne drop on Messina seemed out of the question given the failure of all airborne operations so far. A secondary landing in Calabria would have required that the Allies plan for it from mid-July. But no decision on an operation after Husky had been taken, and neither Eisenhower nor Alexander took the initiative to see that this happened.[86] The air force had some success delaying the ferry traffic at night. But the daytime flak was too thick and the targets too small for air power to have a decisive effect. Tedder argued that strategic targets on the Italian mainland were more profitable. Brave attempts to fly through the flak barrage in the last week of the evacuation succeeded in damaging only five Siebel ferries and a few barges.[87]

No repetition of the "Sink, burn and destroy. Let nothing pass" order issued by Cunningham during Retribution, the final stages of the Tunisia operation, occurred in Sicily. The British admiral argued that he had no intention of repeating the World War I fiasco of the Dardanelles at Messina. Maintaining a surface fleet in a narrow, ten-mile-long strait with a six-knot current, swept by searchlights and artillery, "would be a gift to enemy submarines; and destroyers, as usual, were hard to come by. Very accurate spotting would have been required, and the spotter wouldn't have lasted five minutes over the Straits." More likely, Cunningham's biographer concludes, the admiral was distracted by planning for Avalanche.[88] Eisenhower failed to intervene to force Tedder and Cunningham to prevent the "sorry spectacle" of an Axis getaway.[89] Therefore, only feeble attempts were made to intercept the evacuation.

On 6 August, Montgomery finally cracked the Etna line. By 11 August when the final evacuation began, 13,000 German and numerous Italian troops had already been ferried to the mainland. By 17 August, when Patton made his triumphal entry into Messina to take the formal surrender, 55,000 German and 70,000 Italian soldiers had reached the mainland, along with almost 10,000 vehicles, 51 tanks, and 163 guns. Allied efforts to interdict this evacuation had been halfhearted and ineffective. Bradley complained that Patton's obsession with entering the city himself had delayed its capture and allowed yet more Germans to escape. On 17 August, Patton received a letter from Eisenhower admonishing him for "brutality, abuse of the sick, [and] exhibition of uncontrollable temper in front of subordinates." On Eisenhower's orders, Patton began his tour of Seventh Army units to apologize "for any occasions when I may have harshly criticized individuals."[90]

"A THIRTY-EIGHT-DAY RACE WITH
THE ITALIANS IN THE LEAD"

Carlo D'Este has called Sicily a "hollow victory," characterized by "military blunders, controversy and indecision." Sixty thousand Germans had managed to hold off eight times their number of Allied troops as they organized a successful evacuation from the island.[91] Strategically, Sicily produced several pluses for the Allies, however. The operation precipitated Mussolini's overthrow and began a process that knocked Italy out of the war, thus realizing one of the important goals of the Allied Mediterranean strategy. The Sicilian campaign brought seething relations between Italians and Germans to the point of breakdown. "At first, when they came, the Germans are saluting, laughing, and they are friendly," Richard Tregaskis was told by the mayor of Catania. "To see them drilling in the square was wonderful." Mussolini's ouster and the spectacle of mass defections of Italian forces in Sicily pushed German troops beyond the brink of contempt. They began mistreating Italian civilians, seizing food, and looting houses at gunpoint. Tregaskis was told that Italian soldiers trying to protect civilians had even been drawn into firefights with German troops. As they evacuated Sicily, the Germans blew up all public buildings that might be of use to the Allies.[92] One journalist described Husky as a thirty-eight-day race with the Italians in the lead. Indeed, GIs entering Sicilian villages received phone calls from Italian soldiers in the villages ahead asking to surrender. Italian troops attempting to surrender did not know where to turn, as they were fired on by both the Allies and the Germans.[93] Axis forces were driven from the island, 147,000 Italians were killed, wounded, or captured, while the Germans absorbed an estimated 29,000 casualties (4,325 killed, 6,663 captured, and almost 18,000 wounded). The British, in contrast, took just under 12,000 casualties and the Americans 7,402.

Husky opened the floodgates of Lend-Lease aid to the Soviet Union. Clear Mediterranean sea lanes economized shipping and allowed for the year-round supply of the Soviet Union through Persia (Iran). Indeed, Persia was nicknamed the Bridge of Victory after over four million tons of supplies, or 23.8 percent of the total Lend-Lease aid sent to the Soviet Union, was funneled through Persian ports and the trans-Iranian railway to the Caspian Sea. The Mediterranean campaign even contributed to the success of the Arctic convoys, which funneled 22.7 percent of Lend-Lease supplies around the North Cape through Archangel and Murmansk.[94] The requirement to shift planes from northern Norway to defend the Mediterranean and the subsequent attrition of the Luftwaffe meant that disasters like that which befell convoy PQ 17 in July 1942 were not repeated. Large numbers of Axis troops had been diverted from the Eastern Front to occupy Italy, the Balkans, and Greece, forcing the abandonment of the Kursk offensive.

On the operational level, surprise was achieved on both the strategic and tactical levels. Apart from the disastrous airborne operations, the amphibious invasion plan was flawlessly carried out. The Luftwaffe was on its way to becoming history. Henceforth the Allies effectively dominated the air over the Mediterranean. The U.S. Army demonstrated a marked improvement in performance over that in Tunisia. It had fielded four new divisions as well as its first army in World War II. Allied divisions, especially American ones, evidenced solid combat qualities and a capacity to learn which would prove extremely valuable in the Italian and Normandy campaigns.[95] Division-level combat leaders that the U.S. Army had identified in Tunisia continued to demonstrate their value in Sicily. A firming up in the quality of senior army leadership combined with operational improvements in U.S. forces to advance Roosevelt's goal of asserting American domination of the Western Alliance. "We had learned a great deal more about fighting a war," Bradley concluded.[96] U.S. Army leadership concluded that American drive and aggression should be accorded pride of place in the invasion of Italy.[97]

But problems remained. On the debit side of the ledger, senior Allied leadership—Eisenhower, Alexander, and Montgomery—continued to display their limitations. Each was stalked in turn by a lack of assertiveness that sprang from a sense of intellectual inadequacy, overconfidence bred from conceit, and impetuosity born of ambition. Faulty command decisions, combined with Allied inability or unwillingness to cut the strait, had allowed the better part of four German divisions to escape with most of their equipment to fight another day.[98] The campaign plan, from its inception a conservative one that reflected the risk-averse attitude of both Montgomery and Eisenhower, became a tangle of improvisation for both sides. The absence of clearly defined campaign objectives among the Allies, the side on the offensive, bought time for Kesselring.

Eisenhower's performance as a commander had been "minimal and indecisive." The result was that both Patton and Bradley decided to take a page out of Montgomery's book, and would in future ignore Ike's orders if they did not suit their own purposes.[99]

Alexander demonstrated that the task of leading the Fifteenth Army Group exceeded his capabilities. In part, Alexander's inadequacies reflected those of a British system of command in which "suggestions" failed to translate into clear and definite orders for subordinates.[100] But they were also a reflection of Alexander's personality. Montgomery complained that Alexander was hardly more than a charming nonentity, and that he and his bloated headquarters staff were "out of their depth."[101] He failed to define a clear plan of campaign, and then reigned as an absentee commander from Tunis. With no one to coordinate operations, the invasion quickly lost focus. Alexander's vacillation and subservience to Montgomery's demands allowed alliance friction to develop to potentially campaign-compromising levels. He permitted his two strong-willed army commanders to follow their individual, and competitive, conceptions. His failure even to attempt to interdict the Axis escape from Sicily displayed both a lack of energy and a lack of character. The unfortunate combination of absence of focus and Alexander's inability to "grip" the campaign would set a pattern for subsequent operations in Italy. Two Allied armies would fight their separate battles without a single commander with the military genius and strength of character able to coordinate their separate national wills.[102]

Montgomery's command shortcomings revealed in Sicily were temporarily masked by his reputation as Rommel's conqueror and by the fact that his concern for the welfare and morale of his troops made him genuinely popular in the Eighth Army.[103] However, the ace of sweeping desert warfare seemed to lose his touch on the tight battlefields north of the Mediterranean. His tactical judgment had been clouded by his arrogance and overconfidence. Catania was his for the taking on the evening of 12 July. Its fall would have collapsed weak German positions south of Etna and opened the way to Messina. His decision to shift his advance to Leese's Thirtieth Corps, in the process "stealing" Second Corps's road, at a stroke took pressure off the German defenders at their two most vulnerable points and allowed them precious time to recover. This stopped the momentum of the U.S. advance and momentarily deprived the Seventh Army of any meaningful role to play in the campaign. Once his advance bogged down, Montgomery relied on an unimaginative frontal assault against German forces south of Catania, planning but failing to carry out an amphibious "end run." His ill-fated "left hook" at the foot of Mount Etna was both unsuitable to the terrain and violated his oft-stated principle of concentration of force. After that, the Sicilian campaign came down, in the words of the U.S. official history, to "little more . . . than digging the enemy out of strong-points and knocking him off mountain tops."[104]

Patton had emerged as the hero of Husky. But in the process, his legendary cavalryman's audacity had passed over into recklessness and lack of self-control. His strengths and weaknesses as a commander were brought out by the psychologically unsettling conviction that the British had stacked the cards against the Seventh Army and by Alexander's weakness and subservience to Montgomery's uncharacteristic tendency to react to German moves. Patton's flair for public relations, his showmanship, helped to create an image of an aggressive, resourceful American commander in the flamboyant cavalry tradition of J.E.B. Stuart and Phil Sheridan. He single-handedly crafted a meaningful role for the Seventh Army and gave it the impetus to seize Messina. Unlike Montgomery, he demonstrated a flair for operational experimentation, especially with his end-run amphibious assaults. Fundamentally, however, Patton was a desperately unstable and insecure man. His ambition, his quasi-mystical conception of his personal destiny, his haunting fear of death that had constantly to be mastered, meant that he lived on a psychological precipice. To his subordinates, generals and privates alike, Patton was like an abusive father, alternating flashes of cruel rage with declarations of maudlin affection. "Canny a showman though George was," Bradley believed, "he failed to grasp the psychology of the combat soldier."[105] For his superiors, he was a loose cannon who obliged them to expend a great deal of political capital to salvage his career. While Montgomery's professionalism and eccentricities embellished the reputation of the Eighth Army, Patton's excesses of temperament overshadowed the legitimate successes of the Seventh Army. Eisenhower's disciplining of his old friend following the infamous slapping incidents constituted "the strongest words of censure written to a senior American during World War II."[106] American attitudes were deeply ambivalent toward a man so obviously a winner, and a colorful one at that, but whose imperious conceit personified the antithesis of the democratic values they believed they were fighting for. Patton was struck from the list of potential commanders to lead the cross-Channel invasion, and Eisenhower vowed to place him in a position where his recklessness could be kept under control.[107] Bradley hurdled Patton to lead American forces in Overlord, an unfortunate decision, some argue, that led to many missed opportunities in Normandy and Northwestern Europe in 1944.[108] The imperious Patton sulked like a scolded puppy, able only to comprehend the consequences of his action, not that he had done wrong.[109]

Husky was hailed by the British official history as "the coming-of-age of British combined operations . . . professionally recognized to be all-or-nothing affairs, inter-Service and technical to the last degree."[110] In many respects this is true. The Mediterranean in general, and Sicily in particular, offered the theater *par excellence* for the Allies to practice interservice cooperation. The original amphibious landings were models of planning and joint interoperability. Low ship losses were a tribute to a thorough plan of suppression of Axis air power on the island. The Luftwaffe was reduced to night operations and the Italian air force effectively eliminated from the war. Naval gunfire rescued the American beachhead at Gela, and ensured the survival of troops placed by Patton behind German lines at Brolo during the advance to Messina. Guns mounted on shallow-draft vessels gave fire support to the Eighth Army as it advanced up the coast toward Messina. Patton's use of amphibious operations to bypass opposition was inventive, if on too small a scale to be decisive.

In other ways, however, Sicily demonstrated the many limitations of interservice and inter-Allied cooperation, ones that foreshadowed problems that the Allies would encounter in Italy. Allied air forces proved reluctant to provide close air support to ground troops, especially early in the campaign, insisting that their mission was to fight the Luftwaffe and bomb strategic targets. Toward the end of the campaign, the "rover" system of air-ground coordination via mobile forward air controllers attached to ground units able to communicate to planes by radio was developed. But on the whole, the system to call in close air support was cumbersome, while the lack of accuracy made Allied troops reluctant to order air strikes.[111] Allied airborne operations almost died on Sicily, much as Crete had spelled the demise of German airborne operations. The disastrous failure of four airborne operations on Sicily was blamed on the poor training of air crews and the policy of the navies to fire on all planes at night, even friendly ones, despite being forewarned that the transports would be flying overhead.[112]

Naval gunfire from high-velocity, flat-trajectory guns firing from unstable platforms had its limitations in support of ground operations. Amphibious "end runs" like those carried out by Patton depended on the availability of limited numbers of landing craft and suitable beaches.[113] Close air support of ground forces, which the Desert Air Force had developed to a relatively fine art in North Africa, proved much more difficult in Sicily's mountainous terrain, where targets were difficult to identify and even more difficult to hit. Kesselring noted that his daring maneuver of landing German paratroops on Primosole Bridge to block Montgomery's advance toward Catania had been possible only because "the British fighters' rigid time-table gave us repeated opportunities to risk the move."[114]

Kesselring faulted the Allies for "the absence of any large-scale encirclement of the island or of a thrust up the coastline of Calabria [which] gave us long weeks to organize the defense with very weak resources."[115] Allied leaders argued that the technical capabilities of both their air forces and navies were insufficient to sever the narrow, heavily guarded Strait of Messina. Kesselring disagreed. While he praised "the unique success of the flak defense of the straits," he believed that it would not have withstood a determined Allied assault. Even so, Kesselring conceded that German success at Messina was purchased at the expense of other targets of Allied bombers, especially Axis airfields, harbors, and railways.[116] Nevertheless, Kesselring believed that in Sicily he had taken the measure of Allied forces and found them wanting. Roughly 60,000 German troops had held at bay thirteen Allied divisions for thirty-eight days. He concluded that tough rear-guard actions fought by tenacious troops in the difficult Italian terrain more than compensated for Allied technological superiority. As a bonus, on the Italian mainland he would no longer have to worry about organizing his erstwhile Italian allies. All Kesselring had to do was to convince his superiors that Italy was worth defending.

CHAPTER TEN

"The Mediterranean Year"

MESSINA TO REGGIO was a short skip across a sleeve of water that the Allies, now experienced in amphibious operations, might hurdle in stride. The 6,500-foot Aspromonte Massif on the Calabria shore shimmered slate gray in the late August heat. Beyond, Naples and Rome beckoned to Churchill. Momentum belonged to the Allies. Success must be relentlessly exploited. The Mediterranean slashed like a fault line through the Axis, one that begged for exploitation. The capture of Rome, he believed, offered a fitting culmination to "the Mediterranean year," a symbol of the success of Allied strategy and of Britain's future strategic monopoly in the Mediterranean.[1] Churchill, the military historian, searched for analogies that fell within the limited grasp of a parochial American Congress. Tunis had been the Gettysburg of the Mediterranean War, he told them. "No one after Gettysburg doubted which way the dread balance of war would incline. Yet far more blood was shed after the Union victory at Gettysburg than in all the fighting that went before."[2] For George Marshall, however, Tunis, then Operation Husky, had been more like the fall of Chattanooga or Atlanta, gratifying victories, but frontier engagements, triumphs achieved far from the main theater. And he had no desire to go marching through Georgia, swinging like Sherman through a pliant and ill-defended hinterland to peel off enemy resources and support, lay bare vulnerabilities, sap the will to resist, macerate the enemy in preparation for the kill. With the conclusion of

Husky, maximum advantage had been squeezed from the peripheral theater. The time had come to shift resources to a theater that mattered. It was time to mount a cross-Channel invasion.[3]

The revival of this inter-Allied strategic debate was inevitable, as the alliance transitioned from a defensive to an offensive posture. The "backs to the wall" mentality that had forged a unity of purpose in the late summer of 1942 unraveled a year later in a confusion of strategic choice and conflicting political goals. From the beginning, the Mediterranean had been a *pis aller*, part of Churchill's ad hoc vision that Roosevelt, for his own reasons, had bought into. Nor must this inter-Allied tension be exaggerated. Even Churchill had never conceived of the Mediterranean strategy as a substitute for an invasion of Northwestern Europe. The Middle Sea was merely a placeholder until the preconditions for a successful cross-Channel invasion could be met.[4] Churchill's argument was about timing. Germany was on the road to defeat. With the Soviet Union out of danger, there was no need to rush an invasion of the Continent. The continued diversion and attrition of German forces on Hitler's southern flank bolstered Overlord's prospects of success. "I wished also to have the options of pressing right-handed in Italy or left-handed across the Channel, or both," he explained in his memoirs. The cross-Channel assault would deliver the final blow to a debilitated German army.[5]

The immediate problem, however, was how to dispatch Italy. The disintegration of Italian divisions in Sicily and the overthrow of Mussolini suggested that an invasion of the peninsula would be like kicking in an open door. Italy's defection from the Axis promised a tangible political dividend to leverage the Mediterranean investment. With speculation about Germany's imminent collapse rife in the Allied camp, policy makers also began to think in terms of the postwar settlement. Italy became the first step along the road to Yalta, a tacit agreement struck among the Big Three that the Anglo-Saxons' pre-emptive negotiation of Italy's surrender yielded to Stalin the liberty to dispose of Poland. The following year, the future of Romania was bartered in similar fashion against a guarantee of supremacy of British influence in Greece. Europe was being carved up even before it was conquered. The Mediterranean was the whetstone.[6]

The desire to preempt the Soviets in the Mediterranean, combined with the optimistic assumption that Hitler would invest little to salvage his ungrateful ex-partner, tempted the Allies into risks they would have shunned in Northern Europe. The fact that Allied forces in the Mediterranean were in drawdown in preparation for Overlord encouraged a gambler's mentality at AFHQ. Therefore, Allied strategy toward Italy was guided by opportunism mixed with a touch of euphoria, rather than by caution. On 27 July 1943, the Joint Intelligence Committee, in keeping with the mood of the moment, predicted that an Allied landing on the Italian mainland would induce an Italian surrender and precipitate a German withdrawal.[7] Italy's defection would cleave the Axis and signal Hitler's reluctant allies in Hungary and Romania that they, too, should reconsider their options. Allied armies could surge northward toward the Alps, thereby depriving the Germans of much of Italy's economic and manpower resources. The peninsula would provide a solid base for air attacks on Germany and for an invasion of southern France. "I call this the Mediterranean year—where we exploit our advantage," Richard Tregaskis was told by Air Marshal Sir Arthur Coningham. "It's obvious we must try and do something—and go on . . . The German is playing for time now. He's holding us up while he's building up back here [pointing to a map of Italy]."[8]

Mediterranean success encouraged Churchill's tendency, in Brooke's words, "to settle on some definite part of the canvas" and forfeit the larger strategic picture.[9] In fact, it was by focusing on "some definite part of the canvas" that the prime minister sought to multiply military triumphs that could prolong British influence in the alliance. In the summer of 1943, Britain stood at full stretch, with over five million men mobilized, the RAF the equal of the Luftwaffe, and the Royal Navy rated as the world's second most powerful.[10] The inevitable consequence for the future was that British influence in the alliance would decline along with its relative strength when measured against that of the United States and the Soviet Union. Churchill understood that the cross-Channel invasion would be largely an American show. In the Continental warfare that followed Overlord, Britain's dwindling divisions would be dwarfed in great land battles by the American and

Soviet juggernauts. The Mediterranean was a theater made to Britain's measure, tailored to the strengths of her versatile force structure. The British would control the vast majority of military assets there.[11] An invasion of the peninsula appealed to Churchill's sense of strategic expediency. The British prime minister retained an emotional commitment to the "liberation" of Italy. He had wept at the Tripoli victory parade. The spectacle of his vaunted Eighth Army striding triumphantly through Rome would release a warm surge of vengeful contentment.[12] Even Marshall, understanding the advantages of Italian air bases and eager to capitalize on Mussolini's downfall and rock-bottom Italian morale, urged an amphibious invasion of Naples. Brooke "produce[d] countless arguments to prove the close relationship that exists between cross-Channel and Italian operations"[13] to reinforce the American chief of staff's momentary willingness to pursue Mediterranean options. So Italy was to be dealt a *coup de grâce*.

Offensive success allowed Churchill's fertile strategic imagination to conjure up a smorgasbord of Mediterranean targets. The prime minister argued that Italy could become a stepping-stone to the Balkans, Greece, and the Aegean, with the goal of enticing Turkey into the war. Brooke complained in the autumn of 1943 that Churchill's obsession with seizing Rhodes and attacking the Balkans with the aim of enlisting Turkey both endangered relations with the Americans and threatened the success of the Italian campaign. "The Balkan ghost in the cupboard made my road none the easier in leading the Americans by the hand through Italy!" the British general staff chief complained.[14] And he was correct. Even sympathetic "Mediterraneanists" like Roosevelt never envisioned the sea as an objective in its own right. It was a corridor to Europe, a means to an end, a transition phase from weakness to strength. Churchill's strategically eclectic shopping list appeared a dalliance designed to utilize U.S. forces to further British imperial interests, or to impede those of Stalin, rather than expeditiously to defeat Germany. Moscow and Washington now began to perceive the Mediterranean as a potential source of disunity rather than as a theater to showcase and further alliance solidarity. In the process, Churchill inadvertently supplied ammunition to those hostile to the Mediterranean strategy like U.S. Secretary of War Henry

L. Stimson and George Marshall. Montgomery, too, appeared to be wavering, arguing even before the invasion of Sicily against the extension of the Mediterranean war into Southern Europe.[15]

Allied planning was hampered by at least three problems. The first was the competing priorities and perspectives among Washington, London, and AFHQ in Algiers, not to mention differences among the respective armed services. Marshall led a chorus that argued that the Allies must stick to their game plan to move rapidly to pierce the heart of the Axis. Churchill, on the other hand, favored a flexible strategy to exploit opportunity in the Mediterranean. Second, the complex geography and politics of the Mediterranean translated into an abundance of options, each with its strengths and weaknesses, all of which found their champions. Third, the rapidly unfolding political and military situation in the Mediterranean during the summer of 1943 made it very difficult to predict with any degree of certainty which military option would translate into the greatest strategic benefit.

The Trident Conference, held in Washington in May 1943, had established in principle that the Mediterranean would become a subsidiary theater to northern France. Overlord was to occur on 1 May 1944. In the meantime, much of the huge force that had been collected for Husky would be returned to Great Britain to prepare for Overlord. This included three British and four U.S. divisions, twelve U.S. and three Canadian bomber squadrons, and approximately half of the landing craft used in Sicily.[16] In the Mediterranean, the Western Allies hedged their bets, awaiting the outcome of Husky. By mid-July, opinion had congealed around an invasion of the Italian mainland as the best way to capitalize on the momentum of Husky, eliminate Italy from the war, seize air bases for the bomber offensive against German oil reserves in Ploesti and targets in southern Germany, tie down a maximum number of German divisions, and threaten German forces in the Balkans. If Italian resistance collapsed, then the Allies would move on Rome. Sardinia and Corsica would be seized as a prelude to an invasion of southern France. Even though the Quadrant Conference held in Quebec in August reaffirmed that Overlord was to be the main effort for 1944, success in Sicily had definitely shifted the mood, as the British proclaimed optimistically that Mediterranean opportunities had yet to be exhausted. The possibility that the Allies might be committing themselves to a slogging match up the Italian boot was far from the minds of those who now began to define Rome as a minimum goal of Operation Avalanche. Churchill was keen to advance to a line running from Leghorn to Ancona on the Adriatic. Beyond that, the geography of the peninsula broadened so that too many divisions would be required to conquer and occupy it.[17]

On 24 August, the Quebec Conference defined the goals of the Allied invasion of Italy as: the elimination of Italy as a belligerent; the establishment of air bases near Rome and, if possible, farther north; the seizure of Sardinia and Corsica; and the "maintenance of unremitting pressure on German forces in north Italy so as to create conditions favorable to *Overlord*" and the eventual entry into southern France.[18] Churchill also kept open the possibility that an Italian collapse would trigger operations in the Balkans and the Aegean. Quadrant left vague the question of the exploitation of an Italian surrender and the resources to be devoted to the Mediterranean.[19] The drift of Quadrant, one confirmed by the Teheran Conference of November, was a strategic shift away from Churchill's position on the Mediterranean. But the absence of precision in Allied directives allowed for plenty of wiggle room in defining future Mediterranean targets. Vague policy, in other words, would translate into an unfocused strategy that would transform the Italian campaign into an operational nightmare. Best-case Allied assumptions predicted Italian cooperation combined with a German withdrawal from Italy. Therefore, an understrength Allied invasion would not be embarrassed.

The debate in Berlin mirrored that among the Allies. Like the United States, Hitler had backed incrementally into the Mediterranean to bolster a faltering ally. Gradually, Italian weakness combined with a growing awareness that Allied Mediterranean advances actually posed a threat to his southern flank caused him increasingly to view the Mediterranean as a theater that required a significant investment of German resources. The problem for Hitler was that the plethora of strategic options open to the Allies in the Mediterranean made it difficult to know where to bolster his defenses. Viewed from Berlin, the Balkans offered the best Allied option: Allied forces could link up with a thriving resistance movement; it would put them closer to the Ploesti oil fields and cut off Axis sources of bauxite, copper, and other minerals. An Allied force in the Balkans would certainly influence the attitudes of Turkey, Bulgaria, Romania, and Hungary, and put Allied armies in position to join hands with the advancing Red Army. Good communications combined with difficult terrain to mean that Italy would be easier for the Germans to defend than the Balkans. The Ljubljana Gap offered a historic invasion route while the Alps of northern Italy rose as a practically impenetrable barrier for land forces.[20]

The overthrow of Mussolini on 24 July had caused Hitler to activate Operation Achse (Axis). By 9 September, when the Italians surrendered, he had shifted fourteen German divisions into the peninsula. He also placed the Dodecanese under German command and significantly reinforced German garrisons in the Balkans, Greece, and the Aegean. However, German intentions in Italy remained uncertain so long as the Italians had not made a definite attempt to break with the Axis. On one hand, Jodl and Rommel advocated letting the Italians defend southern Italy, with German forces occupying a shortened defensive line based on Pisa and Salonika to save manpower and guard against Italian treachery. Germany simply did not have the resources to battle the Red Army on the Eastern Front, defend the Atlantic wall, and occupy the Italian Peninsula.[21] Kesselring and Dönitz, on the other, espoused a forward defense of southern Italy. They argued that this would protect the Aegean and the economically important Balkans, keep Allied bombers at arm's reach, and use no more troops and matériel than would Rommel's proposed defense of the Apennines.[22] If the Germans surrendered the Italian Peninsula, then the Allies would be free to attack the Balkans or southern France, and ultimately Austria and southern Germany. A southern defense would retain Rome, and place German troops in a better position to attack the Allied flank if they attempted to use southern Italy as a springboard to the Balkans. Hitler liked the idea of a counterattack, and was also impressed by Kesselring's argument that to forfeit southern Italy meant also a withdrawal from the Aegean, a prospect that Hitler refused to accept. Besides, Kesselring's upbeat assessment offered welcome relief from the unremitting gloom of Rommel, whom Hitler had never forgiven for his "unauthorized" withdrawal from El Alamein.[23] Nevertheless, he must have appreciated Rommel's view that a defense south of Rome would not be possible without Italian collaboration, which seemed increasingly unlikely as German-Italian relations plunged into a morass of intrigue and distrust.[24] A southern defense would also make German forces vulnerable to an amphibious end run. For the moment, Hitler deferred a decision, preferring to await events. However, as a sop to Kesselring, on 17 August the Tenth Army was created under Heinrich von Vietinghoff to unite the Eleventh and Seventy-sixth Panzer Corps stationed in central and southern Italy and remove them from Italian command.[25]

Thus September 1943 was a transitional moment when each side decided whether to continue to invest considerable resources in the Mediterranean or to cut its losses there and reduce operations to a minimum. The consequence of the decisions taken in August–September 1943 have imparted an ambiguous strategic legacy to the Mediterranean enterprise. Some, then as now, view the Allied decision to invade the Italian Peninsula as a huge mistake, "tactically the most absurd and strategically the most senseless campaign of the whole war."[26] The assault on the Italian mainland stumbled on divergent Allied strategic priorities. It was anchored in wishful thinking and best-case assumptions about Italian cooperation and German reactions. It was starved of resources and relied for success on the cooperation of pusillanimous Italian leaders conniving at their own survival. It assumed that the combination of an Allied invasion and Italian resistance would precipitate a German withdrawal. The consequences were inevitable: once Allied forces were engaged on the Italian mainland, the advantages of terrain and logistics shifted overwhelmingly to the Germans, who could reinforce and resupply overland more rapidly than could the Allies by sea. Yet the Allies were stuck, unable to reduce their investment, because Kesselring could take advantage of any weakening of Allied forces on the peninsula to launch an offensive of his own. Tenacious German resistance in Italy tied down two Allied armies and significant maritime and air assets in a dead-end theater until the surrender of Germany in May 1945. "Overnight Italy went from German ally to German-occupied country," notes historian David Kennedy. "Now it was about to become a battleground in a grinding war of attrition whose costs were justified by no defensible military or political purpose."[27]

While there is no denying the lack of strategic focus and wishful thinking that informed Operation Avalanche, it is difficult to imagine that the Western Allies, having driven to the doorstep of the peninsula, could simply forsake its alluring promise in September 1943. The prize of Italy was simply too dazzling to be left on the table. Nor, unlike Hitler, could the Western Allies entertain any immediate strategic alternatives. There could be no question of Allied armies taking a winter sabbatical while Hitler hammered Stalin on the Eastern Front. The British ambassador in Moscow, among others, urged that unless a new front was opened in 1943, Stalin might be tempted to conclude a separate peace with Hitler.[28] South African Premier Jan Smuts echoed the ambassador, arguing that if, by the end of 1944, "we have done no better than merely nibble at the enemy's main positions," then Russia's "suspicions" that the Western Allies were unnecessarily prolonging the war would seem justified. The fear of a new German-Soviet rapprochement in retrospect may seem far-fetched, given the oceans of blood spilled between the two adversaries since June 1941. However, Smuts was on firmer ground when he insisted that Anglo-American public opinion would regard a suspension in Mediterranean fighting as a betrayal of its staunch Soviet ally. "We may experience a dangerous revulsion of opinion, and rightly so," concluded the old soldier.[29] Logistics also argued against a wholesale reorientation of forces to Overlord: the simple fact was that British ports lacked the capacity to absorb the divisions deployed in the Mediterranean and also accommodate new U.S. divisions.[30]

Without a doubt, on the operational and tactical level the Italian Peninsula offered a challenging battleground for Allied armies, and allowed the Germans to neutralize Allied superiority in matériel. Nevertheless, just because the Italian campaign was difficult, Avalanche was far from opening the door to a strategic cul-de-sac, as its critics argue. The strategic rewards for the Allies of attacking Italy were considerable. By holding the flank and attriting German forces with relatively few Allied divisions, the Italian campaign facilitated the task of Overlord. The decision to invade Italy was bound to favor the Allies in any case, because superior resources meant that they could threaten both the Channel *and* the Mediterranean. Hitler's decision ultimately to commit fifty divisions to defend the Eastern Mediterranean at the expense of other fronts was a great boon to the alliance. Only in the autumn of 1944 did Hitler begin to withdraw from Greece. Division-sized German units left Italy only in March 1945 in the wake of the 13 February Soviet capture of Budapest. Walter Warlimont argued that "Hitler's Mediterranean strategy threw a far greater strain upon the German war potential than the military situation justified."[31] "By his decision to commit the maximum available resources to the defense of the Mediterranean," British historian Michael Howard concludes, "Hitler thus played into the Allied hands."[32] Even had Rommel and Jodl prevailed, allowing the Allies to absorb most of Italy without a fight, it is doubtful that the Germans could have saved much manpower, given Hitler's obsession with Allied threats to Greece and the Balkans.

What is certain, however, is that at the very least, the ambiguity of that legacy might have been minimized had Allies been able to spare themselves what Carlo D'Este calls "the longest and bloodiest campaign fought by the Allies in the West during World War II."[33] By improvising a campaign to attack Italy with weak forces without clear strategic goals, the Allies forfeited the momentum they had built up in North Africa and Sicily. A halfhearted Allied invasion combined with incompetent and spineless Italian leadership to resolve the debate in the German camp in favor of Kesselring and forward defense. Italy lived out what one Italian historian has called "one of the saddest and most humiliating chapters" of its history as Italian divisions were sacrificed and the country was turned into a battlefield.[34] Finally, the separation and lack of coordination of the Eastern and Western Mediterranean commands prevented the Allies from taking advantage of the Italian surrender to crumble German positions in the Eastern Mediterranean. In this way, Italy joined Tunisia as the second Verdun

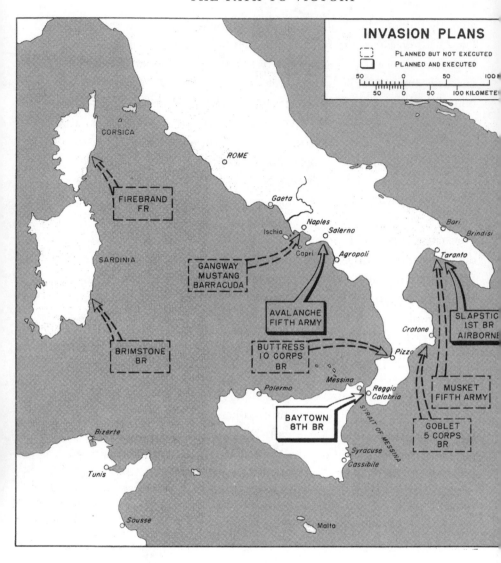

of the Mediterranean theater. Hitler continued to pour in reinforcements to salvage his discredited ally and protect his southern flank, in the process sacrificing a half-million casualties.[35]

THE SURRENDER OF ITALY

The more immediate problems facing the Allies were how to knock Italy out of the war, and at what price. At Casablanca, Churchill persuaded Roosevelt that an Italian collapse would be followed by a German withdrawal.[36] A soft approach toward Italy found some support in the United States, where a large Italian-American community urged a separate peace with Rome based on an exception to the unconditional surrender policy laid out at Casablanca. Roosevelt, always in a vote-collecting mode, was inclined to support this view. He believed Italian participation in the war had been a personal project of Mussolini's, in which Italians had acquiesced without enthusiasm. Nor, unlike Great Britain, did the United States have any fundamental conflicts of interest with Italy. Washington flirted with recognizing the "Free Italy" movement or an Italian government-in-exile led by Carlo Sforza. The ever cautious Eisenhower, aware of the paucity of military resources, always favored a political deal over the risk of a military reversal or the burden of running the country.[37]

This soft American approach was resisted by the Foreign Office, where Anthony Eden argued that concessions proffered to entice Rome to exit the Axis simply revived Chamberlain's discredited policy of "appeasing a minor dictator." Early hopes of a separate armistice with Italy had been dashed by Rommel's February 1941 intervention in Libya. Barbarossa, and the participation of Italian troops on the Eastern Front, had hardened London against compromise with Italy. American entry into the war, and with it a renewed focus on a cross-Channel invasion, worked to diminish Italy's military importance to the Allies. Badoglio had allegedly attempted to contact the British in May 1942, while Italian anti-Fascists had put out peace feelers in 1943. Eden remained deaf to these entreaties, arguing that Italy would prove an ally of questionable worth even if it did switch sides. The British had enough trouble with French exiles, and had no wish to burden British policy with disputes between competing Italian movements. Mussolini's ouster encouraged the view that Italy would exit the war without any special inducements.[38] In any case, Churchill had no desire to fall victim to a Badoglio double-cross.[39]

Different interpretations of unconditional surrender, combined with the bitter experience of the Darlan deal, made it difficult in practice to find a middle ground. The advantage of unconditional surrender as laid out at Casablanca was that it transformed the war into a moral crusade that reassured the USSR that the Western Allies would not make a separate peace with Hitler. It also underlined Roosevelt's intention to rebuild Axis countries from the ground up, rather than walk away from victory as had the United States in 1919. In practice, however, its actual meaning was unclear. The American military interpreted unconditional surrender in the narrow sense of the total surrender of enemy armies. This had been the basis of Clark's deal with Darlan—the Vichy French laid down their arms, but continued to exercise political control in French North Africa. This arrangement had been a source of great controversy at the time, especially in the United States. Was a similar deal to be cut with the Italians? Darlan had been no Mussolini. But neither had Italy produced a Charles de Gaulle. Mussolini's overthrow induced a degree of euphoric anticipation in the Allied camp. But no one knew for certain what the Duce's departure meant for the future of Italian politics. What would a political compromise to get Italy out of the war look like? For the moment, the official line was *plus ça change*—London's Office of War Information called Vittorio Emanuele "a moronic little king," while the *New York Times* complained that Badoglio was simply a warmed-over military despot.

The Allies might be forgiven their inability to gauge the Italian situation, because Mussolini's overthrow had spawned considerable confusion on the Italian side. Mussolini's 24 July departure was not the work of an anti-Fascist clique. On the contrary, his ouster had been an act of desperation by men who continued to grasp at the delusion that a German commitment of resources to the Mediterranean and an Allied defeat would send the United States scampering to the Pacific and thus rescue the European Axis. Husky, the disintegration of many Italian units on Sicily, and stepped-up Allied bombing of Italian cities coincided with increasingly violent confrontations between German soldiers and Italian civilians. These events convinced the nervous, physically infirm seventy-four-year-old King Vittorio Emanuele and his chief of staff Ambrosio, whose mind was judged to be more efficient than intelligent,[40] that Anglo-American military power posed a serious threat. The complaint of the conspirators was that through timidity, Mussolini had sacrificed Italy's Mediterranean interests to Hitler's obsessions with the Eastern Front. Although Mussolini's overthrow was advertised as a military coup against fascism, in fact, the goal of the conspirators was to build a proroyalist coalition of moderate Fascists and traditional conservatives. Badoglio dissolved prominent symbols of the *ancien régime* including the Fascist Party, the Special Court for the Defense of the State, and the Grand Council of Fascism. He also appointed a few anti-Fascists to minor positions. But the core of the new government was concocted from the old-guard military and political elite who had served Mussolini.[41]

Despite cosmetic surgery to remove Italy's most obvious Fascist warts, Badoglio discovered that Mussolini's departure did not suddenly open new diplomatic vistas for Italy—quite the contrary. Dino Grandi, the ex-ambassador to Britain who had proposed the motion that led to Mussolini's ouster, headed a coalition of high officers who called for Italy immediately to switch sides. Some have argued that this was Italy's best hope, one that Badoglio squandered. Six Allied divisions in Egypt and North Africa might have played midwife to an Italian defection while German forces on the peninsula, in the Balkans, and in Greece were relatively weak. Italian control of both the Brenner Pass and petrol supplies might have trapped two German divisions on Sicily and preempted a German invasion of Italy.[42] But initiative and decision no longer counted among Badoglio's character traits, if indeed they ever had. Since his dismissal as chief of staff over the fiasco of the invasion of Greece in 1940, Badoglio had passed his days largely playing cards and medicating his grief over the deaths of his wife and son with magnums of champagne. The collapse of the Fascist regime restored him to prominence. When Harold Macmillian met the seventy-two-year-old marshal in September 1943, he discovered a bald man of slight build, a peasant shrewdness showing through a veneer of dignified but characterless restraint. Badoglio reminded the future British prime minister of French General Giraud minus the ego, a fundamentally honest soldier with limited political sense. Within months, however, Macmillian understood that Badoglio's facade of "stupidity" was merely a Potemkin-like ruse that allowed him better to reduce Allied diplomats and soldiers "to a state of intellectual subjection."[43] In September 1943, however, Badoglio feared a violent German reaction if he asked the Allies for terms.[44] Both he and the king were too closely associated with Mussolini to expect anything but wariness from the Allies. Nor could he count on Italian military leaders to support a decision to abandon their Axis comrades-in-arms.

Badoglio's second option was to slide into neutrality in return for a peaceful turnover to the Germans of Italian-occupied territory in Greece and the Balkans. But the Führer was too enraged by the "betrayal" of Badoglio and the king to let them off the hook.[45] In fact, Admiral Dönitz had to intervene to dissuade the German leader from sending a division to Rome to punish the authors of the coup, fearing that it would precipitate Italian resistance.[46] Nor could the German leader afford to allow Italy's defection to contaminate other allies and satellites like Hungary and Romania, whose search for an exit had already begun. Once Badoglio realized that no soft solutions were open to him, he began to work his third option—dissemble, play for time, ostensibly continue to support the Axis while sending back-channel peace feelers to the Allies. In public, Badoglio declared that "the war will go on" and pretended to prepare the defense of Italy with German help. But to Hitler, Badoglio was about as trustworthy as a Sardinian bandit. He assumed, correctly, that Italian-Allied negotiations were in progress and that the Italians would "rat to the other side" as soon as the time was right.[47] Moreover, Badoglio's cautious attempt to depart the war with a minimum of fuss did not have time on its side. German divisions poured into Italy from the north, while an Allied invasion in the south could only be a matter of days away. Mussolini's ouster triggered strikes and demonstrations against the war that caused the new government to fear a Communist revolution. Badoglio's intelligence told him that the Germans were working with disgruntled Fascists to reinstate Mussolini or install by force a Quisling-style government under Roberto Farinacci, ex–party secretary and one of the *gerarchi* of the regime. This caused him to arrest several Fascist leaders, including Ugo Cavallero, in an attempt to stave off a coup. But this only worsened relations with the Germans. Friction between German and Italian forces increased in southern France, Yugoslavia, and around the Brenner Pass. On 31 July, Badoglio belatedly decided to initiate exploratory contacts with the Allies through the British ambassador to

Lisbon. But, still under the delusion that he held the whip hand with the Allies, he instructed his emissary not to ask for peace terms.[48]

The hesitation of Badoglio and the king to face up to an untenable situation of their own making laid the groundwork for a catastrophe of unprecedented dimensions in modern Italian history. Rather than grasp the peril they courted, however, they basked in delusional miscalculations of both German intentions and Allied capabilities. They shared the Anglo-American belief that an Allied invasion combined with an Italian request for an armistice would precipitate a German withdrawal. They also concluded that the Allied invasion, when it came, would be massive. They failed to realize that of the immense army camped out in Sicily that appeared poised to assault the Italian mainland or the Balkans, seven divisions were in fact destined to be shifted to Britain to prepare for the invasion of Normandy. Even had Italian leaders known this, they would probably have persisted in their erroneous certitude that Italy's military assets, intelligence on the German positions, and potential to cooperate with Allied forces in the Balkans could be used as leverage to suspend the requirements of unconditional surrender.[49]

Italian delusions were abetted by Eisenhower, who, concerned by Allied military weakness, greeted news of Mussolini's overthrow with the hope that "honorable" conditions might be arranged for Italy's surrender. But the truth was that neither Churchill nor Roosevelt felt compelled to rush into an agreement with the new Italian government because they assumed that Italy was now de facto out of the war and because they, like the Italians, underestimated German ability to seize control of the peninsula. However, the Allied leaders did warm to the idea proposed by the anti-German Brigadier General Giuseppe Castellano, sent to Lisbon on 12 August, that Italy bolt from the Axis and join the Allies.[50] At Quebec on 21 August, the two Allied leaders approved a "long armistice" that called for the total surrender and disarmament of Italian forces, Allied control of Italy, and stringent economic conditions imposed on the defeated country. Mussolini was to be surrendered to the Allies to be tried as a war criminal. At Eisenhower's insistence, this "long armistice" was not made public for fear that it would undermine efforts to gain Italian compliance. The subsequent Quebec Declaration stated that Italy's treatment was to depend "on how far the Italian government and people do, in fact, aid the United Nations against Germany during the remainder of the war."[51]

The armistice signed on 3 September at Fifteenth Army Group headquarters at Cassibile in Sicily between Bedell Smith and Castellano, after almost a month of haggling, was precipitated by events. For his part, Eisenhower, aware of the weakness of his forces landing at Salerno, was eager to secure an Italian signature before the armistice could be sabotaged by the British Foreign Office. The success of Avalanche, Ike believed, turned on the question of Italian support. He promised to drop the Eighty-second Airborne Division on Rome— Giant II—to secure the Italian capital and block German reinforcements until the arrival of Allied forces.[52] The 3 September news that Montgomery's Eighth Army had crossed the Strait of Messina to begin the conquest of the Italian mainland convinced the Italians to drop their demands for a strong Allied landing near Rome and sign. The Allies had, in effect, offered the Italians a de facto alliance, because their plan presupposed cooperation with the Italians to gain control of most of the peninsula. The surrender of Italy prior to the Allied invasion would encourage the aid of twenty-four Italian divisions within Italy, including six around Rome, and reduce the requirement for large numbers of Allied troops to be committed to an invasion.[53] And although Italian military cooperation was not guaranteed, the optimistic assumption remained that a combination of Italian resistance and the psychological shock of Giant II would prompt a retreat of the estimated 400,000 German troops in Italy to a line running from Genoa to Ravenna.[54] Rome would be liberated at the very latest by October.

These hypotheses began to unravel almost at once. On 7 September, American General Maxwell Taylor traveled secretly to Rome to ascertain the state of Italian preparations for Giant II. Taylor reported to Alexander that, despite assurances by Castellano, passivity, indecision, and duplicity reigned in Rome. Badoglio planned neither to secure the airfields for the arrival of the Eighty-second nor to defend his capital. On the contrary, when Taylor pulled a startled Badoglio from his bed at midnight, the Italian general disavowed the commitments made by Castellano at Cassibile. He laid out, in what Taylor insisted was "the voice of an actor,"[55] a list of impediments—most of them imaginary—to effective Italian cooperation with an Allied invasion. It was clear that Badoglio and the king expected to be rescued, and were too frightened of the Germans to fight in their own defense. On this news, Taylor forced Badoglio to send a request at two o'clock on the morning of 8 September to cancel the parachute drop on Rome, a message that catapulted Eisenhower into an apoplectic rage.[56]

At 6:30 on the evening of 8 September, as Allied troops stood poised to invade the Italian mainland, the BBC announced the armistice between the Allies and Italy. Badoglio, who had pleaded in vain with Eisenhower for a postponement of the armistice announcement until he was certain that they could take Rome, dithered as a confused and surprised Italian military leadership asked for guidance. On orders from the king, he confirmed Italy's surrender in a 7:45 broadcast to the Italian people. His indecision prevented military leaders from preparing instructions for resisting the inevitable German retribution. Instead, Italian soldiers were ordered "in no case . . . to take the initiative in hostilities against German troops."[57] The questionable rationale for the "no resistance" order was that the Germans would withdraw quietly if Italian forces did nothing to impede their retreat. Even when they received news of the 9 September landing at Salerno, Badoglio, the king, and Ambrosio assumed that this was a secondary beachhead, with the main—nine-division!—landing to come near Rome.[58] Their precipitous flight from Rome at 5 a.m. on 9 September to Pescara on the Adriatic and then in an Italian corvette to Brindisi would be only temporary, they assumed, because they would return to the capital in the baggage trains of the Allies in a matter of days. Most of the Italian high command joined this stampede to safety. When the civilian members of the government met on the morning of 9 September, they were astounded to find that the palace was guarded by only a doorman, even the *carabinieri* having decamped.[59]

The results of this complete abdication of responsibility were an unmitigated disaster for Italy. An initially weak three-division Allied invasion at Salerno combined with Italian passivity decided the argument in the German camp in favor of forward defense. Kesselring's discovery on the morning of 9 September that the Italians had no intention of defending Rome steeled him in his determination to occupy the peninsula. Operation Achse, which called for the disarming of 1,700,000 Italian troops and the German occupation of important northern Italian cities, naval ports, and air bases, was launched by Kesselring on the announcement of the armistice. Italian troops guarding the Brenner Pass, surrounded by a German-speaking population whose sympathies were clearly on the side of the invaders, surrendered. Even though the Italians had clear numerical superiority in Rome and Naples and German diplomats had begun to burn their files in preparation for flight, Badoglio, the king, and Ambrosio were preoccupied with saving their own skins and desperately fearful of tumbling into German hands. Their pusillanimous flight, combined with orders not to oppose the Germans, meant that Italian troops, demoralized, leaderless, and bewildered by the rapid pace of events, allowed themselves to be disarmed. Once it became apparent that the Germans, who cleverly appealed to the honor of Italian soldiers as former comrades and who promised no retribution, were in fact dispatching their erstwhile partners as POWs to Germany, some Italian units resisted, which brought harsh German retribution. In the south, the Italian Seventh Army did nothing to stop German soldiers who took the announcement of the armistice as a signal to plunder the civilian population. On the contrary, many Italian generals willingly turned over their equipment to the Germans.[60] Italian police and soldiers guarding Mussolini failed to lift a finger to prevent a dramatic rescue of *Il Duce*, confined at Gran Sasso in the Alps, by German airborne troops on 12 September. On the contrary, the Italian colonel in charge of Mussolini's guard invited the commander of the glider-borne German troops, Otto Skorzeny, to share a flask of wine. Mussolini was packed into a small plane and flown off to a velvet exile as titular head of the Republic of Saló.

A depressingly similar fate attended the thirty-five Italian divisions stationed outside the peninsula. Some 40,000 soldiers of the Italian Fourth Army in southern France and Liguria surrendered with minimal resistance. The British commander in the Eastern Mediterranean, Maitland Wilson, broadcast instructions to Italian soldiers in Greece and the Balkans to make for the ports, where they would be transported by Allied ships. But Germans and the partisans combined to block this "race to the ports," while those who actually reached the coasts searched the horizon in vain for promised Allied rescue. In Yugoslavia, the Taurinense Alpine Division and the Venetia Infantry Division defected to the partisans. Italian troops fought a brush war with Germans on Corsica. The most determined acts of resistance occurred in the Ionian Sea on Cephalonia and Corfu, where several thousand Italian soldiers died fighting Germans or were executed after surrendering. On Sardinia, in contrast, vast numerical superiority should have enabled Italian soldiers to overwhelm their German counterparts. Instead, they chose to interpret the armistice as a betrayal of Italian honor and continued to serve the Axis loyally. A similar confusion prevailed in the Italian navy, where shock and shame at the news of the armistice prevailed. The fleet at Taranto followed orders to sail for Malta. But only when it was realized that the battleship *Roma* on the way to Malta had been sunk by a German glider bomb, and not by the British, did the portion of the fleet stationed at Tirreno set sail for Bizerte. A handful of Italian captains who scuttled their ships at La Spezia were executed by the Germans. Anguish over the navy's defection was eased by the Allied concession that the fleet was not to be demobilized and that it could continue to fly the Italian flag. Nevertheless, a few captains elected to sail to the Balearic Islands. Overall, the Allies managed to recoup only about half of the Italian fleet.[61]

Churchill's eagerness to exploit the Italian surrender to gain strategic advantage in the Eastern Mediterranean led to a minor disaster for British troops in the Dodecanese. Churchill had long been obsessed with drawing Turkey into the war, a fixation many believed stemmed from a desire to prove that he had been correct to champion the ill-fated Dardanelles campaign of 1915. In his view, Turkish belligerency would outflank the Axis position in Greece and the Balkans, forcing Berlin to divert troops to yet another front; cut their Black Sea route to the Eastern Mediterranean; threaten Germany's Balkan satellites; and provide a direct link with the USSR. Turkish airfields would offer a useful vector of attack against Axis targets, especially Romanian oil, for Bomber Command. Moscow, too, reckoned that Turkish belligerency would divert at least ten German divisions. Nevertheless, Churchill and Brooke could raise no flicker of enthusiasm among the Turks with promises of RAF squadrons, troops, and artillery. Ankara believed that it had been deceived into entering World War I, and that it had nothing to gain by joining the latest European fray. Turkey had gone through its revolution in the wake of World War I. A secular government supported by the military was in power. No dissident political factions waited in the wings to exploit the inevitable disruptive consequences of the war, as in most other Mediterranean countries. A potential fifth column of Greeks and Armenians had been exterminated or expelled by 1922. No significant irredentist faction argued for a reclamation of Ottoman imperial frontiers. A defeat would open Turkey to German retaliation, while victory could only benefit the USSR, of whom the Turks were equally wary. Nor was Washington eager to add forty-six Turkish divisions to the list of armies to be put in working order, a list that already included the Soviet, British, French, and Chinese forces, as well as other odds and ends. No enthusiasm for a Dodecanese operation, code-named Accolade, had been in evidence at either Casablanca or Quebec in August 1943. Accolade languished near the bottom of Cairo's list of operational preferences.[62] Eisenhower informed Churchill in late August that he had no ships to spare for Accolade. When Churchill appealed over Eisenhower's head to Roosevelt, the American president supported his military commander.[63]

Nevertheless, Churchill believed that an audacious operation could produce a dramatic strategic shift in the Eastern Mediterranean, even though his American ally refused to cooperate. The prospect of an Italian surrender combined with a general collapse of Axis fortunes in the Mediterranean in the late summer of 1943 to encourage him. "This is the time to play high," the prime minister cabled General Maitland Wilson, Middle East commander, from Washington on 9 September 1943, as Allied troops stormed ashore at Salerno. "Improvise and dare." Both strategic and mathematical calculations argued well for Accolade. Churchill concluded that the island of Rhodes offered the key to the command of the Aegean and ultimately to

Turkey's decision to enter the war. A relatively small British force with sea control, making common cause with two Italian divisions on Rhodes and its neighboring islands, could overwhelm the single German division in the area. The Dodecanese would then be offered to Ankara as the prize for entering the war. This would give the Allies access to Smyrna as a base from which to carry out operations in the Eastern Mediterranean.[64] Unfortunately for Churchill, Hitler, too, believed German control of Rhodes kept Turkey in line. His generals, contingency plans in hand in case of Italian defection, pointed out that as they had no means to evacuate German troops in the Aegean in any case, they might as well act aggressively. As a consequence, when a small party of British troops landed on Rhodes on 9 September, the Germans pounced on the Italians. The Italian commander surrendered when he learned that the main British reinforcements would not arrive before 15 September. By 13 September, German troops controlled Rhodes and its vital air base. The British subsequently landed forces on Cos, Leros, and Samos as well as other, smaller islands in the Dodecanese chain as a prelude to what they envisaged would be the conquest of Rhodes. Small Italian garrisons on these islands were cooperative but demoralized and ill-armed.

Almost immediately, Churchill's bluff was called. He quickly discovered that Hitler had no intention of allowing his flank to be turned by Turkish defection. The Luftwaffe massed over four hundred planes on airfields in Crete, Rhodes, and Scarpanto, forty-five miles from Rhodes. The nearest British airfield was on Cyprus, 270 miles distant. North African airfields were beyond the range of single-engine fighters. A small airfield on Cos, which in any case could accommodate only seven Spitfires, was put out of action by German bombers by 18 September. Obsolete Beaufighters that courageously flew in from Cyprus were decimated by Bf. 109s. British destroyers were forced by German domination of the skies to resupply the British-held islands only at night. Furthermore, Roosevelt refused to commit U.S. assets to what he declared was a futile operation, especially as Allied troops were fighting tooth and nail to hold on at Salerno.

On 3 October, German paratroops descended on Cos, combining with a primitive seaborne invasion that succeeded largely because it caught British intelligence completely by surprise. British destroyers had withdrawn to refuel, leaving 1,600 troops of the Durham Light Infantry, veterans of the Western Desert and Syria, plus Italians who had rallied to the British, virtually defenseless. At the cost of eighty-five casualties, the Germans reoccupied Cos. The Italian commander and many of his officers were executed. Leros and Samos held out a few weeks longer, mainly because the Germans lacked the ships to land troops there. On 2 November, the British and Soviet governments formally asked the Turks to join the war. But Ankara, fearing German reprisals and distrusting Soviet ambitions in Southeastern Europe, declined. On 18 November the garrison at Leros, reinforced by the Royal Navy with a battalion from Samos, surrendered after a five-day battle. Samos and other small islands were subsequently evacuated by the British.

Eden compared the Dodecanese debacle to the fall of Tobruk in June 1942. Accolade had failed at the cost of over five thousand soldiers and twenty-six ships because Churchill had undertaken it with inadequate resources, especially air power, without U.S. support, and in the absence of any realistic hope of influencing Turkey to join the Allies. Indeed, even had Rhodes been secured, it would have become another Malta, a forlorn insular backwater under constant attack by German forces based in Crete and on the Greek mainland. The fact that the Americans had refused to rescue the prime minister's strategic miscalculation signaled Churchill's waning influence in the alliance, and left a residue of hard feelings between the Western Allies.[65]

One result of the Dodecanese fiasco was to push the Allies into creating a unified command for the Mediterranean under Maitland Wilson, an organization capable of seeing the Mediterranean as a unified theater. The British also hoped that it would affirm their "executive direction" of the theater. General Kenneth Strong, Eisenhower's intelligence chief, complained that the British takeover of AFHQ meant that "champagne and oysters gave way to beer and cheese."[66] But Wilson's refusal to become Churchill's Trojan horse for the takeover of AFHQ, combined with American logistical control of the theater, meant that the PM's scheme for British domination of the Mediterranean was never fully realized.[67]

Churchill's Aegean gambit typified the strategic dispersion and wishful thinking that characterized Allied strategy in the late summer of 1943. Operation Baytown, the landing in Calabria by the Eighth Army, and Operation Avalanche, the Fifth Army's assault on Salerno, were too far south either to cut off the German Tenth Army or to link up with Italian units guarding Rome. Kesselring realized that conservative, operations-driven Allied planning might have forfeited their last opportunity rapidly to wrap up Italy. One Italian historian has argued that Giant II offered the Allies their best chance to avoid a nine-month campaign to capture Rome. The appearance of the Eighty-second Airborne Division in the Italian capital might have galvanized Italian action and precipitated a German withdrawal.[68] But this was unlikely. The inescapable conclusion is that a combined Allied air and sea invasion close to Rome would have been a long-shot gamble. The obvious intention of the Italian leadership to flee, the lack of an Italian military plan to take over Rome, the demoralized and confused state of the Italian army, and the absence of orders requiring the Italians to cooperate with the Americans would have produced massive confusion among the invaders. Kesselring would have acted resolutely, massing well-trained German divisions against a relatively inexperienced Allied-Italian force deprived of air cover. Even a beefed-up Giant II would have made Accolade look like a Sunday school picnic.

Algiers failed to grasp the degree of confusion and equivocation that prevailed in Italy. Indeed, the refugees who collected at Brindisi led by a "pathetic, very old, and rather gaga"[69] seventy-four-year-old king and his vacillating prime minister had been stripped of all credibility by their criminal negligence. Nevertheless, the prospect of the long campaign ahead and his disinclination to take over the governance of Italy caused Eisenhower to recommend that the Badoglio regime be accorded the status of a "cobelligerent." Roosevelt and Churchill reluctantly agreed. The Italian prime minister signed the official surrender on 29 September on a British battleship off Malta. But Vittorio Emanuele III, who continued to insist on being addressed as "His Majesty the King of Italy and Albania, Emperor of Ethiopia," resisted a declaration of war on Germany as well as attempts to introduce democratic reforms in his government.[70] The mishandling of the surrender together with the acquisition of an ally of doubtful value produced a doleful effect on the alliance. It helped to transform the Mediterranean from a source of Allied unity into one of division. Churchill bellyached that poor management of the Italian surrender had caused the alliance to forfeit brilliant opportunities to exploit German weakness in the Balkans, Greece, and the Aegean in conjunction with Italian garrisons. Roosevelt began to see Churchill's obsession with the Mediterranean and the Balkans as a distraction, and made common cause with Stalin at Teheran to shift the focus of Allied efforts back to Northern Europe.

THE BALKAN WAR

The Italian surrender changed the dynamic of the conflict in the Balkans and Greece. By late 1942, as his offensive stalled before Stalingrad and Rommel was thrown back from Egypt, Hitler began to understand that he had a serious rebellion on his hands in the Balkans. His great fear that a "catastrophic" Allied landing in Greece or the Balkans, "where the enemy can count on the goodwill of the population and the support of those bands which infest the Balkans," helps to explain his questionable decision to keep the Allies penned down in North Africa, to reinforce his Balkan and Greek garrisons rather than Sicily, and to launch an all-out counterinsurgency in Yugoslavia in 1943. Fear of a Turkish defection as prelude to an Allied Balkan invasion, possibly with Italian connivance, also stimulated distrust in the Axis.[71] Tito, too, worried that Allied landings in the Balkans would short-circuit his revolution before he could finish off Mihailović. Both were correct to fear a British landing, which would certainly have come had the Americans not vetoed the enterprise.[72]

On the verge of forfeiting North Africa, the Germans understood that they needed to destroy the insurgency before the Allies could take strategic advantage of it.[73] However, having orchestrated the conditions for a Balkan uprising, the Germans proved remarkably ill-equipped to deal with an insurgency on such a scale. Overlapping Axis jurisdictions, bureaucratic and strategic feuds between Nazi party and military officials, Italian passivity and defeatism, and Croat brutality combined with the savage enormity of the country to compromise the repression. News of German failure at Stalingrad and in Africa had emboldened the partisans, whose tactics were to build tank traps, mine roads, and sabotage bridges and railway lines to oblige the Germans to commit large forces to antipartisan operations.[74]

Even so, 1943 began well for the occupiers. Tito had to contend with two massive Italo-German offensives, Weiss (January–March 1943) and Schwartz (May–June), which drove his 20,000-strong force, carrying their wounded and followed by swarms of refugees, back into southeastern Bosnia. "The Germans crushed our defenses with tanks and artillery, set our villages afire, and shot hostages and prisoners," remembered Milovan Djilas. "From morning till night their aviation pounded everything in sight."[75] Weiss, carried out in the depths of winter in the rugged terrain of eastern Bosnia, was particularly grueling, as partisans destroyed bridges and roads, complicating German supply. "When I was in Rogatice, it was reported to me that a unit of about 100 Communists was situated in the neighborhood," reported one German commander. "I therefore ordered my battalion to surround the village at a distance at night. Before dawn penetration was made from all sides. The whole band, approximately 100 men, was destroyed. However, such operations are only successful at night. I needed the whole battalion to clear the village!" Despite German success and a relatively low casualty rate of around 14 percent, the psychological stress of being scattered in small, vulnerable garrisons in the midst of a hostile population took its toll on German morale. Yugoslavian service remained unpopular in the Wehrmacht, whose soldiers often requested a transfer even to the Eastern Front in preference.[76]

The Weiss offensive also witnessed the epic battle on the Neretva River in Herzegovina, which went down in partisan lore as a psychological turning point when "the mythical fear of the German army vanished," Chetnik collaboration was exposed, and Churchill, impressed with partisan resistance, opted to send a military mission to reevaluate Britain's policy in Yugoslavia.[77] The casual brutality of these battles was memorable. After an entire battalion of Italian POWs was executed and tossed in the Neretva River by the partisans, Djilas "shared with our officers a malicious joy at the thought of Italian officers on the bridges and embankments of Mostar stricken with horror at the sight of the Neretva choked with the corpses of their soldiers." In most cases, however, Italian POWs were impressed to carry wounded.[78] OSS operative Franklin Lindsay noted that both the barber and the doctor in his unit of Slovene partisans were Italians. After their leaders were shot, "collaborators" were usually offered the choice of execution or enlistment. Even if this tactic filled partisan ranks with unenthusiastic recruits, in Lindsay's view at least it removed a source of support for the Western Allies should they attempt to deny Tito domination of postwar Yugoslavia. Ethnic Germans and older auxiliary troops were often stripped to their underwear and turned loose, an exercise in humiliation that allowed the partisans to joke that captured Germans were frequently their primary source of uniforms. POWs from line units that bore the brunt of the offensives against the partisans could expect execution—"There was no way to hold those captured as prisoners," Lindsay observed.[79]

For Schwartz—called the Fifth Offensive by the partisans—the Axis brought twelve divisions and considerable air power against partisan forces encircled in the mountains. Tito sacrificed 7,000 troops, or almost one-half of his main force, to break out of encirclement.[80] So desperate was the partisan condition that Tito requested an armistice from the Germans while the two sides carried out negotiations in Zagreb aimed at achieving cooperation to eliminate the Chetniks. Tito even offered to make common cause with the Germans in case Allied armies landed in the Balkans. As a gesture of good faith, he ordered a cessation of attacks on German communications. However, these negotiations collapsed for a number of reasons: Hitler opposed them, Tito realized that once Weiss had run its course, he could deal with the Chetniks and the Axis simultaneously, and the British were knocking on his door.[81]

A British military mission under the thirty-two-year-old Conservative member of Parliament Brigadier Fitzroy Maclean parachuted to the partisans in September 1943. One member, the Earl of Birkenhead, described an atmosphere of "Cromwellian austerity" that reigned at Tito's headquarters. "There were many women in the ranks, and although their appearance was not of the sort that makes men forget themselves, there were severe penalties for sexual promiscuity." The spectacle of a celebratory dance performed by the League of Anti-Fascist Women became a regular highlight of partisan festivities. The British writer Evelyn Waugh, included in Maclean's mission, noted that as they danced, "these unsexed creatures, ferocious in appearance . . . clad in battledress . . . wore girdles of live Mills bombs around their waists, which joggled up and down as they moved." Nevertheless, he acknowledged that "the Partisans fought with Balkan courage and took few prisoners."[82] According to Djilas, "Cromwellian austerity" was a virtue unpracticed in the leadership, where Tito and his major lieutenants "were followed about by pretty young secretaries who were obviously more intimate with them than their duties required." When Djilas, fresh from the butchery and sexual repression of Montenegro, inquired about this double standard, he was told, "It goes with power. In Serbia, a minister without a mistress is unthinkable."[83]

The surrender of Italy in September 1943 swung the pendulum back to the resistance. Although the Italian capitulation took them by surprise, both partisans and Chetniks took quick action to rearm themselves courtesy of six Italian divisions. It also began to dawn on many fence sitters and deserters from Pavelić's Croat army that Germany would lose the war. Some may have also reasoned that the Croat Tito would end Serbian hegemony in Yugoslavia,[84] and were lulled into the self-delusion that he was more patriot than Communist. The writ of the NDH, the Axis-created Croatian state, hardly extended beyond the city limits of Zagreb. The arrival into partisan ranks of young Croat peasants, "without song and music, but with an anxious sobriety,"[85] enabled Tito to organize four new 4,000-person "divisions" with captured Italian weapons. Enough Italians also escaped the German roundup to create a "Garibaldi Division," raising partisan strength to around 200,000 persons, according to Churchill's exaggerated estimates.[86] The partisans also beat the Chetniks in the race to seize Split and much of the Dalmatian coast, hitherto part of the Italian zones.

In response, the Germans rushed in new divisions, including mountain and antiguerrilla *Jagdkommando* units made up of young, energetic veterans of other fronts. With these they launched a major offensive to recover most of the coast, with the exception of the island of Vis. But the flood of Allied matériel through Vis, some of it arriving in the fishing boats of the OSS-organized "Splinter Fleet," augmented with the creation on 1 June 1944 of the Balkan Air Force, which, guided by OSS and SOE operatives, parachuted tons of supplies to the partisans, gave Tito a base of support the Germans could not overcome.[87] Lindsay discovered that although the British Bren light machine gun was the favorite weapon among the partisans, most were armed with a motley of German and Italian small arms, either captured in the Balkans or supplied by Allied air drops from Axis stocks captured in North Africa and Italy.[88] Twenty German or German-controlled divisions totaling 700,000 men plus eight Bulgarian divisions in Greece and Yugoslavia—as many as were required in Italy to stop two Allied armies—eventually settled on the Balkans. However, they were often made up of scrapings from other fronts, while the land was simply too large and too wild for the Germans effectively to control more than a few key points.[89]

By late 1943, Allied supplies to the Chetniks had dried up, about the time that the Chetnik staff concluded a nonaggression pact with the Germans. In January 1944 the British took the decision to withdraw their mission to Mihailović after Ultra revealed evidence of his duplicity.[90] The second session of the Anti-Fascist Council meeting in Jajce in November 1943 declared Tito a "marshal" and named him prime minister and defense minister of the provisional government, the National Committee for the Liberation of Yugoslavia. The king's exile became permanent.

While the Greek partisans never achieved the level of organization of the Yugoslav resistance, four factors influenced the transformation of the scattered *andartes* into a resistance movement on a national scale. In November 1942, a detachment of British SOE operatives under Colonel C. W. Myer, aided by *andartes* from both ELAS and EDES, blew up the Gorgopotamos railway viaduct ninety miles northeast of Athens. This caused electricity and fuel shortages in Athens, made the Tsolakoglou government appear vulnerable, and brought the *andartes* to public notice at the very moment that Rommel's defeat at El Alamein signaled that the Germans had reached their high-water mark in the Mediterranean. Demonstrations and strikes against harsh conditions, swelled by adolescents whose schools had been shut down for lack of funds, began to take on a distinctly anti-Axis flavor, especially as the German debacle at Stalingrad unfolded. Myer and his second-in-command, Major Christopher Woodhouse, remained in Greece as the nucleus of a British military mission to coordinate Greek resistance activities and to distribute some arms, but mostly food and gold sovereigns supplied by SOE-Cairo.[91]

A second factor that encouraged growing resistance arose in early 1943, when the Germans decreed a "civil mobilization" of Greek workers to be transported to Germany. As in other countries under German occupation, "civil mobilization" transformed the resistance from a movement of anti-fascist ideologues into the option of choice for thousands of young men. Overnight, the numbers of resisters grew from around 5,000 to between 30,000 and 50,000, as many succumbed to the EAM slogan "Mobilization = Death: *Andartes* Everyone!" The third event that bolstered the resistance was the Italian surrender of September 1943. This proved to be a mixed blessing for EAM/ELAS. On the plus side, Italy's defection from the Axis offered a psychological boost, further evidence that Germany would lose the war, which motivated yet more recruits; also, the windfall in weaponry captured from some of the 160,000 Italian troops stationed in Greece enabled ELAS to form a new brigade and a new division, which they subsequently turned against their EDES rivals. The Pinerolo Division and the Aosta Cavalry Brigade defected en masse to the insurgency. Elsewhere, Italians sold their weapons to the *andartes* before marching into internment by the Germans.[92] The drawback for the resistance was that the Italian defection made Churchill aware that the balance of power in Greece had shifted irrevocably to EAM/ELAS. This confirmed him in his determination to intervene upon the German withdrawal.[93]

The final act in the transformation of the resistance was the effort of Saraphis and Velouchiotis to incorporate these dispersed bands of bearded insurgents—dressed in bits and pieces of uniform, shepherd's coats, woolen hats, and armed with an assortment of weapons—into a coherent movement. By February 1943, attacks on trains, convoys, and even isolated military garrisons had become a frequent occurrence.

Andartes installed their own officials in towns, organized their own justice system, or forced local officials and gendarmes to cooperate with them in secret or pay the penalty. Resistance *kapetanoi* often behaved with great brutality, running their own terror camps where arrested suspects were tortured and murdered. Much of this violence occurred between rival *andartes* groups fighting over territory, especially in areas where food was scarce, making it delicate for villagers to know whom to support.[94] Bands who refused to be incorporated into ELAS had their leaders assassinated or were wiped out. Such was the fate of Colonel Psarros of the EKKA, killed on Velouchiotis's orders along with perhaps as many as four hundred of his guerrillas in an April 1944 ELAS attack and subsequent purges in Roumeli. These attacks were counterproductive, for they spread fear in the resistance and among the British that EAM's main goal was to take power after liberation, not to battle Germans. This ultimately gave credibility to Churchill's claim that British intervention in October 1944 had forestalled an EAM coup.[95]

Having created the conditions for widespread rebellion, the Axis proved remarkably unprepared to deal with it. The occupiers had settled into the major population centers, leaving the task of policing the countryside to the lethargic agents of a Greek government reluctant to crack down on their countrymen. The Italians, responsible for the administration of most of the country, attempted from the summer of 1942 to introduce informers into resistance groups and to arrest former Greek officers whom they saw as potential resisters. These measures failed as resistance groups became more adept at sniffing out treachery and as Greek officers fled into the sanctuary of the insurgency. The Italian surrender in September 1943 shifted the burden of managing the counterinsurgency to German commander Alexander Löhr. It could not have come as a welcome assignment to the Luftwaffe general, a fluent Russian speaker whose solid understanding of the complexities of Balkan history made him aware of the daunting nature of his task.

The Germans followed a two-pronged strategy. The first and most successful element was to promote Greek discord. In April 1943, the Axis organized a collaborationist government under Ioannes Ralles, a politician from an old political family celebrated for his visceral anti-Bolshevism, but who otherwise enjoyed no significant political following. Ralles's chief advantage in German eyes was that his "Security Battalions," which grew to include between seven and eight thousand men by February 1944, could spearhead the counterinsurgency movement and protect local authorities loyal to Athens. Ralles's weakness was that his anti–EAM/ELAS views did not necessarily make him pro-Axis. Instead, he hedged his bets by maintaining covert contacts with the British, while he also reached across the chasm of the national schism to establish links with Venizélists. Because the Germans distrusted Ralles, they increasingly took control of the Security Battalions from October 1943, so that they soon operated almost exclusively under SS direction.[96] This did little to increase the efficiency of an organization recruited in the main from the scrapings of taverns, prisons, and the traditionally royalist areas of the Peloponnese and Euboea, and from men driven to enlist out of fear of reprisals against their families, led by officers whose bonds of loyalty reached back to the Metaxas dictatorship. In Thessaly and Macedonia, the Security Battalions were supplemented by freelance profascist bands that one historian has called "death squads," recruited among ethnic minorities or victims of EAM/ELAS violence, men whose brutality, hostage taking, and indiscriminate killing were so horrific that even the Germans felt obliged to execute some of them. Some of these groups managed successfully to run for the cover of Zervas's EDES at war's end.[97]

Greek discord, inefficiency, and disloyalty meant that the burden of the repression would fall to the Germans, who, as in Yugoslavia, were ill-placed to carry it out. The Germans built strong points and blockhouses at key points surrounded by mines and barbed wire. They occupied the main towns and the coast. But this was a defensive strategy that left to the resistance the run of the countryside. A department of Army Group E headquarters outside Salonika, in which Lieutenant Kurt Waldheim served, provided intelligence on the *andartes*. But the effectiveness of these operations was limited by the imprecision or untimeliness of this information; the failure of the SS, Abwehr, and the Secret Field Police to cooperate; lack of fuel; the slow and predictable nature of the process of massing and moving troops; and the rugged

terrain, which made the cohesion of counterinsurgency sweeps difficult to maintain and offered guerrilla units many opportunities to escape. The Germans resorted to the wholesale destruction of villages.
On their own entrepreneurial initiatives, individual "Germans"—
including Serbs and Russians incorporated in Wehrmacht formations,
soldiers otherwise paid in worthless drachmas—would seize hostages
and ransom them back to their families. The savagery of these measures came naturally to the divisions sent from the Eastern Front and
Yugoslavia to repress the *andartes*. By the liberation, it was reckoned
that around 1,700 villages had been destroyed, 21,000 civilians killed,
similar numbers arrested, and over a million left homeless, all at the
relatively light cost to the Germans of 8,383 casualties.[98] The most serious depredations were carried out in central and northern Greece.
But these savage acts only served to stimulate resistance recruitment
and spread the famine to the countryside. Haiari, a large SS internment center outside of Athens staffed by *Volksdeutsch* from Hungary
and Romania, served as a way station for deportation and a repository
of hostages to be shot in retaliation for resistance attacks.[99]

The British response to the savage cycle of resistance and repression was rather ambivalent. So long as Rommel rampaged in Egypt
and Tripolitania and the Germans threatened Turkey and the Middle
East, Greece was viewed as an important conduit of supplies and reinforcements. Much of the oil traveling from Ploesti to North Africa
transited through Greece. Cairo was also keen to stimulate resistance
activity that would encourage the Axis to commit troops to the defense
of Greece and the Balkans. Prior to the Sicily invasion, the British ran
Operation Animals, a deception operation that involved stepped-up
guerrilla activity and the creation of a fictitious army in Egypt to promote the idea that Greece was a prime target for Allied invasion.
Hitler took the bait and transferred five fresh German divisions to
Greece, including the crack First Panzer and the First Mountain Divisions. Operation Animals constituted, in Churchill's view, "the last
direct military contribution which the Greek guerrillas made to the
war."[100] Churchill and the Foreign Office also sought to reinstall
George II on the Greek throne upon liberation. But fundamentally,

British policy proved to be confused and even counterproductive. Members of the British military mission in Greece—which became the Allied military mission when the Americans joined it in September 1943—pointed out that Greek support for the monarch and his government-in-exile was nonexistent. Once Anvil, the August 1944 invasion of the French Riviera, demonstrated conclusively that Greece would be bypassed by Allied armies, the policy of supplying ELAS appeared to be setting up a positively dangerous post-liberation situation.

But London's attempts to force a shotgun marriage between the exiled royal government and the internal resistance backfired badly: it actually served to strengthen the Communist hold on the population. King George and his entourage of émigré courtiers and nonentities, who lived in indolent splendor at Claridge's and in Cairo, were associated with the discredited Metaxas dictatorship, which delegitimized them in the eyes of most Greeks. In July 1943 the three principal Greek resistance groups met in Cairo and agreed to coordinate their activities under a headquarters set up by SOE. London's attempt in August 1943 to force the resistance to agree to the king's return after liberation led to the "Cairo crisis," sometimes called the first act of the Greek Civil War. EAM/ELAS insisted that the king should only return after a plebiscite, and that the resistance movements be given the justice, war, and interior portfolios in the Greek government-in-exile. When the king rejected this, the EAM representatives broke off relations and returned to Greece.

AVALANCHE

Operation Avalanche was born in the confusion of the Italian surrender. Its problems began at the top. Allied misgivings about the advisability of invading the Italian mainland only increased after the successful Axis evacuation from Sicily.[101] Marshall was eager to redeploy troops, landing craft, and bombers to Great Britain for Overlord. His protégé Eisenhower must invade Italy with the resources at hand, which, among other deficiencies, meant that he could count on roughly half the small craft that had been available for Husky.[102] Eisenhower, distracted by the negotiations with the Italians and un-

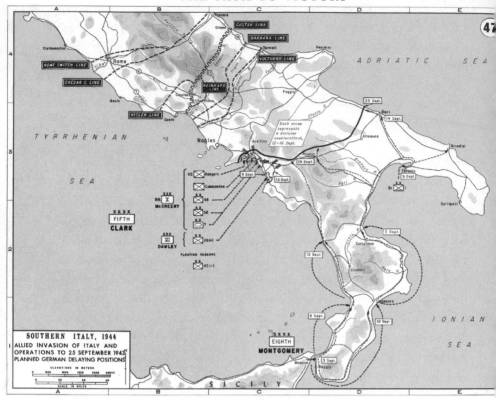

SOUTHERN ITALY, 1944
ALLIED INVASION OF ITALY AND
OPERATIONS TO 25 SEPTEMBER 1943
PLANNED GERMAN DELAYING POSITIONS

able to adjudicate the competing priorities of the British and Americans, allowed AFHQ planners to concoct no fewer than four separate, widely scattered assaults on Italy that could not be mutually supporting. The inevitable result was that already meager forces became dangerously stretched as they were parceled out over separate, often rival, objectives.

The main invasions were left to Montgomery's Eighth Army and the U.S. Fifth Army under Mark Clark. The farther up the peninsula the assault could be landed the better, Rome, or at the very least Naples, being the primary objectives. Unfortunately, Salerno, fifty miles south of Naples, offered the most northerly site within the maximum range of fighters operating out of Sicily. Montgomery argued that the two armies should hit the same beach, side by side, as during Husky. This assessment was probably informed by Allied intelligence reports from late August of the buildup of eighteen German divisions on or near the peninsula, and of Rommel's appointment as commander-in-chief of Army Group B in northern Italy, although there was no indication of how Germany planned to use its forces.[103] Montgomery foresaw that Kesselring could rapidly concentrate superior force against the four divisions of the Fifth Army. In Montgomery's view, a two-army invasion at Salerno would bypass any German troops in Calabria, who must either fight their way back up the peninsula or risk becoming marooned in the south. This otherwise sound idea was rejected largely because Marshall had recalled the landing craft required to transport two armies simultaneously to the beaches at Salerno. Therefore, the Eighth Army was to be ferried across the Strait of Messina—Operation Baytown—so that landing craft could be freed up for Avalanche, scheduled for 9 September. The planners' justification for two widely separated invasions was that two Allied armies storming ashore 250 miles apart would split German defenders between Salerno and Calabria. Montgomery ranted in vain that this violated the principle of concentration of force and divided logistics and air power between two widely separated fronts.

On 3 September, six hundred artillery pieces on the Sicilian shore opened fire on Calabria, joined by the guns of a naval armada led by four British battleships, and lashings of explosives dropped from British and American bombers. Intelligence showed that German divisions near Salerno did not take the bait by moving south to defend the toe of Italy, precisely because both German and Italian intelligence anticipated a second invasion in the Naples-Salerno area.[104] A few dazed Italian soldiers emerged from the rubble to help the British disembark. The only opposition to Montgomery's two-division assault across the strait came from a puma and a monkey freed from their cages in the Reggio zoo by the massive British bombardment. These two animals attacked soldiers of the Canadian Division before being frightened away by rifle fire. Montgomery, made unhappy by the anticlimactic arrival of Allied troops in Western Europe, complained that Baytown had no strategic objective beyond a leisurely stroll up the boot and railed against Eisenhower for failing to "grip" the campaign. A secondary seaborne assault—Slapstick—by the British First Airborne Division on Taranto on 9 September helped to persuade a portion of the Italian fleet to sail for Malta. These troops then joined with the Eighth Army's main thrust north to capture the airfields around Foggia on the Adriatic coast.

Giant II, canceled at the last minute, freed up the elite Eighty-second Airborne Division to serve as a strategic reserve for Salerno, which helped to tip the balance between success and failure for Mark Wayne Clark, the Avalanche commander. Tall, slender, with an angular face and prominent nose that earned for him Churchill's nickname "the American Eagle,"[105] Clark first came to public notice in 1918, when, one year out of West Point, he commanded a battalion on the Western Front, and in the process collected a life-threatening wound. Such was Clark's reputation in the interwar army for physical bravery, forcefulness of character, and administrative flair that, in 1941, he was catapulted directly from lieutenant colonel to brigadier general in order to second General Lesley McNair in the huge expansion of the U.S. Army. Clark, who with Patton and Eisenhower emerged as the stars of the 1941 maneuvers, had used his influence to ease his friend Eisenhower onto McNair's promotion list to brigadier general and chief of the operations division of the War Department. Marshall had sent both men to London to take charge of the U.S. observer group, a pretext to promote them to major generals. Once in place, they became the leaders of the growing American force in Britain.[106] Eisenhower called on "Wayne," as he was then known to his friends, to supervise the details of the invasion of North Africa from his London headquarters, because Marshall considered Clark "the only man who knew about amphibious operations."[107] He played a vital role in the eventual success of Torch, first by landing in a submarine to contact officers favorable to de Gaulle, and finally by negotiating the controversial cease-fire in Algiers with French Admiral Darlan in November 1942 that ended French resistance. But Eisenhower's friendship with Clark, and Marshall's confidence in him, began to erode early in the new year as they witnessed what George Patton referred to as Clark's indefatigable quest for "cheap publicity."[108] Indeed, Clark's vanity was such that he was followed around by an official photographer who was allowed to photograph him only from his "best" left profile.[109] Once Eisenhower settled on Bedell Smith as his chief of staff, Clark successfully campaigned for command of the Fifth Army. Clark's promotion deeply disappointed Patton, chagrined that a man eleven years his junior had beaten him to a third star.

At Salerno, Richard Tregaskis discovered Clark to be "a surprisingly young man. I would never have guessed his age at more than thirty-five."[110] Even at forty-seven (his true age), Clark was the youngest lieutenant general in the U.S. Army. Harold Macmillan declared Clark the most intelligent general that he encountered in any army in the Mediterranean theater. Clark was also demanding, despotic to the point of tyranny, and ruthless with subordinates who he deemed had failed. These traits had served Clark well when, as McNair's hatchet man, his job had been to weed out incompetent officers. Clark's admirers argue that "the American Eagle" combined intelligence and determination with an ability to learn from his mistakes to merit a place among the war's leading commanders. His merciless drive fueled Allied success in Italy, the motor that propelled a diverse coalition forward in campaign conditions as difficult as those encountered in any theater of the war. He eventually replaced Alexander as Fifteenth Army Group commander, thus equaling in rank Omar Bradley and Bernard Montgomery, testimony to Clark's suitability for the highest commands.[111] However, Clark was too ambitious to be a team player. He thirsted to be a star. "He seemed false somehow," Omar Bradley wrote of Clark, "too eager to impress, too hungry for the limelight, promotions and personal publicity."[112] Even Eisenhower's initial enthusiasm for his old friend cooled after Clark refused to step down from the still-building Fifth Army in the wake of Kasserine to take command of the shaky Second Corps in Tunisia, because he felt that it would be a demotion.[113]

Nor would the transition from staff officer with a brilliant reputation for planning and training to battlefield commander in an alliance framework prove an easy one for Clark, for at least three reasons. First, critics claimed that, though intelligent, Clark lacked a feel for battle, that *je ne sais quoi* of command that enables all great generals to adjust instinctively to the ever-evolving circumstances of the front line. His approach to combat was mechanical, plan-driven, formalistic. Patton believed that Clark lacked a big-picture mind. He thought small-scale, in terms of battalions rather than army corps. There was also a whiff of the château about a general who issued orders from his headquarters at Caserta fully three hours' drive from the nearest point of the Cassino line, with a finality that permitted no discussion. Clark believed that his "lay down the law" command style enforced his authority, that discussion and debate produced only drift and death in combat. But his subordinates perceived Clark to be at once close-minded, arrogant, and insecure.[114]

Clark's second blemish followed fatally from the first. Once he settled on a plan, he drove his men mercilessly toward the objective regardless of the costs. His willingness to absorb heavy casualties, his lack of flexibility, his rejection of alternative suggestions, his habit of shifting the blame for failure onto subordinates, won him few admirers. He became identified in the popular mind with an Italian campaign increasingly perceived as futile, costly, poorly managed, and superfluous. Finally, Clark appeared to suffer from a particularly debilitating case of Anglophobia, one that made his actions irrational and increasingly paranoid. This was not instinctive or inherited, but the product of a crippling combination of ego, ambition, and the Allied character of the Italian campaign. Clark's obsession with publicizing the exploits of "Mark Clark's Fifth Army" translated into a determination not to let the British steal a march on him. This created bad Allied chemistry in Italy, where the British found Clark to be a dissembler who did not deal honestly with them. He made no attempt to be convivial, to establish a social relationship as the foundation for a professional understanding. Instead, he preferred to work out his own plan in secret and then dispatch underlings to make unpopular requests or issue controversial directives. McCreery, Kirkman, and Freyberg, all of whom served as corps commanders in the Fifth Army, found that the ordeal of working for Clark stretched their alliance loyalty to the limit. So disgusted was Oliver Leese, Montgomery's successor as head of the Eighth Army, when Clark dashed to Rome in June 1944 rather than cooperate with the Eighth Army to round up the German Tenth Army in full retreat from the Gustav line, that thenceforth each of the Allied armies fought its separate battles in Italy with only the merest pretense of cooperation. As the campaign progressed, Clark publicly complained that the British were not fighting hard enough. A more forceful leader than Alexander might have contained the damage. But the Fifteenth Army Group commander was cut to lead a coalition of gentlemen. Clark instinctively sensed Alexander's weakness of character and assumed that his "suggestions" were concocted to advance British interests.[115]

Even though he had initially been passed over for Fifth Army command in favor of Clark, Patton's subsequent success in Sicily at the head of the Seventh Army seemed to make him the general of choice to lead Avalanche.[116] But even before the infamous slapping incidents at the end of Husky caused Patton to be seen as damaged goods, it had been Omar Bradley's, rather than Patton's, performance in North Africa and Sicily that had attracted the attention of Eisenhower and Marshall.[117] Montgomery, for one, was baffled when Eisenhower designated the green Fifth Army assembled in North Africa and its inexperienced commander to lead the major assault on the Italian mainland. At the very least, in Monty's view, the Fifth Army should have been assigned Baytown and the Eighth Army given Avalanche.[118] Patton's view that Clark was "too damned slick," did not know how to organize a headquarters, and needed "to learn the facts of life" about warfare, seemed to be borne out during Avalanche.[119] Clark's near panic at Salerno and increasing criticism of his stubborn, poorly conceived, and inadequately supported attacks on the Cassino line in the winter of 1943–44 caused Eisenhower to consider relieving him, a step he never took. So disappointed had Eisenhower been in Clark, however, that he was never included on Ike's shortlist for a command in Overlord.[120]

For Avalanche, Clark's Fifth Army was organized into two forces. A Northern Attack Force made up of the British Tenth Corps, lifted from the Eighth Army, was composed of two British divisions that had fought in North Africa, the Forty-sixth and Fifty-sixth, together with British commandos and U.S. Rangers. The Seventh Armoured Division served as their reserve. These were to be commanded by an Anglo-Irish cavalry officer, an experienced horseman and pioneer in armored warfare who had served brilliantly as Alexander's chief of staff in the Western Desert, Lieutenant General Richard McCreery. A severe wound in the Great War had left McCreery with a limp, which invariably earned him the nickname of "Hopalong Cassidy" from his troops. Otherwise, McCreery was a pious, intensely private, but otherwise open-minded (Alexander thought inspiring) commander, extremely popular with subordinates, but less so with superiors who found him blunt, occasionally cantankerous, even argumentative.[121] Needless to say, his relationship with Clark would become tempestuous. Tenth Corps's task was to land at the northern end of a thirty-five-mile-long coastal plain that stretched from the town of Salerno south to Paestum, and then strike north toward Naples. The Rangers and commandos would seize the high ground northwest of the beach to block German attempts to reinforce along Route 18 or via the coastal road that connected Salerno with Naples.

A Southern Attack Force, made up of the U.S. Sixth Corps under Major General Ernest Dawley, like Clark a staff officer as yet inexperienced in combat, was composed of the Thirty-sixth and Forty-fifth Divisions, with the Eighty-second Airborne Division in reserve. This force would land south of the Sele River at Paestum. The Third and Thirty-fourth Divisions waited in North Africa to be fed into the battle. Their task was to guard the southern flank of the beachhead and eventually make contact with Montgomery's Eighth Army driving up from the south. Together, under the command of Alexander's Fifteenth Army Group, they would wheel north and roll toward Rome.

For a man praised by Eisenhower as the U.S. Army's preeminent planner and amphibious assault specialist, Clark came up with an attack scheme shot full of weaknesses. On paper the plan looked straightforward and powerful, supported by 150 Sherman tanks, an abundance of antitank guns, artillery, and naval artillery, as well as a tempo of air operations that could outpace Luftwaffe sorties by a ratio of ten to one. In practice, however, Avalanche was complicated by geography, organizational constraints, and the probable reaction of the enemy. To the casual observer, the Bay of Salerno appeared idyllic, a scythe of pale pink sand that curved for thirty miles from Salerno, a small harbor at the base of the Sorrento Peninsula, south along a verdant shore through Paestum, an ancient Greek city discovered by chance by road builders in 1750, to Agropoli. The beaches of the sweeping bay eased into a triangular coastal plain of ochre farmhouses, olive groves, and fields engorged with tomatoes, melons, hemp, and tobacco, and cubed by stone walls. Numerous streams and two significant rivers, the high-banked Sele and its tributary the Calore, flowed out of the mountains of the Campania, some of them reaching four thousand feet, past Eboli and Battipaglia to the bay. The main rail line from Messina to Naples, and a coastal highway cut the valley from north to south. As a tourist destination, Salerno appeared enticing. The castle keep, a picturesque fragment of the medieval town, and the duomo or cathedral consecrated by Pope Gregory VII in 1085, gave ev-

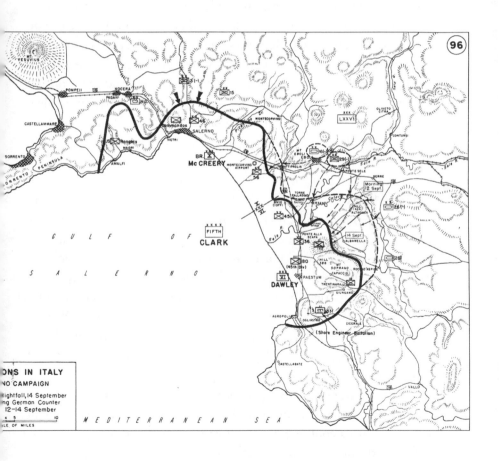

idence that in the Middle Ages Salerno had been a rich trading city that rivaled Naples in influence. Its celebrated medieval university had earned for the town the nickname "City of Socrates."

As a military project, however, Salerno's shallow hinterland presented significant challenges. The beaches were DUKW-compatible, and Salerno had a small harbor and airfield that might prove useful. However, the plain was dominated by high, gunner-friendly mountains that the Germans would surely control. Furthermore, sandbars at the mouth of the Sele forced the invaders to split their force to the north and south of it, leaving a ten-mile gap between the two Allied corps traversed by the Sele-Calore corridor. Not only would this prevent communication between the two attack forces, but also, as Patton pointed out when, as reserve commander for Avalanche, he was briefed on the operation, it offered an undefended passage splitting the beachhead that beckoned the German defenders to attack. The only exit north off the plain was through the Salerno bottleneck to easily defended gorges of the Sorrento hills and Naples beyond. The quality and quantity of the attacking force was also suspect. The British divisions, a mix of regular and territorial battalions, had seen action in the final stages of the Tunisia campaign, earning reputations as solid if unenterprising units. The shortage of landing craft meant that, of the American contingent, only the Thirty-sixth Division could be put ashore in the first wave of the Southern Attack Force, making the initial three-division insertion vulnerable to a rapid German buildup by land. Inadequate means to reinforce and provision the beachhead was particularly worrisome, as the Thirty-sixth Division, under Major General Fred Walker, was made up of Texas National Guardsmen, as yet uninitiated in the rigors of combat. The Forty-fifth Division was commanded by Troy Middleton, who had been the youngest and most promising colonel in the American Expeditionary Force in World War I. He had nevertheless left the army for an administrative job at Louisiana State University in the 1930s. Middleton returned on the outbreak of war, eventually to become one of Eisenhower's best corps commanders. In September 1943 his division had seen some combat in Sicily. But its contingent of National Guardsmen drawn from several Western states was inadequately trained.

Lessons learned from Husky offered limited guidance for Avalanche planners. On Sicily, seven experienced Allied divisions had been inserted side by side against defenders that included only two German divisions. By the time Kesselring had been able to funnel reinforcements across the Strait of Messina, the Allied beachhead had become too strong to eject. All Kesselring could do was to execute a fighting retreat. One lesson the Allied planners could legitimately conclude from the Husky experience was that a concentrated invasion was unnecessary.[122] If the Husky planners had overcompensated by landing the Eighth and Seventh Armies side by side, those who dreamed up Avalanche had seriously underestimated the German response. Betting on active Italian assistance, they had failed to allocate adequate reserves. The three Allied divisions of less than 70,000 men put ashore on Salerno beaches ten miles apart would basically be left to fight their separate campaigns. Bradley, who was asked by Eisenhower to review the planning for Avalanche, argued that mixing British and U.S. units in the same army had worked badly in Tunisia and predicted in private that "the situation seemed ripe for disaster."[123]

Probably the greatest defect of Avalanche was that the element of surprise belonged to the German defenders. Albert Kesselring needed neither an intelligence staff nor the tip-off of an introductory bombardment to divine that the limitations of Allied fighter range made Salerno the most likely invasion point.[124] Salerno was garrisoned by the Sixteenth Panzer Division, hardened in the intense fighting around Stalingrad and considered one of the strongest units in Italy. Its 17,000 men and one hundred tanks had already rehearsed antiinvasion exercises on the beachhead. Artillery had been prepositioned in the hills above the plain. Reserve divisions were near. Clearly, this was going to be no rehash of Sicily. Eight defensive strong points linked by a web of heavy machine-gun nests, mortars, artillery, and mines sprouted on the plain. German air reconnaissance had little trouble locating the 500-ship sprawl of the Allied fleet as they sailed north on 7 September, in time to allow the Sixteenth Panzer Division to put the final, lethal touches on their defenses.

The concluding indication that invasion was imminent was Eisenhower's 8 September announcement over Radio Algiers that the Italians had surrendered, followed by a bombing raid on Kesselring's headquarters south of Naples. The announcement caught both Clark and his naval chief, corpulent, rumpled, fifty-five-year-old New Jersey native Vice-Admiral H. K. Hewitt, by surprise. The tension among the invaders snapped. Soldiers jostled onto the decks, cheering, shouting, slapping each other on the back. On British ships, celebratory drinks were ordered. Salerno would be a Sunday outing, a practice landing into an admiring throng of Italian spectators. Clark had left to Major General Walker the decision on whether to order a preliminary naval bombardment of his Thirty-sixth Division's beach. Walker had been unimpressed with the target list and had no desire to alert the Germans to the coming invasion. Eisenhower's announcement seemed to vindicate his decision not to kill "a lot of peaceful Italians and destroy their homes."[125] This proved to be a desperate miscalculation, for it spared the German defenders a preparatory softening up.[126]

Although criticized for his armistice announcement prior to Avalanche, Eisenhower's move avoided two potentially campaign-ending consequences: active Italian resistance and a more rapid, and possibly overwhelming, German reaction to the Allied invaders at Salerno. The combined number of Axis divisions in Italy stood at thirty-five. Had the Axis been able to concentrate even a portion of them, the four-plus divisions of Avalanche, two of Baytown, and one slated for Slapstick would have stood little chance. At the very least, the armistice announcement caused the Germans to turn on Italian units that might otherwise have opposed the invasion. It also introduced temporary confusion into the German response at a time when the invasion was extremely vulnerable.[127] German troops throughout Italy, the Balkans, Greece, and the Aegean were busied disarming Italian garrisons while German airborne forces were diverted to secure Rome. Hitler ordered the rescue of Mussolini, carried out on 12 September by Otto Skorzeny, as the first step in creating the Republic of Salò in the north of Italy. On the eighth, 18,000 German troops evacuated Sardinia via Corsica, which itself was evacuated from the twelfth. Nor is it likely that the (temporary) impact of the announcement on the psychological preparation of Allied soldiers for the invasion influenced the outcome. Instead, Eisenhower's announcement added to the confused, improvised nature of the Axis response to the Allied invasion and contributed the critical difference between the success and failure of Avalanche.

While German reinforcements had been pouring into the Italian Peninsula since Mussolini's July overthrow, disputes in the German high command over how Italy was to be defended combined with uncertainty over Italian sentiments to make the defense of Italy ad hoc and improvised.[128] The two-corps-strong German Tenth Army at Naples had only been organized on 22 August, and as yet lacked many of the accoutrements of command, including a signals and logistical structure, which impaired its response to Avalanche. Kesselring's plan was to defend a line south of Rome running from the mouth of the Garigliano River, along a ridge line that bisected the historic Benedictine abbey at Monte Cassino, to the mouth of the Sangro on the Adriatic. The job of von Vietinghoff was to hold up the invasion at Salerno long enough for his engineers to put the finishing touches on his defenses. If, in the process, he could mass the scattered divisions of his two corps to counterattack the beachhead and hurl Avalanche into the sea, then this would constitute a huge embarrassment for the invaders. But von Vietinghoff would have only a narrow window of opportunity to inflict a stinging reverse before the besiegers were taken in the rear by Montgomery's Eighth Army advancing from the south. To buy time, the defenses at Salerno were arranged in a classic German army fashion. A thin, elastic front line of machine guns and antitank weapons sited behind belts of antipersonnel mines and covered by artillery would slow down attacking forces before they encountered a main line of resistance sited two to five miles to the rear. A third or reserve line concealed beyond artillery range received reinforcements who, when the attackers became overextended and exhausted, would counterattack in strength with tanks and heavy weapons. As in all amphibious invasions, Avalanche would be a race between invaders building up the beachhead and defenders pulling in their scattered reserves to counterattack.

In the event, to those who observed the countless ships that massed in the sea before the crescent-shaped shore in the dawn of 10 September 1943, Avalanche appeared irresistible, "as if some corporation gone massively astray was floating in on waves from the standing ships," recorded American poet Bruce Cutler.[129] But as LSTs, interspersed with rocket-firing landing craft able to fire 800 three-inch rockets practically simultaneously, began their run to the beaches from ten miles out, they met a gauntlet of exploding artillery shells and Luftwaffe fighters, which transitioned to mortar, antitank, and machinegun fire as they approached beach defenses left pristine by the lack of a preliminary bombardment. Landing craft erupted as they touched mines anchored in the surf. While the two divisions of Tenth Corps came ashore with relative ease, some of their units having the leisure to land a piano and a pig destined for the officers' mess, those of the neophyte Thirty-sixth Division were nailed to the sand by intense fire and had to be prodded off the beach and into the stands of pine. A dozen or more panzers paraded up and down the beach northwest of Paestum, sending the Texans scurrying for cover. Men edged forward along the stone walls, dragging bazookas and grenades to silence the German machine guns and encourage the tanks to depart.

Farther north, in the Tenth Corps sector, troops of the Fifty-sixth Division were bludgeoned by panzers and 88 mm guns as they untangled on the beach and moved inland up narrow, easily ambushed lanes. A British destroyer moved dangerously close to shore, swung sideways, and unleashed broadsides at German batteries. Only the Rangers and commandos at the northwestern end of the beachhead encountered little resistance and appeared to reach their objectives with few losses. As troops from Heinrich von Vietinghoff's Tenth Army (Nineteenth Panzer Grenadier and Twenty-sixth Panzer) filtered in from the south to reinforce the Sixteenth Panzer, overall control of the battle broke down in a confusion of skirmishes to dominate sand dunes, olive groves, and half-demolished farmhouses. A few Allied landing craft filtered through the intense fire carrying tanks and artillery, but not enough to redress the superiority in firepower held by the defenders over the lightly armed Allied infantry. Air strikes, destroyers that ventured suicidally close to the beaches to redress the balance with devastating naval gunfire, and the fact that for once the Germans counterattacked in ad hoc and uncoordinated formations, kept the invaders from being crushed beneath the weight of German resistance.

By the end of the first day, the best thing that could be said was that the invasion had not yet failed. The Thirty-sixth Division clung to a beachhead less than five miles deep, separated from that of the Tenth Corps by a gap of seven miles through which the Sele River ran like a barrier between the two Allied toeholds. The Tenth Corps had pushed farther inland. But even their relative success caused problems. The Fifty-sixth Division had seized the Montecorvino airfield, but in doing so had acquired a fifteen-mile front to defend. The advance of the Forty-sixth Division had failed to link up with Rangers and commandos. Inadequate reserves had been allocated to making a breakout. The entire beachhead was dominated by German guns sited on the high ground. The only good news, had the Allies realized it, was that German reinforcements, especially three panzer and panzer grenadier divisions, were slow to arrive because of fuel shortages and because von Vietinghoff continued to expect a second landing near Naples. Clark, who had yet to come ashore and who had only a vague idea of the disposition of his forces, tried to convey a quietly optimistic forecast of success to Eisenhower, who was worried that failure at Salerno would mean the end of both their careers.

The next two days were employed by each side in reinforcing the beachhead and maneuvering for advantage. On 10 September, the Royal Fusiliers were ejected from Battipaglia, leaving 1,500 POWs behind. Elements of the U.S. Forty-fifth Division landed, but were unable to close the gap along the Sele between the Tenth and Sixth Corps. On 11 September high-altitude Luftwaffe planes dropped radio-controlled glider bombs that flew at over 600 miles per hour and packed an explosive warhead capable of penetrating several layers of steel decks; they sank thirteen Allied ships, including a hospital ship, and damaged two American cruisers. American troops seized Altaville. Clark dispatched Brigadier General John "Iron Mike" O'Daniel to bring order to the logistical chaos on the Thirty-sixth Division beach by organizing the plethora of supplies into dumps, grouping vehicles into parks, and speeding the flow of supplies inland. He also became Clark's eyes at the front, radioing the changing tactical situation back to the Fifth Army commander aboard the USS *Ancon*, until Clark could establish his own command post ashore on 12 September.

But otherwise, an unnatural calm seemed to prevail in the beach-head among abandoned farms, olive trees heavy with fruit, and brightly colored butterflies and grasshoppers. Between bombardments, high-spirited Italian soldiers, ragged and barely shod fugitives from the war, scuttled south down the railway line as they sang "Figli di nessuno" or "Bella ciao." Occasionally one would stop to accept a K-ration kit that had been pillaged for its Hershey bar, bestowing on the giver a *"Cient' anni!"* ("May you live a hundred years!") or a bless-ing from the Madonna of Pompei.[130] For those out of bayonet range of the Germans, the most egregious threat, according to Norman Lewis, member of a British security service detachment assigned to Fifth Army headquarters, came from "armed hillbillies . . . constantly jump-ing out from behind a hedge to point their rifles at us and scream a demand for an answer to a password that nobody had bothered to give us."[131]

On 12 September, Kesselring piloted his Ju52 to the battlefield to inform von Vietinghoff that time was running out. Unless the Salerno beachhead was overwhelmed soon, the inexorable Allied buildup and the crushing weight of naval gunnery and Allied air power, combined with the arrival of the Eighth Army, slowly plodding up the peninsula from Calabria, would fatally compromise the defense. He blessed his subordinate's plan to launch three divisions at the beleaguered Sixth Corps while the Hermann Göring Division and the Fifteenth Panzer Grenadiers, veterans of Sicily, with the Third Panzer Grenadier Divi-sion in reserve, would slash at McCreery's Tenth Corps.

The German offensive, launched on the afternoon of the thir-teenth, failed to dent the front of the 201st Guards Brigade, which lashed out at its attackers with a massive artillery bombardment. It was a different story on the American front, where panzer and panzer grenadiers regiments, all guns of the twenty-one tanks in the spear-head blazing, raced down the Sele River valley toward ill-sited U.S. positions. Rockets from Moaning Minnies—*Nebelwerfers*—thudded into the foliage, 88s screamed past. The smell of cordite mixed with that of excrement, a sign that stomach wounds were plentiful. Most of the Second Battalion of the 143d Infantry, stunned by the fury of the attack, surrendered, while the rest bolted for the rear. Two other battalions were virtually annihilated. Norman Lewis witnessed "a rabble of shocked and demoralized soldiery—officers separated from their men and men from their officers," wash down to the beach.[132] As night fell, platoons and battalions, illuminated by the alien incandescence of phosphorus flares, opened fire on one another. Little stood between the German attack and Fifth Army headquarters, which seemed to be in a complete funk. Men ran in all directions, many panicked into wearing gas masks. It looked as if the Fifth Army was about to relive the experience of Kasserine, this time in Italy, as troops fell back under the weight of the German armor. Clark, prowling the battlefield, threw in his last reserves—cooks, clerks, drivers, anyone who could tote a rifle. In desperation, he sent a personal order to Matthew Ridgway to drop his Eighty-second Airborne Division within Allied lines that night. But even this might be too late. Once the panzers reached the sea a mere five miles distant, they could turn south toward Paestum and roll up the Sixth Corps. Smelling success, von Vietinghoff informed Kesselring that the Fifth Army lay on the very verge of annihilation. Goebbels's propaganda machine cranked out predictions that the Fifth Army was about to reembark, while Lord Haw Haw taunted the Allied troops and wished them *bon voyage*.

Clark initiated plans to consolidate his faltering beachhead by withdrawing the Sixth Corps by sea. His scheme was to reinsert the evacuees on the Tenth Corps sector. But his subordinates, who had not been let into his secret, were livid when they heard the news of this tactical Dunkirk. "No one we spoke to believed this operation was feasible," Norman Lewis remembered of this confusion, "the feeling being that at the first signs of a withdrawal the Germans would simply roll forward and drive us into the sea." Rifles were distributed to headquarters staff who had not fired a weapon since basic training. "In the belief that our position had been infiltrated by German infantry they began to shoot each other, and there were blood-chilling screams from men hit by the bullets."[133] Shivers of apprehension went through AFHQ in Algiers as senior commanders realized that they faced, in Admiral Cunningham's words, "a reverse of the first magnitude—an Allied defeat which would have completely offset the Italian surrender, and have been hailed by the Germans as a smashing victory." Ike muttered platitudes about Stalingrad, admonished Clark to go down with his ship, and cursed the day he had not given command of Avalanche to Patton.[134] Brooke predicted doom, for which he blamed Eisenhower and Alexander, who "will never have sufficient vision to be big soldiers . . . It is maddening not to be able to get the Americans to realize that they are going to burn their fingers *before* they do so."[135] Frantic efforts were made to assemble more planes and ships at the beachhead.

At this point in the battle, two factors intervened to rescue the Allies. The first was that the German attack, which seemed unstoppable, in fact guided itself into a cul-de-sac formed by the confluence of the Sele and Calore Rivers. As the German commander contemplated the narrow peninsula between two rivers whose steep sides offered no recourse except withdrawal, naval artillery, Sherman tanks, tank destroyers, and 105 howitzers arranged wheel to wheel, their gunners stripped to the waist, poured more than 4,000 rounds into the stalled Germans. "The ford beside the bridge and the road leading to it simply went up in dust," Clark remembered. "The fields and the woods in which the enemy tanks took cover were pulverized."[136] Even though he was a mile and a half distant, Lewis found that "our uniforms fluttered in the eddies of the blast." The noise even drowned out the singing of the Italians who continued to trudge down the railway line.[137] Unable to go forward, pounded mercilessly by the American artillery, the Germans had no alternative but to retreat. The momentum of their attack was broken. The Americans had bought time, but Clark was not yet off the hook.

The second factor kicked in when the Germans renewed their attack on 14 September. By then, the hard-pressed Thirty-sixth Division had been reinforced by a night drop of 1,300 tough U.S. paratroops of the 504th Parachute Infantry Regiment. "And just at dawn the naval batteries began to take out city blocks of landscape," recorded Bruce Cutler.[138] Amid the shredded trees and oily gray smoke that swathed the Bay of Salerno, the Americans had recovered their poise. By the night of 14–15 September, as the Germans dug in on their advanced positions, 2,200 more paratroops floated down into the beachhead. German commanders began to complain that naval gunfire and Allied air strikes were taking an unacceptable toll on their exhausted troops. The Sixteenth Panzer Division had ceased to be an effective force. The British Seventh Armoured Division as well as more regiments of the Forty-fifth Division landed on the beaches. Von Vietinghoff asked for, and was accorded, permission for a climactic offensive on 16 September, this time directed at the Tenth Corps. It went nowhere. The Twenty-sixth Panzer Division was decimated by artillery fire and then counterattacked by the Royal Scots Greys. On the next day, German troops began to filter north, demolishing bridges, canals, and culverts, and sowing mines and booby traps in their wake. On 1 October, Clark rode in triumph into Naples.

MONTY TO THE RESCUE

Even though he felt that Hitler's meddling in Italian affairs had forfeited a potentially "decisive victory,"[139] Kesselring had reason to be satisfied with the result of Salerno. From the German viewpoint, the Allied invasion of Italy had spared the strategically more important Balkans and committed Allied armies to an area far easier to defend. The German commander had taken advantage of a poor Allied net assessment and incautious strategic assumptions, beginning with a presumption of Italian assistance. By foresight and rapid decision, Kesselring had preempted Italian treachery, in the process creating an Italian strategy for Hitler who, until then, had none.[140] As Kesselring had calculated, the limitations of Allied air power and amphibious lift had resulted in a dispersed invasion. It had attacked no center of gravity that might, at a stroke, alter dramatically the situation on the peninsula. The fragmented and tentative nature of the invasion with slender resources telegraphed a lack of resolution that allowed Kesselring to prevail in his argument with Rommel over how Italy was to be defended. "Had Clark been provided with two full corps, strong in armor, able to burst out of the ring of hills and in the process smash the game but skeletal German divisions, Kesselring and his strategic arguments would have been discredited and the campaign in Italy have taken a completely different course," conclude two historians of the Italian campaign.[141] But that was not going to happen on Marshall's watch.

The "Italophile" Kesselring had proved to Hitler's satisfaction that chaotic Italian geography, combined with the fighting powers of German soldiers, favored the defense and neutralized Allied "brute force." As a reward, Rommel's Army Group B was disbanded and all German troops in Italy were placed under Kesselring's command. Although the Fifth Army escaped disaster at Salerno, Kesselring had inflicted 8,659 casualties and taken 3,000 Allied POWs, while absorbing 3,472 casualties, despite the fact that he had taken the offensive against overwhelming Allied firepower. The panic induced in the Thirty-sixth Division during the attack of 13 September by what turned out to be no more than four reinforced German battle groups (battalions) caused Kesselring to conclude that the Americans in particular were soft, easily demoralized, and shy of close combat. He discerned that beneath a veneer of impressive firepower and amphibious capability, Anglo-American forces were hardly more than collections of militias that would be no match for his Wehrmacht.

Had he but known it, Kesselring's stout defense at Salerno had reopened that breach of suspicion within the Anglo-American camp over the relative fighting abilities of the two armies that Sicily had begun to close. By selecting the unblooded, understrength Fifth Army and its inexperienced commander Mark Clark to lead the invasion, Eisenhower simply confirmed the suspicions of many British that the U.S. Army had scarcely progressed since Kasserine. On the other hand, discipline and morale in the British army were revealed to be shaky when 700 British replacements, most of them veteran troops, landed on the beach at Salerno on 16 September in the midst of von Vietinghoff's final push against the beachhead, but refused to report to the front.[142] On the strategic level, Salerno had bought the Germans time to establish formidable defensive positions on the Gustav line north of Naples. Salerno dispelled early Allied illusions that the conquest of Italy would be a cakewalk.

Kesselring's elation was matched by a sense of foreboding that gripped the Allied camp. The Allied command, though victorious, had been revealed as a collection of insecure, distrustful, sometimes disputatious generals. Eisenhower was taken to task by Marshall, somewhat unfairly, for poor planning.[143] Alexander's aloof command style came to be seen as an indication of casual indifference rather than as a hitherto courteous display of *noblesse oblige*. He had approved a plan of attack that had obvious flaws. The Fifteenth Army Group commander had proven able neither to muster more resources for the beachhead nor to lash Montgomery forward to rescue the beleaguered Fifth Army. Alexander's patrician detachment sealed Brooke's opinion that Montgomery, rather than Alexander, should lead Overlord. Montgomery, who never believed in the Italian invasion in the first place and who felt personally slighted that his glorious Eighth Army had been relegated to a secondary role in the campaign, truculently slowed his pace before negligible German resistance as Allied soldiers were dying at Salerno. As a consequence, the Eighth Army press corps arrived at Salerno ahead of the main body of British troops to inform Alexander than nothing stood in the way of a more rapid advance by Monty. None of this, however, squelched the myth that the Eighth Army had saved the Fifth from extinction. Montgomery's patronizing attitude toward Clark, Alexander's orders that the press office play up the arrival of the Eighth Army, the widely distributed picture of Monty leaning down from his tank to shake hands with the "rescued" American commander, only added to Clark's paranoid belief that the British were intent on humiliating the Americans and stealing his thunder.

Clark's debut as a field commander drew mixed reviews. His energetic battlefield tours to bolster morale reaffirmed his reputation for personal courage. However, his unsteady behavior when the chips were down undermined the confidence of his superiors in his abilities. Poor staff work, his tendency to preempt the tasks of his division commanders, whom he treated with imperious disdain, and his unwillingness to listen to their ideas brought relations with them to the point of breakdown. Lyman Lemnitzer, Alexander's U.S. deputy, believed that Clark should be relieved.[144] Instead, Clark preempted his dismissal by reducing the unfortunate Sixth Corps commander Major General Ernest J. Dawley to the rank of colonel and packing him home after the two argued violently over Clark's conduct of operations. He publicly called McCreery a "feather duster," an accusation supported by what Clark saw as McCreery's timid advance toward Naples and the

Gustav line to the north.[145] Clark fell into the mindset of a World War I commander, refusing to analyze the battle for tactical and operational lessons, and instead blaming setbacks on inadequate resources, shortcomings of subordinates, and lack of courage in his troops. Problems with combat performance at Salerno simply reinforced Clark's natural inclination to hound incompetents and drive his men forward no matter the casualties until his force became battleworthy. Above all, Salerno made Clark cautious—operationally conservative, risk-averse, distrustful of his British ally, and overly concerned with his own reputation.[146]

CHAPTER ELEVEN

The Incomplete Victory

B Y OCTOBER, Italy, which barely a month earlier had beckoned Anglo-American forces with bright promises of facile strategic dividends, offered somber confirmation of Clausewitz's dictum that the defense offers the stronger form of warfare. At Salerno, Kesselring confirmed a strategy for Italy, even if it was only one of delayed defeat. He also won the unified command for which he had battled for so long. The defection of Badoglio and the king to the Allies was a godsend, for it allowed the Germans willy-nilly to requisition food and labor in Italy without the requirement for tedious negotiations with an unpopular government. "Our hands were no longer tied," the German commander recalled, "and the fortification-in-depth program in the rear of the Gustav Line, with Monte Cassino as its central point, as well as the construction work ordered by Rommel, was now adapted to my needs."[1]

Conversely, Eisenhower's strategy, based on wishful thinking and best-case scenarios, had drawn the Allies into a campaign without clear strategic objectives beyond a vague desire to capture Rome and tie down German divisions. But with Overlord looming and Italy out of the war, Rome became a "nice to have" but hardly critical objective—the war would be decided on other fronts. Furthermore, the requirement to tie down German divisions, while laudable in itself, required the Allies to carry out offensive operations in terrain that goats would find difficult to negotiate. Psychologically unable to adjust to the reality that they had cast themselves into an open-ended campaign with nebulous goals, and despite intelligence warnings to the contrary, Allied planners continued to bask in the complacent illusions of summer that the Germans were withdrawing up the peninsula by phases and that Berlin was on the verge of implosion.[2]

The truth was somewhat different. The Germans reinforced to between twenty and twenty-five divisions, led by some of the toughest and most experienced commanders in the Wehrmacht. The Allies had already made the acquaintance at Salerno of the commander of the German Tenth Army, now occupying the Gustav line,[3] General Heinrich von Vietinghoff, who had earned his spurs on the Eastern Front as an understudy of the formidable panzer commander Heinz Guderian. Colonel General Eberhard von Mackensen led the Fourteenth Army, which would duel the Allies at Anzio.[4] The aristocratic son of a World War I field marshal, von Mackensen represented the epitome of the Wilhelmine military elite. A member of the socially exclusive pre–World War I Death's Head Hussars, whose officers were elected to membership, von Mackensen manifested a minimum of deference toward his superior, the bourgeois Bavarian Kesselring, who returned von Mackensen's contempt with interest.

The Fourteenth Panzer Corps was led by General der Panzertruppen Hans Hube, another alumnus of the Russian front, who was replaced in November 1943 by Lieutenant General Frido von Senger und Etterlin. A descendent of senior civil servants and the Baden *haute bourgeoisie*, devout Catholic, whose flawless English had been perfected during his two-year passage just before World War I at St. John's College, Oxford, as a Rhodes scholar, the gaunt, ascetic von Senger had come reluctantly to a military career when the war and his family's impoverishment in its aftermath forced him to remain in the Reichwehr. Though a passionate anti-Communist, he was greatly troubled by Hitler's murderous ascension to power. But his undisguised contempt for Hitler did not harm his career. Guderian selected von Senger to be one of the pioneers of the new panzer arm in 1938. SS excesses against the Poles and the collapse of France, which he applauded as a professional soldier but which saddened him because it bolstered the Nazi regime, left him with a deep pessimism about Germany's future, one undiminished by command on the Eastern Front in 1942–43, where his Seventeenth Panzer Division participated in the unsuccessful attempt to relieve Paulus's Sixth Army at Stalingrad. Called to Sicily in July 1943 to evacuate the Fourteenth Panzer Division across the Strait of Messina, von Senger continued to earn Kesselring's admiration by safely withdrawing 40,000 German troops with their arms and equipment from Sardinia and Corsica in September 1943. Von Senger's corps would be given the critical job of holding the Rapido River and the Liri Valley against Allied attacks.

As Kesselring completed a formidable barrier across Italy to deny access to the north, seven Allied divisions, 170 bombers, and troop-carrying ships and amphibious craft, not to mention some of the more experienced Allied commanders, were spirited back to England to prepare for Overlord, in strict adherence to the decisions made at Quebec. Back-to-back conferences in late November and early December 1943 at Cairo and Teheran relegated Italy to the bottom of Allied European priorities, behind Overlord and Anvil, the invasion of southern France. The capture of Rome became an old-fashioned campaign of strategic diversion in an Allied strategy that focused on Northern Europe. Allied staffs subsequently met in Cairo to consume vast amounts of alcohol, cigars, and eggs (rationed in Britain) while they matched resources to priorities. At Teheran, Roosevelt designated Eisenhower to lead Overlord, with Tedder as his deputy. Several of the most experienced Allied commanders followed Ike and Tedder to England, including Patton, Bradley, Montgomery, Coningham, and Cunningham. Six-foot-seven-inch General Sir Henry Maitland "Jumbo" Wilson succeeded Eisenhower as commander in the Mediterranean.[5] The irony was that as the Mediterranean was culled of men and resources, pressure built to secure Rome, especially from Churchill, who complained to his commanders in December about the "scandalous" stalemate in Italy.[6] No one felt this pressure more keenly than did Mark Clark, who burned to seize Rome ahead of the British. Unfortunately for Clark, the operational resources devoted to the Mediterranean failed to equal his ambitions in Italy.

The advantages of terrain allied with what Churchill described as "shocking" weather to reduce the Anglo-American advance to a laborious slog in the autumn of 1943. Unlike North Africa and even Sicily, where there were lulls between battles, combat in Italy was continuous, casualty-heavy, and physically and psychologically exhausting. Months of training that had emphasized initiative, maneuver, and surprise attacks gave way before the reality that combat against Germans who occupied the high ground must be a deliberate, step-by-step exercise that began with meticulous planning, careful reconnaissance, anticipation of German countermoves, coordination with flank units, and provision for logistical needs.[7] Allied troops crawled along narrow roads and battled through a series of German strong points. Destroyed bridges, tenaciously defended villages and defiles, and abandoned towns seeded with diabolical booby traps and lethal Teller mines, to which antihandling devices were affixed, became a day at the office for Allied forces. The advance was reduced to a huge traffic jam behind sappers who, usually under fire, de-mined the roads and rebuilt or reinforced damaged bridges to carry tanks, petrol, and ammunition trucks forward to the next roadblock. The mountain range that bisects the Italian "boot" lengthwise invited each Allied army to advance up the narrow coastal plains to the east and west and made cooperation between the Allied Fifth and Eighth Armies problematic. Even were the Eighth Army, operating along the Adriatic, to crack the German defenses, the combination of mountains and mud, force multipliers for the defense, kept it from exploiting westward to capture Rome. This is precisely what happened to Montgomery on 3 October, as he landed a commando force by sea behind German lines at Termoli on the Adriatic, and then fought the Eighth Army through to rescue it. Casualties mounted as the Fifth and Eighth Armies battered through a series of defensive belts created by Kesselring, to which Allies and Germans gave various names like the Bernhard line and the Winter line. In London, British planners, who were acutely aware that their manpower reserves stood at full stretch, began to view mounting casualties with grave concern.

Shorn of numerical advantage, the terrain and weather strongly tilted in favor of the defense, the attackers came to rely increasingly on air power and artillery to punch forward. And while these massive demonstrations of firepower traveled under different names depending on the arm or service that delivered them, American soldiers conflated these technically distinct but single-purpose marketing tools into a single term—"stonk."[8] Unfortunately, the tormented terrain combined with dismal weather, which made it virtually impossible to see, much less calculate angles and ranges, reduced the "stonk" to an intimidating but nevertheless approximate science. "Stonks" did aid the Fifth Army's laborious advance in early December to Kesselring's main defensive line, called the Gustav line. But there it halted, before the town of Cassino, nestled on the north bank of the aptly named Rapido River at the foot of Monte Cassino.

The Allies faced a seamless and near-impregnable string of fortifications that ran from the mouth of the Garigliano on the Tyrrhenian Sea, along the jagged ridges and peaks of the Aurunci Mountains, which followed the Garigliano, to the confluence of the Gari (an extension of the Rapido) and Liri Rivers about a mile and a half south of Cassino town. Route 6 wound southwest through the town of Cassino, round the foot of Monte Cassino (called Monastery Hill by the British), crowned by the majestic medieval mother abbey of the Benedictine order, before it turned in a northwesterly direction toward Rome. Unfortunately, to exploit this most practical route toward the Italian capital, the Allies would have to cross the Rapido and charge up the funnel of the Liri Valley. To do so would expose their flanks to the Aurunci Mountains to the south and, to the north, to Monte Cassino, a shoulder of rock that stretched southeast from the 5,000-foot pinnacle of Monte Cairo. Recognizing that Monte Cassino and the Liri Valley offered the most obvious passage to Rome, Kesselring took care to concentrate his strongest defenses there. To the northeast, the Gustav line curved through a series of spurs and ridges dominated by Monte San Croce and Monte Belvedere before it joined the Sangro River as it dropped out of the mountains to the Adriatic. This tortured landscape became home to 60,000 German defenders ensconced deeply behind ridges and on reverse slopes. They remained difficult to spot, much less "stonk." Ridge lines that appeared from a distance to offer smooth routes of advance were, in fact, shattered into irregular knolls and outcroppings transformed by the defenders into bunkers reinforced with concrete and railway tracks and ties, protected by kilometers of barbed wire and mines. For this reason, Allied attacks launched in the wake of truly awe-inspiring "stonks" were met by the fire of mobile artillery batteries alternating among narrow valleys on the rear slopes, guided to their targets by forward observers sited on mountain crests. In the end, the Allied forces had no option but to send infantry up slopes fit only for goats to shove the Germans out of their positions *mano a mano*.

The Allied force ranged before the Gustav line in January 1944, while formidable, did not outmatch the Germans in any significant way except in intelligence capabilities[9] and firepower.[10] The weaknesses of the German position in Italy were two: they could be outflanked by sea, while the massive extension of the front caused by the sheer size of the mountains meant that the Germans could not be strong everywhere. But neither of these weaknesses was immediately exploitable by the Allies. A combination of the repatriation of maritime assets after Husky and a dearth of adequate landing places along the Italian coast meant that landings like that at Anzio were too weak to pry Kesselring out of his positions. In fact, it was the attackers who rapidly became the besieged, as Kesselring was able to rush reinforcements to the beachhead by land faster than the Allies could build up by sea. Only gradually did the Allies understand that infiltration by light infantry supported by a mule-based logistical system through the highest, most remote, and consequently least heavily defended sectors of the German lines, rather than classic infantry-armored thrusts up narrow river valleys supported by massive air and artillery support, offered the way forward in Italy. But this required the expansion or creation of units specializing in mountain warfare, not easy to do in armies that had hitherto relied for success on more classic infantry-armor-artillery-air collaboration.

This adaptation proved especially difficult for the Eighth Army, where, on 1 January 1944, Lieutenant General Sir Oliver Leese succeeded Montgomery in command. A Coldstream Guards officer and decorated World War I veteran, Leese had been summoned by Montgomery from the Guards Armoured Division to take command of the Thirtieth Corps on the eve of El Alamein. Leese had gained a reputation as Monty's dependable "battering ram" at El Alamein, Mareth, and Wadi Akarit, "1st class . . . easily the best [corps commander] I have," Monty insisted.[11] Leese's job was to pulverize Axis fronts while the Thirteenth Corps under Brian Horrocks performed the more athletic flanking maneuvers.

At first sight, Leese's accession to leadership of the Eighth Army offered a welcome promise of command continuity. An archetypal graduate of Monty's Eighth Army, Leese applied in practically adulatory fashion the Montgomery ritual of massive artillery barrages on a narrow front as a prelude to a combined infantry-armor offensive. Leese's admiration for his former boss was such that he replicated Montgomery's command style down to the small mobile headquarters separate from the main HQ, eccentric dress, and Monty's habit of doling out cigarettes to British soldiers he encountered on the road. Harold Macmillian found Leese to be the very model of a modern major general, "a very nice fellow, a big, burly, efficient solid Guardsman," who conducted himself more like a politician running for office than a general. Dressed in shorts and an open-necked shirt, Leese waived cheerfully to the troops, like a squire touring his estate, as he steered his own jeep past tanks, trucks, and guns along the muddy roads of Italy. Indeed, the youthful Leese seemed the very antithesis of his Blimpish World War I predecessors.[12]

But others saw the new Eighth Army commander as a Monty understudy struggling to replicate his mentor's tired "playing to the prols" pantomime. This worked poorly in an army that was no longer a collection of irreverent colonial exiles amused by Monty's tireless exhibitionism. Indeed, Lieutenant General Richard McCreery found that in Italy the Eighth Army had lost its desert pluck and become like "an old steeple-chaser, good for one more race if it were carefully handled."[13] The British national servicemen, earnest Poles, high-strung Greeks, Palestinian Jews, and straitlaced Canadians who peopled the Eighth Army in Italy appear to have found Leese's cheery eccentricity and Bohemian dress contrived, even disconcerting. Officers able to locate Leese, often after great difficulty, in his elusive, Monty-like tactical headquarters, might find a man dressed in plus fours, sheepskin jacket, and straw hat, carefully watering tulips. His most distinguished subordinates sometimes found it awkward to hold military conferences heavy with implications for men's lives with a commander soaking naked in a tub. The expression of quizzical bemusement permanently etched on Leese's face in fact hid a sensitive, taut personality who became difficult and irritable when under stress.

Nor was continuity with the Eighth Army's illustrious North African past necessarily the required component in 1944 Italy. Leese's inability to find his own voice, to develop his own vision for the Eighth Army, led to stagnation and a failure to adapt. The closed, mountainous terrain of Italy canalized routes of advance and restricted strategic options. Even after French North African troops demonstrated the possibilities of infiltration by light infantry, Leese never abandoned his overreliance on armored thrusts up the Liri Valley or along the narrow, river-sliced Adriatic Plain. Leese's inadequate road management meant that Eighth Army became entangled in traffic jams and was increasingly outdistanced in the advance by the Fifth Army. As the campaign progressed, Eighth Army operations became increasingly predictable, roadbound, stilted, and ponderous, which caused British general staff chief Alan Brooke to conclude that Leese "is certainly not anything outstanding as a commander."[14] Nor did Leese have a brilliant chief of staff like Montgomery's Freddy de Guingand, able to negotiate misunderstandings, smooth over gaps in operations, and counterbalance Monty's most obvious imperfections of character. Even Leese's admirers conceded that he was an able, straight-arrow soldier who lacked the political instincts for high command.[15]

The military obstacles posed by the Germans and by the Italian terrain obliged the Allies to construct a logistical base to support two armies. Until Avalanche, the problems of prolonged military campaigns in populated areas had not affected the Allies. Fighting in the Western Desert had taken place among a scattering of nomads. The Darlan deal had arrogated to the converted acolytes of Vichy France the continued administration of North Africa. Likewise, although the Allies created the Allied Military Government of Occupied Territories (AMGOT or AMG) to ensure that civilians did not impinge on the lines of communication, the transformation of Italy from enemy to "cobelligerent" at the stroke of a pen was expected to alleviate the most onerous tasks of military government. Husky had offered minimum indication of the complexities now faced by Allied armies campaigning in populated areas. The short duration of that campaign, the friendly population, and the fact that even Sicilian urbanites had friends and relatives on farms where summer vegetables were in generous supply, helped to mitigate the food problem.[16] AMGOT's main role in Sicily was confined to helping Italian mayors to redistribute captured German stores to the population and to get schools and other municipal services running in the wake of the advancing Allied armies.

Mark Clark expected an outpouring of delirium from Neapolitans grateful to be liberated. Instead, his jeep pushed past bombed-out buildings to enter "a city of ghosts." The occasional *carabiniere* stood sentinel over streets clogged with debris and charred vehicles, while the half-submerged hulks, smashed docks, and destroyed warehouses in the harbor made Pompeii appear by comparison like a turnkey community.[17] Only gradually did the Allies understand that they had invaded a country that required emergency life support. Macmillan found Naples stinking of raw sewage, "squalid and dirty . . . in terrible condition." Destruction caused by Allied bombing had been compounded by the depredations of the Germans, who had carried off most of the livestock in the south, planted booby traps everywhere,[18] and even sabotaged the main aqueduct, adding the torment of thirst to a city that already stood on the verge of starvation. At the best of times, Sicily and southern Italy could not feed itself. However, the Italian merchant marine had been destroyed trying to supply Axis troops in North Africa, and the Allies had little shipping or berthing capacity to spare for civilian commodities. As Allied plans had failed to factor in feeding the Italian population, no extra food stocks had been called forward from the United States. Once on the peninsula, "reckless and indiscriminate" Allied requisitioning absorbed transport and fuel, up to a third of the electricity generated, enough machine tools to force plants to close, and over a million tons of commodities, including soap and food stocks, normally destined for civilians. The arrival of U.S. soldiers willing to pay top dollar for scarce commodities and pay civilian labor with occupation script printed with reckless abandon, drove inflation through the roof. Farmers, who often trudged miles along roads clogged with military vehicles, carts, wagons, and bicycles to bring their crops to market, refused to sell their production for worthless lire[19] at government-pegged prices. Instead, they turned to the burgeoning black market. To compound the problems of Naples, the 1943 harvest had been disappointing, causing officials in grain-producing areas to hold back for local consumption supplies normally shipped to the city.

While Eisenhower acknowledged that the Allies had a responsibility to feed the Italian population, frontline commanders, their hands full with Kesselring, considered rear-area problems an unwarranted distraction. Allied commanders regarded AMGOT as "nothing but an unmitigated nuisance."[20] One must not ignore the successes of Allied Military Government, especially given the considerable handicaps under which it worked.[21] The AMGOT was understaffed, top-heavy with military police rather than transportation, public works, and government affairs specialists required to rebuild the Italian economy and political life, and otherwise composed largely of men considered too old for combat.[22] Indeed, AMGOT, according to the combat commands, stood for "Aged Military Gentlemen On Tour." AMGOT arrived in Naples behind a vanguard of "interpreters" recruited in Sicily, men who had spent a few years in Brooklyn or Cicero and who, too often, exploited their positions for personal gain.[23] AMGOT was put into the surreal position of enforcing a rationing system inherited from Mussolini for products available only on the black market in any case.[24] "When the Germans were here, we ate once a day," a suspect brought before an Allied tribunal for stealing military clothing shouted at the judge. "Now that the Americans have come, we eat once a week."[25] By November 1943, Patton predicted that "riots and bloodshed" would erupt on Sicily unless grain was imported to feed the population, while Harold Macmillan noted in his diary that food shortages had made Naples "restless."[26] In the autumn of 1944, following the capture of Rome, Mark Clark expressed similar fears that indifferent administration of the rear areas might compromise the progress of the military campaign.[27]

Even by Italian standards, Naples had always been considered in a class by itself—"the only Oriental city," the Italian journalist Scarfoglio wrote, "without a residential European quarter."[28] But the Allied invasion combined with the collapse of fascism added a layer of creative desperation to the city's normally calibrated histrionics. The reason was hunger. Food became the city's daily obsession. The competition to eat transformed Naples into an odeum where no performance was too immoderate, no act of self-abasement too abject, no crime too brazen, so long as the payoff came in calories. To enter Naples in 1943, Bruce Cutler recorded, was to fall "five hundred years downward in time—back to Boccaccio, the plague raging, a Court of Funereal Miracles about to form." Cutler described an outmatched black GI armed with a cracking bullwhip unsuccessfully defend a food dump against a surge of famished Neapolitans. To dine at an outdoor restaurant or cafe was to attend a medieval spectacle of blind, maimed, or otherwise debilitated human forms propped up on makeshift conveyances bumping between tables, hunchbacks offering a lucky touch of the hump to purchasers of lottery tickets, or dwarfs hawking cut-price coffins. Street urchins, the ubiquitous Neapolitan *scugnizzi*, camouflaged in clothes fashioned from GI blankets, "moved like ragged afterthoughts among us" to snatch unfinished meals off tables, when they were not swarming the tailgates of army trucks to relieve them of their cargo.[29] "Nothing has been too large or too small—from telegraph poles to phials of penicillin—to escape Neapolitan kleptomania," recorded British counterintelligence officer Norman Lewis. Statues disappeared from public parks, tombstones from cemeteries, even manhole covers were found to have value, so that suddenly a drive down the street became a life-threatening experience. One orchestra returned to the stage to perform the second half of a concert only to discover that their instruments had been lifted during the intermission. Telephone wire was a favorite target of thieves: it was ripped down by the kilometer for its copper content, an act that severely disrupted military communications. When hauled before Allied courts, the miscreant's plea was invariably "innocent" based on the claim that the wire was German (which was true, but the Allies communicated on it nonetheless). Allied military engineers had performed such prodigies in reconstructing the destroyed harbor that by March 1944 Macmillan could boast that Naples had a higher volume of maritime traffic than New York.[30] However, the principal benefit went to the Camorra, the Neapolitan underworld, rather than to the Allied war effort. Lewis recorded that the contents of one ship in three that arrived in Naples harbor were pilfered, although he probably underestimated by about half.[31] German air raids provided the distraction required by well-organized criminal bands to sweep docks and warehouses.

While the Americans complained that the British treated Italians like "Indian colonials,"[32] Lewis joined a chorus of critics who claimed that thievery of epic proportions was facilitated by Italian-American officers in the AMGOT and in U.S. counterintelligence in cahoots with Lucky Luciano and the Genovese crime family.[33] The resurgence of criminal activity in southern Italy undoubtedly benefited from a degree of encouragement by misguided U.S. efforts to employ the Mafia to build support and acquire intelligence. However, the collapse of the Fascist administration and invasion-induced chaos created a vacuum that organized crime simply rushed to fill, no doubt with the help of some corrupt or venal officers. The economy of post-liberation Naples was driven by the black market. Makeshift stalls throughout the city brazenly displayed stolen military articles beneath signs such as "If you don't see the overseas article you're looking for, just ask us and we'll get it!" Catalogs of articles available for order read like the inventory of a National Rifle Association gun show, and included even machine guns and light tanks. Even the papal legate, whose car was detained at a roadblock, was discovered to be riding on stolen tires. Outside Naples, armed bands, many made up of army deserters (Moroccan *goumiers* prominent among them), joined with local bandits to vie for the privilege of pillaging Allied supply trains.[34] Many of these problems would recur in northern Italy following the Allied seizure of Rome in June 1944.

A favorite target for thieves was penicillin, to the point that military hospitals faced shortages. This was a dire situation because the rate of venereal disease among Allied troops soared to "alarming altitudes"[35] as an estimated 42,000 Neapolitan women, faced with shortages and inflation, turned for survival to prostitution. Hardly had the Battle of Salerno finished than Norman Lewis discovered in the municipal hall of a small town south of Naples a row of women with "the ordinary well-washed respectable shopping and gossiping faces of working-class housewives," offering to copulate with GIs for a tin of C-rations. Many of the women were married to Italian soldiers who had failed to return from distant theaters or who had been interned by the Germans. Others hoped to snag a British or American soldier as a husband. "I didn't ask to live like this," they told military interrogators dispatched to check on their suitability for marriage. "Give me the chance to get away from it and I'll be as good a wife as anybody else." While most of these women were working-class, even Neapolitan aristocrats strapped for cash were not above offering their sexual services. Lewis was astonished when a prince with a large estate in the south appeared in his office with his twenty-four-year-old sister, whom he wished to place in a British army brothel. When Lewis explained that the British army did not have brothels, he turned to his sister and said in flawless English: "Ah well Luisa, I suppose if it can't be, it can't be." By the spring of 1944, "as many hospital beds in the Naples area are occupied by sufferers from the pox as from wounds and all the other sicknesses put together," Lewis recorded.[36] Each month 3,500 new cases kept beds fully occupied in the nineteen military VD hospitals set up in Italy by the summer of 1944.[37]

Allied authorities placed licensed brothels off limits. But this restriction merely prevented them from controlling the sex trade, as no law allowed them to detain the shoals of freelance prostitutes that surged onto the streets. Attempts to discourage soldiers from frequenting prostitutes bordered on the ridiculous. Leaflets were distributed to soldiers to be handed to Italians who approached them that read, "I'm not interested in your syphilitic sister," a gratuitous insult calculated to produce casualties. "Remarks about sisters are strictly taboo to southern Italians," Lewis wrote.[38] Barely three months into the Allied occupation of Naples, a British medical officer told Harold Macmillan that uninfected women were now a rarity.[39] Following the logic of this pronouncement, MPs began at random to snatch gaggles of women off the streets, many while standing in food queues, for an involuntary trip to the hospital for a medical examination. "Panties down girlies, the Americani want to look at what you've got," the orderlies would shout as they pushed the protesting women into chairs, raised their skirts, spread their legs, and locked their feet into stirrups for examination by a diminutive Italian doctor. "Not even the Germans picked up housewives for a thing like this," Cutler believed.[40] But this amounted to no more than a temporary humiliation that did nothing to stanch the VD epidemic.

The appalling situation in Allied-occupied southern Italy had several causes: poor planning, the ineptitude, inefficiency, and small size of the AMGOT, the resilience and adaptability of the Neapolitans, Churchill's desire to punish the Italians, and, finally, British fears that an Italian economic recovery would lead to economic competition.[41] Although Joseph Heller claimed that his novel *Catch-22* was really about the Cold War or even Vietnam, or perhaps not even a war novel at all,[42] it captures well the atmosphere of wartime Italy produced by the amoral neutrality that reigned behind the front and the relative stalemate of the military campaign. Rather than the ever-shifting fronts that characterized World War II combat elsewhere, the Italian theater recalled the static and futile infantry battles of World War I. Soldiers might easily conclude, as did Heller's character Yossarian, that they were pawns hurled into bloody assaults to seize strategically meaningless objectives to assuage the egos of generals irritated that they had been left to languish in a dead-end Mediterranean theater.[43] Impasse in the military campaign was matched by the arrogant ineptitude of AMGOT policies that, in the quest to cleanse Italy of its fascist past, instead succeeded in transforming a European nation into something that resembled a failed African colony. The absurd futility of a military campaign that seemed to go nowhere combined with manufactured anarchy in the rear to create a perfect Catch-22 situation in Italy. It seemed logical to conclude, as did Yossarian, that soldiers and civilians alike were victims of a bullying and manipulative bureaucracy that urged an energetic idealism on people whom they could not deceive. Wartime Italy turned everyone into Neapolitans, whatever their nationality. The heroism of fighters became a commodity as devalued and expendable as the sexual favors of Italian women. Too weak to overthrow their oppressors, everyone fought back as best they could against a system incapable of self-criticism and convinced of its moral rectitude, in the process turning themselves into misfits, outcasts, and antiheros. Yossarian's defiance mirrors on the military side the anarchic individualism, the absence of ideals, the sense of Falstaffian irresponsibility of the Neapolitans. The only important objective, however, was survival. And to achieve this, the individual must withdraw his cooperation.[44]

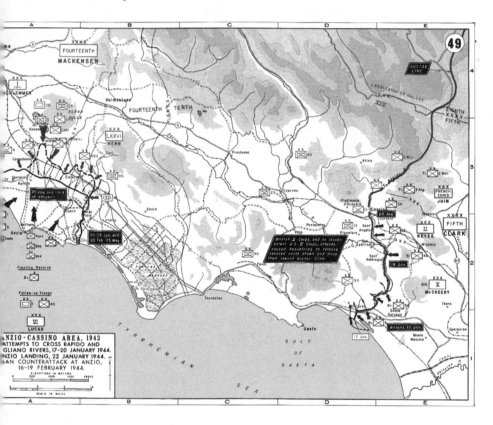

"HURL A WILDCAT ONTO THE SHORE": CASSINO AND ANZIO
Monte Cassino would become synonymous with the futility of the Italian campaign. Battles raged at the foot of that mountain from December 1943 until the final breakthrough toward Rome in May–June 1944. Clark's plan in January 1944 called for a progressive assault on the Gustav line beginning on the seaward side of the Allied line running along the Garigliano by McCreery's Tenth Corps, made up of the British Fifth, Forty-sixth, and Fifty-sixth Divisions. This, he hoped,

would draw off von Senger's panzers so that General Fred Walker's Thirty-sixth Division could vault the Rapido to break into the German lines. This would open the way for Ernest Harmon's First Armored Division to move through the Texans and charge up Route 6, which led north through the Liri Valley toward Rome. The Thirty-fourth Division would cross the Rapido and attack the abbey and the town from the north. A two-division attack by Algerian and Moroccan soldiers of the French Expeditionary Corps (CEF) under the command of General Alphonse Juin on the Belvedere almost four miles to the north of Cassino would complete the outflanking movement on German positions at the mouth of the Liri Valley. Clark's theory of victory was that Monte Cassino, too difficult to storm head on, would be abandoned when outflanked in the Liri Valley to the south and in the mountains to the north. Walker's breakthrough across the Rapido would combine with a two-division amphibious assault by Major General John P. Lucas's U.S. Sixth Corps at Anzio, thirty-five miles south of Rome, to lever Kesselring out of the Gustav line. Kesselring gave his assurance to the Vatican on 11 December 1943 that the famous abbey would not be occupied by his soldiers. The magnificent library and many works of art were evacuated to Rome.

There were several things wrong with this plan. In the first place, it bore the defect of most U.S. efforts in that it was prepared by staffs and approved by a barely experienced general, with minimal feedback from the commanders expected to carry out the operation. Few of Clark's subordinates believed in it, and this included Walker, whose Thirty-sixth Infantry Division was assigned the main assault into the teeth of strong German defenses at the mouth of the Liri Valley. Even at the best of times, the task of an opposed crossing of a swift-flowing river in full winter flood in the teeth of the Fifteenth Panzer Grenadier Division, with which the Americans had become acquainted in Sicily and which now held the well-fortified high ground at Monte Cassino, exceeded the capabilities of a single division. It certainly exceeded the capabilities of the Thirty-sixth. Built around a core of Texas National Guardsmen, the Thirty-sixth had failed to find its equilibrium since it crossed the beaches at Salerno. Its reputation as a hard-luck unit had abraded the morale of soldiers who had been badly beaten up in the December approach battles before the Gustav line and who were short of trained replacements. Because the Germans had opened the sluices and turned the banks of the Rapido on the U.S. side to a marshy soup, the First Armored Division, whose job was to exploit the breach made by the Thirty-sixth, would more likely be swallowed up by this sump. Walker tried without success to persuade Clark to move the attack two miles farther up the Rapido to a more fordable, less bog-ridden sector.[45] In short, Cassino was shaping up to be a repeat of the 1917 Battle of Passchendaele in the mountains.[46] The planners seemed to be oblivious to the strength of the German positions anchored by the imposing mass of Monte Cassino, which ascended precipitously out of the Liri Valley to dominate the battlefield. Thirty-sixth Division troops would carry out their maneuvers in full view of the German troops dug in on the steep slopes. And any armored thrust up the Liri would be outflanked and vulnerable to counterattack. Nor had planners considered what to do if poor weather reduced the effectiveness of Allied air superiority.

General Alphonse Juin, commander of the French Expeditionary Corps (CEF), immediately put his finger on the weaknesses of Clark's plan. The World War I veteran recognized that an offensive force needed clear numerical superiority to succeed. Clark's plan required ten more divisions than he had to execute with any hope of success. Nor had Clark made an effort to coordinate his advance with that of the Eighth Army.[47] The Fifth Army plan of attack came down to a series of inchoate and poorly supported local operations backed by inadequate reserves. Operationally, Juin, an expert in North African mountain warfare, recognized that Allied forces were overly armored and too roadbound. In preparation for his attack, Juin's CEF left their U.S.-supplied Dodges, GMCs, tow trucks, and trailers groaning with radios and heavy weapons like antitank guns, mortars, and machine guns at the foot of the mountains. The mule, not the jeep, was the monarch of mobility in Italy. The tactical situation tilted heavily in favor of the enemy, who was virtually invisible to the attackers, had good observation, and was backed by heavy mortars and artillery. Attacks, especially successful attacks, could not be sustained unless they could be supplied. For this reason, every available mule had to be used to carry munitions. Victory in Italy would be an affair of mountain troops able to infiltrate and overwhelm remote and lightly held enemy positions, supported by a flexible, responsive, four-legged logistical system to shuttle supplies to the most remote ridges and mountain peaks.[48]

As the siege of the Gustav line stretched toward the summer of 1944, Clark came to realize that he had a potential battle winner in the French Expeditionary Corps. But in January 1943, the French occupied the basement of the Allied pecking order, their presence in the battle line considered an act of charity by the Anglo-Americans. A two-division vanguard of the CEF disembarked at Naples in the waning weeks of 1943. Lean, bronzed Algerians and Berbers recruited in the Atlas Mountains of Morocco, their American-supplied uniforms camouflaged under striped North African burnooses, moved toward the front along muddy roads, through swarms of begging children and women reduced to prostitution by Allied failure to include the civilian population in their logistical calculations.

At first sight, the division of Moroccans, the other of Algerians, under Juin's command, hardly inspired confidence among Allied generals raised in the traditions of armored warfare and mesmerized by German blitzkrieg methods. The French disembarked with the baggage of contempt that had been bestowed upon them by the Allies in North Africa. Undergunned, armed with World War I vintage bolt action Springfield and Enfield rifles, their divisional structure a quaint amalgamation of traditional regiments with North African *tabors* (brigades) and *goums* (battalions) of Moslem irregulars, the CEF appeared in Allied eyes a study in anachronism. The seeming docility of the North Africans barely masked an ardent love of hard steel, and a capacity for ferocity, even cruelty, born of a fundamental contempt for human life. "Goons" (G.I. shorthand for *goumiers*) struck GIs as remarkably careless soldiers, perpetually wandering into minefields and roasting goats in full view of German lines, which invariably brought down a hail of artillery fire. Clothed in a tatterdemalion of French, British, and American hand-me-downs, invariably topped off by a burnoose, these pigtailed troops struck GIs as "savages," "mercenary degenerates" as much to be feared by their own side, and by the Italian population, as by the enemy. The contrast between these Moslem fighters, who made up about half of the CEF, and the aloof, musta-chioed French officers who led them could hardly have been more striking. Many of these officers, who seemed to have stepped directly out of Belle Époque Paris, carried canes and walking sticks in place of weapons on the theory that their task was to lead the combat, not participate in it. Anglo-Americans tended to regard the French practice of sitting down to long midday meals as effete, and bestowed the same racially motivated disdain on French North African troops as they reserved for colored forces in their own armies.[49]

As the Allies had no frame of reference that would allow them to judge the capabilities of the CEF, so they were equally unsure how to evaluate its leader, Alphonse Juin. That Juin's greatest success should come in command of a French expeditionary force composed primarily of North Africans followed naturally from his own *pied noir* origins and his extensive service with Moslem troops. Son of a French gendarme serving in Algeria and a Corsican mother, Juin had graduated top of his class from the French military academy Saint-Cyr in 1911. His signature was his left-handed salute, permitted after his right arm was badly wounded in the Great War. Juin lacked the theatrical elegance of his rival Jean de Lattre de Tassigny or the austere brilliance of his Saint-Cyr classmate Charles de Gaulle. His bearing was collected, reserved, understated. With his beret pulled down to his ears, the inevitable cigarette dangling beneath a full mustache, a contorted smile that displayed a mouthful of crooked teeth, and a thick *pied noir* accent, Juin might easily have been mistaken for a Mediterranean peasant who had wandered onto the battlefield, were it not for his insignia of rank. But those inclined to underestimate him soon discovered a man who succeeded through personal bravery, an intuition for the right answer, and more than a touch of cunning. In 1940, Juin was found in command of a motorized division. Captured by the Germans, he had been released to organize the rump of French forces left in North Africa. He broke out of the pack of discredited Vichy generals in November 1942 when he shouted down those who wanted to resist the Anglo-Americans and almost single-handedly imposed a cease-fire on a factious and confused French high command. This caused Juin to be seen as one of the few generals upon whom the Allies could rely for judgments uncluttered by the usual baggage of internecine French discord. Juin helped to build the foundation of later French success by acting as a calming influence on the French army after the Allied landings in North Africa.[50] In 1944, de Gaulle named Juin chief of staff in part because he was the only general acceptable to both the Gaullist and Vichy factions of France's riven army.[51]

Allied appreciation of Juin's political astuteness was quickly matched by his obvious skill on the battlefield. In February 1943 he restored order to a crumbling front in Tunisia, and helped to calm the nerves of green American commanders rattled by the drubbing they had received at Kasserine. Tunisia enabled Juin to showcase the quality of French cadres and staffs, and the obvious strengths of their Moslem soldiers, who, despite being poorly armed, displayed a tough resilience utterly lacking in barely blooded British First Army and American Second Corps troops. His reconciliation with de Gaulle, who required the support of a general of Juin's stature, assured his position in the newly aggregated French forces. Juin's strengths resided in his understanding of the capacities and limitations of the mainly illiterate North African troops who formed the backbone of his command, and his reliance on a carefully prepared plan that combined simplicity with a robustness that could withstand setbacks. Juin's experience of mountain combat as a veteran of the Rif War of 1924–25 would prove invaluable, and ultimately decisive, in shattering the Gustav line. Aficionados of de Lattre, the French general with whom Juin is most often compared, found Juin workmanlike rather than brilliant, methodical rather than inspired. But spontaneity and opportunism were seldom rewarded in Italy, where rugged terrain, the steel band of German defenses that had to be cracked head on, and the diminutive size and fragile composition of his force imposed tight operational constraints.

Shingle, as the Anzio operation was code-named, had its origins in the tough fighting between Salerno and the Gustav line in November and December. Eisenhower's growing realization that the Germans intended to fight south of Rome, combined with Churchill's hectoring insistence that Alexander accelerate the Italian advance before much of his sea lift was repatriated for Overlord, had the Allies searching for an amphibious shortcut. Clark, impressed and not a little envious of

Troops bound for Salerno cheer news of Italy's surrender.

ABOVE LEFT: An American spitfire in the surf at Salerno, September 1943
OVE RIGHT: Badoligo and Eisenhower sign the "Long Surrender" on 29 September 1943. In the background are Lord Gort, Air Chief Marshal Tedder, Lt. Gen. Sir Noel Mason-MacFarlane, and General Alexander.

ABOVE: Retreating German troops in Italy were able to delay pursuit with demolitions, mines, booby traps, and ambushes.
BELOW: LSTs load supplies in Naples for Anzio.

German POWs file toward the beach at Anzio.

General Lucian Truscott

ABOVE: Monte Cassino smolders after 1,200 tons of bombs and 195,000 artillery shells were fired at it on 15 March 1944.
BELOW: French North African troops at Monte Cassino

OVE LEFT: Generals Oliver Leese, Harold Alexander, and Mark Clark; ABOVE RIGHT: U.S. B-24 "Liberators" pound Ploesti oil field in Rumania, the source of 60 percent of Axis oil.

The Fifth Army enters Rome in June 1944.

ABOVE: "Marshal" Tito and Churchill meet in Naples, August 1944.
BELOW LEFT: Chetniks; BELOW RIGHT: General Draja Mikhailovitch, Chetnik leader

ABOVE: French General Philippe Leclerc de Hautecloque; BELOW: French partisans

ABOVE: Anvil meets Overlord in Saulieu, France, on 11 September 1944.
BELOW: General Frido von Senger surrenders to Mark Clark.

could virtually match the number of Allied invaders at Anzio within three days.[60]

This pessimistic prognosis hardly improved the morale of a man who, by his own admission, was temperamentally unsuited to combat command. A graduate of the West Point class of 1911, Lucas, aged fifty-four, had probably envisaged finishing out his career as a peacetime colonel, perfectly content to shuffle papers in a backroom bureau. Instead, Marshall recognized Lucas as a man of "military stature, prestige and experience." And, indeed, with close-cropped hair, mustache, rather large ears, and the habit of leaning toward his interlocutor and fixing him with his large, intense eyes, Lucas seemed to be a man habituated to command. He trained the Third Infantry Division in the United States, which under the able Lucian Truscott came to be regarded as one of the best U.S. infantry divisions in Italy. Bradley declared Lucas "first rate," which was probably why he was dispatched to North Africa and Sicily to act as Ike's "eyes and ears."[61] Lucas's debut in Italy had been a promising one, earning him Alexander's praise as "the best American corps commander." He knew how to combine units to achieve balance, husband a reserve, and keep his logistics shipshape.[62] But Lucas recognized his limitations, which were considerable. He was a fundamentally shy man, "too tender hearted ever to be a success in my profession," he confessed to a friend. He felt most comfortable when the operational parameters were strictly defined for him. In that way, he was liberated from the need to take strategic initiatives, especially to give orders that sent men to their deaths. He reflected in full measure the suspicion of Patton and Clark that the British were eager to steal the thunder of the U.S. Army.[63] The British complained that Lucas's "unbounded admiration for the American soldier" made him "incurious" about his British ally, whose capabilities he tended to underestimate. By January 1944, Lucas had adopted a fatalistic, resigned, even tragic outlook. His hair and mustache had gone gray. Behind his wire-rimmed glasses, he looked small, withered, more like a tax accountant than the impresario of a bold plan to turn Kesselring's flank. Irish Guards whom Lucas inspected before the expedition set sail discovered "a pleasant, mild, elderly gentleman being helped out of layers of overcoats." The formalities quickly dispatched,

Lucas declared the Irish "mighty fine" and drove away, "leaving the British slightly puzzled."[64]

Clark later attributed what he called Lucas's subpar performance at Anzio to the fact that he was "ill—tired physically and mentally—from the long responsibilities of command in battle."[65] But Lucas seemed to sense that the more the Mediterranean sank toward secondary status, the more those in charge seemed determined to inflate Italy's prominence in the public mind by taking insane risks. The Mediterranean had been cherry-picked of its most illustrious commanders for Overlord. Alexander and Clark had obviously been passed over, their hopes for a conspicuous role in the soon-to-be-initiated Northern European theater temporarily dashed.[66] The damage went deeper than the top commanders, for, as they departed, they took with them most of their favorite support staff. Bradley, for instance, gutted Second Corps of its most experienced staff officers.[67] Shingle metabolized the same capricious optimism that had informed Allied planning in Italy from the outset. The plan called for the British First and the U.S. Third Divisions supported by tanks, parachute infantry, and U.S. Army Rangers to land on 22 January, only days after the initiation of the attack at Cassino. Although Churchill chortled that Shingle would "hurl a wild cat on to the shore," in private Allied commanders conceded that the invasion force was too small, but they lacked the sea lift to support a larger force.[68] When Lucas, after doing his sums, protested that the ships designated for Shingle could transport less than a third of required supplies, he was told by Admiral Cunningham not to worry, as the Germans would be north of Rome by the time he hit the beach. Alexander predicted that the anticipated collapse of the Gustav line and the subsequent German retreat would make Overlord unnecessary.[69] Only Patton demonstrated his flair for the summary *mot juste*, predicting that his friend Lucas would never "get out of this alive."[70]

The Allies launched the January attack on Cassino with high hopes. McCreery's Tenth Corps kicked off its assault a day late, but caught the Germans by surprise. In a carefully choreographed operation, the Fifth Division crossed the mouth of the Garigliano by stealth on the night of 17–18 January 1944, followed by a thunderous attack carried out by the Fifty-sixth Division on its right flank the next morning. Within two days, with the aid of close support from the U.S. Twelfth Air Force, the British had climbed the steeply terraced hillsides to dig a deep divot from the German flank. As Clark had hoped, Ultra revealed that Kesselring, his Tenth Army commander screaming that his troops were holding on by the slenderest margins, took the bait and committed his reserve of two panzer grenadier divisions and an air group to block the British advance which he correctly perceived had the objective of outflanking the Liri Valley from the south.[71] At this point, however, Clark lost the battle, basically because he decided to adhere strictly to his plan centered on a breakthrough by U.S. forces up the Liri Valley, rather than reinforce McCreery's success at the mouth of the Garigliano. His best bet for victory was to call off the attack of the British Forty-sixth Division and hand it over to McCreery's badly battered Tenth Corps as a reserve. But this he chose not to do.[72] To protect the assault of the U.S. Thirty-sixth Division on the Liri, Clark required the British Forty-sixth Division to guard the flank of his Texans. Therefore, on 19 January, the Forty-sixth was pitched with inadequate assault craft across the Garigliano, transformed by the winter weather and by open sluice gates on the irrigation dams into a rushing torrent. Swimmers were unable to carry lines to the far shore. Boats were smashed or carried downstream as the Germans, now fully alert to the attack, reacted fiercely. Only one battalion managed to reach the west shore, and it was decimated, a few survivors straggling back in water-logged boats. Clark attributed the failure of the British river crossing to "lack of strong aggressive leadership at the divisional level."[73]

As Fred Walker realized, the Forty-sixth's failure to cross the river at a relatively weakly defended sector offered a terrible omen for his Texans. On the night of 20 January, fatalistic soldiers of the Thirty-sixth Division, carrying their 12-man plywood assault boats or 24-man rubber dinghies, were guided through the marshes that bordered the Rapido along narrow approach lanes cleared through minefields and marked by white engineering tape clearly visible to the Germans on Monte Cassino. Morale, already low, predictably collapsed when the attackers were slammed by a ferocious preregistered artillery barrage, mortars, and machine-gun fire that destroyed assault boats and ammunition dumps on the Allied shore. Many inexperienced soldiers tossed directly from poorly managed replacement depots into battle simply broke and ran. About a thousand men managed to get across. On the east bank of the river, trucks bringing forward girders for the Bailey bridge bogged down in the mud. Engineers threw four small foot bridges over the Rapido, which another 350 or so GIs managed to cross. Germans moved tanks to seal off the U.S. bridgehead, while German artillery observers ordered down a hail of phosphorus shells. The bridges became slick with blood before they were destroyed by artillery fire. The American fire support plan broke down because smoke and fog obscured observation. Cooperation between infantry and engineers who had never trained together was a shambles. GIs who eluded German artillery barrages refused to cross the river, or jumped into the water for shelter. Others wandered off into unmarked minefields and triggered "Bouncing Betties," mines that sprang up before exploding. Those GIs still alive fled the north bank by 1000 on 21 January.

Despite horrific losses, Clark ordered a renewal of the assault that afternoon. Five hundred GIs who managed to cross the river were cut off as every bridge and boat was destroyed. "I saw boats being hit all around me," one American sergeant remembered, "and guys falling out and swimming." Many drowned in the deep, frigid, swift-running water. On the German side of the river, bodies lay everywhere. "I remember this kid being hit by a machine gun; the bullets hitting him pushed his body along like a tin can . . . Just about everybody was hit."[74] Radios went down, most of the officers were killed or wounded, and men dodged from foxhole to foxhole stripping C-rations and water off the dead. Slowly, the defensive fire died out, as the Americans exhausted their ammunition and were rounded up by the Germans. On the twenty-fifth, a truce was organized so that the Americans could cross the river and collect their dead. Limbless, headless torsos were stacked like firewood on the banks of the Rapido to await collection. The Thirty-sixth Division counted 1,681 casualties, and the Rapido earned the nickname "Bloody River." Walker, like Dawley before him, characterized Clark's dogged persistence in a catastrophically failed operation as "stupidity." Typically, Clark shrugged off accusations of "mass murder" and instead set about designating scapegoats among the senior officers in the Thirty-sixth, whom he blamed for the division's low morale and poor performance.[75]

The one breath of promise and suggestion for a way forward came on Clark's right flank. Juin had kicked off his attack on 12 January against the German Fifth Mountain Division, which, within two days, was so decimated that Kesselring was forced to replace it with the Third Panzer Grenadier Division. Juin renewed his offensive on the twenty-first, his agile Moors scaling the most difficult routes in the hope that these would be the least well defended. By 26 January the CEF had seized the 2,364-foot-high Monte Belvedere. The mist-shrouded Belvedere changed hands several times before the French finally secured it that day against repeated German counterattacks. Only two of eighty mules sent to resupply the French defenders reached the summit. The French advance placed the defenders in crisis mode. After von Senger warned that Juin's advance threatened to cause "the Cassino block to cave in from the north," Kesselring milked his divisions for reserves.[76] On 30 January, the French seized Monte Abate, where squads of Moslem troops cautiously approached German bunkers from the flanks to push grenades through the embrasures. Peaks and ridges were taken, surrendered, and retaken as men fought for days without food, their weapons often frozen in their hands, depending on captured German rations and munitions to continue the struggle. *"Pas bu et pas mangé depuis le départ"* (haven't eaten or drunk since we set out) read a note taken off one dead French officer. Time and again German counterattacks were shattered by American and French artillery. On 29 January, the U.S. 142d Infantry Regiment was lifted from the Thirty-sixth Division and thrown into the fight for Monte Abate to bolster the French, who were at the end of their tether. Captured German POWs were dispatched to the rear, their only escort the wounded Moslems they were ordered to carry back. One group of twelve POWs caused a panic when they stumbled into the command post of the Moroccan Eighth Infantry Regiment, whose officers sheepishly lowered their arms as they realized the Germans were without weapons. By the first week in February, however,

the German defenses had hardened, and lashing rain, logistical problems, and sheer exhaustion had halted the Allied advance. The CEF
had taken almost 8,000 casualties, the Tenth Corps over 4,000, while
10,000 GIs had become casualties. Loss rates for the Germans were
unclear, but included 1,200 POWs captured by the CEF alone.[77]

It was generally conceded that, for the visiting team, the CEF had
snatched the honors of the battle.[78] Juin reported that the Germans
had required seventeen battalions to halt the CEF, or 44 percent of
their forces. "One can say that the French army has recovered its reputation," he claimed. However, a setback was a setback. Juin's desire to
restore France's martial reputation did not blind him to the serious
problems the Allies faced in Italy. Tactically, he had been unhappy
with the performance even as the combat raged. He felt that the
strengths of his troops—mobility, fluidity, the ability to maneuver and
infiltrate—which had been displayed to their advantage in the extended fronts of Tunisia, were a liability against a tightly constructed
German defensive system like that at Cassino. He feared that their
morale was likely to crack as their cadres were decimated. On the
strategic level, he noted that the Allies suffered from a dearth of resources. The Germans actually outnumbered the attackers, who were
temporarily exhausted by the mountain combat.[79] For his part, Kesselring did not see French infiltration tactics as a threat to the Gustav position. Rather, he concluded that the Allies could not continue such a
"reckless" expenditure of men indefinitely. He attributed their gains to
shortages of winter gear, divergences over mountain warfare tactics
"which it took me some time to sort out," and the requirement to pit
only "picked German units under proven commanders" against "the
excellent troops of the French Expeditionary Corps."[80]

Clark was obliged to grind out his bloody Cassino offensive to take
pressure off Anzio. Although Kesselring claimed to have nurtured a
"hunch" that the Allies would coordinate an amphibious landing with
a major push on the Garigliano, one that had caused him to hesitate
before dispatching reinforcements to the Tenth Army front, his military intelligence failed to detect the departure of the invasion fleet
from Naples.[81] Therefore, he was caught completely by surprise in the
early hours of 22 January when a German railway corporal stationed at

Anzio escaped by motorcycle to report that Allied troops were streaming ashore under a thunderous naval barrage.

The actual invasion went far more smoothly than had the confused rehearsal at Salerno. Two small ships were lost. But otherwise, within twenty-four hours, the entire invasion force of 36,000 men together with over 3,000 vehicles was ashore at the cost of thirteen Allied soldiers killed. Critics of Shingle argue that Lucas's pessimism combined with Clark's caution to compromise fatally an operation that might have brought the Allies stunning strategic success. Anzio had been seized, which allowed the British First Division to disembark at the harbor rather than across problematic beaches. Allied troops fanned out to seize bridges over the Mussolini Canal and pushed seven miles inland without encountering an enemy soldier. However, Lucas, guided by Clark's admonition not "to stick your neck out," squandered tactical surprise and instead concentrated on fortifying his beachhead in expectation of the inevitable German counterattack. In this way, Shingle extended what was becoming an Allied tradition in Italy of launching operations based on best-case strategic assumptions with inadequate operational resources. Lucas understood that his options at Anzio were severely limited. Ultra revealed that the German high command was transferring units from the Replacement Army in Germany to Italy, and that as early as 26 January, Kesselring had assembled elements of five divisions at Anzio.[82] Sixth Corps was too small to advance without opening itself to devastating counterattack. Every mile inland Lucas advanced gave him seven more miles of front to defend. Even had Lucas's force been large enough to seize the Alban Hills, only an army could have surged beyond them to cut the railway and Route 6 to Cassino. To hunker down, on the other hand, was merely to hand Kesselring the opportunity to mass overwhelming force against a fragile beachhead whose survival depended on a tenuous sea link.[83] Lucas chose a cautious middle course, which was to push against the tightening German noose to gain a little breathing room and keep the Germans off balance.

Lucas's caution allowed the Germans to perform what the British official history described as "a brilliant and swift, if higgledy-piggledy, feat of improvisation."[84] Kesselring called in units from as far away as

Yugoslavia and France as well as northern Italy. Lucas's passivity combined with Clark's sputtering offensive at Cassino permitted Kesselring to withdraw troops from the Gustav line to concentrate them at Anzio. "Every yard was important to me," Kesselring asserted. He first installed antitank guns to confine Allied armor to the beachhead. Then, as German reinforcements arrived, he drew a defensive cordon around Sixth Corps. By the afternoon of the twenty-second, despite the successful landing, Kesselring claimed to have "the confident feeling that the Allies had missed a uniquely favourable chance of capturing Rome and of opening the door on the Garigliano front. I was certain that time was our ally."[85] If the Allies required proof that this was so, on 23 January German bombers armed with radio-guided bombs sank or damaged several Allied ships standing off Anzio and forced the others to retreat during the night. By 30 January the German Fourteenth Army under von Mackensen had solidified a strong defensive ring around Sixth Corps, complete with flak and air cover "reminiscent of past glories," Kesselring effused.[86] All this meant that when on 29 January, at Clark's urging, Lucas sent the British First and U.S. First Armored Divisions toward Campoleone and the U.S. Third Division in the direction of Cisterna, Kesselring felt confident of success, despite the fact that German units were unbalanced and many of their troops inexperienced. The British advance toward Campoleone made good progress on the twenty-ninth, until it was vigorously attacked and hurled back with heavy losses on the thirtieth. Truscott's attempt to infiltrate Cisterna was embarrassed when 767 Rangers were surprised and captured as they filed up the "Pantano ditch," a dry irrigation canal. When the Third Division launched an all-out attack on the Hermann Göring Division occupying Cisterna on the thirty-first, they were thrown back with 3,000 casualties. Although the attack had given the Germans some anxious moments,[87] Lucas had had enough. He went over to the defensive.

Kesselring boasted that he had Lucas at a huge disadvantage: penned in on low ground, constantly pummeled by artillery and the Luftwaffe. If they thinned out their garrison, they risked being overwhelmed by von Mackensen's Fourteenth Army. So the Allies shoehorned reinforcements into the crowded beachhead, which simply multiplied Kesselring's targets. Axis Sally boasted that Anzio had become "the largest self-supporting prisoner-of-war camp in the world." "It must have been damned unpleasant," Kesselring opined.[88] It was. Daylight movements were invariably accompanied by a symphony of sniper or machine-gun fire, the crash of an incoming barrage from 372 guns guided by observers on the Alban Hills, or the scream of a Luftwaffe strafe. The northern part of the salient, known as "wadi country" because it was traversed by veins of bramble-choked gullies, was ideal for infiltration and so witnessed constant raids and skirmishing. Despite the continuous fighting, soldiers preferred the relative security of frontline fortifications rather than risk their survival in the "rear area," where mountains of equipment and vehicle parks drew persistent shelling.

During the day, the salient appeared lifeless as Allied soldiers crowded into old wine cellars transformed by sandbags, lumber, or any available material into bunkers. There they read or organized beetle-racing competitions, which became a favorite leisure activity among the British. Hospitals under canvas were particularly dangerous places to be, as they were unprotected from the indiscriminate German shelling. At night, Anzio sprang to life as scarce LSTs and DUKWs, dodging mines sown by the Luftwaffe, ferried supplies and reinforcements from ships standing three miles offshore, beyond artillery range.

On 2 February, Ultra collected a decrypt that listed the German order of battle at Anzio, complete with their commanders.[89] By 3 February, Lucas had compacted four divisions, two infantry brigades, and a three-regiment Canadian-American special service force into the beachhead.[90] Ultra told him repeatedly from early February that Kesselring was planning a big offensive, one delayed only because the Germans were having supply problems due to railway bottlenecks and lack of motor transport south of Rome.[91]

Urged on by Hitler, who wished to use the annihilation of the Anzio beachhead as a predictor of the fate that awaited an Allied invasion of Northern Europe, Kesselring initiated a series of local attacks to seize important jump-off points in preparation for a major push that, he hoped, would drive the Sixth Corps into the sea. Fighting was especially hard in the Campoleone salient on the First Division front, where the British took 1,400 casualties but were forced to fall back nonetheless. Attacks on Truscott's Third Division at Cisterna were blunted by U.S. tanks and massed artillery. As each side infiltrated porous positions in mainly night fighting, front lines exchanged hands and became intertwined and confused and casualties mounted on both sides. Kesselring brought up two monster 218-ton railway artillery pieces: "Anzio Annie" and "Anzio Express" would emerge briefly from caves in the Alban Hills to lob 280 mm shells at the beachhead before retreating to cover. Tracked by Ultra, Kesselring continued to funnel reinforcements toward von Mackensen's Fourteenth Army until he had massed almost 120,000 men around the beachhead.

At dusk on 16 February, von Mackensen directed an infantry division and a panzer grenadier division down the main highway straight at the badly mauled British Second Brigade (part of the Fifty-sixth Division) and the U.S. Forty-fifth Division, behind an overwhelming artillery "stonk." What followed was a "soldiers' battle," as U.S. and British units mingled in a desperate defense of the bridgehead. The celebrated Berlin-Spandau Infantry Lehr Regiment, sent by Hitler to lead the attack, was ignominiously put to flight by the Forty-fifth Division. American artillery spotters in L-4 cub planes circled overhead to call down lethal barrages on German troop movements, which because of the mud were confined to the main roads. By 18 February the Allied line had been driven back, two battalions of the 157th Regiment of the U.S. Forty-fifth Division had been surrounded, and the entire line appeared to be on the point of cracking. Von Mackensen threw his last reserves at a battalion of the Queen's Royal Regiment, a territorial unit from North Lancashire, and a company of Gordon Highlanders, who, aided by tanks from the U.S. First Armored Division, had been sent to rescue the surrounded Americans. Alerted by Sigint as to the time and axis of the attack, Lucas was able to mass 224 guns at the narrow German salient to shatter Kesselring's offensive.[92]

On 20 February, von Mackensen called off the offensive after advancing two and one-half miles at the cost of more than 5,000 casualties. Allied air strikes had limited the supply of German shells and disrupted German communications, throwing off the coordination of their attacks. Kesselring blamed the failed offensive on the use of inexperienced troops unfamiliar with the terrain who were forced to attack at night.[93] Nevertheless, he consoled himself that the Sixth Corps had only narrowly avoided extinction and was short of reserves.

At Hitler's insistence, Kesselring renewed his attack on 29 February, this time against the Americans at Cisterna. But, alerted by Ultra,[94] Truscott organized the guns and tanks of the U.S. Third Division, backed by naval artillery and air strikes, into a formidable resistance. Allied firepower combined with rain to bring operations to a halt by 1 March. Kesselring concluded, and Ultra confirmed, that his divisions had suffered significant casualties and that he lacked the reinforcements to eliminate the Anzio beachhead.[95] Now it was the Germans' turn to go over to the defensive.

The battle's last casualty was John Lucas. The Sixth Corps commander was accused of faulty strategic planning and the inadequate allocation of resources, misdemeanors that rightly belonged to Alexander, Clark, and Churchill. Although he had presided over a significant defensive victory, his division commanders complained that he failed to coordinate the battle from his cellar headquarters, derisively called "the catacombs under the Nettuno." Clark complained that Lucas "had no flash," and Alexander that Anzio required a "thruster like George Patton." On 22 February, Clark flew into Anzio to put Sixth Corps under Lucian Truscott.[96]

Churchill put a brave face on the failure of Anzio, insisting that "even a battle of attrition is better than standing by and watching the Russians fight," and that Shingle had caused the Germans to shift eight more divisions to Italy, eight less to face Overlord.[97] Although Anzio had survived, the Allies, their forces divided over two separate fronts, were unable to concentrate their resources. Von Mackensen's offensive, coming within a hair of success, had made the Allied command practically desperate to break the Gustav line and relieve the beachhead. Unfortunately, Clark had exhausted his forces in his January 1944 assault on the Gustav line, while Anzio had gobbled up the Forty-fifth Division, which was his reserve, and absorbed much of his air power.

On 1 February, Clark ordered the Thirty-fourth Division to renew its attack across the Rapido north of Cassino town. Once across the river, his troops would divide into three prongs to attempt to break into the Liri Valley from the north. One prong would turn south and attack Cassino town. A second would move up the ridgeline of Monastery Hill (Monte Majola) toward the abbey, while a third would seize the village of Caira, then turn south to follow the ridgeline to Monte Castellone and beyond toward Point 706. Aided by a mist and devastating artillery barrage, the Americans seized both Montes Majola and Castellone, which dominated the abbey, and even entered Cassino town before they were hurled back by a counterattack. So worried was Kesselring by the American advance that on 3 February he transferred the Parachute Division from the Adriatic coast to block the advance of the Thirty-fourth Division. The next days saw ferocious hand-to-hand combat between German paratroops and American infantry at Cassino and in the mountains above. Peaks and ridges changed hands several times. When the Americans came within a few hundred yards of the crest of Monastery Hill and only one and a half miles from Route 6, Ultra decrypts revealed desperate pleas that the Allies were on the verge of turning the Cassino position from the north and west.[98]

When, on 12 February, the Thirty-fourth was finally relieved by the Fourth Indian Division, a Gurkha officer was awestruck at what they had accomplished: "How the hell you chaps did it, I can't imagine," he intoned. The answer was, with extreme difficulty. Men could only advance in small groups over the flinty and ice-hard mountainsides, seeking fragile and inadequate shelter in ravines and behind boulders from the probing artillery fire. Soldiers felt that every artillery piece in Germany was aimed at them. "The ground all around us shook with gigantic explosions," one lieutenant remembered. "Huge showers of earth rained down on top of our canvas. The air was full of flying dirt and shrapnel. There was the frightening smell of gunpowder and crash after crash." A canteen cup inadvertently left on the lip of the foxhole was jagged with shrapnel marks. Each man, isolated in his own terror, fully expected that the next shell had his name on it. It took an enormous act of will to advance. Officers posted on trails with drawn pistols heard every imaginable excuse from soldiers trying to filter toward the rear. "Go back, goddamn you! My orders are that nobody goes out of here unless he's seriously wounded. Go on! Get back!"[99] Those advancing into Cassino town at the foot of Monastery Hill found that bazookas and even 105 mm shells failed to dent the thick walls of the Italian houses, which German engineers had integrated into a maze of steel-reinforced bunkers linked by trenches and tunnels.

As the Germans mustered troops and artillery ammunition for a major counteroffensive to drive the Americans off Montes Castellone and Majola, Second Corps commander Keys brought up the Thirty-sixth Infantry Division and Combat Command B, detached from the First Armored Division, which together with the Thirty-fourth Division were to drive into the Liri Valley from the north. The New Zealand Division and the Fourth Indian, joined in the New Zealand Corps under Freyberg, would exploit. The renewed attacks began on 8 February as the weather turned to sleet and snow. The Germans gave a few grudging yards but refused to break. A Second Corps offensive on 11 February had the Germans down to their last reserves. But the Americans, too, were feeding drivers and typists as replacements into the rifle companies that were down to a quarter strength. A counteroffensive by the 200th Panzer Grenadier Regiment on 12 February briefly gained the summit of Monte Castellone, only to abandon it under an annihilating American artillery barrage. Each side was too exhausted to continue. Von Senger announced that the Americans had come "within a bare 100 meters of success."[100] During their three-week struggle to take Cassino, 2,200 men of the Thirty-fourth Division became casualties.

Alexander, feeling heat from Churchill and aware that the Germans were massing against Anzio, was determined to keep up the pressure. He decided to throw the New Zealand Corps at the reeling Germans. Had he done so on 9 February, when the two divisions of the New Zealand Corps would have augmented, rather than replaced, those of Second Corps, he might have finished off the Gustav line then and there. He had not because he believed that Second Corps was on the verge of breakthrough, and wanted to hold the New Zealand Corps in reserve to exploit up the Liri Valley. However, delay resulted in a piecemeal effort by a corps commander inexperienced in mountain warfare.[101] Worse, it culminated in one of the most enduringly controversial actions of an Italian campaign already pockmarked with poor decisions. As a condition for his attack, Freyberg, egged on by Fourth Indian Division commander Major General F.I.S. Tuker, insisted that the abbey be bombed because, he argued, it was occupied by German artillery spotters and in any case he lacked the means to subdue a strong fortress that the Germans would surely defend. When Clark opposed the request, the New Zealand general took it straight to Alexander, who reluctantly assented. On 15 February, waves of B-17s, interspersed with artillery, obliterated the ancient abbey, killing an estimated 300 to 400 civilians who had taken refuge inside. Tuker, who had requested the strike, was still not in a position to attack. For their part, the Germans now felt no reluctance to occupy the destroyed building, which they proceeded to fortify. When the Fourth Indian Division's attack against German paratroops on Monastery Hill finally kicked in on the night of 17–18 February, it was repulsed with heavy losses. Maoris of the New Zealand Division broke into the Cassino town but were chased out by panzers.

Unfazed by his setback, on 15 March Freyberg renewed his attacks on Cassino, preceded by 455 bombers and followed by almost 200,000 rounds fired by 892 guns. One journalist described the plumes of dark smoke that sprouted above the town as like the spontaneous germination of a dark forest from seeds sown by "beautiful, arrogant, silver-grey monsters."[102] These were followed by fighter-bombers that plunged busily on the smoldering and broken buildings. Miraculously, German paratroops, dazed and thrown into darkness by the massive bombardment that killed half of the defenders, nevertheless survived in their deep tunnels and steel-reinforced bunkers. Infantrymen of Freyberg's New Zealand Division, equipped with web gear and ammunition for what was expected to be "merely a walk through the battered town,"[103] infiltrated the rubble unaccompanied by their tanks, which were blocked by the destruction from advancing. The "mere walk through" failed to materialize. Germans seemed to be everywhere — snipers felled officers as they peered toward German bunkers, while MG42 "Spandau" machine guns, able to fire 1,200 rounds a minute, forced units to shatter into small, isolated, difficult-to-coordinate patrols. Without tanks, some soldiers lurked about on the outskirts, reluctant to enter the killing field. It was difficult to organize an advance. Although the Germans were few in number, the shattered town gave them an excellent defensive position. A week of fierce but uncoordinated fighting across the rain-drenched ruins and in the hills above the town failed to dislodge the German paratroops. On 23 March, the attack was abandoned, six days after it was clear that it was going nowhere. Because Freyberg was fighting, in Brooke's view, "with a casualty conscious mind," he held back men who might have turned the tide.[104] For their part, the Germans were amazed at the asymmetry between massive Allied firepower and the paucity of troops committed to exploit a bombardment.[105] Stalemate settled over Cassino and Anzio, a stalemate that favored German, rather than Allied, designs.

Mammoth Allied efforts to crack the Gustav line had met defeat, and in the process cast doubt on Allied strategy in the Mediterranean. Italy had been knocked out of the war, and the Allies continued to wear down German forces. But the capture of Rome, the third goal of the invasion of Italy, remained elusive. Indeed, with Overlord looming, only Churchill and perhaps Mark Clark, who feared for his career in the aftermath of his defeats at Cassino, persisted in considering the Italian capital a "glittering prize." Otherwise, pressure was growing from the Americans in particular to reduce operations in Italy to a minimum and skip to southern France.[106]

In the four months of stymied Allied endeavor before Monte Cassino, the war had progressed elsewhere. In December 1943, as the siege was beginning, the *Scharnhorst* was sent to the bottom off Norway with practically her entire crew by the *Duke of York*, removing virtually the final impediment to the Arctic convoys. In February 1944 the Norwegian resistance blew up a ferry carrying a stock of heavy water from the Ryukan hydroelectric plant to Germany for use in atomic research. In the first three months of 1944, sixty U-boats were destroyed in the North Atlantic. Soviet forces lifted the German siege of Leningrad, advanced inexorably in the Ukraine, forced the Germans to begin an evacuation of the Crimea after vicious fighting around Odessa, and kicked open the doors to Poland, Romania, and Estonia. British and

American air forces continued to pulverize German cities and targeted the aircraft factories and V-weapon sites in France and the Low Countries. In the Pacific, Australians and Americans swept New Guinea and New Britain, cleared Kwajalein in the Marshalls, and had the Marianas in their sights. In Burma, the Battle of Imphal raged.

The siege of Cassino had not been completely wasted. Kesselring had suffered heavy casualties. However, the German commander seemed far more concerned by the enfeebled state of the Luftwaffe, down to 300 planes, than by the solidity of his Cassino position. He devotes barely a paragraph to the March assault on Cassino in his memoirs.[107] Even if the Allied campaign in Italy was tying down German troops that might have been used better elsewhere, it was clear to the Germans that the Balkans were now an unlikely target of an Allied invasion, while the diminished amount of shipping in the Mediterranean indicated that the invasion of Northwestern Europe was imminent.[108] Operationally, Allied failure at Cassino and Anzio had strengthened Kesselring's certitude that his soldiers had their measure. Clark and Alexander had failed in their assaults on the Gustav line because they had spread their forces over wide fronts, declined to reinforce success, and instead frittered away their strength in piecemeal assaults against a tenacious, even heroic, defense. Pressure to succeed, much of it coming from Churchill, caused commanders to persist in attacks long after any promise of success had evaporated. The senior leadership stood accused of château generalship, ordering troops to attack over ground which they themselves had reconnoitered only on maps, and whose texture of sharp escarpments, boulders, and blind ridges they little appreciated. The U.S. Thirty-fourth Division had gained most of the ground won by the Allies on Monastery Hill during January. Viewed on a map, success seemed only a "stonk" away, an affair of an advance of a hundred yards. Commanders little understood that the last few yards were often the most difficult, because a machine gun well sited across a narrow ridge line could balk a battalion, which could attack only one squad at a time. Troops who advanced over mountains required hundreds of mules to keep them supplied with munitions, water, and food, and to evacuate wounded. Without mules, the most promising advance sputtered for want of ammunition.

Brute force demonstrated its limits at Cassino. Prolonged and inaccurate air and artillery bombardment failed to intimidate the defenders of Cassino town, but instead turned it into a mini-Stalingrad where British, Indian, New Zealander, and German competed for advantage amid a chaotic tumble of rubble, rats, feces, plagues of mosquitoes, and decaying corpses. The Germans allegedly awarded an Iron Cross to any soldier who could endure two weeks there.[109] It was clear that massive bombardment as a technique for breakthrough was not working, especially when the follow-up by infantry and tanks was delayed or too weak to succeed. The greatest success had been achieved by large numbers of mobile troops infiltrating by wide flanking maneuvers through the least accessible terrain. The Allies needed to draw lessons from their failures and evolve new techniques to smash the Gustav line.

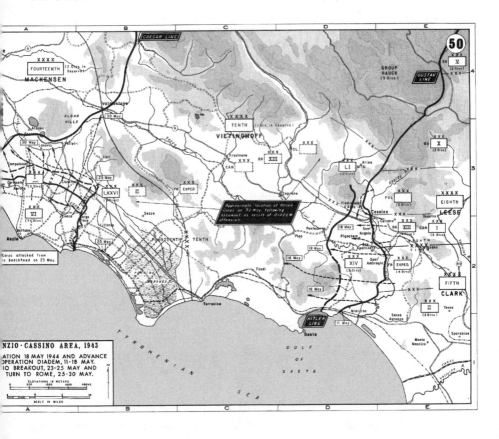

DIADEM: THE BATTLE FOR ROME

With Allied troops in Italy exhausted and Overlord in the offing, Alexander sought to fill the time before the next ground offensive by launching Operation Strangle—a massive air campaign designed to inhibit German supply through Italy and to test air interdiction methods in preparation for Overlord. Strangle, aimed principally at central Italy, did succeed in creating shortfalls in German supplies, although not at the front and not of fuel or ammunition. Lack of aircraft and poorly thought-out targeting policies combined with excess capacity on the Italian railways, capable of carrying eight to twelve times German requirements, to frustrate Strangle. Indeed, the chief of staff of OKH transportation, General Karl Koerner, later claimed that had the Allied air offensive targeted choke points like the Brenner Pass or the Po River bridges rather than marshaling yards, then German resistance might have collapsed in Italy in 1943.[110] The Germans proved adept at avoiding heavily bombed marshaling yards, rapidly repairing damaged track and embankments, unloading goods north of Rome or even north of Florence and continuing by road, and sending supplies by coastal shipping. Plans for Strangle also underestimated German requirements for mounting an effective defense.[111]

Meanwhile, Brooke, badgered since the spring of 1943 by Montgomery, who wrote incessantly to his mentor that Alexander's college master management style required an organized chief of staff to whip it into shape, dispatched Lieutenant General and future Field Marshal A. F. "John" Harding to put some order into Fifteenth Army Group headquarters.[112] Harding was an uncommon commodity in the imperium of the British army. A grammar school boy, son of a humble Somerset solicitor's clerk, Harding was yanked from his civil service job and commissioned in the territorial army in 1914. He finished the war as a temporary battalion commander, a performance that earned him a transfer to his county regiment, the Somerset Light Infantry. He had climbed up the military ladder by dint of application rather than social or regimental connections. Harding was one of those relatively rare officers who combined a flair for frontline leadership with solid administrative ability. His shy smile and modest demeanor belied an inner certitude born of his religious upbringing. The DSO awarded Harding in 1941 during Crusader, when, as chief of staff of the Thirteenth Corps, he had stanched the confusion caused by Rommel's attacks and temporarily stabilized the situation, described him as "a fighting staff officer." Crusader earned him a promotion to command the Seventh Armoured Division, the celebrated "Desert Rats," whom he directed with great vigor in the pursuit of Rommel after El Alamein until severely wounded by a German shell in January 1943 as his division advanced on Tripoli.

In December 1943, Brooke dispatched a now recovered Harding to Italy to fill the "ghastly void" in Alexander's headquarters and impose order on the Fifteenth Army Group commander's casual management style. Harding had his strengths: he was a hardnosed, calculating strategist who understood the role played by the Italian front in overall Allied strategy. He was also good at defining a problem and matching means to resolve it. Still, Brooke's decision to feed a man whom he did not consider "a high class pony" or one "used to first class polo" into the intellectual vacuum of Alexander's headquarters proved detrimental to the CIGS's plan to encourage Alexander to "grip" the Italian campaign. The "loyal" Harding, who Brooke increasingly came to believe was "not up to his appointment," changed the way Alexander's headquarters did business. Where before, Fifteenth Army Group's plans simply emerged over time as Alexander discussed options with his subordinate commanders, now Harding began to drive the Italian campaign train. In the summer of 1944, Harding, probably encouraged by Churchill, fleshed out the scheme to push the Eighth Army through the Ljubljana Gap to capture Vienna on the basis, Brooke believed, of the most "fantastic" operational assumptions.[113] Harding was also to become the *éminence grise* of Leese's ill-fated Olive offensive.

But that was in the future. In the short term, Harding was able to capitalize on Clark's weakened reputation following his failures at Cassino to restore a prominent role for Leese and the Eighth Army in the plan to break the Gustav line, code-named Diadem. In the grand Allied strategic scheme, Diadem was to suck German strategic reserves away from Overlord to fight a battle of attrition on the Gustav line. To simplify the command and logistical structure, Harding's plan called for the massing of the Eighth Army before Cassino. The Fifth Army would be shifted south and west to the Garigliano. The Tenth Corps would rejoin the Eighth Army, its place on the Garigliano taken by Second Corps and the U.S.-equipped CEF. The Polish Second Corps, kitted out by the British, would relieve the CEF north of Cassino. On paper, Diadem appeared to be not so much a conceptual departure from the earlier failed offensives as a renewal of those offensives on a grander and more synchronized scale. Diadem was vintage Eighth Army, an operation reminiscent of El Alamein — a meticulously planned offensive on a narrow front behind irresistible firepower. However, where El Alamein had been a twelve-day battle by three corps of eleven divisions, Harding massed twenty-eight divisions split between two armies of seven corps for an attack that was to last for three weeks. The plan called for Leese's Eighth Army, composed of the British Thirteenth, Canadian First, and Polish Second Corps, to assault the Gustav line at Monte Cassino with the goal of seizing control of Route 6. Responsibility for the capture of Monastery Hill would be handed to the two-division-plus armored brigade, the Polish Second Corps, backed by 300 guns. Once this was done, the Thirteenth Corps with four divisions and the Canadian First supported by seven hundred guns would surge up the Liri Valley.

Clark's Fifth Army on the Garigliano, composed of two divisions of Second Corps and Juin's French Expeditionary Corps (four divisions plus three *tabors* grouping 10,000 *goumiers*), would attack southeast to northwest behind 600 guns, successively crossing the rocky and scrub-choked Aurunci, Ausoni, and Lepani mountain ranges. In an area whose only decent road was Route 7 along the coast, Clark was expected to play only a secondary, flank-holding role in Diadem. Once through the Gustav line, Allied troops would sustain the momentum to overrun the Hitler line, a series of *Stellungen* or fortified points organized around dismantled tank turrets set in concrete behind barbed wire. The "line" that backed up the Gustav position began near Piedimonte, four miles west of Cassino on the north side of the Liri Valley, and curved west and south through Quinto and Pontecorvo to Terracina on the coast. While potentially formidable, many of these positions were poorly sited and suffered from a shortage of matériel, a lack of depth, and a lack of troops to man them.[114]

The simple ejection of Kesselring from the Gustav line was not Harding's sole objective, however. Harding sought to entrap and annihilate him. This would be the job of the Sixth Corps at Anzio, the "cocked pistol" pointed at Kesselring's back door.[115] Operation Buffalo, a separate but coordinated plan, called for Truscott to surge out of Anzio at the head of the seven and a half divisions of the Sixth Corps to cut Route 6 at Valmontone, a choke point that would disarticulate the retreat of the German Tenth Army from the Gustav line. Harding scheduled the operation for May, when good weather would assure air dominance based on the "Rover" system, in which rotating formations of fighter-bombers directed by a forward air controller would deliver close air support. "Horsefly" observers in small Cessna aircraft hovering over the battlefield would direct precision artillery fire.

Harding's plan had several strengths. It viewed the Gustav and Hitler lines as a whole articulated front rather than as separate positions. Attacks were to be coordinated across the front, unlike the piecemeal affairs of the January–March attacks. Diadem provided for a better concentration of force, because it assigned to corps tasks earlier undertaken by divisions. It caught the Germans off balance. Although the Germans counted 82,000 men on the Gustav line and a further 76,000 in the Fourteenth Army at Anzio, many divisions were understrength and had their movements and logistics restricted by Strangle. While he continued to deepen and integrate his defensive lines, Kesselring was short of reserves and in the process of reorganizing his defenses, which led to confusion about boundaries between units. He also complained to Hitler that the classic German counterattack tactics were piling up unacceptable losses in the face of Allied air and artillery superiority. Elaborate Allied deception, including dummy signals traffic and night movements, had blinded German intelligence, which proved unable to give Kesselring a clear picture of Allied intentions or order of battle. Indeed, the apparent lack of activity on the Allied side convinced many Germans until the day of the attack that their enemy had gone into hibernation. Ultra revealed that the

German command was far from complacent, however. They continued to strengthen their reserve lines and held back several divisions to guard against the possibility of an amphibious descent behind their lines.[116] Alexander encouraged this belief with an elaborate deception plan—Dunton—that had his divisions practicing amphibious operations at Salerno and creating radio traffic patterns that suggested that Civitavecchia or Leghorn were their targets. The Allies also took elaborate precautions to camouflage preparations for their offensive: canvas screens along roads obscured the buildup of the Poles before Cassino, British helmets were distributed to the French Expeditionary Corps to hide their replacement of the British Tenth Corps on the left of the Fifth Army line, while the buildup of the Anzio beachhead to a strength of seven and a half divisions occurred mostly at night.

Diadem also counted numerous weaknesses, however. The most obvious was that it offered a recipe for Pyrrhic victory rather than for a campaign of encirclement and annihilation. Alexander, Leese, and Harding continued to underestimate the difficulties of forced river crossings and overestimate the value of air interdiction of German supply routes. As in earlier offensives, the Germans held the high ground, from which they commanded an unobstructed view of Allied preparation. Harding hoped to mitigate this German advantage with a meticulous fire plan that included bombarding the summits with smoke shells to blind German artillery observers, as well as swathing crossing sites with lashings of smoke. However, Kesselring understood that the Adriatic sector offered a dead end for the Allies. Therefore, he thinned out his lines there and concentrated his best troops against the principal Allied thrust at Monte Cassino and the Liri Valley. His Fourteenth Army, he believed, was strong enough to contain a breakout at Anzio. He had ample stores and antiaircraft artillery.[117] Harding's plan saturated the seven-mile-wide Liri front with two corps' (the British Thirteenth and the Canadian First) worth of troops and ironmongery that would severely restrict maneuverability and require meticulously coordinated staff work to succeed.[118]

The Poles, composed of the Third Carpathian and the Fifth Kresowa Divisions, which combined 50,000 men under Lieutenant General Wladyslaw Anders, were assigned the task of taking the abbey.

Enthusiastic, brave, fiercely determined to exact, in Anders's words, "revenge and retribution over our hereditary enemy,"[119] the Poles were also inexperienced. Oliver Leese, grown weary of Anders's passionate speeches about Poland's future, feared correctly that the Polish Corps's quest for national regeneration through heroic sacrifice caused them to regard the Eighth Army's insistence on professional standards as an ignoble obligation beneath the dignity of Poles.[120] They would have the mission—unenviable to soldiers of a less reckless disposition—of overrunning an elaborate system of foxholes, bunkers, and pillboxes, protected by wire, antipersonnel mines, and interlocking fields of fire, backed by over 200 guns of various calibers, and occupied by tough German paratroops.

A final weakness of the plan was that Clark never signed on to the basic concept of Diadem, for two reasons. First, the American general viewed Diadem as a perpetuation of a British conspiracy apparent since Salerno to assign the Americans a secondary role in the Italian campaign. Clark was convinced that Alexander, Harding, and Leese aimed to defraud the Fifth Army of the honor of capturing Rome, and in the process to shatter his career.[121] "The capture of Rome is the only important objective," he informed Truscott. In fact, the capture of Rome was incidental to the outcome of Diadem, not its objective. The goal of Harding's plan was to force the Germans to fight south of Rome and to inflict as much damage as possible. But this raised Clark's second objection, which was that a battle of envelopment as Harding envisioned it was no longer possible, given the firepower available to World War II armies.[122] Clark insisted after the war that Sixth Corps was too weak by itself to halt the German Tenth Army, even in full retreat. In this he was supported by Juin, who argued on the eve of the attack that Sixth Corps would not have the strength to trap the Germans.[123] Clark's unwillingness to sign on to Diadem, combined with Alexander's unwillingness, or inability, to control Clark, led to the greatest controversy of the Italian campaign.[124]

Diadem opened badly on 11 May. For three days, neither the Polish Second Corps nor the British Thirteenth or Canadian First Corps were able to get any traction at Cassino. Though taken by surprise, the German paratroops fought with their accustomed ferocity on the terraced hillsides beneath the abbey, inflicting terrible losses on the Poles, whose reconnaissance had been inadequate and whose infantry attacks were poorly coordinated with preparatory artillery barrages. "Many were killed through their carelessness," one Polish officer recounted. "I noticed that the Germans very wisely stayed under cover at all times, whereas our men would suddenly stand up to hurl defiance at the enemy. They paid dearly for these and similar acts of bravado." One sergeant even stood up to dance a folk dance in full view of the Germans.[125] Attacking troops, searching desperately for cover from German fire, hunkered down in makeshift shelters beside the putrefying remains of earlier battles. The ground shook with exploding shells, and men gasped for breath in the smoke and rotting stench of death. Entire battalions ceased to exist. Soon, the mountain was covered with body parts, misshapen corpses, and well-fed rats. Even Polish courage could not endure such fire, forcing Anders to suspend his attack. He kicked off again on 16 May with the same desperate courage. By evening on the next day, the Col Sant' Angelo was in Polish hands.

On the Rapido, the smoke calculated to blind German artillery and reduce Allied casualties was so thick that British and Indian troops found their crossing points only with difficulty. This threw the crossings, timed to coincide with prearranged artillery barrages, hopelessly behind schedule. Engineers discovered that the fire from the German-controlled west bank made bridge building a dangerous and slowgoing task. Infantry and tanks that crowded into the bridgeheads were vulnerable to multibarreled *Nebelwerfers*, whose shells screamed like Valkyries descending from Monastery Hill. As a consequence, the crossing of the Rapido was attended by the same confusion, capsized boats, air alive with sniper bullets, and wounded and stragglers streaming to the rear with panic-inducing tales of slaughter as had accompanied the U.S. Thirty-sixth Division's "Bloody River" fiasco in January—indeed, many feared that they were reliving that event. Eighth Army veterans of El Alamein declared that Cassino "makes Africa seem like a picnic."[126] Eventually four battalions crossed the Rapido, but were able to control only a space "the length of a cricket pitch."[127] On the extreme left flank at the mouth of the Garigliano,

Second Corps attacks found the green Eighty-fifth and Eighty-eighth Divisions poorly prepared for mountain warfare and easily discouraged by German opposition.

But Kesselring, too, was having his problems. Although his commanders remained confident through 16 May that Monte Cassino could hold, Allied air strikes had put the headquarters of both the Tenth Army and the Fourteenth Corps out of commission. Nor was the German commander able immediately to get a clear picture of what was happening on the Fifth Army front. By 15 May, some of Kesselring's reserves were not reaching threatened sectors, while the CEF had clearly bowled past his defenses and opened a "clear path" to his rear.[128] For their part, the Allied Sigint provided commanders with a plethora of tactical intelligence, supplemented by POW debriefs and air reconnaissance that identified German troop movements.[129] By 16 May, Leese's Thirteenth Corps and the Canadians had driven three miles up the Liri Valley. With Monastery Hill threatened with isolation, Kesselring personally had to order the German paras to abandon "their" Monastery Hill, an order they could not execute immediately because of another profligate, but unsuccessful, Polish attack. On the morning of 18 May, the Poles discovered that the positions to their front had been abandoned. By 1020 hours the Polish flag flew over the ruins of Monte Cassino. The price had been 860 dead and 3,000 wounded. But Cassino town required another day to flush out the snipers and para fanatics who refused to retreat. The fall of Monastery Hill eased the way for the Thirteenth Corps and the Canadians to move farther up the Liri Valley on 17–18 May. On the nineteenth, Sigint picked up Kesselring's order to fall back to the Hitler line (renamed the Senger line to avoid embarrassing the Führer), which he reinforced with two divisions pulled from the Anzio perimeter.[130] On 23 May, Leese unleashed Canadians on the Hitler line at Pontecorvo behind a massive artillery barrage, which they cracked in twenty-four hours. Kesselring's troops began to pull out of the Gustav line and streamed back toward Rome as Sigint intercepted reports of high losses, damage, and delays inflicted by Allied fighter-bombers.[131]

A major reason that the German defenses collapsed was that they were outflanked from the south by the CEF. This came as a surprise to

Clark and Alexander, who, despite a very creditable French performance north of Cassino in January, continued to view the CEF as a motley of cutthroat colonial mercenaries in the service of a nation whose military reputation had taken a tumble in 1940. However, following the January 1943 offensive, Juin realized that he must restructure his forces. First, he required more firepower and heavier units, a "balanced corps," so that the French could combine mountain troops on the heights with heavier motorized thrusts up the valleys. Two more French infantry divisions arrived to raise the number in the CEF to four. Second, he needed to retrain all of his troops to fight in the mountains. A lengthy report on the tactical challenges of mountain warfare produced by the CEF operations bureau in April 1944 emphasized the importance of infiltration, avoiding "hard" positions like road junctions, the need for converging and mutually supporting advances, and the liberal use of smoke screens. In the almost total absence of tanks and given the imprecision of air support on the slopes, artillery and mortars must suppress enemy defensive fire so that the infantry could close on fortifications before uncovering themselves. Engineers must advance with the infantry to de-mine and rapidly open roads and trails so that mules could feed the advance. Finally, Italy was scoured for mules, without which no breakthrough could be sustained: "No mules, no maneuver," Juin declared.[132]

Third, Juin moved to operationalize his tactical concepts. He found Clark's battering-ram approach at Cassino unimaginative, and told him so. Allied progression occurred in fits and starts because, as in World War I, advancing infantry had to halt periodically to allow logistics, reinforcements, and artillery support to catch up. The key to warfare in the mountains was surprise and a seamless advance that denied the enemy the leisure to react. Juin's assignment was to attack the Aurunci Mountains, a roadless tangle of peaks rising to 4,500 feet, alternating with narrow valleys, between Cassino and Gaeta on the Tyrrhenian. German defenses there had little depth and few reserves precisely because the absence of roads and the mountainous terrain led Kesselring to believe the sector too difficult to attack. It was a fair conclusion had the German commander been dealing with anyone else besides Juin and his North Africans. Rivers slashing through narrow valleys created a chaos of cliffs and crags, inventing a maze of stark hillsides bewildering to all but the goats that inhabited them. True to form, the Germans had improved on nature with a solid belt of well-sited bunkers and machine-gun nests, supported by artillery well out of Allied view.

In the original version of Clark's plan, the CEF was to break into the Gustav line and then make way for the Second Corps, which would exploit the breakthrough. Where others might see a thankless task, however, Juin perceived a seam rich with opportunity. He convinced Clark that rather than stop to allow Second Corps to move through his position, the CEF must keep moving, *"exploiter à outrance"* without concern for liaison with units on the flanks, bypassing strong points and not allowing the Germans time to settle into new positions. By concentrating his four divisions against the overstretched German Seventy-first Infantry Division on the Garigliano front, Juin could seize the high ground, move along ridges and crests, threaten flanks, then work down into the valleys to attack the Liri Valley from the south. In this way, he could appear in the rear of a surprised Fourteenth Panzer Corps and cut Route 6 from the south, preventing the Germans from reinforcing the Liri Valley. The only thing that could stop the French advance was lack of ammunition (food and water were considered superfluous in North African divisions). With Alexander and Leese fixated on Cassino and the Liri Valley and Clark banking on a breakout at Anzio to get him first to Rome, Juin's plan was approved. However, Anglo-American wisdom wrote off the French effort as difficult to coordinate in tempestuous terrain, too slow in execution to favor surprise, and logistically unsustainable.[133]

Preparations for the French operation were carefully camouflaged. Because the selected point of attack was in a sector held by the British, Juin's troops, British helmets incongruously sprouting like mushrooms over the Moroccan robes, were transferred over roads obscured by smoke screens and camouflage nets. Despite these precautions, the genesis of what was called the Battle of the Garigliano, launched on the night of 11 May, was a complete failure. Prearranged artillery targeting failed to silence enemy guns. The three attacking French divisions, the North Africans among them armed only with bolt-action rifles and long knives, became entangled in minefields, were subjected to heavy bombardment and counterattacks, and were driven back to their start line after suffering severe casualties. On the morning of 12 May, Juin picked his way forward through a slaughter of dead mules and mutilated men and called a temporary halt to his offensive to reassess the situation. Despite the carnage and lack of success, he had several incentives to renew his offensive. First, he was convinced that tenacious German resistance was a certain indication that they were overstretched. Second, his offensive had advanced on the southern part of his sector, where the Third Algerian Infantry combined with the newly arrived Eighty-eighth Infantry Division of Second Corps to attack up slopes seeded with mines and booby traps and swept by mortar and machine-gun fire to take the strong point of Castelforte. Third, the honor of France and his own *amour propre* would not admit defeat. Juin took the calculated risk of renewing the attack with his single remaining reserve division. Units were mixed and matched into battle groups to conform to new tactical challenges. Clark shifted his artillery to support a promising French initiative, just in time to catch two German counterattacks in the open and stop them cold.

By midafternoon on 13 May, the Moroccans had succeeded in opening a two-and-a-half-mile gap in the German front. German POWs were so intimidated by the bunker-busting techniques of the Moslems that they declared the experience worse than Stalingrad.[134] The hard-pressed Seventy-first and Ninety-fourth Infantry Divisions to Juin's front were thrown into such a funk that they set a record for wireless traffic intercepted by Allied Sigint.[135] The French took the peaks and ridges and dug in for the inevitable counterattack. It did not come. Wireless intercepts revealed that the Seventy-first had been ordered to retreat. The Germans were spent and Juin resolved to forge ahead. Unlike the British and Americans, whose advances came in hiccups, Juin did not stop to regroup. He gave the Germans no respite. This came as a particular surprise to the Germans, who had not taken the French seriously as opponents, and who, as a consequence, were at a loss as to how to defeat them. On Monte Maio, the highest peak in the eastern Auruncis, Juin unfurled a huge tricolor, visible for miles.

The sudden collapse of his Garigliano front caught Kesselring, his attention focused on Cassino and Anzio, off guard and forced him to feed precious reserves, kept back to guard against an amphibious landing, into the Hitler line. "Ability to cross country is especially notable among French and Moroccan troops," Kesselring reported. "They have quickly surmounted terrain considered impassable, using pack-animals to transport their heavy weapons, and have on many occasions tried to turn our own positions (sometimes in wide encircling movements) in order to break them open from the rear."[136] Only on 18 May, however, did Kesselring order the Hermann Göring Panzer Division to move south. Berlin ordered a division moved from Hungary, one from the Eastern Front, and the Twentieth Luftwaffe Field Division from Denmark to Italy. Kesselring's normally optimistic disposition began to fray as his front disintegrated. He grew increasingly vituperative and short-tempered, berated his subordinate commanders, and dictated their tactical dispositions, which confused, rather than aided, the defense.

By 17 May the CEF had outdistanced its mules, and hence its ammunition. Boston bombers of the Twelfth Air Force's Tactical Air Command dropped water, ammunition, and food to the lead French units. Though his men were exhausted, Juin realized that they had to pursue the remnants of the retreating German forces, infiltrating their positions, turning their flanks, focusing resources on weak points, ambushing unsuspecting units, giving them no time to recover their composure. The French advance also served to give momentum to Second Corps, lashed forward by Clark and propelled by lavish artillery preparation. On 18 May, the French submerged the seasoned Ninth Panzer Grenadiers, capturing forty guns in the process. This feat of arms shook the confidence of a German command disorganized by Allied air strikes and demoralized by the shredding of the Fourteenth Panzer Corps. By 22 May the CEF and Second Corps had pierced the Hitler line and closed in on the Liri Valley from the south, facilitating the advance of the Canadians up the valley.

The beginning of the German retreat triggered the breakout from Anzio, and with it one of the greatest inter-Allied controversies of the Mediterranean campaign. Lucian Truscott, a cavalryman, vigorous polo player, Marshall protégé, and perhaps the only general officer in the U.S. army to rival George Patton in sartorial elegance, was the man to impart vigor into a long-dormant Anzio beachhead. On paper, von Mackensen counted five divisions to Truscott's seven. But Kesselring had harvested the Fourteenth Army for reinforcements, while the British First and Fifth Divisions in Sixth Corps were used up and functional only to mount feint, but important, attacks up the coast.[137] On Alexander's (not Clark's) orders, Buffalo kicked off with a thunderous cannonade, which included naval artillery, on 23 May. Von Mackensen begged Kesselring in vain for permission to withdraw his troops from Cisterna. However, Kesselring insisted that the Fourteenth Army hold to allow his Tenth Army to escape from the Gustav line. The U.S. Third Division, too, paid the grievous price of almost 3,000 casualties to seize Cisterna, transformed into a maze of tankproof ditches, embankments, tunnels, and bunkers by the defenders, while the First Armored forfeited eighty-six tanks to the numerous self-propelled guns stationed along the road to Albano. On 23 May, as his embattled units were absorbing 50–60 percent casualties and Second Corps was closing on his flank from the south, von Mackensen defied Kesselring to order a withdrawal of the Seventy-sixth Panzer Corps, a decision that cost him his job.[138] Stranded German infantrymen held on grimly for two more days in the reeking ruins of Cisterna before they were overwhelmed.

By 25 May, Diadem was on a roll. The Canadian corps, though disappointingly slow, had cleared the Hitler line while Truscott's Third Division reached Cori to join hands with Second Corps. The Hermann Göring Division, the last of Kesselring's reserves ordered south from Leghorn, straggled onto the battlefield on 26 May to be plastered by Allied air power and to squander its force in an ill-conceived attack on U.S. troops near Valmontone on the twenty-seventh. Truscott was euphoric. The "Cisterna-Valmontone gap" at the north end of the Liri Valley, through which ran Route 6, seemed to U.S. General John O'Daniel, commander of the Third Division, "very soft" and ripe for exploitation.[139] As the Sixth Corps commander prepared to aim his U.S. divisions toward Valmontone to prevent the Fourteenth and Tenth German Armies from linking up to defend south of Rome, he received an order from Clark to send the Thirty-fourth and Forty-fifth Infantry Divisions together with the First Armored along Route 7 northwest toward the Alban Hills and Rome. This went against Alexander's directive and would allow the Tenth Army to escape. A stunned Truscott and his division commanders opposed the change of plan, but true to form, Clark refused to discuss his order with them.[140]

Clark's decision to shift the axis of his attack toward Rome has added to the mainly negative evaluations of his generalship, and of his personality. Clark's explanation—that Sixth Corps was not strong enough to block the junction of two German armies[141]—was rejected by a "dumbfounded" Truscott, who protested in vain that he still had strong German forces around his perimeter and that his task was to cut off the German retreat. Alexander, although plainly put out by Clark's action, passed up the opportunity to force the American general to adhere to the spirit of Diadem, because it would have been inconsistent with Alexander's limp command style. Nor has Clark's explanation found much favor since. In his memoirs, Alexander assumes that Clark decided to switch the direction of his advance because of the "publicity value" bound to accompany the seizure of Rome.[142] Churchill wired Alexander urging him to force Clark to adhere to Diadem/Buffalo, but in vain.[143] Clark was clearly eager to capture Rome before Overlord would drive Italy off the front pages. The historical verdict on Clark's action has been equally damning. By dividing Sixth Corps on two different axes of advance, he both allowed the escape of the Tenth Army and did nothing to advance the capture of Rome, while at the same time taking heavy casualties.[144] On the contrary, Clark actually retarded the capture of Rome because von Mackensen had anticipated that the Anzio forces would break out along the coast west of the Alban Hills and arranged his defenses accordingly.[145] At the very least, Clark can be accused of deliberate deception, sending a token force toward Valmontone to fulfill the letter of Buffalo, while pursuing his renegade strategy for his own personal ends.[146]

At first glance, Clark seems to have been on solid ground when he argued that the Sixth Corps did not have the ability to block the retreat of the Tenth Army. Furthermore, the dilatory pursuit by the Eighth Army, slowed by traffic jams in the Liri Valley caused by poor road discipline, also facilitated the German escape, as did Alexander's refusal to allow Juin's CEF to cut Route 6. Nor did Allied air power do as much as it might have to impede the German retreat.[147] However much soldiers at the time, and historians since, might decry the escape of the Tenth Army from the Gustav line, the simple truth was that it confirmed a general rule of World War II combat. The firepower available to World War II armies meant that battles of encirclement and annihilation were extremely rare, occurring mostly in the early days of the war in France, in North Africa against the Italians, and during Barbarossa. Apart from Stalingrad and "Tunisgrad," both the direct result of Hitler's insistence on holding ground at all costs, and the final encirclement of German forces in northern Italy in May 1945, German armies repeatedly confirmed their ability to evade entrapment. Rommel's retreat from El Alamein, attempts by Montgomery and Patton to cut off Rommel in southern Tunisia, Kesselring's exit from Sicily, the escape of German forces from southern France after Anvil, together with their breakout from the Falaise pocket in Normandy in August 1944, simply served to confirm this general rule. The best that could be hoped for once firepower and organizational ability were more or less equalized was to shred retreating Axis forces so badly that their fighting power would be significantly diminished.

What can be held against Clark is that he deliberately sabotaged the basic concept of Diadem/Buffalo to seize a political objective of fleeting value.[148] This was because Clark saw the Italian campaign as being fought as much against the British as against the Germans. In this, the Fifth Army commander resurrected and intensified Anglo-American competition for prominence in theater. Since El Alamein, Mediterranean battles had been fought as much between the Allies as with the Axis. Tunisia, the "Race for Messina," and the Baytown/Avalanche controversy and the subsequent "rescue" of Clark's Fifth Army by Monty's Eighth, were all about establishing an Allied pecking order in the Mediterranean. Most of these disputes were press-centered, ego-driven, and petty. Therefore, while Clark's motives may be viewed as a crass and even extreme manifestation of personal and national ego, the simple fact was that he was acting within the norms of inter-Allied competition. The consequences for the Italian theater were significant, however, as henceforth Clark and Leese cooperated with each other as little as possible.[149]

As a strategic concept, Cassino might be said to have succeeded because it tied down German divisions that could have been better utilized elsewhere. However, Cassino left Allied hopes unfulfilled. The acrimony caused by Kesselring's escape was exacerbated because, for many, especially in the American camp, it seemed to confirm the futility of Allied strategy in Italy. Those like Marshall who continued to seek the silver bullet that would bring about the collapse of Hitler, for whom the concept of a long war of attrition in a distant theater remote from any identifiable German center of gravity was difficult to conceptualize, Clark's behavior, combined with the dramatic losses incurred in the capture of Rome, confirmed their deepest prejudices. Diadem had succeeded in battering the German front, inducing a withdrawal, and capturing a city of marginal strategic value. But the cost of 40,205 casualties, 28,556 of them in the Fifth Army, was considered excessive. The fact that German casualties were practically equal was lost in the controversy that swirled around the capture of Rome and the escape of the Tenth Army.[150]

The Fifth Army arrived in Rome on the morning of 4 June to be greeted by a population practically hysterical with joy. But when Clark rolled into the city the next morning, he became hopelessly lost. When, at last, he found city hall, where he hoped to establish his headquarters, he discovered that it was locked against him. "I pounded on the door again," he remembered, "not feeling much like the conqueror of Rome."[151] The fall of the capital of a former Axis power captivated the press for barely forty-eight hours. On 6 June, news of Overlord pushed Italy to the back pages, where it remained for the rest of the war, causing deep resentment in soldiers condemned to serve in a forgotten theater. "Sons of bitches!" Clark raged when the news of the Normandy invasion arrived in Rome. "They didn't even let us have the newspaper headlines for the fall of Rome for one day."[152]

In the Mediterranean, pressure to bypass the blood-soaked mountains of Italy in favor of an end run for southern France—Anvil— became irresistible. Juin chafed that the contribution of the CEF had not been properly acknowledged, while the Poles feared that their heroic sacrifice at Cassino was not price enough to purchase Poland from Stalin's clutches. Clark grumbled that he was now stripped of his Sixth Corps and the CEF for the "dead end street" of Anvil.[153] He was loath to admit that he had strengthened the arguments for Anvil with his poor management of the Cassino campaign and his controversial decision to snatch Rome ahead of the British.

CHAPTER TWELVE

The Mediterranean Road to France's Resurrection, 1940–45

For the french armed forces, World War II was, from beginning to end, a protracted humiliation. The collapse of 1940 chiseled German contempt for the French in stone. German generals refused to surrender at the close of the war to General Jean de Lattre de Tassigny's French First Army, insisting that they would deal only with American commanders. Field Marshal Wilhelm Keitel was openly dismissive of de Lattre's presence at the Berlin surrender ceremony of 8 May 1945: "*Auch!*" Hitler's chief of staff muttered as he entered the room where the surrender was to take place. "The French are here too! It only wanted that."[1]

Allied attitudes toward the French were scarcely less dismissive. The French army remained the Cinderella of the Allied cause, one whose fairy Godmothers even seemed intent on keeping from the ball. The French had been excluded from the great wartime conferences, including Yalta, which adjudicated the fate of postwar Europe sans French input. The exception was Casablanca in January 1943, where Roosevelt and Churchill supervised a frosty but symbolic handshake between Charles de Gaulle and his Allied-sponsored rival, General Henri Giraud. No place was reserved for France at the surrender table on 8 May, nor was a French version of the surrender documents prepared. When the French representative, an offended General de Lattre, insisted on a seat, one American brigadier general tactfully shouted, "And why not China!" The Soviet hosts scrambled to improvise a French flag, but clearly had no idea what it looked like: seamstresses experimented with several versions of the *tricouleur* stitched from pieces of Nazi banner, sheets, and workmen's overalls until de Lattre was satisfied that the result resembled a French, rather than a Dutch, flag. After much wrangling, de Lattre was allowed to sign the surrender document, but only as a witness. The French representative refused to eat at the celebration banquet until France's role in the victory was officially toasted by Soviet Marshal Zhukov and the orchestra instructed to play the *Marseillaise*.[2]

But the French did not have to await the victory ceremony to feel the icy winds of Allied contempt. General Montgomery viewed French units under his command with much the same dismissive hauteur that Rommel reserved for his Italian allies. So displeased was Montgomery by the performance of Gaullist units in the Eighth Army at the Battle of El Alamein that he relieved them. "[The French] do not understand how to train for battle and how to employ a special technique to fit a special problem," he wrote to the chief of the Imperial General Staff, Sir Alan Brooke, in January 1943. "They are in fact quite useless, except to guard aerodromes." Montgomery later conceded that French forces might fight creditably if cosseted by a solid army (his own) and well led by a "magnificent" commander like Philippe Leclerc. Nevertheless, Monty believed the French lacked the fortitude he so admired in ANZAC, Canadian, and Scots troops.[3] George Greenfield, who fought with the Eighth Army at Alamein, equated the French performance in that battle with that of the Earl of Cardigan in the Crimean War, a combination of "idiocy and bravery to match the charge of the Six Hundred."[4]

American veterans of Torch, the November 1942 invasion of North Africa, were exasperated beyond patience by the squabbling between partisans of Charles de Gaulle's Free French and the rump of Marshal Philippe Pétain's Vichy government. The inglorious debut of U.S. troops at Kasserine moderated Eisenhower's irritation at the collapse of the French front in Tunisia in January 1943 — Ike graciously attributed the poor performance of "undernourished"[5] French troops to the fact that they had "practically no modern arms."[6] However, when the decision was taken at Anfa, a wealthy seaside suburb of Casablanca, in January 1943 to organize and upgrade eight French divisions, Brooke objected that the Americans were about to lavish perfectly serviceable equipment on troops capable only of "garrison work."[7]

This glacial attitude thawed somewhat in Italy, where Allied soldiers admired the skill of French troops in mountain warfare as much as the Germans feared them.[8] Still, Allied admiration was tempered by the fact that the French units, composed mainly of North African soldiers, were as much a danger to Italian civilians as they were to the enemy. "The French colonial troops are on the rampage again," Norman Lewis, a member of British military intelligence in Italy, recorded in his diary in May 1944. "Whenever they take a town or a village, a wholesale rape of the population takes place."[9] The Americans were also appalled when, following Anvil, the invasion of southern France in August 1944, de Gaulle stood down his battle-hardened North African and Senegalese units to make room for tatterdemalion, untrained French resisters, up to 140,000 of whom enlisted in the regular army and whose inexperience was purchased in blood during the tough fighting in Alsace and the invasion of Germany. This *blanchissement*—or "whitening"—of de Lattre's French First Army caused a dip in military efficiency and speed. It also ignited quarrels between de Gaulle and the Americans over equipping this force. French field commanders in France and Germany were apt to treat orders from their Anglo-American superiors as mere suggestions to be disobeyed if they failed to further de Gaulle's stiff-necked crusade to uphold French "rights" and "honor." This added tension to an already brittle relationship among the Western Allies.

Despite these negative Allied judgments on the quality of French troops in the later stages of World War II, their successes were considerable, and France undoubtedly produced three of the war's best commanders in Alphonse Juin, Philippe Leclerc de Hautclocque, and Jean de Lattre de Tassigny. This was especially remarkable given the small size of French forces and the fact that they reentered the conflict in significant numbers only in 1943 with an army that was little more than an antiquated colonial constabulary. These men had to learn quickly about modern war, often while operating under significant political constraints.

It is equally true that the Mediterranean offered a theater where French forces could register some brilliant battlefield successes, triumphs that translated into political dividends for de Gaulle. Free French forces fighting with the Eighth Army in the Western Desert distinguished themselves at Bir Hacheim in June 1942 and at Ksar Rhilane in March 1943. Mark Clark accorded Juin the place of honor in the victory march into Rome precisely because the French Expeditionary Corps (CEF) was almost single-handedly responsible for the rupture of the Winter line south of Monte Cassino. De Lattre's French First Army demonstrated great aggressiveness in the assault on Elba that preceded Anvil and in clearing Marseilles and Toulon of large German garrisons, operations vital to the success of the campaign in France. The campaign in Alsace against extremely stiff German resistance in the Colmar Pocket was efficiently, sometimes brilliantly, directed by de Lattre, even though his army was in the throes of reorganization and often lacked vital equipment.

Despite these obvious successes, the general Allied view of the French was at best ambivalent, at worst dismissive. How does one account for this? The first reason was that the French brought with them the stigma of the 1940 debacle. France's defeat in the short space of six weeks could be most easily explained, even in the minds of the French themselves, in moral terms—as the product of an army rotten with defeatism led by men incapable of understanding modern, mechanized warfare. For this reason, the first task of French soldiers was to dispel the barrier of skepticism and persuade Allied generals to take them seriously as soldiers. The future general, André Lanquetot, second lieutenant in the Eighth Moroccan Rifles in 1943, noted that American troops with whom he served in Italy greeted the French as "the vanquished of '40." However, after the French had proven themselves in combat, "we were admitted as companions in arms."[10] But those tests in Italy were a long time in the making. To reach that point, France had to recover from the devastating humiliation of 1940. That task fell to Charles de Gaulle and the Free French.

France's military revival could not take place before the political foundation for France's resurrection was laid, however. This brings one to the second reason for the poor Allied opinion of French performance: the specter of political disarray in the French camp. De Gaulle's inflexible character, his incessant bickering with his French rivals, appeared unfathomable and arcane to Anglo-American military men who nurtured a natural aversion to politics and who found far too much of it in the Mediterranean. For them, French attitudes complicated immensely an already complex military task in a peripheral theater where they seemed, despite immense exertions, to be making a minimal contribution to the defeat of Hitler. They considered their French allies quarrelsome and difficult. American veterans of Torch were especially bitter at the losses they had suffered in French North Africa, "and [they] gave us proof of it as soon as we landed in Italy," Lanquetot remembered. "The clans, the Franco-French backbiting, the incoherence which flowed from contradictory desires . . . all this was Byzantine and incomprehensible to the young Americans, confident in their power and their cause, brusquely transported thousands of miles from their home. Their territory had never been invaded."[11] Nevertheless, even though the French gained the admiration of soldiers who served with them, especially in Italy, they remained an undecipherable hieroglyphic for most Allied combatants. "It seems unlikely that either British or Americans will ever clearly understand what was going on in the minds of Frenchmen during the years of their country's occupation," the British official history diplomatically concluded.[12]

Allied soldiers failed to grasp two essential characteristics of their wartime allies. The first was that far from undermining French military performance, French political rivalries actually inspired and sharpened it. The second was that the French employed the Mediterranean campaigns as a springboard for the revival of the French army and as a way to prepare France to assume an important role in postwar Europe.[13] De Gaulle understood that Hitler was going to lose the war. His task was to put France in the best position to recover its influence once the fighting stopped. The measured Allied advance through the Mediterranean allowed him to achieve military successes so important for that nation's *amour propre*, identify military commanders, settle po-

litical disagreements among competing factions, and acquire a political base in the French empire as a preparation for the invasion of
France. That process was a laborious, even torturous one in which his
forces were used as means to gain political leverage with his allies.
The ultimate triumph of Charles de Gaulle, a man central to the postwar history of France and Europe, is difficult to imagine without his
Mediterranean passage.

Born in obscurity, the Free French might easily have become a
failed cult were it not for the tenacity of their leader and the fanaticism
of de Gaulle's acolytes, men who burned to restore the reputation of
French arms. Most French were reluctantly reconciled to 1940 as a
downturn in national fortune that, although humiliating, was neither
unprecedented nor irreversible over time. The handful of men who
rallied to de Gaulle's 18 June 1940 challenge rejected that premise.
Some were refugees from the failed Narvik expedition stranded in
Britain. Others fled French colonies for the sanctuary of British ones.
In any case, by the end of August 1940, de Gaulle had collected 2,721
disciples eager to bear the torch of La France libre.

The stern determination to reverse the verdict of 1940 gradually
hardened into an attitude that bordered on fanaticism among these
men, as they took in the full impact of their courageous, some would
say foolhardy, decision to fight for French honor. In 1940 the Germans
recognized a French government led by World War I hero Marshal
Philippe Pétain at Vichy in central France. By tolerating a suspicion
of Vichy independence, Hitler sought to ensure that the French
colonies, the French navy, and the rump of the army would not teeter
into the British camp. This Vichy regime, which the vast majority of
French people regarded as the legitimate government, became the
main stumbling block to de Gaulle's goal of resurrecting French
power and reversing the verdict of 1940. From the beginning, therefore, the primary enemies for the Free French were not Germans, but
collaborationist French.

Vichy accused the British, aided by what Pétain's government
termed Free French "mercenaries," of profiting from France's temporary embarrassment to weaken France. The Vichy regime's charges
were lent plausibility in the minds of some Frenchmen by the British

attack on the French fleet at Mers el-Kébir, its internment of a squadron at Alexandria, and the invasion of French possessions in Syria and Madagascar. To the Free French, Vichy collaboration with Hitler was intolerable, a national insult. They became increasingly disgusted as Vichy absorbed humiliation after humiliation without lifting a finger to protect French honor. The agitated confusion that Torch engendered in French North Africa in November 1942 was matched only by the extraordinary passivity of Vichy, which confined its 100,000-man "Armistice Army" to barracks rather than oppose the German invasion of its *zone libre*. In November 1942, only the navy shook off its torpor long enough to scuttle itself in Toulon harbor.

De Gaulle's goal of undermining Vichy legitimacy was compromised by his tributary status *vis-à-vis les Anglo-Saxons*. After all, the Germans had only been enemies since 1870. But the English had burned Joan of Arc. The Free French dilemma, therefore, was: How de we stand up for France's long-term interests while fighting for allies fixated on the short-term goal of defeating the Axis? The answer, of course, was to apply de Gaulle's "I am too poor to afford bending"[14] formula with a vengeance. This went down poorly with FDR, who had no love for the French in any case, especially one as brittle and severe as dc Gaulle. Roosevelt had discounted de Gaulle when he failed to deliver Dakar to the British in September 1940.[15] As the war progressed, Roosevelt saw himself as France's liberator, and hence came to view de Gaulle as a competitor, an imperialist, and a tool of Churchill's ambition. The American president resented the fact that de Gaulle remained impervious to his legendary charm. Rather than show deference and gratitude to the Americans, de Gaulle instead displayed undiplomatic contempt for FDR's plans for a postwar Europe run as an Anglo-American/Soviet condominium, with a disarmed France.[16] The leader of Free France repaid Allied condescension by applying the little leverage he commanded. He did so, for instance, when the British seized the French island of Madagascar in May 1942 to forestall a Japanese takeover. Philippe Leclerc halted all traffic on the Takoradi air route across Africa to Suez and prepared to intern British troops in Chad, where he was military governor.[17]

Free France was a refuge neither for the faint of heart nor for the conventional soldier. The Gaullist attitude of defiance and fanaticism percolated down to unit level. Traditional notions of hierarchy and discipline were of trifling importance to Free French soldiers who had taken French leave from Vichy "legality." They cultivated a style that reflected their status as outcasts and brigands. *"Une atmosphère de li- berté violente"* reigned in Free French units, some of which elected their own officers, much to de Gaulle's dismay. Intolerance for Vichy, rusticity, and austerity were the pillars of Free French military life. In March 1941, Leclerc's soldiers asked if they could take wine on their desert raid against the Italian base at Koufra in the Fezzan, only to be told by their leader: "War isn't a profession, a public works enterprise. It's a total commitment, a passion, the adventure of the resurrection. Now, who came here to talk about wine?"

Allied commanders barely knew how to deal with soldiers whose mental state hovered somewhere between the Inquisition and the nursery, whose *métier* seemed to be acting out—always whining, de- manding something as if it were owed them, usually in a highly inso- lent tone. They cultivated a style that even the British Eighth Army, which prided itself on taking liberties with the uniform, found exces- sively waggish. "In British eyes, the Free French had three defects," one non-Gaullist French officer explained. "They always gave the im- pression that the (other) French were losers, they disdained comfort, and were constantly posing problems in political or moral terms. How do you fight in those conditions!"[18] How the Free French fought was a problem indeed. It is hardly surprising that Montgomery concluded that the Free French were not team players, but unreliable men whose ideas of heroic self-immolation risked the success of the battle plan. The goal of Free French soldiers was not to burnish the reputation of the Eighth Army, much less that of Montgomery. Rather, their aim was to revive France's atrophied martial traditions by spectacular, even futile—especially futile—gestures. The Axis be damned! Their battle was an exhibition of contempt for those French who had quit the fight.

Shut out of the continent, with North Africa bolted against them, Free France singled out those colonies that offered the softest targets for their diminutive forces. De Gaulle was severely embarrassed when the expedition put together by Churchill failed to rally Dakar in French West Africa in September 1940. However, the French Congo, Gabon, Cameroon, and Chad surrendered, practically without bloodshed. New Caledonia in the Pacific and the Pondicherry in India came over to the Gaullist camp, adding éclat, if little else. At that point, the period of facile success came to an abrupt end, as the fledgling movement was alerted that their crusade was likely to be more arduous than they had imagined for two reasons. First, the British, their hands full with the Battle of Britain and unsettled by Italian threats to Egypt, proved reluctant to add Vichy to an already significant list of enemies. Therefore, they called a halt to the Free French colony collection campaign.

Second, if the Gaullists believed that they were benevolently viewed by their erstwhile colleagues, vituperative Vichy denunciations demonstrated that the split of 1940 was rapidly escalating into a bitter civil war. Vichy loyalists repatriated from Africa identified Gaullist soldiers masquerading behind their *noms de guerre*, selected to protect their families from reprisals. Vichy tribunals stripped Free French soldiers of their regular army ranks and decorations as well as their citizenship and condemned many, including de Gaulle and Leclerc, to

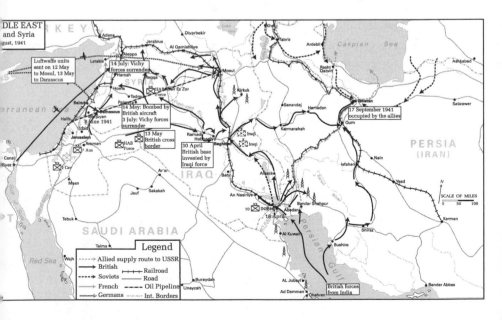

death in absentia. With irrefutable proof that official France considered them traitors and felons, and not simply AWOL ex-colleagues who made a different choice, Gaullist soldiers were left in no doubt that their cause must succeed, or they must die in its defense. Temporization was no longer an option.[19]

IRAQ AND SYRIA

The dual problems of reconciling Anglo–Free French interests and the yawning chasm of animosity between the two French camps came to a head in the spring of 1941 in Syria. The Anglo–Free French invasion of Syria was a spin-off campaign that originated in neighboring Iraq. In 1932 the British accorded sovereignty to Iraq, making it the first of the former Turkish colonies in the Middle East to gain independence. However, because of Iraq's important geographic position as an air link and alternative land passage via Basra and Baghdad between India and British-controlled Palestine and the Suez Canal, an Anglo-Iraqi treaty allowed London to transit troops through Iraq, and required Baghdad to "give all aid, including the use of railways, rivers, ports and airfields," in the event of war. Baghdad also undertook to provide internal security, especially to protect the vital pipelines that ran from the Mosul and Kirkuk oilfields of northern Iraq to Haifa on the Mediterranean coast. By 1937, British presence in Iraq had been reduced to two RAF bases, one at Shaibah, close to the southern port of Basra, and the other at Habbaniya, on the Euphrates about twenty-five miles west of Baghdad.

Despite Britain's reduced profile in Iraq, anti-British sentiment persisted, especially in the army, where nationalist officers resented Britain's residual influence in their country, took offense at London's refusal to arm their forces adequately, and opposed Jewish immigration into Palestine. But little could be done because Iraq's Hashemite monarchy, imported from Saudia Arabia after after World War I, with shallow roots in the Iraqi population and weakened by its association with the British, was utterly dependent on the army to keep order, especially after the military crushed both the 1933 Assyrian rebellion and those of the tribes in 1935–36. In the tumultuous politics of Iraq in the 1930s, Iraqi army officers, organized into a secret association known as the Golden Square, kept a wary eye on the monarchy, sensitive to the slightest pro-British tilt. The logic of Iraqi distrust of London caused many in Baghdad to attribute King Faisal's 1939 death in an automobile accident to British agents. Faisal's death cleared the way for the Golden Square to act as Iraq's principal power broker.[20]

By treaty, Iraq should have sided with Britain on the outbreak of war in 1939. But the government of the four-year-old king of Iraq, led by his uncle, who served as regent, proved too feeble to surmount the opposition of Prime Minister Rashid Ali el Gailani. A lawyer and co-founder of the Moslem Brotherhood, whose cells were active throughout the Middle East, Rashid Ali spoke passionately in support of the "Arab cause" in the face of Zionist penetration of Palestine. Axis triumphs early in the war and the arrival of an Italian armistice commission to monitor Vichy French forces in neighboring Syria emboldened Rashid Ali's defiance of the British. London's insistence that Baghdad break off diplomatic relations with the Italians brought Anglo-Iraqi relations to the brink of crisis by February 1941. When Churchill's war cabinet recommended the precautionary dispatch of a division from India to occupy Basra, Wavell objected that the appearance of British troops would only inflame hair-trigger Iraqi nationalism. Wavell's obstruction left Iraq's vulnerable Royal Air Force bases guarded only by a locally recruited constabulary backed by armored cars.

For London, Iraq was just one piece of a complex Middle East jigsaw that stretched from Cairo to Teheran. Of particular concern to Britain were the intrigues of Amin al-Husseini, the grand mufti of Jerusalem, who had eventually sought refuge in Baghdad after being exiled from Palestine in October 1937. By the spring of 1941, the combination of Arab nationalism among Iraqi officers, the grand mufti's intrigues and propaganda, and tensions created by Rashid Ali's anti-British posturing had brought Iraq to the brink of civil war. On the night of 31 March–1 April 1941, tipped off that army officers planned to move against him, the regent escaped across the Tigris in a motorboat and made his way to the RAF base at Habbaniya, from which he was flown to Basra and the asylum of the HMS *Cockchafer*. On 3 April, Rashid Ali seized power with the help of army and air force officers of the Golden Square and proclaimed the National Defense Government. He sent a note to the British ambassador warning against any intervention in Iraq's internal affairs and dispatched a force to Basra to deny British troops landing rights there.

The coup in Baghdad threatened British interests for at least three reasons. It severed the vital air link, and a supplemental land route, between India and Egypt. It endangered the vital oil supply from the northern Iraqi oilfields, upon which British defense of the Mediterranean depended. Finally, an Arab nationalist success in Iraq could prove contagious and subvert Britain's tenuous political position in Egypt and Palestine. Against a military response to these threats the harassed British commander in the Middle East, General Archibald Wavell, argued that he had his hands full with four genuine crises in the spring of 1941. He had to coordinate the evacuation of three divisions and an armored brigade from Greece and prepare Crete's defenses to withstand an imminent German airdrop predicted by Ultra intelligence. A British offensive against Italian forces in East Africa was ready to kick off. Furthermore, Rommel had launched a surprise March offensive into Cyrenaica with one reinforced German and four Italian divisions, driven to the Egyptian frontier, and invested 36,000 British troops at Tobruk. In Wavell's view, even if he had the troops to spare, this was hardly the moment to stoke volatile Arab opinion with an ill-advised intervention in Iraq.

But in the spring of 1941, Churchill was beyond temporizing. "War," he believed, "is a contest of wills."[21] He had chosen to make a major military commitment to the Eastern Mediterranean, against the advice of his service chiefs, because that was where Britain could take the offensive, showcase its value as an ally for the United States, and where, by vigorous military action, he could distance Britain from the appeasement policies of his predecessor, Neville Chamberlain. An invasion of Iraq would, in Churchill's view, forestall Axis intervention and force Baghdad to break with Italy, eliminate Rashid Ali and al-Husseini, reinforce British rights of transit through Iraq, and, finally, bring Turkey into the war with Mosul as the prize.

On the orders of the chiefs of staff, Delhi landed a brigade at Basra on 30 April, the vanguard of the Tenth Indian Division, whose troops were already at sea en route for Iraq. Rashid Ali, who preferred to avoid a showdown with the British until he could solidify Axis support, now concluded that time was no longer on his side. As a consequence, he assembled a brigade armed with artillery to eliminate the British air base at Habbaniya before it could be reinforced. In London, the 30 April news that a large Iraqi force had invested Habbaniya caused the chiefs of staff to exult that their intervention in Basra had caused Rashid Ali's "plot" to "go off at half-cock" before the Axis could organize military support for the Iraqi regime.[22] But in the short term, it was unclear who had preempted whom. Habbaniya was an airfield that housed a flying-training school of 1,000 airmen, supported by 9,000 civilians, many of them British dependents. Its defenses consisted of a seven-mile-long iron fence and a constabulary of 1,200 Iraqi and Assyrian levies, backed by a fleet of armored cars, under the command of a British lieutenant colonel. Any attacker with even a poor command of tactics must realize that the elimination of Habbaniya's single conspicuous water tower or its power station would instantly compromise the garrison's powers of resistance.

Habbaniya's best defense lay with air power. But even this was limited by the abilities of half-trained students piloting a fleet of seventy-eight mostly obsolete biplane trainers, some hastily rigged to carry bomb loads as small as twenty pounds, hardly more than air-launched grenades. Fortunately, eight Wellington medium bombers, capable of delivering a 4,500-pound bomb load, and a few biwing Gladiators and monoplane Hurricane fighters, the warhorse of the Battle of Britain, arrived from Egypt. These, added to 300 soldiers of the king's own Royal Regiment, airlifted from the RAF base at Shaibah, gave some measure of protection against the two battalions of Iraqi troops that invested the base on 30 April. The steady buildup of Iraqi forces outside the base to brigade size led the commander at Habbaniya, Air Vice Marshal H. G. Smart, to conclude that attack was the best form of defense. At 0500 on 2 May, the Wellingtons and fighters attacked Iraqi forces, which replied by unleashing an artillery barrage on Habbaniya. Planes of the Iraqi air force, stationed at Rashid outside Baghdad, gave a good account of themselves, especially against half-trained student pilots in their trainers. Smart directed subsequent attacks at the Iraqi base at Rashid and against the lines of communication of the besieging force. Small, fast, twin-engine Blenheim medium bombers carrying 1,000-pound bomb loads escorted by long-range Hurricane fighters arrived from Egypt, to pound airfields at Baghdad and at Mosul, where a small Luftwaffe contingent had set up. After four days of constant bombing and raids by troops of the king's Royal Regiment, the besieging Iraqi troops decamped, leaving a wake of burning trucks and exploding ammunition dumps along the Baghdad road courtesy of the RAF.

The Defence Committee in London, armed with Ultra intercepts of Iraqi pleas for Axis support funneled through the Italian embassy in Baghdad, and worried by the mufti's broadcasts calling for a Moslem *jihad* against "the greatest foe of Islam," obliged a harassed and reluctant Wavell to invade before the Axis could organize support for Rashid Ali. For his part, Wavell argued that London should accept a Turkish offer to mediate the crisis on the basis of a cessation of hostilities in exchange for Rashid Ali's promise that Axis forces would not be allowed into Iraq. Churchill rejected this option out of hand, but left open the possibility of ceding Mosul to Turkey as an enticement to encourage Ankara to join the war at Britain's side.[23] "Profuse Axis propaganda" extolling Rashid Ali gave the impression that the new Iraqi prime minister had coordinated his coup with Berlin and Rome.[24] The British prime minister had no intention of allowing the new regime the leisure to pull in Axis reinforcements or to encourage imitators among nationalist army officers and the grand mufti's supporters in Egypt. Wavell argued the risks of denuding Palestine and the Transjordan of its already overstretched and underarmed garrison to invade Iraq to no avail. Reluctantly, the Middle East commander assembled a 5,800-strong intervention force in Palestine (Habforce), commanded by Major General J.G.W. Clark, for a march on Baghdad. However, so annoyed was Churchill at the exasperated tone of Wavell's dispatches and the lack of preparation for combat of the First Cavalry Division in Palestine, much of it still horse-mounted and lacking antiaircraft guns, he came close to sacking his Middle East commander.[25]

Churchill's preventive invasion of Iraq caught Berlin without a ward the Arabs, mainly because German diplomats and soldiers were divided over the issue of exploiting Arab nationalism. The German Foreign Office had been in contact with the mufti, but in keeping with Hitler's views, preferred to relinquish the formulation of policy for the Mediterranean and Middle East to the Italians. The Wehrmacht high command, whose views on Italian competence are unprintable, generally favored active support of Arab nationalist movements to undermine Britain's military position there. Nevertheless, the Iraqi rebellion surprised the German generals as they labored to wrap up the campaign in the Balkans and Greece, organize the paratroop drop in Crete, and put the finishing touches on Barbarossa, the German invasion of the Soviet Union scheduled for June 1941.[26] French Admiral Darlan, still burning with resentment over the Royal Navy's July 1940 attack on the French Mediterranean fleet lying at anchor at Mers el-Kébir, offered to release Vichy war stocks in Syria, including aircraft, permit passage of German war matériel across Syria, and provide a Syrian air link so that the Germans could support Rashid Ali from Axis-occupied Rhodes.[27] Unfortunately for Berlin, by the time Hitler was moved to declare that "the Arab liberation movement is our natural ally," Churchill had preempted Axis intervention. Nor did the Iraqis further their own cause when they mistakenly shot down the plane of Major Axel von Bloomberg, the German negotiator sent to coordinate military support.

Dr. Rudolf Rahn, the German representative on the Italian armistice commission in Syria, made energetic efforts to run trains of arms, munitions, and spare parts to the Iraqis through Turkey and Syria, and approximately thirty German and a few Italian planes intervened.[28] Despite this assistance, Iraq's five divisions and sixty serviceable aircraft proved no match for Habforce. This scratch British force, backed by about 200 aircraft and spearheaded by the Arab Legion, reached Habbaniya on 18 May after crossing almost 500 miles of searing desert in a week. By this time, RAF bombers had virtually annihilated the Iraqi air force and extended their attacks to Syrian air bases that serviced Axis planes. Many in the Iraqi government had applied for Syrian visas.

By mid-May 1941 the British had occupied Basra, thereby exercising their rights under the 1930 treaty, lifted the siege of Habbaniya, and at least temporarily forestalled Axis intervention. But how to proceed in Iraq became a subject of intense debate. The chiefs of staff in London argued for the continued pounding of Iraqi forces, avoiding civilian casualties as much as possible, to "defeat and discredit the leaders in the hope that Rashid's Government would be replaced."[29] For its part, Delhi made a case for a march to Baghdad followed by the military occupation of northern Iraq, which offered the only long-term guarantee against Axis intervention. Churchill compromised: he ordered General Clark to march Habforce to Baghdad, but at the same time assured Wavell that he would not have to commit scarce forces to the long-term occupation of northern Iraq until Rommel was defeated in Libya.

The Iraqi army, fighting from behind defensive lines organized along canals and fields flooded from water unleashed from tributaries of the Euphrates, put up a respectable resistance against Habforce, which divided into separate columns to advance on Baghdad from three directions. On 30 May, Habforce scattered Iraqi units supported by Italian aircraft on the outskirts of Baghdad. To avoid the prospects of a house-to-house street battle, Clark opted for bluff. An interpreter phoned Rashid Ali's headquarters with exaggerated reports of British strength. The Iraqi leader, demoralized by the absence of Axis support, panicked, and, with the grand mufti in tow, scuttled to Persia with the rump of the Golden Square. The British signed a lenient armistice that allowed the Iraqi army to retain its arms and return to its peacetime garrisons. Wavell left the administration of Baghdad to Iraqi authorities. The pro-British regent regained the throne on 1 June.[30] Order disintegrated in Baghdad, as Jewish merchants in particular became the target of outraged nationalists and freelance looters.[31] The British army, camped outside Baghdad, failed to intervene.[32]

Regime change in Iraq created other dominoes. On 25 August 1941, British and Soviet forces invaded Persia, overthrew Reza Shah, and replaced him with his son, Mohammad Reza Pahlavi. Iran might have been the only casualty of the Iraqi affair, had it not been for de Gaulle and the Free French. De Gaulle, eager to pick off another colony and angered by the eagerness of the Vichy commander in Syria, General Henri Dentz, to collaborate with the Germans, flew to

Cairo in April to press Wavell to invade Syria and Lebanon.[33] The Free French painted a picture of a Syrian garrison eager to bolt for the Allied camp at the mere sight of the Cross of Lorraine. In May, as Habforce advanced on Baghdad, General Georges Catroux, an ex–governor-general of Indochina who served as de Gaulle's deputy in the Levant, proposed leading a small Free French force to Damascus. But Wavell, much to de Gaulle's fury, refused to be seduced by Free French fantasies that the Syria garrison was ripe for rebellion. Nevertheless, when Luftwaffe planes landed on Syrian airfields on 14 May in transit to Baghdad, and with the German invasion of Crete pending, even a skeptical Wavell was tempted to give at least partial credence to Catroux's claims that the Germans intended to use Crete as a springboard to Syria, which would be handed over to them by Vichy forces, and then attack Palestine and Suez from the north. Nevertheless, he deferred the decision to invade Syria to the Defence Committee in London. On 20 May, Wavell was told to add Syria to his "to do" list. It could not have come at a worse time for the British commander. The German invasion of Crete had begun, as had the arrival of intelligence of German reinforcements to the Afrika Korps. Habforce, his only reserve, struggled toward the gates of Baghdad. Wavell curtly condemned nefarious Free French influences on British strategy. Intelligence reached him on 21 May that the Vichy garrison had no intention of turning over Syria and Lebanon to the Germans. He contemplated resigning in protest, but grudgingly, on 25 May, began to scrape troops together for an invasion of the French mandates.[34]

Operation Exporter was launched on 8 June with a scratch force of 34,000 British, Australian, Indian, and Free French troops attacking out of Iraq, Palestine, and the Transjordan. The request of General Dentz for Luftwaffe support brought down attacks on the oil pipeline terminal at Haifa by German planes based in Greece and Rhodes. Hitler ordered seven trains of French reinforcements to transit to Salonika. But the British naval blockade combined with Ankara's obstinate insistence on neutrality meant that they went no farther. There was little else Hitler could do to help the Vichy French in the Levant. He lacked the sea power to break the British blockade. His fighters were operating at the extreme limit of their endurance. He had sacrificed his paratroops in Crete. He ignored Rahn's suggestion that the French be shifted to Syria in German transport planes, probably because to assist the French in such a blatant way would undermine Axis standing with the Arabs.[35]

However, the Vichy garrison of between 35,000 and 45,000 troops backed by ninety tanks and fighting from well-prepared defensive positions managed to produce a stalemate by 13 June, and even to counterattack. But the disappointing conclusion of the Battleaxe offensive in Cyrenaica in mid-June allowed the British to transfer reinforcements to Syria. Habforce and part of the Tenth Indian Division were marched in from Iraq. On 11 July, with Beirut and Damascus in British hands, the RAF in complete control of the skies, his supplies and troops exhausted, Dentz requested an armistice. From Wavell's perspective, the dispersal of his forces among Crete, Iraq, Egypt, East Africa, and Syria had prolonged the Syrian campaign and contributed to the defeat of Battleaxe.[36] Nor, he suspected correctly, had the Iraqi invasion bolstered Britain's long-term prospects in the Middle East. In the short term, however, Suez and the Nile Delta, Iraq and its oil remained in British hands, while the prospect of an Axis descent on Syria with Vichy complicity had been balked. Churchill had also seized another opportunity to strut his determination, chutzpah, and sangfroid.

De Gaulle was also ahead on points, although this was not altogether apparent at the time for two very predictable reasons. The British, eager to curry favor with Arab nationalists, refused to allow the Free French to be signatories to the Acre Convention of 14 July, Bastille Day. Instead, they set Syria and Lebanon on the road to independence, lending credibility to Vichy charges that Free France was merely Perfidious Albion's Trojan horse. Once inside French colonies, Britain would "open the gates" and thus dismantle parts of the empire.[37] Second, the British were not eager to acquire more French soldiers that they would have to equip and train, much less inflate a Free French movement that was proving difficult to control. Obstacles placed in the way of a Gaullist recruitment drive among the vanquished Vichy garrison combined with deep resentment over casualties to yield only 1,286 recruits out of the 35,000-man Syrian garrison, almost evenly split between Foreign Legionnaires with an imperfect grasp of the political stakes involved and Moslem soldiers.[38] Although de Gaulle ordered that Vichy and Free French dead in Syria be buried side by side and that no medal be struck for the campaign, the significant bloodletting—3,300 British, 1,300 Free French, and around 6,000 Vichy casualties[39]—further poisoned relations. The Vichy commander in Lebanon urged his men not "to trample on the corpses of so many of our brave, fallen comrades" by defecting to the Gaullists. The Germans were only too delighted to repatriate Syrian veterans eager to propagate hostile opinions of their renegade Gaullist colleagues throughout North African messes. The pro-Vichy press in North Africa fanned the flames of resentment. Syria became an addendum to a lengthening list of Anglo-Gaullist treachery that included Mers el-Kébir and Dakar. Free France was a collection of adventurers and "disobedient hotheads," who fought not Germans but other Frenchmen.[40] General Maxime Weygand, Vichy's *délégué général* in Africa, known to be uncomfortable with Darlan's collaborationist policies, refused to reply to a letter from de Gaulle calling on the ex-commander-in-chief of the French forces to rally to Free France.[41] Gaullists in North Africa became as rare as hens' teeth. The flickering admiration for de Gaulle in the post-capitulation officer corps appeared to have been completely extinguished by Syrian fratricide. The prewar camaraderie of the mess would prove difficult to piece together again.

In another sense, however, de Gaulle emerged the big winner in a Syrian campaign that had made it ever more apparent that "legitimate" France had backed the wrong horse in the war. Darlan's willingness to collaborate with Hitler endangered the British position in the Mediterranean. "When you deal with Vichy, you deal with Hitler," de Gaulle told Churchill.[42] Free French soldiers became even more fanatical, more ruthless, more determined to succeed. Syria made it more difficult for the Allies to find an alternative to de Gaulle, and to resurrect a French army that shunned its Free French element.

But these trends were not immediately apparent to the Allies, who seemed unaware that their French options had narrowed. In the battle for control of the French government-in-exile, 1943 was a crucial year, and North Africa a decisive theater in the struggle between de Gaulle and American-backed General Henri Giraud. Eisenhower's attempt to hand over North Africa to Admiral Darlan backfired badly with Allied public opinion, and benefited de Gaulle in the long run because it boosted his credibility and forced him to conquer the leadership of France's resistance movement. One of the strongest arguments for Torch was that French North Africa offered a repository of 120,000 French troops who could be bonded to the Allied cause, and a stepping-stone to a cornucopia of manpower in Continental France.[43] However, Allied attempts to resurrect the French army from January 1943 were retarded by intramural feuds between supporters of Giraud and de Gaulle—known at the time as "Star Wars"—that left France's Anglo-American allies gape-jawed in disbelief and nourished what de Gaulle biographer Jean Lacouture called "Washington's stubborn contempt" for the French.[44]

But gradually, Free French forces conquered the grudging esteem of Allied generals, even ones as parsimonious with praise as Montgomery. One reason for the poor opinion of Free French military performance, especially before 1943, was not so much underachievement as the fact that there were so few engagements that their failures were instantly noticeable, while their successes were often subsumed in the tide of Allied victory. It is also fair to note that the Free French fought better in defensive than in attacking roles. That said, however, Montgomery's poor opinion of Gaullist troops, which he communicated to Brooke, was based on a single lapse during the Battle of El Alamein, when Pierre Koenig's Free French Brigade had faltered during a diversionary night attack upon Axis positions at El Himeimat, a strongly fortified ridge 1,300 feet high that overlooked the sandy Qattara Depression and anchored the southern extremity of Rommel's defensive lines at El Alamein. The attack became a shambles as French halftracks, attacking into a smoke screen, failed to follow the path that had been cleared for them through the minefield. Instead, they fanned out, became bogged down in sand, and set off mines as they came under heavy artillery fire. Because the command radio went down, one battalion could not inform the other that it was withdrawing when it was attacked by eight captured "Honeys" (light Stuart tanks) because it had no antitank guns.[45] The second battalion continued to thrust forward under heavy fire, losing its commander in the process. A German counterattack drove the French back to the starting line. Montgomery complained that the French had failed to push their antitank guns forward to take care of the tanks and that their artillery was poorly coordinated with their infantry attacks. He relieved the Free French Brigade and consigned it to secondary duties for the remainder of the North African campaign.

Montgomery's reaction becomes more comprehensible when one understands that Montgomery's, and the British Army's, reputation was on the line at El Alamein.[46] The general who was fast ascending into the pantheon of British arms concluded that the low casualty figures suffered by the French at El Himeimat suggested a loss of nerve as well as a lack of skill, both unpardonable sins in Monty's view. The Free French Brigade had failed the Montgomery test, and he registered the failing grade with his superior Alan Brooke.

Of course, what Monty had missed was the Free French success at Bir Hacheim during the Battle of Gazala, which had occurred two months before his August 1942 arrival in Egypt. The Free French celebrated Bir Hacheim as a great victory, its first against Germans. The BBC's Radio Londres extolled the *"rendez-vous d'honneur"* of a handful of Frenchmen, which it compared, presumably without blushing, with the 1916 defense of Verdun. For de Gaulle, Bir Hacheim became payback both for the British, who had "abandoned" Bir Hacheim (a claim that German radio was happy to confirm), and for Vichy, whose soldiers were consorting with the occupier while his men won laurels fighting them.

To be fair to Montgomery, even though the brigade had failed at El Alamein, he was perfectly willing to offer a chance to another Gaullist officer who joined him in Tunisia. Captain Philippe de Hautclocque was probably de Gaulle's most gifted military recruit. A 1924 graduate of Saint-Cyr and of the prestigious École de Guerre, de Hautclocque was considered one of the French army's "comers" until July 1940, when he transited through Spain on a false passport, presented himself to the British military attaché in Lisbon for passage to London, and quickly adopted the name Leclerc. De Gaulle and his young protégé shared many characteristics. Both were brilliant mavericks, sons of conservative, Catholic minor gentry in northern France. Both were men of uncompromising principle, crusaders for France's resurrection, whose bond was practically a feudal one. Each projected a cool, distant, austere, even intimidating veneer that concealed a passionate nature. When primed, each exploded into intemperate tirades.

There were differences. Where de Gaulle's cold formality left people unsettled and overawed, Leclerc appeared approachable and generous—to all, that is, except Marshal Pétain's men. Americans who served with Leclerc did not quite know how to take him. George Patton, Francophile and fellow cavalryman, reveled in Leclerc's flamboyant, open-warfare style. On the other hand, Bradley, the careful Midwestern infantryman, found the combination of Leclerc's nervous impatience and his quasi-mystical fanaticism mildly repulsive.[47]

After helping to bring Cameroon into the Free French fold, Leclerc was chosen to command French forces in Chad, where, cooperating with British Long Range Desert Patrol (LRDP) groups, the acclaimed "Desert Rats," Leclerc seized the Italian base of Koufra in the Libyan Desert in March 1941. At this point, Leclerc and his men took what became known as the Vow of Koufra, the most widely accepted version of which runs: "We swear not to lay down our arms until our colors, our beautiful colors, again fly from the Strasbourg cathedral."

Leclerc languished for almost a year and a half in the obscurity of central Africa, although he earned a promotion to brigadier general. In November 1942, with the Eighth Army closing on Tunisia and Koenig's Free French Brigade languishing in Montgomery's bad books, de Gaulle ordered Leclerc to march across the Libyan Desert to Tripoli, installing French administrators in the oases along the way to prevent the British from taking control. Leclerc left Chad on the thirteenth with a ragtag band of 4,375 men and 543 vehicles, arriving in Tripoli at the end of January 1943. There, Leclerc presented himself to Montgomery and asked to be incorporated into the Eighth Army. The British, fully expecting that Leclerc would make extravagant demands on the Eighth Army's logistics, asked what he needed. They were stunned when Leclerc produced a very small piece of paper on which was written, "2 trucks, 5 machine guns," and a few other modest requests.

Indeed, the British soon realized that Leclerc's demands were so modest because his expectations were so low. So antiquated was Leclerc's "Force L" that its inclusion in what was in late 1942 the Western Allies' most successful army was practically an act of charity. Monty kitted out Leclerc's men in British uniforms, installed new motors in their trucks, and gave them thirty antitank guns, generally regarded as a requirement to fight panzers. He also attached eighty British sappers to initiate the Frenchmen into the mysteries of mine clearing. Leclerc was reinforced with a group of Greeks organized on the "Desert Rat" model, as well as the "French Flying Column," the only French troops that Monty had retained in his vanguard, composed of some Moroccan spahis and a French tank regiment. While this influx of matériel and reinforcements represented a considerable upgrade for the French, it only served to make Leclerc, who had dreamed of commanding a light division, aware that he was no longer skirmishing against lightly armed Italians in the desert, but was now integrated into a modern army whose system was based on strong artillery, air support, and mobility.

Monty, too, was aware of the "light" nature of Force L. Nor, as has been seen, did he have great faith in the fighting qualities of the French. "There is great pressure to employ the French troops in the fighting here," he wrote to Brooke in January 1943. "But perhaps it is not realized that they are no good; I have had them once in battle and never want them again."[48] So, most likely to keep them well away from the main action, he assigned Leclerc as flank guard attached to the New Zealand Division. In early 1943, the Eighth Army advanced on the Mareth line, old French fortifications, similar to the Maginot line, built in the 1930s to protect Tunisia from an Italian attack and updated by Rommel's engineers. Before Montgomery could reach them, however, Rommel lashed out at American troops at Kasserine in mid-February, and then turned to spoil preparations for Montgomery's assault on the Mareth line. When Rommel attacked on 6 March, Montgomery was waiting for him, and repulsed the Germans with significant losses. Four days later, Rommel returned to attack a section of the front held by Leclerc at Ksar Rhilane. Montgomery offered to allow Leclerc to withdraw in the face of the German Ninetieth Light

Division. However, the Frenchman insisted he could hold if he received adequate air support. Montgomery gave it, and Leclerc repelled the German attack. "This was a fine performance," Montgomery noted in his diary. Sir Charles Richardson observed Leclerc coolly beside his radio directing the defense. The Free French appeared to have earned some respect. Unfortunately for Leclerc, that was the last action his troops saw in the Tunisia campaign. But his advance with the Eighth Army toward Tunis was a valuable experience during which he learned how to adapt and reconfigure his forces according to terrain and enemy opposition, how to handle minefields, and how to utilize air support.

The liberation of Tunisia was a real turning point in de Gaulle's struggle to gain control of the French government. Leclerc's troops were welcomed with enthusiasm by a white population that knew only the name of de Gaulle, not Giraud. The first indication that the Allies might be in for trouble occurred at the end of the Tunisian campaign, when Free French fighting with Montgomery's Eighth Army coming up from Libya met former Vichyites from Algeria. According to Giraud, Eisenhower and Alexander were stupefied when the Free French refused to march in the victory parade alongside their North African colleagues, choosing instead to march with the British. Senior Free French officers also boycotted the post-parade victory luncheon hosted by General Alphonse Juin, who had commanded Vichy forces in North Africa. But Free French contempt for the ex-Vichy, now pro-Giraud Armée d'Afrique did not stop at mere snubs. Eager to create two divisions to increase de Gaulle's political clout with the Allies, Free French soldiers launched an intensive recruitment campaign— Giraud called it "kidnappings"—among soldiers from the Armée d'Afrique. These "desertions" to Free France soon achieved epidemic proportions. Nor were some of them prepared to stop there. In May 1943 the Americans learned that Free French soldiers were making plans to "clean out the [French] high command" in Algiers. They threatened to cut off all rations to the Free French First and Second Divisions unless they withdrew to Libya. Those forces that had fought so valiantly in East Africa, Syria, and since El Alamein were exiled to the sand wastes south of Tripoli. The British in Libya complained that discipline had seriously deteriorated in Free French forces, a decline that is hardly surprising.[49] But by then, opinion in the French population of North Africa and the French resistance had turned toward the Gaullist camp.[50]

In August 1943, "Free France" became "Fighting France." Even the most sectarian Gaullist was forced to accept the logic that now that the French had decided to fight, there was no point in maintaining a divided army. Besides, not only was de Gaulle consolidating command of the French government-in-exile, but American equipment, the result of the Anfa agreement of January 1943 to reequip French forces, was arriving in North Africa by the boatload. The price of access to recruits and matériel was for the various factions of the French army to bury the hatchet. For the equipment-starved French, it seemed a price worth paying. André Lanquetot's Moroccans stood like spectators at a bicycle race as the first convoy of Dodges, GMCs, tow trucks, trailers groaning with radios, antitank guns, mortars, and machine guns roared into their camp south of Fez in June 1943. "We were drunk with joy. How we loved and polished this matériel. Some bonded with their jeeps . . . We were euphoric! We were no longer poor!" They quickly, and as it was to transpire prematurely, shed their mules, regarded as "companions of our poverty."[51] However, the Gaullists were too invested in a culture of rebellion, too bitter at the refusal of the Armée d'Afrique for almost two and a half years to fight anyone but Gaullist and British forces to surrender to a spirit of reconciliation. They were especially annoyed that the commanders selected to lead Armies A and B respectively, which were to form the nucleus of the French military revival, were ex-Vichy generals Juin and de Lattre.

The remainder of the war failed to measure up to the heady early years of Free France. Gaullist soldiers were ill at ease occupying barracks where pictures of Marshal Pétain were still prominently displayed. The regular army refused to acknowledge many of the rapid promotions achieved under de Gaulle. Gaullists reciprocated by neglecting to salute "Pétainist" officers. Fisticuffs between veterans of the two sides in Syria became a regular feature of mess nights. The Free French First Division never adapted to the enforced amalgamation. It served under Juin in the final Battle of Cassino under protest, and had to be removed from the French First Army in Alsace in 1945 after its Gaullist officers traveled to Paris to complain about de Lattre's leadership.

The French Second Armored Division was more of a success, due in part to Leclerc's dynamic leadership, and because it had the better part of a year to sort out its personnel problems in a remote training area of Morocco. The unit and its commander were unrelentingly promoted by Gaullist propaganda. It avoided Italy and fought most of the campaign for France integrated among U.S. forces. However, once Leclerc was paired with de Lattre, the Second Armored Division fared little better than its sister Gaullist division, the Free French First Division. Leclerc insisted that building his division into a cohesive force was the toughest task of his career. The adoption by the French of the U.S. system of "combat commands" obliged Leclerc to mix and match units from the two camps, not always with success. For instance, Gaullists in the Second Armored Division undiplomatically referred to the Twelfh Algerian Cavalry Regiment, an Armée d'Afrique unit assigned to their division, as the *"Royal-Nazi."* Even Leclerc protested when a regiment of French marines was assigned to his division, so passionately did he despise the French navy's unstinting loyalty to Pétain. Many Armée d'Afrique officers persisted in calling him "Hautecloque," pointedly ignoring his accomplishments under his Free French *nom de guerre.* In Alsace in the winter of 1944–45, the Americans became so fed up with the perpetual disputes between de Lattre and Leclerc that caused the French Second Armored Division to bounce between the U.S. Seventh Army and the French First Army that Leclerc's division was eventually dispatched to attack German troops blocking the Gironde Estuary at Royan, near Bordeaux.

ANVIL[52]

The invasion of southern France had been, from its inception, an orphan idea. The possibility of a Riviera invasion was first proposed at the Washington Trident Conference in May 1943, but rejected in favor of an invasion of Italy.[53] However, the concept of a southern France landing, code-named Anvil in August 1943, was kept alive by several factors: the reconstitution of a French army, which meant that twelve to fourteen divisions were available for offensive operations in the Mediterranean even after deducting resources for Overlord; a realization that it was easier to shift assets for Overlord directly to England from the United States rather than transfer them from the Mediterranean; and finally, a U.S. desire to checkmate Churchill's schemes for operations in the Eastern Mediterranean combined with Stalin's wish to keep the Western Allies out of the Balkans. Even some Anvil agnostics, like Eisenhower's chief of staff Bedell Smith, Montgomery, and Brooke, had supported a Riviera assault as a strategy to retain resources, especially landing craft, in the Mediterranean.[54]

The Allied breakthrough at Cassino and the capture of Rome reignited a bitter debate in the Allied high command over an operation that, although left for dead on several occasions, sprang to life with every new alteration in Allied Mediterranean fortunes. The original conception called for Anvil to coincide with Overlord, thus forcing the Germans in France to split their forces between two fronts. Its success was premised on the assumption that Allied armies would be camped out in northern Italy by May 1944. However, German resistance at Cassino and the requirement to use landing craft earmarked for Anvil to sustain the Anzio beachhead, combined with the success of Overlord, called the logic of Anvil into question. Alexander argued that it made no sense to divert manpower from Italy, where the Allies were "bleeding and burning the German divisions." The long struggle for Cassino had gutted the German forces, he insisted, leaving them with too few divisions to hold the Pisa-Rimini line without a fresh infusion of eight to ten divisions from France or the Balkans. Anvil and Overlord were too distant to be mutually supporting. Anvil had no geographic objective. Nine German divisions could easily block Allied progress north up the Rhône Valley. The best Allied option was to capitalize on the momentum of the Fifth and Eighth Armies backed by massive air power to attack the Pisa-Rimini line by 15 August, and then turn either west toward France or east to Venice and Austria.[55]

However, the arguments for Anvil were more compelling for the American chiefs of staff. They had surged into Italy in September 1943 *faute de mieux*, in a spirit of optimism inflated by the expectation of discounted victories against an enemy in retreat. Nine months later, a chastened high command was keen to cut their losses in a marginal theater, bypass fierce German resistance in Italy, and redirect their energies toward the main front in Northwestern Europe. For Eisenhower, the principal justification for Anvil was logistical: he required ports to disembark the divisions still languishing in the United States and North Africa, and to supply the main front. The French Channel ports were too small, and too devastated, to support single-handedly large Allied armies in Northern Europe. Therefore, the prospect of seizing the major Mediterranean ports of Marseilles and Toulon was, in itself, a compelling justification for Anvil. The Allied commanders in Italy had not kept systematic pressure on the Germans, which gave Kesselring time to recover between Allied offensives that lurched up the peninsula. Even if Alexander managed to crack the Pisa-Rimini line, there was no guarantee that the Germans would withdraw beyond the Alps. The British proposed no concrete alternatives to Anvil beyond speculative pronouncements about an attack through the Ljubljana Gap into southern Germany.[56] The German Nineteenth Army grouped approximately ten divisions in southern France. If these were not attacked, they might be shifted to either Italy, Normandy, or a combination of both.[57]

For Roosevelt, the clinching arguments in favor of Anvil were political. Roosevelt was loath to renege on a commitment to Anvil made to Stalin at Teheran in December 1943. Churchill's emotional pleas that to adopt Anvil was to "cast aside" Italy's "dazzling possibilities" failed to sway the American president. Relations between the two men had cooled considerably since the debacle at Anzio, which FDR blamed on Churchill's micromanagement of the Mediterranean campaign. Roosevelt was also planning for the *après guerre*. Overlord had transformed Italy, indeed the entire Mediterranean, into a strategic corpse, one into which the British tried to breathe life because this was where, in Churchill's mind, London retained an illusory alliance "seniority." Roosevelt made it clear that he would not commit U.S. forces to an advance in the Ljubljana while Allied troops appeared to be stalemated in Normandy. To cancel an invasion of southern France

was to invite justified rebellion among the French. Wary of earlier assurances of facile victories in Italy, the American president feared that
a campaign through the Po Valley and Slovakia into Hungary, Austria,
and southern Germany might drag on for months because of logistical
difficulties, a delay that would most certainly complicate his reelection campaign. Even if such an advance were successful, its momentum would rapidly dissipate as troops would be peeled off for
occupation duties in hostile territory. "Finally, for purely political considerations over here, I would never survive even a slight setback in
'Overlord' if it were known that fairly large forces had been diverted to
the Balkans," he told a disgruntled Churchill. On 14 June, the chiefs
of staff ordered Alexander to halt at the Pisa-Rimini line and release
seven divisions and 70 percent of Allied air power in Italy for Anvil.
Meanwhile, Hitler tossed a further eight divisions into Italy.[58]

Although Mark Clark later claimed that Anvil constituted "one of
the outstanding political mistakes of the war,"[59] he was especially disappointed at the departure of Juin and the CEF, which had been responsible for his successes. The truth was, however, that the CEF had
shot its bolt. "Juin's operation was one of the most remarkable feats of
a war more remarkable for bloody attrition than skill, and deserves to
be better known," write historians of the Italian campaign Dominick
Graham and Shelford Bidwell, "instead of being a briefly noted incident of the secondary Italian campaign, or ignored altogether. It was
orchestrated with extraordinary skill."[60] However, rather than being
praised for his operational finesse, Juin instead was criticized for a casualty rate that threatened the CEF with annihilation. Estimates of
battle casualties vary. But between November 1943 and August 1944,
the CEF lost over 6,500 officers and men killed, around 25,000
wounded, 8,000 captured, and 2,000 missing out of a corps of around
105,000 men. Some Moroccan units lost half of their strength.[61] De
Gaulle also recognized that the CEF's overwhelmingly Moslem recruitment formed an inadequate basis on which to construct France's
military, and hence its political, renaissance. Of 560,000 men serving
in the French Army on 1 September 1944, 295,000 were colonial subjects.[62] The initial wave of conscription in 1943, combined with those

North Africans already in uniform at the time of Torch, accounted for most of the Moslems willing to serve. North Africans had begun to evade the draft in droves. The French, reluctant to promote Moslem officers and NCOs beyond subaltern roles, were running short of cadres. U.S. commanders carped that the French were living rent-free on an already overtaxed Allied support base that armed, clothed, fed, and provided medical services for French troops, and that they needed to direct more troops into logistical and service jobs. Clearly, the French army needed to regain control of its own country and tap into its deep reserves of manpower and patriotism if it was to remain militarily effective.

De Gaulle had no interest in retaining his troops in Italy. On the contrary, his primary goal was to reach France and establish his authority there. Anvil was vital to the realization of that goal. The Allies had room to insert only Leclerc's Second Armored Division into Overlord. For the remainder of the French army, exile would end only when they returned to France across Mediterranean beaches. Without French troops on the ground, De Gaulle's capacity to grasp power in mainland France would be curtailed. The Allies would be free to impose AMGOT on Allied-occupied France and arbitrate a political settlement there, much as they had done in Italy. This might be dangerous, not only for de Gaulle's future, but also for that of France and Mediterranean Europe in general. The northern arch of that sea running from the Pyrenees to the Bosporus seemed to be in danger of falling under Communist control. Nazi occupation and fascist governance had laid waste to the economic and social fabric of Mediterranean Europe, and discredited traditional ruling elites. Everywhere political power seemed to be up for grabs in the wake of liberation. In France, resistance to German occupation was by no means an exclusively Communist enterprise. However, from the German attack on the USSR in June 1941, Communists had been quick to resurrect anti-German patriotism as a way to dissipate the shadow of their collaborationist stance before Barbarossa. Years of persecution allowed the politically savvy Communists to adjust with relative ease to the clandestine life of the resistance. A revolutionary message came naturally to them. The Communists seemed the party best placed to make a credible case for leadership of the resistance, and for resistance leadership of postwar France. The resistance challenged Vichy legitimacy and promised a moral regeneration of France based on a new social order. Indeed, a return to the prewar status quo after the trauma of defeat and occupation seemed unimaginable. But how far an armed and war-hardened resistance would challenge the bounds of established social order remained an open question in 1944. The withdrawal from Europe of U.S. troops after the defeat of Nazi Germany was assumed. What might occupy the vacuum left by an American withdrawal if not a government based on leaders drawn from the resistance?

Resistance in France had developed slowly from 1940, a largely spontaneous reaction by the young, the restless, and the politically active to the humiliation of the French debacle of 1940. It was given a huge boost in February 1943 when the Germans imposed *Service du travail obligatoire* (STO, or forced labor) in France. At a stroke, thousands of young men bolted for the hills, and into the arms of the resistance, to avoid deportation to Germany. The Gaullist movement in London had been slow to detect the growth and importance of the resistance in occupied France. De Gaulle had a natural aversion, even disdain, for the type of vigilante politics represented by the resistance, as well as for the advanced opinions of many of its leaders. The Free French intelligence service, the BCRA, struggled to organize the resistance as a special operations and intelligence service to facilitate the Allied invasion. However, political control from London, and eventually Algiers, was difficult to achieve because of the anarchical growth and competitive nature of resistance groups; the problematic independence of their leaders; competition with the British Special Operations Executive (SOE) and eventually the American OSS, which commanded far more resources than did the BCRA; and the intensity of German and Vichy repression, which imposed a fragmented and decentralized structure on the resistance. In 1943 Jean Moulin, a socialist and ex-prefect, was parachuted into France to cajole the various resistance organizations into a united front behind de Gaulle's leadership. But the Conseil National de la Résistance (CNR) was a fragile organization with shallow roots whose main purpose was to give legitimacy to the Gaullist movement vis-à-vis the Allies, and to abort Giraud's attempt to seize control of the exile government. Communist influence in the CNR remained strong, as did resistance of the "interior" to control by the "exterior."[63]

With the advantages of hindsight, it requires a great deal of imagination to invent a scenario whereby the Communists could have seized control in France or Italy. The presence of Allied troops in both countries would have made such a power grab suicidal. Furthermore, it is clear in retrospect that Stalin would not have supported such a move. Non-Communist resisters deeply distrusted their Communist colleagues. But Communist leaders, in the firm belief that they occupied the moral high ground, accustomed to a fair degree of independence from Moscow since the Spanish Civil War, and whose followers were armed to the teeth, talked as if political power were theirs for the taking.[64] For this reason, it remained vital that French troops be inserted into France to back up de Gaulle's claims for leadership. The French portion of Anvil was entrusted to Jean de Lattre de Tassigny. De Lattre was the spiritual antithesis of Juin as theatrical, spontaneous, and volatile as his rival was blunt, careful, and concentrated. A fastidious cavalryman, de Lattre lived on stage, as gracious to dignitaries, whom he received with Bourbon éclat, as he was severe with subordinates, whom he slaved to exhaustion. Like Juin, "Le Roi Jean" redeemed his Vichy service with a late conversion to the Allied cause. His abortive attempt to muster the 100,000-man Vichy army to resist the German occupation of the *zone libre* in November 1942 earned him a Vichy court martial for "abandoning his post," which resulted in a ten-year prison sentence. However, the British SOE (Special Operations Executive) sprung de Lattre from jail and flew him to North Africa in September 1943.

In Algiers, de Lattre resumed his thespian career, alternating hostility and charm in the pursuit of building the Army B. "Ardent to the point of effervescence, as sensitive as he was brilliant, de Lattre was extremely anxious that nothing should fail, regarding each vicissitude as a personal matter," de Gaulle wrote of his Saint-Cyr senior, who now fell under his authority. "Those who served under him received many rebuffs and pinpricks. But so forceful was his excellence that their re-sentiment was always short-lived . . . [His] faults . . . were rather the excesses of his virtues."[65] To be fair, de Lattre had been dealt a poor hand. Of eight French divisions initially approved for rehabilitation by the January 1943 Anfa accord, the Second Armored Division had been assigned to Overlord, and four committed with Juin to Italy, leaving de Lattre a nucleus of only two armored divisions and one infantry division for his new army. And these were continually picked over for men to replace the CEF's horrific losses. Juin protested bitterly when his four CEF divisions were transferred to de Lattre for Anvil. De Gaulle, however, ignored Juin's protests, probably because he was reluctant to see a single military hero emerge around whom his many enemies might coalesce to challenge his authority. Therefore, Juin was "demoted" to chief of the general staff, while de Lattre grasped the honor of liberating France.

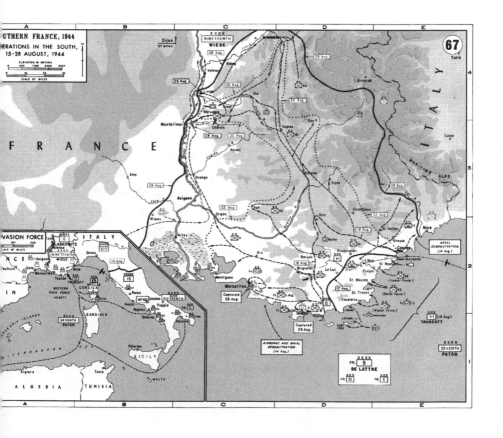

Despite the stunning success of French arms in Italy, and de Lattre's rehearsal during which, on 16–17 June, the French Ninth Colonial Infantry Division seized the strongly fortified island of Elba, the Americans still believed the French too inexperienced to be included in the first invasion wave of Anvil. Although the Germans counted up to ten divisions in southern France, the 15 August 1944 invasion by Lucian Truscott's Sixth Corps, whose troops came ashore between Cannes and Cavalaire in the vanguard of Lieutenant General Alexander Patch's Seventh Army, caught them by surprise and poorly placed to offer much more than token opposition. The Mediterranean Allied Air Forces (MAAF) had destroyed many bridges over southeastern France's main rivers. Airborne troops of the Anglo-American First Airborne Task Force (the only British and Canadian land forces involved in Anvil) seized the Le Muy to block the main road to the invasion beaches. French resistance forces, collectively known as Forces Françaises de l'Intérieur (FFI), increased sabotage attacks, forcing the Germans to deploy troops to guard supply dumps, bridges, headquarters, and lines of communication. Determined to avoid an Anzio-like beachhead stalemate, Truscott whipped his forces north and west through the coastal Monts des Maures. De Lattre landed the next day with seven divisions of the 256,000-strong Army B and began to push his advanced element toward Toulon and Marseilles in the wake of Truscott's Sixth Corps. De Lattre ignored Patch's caution that these strongly held ports might be too tough for the French to take unassisted, especially as all of his heavy equipment was yet to be landed from Corsica. De Lattre insisted that his "Berber cavalry" in their stripped djellabas, their boots hanging around their necks as they marched in sandals from the invasion beaches toward the French ports, were fully up to the task. The future general Raoul Salan reported to de Lattre near Saint-Tropez on 18 August to ask for orders. He was merely told, "Toulon awaits you."[66]

German defenses in Normandy began to crumble in late July. On 7 August, Hitler launched the Mortain offensive, which attempted unsuccessfully to cut off Patton's Third Army as it curled through Avranches around the German left flank and into the rear. By 11 August the Germans had begun to evacuate forces through the Argentan-

Falaise Gap. The Allied breakthrough in Normandy combined with the shock of the Anvil landings to cause OKW, with Hitler's assent, to order a general withdrawal of German forces in Normandy on 16 August, the beginning of a strategic repositioning of German forces in France.

Nevertheless, ports on the Atlantic coast, as well as Toulon and Marseilles, were designated by Hitler as "fortresses" to be defended to the last man. But the rapid Franco-American advance stripped the defenders of prep time. The tough North African veterans of Italy made quick work of German garrisons in the southern ports. On 26 August, Toulon fell, a full week before Allied planning calculations, freeing up troops who seized Marseilles two days later, yielding a bag of 37,000 German POWs at a cost of 4,000 French casualties. Army B then turned north in the wake of Truscott, who was determined that the German Nineteenth Army not be accorded the leisure to organize a stand in the narrow Rhône Valley. On 21 August, Truscott's forces, cutting west along the Drome River, grabbed the high ground north of Montélimar in an attempt to block the German retreat up Route N-7, which paralleled the Rhône. The Americans pushed the "hard-luck" Thirty-sixth Division toward Montélimar from the east, while the Germans reinforced from the south. Heavy fighting began on 23 August and continued until the end of the month, as the Thirty-sixth Division struggled unsuccessfully to stem the flow of German troops and vehicles northward. The road was periodically cut, but the Americans were too thin on the ground, too undersupplied, and the Thirty-sixth Division commander, Major General John E. Dahlquist, was too inexperienced to check the German retreat completely.

Despite Truscott's disappointment that, as at Cassino, Sixth Corps had failed to cut off and annihilate a German army, German troops abandoned about 20 percent of their strength at the Montélimar choke point.[67] The Thirty-sixth left Route N-7 a charred, twisted queue of over 2,000 vehicles, 80 artillery pieces, and 5 mammoth railway guns. Truscott again tried unsuccessfully to entrap the retreating Germans at Lyons, but they moved too fast for him. Nevertheless, the French bagged the rear guard of the Fourth Luftwaffe Field Corps about twenty miles north of that city. On the afternoon of 11 September,

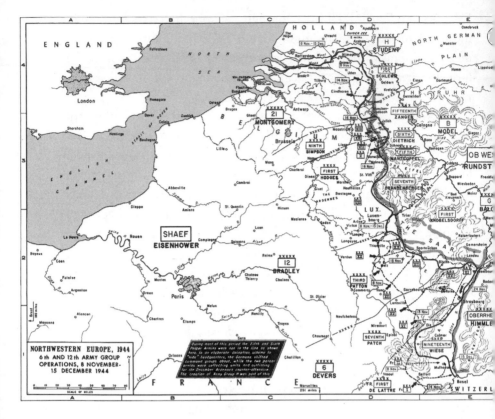

Overlord met Anvil at Saulieu, about twenty-five miles north of Autun, in the form of an encounter between the Second Dragoons of de Lattre's French First Armored Division and the U.S. Sixth Armored Division of Patton's Third Army.

The Germans finally called a halt to what GIs had begun to call the "champagne campaign" in the second week of September, and settled three corps, backed by reinforcements of men and matériel from Germany, into a defensive position running from Chaumont through Belfort to the Swiss border. This interdicted the approaches to the Belfort Gap, the obvious invasion route into Alsace between Switzerland and the Vosges Mountains to the north. Anvil had cleared southern France, in the process capturing two major harbors vital to sustaining Allied operations in France and the advance into southern Germany. In the process, 131,250 German soldiers, or about 40 percent of Army Group G's strength on 15 August, had been rounded up in the retreat or isolated on the Atlantic coast. In fact, more German troops had been put out of action by Anvil than at "Tunisgrad."[68]

But the stunning advance out of the southern beaches now ground to a halt for several reasons. Patch's Seventh Army and de Lattre's Army B, now christened the French First Army, were united in the Sixth Army Group under General Jacob Devers, a handsome, athletic man, a West Point classmate of George Patton. Devers's administrative skills had singled him out for rapid promotion early in the war. From 1943 he commanded the headquarters that orchestrated the buildup of U.S. forces in Britain. However, Devers fell from favor in the eyes of Eisenhower and Bradley after they crossed swords over the transfer of bombers to the Mediterranean from Britain. In Bradley's view, Devers was "overly garrulous, egotistical, shallow, intolerant, not very smart, and much too inclined to rush off half cocked."[69] Eisenhower called Devers ".22 caliber," and dispatched him to become Maitland Wilson's deputy in the Mediterranean.[70] Indeed, Marshall, surprised that Devers had not been offered an Overlord command, suspected that Eisenhower had recommended him as Wilson's assistant to eliminate Devers as a possible command rival. Sixth Army Group was Devers's first combat command. His lack of campaign experience would leave him poorly placed to argue his case for the southern front with combat-blooded generals like Eisenhower, Bradley, and Patton. Eisenhower rated Devers poorly as a commander, complaining that he did not inspire "that feeling of trust and confidence that is so necessary to success." But this was probably because Devers, Eisenhower's senior in age, frequently angered the supreme commander by pointing out the flaws in his strategic logic and by practically refusing to abandon Strasbourg in December 1944 in the face of Hitler's Ardennes offensive. More dispassionate assessments rate the Sixth Army Group leader as a skilled and dynamic commander.[71]

The absorption of the forces in southern France into Eisenhower's command at Supreme HQ Allied Expeditionary Force (SHAEF) on 15 September ended the operational freedom that Patch, Truscott, and de Lattre had hitherto enjoyed, and forced them to conform to Ike's priorities. These focused on a push into the Ruhr by Montgomery's Twenty-first Army Group, composed of the British Second Army and the Canadian First Army in Belgium, and the U.S. First Army in the Ardennes, which ended with the failure of Operation Market Garden on 17–24 September. After this, Eisenhower ran out of ideas, merely pushing forward on a broad front in the attempt to wrest territory from the Germans, rather than destroy enemy forces or concentrate on vulnerable points like the Belfort Gap to break onto the Alsace Plain and turn the Vosges from the south. Brooke fumed at "Eisenhower's complete inability to run the land battle . . . It is an excellent example of the American doctrine of attacking all along the line." The Vosges offered "impossible country," he noted in his diary. "All he will do there is lose men."[72] To be fair to Eisenhower, Montgomery's alternative of concentrating forces on a particular section of the line had also failed. Logistical problems and a lack of U.S. reinforcements reduced the Seventh Army to the three-division Sixth Corps. Although Patch was reinforced by transferring the 50,000-strong Fifteenth Corps from Patton's Third Army, which included Leclerc's French Second Armored Division, most units were seriously understrength, tired, and their vehicles were in poor mechanical shape after pursuing Germans across France from Normandy. As Brooke had predicted, attacks in the heavily forested Vosges yielded only grudging advances against high casualties, especially among experienced junior officers and NCOs. Without strong leadership, exhausted U.S. troops, sensing that the war would soon be over, lost their aggressiveness.[73] Truscott departed Sixth Corps on 25 October to take over the Fifth Army in Italy from Mark Clark, thus removing a commander who had whipped the Franco-American advance forward from the Riviera. Furthermore, the Americans discovered that de Gaulle had priorities other than the rapid defeat of Germany.

L'AMALGAME

August 1944 was almost as euphoric a time in the Allied camp as the previous August, when North Africa and Sicily had been cleared of Axis forces and Italy stood on the brink of surrender. With the Normandy front in collapse and the Germans reduced to a few delaying actions in the Rhône Valley, the war's finale suddenly seemed days, rather than months, away. It was precisely at this point, however, just as the French appeared capable at last of contributing an entire army to the Allied *coup de grâce* on Germany, that de Gaulle ordered what Allied generals believed to be the most incomprehensible of the many impenetrable French actions of the war: he began to stand down his experienced, battle-hardened imperial units and replace them with raw levies drawn from the French resistance.

Yet what became known as *l'Amalgame* (the Fusion) or *le blanchissement* (the whitening) had roots deep in French war aims. Those of de Gaulle, while parallel to Allied goals, did not always converge. From de Gaulle's perspective, the overwhelming power of the Anglo-Americans and the complete annihilation of Germany appeared as a threat to French sovereignty, and to French postwar aspirations, almost as serious as had been the annihilation of 1940. De Gaulle, desperate to establish France's preeminence in postwar Europe, feared that "victory" might merely exchange a German occupation for a benign but nevertheless (in French eyes) humiliating Allied one. Therefore, the French leader sought to use the closing months of the war to expand and restructure French forces at Allied expense. This reequipped and revivified army would become an instrument to recoup France's vanished prestige and guarantee Paris a voice in postwar Allied councils through an occupation zone in Germany. In this way, the French president could ensure that the war would finish, as far as possible, on French terms. De Gaulle's use of French forces in ways that did not always directly contribute to Germany's rapid defeat frequently placed him at odds with American generals eager to bring the conflict to a rapid conclusion: "For many months we have fought together," Devers wrote to de Lattre at the war's end, "often on the same side."[74]

Imbued with a profound sense of history, de Gaulle realized that few terms from his nation's past were more potent, or more timely, in the autumn of 1944 than *l'Amalgame*. Like its 1794 predecessor, which fused the old royal army with the Revolution-spawned National Guard, *l'Amalgame* linked the martial virtues of France's regular army with the popular will and patriotic ardor of the French resistance fighters (FFI). *L'Amalgame* once again offered the promise of French national unity after four divisive years of defeat and occupation. It united the "external" resistance with those who had battled the occupiers from within. However, *l'Amalgame* was far from an innocent morale-boosting exercise. One of de Gaulle's goals was to master and disarm the estimated 400,000 resisters, many of them Communist-led, who might have political ambitions of their own. Either the FFI must join the army and fight for the defeat of Germany, de Gaulle calculated, or they would be politically discredited as shirkers with political ambitions.[75]

L'Amalgame inevitably touched off a row between the Allies, who wanted to get on with killing Germans, and de Gaulle, who sought to secure his government and lay the foundation for France's postwar resurrection. At first, Allied leaders accepted the view pressed hard by the French that their "reorganization" was really a question of internal security, one that should concern American generals as well. And in truth, resistance bands, known derisively as *fifis*, had taken the law into their own hands in several areas. With black berets, home-stitched FFI armbands, armed with everything from submachine guns to hunting pieces, exuberant *fifis* rampaged through the French countryside clinging to the running boards of black Citroëns, taking over town halls, breaking into houses, and organizing autos-da-fé of public humiliation whose centerpiece was shaving the heads of female "horizontal collaborators." At best they had become a nuisance, at worst a threat to the Allied advance. U.S. Chief of Staff George Marshall agreed in September to the formation of lightly armed security and labor battalions from resisters.[76] But de Gaulle wanted more than a token absorption of resistance manpower. De Lattre insisted that resisters were flocking to join his army as he advanced up the Rhône Valley, and that they needed to be equipped. Salan reported that *fifis* asked to enlist in his Senegalese unit as soon as Toulon was liberated in late August. Without equipment or uniforms, the only way to incorporate them was to stand down the Africans and give their uniforms to the FFI. "The exchange of uniforms was often comic," Salan noted, "because our Senegalese were big chaps" whose American overcoats were several sizes too large for the small, undernourished French teenagers who made up the bulk of the volunteers.[77]

As the battle lines hardened in October and the warm optimism of quick victory dissipated in the chill of a premature winter, the American argument that the approaching end of the war made it unnecessary to expand the French army began to lose credibility. Eisenhower agreed in October to create two new French divisions, bringing the French total to ten. But Juin wanted their numbers doubled to sixteen and won over the Combined Chiefs of Staff, who were increasingly concerned about declining Allied manpower reserves. However, on 1 January 1945, de Gaulle dropped a bombshell: he wrote to Roosevelt to insist that France needed fifty divisions by the war's end. De Gaulle's demand forfeited what little remained of the French leader's credibility with SHAEF. Without a massive mobilization, de Gaulle could not have produced the 1,275,000 men his fifty divisions required. It was certainly beyond anyone's ability, much less that of France, to train, equip, and staff such large numbers. Allied leaders denounced de Gaulle's request as "utter folly."[78]

A negative side of *l'Amalgame* was that it provided yet another excuse for a mammoth spat between de Gaulle and the Americans. The French general accused the United States of bad faith, of seeking to deny France an important, "perhaps decisive," role in the war and a voice in the postwar settlement. To arm France, de Gaulle lamented, "we were obliged to depend on the good will of the United States. Their good will was scanty."[79] De Gaulle's criticism of the Americans was, of course, desperately unfair. That said, however, it is equally true that the positive effects of *l'Amalgame* far outweighed its negative consequences. First, *l'Amalgame* helped to resolve France's internal security problem. While in retrospect a coordinated uprising of the Communist elements in the resistance was unlikely, especially as Stalin opposed it, the continued presence in many communities of armed gangs affiliated with an avowedly revolutionary political party would certainly have retarded the return of political stability in France and perhaps even compromised the war effort. Of an estimated 400,000 resistance fighters, around 190,000 eventually volunteered for the army or to besiege German garrisons that held out along the Atlantic coast. Some saw this tepid response as evidence of a popular failure to respond to the liberation, and of a French willingness to allow "*les Anglo-Saxons*" and the Russians to pay the blood tax of defeating Germany. Only 10 percent of Communist resisters volunteered to fight.[80] On the other hand, the French army probably could not have effectively absorbed many more than this. Furthermore, on the internal security level, *l'Amalgame* achieved de Gaulle's goal of taming the resistance—under orders to disband or enlist, most *fifis* elected to return home. Those who remained were young, ill-nourished, poorly equipped, and resistant to traditional military discipline. However, they proved willing and patriotic. Brooke described ex-maquis recruits whom he reviewed at a French training camp in Alsace in November 1944 as "good, tough looking boys that promised well."[81]

Second, *l'Amalgame* was at least a partial success in reuniting the army and the French people in a common cause. De Lattre, its chief architect, called *l'Amalgame* "a crusade," a spiritual movement necessary for French self-respect and for "the future relations between the army and the nation."[82] However, even he confessed that the unification of the "external" and "internal" resistance did not pass off without friction. Many resisters denounced their officers as Vichy reactionaries, eleventh-hour converts to the Allied cause. They had not been "amalgamated," the more left-wing resisters complained, but co-opted into a "new concentration camp." For their part, French officers lamented that the new recruits refused to shed their "civilian mentalities," that they adapted badly or not at all to formalized military discipline. The fact that de Gaulle never considered ex-resisters as real soldiers, and was obviously using the army as a dumping ground for potential troublemakers, meant that the First Army preferred to quarantine *fifi* recruits in separate battalions to reduce the danger of ideological contamination.[83] Hardly was the war over than military commissions dominated by professional soldiers began to eliminate former resistance fighters from the ranks.

Third, *l'Amalgame* gave a new impetus to French forces just when they appeared to be faltering. All armies were suffering from battle fatigue in the war's closing year, none more so than those that had fought their way through Italy. De Lattre insisted that his black troops could not endure the winter, while French North Africa's ability—and willingness—to support the war "had reached the limit of its capabilities."[84] While colonial, especially North African, troops continued to make up about one-third of the French forces to war's end, it was clear that if France wanted to continue to field battleworthy units, it would need to integrate Frenchmen. By December, de Lattre was desperate for replacements to restore the "moral equilibrium" and "fighting qualities" of his troops. The FFI was the only manpower reserve open to him.[85] FFI personnel were best utilized in commando-style units or as light infantry attached to armored divisions, or fed as replacements into "Senegalese" battalions. But they suffered from poor training and heterogeneous armament drawn from French, British, and American surplus as well as captured German equipment.

De Lattre's manpower problems were also at least partially of his own making. In late September and early October, he had pressed piecemeal and partially successful attacks into the Belfort Gap and the southern Vosges with forces that lacked adequate logistical support because, de Lattre raged at a visibly angry George Marshall, the Americans were starving him of supplies. Nor had de Lattre's attacks been coordinated with those of Patch's Seventh Army farther north.[86] Eisenhower expected little of his southern flank, still pinning his hopes for an advance into Germany on Montgomery's Twenty-first Army Group with its logistical base at Antwerp. He placed even less faith in de Lattre's understrength First Army, especially after de Gaulle intervened to have the French First Infantry and First Armored Divisions and sundry units—a total of 60,000 troops—redeployed to the southwest for reasons of "internal security" and to clear the Gironde Estuary, La Rochelle, and Saint-Nazaire of German troops.[87]

Nevertheless, Devers began to plan for a supporting offensive that would break past the blockade of the Vosges and into the Alsace Plain. The only good news was that if the Allies had designated the southern sector as lowest priority, so had the Germans, who had stripped the Nineteenth Army bare of reserves and armor to reinforce the Ruhr. Devers's offensive in the north opened on the night of 11–12 November with the U.S. Seventy-ninth and Forty-fourth Divisions attacking north of the Vosges into the Saverne Gap. This sprung Leclerc's Second Armored Division, which broke out onto the Alsace Plain and stormed into Strasbourg on 23 November. The liberation of the city on France's eastern frontier had enormous symbolic value to the French. For Leclerc, Strasbourg fulfilled his 1941 oath taken at Koufra in the

Libyan desert: "Now we can die," he muttered as the tricolor was raised over the cathedral tower. In the center, Sixth Corps, now composed of four divisions, smashed through demoralized German defenders along the High Vosges and spilled down the eastern slopes toward the Rhine.

In the Belfort Gap between the Vosges and the Swiss frontier, de Lattre executed what became known as the Burnhaupt maneuver, a daring sweep that broke into southern Alsace through heavy German defenses. From 14 November, de Lattre slid his First Corps along the Swiss frontier, hooked it north along the left bank of the Rhine to Mulhouse, then turned west toward Burnhaupt, where it met his Second Corps driving in from the west. Confused by French deceptive measures and heavy snow that concealed de Lattre's preparations, and convinced that the French had settled into defensive positions for the winter, the Germans were caught by surprise. By the twenty-eighth, the encirclement had snapped shut, entrapping Germans who fought desperately, but in vain, to break out. According to de Lattre, his tour de force had seized Belfort and Mulhouse, in the process killing 10,000 Germans, capturing 17,000, and destroying 60 tanks and 120 guns.[88] But de Lattre's victory, while stunning, had been dearly bought at a cost of 10,000 French casualties, plus serious losses of matériel. "Twenty days of uninterrupted battles against an enemy whose stubbornness had not weakened for a single hour and whose violent reactions allowed us no respite," de Lattre remembered. "Twenty days of rain, cold and mud. Floods everywhere, streams in spate, sodden earth."[89]

The Sixth Army Group's breakthrough into Alsace had several positive outcomes. The French had proven their worth as soldiers, which not only increased French stature but also justified de Gaulle's demands for more U.S. equipment.[90] This was especially true as the Allies became aware that not only would they need French troops to fill their dangerously stretched Anglo-American manpower reserves, but also, *l'Amalgame* resurrected the French army to play an important role in the postwar era. Ironically, it was the British, who in January 1943 at Casablanca had opposed U.S. plans to waste perfectly serviceable equipment on French "garrison troops," who now most often took de Gaulle's side in the winter of 1944–45 in his disputes with the Americans over rearmament. This was precisely because they realized that they would need French help in policing Germany. By the war's end, the French were on their way to eighteen divisions.[91]

The downside of the Allied offensive was that the failure to set objectives beyond the breakthrough onto the Alsace Plain, combined with the relative weakness of de Lattre's forces in ordnance, signal, engineering, and support units, had allowed the Germans to maintain control of a pocket of territory around Colmar. Relative success also brought relations between Devers and Eisenhower to a boiling point, when the supreme commander intervened in the battle to prevent the Seventh Army from crossing the Rhine at Rastatt. This, Devers argued in vain against Ike and Bradley, would have allowed him to break into the Saar and outflank German defenses on the Rhine, and perhaps shorten the war by several months.[92] Furthermore, Eisenhower's or-

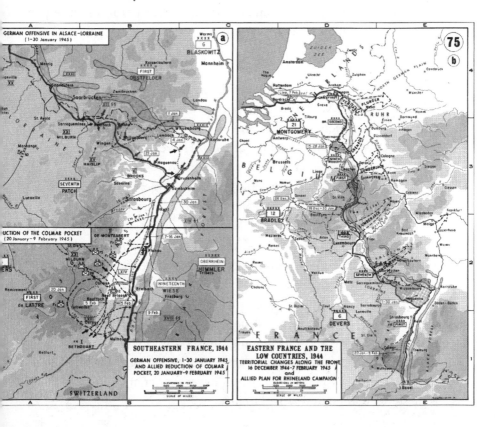

SOUTHEASTERN FRANCE, 1944
GERMAN OFFENSIVE, 1–30 JANUARY 1945
AND ALLIED REDUCTION OF COLMAR
POCKET, 20 JANUARY–9 FEBRUARY 1945

EASTERN FRANCE AND THE LOW COUNTRIES, 1944
TERRITORIAL CHANGES ALONG THE FRONT 16 DECEMBER 1944–7 FEBRUARY 1945
and
ALLIED PLAN FOR RHINELAND CAMPAIGN

ders that Devers direct the Seventh Army to attack into northern Alsace toward the German frontier in support of Patton split his forces between two separate fronts, which gave a much-needed respite to the Germans in the Colmar Pocket. At first, Devers attempted to make the best of an unfortunate situation, assuming that the badly mauled Germans would seize the opportunity to withdraw east of the Rhine, helped on their way by French attacks as soon as de Lattre's troops regained their breath. Instead, Hitler reinforced his Colmar bridgehead, while morale plummeted among the poorly equipped, hastily trained, and undernourished ex-resisters, as the initial patriotic enthusiasm of the liberation gave way to the desperate business of fighting Germans through one of the coldest winters on record.[93] Devers transferred the Thirty-sixth and Third Infantry Divisions and Leclerc's Second Armored Division from Patch to de Lattre. But these units were unable to make much headway toward Colmar before Devers, again on Eisenhower's orders, halted operations on 22 December in the face of a threatened German breakthrough in the Ardennes.

Eisenhower's decision not to unleash the Seventh Army across the Rhine enabled Hitler to prepare a counterblow, one that brought Franco-American relations to a crisis point. On 16 December, Field Marshal Walter Model's Army Group B sliced through American forces in the Ardennes and provoked panic in Paris among a skittish population who feared a replay of 1940. However, within less than a week, the Ardennes offensive had begun to lose momentum. The price of halting the German offensive was to reorient Devers's Sixth Army Group farther to the north and west, freeing up Patton's Third Army to attack the German flank in the Ardennes. Hitler and Gerd von Rundstedt, Commander-in-Chief West, understood that this had greatly overextended the Seventh Army. Desperate to shorten his line and recover two divisions for his strategic reserve and armed with intelligence that predicted a German attack on northern Alsace, on 26 December Eisenhower instructed Devers to pull troops back to the Vosges, in this way abandoning Strasbourg to the Germans. Both Devers and Patch protested the order to surrender hard-won ground. In the French camp, however, Eisenhower's order at first met with an incredulity that rapidly turned to rage.

On New Year's Eve, Operation Nordwind struck into Alsace. "The Americans retreated everywhere," remembered Paul Fussell, second lieutenant in the 103d Infantry Division.

> Whole battalions were wiped out. Many men were captured. Quite a few deserted. The roads were icy and it was snowing much of the time. When the snow let up, the temperature dropped to twenty below zero . . . The retreat in snow and ice was a nightmare: tanks and trucks skidded off the road and had to be abandoned—to the Germans. We had a day or two to slow them down as they pursued us, and at one point someone laid out on the road a number of inverted dinner plates, hoping that when covered with a bit of snow they'd resemble antitank mines and cause a brief German delay.[94]

After de Lattre's emotional appeal to Patch not to abandon Strasbourg fell on deaf ears, the French general vowed to defend it on his own and began to move in reinforcements. Juin informed Eisenhower's chief of staff, Bedell Smith, that if the Americans abandoned Strasbourg, they would be denied use of French railways and the French First Army would be withdrawn from SHAEF control. The issue was resolved on 3 January at a meeting between Eisenhower, Churchill, and de Gaulle at Versailles. Churchill eloquently defended the French position. In any case, the German offensive, hastily planned and poorly executed, made little headway against solidifying Allied resistance. Ike rescinded his order to abandon Strasbourg.

On 7 January 1945, the Gaullist Free French First Division and the U.S. Sixth Corps combined to repulse a serious German thrust. Nevertheless, the Germans continued to hammer at Sixth Army Group until the end of the month. Paul Fussell endured one such attack on 25 January that "followed a really terrifying artillery preparation. We cowered at the bottom of the hole, dreading a direct hit, and dreading equally a German attack during the barrage, which would catch us utterly unprepared to repel it." After weeks of fighting against old men and "pitiful youths who came across willingly, persuaded that the war was lost, and tired and wet and hungry and scared as well," it came as rather a shock to confront troops of the Sixth SS Mountain Division. "Stimulated by schnapps, shouting slogans and abuse, they swarmed toward us—to be torn to pieces by our machine guns . . . On the right the SS burst through our line, capturing a town behind, from which they were finally ejected after a brutal struggle. These SS men were the best troops we ever fought. They behaved as if they actually believed that their wounds and deaths might make a difference in the outcome of the war."[95] In the end, Nordwind blew itself out, in the process inflicting 23,000 German casualties to 14,000 for the Allies. "Ah, these Americans," de Gaulle is alleged to have mused at the end of the Strasbourg crisis. "[They] equate politics with sentiment, the military art with logic . . . Churchill knows better."[96]

De Lattre came out of the Strasbourg episode well, as one who had put the French view across without burning bridges to his American colleagues, whose support and cooperation he needed to continue the war. He would need all the cooperation he could get to reduce the Colmar Pocket, an 850-square-mile bulge with a 130-mile perimeter of territory packed with eight German infantry divisions and an armored brigade organized into two corps. Eisenhower wanted what he called the "sore" on his front reduced so that he could shorten his line and close it up to the German frontier in preparation for a Rhine crossing. The Allies enjoyed superior firepower. But this was nullified by strong German defensive positions and by weather so beastly that Allied planes flew infrequently. De Lattre launched his attack in a blinding 20 January snowstorm, across fields "packed with innumerable glass or plastic mines, which were further protected by the snow and by a layer of glazed ice several centimeters thick." In an action that saw Audie Murphy earn both the Congressional Medal of Honor and the Legion d'Honneur, 400,000 French and U.S. troops fought side by side. U.S. units like the Third Infantry Division distinguished themselves in combined arms combat, helping to supplement the deficiencies of raw French recruits. On 9 February, after twenty-one days of fighting, the Colmar Pocket collapsed, caging 20,000 German POWs and inflicting on the order of 22,000 dead and missing. Probably no more than 10,000 German troops escaped across the Rhine.[97] "How good it was for French hearts to see the defeated columns of yesterday's arrogant victors marching along the roads of Alsace," de Lattre remembered. "Terrible memories were blotted out. In this sight, our men found their surest reward."[98]

The war's end was soured by disputes between de Lattre and his diehard Gaullist commanders. Both the Free French First Division and the Second Armored Division were removed from his command after they complained, unfairly, that their losses had been disproportionately higher than those of other corps, and that tough, high-casualty missions constituted Vichy's revenge on the Free French. The final march to victory was also sullied by disagreements between de Lattre, instructed by de Gaulle to seize strategically placed German towns to get the Allies to grant France an occupation zone, and American commanders eager to destroy the last remnants of German forces. These were usually much less bitter in Germany than in Paris, where Juin complained that the United States had denied the French a voice in the direction of the war and had kept them in the dark about the allocation of occupation zones. Finally, Juin complained, presumably without a trace of irony, the Americans had treated French troops as mere "colonial auxiliaries." He threatened, once again, to deny the Allies the use of French transportation. The U.S. reply was the inevitable one that if the French felt unable to cooperate, then the Americans would simply divert French rations to Belgian, Dutch, and U.S. troops.

For de Lattre, however, the war ended on a high note. The French First Army entered Germany on 19 March and was through the Siegfried line by the end of the week. On 29 March, de Gaulle ordered de Lattre to cross the Rhine by hook or by crook, "even if the Americans are not agreeable and even if you have to cross it in boats. It is a matter of the greatest national interest. Karlsruhe and Stuttgart await you, even if they do not want you." De Lattre had to cross before the Americans seized the vital roads. With great difficulty, his engineers scraped together a few boats and enough bridging material for a single ten-ton bridge. On 31 March he began to infiltrate Moroccan troops across the Rhine. The Germans counterattacked vigorously, but the Moroccans held. The Americans, realizing the French were in a tight spot, allowed them to put troops across U.S. bridges farther north and then strike south to secure their bridgehead. The French crossed the Danube on 21 April, occupied Stuttgart on the twenty-fourth, and took Ulm, the site of Napoleon's 1805 victory over the Austrians. The long march of the French finally came to an end in Constance on 26 April. "For kilometers the roads recalled those of the Rhône valley at the beginning of September [1944]," de Lattre wrote of southern Germany. "There was nothing but abandoned vehicles, scattered equipment, destroyed guns, disemboweled horses—the unbelievable picture of total defeat."[99]

The French army's odyssey from defeat to victory had traversed the Mediterranean. In the war's early days, Gaullist passions, the desire to revive French military fortunes, had more than compensated for the battlefield shortcomings of Free French forces. After Torch welded the Armée d'Afrique to the Allied cause, the French drew on their deep military traditions to adapt rapidly to the demands of a modern, mechanized war. The profound professionalism of Juin combined with the tenacity and resilience of his North African troops to give the French the accolades of the Italian campaign. Anvil had proved vital to the success of Allied fortunes in northeastern France in the winter of 1944–45 by placing two armies combining ten divisions with their own supply links to the Mediterranean on the Western Front. Eisenhower otherwise would have found it difficult to sustain a third army group through Atlantic ports. Bradley's Twelfth Army Group could have held a front stretching from Lorraine to the Swiss border only with the greatest difficulty, especially if the German Nineteenth Army had been able to retreat casualty-free from the Riviera. Hitler's December 1944 Ardennes offensive might have enjoyed greater success had Eisenhower not been able to draw on the reserves of Devers's Sixth Army Group. One possible consequence of canceling Anvil might have been the transfer of the German Nineteenth Army to Italy.[100]

Anvil offered an artery through which to tap France's manpower resources and prepare France for a postwar role. De Lattre's task had been especially complex, because he had to fight a series of bitter winter battles in Alsace while at the same time rebuilding and reorganizing his army. That reorganization was vital not only to maintain the combat efficiency of the French First Army, but also France's internal stability and its credibility as an ally. De Gaulle used his military contribution and France's geographic position as leverage to stake out France's claim to an important role in postwar Europe. This was critical to the Allied cause and the stability of postwar Europe. Even if the Allies were reluctant to acknowledge France's contribution to victory at the surrender ceremony of 8 May 1945, the Mediterranean theater allowed them to reap the significant benefit of France's revival.

CHAPTER THIRTEEN

Cassino without the Monastery: Cracking the Gothic Line

T HE SHIFT OF THE WAR'S axis to France reduced the Mediterranean to a strategic backwater in the war against Germany. The Soviets advanced in the Baltic, Byelorussia, and the Ukraine. On 20 July 1944, conspirators around German Colonel Count von Stauffenberg failed in their attempt to assassinate Hitler. In August the Polish Home Army unleashed an uprising in Warsaw, which the Soviets did nothing to aid, despite prodding by Washington and London. The first of the concentration camps was discovered at Majdanek in Poland. De Gaulle settled into Paris. In early September, Brussels and Antwerp were liberated by the British, as Soviet troops pushed into Yugoslavia and Romania. In the Pacific, the U.S. Navy won the Battle of the Philippine Sea in June, and cleared Guam and Tinian in the Marianas through August. Nevertheless, despite momentum on other fronts, the Mediterranean theater continued to play an important role in the final stages of the war for at least two reasons. First, bitter as Clark, Leese, and Alexander were at the downgrading of the Italian front, their task remained to press Kesselring hard to prevent the Germans from shifting divisions to the more critical Eastern and Western Fronts. This assignment was complicated by the transfer of experienced soldiers of the French Expeditionary Corps and Truscott's Sixth Corps, and air and naval assets toward Anvil, and by the residual fear that the Americans would abandon Italy altogether. British forces in the Mediterranean were already stretched to furnish replacements to the Eighth Army and provide garrisons for an increasingly restive Middle East. In the Levant, the French and the Arabs were at daggers drawn, Jewish extremism had begun to rear its head in Palestine, while in Egypt tensions between Farouk and Prime Minister Nahas Pasha had reached crisis point. Through prodigies of reorganization, Alexander managed to comb the equivalent of six new divisions out of the Mediterranean—antiaircraft units were converted to infantry, many infantry battalions were reduced from four to three companies, POW camps in southern France yielded 5,500 Poles, Italians furnished three divisions, a division was found in Egypt, and six brigades were squeezed out of Greeks, Jews, Gurkhas, Canadians, and Gibraltar. Nevertheless, Alexander was in a dilemma. Churchill pushed for a victory in Italy that "would greatly strengthen our hands in the forthcoming discussions with the Americans." The prime minister hoped to induce Washington to capitalize on the momentum of the 23 August 1944 surrender of Romania and Bulgaria's 8 September declaration of war on Germany to support British aims in the Balkans.[1] On the other hand, British commanders were forced to plan operations with the caution required to conserve their dwindling manpower reserves. This actually diminished their leverage in the coalition, earning the contempt of Mark Clark, who increasingly criticized the Eighth Army as sluggish and battle-shy. But Clark, too, would soon suffer the pinch of insufficient replacements. The only fresh troops immediately available to stand in for Truscott's Sixth Corps, departed for Anvil, were the U.S. Ninety-second Division, black troops under white officers who arrived in September, and an ill-equipped division of Brazilians who disembarked at the end of October. Clark had little confidence in either formation.[2]

A second reason that the Mediterranean theater continued to be important was that the British in particular were already contemplating the postwar situation. The withdrawal of German forces threatened to create a political vacuum in Greece and the Balkans, possibly also in northern Italy, one that promised to be occupied by aggressive resistance movements under Communist domination. Churchill's desire to preempt the growth of Communist influence in the Eastern Mediterranean, an area of traditional British interest, aggravated tensions in the Anglo-American alliance already raw with discord over Anvil, and raised concerns about a dispersion of forces not seen in the Mediterranean since the spring and summer of 1941.

The reorientation and reorganization of Allied priorities joined the increasing difficulties of supply as Allied armies advanced northward. Wrecked cranes, destroyed bridges, harbors choked with the hulks of sunken ships, mines, and blown quays had come to typify Italian ports abandoned in the wake of a German retreat; at Leghorn these were accompanied by 25,000 diabolical booby traps that continued to inflict Allied casualties for weeks after the city had fallen. Berlin's willingness to rush reinforcements into Italy also favored Kesselring, whose Fourteenth Army in particular had been badly chewed up south of Rome. Some of these units were scraped together from

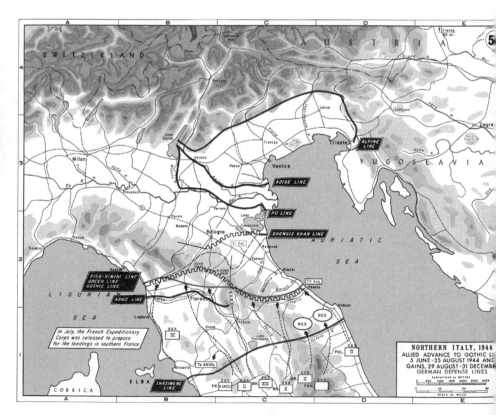

NORTHERN ITALY, 1944
ALLIED ADVANCE TO GOTHIC LI
5 JUNE - 25 AUGUST 1944 AN
GAINS, 29 AUGUST - 31 DECEMB
GERMAN DEFENSE LINES

convalescent troops, underemployed airmen, and even the 162d Tur-coman, former Soviet POWs with German cadres who volunteered to fight to avoid lingering starvation in Hitler's stalags. Kesselring's great-est fear was that the Allies would concentrate on the seam that sepa-rated the Fourteenth and Tenth Armies. But he soon realized that Allied disorganization and hesitation following the breakthrough at Cassino, combined with Italian terrain that allowed his enemy to con-centrate only a fraction of their numerically superior forces against his battered but tenacious troops at any one time, gained him badly needed breathing space. The southern commander met in early July with a surprisingly optimistic Hitler, who emphasized that his task was to buy time until new German weapons systems could come on line, systems that would shift the strategic balance of the war. In return, Kesselring exacted a promise from Hitler—one not always respected—that he would not intervenc, as was his wont, to prevent tactical with-drawals.[3]

Kesselring's plan was to slow and then halt the Allied advance through the winter and prolong the campaign into the spring of 1945. "Our general strategic idea from 7 June remained the same [as be-tween Salerno and Cassino]," the German field marshal wrote. "To gather reserves arriving from the rear and from the side, both armies contesting every step of their retreat, to stop gaps and to effect a firm junction of the inner flanks. It did not matter whether more or less ground was surrendered; the main thing was to surmount our mo-mentary weakness, to pull out our battered divisions and to rest and re-equip them." To further this objective, four Italian divisions had been raised and were training in Germany to serve in Italy as the Army of Liguria under Graziani. The rapid fall of the island of Elba to a French invasion on 17 June raised concerns about further amphibious landings in his rear or airborne descents in support of Italian partisans, who were actively blowing up bridges and ambushing retreating Ger-man convoys, activities that elicited savage German reprisals. But to Kesselring's relief, "the Allies utterly failed to seize their chances."[4]

Ultra revealed to the Allies that German reinforcements arriv-ing in Italy were not shunted forward, but instead were stopped on the Pisa-Rimini line, where Kesselring clearly intended to make his stand.[5] Clark's Fifth Army progressed relentlessly behind the battered Fourteenth Army. However, Leese's advance plodded northward over roads cratered by Allied air raids against a relatively unshaken Tenth Army, which destroyed bridges and roads, laid booby traps, and fought defensive battles. The Germans' slow retreat bought time to transform the Gothic line[6] from little more than a series of light machine-gun posts into a fifteen-mile-deep chain of Cassino-like strong points, tank traps, and lavish minefields. The line cut from the high peaks of Liguria on the Mediterranean coast through ridge lines and promontories like Monte Monticelli and Monte Altuzzo, which bordered the Futa and Giogo Passes north of Florence, before it dropped to the rolling hills along the Adriatic Sea to Pesaro, south of Rimini. Even the British official history concedes that neither Leese nor Alexander exhibited an aptitude for pursuit, or for using their two Indian divisions experienced in mountain warfare in imaginative or innovative ways. Despite detailed intelligence that delivered precise information on enemy strength and dispositions, they contented themselves with a leisurely "partridge drive" while Alexander awaited the opportunity to launch another minutely prepared, set-piece assault against static German positions, at which Eighth Army excelled.[7] By the time the British reached Florence and the River Arno on 4 August, the Allies had absorbed a further 34,000 casualties, many of them in hard fighting around Lake Trasimeno in late June, and were still twenty miles south of the Gothic line. Over Kesselring's protests, Hitler declared Florence an open city, but allowed his southern commander to mine Florence's historic bridges, with the exception of the fourteenth-century Ponte Vecchio, too narrow and fragile to support military traffic in any case.

On 4 August, as Alexander prepared to strike at the center of the Gothic line northward from Florence up Route 65 through the Futa Pass toward Bologna, he was invited to Orvieto airfield, where, hunched beneath the wing of a Dakota, Leese persuaded the Fifteenth Army Group commander to shift his attack from the mountainous center of the peninsula to the Adriatic coast. Four considerations informed Leese's arguments. First, he felt that the center of the Gothic line was too strong, especially as the departure of the CEF had deprived the Allies of their ability to operate effectively in the mountains. Second, he believed that the firepower of the Eighth Army, especially its overwhelming superiority in artillery, could be applied more effectively on the coastal plain, where his tanks would have greater freedom to maneuver. Third, a breakthrough on the Adriatic would allow the Eighth Army to sweep behind the Gothic line and into the Po Valley more easily than would a strike through Bologna. Finally, the unspoken consideration: operations concentrated on his Adriatic flank would obviate the need for Leese to cooperate with Clark and the Fifth Army, and hence to give them any credit for the forthcoming breakthrough. It would be Leese's—and the British's—revenge on Clark and the Americans for Rome.[8]

The Orvieto meeting symbolized how far the atmosphere of competition and condescension that had characterized the Anglo-American partnership since Torch had degenerated into one of barely concealed contempt in the hands of men less sensitive to the diplomatic requirements of inter-Allied relations. The relegation of the Mediterranean to peripheral status increased the unwillingness to cooperate. A pattern had developed in Italy for all to see. At the end of Husky, and after the Cassino breakthrough, every time momentum shifted to the Allies, Italy had been stripped of experienced forces for the benefit of Northern Europe. By August 1944 the three senior commanders of the Fifteenth Army Group had lost their argument against Anvil. They had been passed over for more exalted commands elsewhere, an unequivocal vote of no confidence by their superiors. The war—and the media—had relocated to more lucrative theaters, which hindered their ability to regain the limelight through dramatic feats of arms. Relations between Leese and Clark had failed to recover from their plunge caused by Clark's preemptive capture of Rome. On the contrary, the American commander's vocal criticism of the Eighth Army's sluggish advance, while justified in part, hardly stoked the fires of Allied harmony. Clark, petrified that Fifth Army would be bled for the benefit of Sixth Army Group commander General Jacob Devers and Anvil, was desperate to attack before his army—and his job—were declared redundant.[9] Alexander, temperamentally ill-equipped to deal with Clark's raw ambition, reigned over this ungentlemanly competition with his usual patrician hauteur. Listening to Leese's arguments, Alexander concluded that a shift of the axis of attack to the Adriatic would force Kesselring to split his defenses between Ravenna and Bologna. In any case, Alexander was hardly the man to oblige his subordinate to carry out a plan in which Leese had no faith. In the late summer of 1944, Allied armies were everywhere on the rampage, and a sense of optimism settled on Allied forces. Staff wags erected signposts that read: "DUST—drive carefully or you won't see Vienna." The Luftwaffe remained a memory that lingered only among relatively ancient veterans of the Mediterranean theater. Destruction of the Po River bridges was thought, incorrectly, to have caused a severe ammunition shortage on the German side of the line. One plan seemed as likely to succeed as another. Alexander pronounced his benediction. Operation Olive was born.

Alexander's inability to "grip" the situation, quell the dissension between his subordinates, and impart firm direction to the campaign was to have baleful consequences, for, like so many strategic decisions in Italy, the arguments for Olive were anchored in wishful thinking and optimistic assumptions. Eighth Army's problem was that psychologically it had never left the Western Desert. It longed for the wide-open spaces, the limitless horizons that offered opportunities for bold maneuver. By shifting to the Adriatic, Leese sought terrain better suited to his highly mechanized army, rather than adapting his army to the terrain. In the process, he merely exchanged a mountainous line of advance for a river-laced coastal plain that would challenge the ingenuity of his engineers and logisticians to build new roads, bridges, supply dumps, a pipeline, and airfields, and the ability of his armored units made up of undergunned Sherman and Churchill tanks to maneuver. The Gothic line in the Rimini sector, consisting of tank trenches, Spandau posts surrounded by deep wire, and flamethrower and tank turrets set in concrete, was at its most formidable.[10] Three belts of minefields included circular Teller mines, packed with eleven pounds of TNT, and S-mines ("Bouncing Betties"), whose small prongs when touched shot a shrapnel-filled canister five feet into the air to explode chest-high. By 1943, many of these mines were nonmetallic, making them difficult to detect, and were fitted with fuses that detonated if the mine was lifted. Therefore, the most favored mine-clearing devices included tanks called Crabs or Scorpions, fitted with rotating drums and chains to flail a path through the minefields. Steel pipes crammed with explosives called Snakes were also detonated to make the Betties bounce prematurely. But they frequently failed to touch off the heavier Teller mines. Twenty to thirty percent of tank casualties were mine-induced.[11]

Although initially Leese could concentrate ten divisions against three German divisions, he lacked the LSTs to execute end runs, and thus exploit Kesselring's "Anzio syndrome." Although air support was adequate, only two gunboats and a small destroyer force were present in the Adriatic to give naval fire support. Furthermore, three weeks of exceptionally fine campaign weather were frittered away, weeks that would prove critical in a rain-soaked September, while Eighth Army shifted 52,000 vehicles to the Adriatic coast. These repositioning operations were slowed further because they had to be carried out in great secrecy, by a small staff, in absolute radio silence. Meanwhile, the Germans put the finishing touches on the Gothic line. It also meant that the Allies could not coordinate their offensive to take advantage of Kesselring's temporary disorientation caused by the Anvil landings on 15 August.[12]

No Montgomery was nearby to remind Alexander that, once again, he was violating the principle of concentration of force by dividing his armies between two widely separated axes of advance—in effect fighting two battles instead of one.[13] A stronger army group commander would have understood that the fundamental motivation for the change of plan was the visceral antagonism between Clark and Leese and their disinclination to cooperate. When Clark was presented with the change of plan during a visit to Leese's headquarters on 10 August, he did not object in principle, although Alexander's proposal clearly reduced Fifth Army to a reserve role. However, he requested that Lieutenant General Richard McCreery's Thirteenth Corps be loaned to Fifth Army, ostensibly to maintain a balance of strength between the two armies, but also to increase his chances of making a breakthrough in the center. Leese heatedly objected, until Alexander intervened with Solomonic finality to sever Thirteenth

Corps from Eighth Army for Clark's benefit. By acceding to Clark's request, Alexander compounded his errors, ensuring that neither of his two armies would be strong enough to achieve its objective. The assignment to Clark of the four-division-plus-one-brigade Thirteenth Corps, taken from McCreery and given to Major General Sidney Kirkman, deprived Leese of his strategic reserve. Finally, Olive was to be carried out in the typical Eighth Army fashion of a massive concentration of three corps—Poles, Canadians, and the British Fifth Corps—attacking along a narrow eight-mile coastal plain between Rimini and the foothills of the Apennines. This promised to reenact the congestion of El Alamein and Diadem, which would hinder exploitation of any breakthrough.[14]

Kesselring's Army Group C numbered twenty-six German and two Italian divisions. The eleven divisions of the German Tenth Army occupied the ground from the Adriatic to San Sepolcro, south of Bologna. The Fourteenth Army, consisting of eight divisions, was hunkered down in the mountains running to the Mediterranean coast. Meanwhile the seven divisions of the Army of Liguria both guarded the coast and acted as a reserve. Army Group C kept two infantry divisions in reserve.

Leese's attack opened one hour before midnight on 25 August. Because it caught Kesselring by surprise as the German Seventy-first Infantry Division was in the process of being relieved, it made good initial progress, breaking through German defenses on the Metauro River and pushing up to the Gothic line by the end of the month. Kesselring, fully expecting Clark's Fifth Army to roll into action north of Florence and thinking Olive a diversion, was slow to react despite Tenth Army commander von Vietinghoff's desperate pleas for reinforcement and permission to withdraw into the sanctuary of the Gothic line. Only on 28 August, when German Sigint captured a radio message detailing Leese's admonitions to his troops to make a breakthrough, did Kesselring grasp the importance of the Eighth Army offensive.[15] The tardy German reaction allowed the Canadian First Corps to "gate-crash" the thinly held Gothic line on 30 August, rushing through minefields and over tank trenches to split the Twenty-sixth Panzer and First Parachute Divisions, and moving forward ten miles to seize Monte Peloso and Monte Luro by 3 September. "Rover" teams of artillery spotters pinpointed German artillery positions.

But once the advantage of surprise dissipated, the shortcomings of Leese's plan became apparent, especially the absence of armored reserves to capitalize on the beckoning opportunity opened by the Canadians. Indeed, the rapidity of the Canadian advance caught both Leese and Alexander by surprise as much as it did Kesselring. Belatedly, Leese attempted to bring the First Armoured Division forward to deal with solidifying German resistance. Unfortunately, the First Armoured had been placed over one hundred miles to the rear, ostensibly to keep the roads in the battle area traffic-free. The tanks slowly ground forward along muddy tracks in low gear, many breaking down along the way. By 4 September, as the first tank reserves began to appear on the battlefield, the transfer of German reserves from the Bologna front to the Adriatic combined with German counterattacks to take the wind out of Olive.

For the next three weeks, the Canadian First Corps and British Fifth Corps slogged forward in torrential rain. On 21 September, the Greek Third Mountain Brigade entered Rimini, reduced to a rubble of battered antiquity. In twenty-six days, Leese had advanced thirty miles to the fringe of the Romagna Plain, in the process taking 14,000 casualties that the Eighth Army could ill afford. On 29 September, Leese was promoted, relieved, and sent to command Allied land forces in Southeast Asia, an event, Brooke discovered, that was "greeted with considerable joy" in Italy.[16] McCreery, Leese's successor at Eighth Army, advanced methodically up the Adriatic coast against a tide of autumn rains that transformed roads into mud and coastal rivers into torrents, capturing Ravenna on 4 December.[17]

Revelations by Ultra that the Germans had shifted three divisions from the central sector to stem Eighth Army attacks was the signal for Clark on 12 September to punch at the center of the Gothic line north of Florence with the Fifth Army's three corps. His objective was to break through the Apennine passes at the point where the mountain range was at its most narrow, to reach Bologna and the Po Valley beyond. The good news was that the combination of Olive, air interdiction of German logistics, and activity by Italian partisans had stretched

German strength to the point that only two divisions, filled with green replacements, opposed the U.S. Second Corps and British Thirteenth Corps, with which Clark looked to make his main attacks.

Unfortunately, prospects for the defense were improved by the chaos of brush-covered escarpments, mine-choked ravines, and narrow valleys studded with well-concealed, concrete-reinforced antitank defenses, practically invisible rifle pits, and machine guns nestled behind thick shields of wire, through which the Anglo-American forces had to advance. These static defenses were backed by a mobile reserve of self-propelled antitank guns. The Anglo-Americans assembled mules in great numbers and even created a muleteer academy at Orvieto. But recruitment of Italians willing to pursue degrees in beast management had proven disappointing.[18] Tough Moroccan mountain troops, vital to the success of Diadem, had vanished with the CEF into the maw of southern France.

Ultra intercepts disclosed that Hitler expected the main attack to come against the 1,200-foot Futa Pass astride Route 65. Clark capitalized on this by directing his principal effort against the Giogo Pass, through which ran the small secondary Route 6524, hardly more than a country lane. This would bypass the formidable defenses at the Futa Pass, allowing him to rejoin Route 65 beyond and march toward Bologna or exploit northeast toward Imola. The Giogo route also counted the additional advantage of tearing at the seam between the German Tenth and Fourteenth Armies.

The South African Sixth Armoured Division, transferred from Thirteenth Corps to Lieutenant General Willis D. Crittenburger's Fourth Corps, pressured the right wing of the Gothic line north of Pisa and Lucca to keep Kesselring from shifting reserves toward his center, where the Thirty-fourth Division of Major General Geoffrey Keyes's Second Corps made an effort to advance along Route 65 strong enough to persuade the Germans that the Futa Pass was Clark's principal objective. Meanwhile, troops of the Ninety-first and Eighty-fifth Divisions seized Monte Altuzzo and the 3,000-foot Monticelli ridge, high ground that flanked the Giogo Pass, after almost a week of vicious combat against the Twelfth Parachute Regiment. Although the Germans were desperately outnumbered and outgunned, a well-sited and -concealed machine-gun nest might hold up a battalion and defy the best efforts of the artillery or air force to obliterate it. Allied radios worked poorly in the mountains, making it difficult to coordinate action. Attacks sputtered as ammunition became exhausted and units might wait hours, even days, for mule resupply. Hard-won ground could be lost to counterattacks launched by Germans concealed in concrete shelters hidden on reverse slopes. It was Cassino without the monastery. The Giogo Pass in American hands, the Germans had no option but to abandon the Futa Pass, which fell to the Thirty-fourth Division. On 17 September, Fourteenth Army commander General Joachim Lemelsen, his reserves dispatched to help the Tenth Army stanch Olive and reduced in desperation to arming Lithuanian labor troops, ordered the Gothic line abandoned. The price paid by Second Corps for the passes was a relatively light 2,731 casualties. On the right flank of the Fifth Army, Kirkman's two divisions attacked and broke through the 715th Division of the German Tenth Army north of Borgo San Lorenzo, in the process pinning down German troops that might have shifted to oppose Second Corps.

By 21 September, Clark was through the passes and had Bologna in his sights. Ultra revealed deep confusion and disarray in the German command.[19] The Fifth Army pressed forward, aided by Italian partisans who seized high ground and defended it against German counterattacks. Engineers, helped by Italian laborers, threw Bailey bridges over streams and rivers as German shells rained down on them. On 22 and 23 September, Ultra began to decrypt messages that suggested that the Germans were making plans to withdraw across the Po River to the Alps, and Allied intelligence predicted a general German withdrawal. But Hitler's veto, which became firm on 5 October, combined with sluggish Allied progress caused by rain, poor roads, and German demolitions and Kesselring's decision to rush in two reinforcing divisions to scotch any contemplation of retreat.[20] Clark's troops, exhausted by continuous combat and without reserves to flesh out decimated units, faltered, despite the American general's best efforts to lash them forward. On 1 October, Clark renewed his offensives, sending the Eighty-fifth and Eighty-eighth divisions to take Monte Grandi, which dominated Route 65. When Monte Grandi fell, a jubilant Clark could write, "I could see for the first time the Po Valley and the snow-covered Alps beyond. It seemed to me that our goal was very close."[21] Even though the Germans had shifted their main reserves back to the Fifth Army front, steady if hard-bought progress by month's end brought one mountaintop after another under Fifth Army domination. On 23 October, Kesselring was seriously injured when his automobile collided with a towed artillery piece. Wisdom in the German army held that the field marshal was recovering nicely, but that the gun was a write-off.[22] Pending Kesselring's recovery, command fell to Tenth Army commander von Vietinghoff.

The final days of October brought Clark to within only two miles of the spot where the Apennines begin their descent to Bologna, fifteen miles distant. But Clark's interminable attacks against a seemingly endless succession of Apennine peaks had raised his munitions expenditures—Ninety-first Division artillery alone fired 24,000 shells in a forty-eight-hour period in mid-October—and casualties to unsustainable levels.[23] Fog and rain grounded Allied aircraft, especially the ubiquitous artillery spotters, permitting German reinforcements to arrive unimpeded. Rain-swollen rivers washed away bridges. Clark admitted that he did not end the offensive so much as it ground spontaneously to a halt as energy drained from the Fifth Army advance.[24] His concentration of troops before Bologna opened him to a German counterattack on 26 December against the Ninety-second Infantry, a division composed of black American troops guarding the approaches to Leghorn. Despite ample indications of an impending offensive, including speculation in Allied intelligence that the Germans might seek to repeat in Italy the success of the December 1944 Ardennes offensive, the attack achieved complete surprise. However, its success was short-lived, quickly stanched by air power, by reinforcements composed of two Indian army divisions, and by the fact that it seemed to have no strategic objective.[25] Winter settled onto northern Italy with Second Corps only nine miles from Bologna, but still stuck in the mountains.

The Allies felt that they had come within a hair of achieving a decisive victory in Italy. Eighth Army alone had badly mangled 11 German divisions, destroyed 100 German tanks and 124 guns, and inflicted almost 16,000 casualties. However, there could be little doubt that the Allies had, once again, been outfought and outgeneraled. In his memoirs, Kesselring insists that "the battle of the Apennines" was "a famous page of German military history," one in which his troops had overcome serious handicaps to master technologically superior Allied forces.[26] But that was in retrospect. By the end of September, the threat of a breakthrough by the Fifth Army had caused Kesselring to contemplate a withdrawal to the Alps, a thought nipped in the bud by Hitler, who calculated that if German forces withdrew, they could no longer live off the country, and Germany lacked the supplies to support them. He also had to continue to sustain the fiction of the Republic of Salò, and, above all, continue to exploit Italian industry to supplement the loss of France. Hitler continued to believe that control of northern Italy protected his Balkan flank.[27] After the fact, Kesselring justified this refusal to retreat—Allied intelligence invariably would have detected a withdrawal and would have transformed it into a rout. Even had he succeeded in evacuating the Apennines, his only fallback position was the Po River, which was hardly defendable against the inevitable spring offensive. But in the final analysis, he confessed that retreat ran "against my deepest conviction."[28]

Allied intelligence supplied the counterargument, calculating that a withdrawal of Army Group C north of the Po River would allow them to recuperate twelve badly needed divisions that they could transfer to Hungary to oppose the advancing Red Army, which encircled Budapest in December.[29] Even German commanders saw that the Germans had passed the "culminating point of victory" in Italy. Poor-quality replacements had caused the unprecedented spectacle of voluntary surrenders—8,170 POWs were taken by the Eighth Army—and even of wholesale desertions. Kesselring noted that the deterioration of Germany's military fortunes "meant that a good deal of self-confidence was needed by commanders to inspire the troops with the courage to stick it out. In this critical situation our plans were wrecked by accumulating orders to release divisions, and the troops received the impression that we were only muddling through."[30] Kesselring lauded the obvious improvements in Allied performance: an extensive communications network combined with improved air artillery spotting to achieve better artillery and tank support of infantry, while, over-all, the Allied armies had better adjusted their assignments to their ca-pabilities. But he insisted that on the unit level, where mountain warfare was won or lost, Allied junior leadership continued to lack ini-tiative.[31] On 9 March 1945, Hitler appointed Kesselring commander-in-chief, West, giving command in Italy to von Vietinghoff. General von Senger und Etterlin took over the Fourteenth Army from Lemel-sen, who moved to the Tenth Army.

Despite the impressive advances of the summer and autumn of 1944, the failure of the assaults on the Gothic line left the Allies with a feeling of disappointment and missed opportunities. The successes of an understrength Fifth Army in the mountains caused many to specu-late that the campaign in Italy might have terminated in the autumn of 1944 had the two armies pooled their diminished resources to attack side by side, rather than fight separate offensives. Leese was criticized as unimaginative and lacking in dynamism, a Monty knockoff who lacked Montgomery's enterprise. A general who had learned his trade in the desert, Leese had sought to adapt Italy to his army, rather than take a page out of Juin's book and spearhead his advance by using his mountain-experienced Indian divisions to infiltrate German positions on his flank, as had the French at Cassino. Inadequate staff work made poor infantry–armor coordination and traffic jams a hallmark of Eighth Army operations in Italy. The price Leese had paid in casual-ties had been roughly equal to those inflicted on the Germans, despite his overwhelming matériel superiority.

The British army was short 42,000 replacements, half of them in the Mediterranean. Refugee Poles contributed two new brigades total-ing 10,000 men to the Eighth Army. But this hardly compensated for the fact that the First Armoured Division and two brigades had to be dissolved and all infantry battalions reduced from four to three com-panies. The British Fifth Corps alone had absorbed 9,000 casualties, with a further 6,000 reporting sick, a sure sign of low morale. Some British soldiers had been in the Mediterranean without a home visit for four and a half years. Rising desertion—over 1,000 a month by October 1944, mainly in the infantry—and epidemic self-inflicted wounds and soldiers who preferred the guardhouse to the front line combined to reinforce the widespread impression that the Canadians and the Poles were outperforming British troops.[32] But Canadian divisions were transferred to Northwestern Europe from February 1945, and General Anders had to be persuaded to keep his Polish corps in the line after the confirmation that the February 1945 Yalta Conference had lopped off much of eastern Poland to Soviet advantage.[33]

The Apennine offensive also hardened Clark's opinion that the Eighth Army was an old dog that had forgotten how to hunt. On 14 October, in the midst of the drive toward Bologna, Clark publicly berated Major General Kirkman in front of his staff, insisting that the British Thirteenth Corps had taken half the casualties and roughly one-fifth of the German POWs as had the hard-fighting U.S. Second Corps. Clark's view that some British units at least clearly preferred to allow their artillery to do their fighting for them was not purely a product of his Anglophobia.[34] But it is also true that the unfortunate Kirkman had borne the brunt of Clark's deepening persecution complex and was a victim of Clark's habit of blaming his subordinates for failure. In fact, Kirkman, who was repatriated to England, joined the lengthening list of Clark's scapegoats, one that already included Dawley at Salerno, Lucas at Anzio, and McCreery and Freyberg at Cassino. But as an equal-opportunity scapegoater, Clark was prepared this time to blame his superiors as well for his failure to smash his way into the Po Valley. Alexander, he was convinced, had 50,000 reserves stashed in the Mediterranean that he would not release. "We are caught in the British empire machine," he lamented.

Clark remained practically deaf to criticism that he had attacked on too broad a front and had failed to rest and rotate units, but had instead driven them forward beyond endurance and, hence, beyond combat efficiency. When, on 20 October, Devers, then senior American officer at AFHQ, remonstrated with the Fifth Army commander that his incessant offensives were piling up bodies at an unsustainable rate, Clark complained that even the Americans were shifting troops to France that might be more profitably invested with him in Italy. He conceded that every ten days of combat cost him 5,000 casualties, and that "psychiatric disorders . . . directly related to the length of time in combat"[35] had also begun to bite into his strength. He therefore appealed directly to Eisenhower, who freed up 3,000 soldiers for the Fifth Army at the end of October—too late, Clark complained, to allow him to continue his push toward Bologna. The Thirty-fourth Division, in theater since 1942, had suffered high losses of junior officers and NCOs and was battle-weary. The Eighty-eighth Division alone had absorbed one-third of Fifth Army's 15,716 casualties.[36]

THE BALKANS AND GREECE

Mussolini's surrender, the Allied breakthrough at Cassino, the Normandy invasion, and Soviet advances on the Eastern Front impacted events in the Balkans and Greece. Tito's goal to create a Soviet-style state in Yugoslavia, along with fears in Whitehall that this was part of a pattern of Soviet ambitions in Italy, Yugoslavia, and Greece, eventually led to the so-called percentages agreement concluded in October 1944 by Churchill and Stalin. The British were to yield a "90 percent predominance" in Romania in exchange for gaining the equivalent influence in Greece. Yugoslavia was to be shared fifty-fifty. This forward diplomacy in the Balkans increased tensions between Churchill and the Americans, who denounced it as an attempt to further British imperial ambitions in the Eastern Mediterranean and a return to "discredited forms of pre-war diplomacy."[37] But even the British were forced to concede that the Yugoslav partisans were the stronger, more militarily efficient movement, and the more likely to take power at war's end. Therefore, they urged King Peter to jettison Mihailović to improve his chances of entering into a coalition with Tito.[38] They also hoped that aid to the partisans would moderate Tito's Communism.[39] But Tito's long-term goals matched up poorly with those of Churchill. He feared that by claiming to represent Serbia, where partisan support was weakest, King Peter could become the Trojan horse for Allied landings to settle the fate of postwar Yugoslavia.[40] In the short term, however, two things worked to moderate Tito's behavior, at least on the surface. First, he was brought to realize that the war was not yet over, and he still needed Allied assistance. German military pressure had driven Tito to Drvar in western Bosnia, where he and his staff narrowly evaded capture in a surprise 25 May 1944 German airborne raid. Tito was evacuated by the Balkan Air Force, created to supply the partisans, to Bari in Italy, and then taken by British destroyer to the island of Vis, which had become virtually a British protectorate.

A second moderating influence on Tito was Stalin, who was eager not to frighten the Western Allies into believing that he intended to make Yugoslavia a Soviet satellite. At Stalin's insistence, Tito invited Ivan Šubašać, prime minister in the royalist government, to become foreign minister in his partisan government. This further cut the ground from Mihailović's feet, and many erstwhile Chetniks jumped ship after King Peter praised the partisans in a radio broadcast. Tito sealed his status in the summer of 1944 when he traveled to Italy to meet Churchill. Partisan units had begun to make inroads into Serbia, and Tito came away from his meeting with Churchill with the impression that a British invasion of Yugoslavia, and hence a partition and restructuring of the country, was off the table.[41] In July 1944, Tito wrung agreement from Stalin to train and equip fourteen partisan divisions, complete with armor and artillery, to deal with the counterrevolutionary threat posed by Mihailović. The Red Army was also to take a "shortcut" through Yugoslavia on their way to Hungary, to shore up the partisan position. Unfortunately, the Red Army's habit of raping, looting, and even holding up partisans at gunpoint served to sour relations between Tito and Stalin once Soviet soldiers crossed the Yugoslav border on 22 September 1944.[42]

By late August 1944, Ultra began to reveal that the Germans were preparing to withdraw from Greece and the Balkans, and Bulgaria was about to abandon the Axis. Tito, meeting with Churchill at Caserta in August, agreed to join "Ratweek," the British-inspired plan for the Greek and Yugoslav resistance to assail German soldiers as they retreated up the Balkan Peninsula. Resisters did carry out attacks on bridges and rail lines that, British intelligence estimated, caused delays and disruption. Nevertheless, OSS operative Franklin Lindsay declared partisan attacks on major rail links in Slovenia "disappointing."[43] Partisans also flowed into coastal areas abandoned by the Germans as they consolidated their troops in central Yugoslavia along their axis of retreat. German forces moving out of Greece through Albania into Yugoslavia were held up for two weeks by partisan attacks before they managed a breakout. However, the facts that the Russians switched the axis of their advance north into Hungary, that Tito's primary energies were put into attacks on Mihailović, and that Tito resolutely refused British offers to land forces in Yugoslavia to cut off remaining German troops there,[44] allowed the Germans to consolidate along a Winter line running from Fiume through Mostar and Sarajevo and then north to Vukovar. By then, Ultra intercepts that revealed growing cooperation between Mihailović and the Germans removed any residual sympathy that lingered in London for the Chetnik leader.[45] As the rival resistance groups fought it out, the Germans retired virtually unmolested. On 1 November 1944, the partisans installed themselves in Belgrade. A provisional government, dominated by the Communists but also containing three ministers from the exiled regency, was formed and was recognized by the Allies. Nevertheless, relations between the partisans and the Western Allies had grown decidedly cool in the autumn of 1944, as Tito feared an Allied invasion and advance through Ljubljana might revive antipartisan forces in Yugoslavia and frustrate his territorial goals in southern Austria and Italy.

The August 1943 death of Bulgaria's King Boris in mysterious circumstances after a heated interview with Hitler, followed by heavy attacks on Sofia by Allied bombers, set the Bulgarian government looking for an exit. A small Communist-led resistance movement, the Otechestven (Fatherland) Front, began to swell with recruits as Germany's Eastern Front contracted and the food crisis in Bulgaria caused by German requisitions increased. The 8 September 1944 arrival of the Red Army in Bulgaria sparked a Communist coup in Sofia. The Bulgarian army was reorganized along Soviet lines and supplied with a cadre of political commissars; it joined the forces of the Soviet Third Ukrainian Front to attack Budapest and Vienna.

The approaching end of the war in the Balkans left EAM/ELAS in fear of British intervention in Greece, followed by the imposition of a monarchy. This caused EAM/ELAS to redouble its efforts to eliminate EDES. Throughout the winter of 1943–44, ELAS carried out a series of successful offensives against Zervas's units. But Allied support to EDES and the exhaustion of the ELAS offensive allowed Zervas to counterattack successfully. In February 1944, the Allied military mission brokered a cease-fire between ELAS and EDES, each agreeing to remain within defined areas of operation and to attack only the Germans. In order to increase their leverage and to counter royal promises that George would return when invited by a properly elected governing body, the KKE and EAM organized a Political Committee of National Liberation (PEEA) on 10 March 1944, which promptly set out to organize elections for a parliament as well as establish municipal councils, schools, police, health and postal systems, newspapers, and agricultural cooperatives throughout "free Greece," all funded by public taxation.[46]

On 11 March 1944, a Provisional Government of Free Greece was proclaimed. Greece now had three governments: a collaborationist regime under Ralles, an unelected government-in-exile, and a Communist-dominated PEEA that purported to be democratically chosen. Infighting between the internal and external Greek resistance infected the 20,000 Greek troops stationed in Egypt, several of whose units formed soldiers' committees and mutinied against their officers, disturbances that the British attributed to Communist influence. The mutiny was repressed by the British and by loyal Greek units on 22–23 April 1944. Greek units were purged of republican and Communist sympathizers, and 10,000 Greek soldiers were sent into detention in Libya and Eritrea. A Third Mountain Brigade, composed of royalist sympathizers, was sent first to Italy, where they participated in the capture of Rimini as part of the Eighth Army, and subsequently to Athens in November 1944.[47]

To end this perpetual bickering, the British called together seventeen Greek political parties and resistance groups in Lebanon. The result was the May 1944 Lebanon Agreement, which formed a "Government of National Unity" under the leader of the Greek Social Democratic Party, George Papandreou, with EAM/ELAS accorded one-quarter of the ministerial portfolios. The Greek armed forces in the Middle East were to be reorganized. In a series of complex political maneuvers, Papandreou managed to adopt EAM's political themes and then unite the republican parties and resistance groups to resist EAM's growing power in Greece.[48] In July 1944 a Soviet mission parachuted into "Free Greece" and ordered EAM to join the Papandreou cabinet. As the Germans prepared to withdraw from Greece, Security

Policy chief Walter Blume proposed to apply the "chaos thesis"— the arrest and execution of Greek politicians and civil servants suspected of being pro-British. He was talked out of it by German Foreign Office representative Hermann Neubacher, who argued that the anti–EAM/ELAS attitudes of the Ralles government meant that the Germans still needed them to cover their retreat.[49] Allies gathered the resistance leaders at Caserta to finalize plans for the liberation. EDES, ELAS, and the government-in-exile agreed to place their forces under the command of British Lieutenant General Ronald Scobie, who would occupy Athens with British and Indian units. All military organizations were to be disbanded on liberation, and a new national army was to be formed. But as the liberation approached, EAM/ELAS agents stepped up assassinations in Athens to eliminate their most dangerous opponents.

On 14 October, the first British troops disembarked in Athens. Papandreou arrived three days later at the head of the Government of National Unity, followed by the Third Mountain Brigade from Italy. ELAS and EDES remained in the countryside, where ELAS in particular cleaned out arsenals left behind by the retreating Germans and the Security Battalions. Zervas pounced on the Moslem Chams, killing hundreds, driving over 15,000 into Albania, and installing his men in their ruined villages. Thirty thousand members of Slavic-speaking minorities around Kastoria and Floriana in the north, some of whom were *andartes*, were expelled to Yugoslavia and Bulgaria. Without a political base, Papandreou dared not attack reactionary and royalist elements who had supported Metaxas, Ralles, and the occupation, and who in any case rallied to the Government of National Unity and its British protectors as the best bulwark against an ELAS takeover. When Papandreou attempted to apply the portion of the Caserta Agreement that called for the dissolution of all armed groups and the creation of a new national army composed of all elements, EAM/ELAS cried foul—the Third Brigade and even former members of the Security Battalions were included in the new army, while ELAS veterans were invited to disarm and go home. Former collaborators were given important government posts, while notorious war criminals walked the streets of Athens as free men.

The late autumn of 1944 found the Allies stalemated in Europe. Montgomery's Ruhr offensive had come up short, and the Germans maintained a firm grip on several Atlantic ports and blocked the Scheldt, which made Antwerp useless. Fighting settled down to deadlock in the Vosges of eastern France and in the Ardennes. The Warsaw uprising was extinguished in early October. The Russians were thrown out of East Prussia. The Germans had been allowed to withdraw from Greece and Yugoslavia unmolested, even as the Red Army seized Belgrade. Operation Manna, the British descent on Greece, stripped the Indian Fourth Division and the Greek Third Mountain Brigade from an already overstretched Eighth Army. The Canadian Corps joined the Canadian Army in the Twenty-first Army Group poised to invade Germany. Kirkman returned to Britain, as did Harding. Alexander complained that he could not sustain an Italian front while supplying troops to deal with the deteriorating situation in Greece. However, appeals to Brooke for more men and ammunition drew the reply that France, not the Mediterranean, remained the priority front for the Allies. On 31 January 1945, Brooke informed Alexander that Russian gains in the East made Alexander's Ljubljana Gap proposal both superfluous and politically objectionable to the Soviets.[50]

In another sense, however, failure to make a breakthrough in the Apennines in the late summer of 1944 offered advantages to the Allies. Why hasten to close down a peripheral theater where German troops fought at a disadvantage, one that Hitler continued to reinforce? Despite the crumbling defenses of the Reich, Hitler withdrew only three divisions from Italy, troops that could have bought him time on other fronts. Stalemate prevented the Allies from launching more imaginative operations with a high potential for failure. Marshall, never a fan of the Mediterranean theater, saw the failure of the autumn offensives in the Apennines as confirmation that no decisive results could be attained in Italy, and so opposed plans to reinforce there.[51] Failure to seize Bologna, in the process driving back the Tenth and Fourteenth Armies, scuppered Churchill-inspired AFHQ plans to withdraw six divisions from the Italian front for an amphibious attack on Fiume and Trieste, followed by a march into Venetia to take Kesselring from the rear and occupy a region ripe for Communist takeover. Maitland

Wilson predicted that instead of a triumphal march into Venetia, Churchill's strategy would result in another Anzio.[52] Allied commanders also became aware that the capture of the heavily populated Po Valley, where food stocks were low, would add a humanitarian crisis to their lengthening list of logistical and political problems.[53] The failure to capture Bologna diminished neither Alexander's nor Clark's stars. Maitland Wilson, the commander-in-chief in the Mediterranean, was named to replace deceased Field Marshal Sir John Dill as British representative to the Combined Chiefs of Staff in Washington. Alexander was elevated to field marshal and SACMED—Supreme Allied Commander Mediterranean—over the protests of First Sea Lord Admiral Sir Andrew Cunningham, who insisted he was "unfitted for the job." Brooke's retort was that it mattered little because there were no alternatives and in any case Italy had become a moribund theater.[54] On 24 November, at Churchill's suggestion, Clark received notice that he was to direct Allied armies in Italy, as head of the Fifteenth Army Group, with Lucian Truscott recalled from France to head the Fifth Army.

"A SCOURGE TO DECENT ITALIANS"

The collapse of the Fascist government and the Allied invasion of Italy in September 1943 had given rise to a spontaneous resistance movement in German-occupied northern Italy. Italian soldiers who escaped German internment, Allied soldiers released from Italian POW camps, Jews on the run, urban workers, and radical middle-class opponents of the regime who dared not sleep in the same bed two nights in succession all took to the hills to become the first *ribelli*. They were soon joined by victims of fierce German repression such as that which fell on the village of Boves in Piedmont in September 1943, those impressed as forced labor for the Todt Organization, those evading conscription into the armed forces of Mussolini's Republic of Salò, and veterans of World War I or of the Italian Eighth Army on the Eastern Front who shared a dislike of Germans, in all about 9,000 men. Kesselring called this early resistance movement "a scourge to decent Italians," but assessed it as isolated and "not particularly dangerous."[55] Though the vast majority of resisters were driven by circumstance rather than ideology, this spontaneous movement was given political coherence by committees for national liberation that sprung up in northern Italy, grouped under the central National Committee for the Liberation of Upper Italy (CLNAI). The liberals and Christian Democrats, prominent in the Allied-sponsored government in the south, were notably absent in the north, where the Communists and the Party of Action ruled the resistance movement. However, smaller numbers of resisters affiliated with socialist, monarchist, or Catholic groups also took up arms.

The situation changed by the spring of 1944, as partisan groups in the Alps and Apennines swelled to 20,000 to 30,000 members, and then to more than 80,000 by what was called "the great partisan summer." Many were no doubt enticed to join by Alexander's 6 June 1944 call for Italians to prepare for an uprising. This suited the plans of the Communists, who wished to take power before Allied troops arrived so that the political future of Italy would not be dictated entirely by Washington, London, and Rome. In June, Alexander speculated that the resistance was tying down up to six of the twenty-five German divisions in the country.[56] Partisan-organized "republics" emerged in remote highland areas along the French and Swiss borders and in the Apennines, supplied by air drops of the Balkan Air Force.

From June 1944, with the breakout at Cassino, all partisan groups were coordinated into a coherent command structure known as the Voluntary Freedom Corps (CVL), under General Raffaele Cadorna, who was parachuted in from the south. Cadorna's task in Allied eyes was to create a unitary resistance answerable to Allied command. But to ensure political balance, he took as his two deputies Luigi Longo, representing Communist interests, and Ferrucio Parri, nominated by the Party of Action. Cadorna's reports that the Communists were prominent in the resistance worried the Allies, who began to fear that like Greece and Yugoslavia, Italy was sliding toward postwar instability. Kesselring noted that the fall of Rome made partisans "more aggressive, far more in fact than I had reckoned with, and this date may be called the birthday of the all-out guerilla war." He complained that partisans had become "an actual menace to our military operations and it was vital to remove it."[57] The Allies also found the resistance in the north to be more vocal in asserting the CLNAI's nominations for local government positions against those supplied to Allied Military Government officers by Rome.[58] By October 1944, SOE was running thirty-three missions to the partisans, with a decided bias for non-Communist groups.[59]

Partisan groups split on strategy as well as politics. Some preferred *attendismo*, awaiting the Allied liberation. While this would have caused far fewer deaths, it was a tactic roundly condemned by the Communists, who incited urban terrorists known as *Gappisti* to plant bombs and assassinate German soldiers, a tactic that invariably provoked ferocious reprisals. The Germans also deported two thousand ringleaders of the massive strikes organized in Milan and other large industrial centers in the north in the summer of 1944, causing the strikes to collapse.[60] Allied diaries mention partisan assistance in the advance toward the Gothic line, in the capture of Florence, and even in attacks such as that on Monte Battaglia in the Apennines. To contain the partisans, Kesselring tried the carrot as well as the stick, working through the church, local leaders, and radio broadcasts to curtail partisan attacks, an appeal for calm that he claimed enjoyed some success.[61] From the summer of 1944, with Kesselring fearful that renewed partisan activity might threaten his line of retreat, the Germans lashed out furiously at those "republics" that threatened their control of the north, using mainly ex-Soviet troops of the 162d (Turcoman) Infantry Division under General Oscar Ritter von Niedermayer. In August, elements of the Adolf Hitler Panzer Division massacred 560 people in Santa Anna di Stazzema north of Pisa. On 18 October 1944 it was the turn of the village of Marzabotto near Bologna, where 1,604 men, women, and children were murdered by German soldiers. The Allied failure to break the Gothic line gave the Germans the freedom to launch a major antipartisan offensive in October, which devastated the resistance and substantially reduced their numbers. In all, around 35,000 Italians, including partisans, died, 21,000 were wounded, and 9,000 deported as the result of German reprisals.[62] "In the areas in which they operated there were Partisan-occupied villages, even zones in which every man, woman and child was in some way connected with them, either as combatant, helper or sympathizer," Kesselring wrote. "Whether these people acted spontaneously or under gentle pressure made no difference. When a bullet killed a German soldier it was not possible for us to discriminate." Soon, he noted, German soldiers in the infested areas suspected every civilian of either sex to be a partisan, or at the very least a cog in an elaborate "warning system which placed every German soldier's life in danger."[63]

To save resistance lives, on 13 November 1944 Alexander called on partisans to suspend operations for the winter, to "save their munitions and materiel until further orders." Alexander was criticized for undermining partisan morale at a time when they were hard-pressed by the Germans and for handing a political issue to the Communists, who claimed that it was the British revenge on the Russians for allowing the Warsaw uprising to be suppressed. The Allies, the left argued plausibly, merely wanted to dissolve the resistance, with whom they had no desire to share political power.[64] On the other hand, Alexander's appeal could hardly be equated with Stalin's cynical *attendismo* before Warsaw. In November 1944, Maitland Wilson signed the "Protocols of Rome" with the CLNAI, offering Allied supplies in return for a promise that resisters would obey Allied orders and disband on liberation. The spring of 1945 witnessed the revival of the partisan movement and with it fears expressed by the Foreign Office that, if Allied troops did not remain in Italy, Communists might seize power there. Harold Macmillan was eager to get the AMGOT in place and disarm the partisans so as to strengthen the hand of the Italian government.[65] Otherwise, the dismemberment or partition of Italy might be the result, one that could influence the political settlement in the Balkans and Greece, Macmillan feared.[66] In a country that had been a battlefield for almost two years, the severe devastation, starvation, the bankruptcy of the state, the collapse of national self-respect, the million men deported as POWs or slave laborers, caused others to believe that Communism would take root before reconstruction.[67] In the end, the feared partisan putsch failed to materialize, in great part because Stalin, who had recognized the Badoglio government in March 1944, had no plans to use the partisan movement to seize power in Italy. Palmiro Togliatti, founder and leader of the Italian Communist Party (PCI), was prepared to work through the democratic process as a way to legitimize the PCI within the Italian political system. He was also aware that the presence of hundreds of thousands of Allied soldiers would have made an armed insurrection a suicidal undertaking.[68] Besides, the resistance was fragmented and localized, many of its members were antifascist but otherwise apolitical, and they would have made a poor launching pad for a power grab.[69]

The value of partisan activity is difficult to gauge, because survival, rather than combat, absorbed most partisan energies. Officially, partisans inflicted 2,670 casualties on German forces and another 3,868 on Italian fascist troops, although Kesselring insisted that the figure was far higher.[70] Partisans did coordinate in supplying intelligence to Allied troops before and during Operation Grapeshot (the final Allied offensive against the Winter line) and in carrying out some sabotage missions behind German lines.[71] Some historians agree with Alexander's estimate that the Germans detached as many as six divisions to control the partisans.[72] But as in many other occupied territories, the occupiers generally relied on approximately 100,000 Italian police and fascist militia to contain resistance activity.

THE FINAL OFFENSIVE

By the spring of 1945, as Allied armies pushed into Germany, Kesselring and von Vietinghoff saw the handwriting on the wall. Although winter in the Apennines had been relatively quiet, the Allies incorporated replacements, bolstered their artillery, stockpiled supplies, and carried out limited attacks so as to position themselves better for the cleanup offensives. By March, the Fifth Army had accumulated so many artillery shells that they were ordered to begin firing them off to make room for new shipments.[73] Skirmishing between frontline units of the British Eighth and German Tenth Armies had been a constant feature of the exceptionally bitter winter, as British troops eliminated German bridgeheads across which they would need to advance in the spring. Between 18 February and 10 March 1945, the Tenth Mountain Division, the only unit of the U.S. Army specializing in mountain warfare, supported by the Brazilian Division, advanced six miles across the high ground flanking the Reno River and Route 64, preceded by swarms of rock climbers who scaled the 1,500-foot-high Riva Ridge to

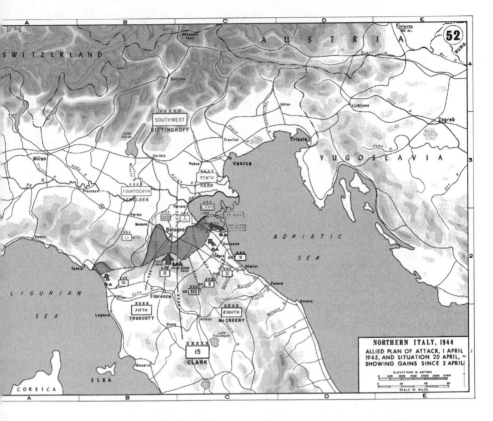

take the thinly held German positions by surprise. This rapid advance caused momentary panic in the German command. "Though success had been only local and not in any way decisive," Kesselring remembered of the Tenth Mountain's attack, "they had blunted the mettle of our troops."[74]

Ultra intercepts enabled the Allies to keep close track of the German order of battle and the deteriorating German supply situation.[75] Between January and March, Berlin transferred three precious divisions out of Italy and culled mountain and paratroop divisions for replacements to shore up the crumbling defenses of the Reich, and rearranged their defenses along the Winter line.[76] Allied air interdiction against the Brenner Pass had reduced trains from Germany to an average of 2.3 per day, half the number needed to keep Army Group C supplied.[77] Even those that got through were plagued by partisan attacks, all of which transformed the German supply situation into a nightmare of logistical improvisation. On 21 February, German fuel and ammunition stocks in Italy were sufficient for no more than two weeks of fighting.[78] In February the Siegfried line was taken and the Rhine was crossed in March. As April opened, large numbers of German troops were surrounded in the Ruhr. Tito's partisans advanced to within thirty miles of Fiume, deepening Kesselring's fears of an amphibious attack combined with a partisan advance north of the Po.[79] There was a case to be made for the Allies simply to do nothing in northern Italy, allowing the war to take its course in Northern Europe. But several factors argued against this option. First, Churchill persisted in his belief that Italy remained a critical theater; he demanded action there, to the great frustration of his chiefs of staff, who were eager to pull Indian divisions out of Italy for the Far East. He persisted in his desire to invade southern Austria through Italy and Yugoslavia, in part to raise Alexander's command profile, but also to preempt Soviet influence there.[80] Like the prime minister, Alexander and Clark were also impatient to exterminate Army Group C. Clark believed that if he waited for the good weather in May, the Red Army and the U.S. Seventh Army would reach Austria before him, concluding the war before he could win the renown that had, so far, eluded him. Finally, a residual fear, fed by false German intelligence reports to OSS agents in Switzerland and Austria, also existed within Eisenhower's Supreme Headquarters Allied Expeditionary Force, SHAEF, that, in a desperate attempt to stave off defeat, the Germans might bolt for the Alps to establish an "Alpine Defense Zone" or "National Redoubt." The Allies were therefore keen to reach the Alps before the Germans could organize a last stand that might take months and substantial casualties to smother.[81]

Though weakened, Kesselring, who returned to command on 15 January 1945, still packed a punch. By the end of February 1945 the Tenth Army counted thirteen divisions and the Fourteenth Army nine divisions, totaling 349,000 men. His 45,000 Italian troops concentrated in the Army of Liguria were largely worthless. But he had a reserve of 91,000 Germans in police and antiaircraft units and 100,000 Italian police. His arsenal included 1,436 field artillery pieces, 450 self-propelled assault guns, and 261 tanks.[82] The German Winter line consisted of well-fortified mountain strong points across the center of the peninsula. On their Adriatic flank, engineers and conscripted Italian laborers had toiled to construct a defense in depth along a series of river lines, the same waterlogged terrain that had confounded Leese in the autumn. Nevertheless, the German commander was reluctant to fight it out on the Winter line, and began to plot withdrawal positions so that Army Group C would be able to retire in an orderly manner when the inevitable blow fell in Italy, protecting Italy's industrial areas for as long as possible before retiring to the Alps.[83] But Hitler had vetoed this option on 5 January, a refusal he repeated on 17 April after von Vietinghoff, in the heat of battle, again pleaded that he lacked the supplies and the reserves to man defenses so far forward in the face of Allied matériel superiority.[84] Ultra left Allied generals in no doubt that Hitler's micromanagement of the Italian front had committed Army Group C to a dangerously exposed forward defense. In any case, serious Allied air interdiction left petrol the most prized commodity in the German forces, and guaranteed that should they attempt to reorganize their front or even retire, they must do so slowly and on foot.

In the absence of any realistic grasp of the strategic situation on Hitler's part, Obergruppenführer Karl Wolff, head of SS Security in Italy, took it upon himself in February to open negotiations with Alan Dulles, who ran the OSS in Switzerland. But "Crossword" made glacial progress, both because the Allies feared leaks to the Russians and because, on the German side, neither Kesselring nor von Vietinghoff was persuaded to enter the conspiracy. The Allies were also alerted through Ultra that Himmler had got wind of the negotiations and that he opposed surrender. Wolff's initiative was propelled by the naive delusion that the Western Allies could be persuaded to sign an armistice with the Third Reich that would allow Germany to direct all its forces against the Red Army. In the event, "Crossword" did provide the eventual framework for the surrender of German forces in Italy.[85]

For the final Allied offensive against the Winter line—Grapeshot— Clark assigned the main thrust to Truscott and the Fifth Army, so convinced was he that the British could not "carry the ball."[86] But Clark encountered three problems in imposing his view. First, the Adriatic sector on the Eighth Army front offered the most promising route of advance into the rear of Army Group C. If "feather duster" McCreery, who commanded the larger of Clark's armies[87] with more armored pursuit potential, could bridge the Reno River near its mouth and charge across a thirteen-mile-wide spit of land known as the Argenta Gap, which separated the Reno from the Comacchio Lagoon, which remained partially dry despite the flooding caused by German destruction of the dike system, he would outflank the series of defensive river lines created by Kesselring's engineers. Clark's second miscalculation was that Lucian Truscott proved to be his own man, determined to stamp his own personality on the Fifth Army. Taking counsel from Clark's change of direction after Anzio in June 1944 to capture Rome, Truscott declined to be railroaded again into a plan aimed to satisfy his superior's quest for headline-grabbing objectives.[88] Rather than hammer up Route 65 in a series of phased attacks aimed first at Bologna, then across the Po, after which the Fifth and Eighth Armies would fan out through the Po Valley as Clark desired, Truscott determined that Fifth Army would strike to the west of Bologna along Route 64, avoiding the two strong paratroop and panzer divisions guarding the approaches to that city. This would give them access to the Plain of Emilia and the south bank of the Po, where he would meet the Eighth Army driving up from the south. Clark's third problem was that this general concept had been developed by Alexander's staff at Caserta, who argued convincingly that, given Hitler's firm order to von Vietinghoff to cede no ground, this would enfold the Tenth and Fourteenth Armies in a double-enveloping maneuver, crush Army Group C, and put the Allies in the best position to wrest control of northern Italy from a potential partisan power grab. In short, Clark had been outmaneuvered and isolated by his own command.

In executing the plan, the Allies would have several advantages. First was the extra muscle of B-17 and B-24 bombers of the Twelfth Air Force, based in Italy but whose targets in Germany had been overrun by the advancing Red Army. These increased the strength of the already powerful U.S. Twenty-second Tactical Air Command and the Desert Air Force. Second, the Allies enjoyed a two-to-one advantage in artillery pieces and infantrymen and a three-to-one advantage in armor. Third, engineers adapted Armored Personnel Carriers (APCs),

Duplex Drive tanks, and LVTs ("Landing Vehicles Tracked") to carry their troops across killing grounds swept by enemy fire. The LVTs, called "Amtracks" by the Americans, "Buffaloes" or "Fantails" by the British, had been developed by the U.S. Marines to carry troops over the coral reefs that kept LSTs from reaching Pacific beaches. McCreery realized that the tracked, triangular vehicles, some fitted with turrets, others simply open troops carriers with mounted machine guns, were perfectly adapted to ferry troops across flooded areas and the sandbanks of the shallow Comacchio Lagoon to catch the Germans guarding the Argenta Gap by surprise.[89] Fourth, the Allies enjoyed the intelligence high ground against an enemy that was practically blinded by its lack of aircraft. Finally, the Germans must cope with roughly 50,000 partisans behind the front, organized in part by 200 Allied personnel. Even before Grapeshot was launched, the Eighth Army front had been well scouted by Italian partisans and fishermen, who traded eels with the Germans for fishing permits that allowed them to map the Comacchio Lagoon area.

At 1930 on 9 April, New Zealanders and Indians of the Eighth Army crossed the Senio River in assault boats, threw kapok bridges over the water, and advanced behind a thunderous artillery barrage and Churchill tanks spitting geysers of flames. Von Vietinghoff tried to counter this expected barrage on his front lines by the classic tactic of thinning out his advanced positions and establishing his main position farther back. But this plan was thwarted by 1,673 heavy and 624 medium bombers that carpeted German troop concentrations between the Santerno and Senio Rivers with fragmentation bombs. Bombing continued through the nights, giving the Germans no respite. Over the course of the offensive, German positions were pounded by almost 150,000 bombs. The infantry was set to mine clearing, freeing up engineers to lay bridges across the rivers. German resistance was sporadic and disorganized. The British advanced through a maze of marshes and rivers on the Adriatic coast, converging on the Argenta Gap, the neck of dry land between the Comacchio Lagoon and the Reno River. McCreery sprung his surprise on the Germans defending the gap by attacking across the Comacchio Lagoon with a brigade of the Fifty-sixth Division in LVTs. This outflanked and collapsed the German line. The Germans rushed the Twenty-ninth Panzer into the gap. But the German line creaked under the sheer weight and momentum of the advance of two British, one Indian, two Polish, and one New Zealand division. Clouds of small Allied observation planes buzzed above the German positions like insects, calling down artillery and air strikes. LVTs carried troops across the flooded areas that the Germans had counted on to guard their flanks. Von Vietinghoff, low on replacements and practically out of fuel, ordered a tactical withdrawal, which brought down dire threats from Berlin. By 23 April, the Sixth Armoured Division was camped on the banks of the Po. There they met elements of the Second Corps pushing up from the south.

Fifth Army's attack had been preceded by a 5 April diversionary attack by the reconstituted Ninety-second Division on Massa, the last surviving position of the old Gothic line on the Ligurian front, in which the aggressive advance of the Japanese-American 442d Regimental Combat Team challenged other units to keep pace. This attack forced von Vietinghoff to commit reserves of the Ninetieth Panzer Grenadier Division to halt the Ninety-second and depleted his fuel even further. The main attack, delayed by bad weather, opened at 0830 on 14 April with waves of over two thousand heavy bombers saturating the front. Behind them, the Twenty-second Tactical Air Command napalmed gun positions, strong points, and troop concentrations. Then came the Tenth Mountain Division of the Fourth Corps, which advanced into a smoky dusk created by the bombardment, picking their way through thinly manned but heavily mined and booby-trapped forward positions toward the German main lines, positions that belched with defensive fire despite the heavy air bombardment. Nevertheless, the Tenth Mountain managed to drive a wedge between the defending German 334th and Ninety-fourth Divisions. The attack caused German radios, so long silent, to crackle with orders, giving the Allies a good picture of the situation on the enemy side, although by the time tactical intelligence could be collected, processed, and disseminated, events had moved so rapidly that it was out of date.[90] So many peaks fell to the Tenth Mountain, recruited largely among college boys on ski teams, that by twilight on 15 April the division stood on the verge of breakthrough. For the next three days, the German Ninety-fourth Division threw up smoke screens and defensive artillery fire to cover their retreats before the Tenth Mountain's relentless advance, which drew the Brazilian Division and the First Armored Division in its wake. The four divisions of Second Corps, advancing on a fifteen-mile front behind heavy tactical air support alternated punches with Fourth Corps. A big push launched by the Tenth Mountain and Eighty-fifth Divisions on the morning of 18 April was like kicking in an open door against a German defense that was only spasmodically effective. Ultra revealed that German divisions were collapsing.[91]

By 20 April, the Fifth Army, attacking across its entire front, had cleared the mountains and flooded onto the Plain of Emilia, despite a desperate attempt by the Ninetieth Panzer Grenadier Division to sacrifice its tanks to prevent it. Fighting was hard, nonetheless. Second Lieutenant Daniel Inouye of the 442d took on a machine gun that had wounded him in the side on the Colle Musatello, one of the ridges that blocked the U.S. advance toward the Po Valley. "I threw a grenade and it cleared the log bunker and exploded," he remembered, "and when the gun crew staggered erect, I cut them down with my tommy gun." He pulled himself toward a second machine-gun nest.

At last I was close enough to pull the pin on my last grenade. And as I drew my arm back, all in a flash of light and dark I saw him, that faceless German, like a strip of motion picture film running through a projector that's gone berserk. One instant he was standing waist-high in the bunker, and the next he was aiming a rifle grenade at my face from a range of 10 yards. And even as I cocked my arm to throw, he fired and his rifle grenade smashed into my right elbow and exploded and all but tore my arm off. I looked at it, stunned and unbelieving. It dangled there by a few bloody shreds of tissue, my grenade still clenched in a fist that suddenly didn't belong to me anymore . . . The grenade mechanism was ticking off the seconds. In two, three, or four, it would go off, finishing me and the good men who were rushing up to help me. "Get back" I screamed, and swung around to pry the grenade out of that dead fist with my left hand. Then I had it free and I turned to throw and the German was reloading his rifle. But this time I beat him. My grenade blew up in his face and I stumbled to my feet, closing in on the bunker, firing my tommy gun left-handed, the useless right arm slapping red and wet against my side.

Inouye was awarded the Distinguished Service Cross and later served as U.S. senator from Hawaii.[92]

Bologna fell to the Poles approaching from the east on 21 April after what their commander, General Anders, described as *"une très jolie petite bataille."*[93] The Poles were particularly elated to have destroyed the First Parachute Division, which had opposed them at Cassino, Anders walking away with the captured divisional flag.[94] When, on 20 April, Hitler's birthday, von Vietinghoff asked permission to withdraw north of the Po, Berlin berated him for his "defeatist attitude" and threatened "serious consequences" if he disobeyed Hitler's orders to defend to the knife. But his army was broken. The Russian crossing of the Oder on 20 April caused Hitler to abandon all hope of persuading the Western Allies to join the Germans in opposing the Soviets. Allied air attacks turned Army Group C's retreat into a *sauve qui peut.*

By 21 April, German soldiers were abandoning their heavy weapons and straggling through the web of secondary roads toward the few crossing points over the wide, sluggish Po River. Allied air attacks transformed these sites into infernos of burnt-out vehicles, dead draft animals, and charred ferries. Germans who managed to reach the northern bank did so without their equipment, and had to run a gauntlet of well-armed and vengeful partisan bands that began to seize the main cities. Truscott reorganized his troops as armor-infantry task forces for the pursuit. The Tenth Mountain reached the Po on the evening of 22 April and crossed the river on assault boats the next morning. On 23 April, Eighth Army's Sixth Armoured Division linked up with the South African Sixth Armoured Division of Second Corps, slamming shut the escape for 100,000 German soldiers caught south of the river. Frido von Senger, commander of the Fourteenth Panzer Corps, ordered his headquarters to disperse and try to reassemble on the Adige River. By 24 April pontoon bridges carried Second Corps units over the Po, followed on the next day by those of Fourth Corps. Allied forces fanned out north of the river. The Tenth Mountain headed to Verona, Lake Garda, and the Brenner Pass beyond to cut off that potential line of retreat. On 27 April resistance ceased in Genoa. British divisions leaped the Adige and ran for Venice and Yugoslavia to block that route into southern Austria through Ljubljana. The Japanese-American 442d met soldiers of the French Twenty-seventh Alpine Division, who had invaded northern Italy from France, at Turin. The greatest threat to advancing Allied troops became their own planes, unable to distinguish friend from foe in the tangled flow of refugees and pursuers.

The committees for national liberation, their numbers swelled by last-minute joiners, emerged in full force, seizing cities like Genoa, Milan, and Turin ahead of the advancing Allied forces and generally assuming political authority throughout the north. Harold Macmillan, who watched partisans liberate Modena, described it as "really quite an exciting little action while it lasted and quite spirited. Of course a lot of partisans fired off their pieces quite aimlessly and threw grenades just for fun. Indeed these gentlemen and their curious assortment of rifles, grenades, tommy-guns, etc., caused me more alarm than our opponents."[95] The Duce fled in a truckload of German soldiers, but was recognized by partisans on 27 April. The next day he was executed, along with his mistress, by a special squad of partisans sent from Milan. Allied Military Government officers arrived to create administrations to rein in the partisans and try, unsuccessfully, to prevent bloody "settling of accounts" with former fascists. Clark, Alexander, and their senior subordinates began to preside over "stand-down parades," ceremonies in which the resister handed over his weapon in return for a "certificate of merit." "I am told that in the black market these certificates command a good price," recorded Macmillan, "which is encouraging."[96] On 29 April, General Wolff's emissaries signed "Instruments of Local Surrender" at Alexander's headquarters at Caserta, near Naples. The fact that local commanders were laying down their weapons infuriated Kesselring, who ordered von Vietinghoff's arrest on 1 May, an order he rescinded the following day after he learned of Hitler's death. In any case, by then the Allies were attempting to manage 200,000 German POWs.

The final action of the Italian campaign occurred on the morning of 4 May, when a gaunt Lieutenant General Frido von Senger, brilliant defender of Cassino, the Iron Cross dangling from a ribbon around his neck, reported to Clark's cramped headquarters outside of Florence for the surrender of German forces in Italy. As von Senger marched into the presence of Clark flanked by Truscott and McCreery, he stepped on Clark's cocker spaniel Pal, causing the dog to yelp and launch a retaliatory strike at the German's ankle. After the ceremony was completed and von Senger had stepped out of the door, a reporter pointed out to Clark that the German still carried a side arm. Clark recalled von Senger and forced him to surrender his pistol. "This was the end. *Finito!*" remembered Clark. "The war in Italy was over."[97]

The German collapse in Italy was repeated in neighboring Yugoslavia. The final partisan offensive against the Germans and their Croat allies was launched on 19 March 1945. On 30 April, Tito's forces reached Trieste, the Adriatic port claimed by Yugoslavia. On 2 May, as German radio broadcast "cease-fire" orders to their troops, Freyberg's New Zealand Second Division reached Trieste for a tense confrontation with Yugoslav partisans who were arresting Italians, cleaning out banks, and generally, in Alexander's understated opinion, "behaving badly." So tense was the standoff that Eisenhower briefly considered sending Patton with five divisions to sort out Tito, but probably realized that Patton's absence of diplomatic skills, combined with his loathing for Communists, would only worsen the crisis.[98] Later, on 9 June, Tito agreed to remain within the pre-1941 Yugoslav frontiers.

The triumphant partisans had scores to settle in Yugoslavia. On 7 May, the Croat forces broke and ran for the Austrian border, but were cut off by British troops coming from the north and partisans from the south. Pavelić and perhaps as many as 40,000 of his soldiers managed to disperse and save themselves. An estimated 30,000 Ustaše were cornered and executed during a four-day march toward Maribor in Slovenia. A further 50,000 Croat soldiers, along with 30,000 refugees, were trapped at Tezna. Few survived. Pavelić found sanctu-

ary in Perón's Argentina. Having annihilated the Ustaše, Tito turned
his attentions to the Chetniks. January 1945 found Mihailović holding
out in Bosnia with the remnants of his followers. In March, one of his
lieutenants took 9,000 men and tried to break out toward Allied lines
in Italy. But they were trapped and decimated by the Ustaše. Mihailović at the head of the rest broke toward Serbia, but was blocked
by strong partisan forces. On 13 March 1946, Mihailović's hiding place
was betrayed by one of his lieutenants. Even his son and daughter denounced him and defected to the partisans. Only his wife visited him
in prison. On 17 July 1946, Mihailović was executed as a war criminal,
after he told the court that "the gale of the world swept away me and
my work."[99] Over a million Yugoslavs had perished in the war. Chetniks captured and deported to Germany returned only to be incarcerated in Tito's prisons. Tens of thousands were executed or jailed in
1946–47. Others became fugitives, hunted down by the OZN—the
Department for the Protection of the People, Tito's secret police. These
persecutions ended only because so many men had been locked up
that the economy was disrupted. Tito was forced to declare mass am-
nesties simply to fill his labor pool.

War's end in Greece was equally unhappy. Papandreou's 1 December 1944 decree that ELAS was to demobilize by 10 December
provoked a government crisis. Police opened fire on a peaceful EAM
demonstration, causing Lieutenant General Scobie to order all ELAS
units out of the Athens-Piraeus area. Instead of leaving, ELAS began
to attack police stations. The British intervened in the civil war on
5 December. Scobie, his forces scattered over the city and the port,
was initially caught in an uncomfortable position. But the arrival of
two divisions of reinforcements from Italy, combined with the fact that
ELAS had exhausted its ammunition, enabled him to stabilize the situation by 18 December. Scobie was also helped by the fact that ELAS
took advantage of British distraction during the crisis to launch an offensive against the EDES that drove Zervas to Preveza, where survivors of his movement were withdrawn by the Royal Navy to Corfu
and disbanded. ELAS had thus eliminated Zervas and EDES. The
problem with this victory was that opposition in Athens combined
with the attack on Zervas to solidify a British-led coalition of royalists

and former collaborationists (the unhappy result, critics claimed, of Churchill's blind support of the Greek monarchists) and to make civil war with the Communists more likely. Worse for the EAM/ELAS, many non-Communists began to jump ship, leaving the opposition strictly in the hands of the KKE. Moscow maintained a diplomatic silence, refusing to support fellow Communists. A British offensive to take control of Athens, spearheaded by airborne forces from 20 December, found EAM/ELAS begging for a cease-fire by the end of the year. Scobie agreed to this on 15 January 1945 after ELAS had abandoned the capital, taking with them almost 15,000 hostages, about a third of whom subsequently died or were executed.

Churchill and Foreign Minister Anthony Eden had arrived in Athens on Christmas Eve to broker a political agreement naming Archbishop Damaskinos as regent to determine whether, and under what conditions, the monarchy would return. At first view, the Varkiza agreement, reached on 12 February 1945, appeared to showcase the Anglo-Saxon talent for compromise. ELAS agreed to demobilize and surrender its weapons. In return, the KKE was to be recognized as a legal political party, and the monarchy would return only after approval by a plebiscite. On the surface, the agreement appeared to offer the basis of a stable postwar settlement, but in fact it weakened the political center, reoriented the prewar national schism to pit the Communist-resistance against the parliamentary-collaborationist parties, and served as a cover for a white terror that swept most Greek institutions. Greek society remained too divided by passions sharpened by the war, passions that the retardation of economic recovery did nothing to placate. Some 700,000 Greeks remained refugees in the cities. Agricultural production had plummeted. The drachma was worthless. Despite massive aid, few Greeks received the 2,000 daily calories considered the minimum for sustenance. Ex-guerrillas found no way to integrate themselves into a debilitated economy. Over a thousand former members of Ralles's Security Battalions received commissions in the new national army. As a consequence, none of the eight weak governments that presided in the fifteen months between the summer of 1945 and November 1946 was able to sustain a political consensus, in large part because they were discredited by obvious

British support. On the contrary, victimization of former resisters was the order of the day, and many were thrown in jail "for their own safety."[100]

This proved the last straw for Aris Velouchiotis, who headed for the hills to take command of the "roaming bands of angry men" whose attacks against gendarmes and government supporters increased in 1946. His *jusqu'au bout* resistance was supported by the pro-Comintern Nikos Zacharidades, liberated by the Allies from Dachau and repatriated to displace the "nationalist" Georg Siantos, who had guided the KKE through the difficult war years. The growing threat of left-wing violence seemed to make the right even less willing to compromise.[101] When elections were finally held in March 1946, the monarchists emerged as the major victors. The KKE, which had mistakenly boycotted the election, denounced it as "a fraud." The new Tsaldaris government suspended civil rights and declared martial law. A September 1946 plebiscite confirmed the return of the monarchy. Armed bands, remnants of ELAS, began to gather in the mountains on the Yugoslav and Albanian borders. In February 1946, London informed Washington that it could no longer support Greece. U.S. President Harry Truman replied with his "two ways of life" speech, the basis of the Truman Doctrine. The U.S. Congress voted $300 million in aid for Greece. The stage was set for a resumption of the Greek Civil War.[102]

"A GREAT HOLDING ATTACK"

Victory in Italy after a campaign lasting 602 days from 9 September 1943 to the surrender of 2 May 1945—the longest sustained Allied campaign of World War II—left many on the Allied side with the inescapable feeling that the decision to invade Italy had been a mistake. The grueling nature of a campaign fought out in impossible terrain, against concealed enemies, in debilitating heat or anesthetizing cold, gave rise to the belief that alternatives to Italy must have existed, ones that would have utilized Allied resources and manpower more efficiently in places of greater strategic significance. Indeed, Italy more often suggested the stalemate on the Western Front during the First World War rather than the sweeping advances and retreats characteristic of the Second. Salerno, Cassino, Anzio, the battles on the Gothic and Winter lines stood as symbols of heroic yet mismanaged and unnecessary sacrifice. Field Marshal Kesselring defended his decision to fight for every inch of the Italian Peninsula: this deepened the battle zone, while it diverted lavishly supplied Allied troops and air assets from attacks on the Reich. Italy continued to be a source of manpower and industrial strength exploited by Berlin until the war's end. To have surrendered Italy voluntarily, as Rommel proposed in 1943, would not have economized German forces. Rather it would have allowed the Allies to use northern Italy as a base to invade the Balkans or southern France. Finally, the tenacity of the twenty-three-month German defense of Italy, despite deficiencies in matériel, constituted a moral as well as a material victory for the Axis. "The Italian campaign must rank as one of the greatest defensive achievements in the history of warfare," writes historian John Ellis.[103] The Allies sustained roughly 312,000 casualties in Italy, 189,000 or 60 percent in the Fifth Army. While serving under Clark or Truscott, 19,475 Americans, 6,605 British, and 5,241 "French" were killed. Eighth Army casualties numbered 123,254.[104] "The conclusion is that the battle for Italy was not only justified, but even imperative," Kesselring insisted. One must do the best for one's theater, "irrespective of the general strategic plan."[105]

David Kennedy has joined a chorus of historians who have called Italy "a battleground in a grinding war of attrition whose costs were justified by no defensible military or political purpose."[106] British military historian Sir John Keegan believes that the campaign in Italy

> might actually be counted as strategically advantageous to the Germans . . . Losses and hardships were made the more difficult to bear, particularly by the Allies, because of the campaign's marginality. The Germans knew that they were holding the enemy at arm's length from the southern borders of the Reich. The Allies, after D-Day, were denied any sense of fighting a decisive campaign . . . No great vision of victory drew them onward, however, as it did their comrades who landed in France. Their war was not a crusade but, in almost every respect, an old fashioned one of strategic diversion on the maritime flank of a continental enemy, the "Peninsular War" of 1939–45.[107]

However, arguments in support of Italy as an Allied success, pivotal rather than "marginal" to Allied victory in Northern Europe, are equally compelling. It would have been very difficult to forgo an invasion of Italy in September 1943. The Italian leadership clearly wanted out of the war, and the Allies could not simply walk away, leaving that country, and its military forces, in the Axis camp. After all, the elimination of Italy from the war was a principal Allied goal in the Mediterranean. And while a premise of Avalanche had been Italian cooperation, the degree of pusillanimity and incompetence of the Italian leadership had been impossible to imagine, much less plan for. That might have changed the way the Allies invaded Italy. But it would not have altered the fact that an invasion was required. A second Allied goal in Italy, asserted by the August 1943 Quadrant (Quebec) Conference, was "the maintenance of unremitting pressure on German forces in Northern Italy and the creation of conditions required for 'Overlord' and of a situation favorable for the eventual entry of our forces, including the bulk of the re-equipped French army and air force into southern France."[108] Kesselring's argument, however, was that he diverted Allied divisions, not vice versa. How credible is this assertion? There was clearly nowhere else for the Allies to fight in 1943–44, months when standing idle was simply not an option. The Soviets required proof that the Allies were not shirking their combat responsibilities. In the autumn and winter of 1944–45, Eisenhower had assembled about as many troops as he could sustain on the Western Front. On the other hand, the 400,000-plus German troops stationed in Italy had to be kept occupied lest they be shifted to other fronts. Indeed, while there was nowhere else in Europe for the Western Allies to fight in the last two years of the war, the Germans had plenty of options that the defense of Italy obliged them to forgo.

It is traditional in assessments of the value of the Italian campaign to compare numbers of Allied and German divisions engaged on the peninsula. The numbers of German divisions in Army Group C consistently matched and even outnumbered those of the Allies.[109]

*   *   *

	ALLIED BATTLE ZONE	GERMAN BATTLE ZONE	TOTAL GERMAN DIVISIONS
1943–44	18	15	23
Diadem	25	18	24
Gothic line	20	22	26
1945	17	19	21

If we add the twenty-four German divisions in Greece and the Balkans, maintained against a potential Allied landing launched from Italy, together with eight to ten German divisions in southern France, then around fifty-five German divisions—more than one-fifth of German ground forces—were tied down defending the central and Eastern Mediterranean at a time when they might have fought on other fronts.[110] For instance, Hitler refused Field Marshal Walter Model's request for more panzer divisions prior to the Ardennes offensive of December 1944, when the Twenty-sixth Panzer Division was idling unemployed in the Po Valley.[111] This hardly constitutes an efficient allocation of forces from a German perspective. Moreover, most of the Allied divisions were already in the Mediterranean in any case. In many respects, the decision to invade Italy was justified by the desire to utilize resources already in the Mediterranean, resources that could not be returned efficiently to England for Overlord.[112]

Kesselring's opinion notwithstanding, both Allied intelligence and Rommel agreed that a withdrawal to the Alps in 1943 or 1944 would have economized large numbers of German troops. It would also have forced the Allies to shoulder the burden of organizing and feeding Italy at a time when their logistical and manpower resources were strained. And while the tenacity of the German defense of the Italian Peninsula invites grudging admiration, Kesselring paid a high price in the form of 536,000 casualties including POWs, of which 48,067 are known dead and another 214,000 listed as missing, probably dead.[113] That is the equivalent of two and a half Stalingrads. Axis attrition was purchased at a relatively low price of 312,000 Allied casualties, even though they were on the offensive. American historian Carlo D'Este calls Italy "the longest and bloodiest campaign fought by the Allies in the West during World War II."[114] It was certainly the longest, but the far shorter campaign in Northwestern Europe, admittedly with far more troops, cost the Allies 766,294 casualties, more than twice the number suffered in Italy.[115] Therefore, if the Spanish campaign of 1808–14 became "Napoleon's ulcer" because it cost Napoleon a hundred men a day, then the "Peninsular War of 1939–45" might qualify as Hitler's hematoma.

The value of the Italian campaign is further enhanced if considered in the context of the Mediterranean theater rather than standing alone. In the final analysis, Italy, when combined with the Balkans, offered huge strategic benefits for the Allies. Hitler invaded the Balkans and Greece in April–May 1941 to bail out his Italian ally, seal his southern flank against British attempts to interfere with Barbarossa, and exploit the economies of the region for the Reich's benefit. In fact, Marita created a debilitating vulnerability for Hitler. The arrival of Axis troops in the Balkans collapsed fragile political structures, reignited barely dormant political and ethnic feuds, and sparked tenacious resistance movements fueled by rapacious and brutal Axis occupation policies. The loss of North Africa followed by the surrender of Italy forced Hitler to commit more troops than he could afford to quell escalating insurgencies, to support incompetent and rapacious puppet regimes, and to defend the Balkan Peninsula against the threat of an Allied attack leapfrogging from Italy. These resistance movements were fragmented and inefficient, were consumed with ethnic and ideological rivalries, and intentionally exaggerated the results of their operations to keep the bounty of Allied supplies flowing.[116] However, from a strategic perspective, the cost to the Allies was the minimal one of a few planeloads of Axis weapons, supplied courtesy of Rommel's Panzerarmee Afrika, a few hundred "liaison officers" who paid their way largely with Reichmarks and lire liberated in North Africa and Sicily, and some deception operations to keep the threat of invasion alive in Hitler's mind. So, in the end, Hitler was forced to underwrite both the Balkan resistance and its repression.

The real price paid by the Allies came at war's end. As everywhere, defeat and Axis occupation had discredited pre-1939 governments. Yugoslavia fell to Communist domination because the Communist party used an appeal to revolution as the only viable alternative to an ethnic bloodbath. And while in the short term this was seen as a defeat for the West in the emerging Cold War context, Tito's ultimate defiance of Moscow offered an early successful defection from the "Communist Bloc." Tito's victory, in retrospect, also postponed the true "liberation" of the Balkan Peninsula until the early 1990s. In Greece, Churchill argued that timely British intervention had prevented a coup by EAM/ELAS *banditti*. "My policy has been vindicated by events," he insisted.[117] EAM/ELAS had no choice after their defeat in December 1944 but to participate in a pluralistic democracy, as had the Communist parties of France and Italy. But they played with a much-weakened hand. The price paid was a high one of ex-resisters jailed sometimes for years, civil liberties curtailed, and the national schism redefined and given a new lease on life in postwar Greek politics.

What can certainly be said of the Allied effort in Italy is that it might have been more efficiently carried out. Until McCreery and Truscott demonstrated in Grapeshot their capacity to organize efficient operations, battles in Italy were seldom conducted with an efficiency that might have brought greater success with fewer casualties. In the initial attacks on the Gustav and Gothic lines, as at Salerno and Anzio, the Allies proved guilty of attempting to achieve too much with inadequate means. Mountain warfare adaptations were not developed in any systematic way, but interrupted by the departure of the CEF, to be revived toward the war's end by the arrival of the Tenth Mountain Division. Leese was particularly remiss in failing to utilize the mountain experience of his Indian divisions. The Italian campaign saw few tactical refinements beyond "Horsefly" air-artillery control techniques and advances in infantry-armor cooperation begun in North Africa. McCreery's imaginative use of LVTs to outflank German positions on the Comacchio Lagoon during Grapeshot stands out as a particularly successful exception. Deception campaigns were effective against an enemy virtually blinded by lack of air power. But surprise was never decisive, and its effects lasted only a few days before the Germans could react. Only at war's end did the Allies manage to assemble an efficient command team in Italy. Until then, poor inter-Allied relations bred mistrust and even distorted the conduct of operations.

That said, however, there seems to have been little that could have been done to speed up or better exploit the opportunities offered by Italy. The nature of the Italian terrain and the limited possibilities for amphibious end runs reduced options to frontal assaults. While some argue that Giant II, the planned airdrop on Rome, might have avoided Cassino, it seems unlikely that Kesselring could have been panicked into a retreat to the Apennines or the Alps. The political stakes were simply too high for Berlin to abandon its Axis partner precipitously. Strategically, Kesselring remained committed to a defense south of Rome. Given the disorganization on the Italian side, Giant II would almost certainly have ended in the needless slaughter of an airborne division whose presence as a strategic reserve at Salerno was arguably the swing factor in that battle. Anvil is blamed for removing seven divisions and sea lift at a time when Diadem had finally given the Allies momentum in Italy. It is possible that keeping intact a Fifth Army whose tandem of Sixth Corps and the CEF had evolved into a formidable force might have pierced the Gothic line, thus avoiding the winter stalemate in the Apennines. But how far Diadem had given the Allies critical momentum in Italy is unclear. Alexander took two months to advance from Cassino to Florence, despite only improvised German resistance. The CEF had suffered about a 30 percent casualty rate, and the Moslem recruitment that had been the basis of its success was drying up. Nor was de Gaulle content to keep his forces in Italy as France was being liberated. Had those seven divisions remained in Italy, Hitler would certainly have matched them with divisions of his own. Nor would keeping these divisions in Italy, even had it been politically feasible, have solved the Allies' command problems. Alexander remained a weak leader, Clark obsessed with capturing publicity-worthy objectives to advance his career, and Leese unable to adapt the overmechanized divisions and underpowered vehicles of the Eighth Army to Italian conditions. In this way, "the hares of the Desert War" were transformed into "the plodding tortoises of the Italian campaign."[118] Nor is it clear what advantage the Allies might have gained from more amphibious operations in Italy. While tempting in theory, amphibious operations posed problems of suitable beaches, adequate sea lift, and the fact that the Germans could reinforce by land against a beachhead faster than the Allies could by sea, as both Avalanche and Shingle demonstrated.[119] It was the threat of amphibious operations, rather than their actual execution, that proved more profitable in the long run by diverting German divisions to guard the coastline.

Anvil complemented Italy, it did not undermine it. Anvil provided the conduit to support an army group in the main theater in the autumn/winter/spring of 1944–45, just as Italy drew off German divisions that might have been used in Northern Europe. Factor out Anvil, and the ability to invade Germany from the west in the spring of 1945 would be problematic for Eisenhower. Italy was a peripheral theater, after all, not the main front. The purpose of a peripheral theater is to support, not rival, the main front. Otherwise, one falls into the trap of strategic parochialism that Kesselring—indeed most Mediterranean commanders—demonstrated when he insisted that, ultimately, one must do the best for one's theater, "irrespective of the general strategic plan."[120] The counterargument is that strategic opportunities were lost in Italy because of Anvil. A simultaneous German collapse in Normandy and Italy would have thrown OKW into consternation. But how advantageous would that have been for the Allies? Why close down a theater where the Germans continued to commit up to a fifth of their troops? And even had the Gothic line been pierced in the autumn, then what? Kesselring's argument was that he had to defend northern Italy lest the Allies turn west toward France or east toward Yugoslavia. Why invade southern France over the Alps when it was far easier to do so by sea? Alexander's Ljubljana Gap option was pure pie in the sky, logistically unsupportable across terrain that made Italy look like a prairie, opposed by Stalin, Tito, Roosevelt, de Gaulle, Brooke, Marshall, and Eisenhower, not to mention Hitler.[121] One can only agree with the verdict of the British official history: a "quicker ending of Kesselring's force in Italy would not have hastened the end of the war."[122]

CONCLUSION

The Pivotal Theater

T HE MEDITERRANEAN STRATEGY in World War II has not lacked
detractors since George Marshall denounced Churchill's dalliance in that sea as a "fundamentally unsound," "prestige" strategy[1]
that attacked no German center of gravity, failed to help the USSR,
and served principally as a venue for a perpetual, acrimonious Anglo-
American spat. Many historians have been no kinder than Marshall.
"The Mediterranean is consistently over-emphasized in most English
studies of the war," British historian John Ellis wrote in 1990. "Indeed,
when one realizes that in March 1943 the Germans had 175 combat divisions (including 29 panzer and panzer grenadier) on the Eastern
Front and only 7½ (4½) in North Africa, and that even in June 1944
the figures for Russia/Italy were 157 (30)/22 (6), then it might well be
thought that the whole campaign barely merits an extended footnote."[2] American historian Robert Love blamed a combination of
Churchill's imperial ambitions and Roosevelt's "vacillation" for "a wasteful peripheral strategy in the Mediterranean" that allowed the Russians to overrun Eastern Europe and gave the Germans two bonus
years to strengthen their Atlantic defenses.[3] John Keegan praised the
"sense of purpose and stoutness of heart" of Allied soldiers fighting in
the "marginal" Italian campaign where no decisive victories were to
be won.[4]

Indeed, the Allied Mediterranean strategy is condemned as a *pis
aller*, opportunistic rather than deliberative, a substitute for strategy

rather than an example of its wise application. "The overall impression is of a remarkable lack of direction in Mediterranean planning," Ellis asserts, "with key decisions taken off the cuff, simply because no one, least of all on the American side, could think of anything better to do."[5] Graham and Bidwell also believe that Italy, and by extension the Mediterranean, rivaled, rather than complemented, other theaters, and served as "a rationalization of jealousies and rival aims."[6]

This book has argued that the Mediterranean was the European war's pivotal theater, the critical link without which it would have been impossible for the Western Alliance to go from Dunkirk to Overlord. There were no "decisive" victories to be won in the Mediterranean. But that was true for all theaters where the objective became to wear down Axis forces gradually, sap enemy strength, shatter his coalition, and push back his armies in preparation for the invasion of Germany. The second charge, that the Mediterranean strategy was opportunistic rather than deliberative, may be true, but it is irrelevant. War, after all, is an interactive process. The Axis decision to open a Mediterranean front was a critical strategic mistake that the Allies would have been foolish not to exploit. This means that far from being taken "off the cuff," strategic choices were the product of an elaborate and remarkably effective mechanism of reassessment that involved both political and military leaders. Mistakes were made, but they were political and operational rather than strategic. Overall, the process of periodic conferences produced balanced evaluations that led ultimately to success. For this reason, the third charge, that the Mediterranean rivaled rather than complemented other theaters, is suspect. Ellis is correct in his assertion that the Americans could think up no better alternatives than to hitch a ride on Churchill's Mediterranean strategy. He fails to add that this occurred precisely because no better alternatives existed until 1944. Thereafter, the Mediterranean continued to fulfill a vital supporting role for the Eastern and Western Fronts.

There are at least three arguments—geographic, strategic, and operational—to support the central role played by the Mediterranean in the Allied victory. The geographic advantages of fighting in the Mediterranean are too often ignored because critics of the Mediterranean strategy narrow the geographic scope of the Mediterranean and hence underplay the strategic significance and global impact of that theater on the outcome of World War II. This book has incorporated the vision of the great French historian of the Mediterranean world of Philip II, Fernand Braudel, who argued that the Middle Sea was more than a self-contained lake. Rather, it formed a critical geographic, economic, and strategic link between and among several continents, one whose influence ran far beyond its shores and deep into the hinterlands of the continents it bordered.

Braudel's view of the strategic impact of the Mediterranean, of the interrelationship between events there and those in other theaters of conflict, is especially applicable to World War II. The Mediterranean offered a critical rendezvous, a maritime corridor where the sea power of the Western Alliance could unite the manpower of America and the British and eventually the French empire, the industrial resources of the United States, and the oil reserves of the Middle East to attack a critical Axis flank. The Mediterranean was both the epicenter of the Western Allied effort against the Axis until June 1944 and a vital geographic, strategic, and economic link between the Western and Eastern Fronts. The Eritrean campaign opened the Red Sea so that U.S. merchant shipping could supply Suez. The opening of the Mediterranean with Husky in August 1943 released a flow of Lend-Lease aid, considered by Roosevelt critical to demonstrate the benefits of American capitalism, build trust in the Western democracies, and secure Stalin's adherence to the alliance. Of U.S. Lend-Lease aid to the USSR, 23.8 percent reached it through Persia, much of it through the Mediterranean. The invasion of Sicily also forced the Germans to withdraw air assets from Norway, which allowed the Arctic convoys to proceed with lower losses; 22.7 percent of Lend-Lease aid destined for Russia arrived at Murmansk via the northern route.

Although Hitler had little desire to invest substantial forces there, he understood in his idiosyncratic way that the Mediterranean formed the southern extension of his vital Eastern Front. Forty-plus German or German-controlled divisions were assigned to Italy, Greece, and the Balkans from the Italian surrender in 1943, in part to keep the Allies at arm's length from his vital Eastern Front, and hence prevent a linkup between the two through Italy, the Adriatic, and the Aegean. Nor should the relative scarcity of panzer and panzer grenadier regiments in the Mediterranean, as Ellis suggests, be taken as a measure of the Mediterranean front's diminished status. Axis logistics simply could not have supported more armored and mechanized units in North Africa. Nor were mechanized forces suited to counterinsurgency operations in the Balkans or mountain warfare in Italy. On the contrary, the fact that the Germans nevertheless committed these precious units to Italy when they might otherwise have increased their mechanized strength on the Eastern Front by 20 percent further enhances the relative importance of the Mediterranean to events elsewhere.

The Mediterranean directly supported the Western Front as well. Anvil/Dragoon, the 15 August 1944 Riviera invasion, was decried as a mistake, one that diverted troops into a strategically vacant area and broke the momentum of the Allied advance in Italy following the Cassino breakthrough of May–June 1944. It also came too late to help Overlord, because vital shipping and troops had been tied up at Anzio. The good news was that between eight and ten German divisions were stationed in southern France to guard against an Allied invasion, divisions that might have made a vital difference in Normandy or Italy. Some 57,000 German POWs were rounded up in Toulon and Marseilles at light cost to French forces. Army Group G lost an estimated 20 percent of its strength at the bottleneck of Montélimar. When Overlord met Anvil at Saulieu in September, 131,250 German soldiers, or about 40 percent of Army Group G's strength on 15 August, had been killed, captured, or simply cut off. In all, Anvil cost Hitler more troops than he lost at either Stalingrad or Tunis.[7]

Nor did Anvil's contribution to victory on the Western Front cease in September 1944. The simple truth was that the Channel ports could not keep three army groups supplied in France and the Low Countries in the autumn and winter of 1944–45. The first Liberty Ships began to arrive at the two southern French ports on 15 September. By October, southern France was handling one-third of supplies and reinforcements reaching the European continent. The Riviera offered a gateway and supply point to support the advance of two Allied armies combining ten divisions into Alsace and southern Germany, terrain that would otherwise have been fought over and occupied by Bradley's Twelfth Army Group. The Seventh Army Group extended the Western Front to the Swiss border in the autumn and winter of 1944–45, absorbed German divisions economized by Hitler's withdrawal from Greece and part of Yugoslavia in October 1944, and provided the vital blocking force that freed up Patton's Third Army to stanch the December 1944 German Ardennes offensive. For these reasons, this book has offered a counter to the view put forward by Ellis, Robert Love, and Corelli Barnett, among others, that the Mediterranean was little more than a series of discrete campaigns limited to North Africa and Italy, fought on the margins of a great conflagration upon which it exercised at best a minimal impact. Rather, the Mediterranean was a vast theater that encompassed India, the Middle East, Greece and the Balkans, East and North Africa, France, and southern Germany. In short, the Mediterranean was both the epicenter of the Allied effort against the Axis for the first four years of the war and a vital geographic, strategic, and economic link between the Western and Eastern Fronts.

The strategic arguments for the benefits of the Mediterranean are equally compelling. The "brute force" argument is that the disparity of resources available to the two sides made World War II a relentless march toward an inevitable conclusion. According to this scenario, the Mediterranean was little more than "mere byplay in the conclusion of a war that had been won in mass battles on the Eastern and Western Fronts."[8] But this view ignores the incremental nature of the Allied victory, and the possibility that bad strategic decisions on the part of the Allies might easily have produced a different outcome. The fundamental argument of this book has been that the Mediterranean was a pivotal theater for the Allies, one that made the difference between victory and defeat. The Axis decision to open a theater in the Mediterranean was a critical strategic error that Churchill was wise to pounce on. It forced Hitler to support operations where he had no fundamental strategic interests except to salvage the mistakes of his incompetent ally. But in doing so, he simply threw good money after bad. In this way, the road from Dunkirk to Normandy traversed the Mediterranean.

The Mediterranean advanced Allied strategic aims in World War II in significant ways. Vigorous British action in the sea, followed by U.S. intervention, helped to keep the Axis from expanding to include Spain and Turkey, with potentially fatal consequences for Allied fortunes in that region.[9] The Mediterranean evolved into a bona fide "second front" both in its strategic impact upon the war in other theaters and in terms of the size of forces committed there. In late 1940, Hitler calculated that he could not fight Britain in Greece while the untrustworthy Stalin threatened his rear. Therefore, events in the south hastened Hitler's decision to attack the USSR and influenced the timing of Barbarossa.[10] Hitler's Mediterranean account, opened with a relatively minor investment of German divisions to bolster Italian garrisons in Greece, the Balkans, and North Africa, soon escalated into a major commitment, as Operation Torch forced him to dispatch seven and one-half divisions to Tunisia, plus significant Luftwaffe assets. "Tunisgrad" and the subsequent threat posed by the combination of Allied sea, air, and land power to his southern flank began a process through which Hitler had to spread his forces over the northern Mediterranean both to control growing Allied-supplied resistance movements and to protect his southern flank.

The increasing commitment of German forces to the Mediterranean accelerated once the Allies' Mediterranean advance eliminated Hitler's major ally in the autumn of 1943, and German divisions were forced to replace Italian ones in Italy, France, Yugoslavia, and Greece. The Allied Mediterranean advance impacted operations on the Eastern Front as well as Soviet resolve at critical periods, as in July 1943, when Operation Husky obliged Hitler to curtail his offensive before Kursk. But more important, the fall of Mussolini forced a basic reorientation of German strategic priorities from east to west. Not all of these forces were committed to the Mediterranean. But it was the deteriorating situation in the Mediterranean that motivated this shift. New and fresh forces, especially armor, tended to flow west, not east. The Italian campaign soaked up German divisions available for the Eastern Front in general, and for the Kursk offensive in particular.[11] A fifth of German troop strength was tied up in Italy alone by 1944, more when German garrisons in Greece, the Balkans, and southern France are factored in. While the military strength of resistance movements in Greece, Yugoslavia, France, and Italy was overestimated at the time, they certainly drew off Axis troops and were seen as evidence in Allied nations of a popular desire in occupied countries for liberation. For the modest investment of a few hundred advisers and a few plane-loads of supplies, the Allies encouraged the growth and military profi-ciency of resistance movements that, together with the threat of an Allied invasion, tied down approximately twenty Axis divisions in Greece and the Balkans. This prevented Hitler from amassing a strate-gic reserve that might have swung the balance in Normandy in 1944.

Likewise, the Mediterranean made its contribution to breaking the economic power of the Reich. From bases in the Mediterranean, Allied bombers attacked Germany and seriously disrupted vital sup-plies of Romanian oil. France's resurrection as a member of the West-ern Alliance was managed in the Mediterranean, another beneficial outcome bought in that theater, without which responsibility for the defeat in the west and postwar occupation of western Germany would have fallen entirely on Britain and the United States. It requires only a modest stretch of the imagination to envision a different strategic out-come on the Eastern and Western Fronts had Churchill, supported by Roosevelt, not engaged the Axis in the Mediterranean.

This was equally true on the operational and tactical level, a third measure of the Mediterranean's importance. Early German opera-tional success had been built on a lethal combination of air power and mechanized forces in the service of an offensive strategy. The Werhmacht was an army configured for Continental warfare, not for maritime campaigns where naval power proved to be the critical ele-ment. The Luftwaffe was able to power its way through to Crete in 1941, because the British were unable to sustain an air umbrella, and because of Freyberg's poor tactical dispositions at Maleme. However, the costs of Herkules discouraged an airborne encore on Malta. Thereafter, the Royal Navy could harass supply lines, snatch stranded forces from the jaws of encirclement, and deliver amphibious landings in unexpected places. Rommel campaigned at the end of a lengthy supply line that was threatened at critical periods by interdiction. Malta-based planes and submarines sank one-third of Rommel's supplies and 41 percent of his fuel in August 1942 as he knocked on the door of Egypt. No fuel reached Rommel in October 1942, the month of El Alamein. Furthermore, the Wehrmacht was forced to campaign with an Italian ally that was poorly led, indifferently equipped, and lacking in mobility. Much German power was shattered in the Mediterranean, where the Luftwaffe in particular was seriously overextended and worn down, in great part because it was forced to compensate for the lack of a viable German navy. Twenty percent of Luftwaffe strength was committed to the Mediterranean between May 1942 and June 1943 alone. The Luftwaffe, configured and trained as a tactical support force, lacked the equipment and the incentive to adapt to the multiple tasks of Mediterranean combat.[12] In 1943, as Ellis concedes, one-third of German aircraft losses were inflicted in the Mediterranean, including much of its formidable fleet of transports, sacrificed in a vain attempt to supply the beleaguered Axis garrison in Tunis.[13] But by 1943, the days when the Wehrmacht could seize and sustain "islands" in the Mediterranean were well and truly over. This offers one more instance of Axis inability to adapt to the multidimensional operational environment of the Mediterranean, and hence indicates the wisdom of choosing to fight there, especially when Hitler and Mussolini were defending Europe from North Africa.

Churchill estimated that North Africa cost the Axis almost a million casualties, 6,200 guns, 2,550 tanks, 70,000 trucks, and most of the Italian navy and merchant marine.[14] And even if these figures may have been inflated for wartime purposes, Axis losses in North Africa remained significant. According to the British official history, 238,243 Axis troops, including over 100,000 Germans, surrendered in Tunis and Bizerte in May 1943 against an investment of slightly more than 31,000 Allied casualties.[15] Another 167,000 were suffered in Sicily, of whom 10,000 were German. This strategic and logistical advantage changed somewhat as the fighting moved to the Mediterranean's northern coasts. Many histories of the campaigns in Sicily and Italy have emphasized the ability of Kesselring to utilize Italy's chaotic terrain and appalling weather to fight a brilliant two-year defensive campaign against better-armed Allied forces. But one must not lose from view the Mediterranean's importance in breaking the offensive power of German arms, and forcing the Reich onto the defensive, after which any hope of victory eluded them. In the process, Kesselring suffered 60,000 killed and missing, 163,000 wounded, and 357,000 captured.[16] In the task of wearing down German forces, therefore, the peripheral Mediterranean theater complemented and supplemented the main Eastern Front and prepared the terrain for the success of Overlord.

While operationally and tactically the Mediterranean worked to Axis detriment, campaigning there benefited the Allies immensely. Despite the arguments of Ellis's "brute force" school that Allied preponderance in matériel was the critical factor in victory, in fact, had the Western Allies passed up the Mediterranean option for a direct assault on the Continent in 1943 as Stimson, Marshall, Eisenhower, and others advocated, strategic disaster would certainly have followed. One only has to contemplate the odds for success of hurling an immature collection of forces, under unproven leaders, with rudimentary and untested weapons poorly integrated into an ineffective operational system, into the teeth of Luftwaffe superiority, with U-boat wolf packs ranging among the assault fleet and a defending army that had not to commit significant forces to prop up Italy and garrison Greece and the Balkans, to shudder at the thought of its military consequences.

One major benefit of the Mediterranean theater, as John Ellis and others acknowledge, was that it bought time for the Allies to master the intricacies of their profession[17]—to identify their most successful generals and to perfect joint and combined operational and tactical systems. When one considers the steep costs of this learning process on the Western Front in World War I, or on the Eastern Front in World War II, then the benefits of acquiring expertise in a theater where the consequences of failure were limited to subcatastrophic proportions becomes easier to appreciate. The procession of failed or simply mediocre British and American generals who commanded in the Mediterranean validated the Mediterranean's reputation as the graveyard of generals, a process ultimately vital to Allied success. One only has to contemplate Operation Sledgehammer under the command of a senior leadership selected from a cast that included Wavell, Auchinleck, "Jumbo" Wilson, Neame, Gambier-Perry, Beresford-Peirse, Alan Cunningham, Ritchie, Anderson, Fredendall, Lucas, and Dawley, to doubt its success. The Mediterranean careers of generals who later proved to be the stars of the Allied command in Northern Europe—Eisenhower, Bradley, Patton—or who arguably developed into competent leaders in the Mediterranean—Clark, Alexander, Truscott, McCreery—were remarkable initially for their energy rather than their operational and tactical competence. Even generals who hit the ground running, like Bernard Montgomery, only gradually developed the staff and intelligence systems to coordinate intricate operational and tactical systems and evolve mechanisms and procedures to prosecute joint and combined operations. Therefore, the Mediterranean offered a venue where the Western Allies could warm up against the Axis B team, which nevertheless contained some first-class players; this too proved vital to ultimate Allied success.

Allied armies took time to bring the weapons on line, acquire enough radios to coordinate operations, evolve an intelligence structure to inform commanders and to acquire the experience and toughness required to defeat the Axis. James Doolittle contrasted the Twelfth Air Force's hand-to-mouth days of 1942–43 in North Africa, Sicily, and Italy with the proliferation of equipment at the disposal of the Eighth Air Force in 1944–45. "Down there the problem was to make something out of nothing," he wrote to Patton. "Up here it requires an equal or greater amount of ingenuity to effectively utilize almost unlimited resources at one's disposal. Down there, when you were not 'under the guns,' any modest success was apparently appreciated. Up here miracles are confidently anticipated."[18] In short, "brute force" never applied in the Mediterranean, and would not have applied in Northwestern Europe in either 1942 or 1943. However, the process of building equipment and expertise was an expensive one, especially for the British, who were slow to master the techniques of modern warfare, and paid a high price in the sacrifice of too many soldiers in poorly conceived operations against Rommel. This reflected on the poor quality of British military leadership, the absence of a strong staff and training system that could bind together a multinational, quasi-colonial Eighth Army, and the slow evolution of the Allied intelligence apparatus. The genius of Montgomery was that he was able to create a system that forced the disparate elements of the Eighth Army to work in unison. Critics claimed that it was inflexible, a knockoff of the rigid system that characterized the British approach to the trench warfare of World War I rather than to the mobile combat of World War II. Nevertheless, it was adapted to the nature of his army, and put the British army firmly on the road to victory.

The major argument in favor of the Mediterranean is that there was no other ground on which to engage the European Axis successfully before 1944. The vital ingredient of Allied success was the coherence of the Western Alliance. The Mediterranean was the place where the alliance was advertised, constructed, nurtured, and finally where it bore the fruits of strategic success. Beginning with the British attack on the French fleet at Mers el-Kébir in July 1940 and continuing with Churchill's forlorn defense of Greece and Crete, his invasion of Syria and Iraq, and the battles to protect the Suez Canal, the Mediterranean offered an arena where Britain could reinforce the determined spirit of resistance so eloquently expressed by Churchill during the Battle of Britain. In the Mediterranean, as in the skies above the home islands, Churchill publicized the fact that this was no longer the Britain of Chamberlain and appeasement, the country that sold out Czechoslovakia in 1938 and stood by the following year as Poland was overrun. Churchill's rhetoric and his actions were those of total war, not of a leader prepared to strike a compromise with Hitler. In the early months of the war, the Mediterranean together with strategic bombing provided the offensive complement to Britain's defensive stance on the Channel. Even when these operations failed—indeed, especially when they failed—they nevertheless projected the image abroad of a courageous but beleaguered Britain, a worthy and valued ally whom the United States would allow to succumb only at its peril.

Roosevelt's refusal to engage U.S. troops in the Mediterranean in 1942 would have been viewed as a betrayal of an ally's valiant sacrifice, a vote of no confidence in Winston Churchill, and a mediocre initiation for the Anglo-American alliance. Without the Torch landings in North Africa, El Alamein, even had Montgomery won the battle, would have been divested of much of its strategic impact. Even George Marshall, who argued vigorously against Roosevelt's 1942 decision to commit American forces to the Mediterranean, never believed that Sledgehammer enjoyed the ghost of a chance of success.[19] The remarkable thing is that Marshall failed to contemplate the potentially disastrous consequences that a premature cross-Channel assault would have on the alliance, on Churchill's and Roosevelt's credibility as political leaders, and on U.S. civil-military relations. A Dieppe on a grand scale would not have helped the USSR, which was Marshall's purpose. Instead, it would have exhausted British stamina, fractured fragile Anglo-American solidarity, and sent U.S. strategy careening off to the Pacific to maroon Great Britain with its shattered army in Europe. Arab nationalists, collaborationist governments, and Axis allies would have been emboldened, possibly even expanded to include Turkey and Spain, and resistance movements would have been demoralized and marginalized. Stalin would have had to calibrate his political options to new strategic realities, to include a separate peace with Hitler. Churchill and Roosevelt, even had they survived politically, would have been finished as effective wartime leaders. As Abraham Lincoln's 1864 election victory had hinged on Sherman's seizure of Atlanta, so Roosevelt might well have lost his 1944 reelection bid had catastrophic defeat in Northwestern Europe in 1943 substituted for evidence of steady progress in "the Mediterranean year." His strategic judgment would certainly have been called into question by a feisty Congress and by soldiers keen to assert their independence over civilian control. The very fabric of democracy in these two great nations would have been threatened as the defeated commanders of Sledgehammer had sought to blame their failure on politicians, the media, their weapons, even faulting the courage of their soldiers, much as Wavell and Auchinleck were inclined to do after their unsuccessful operations in the Western Desert in 1941 and 1942. A stab-in-the-back mentality would probably have settled on soldiers and politicians eager to blame Roosevelt or "our Italians" who lacked "the light of battle in their eyes" for the invasion's inevitable breakdown. The reputation of the "greatest generation" for courage and steely resolve was forged in North Africa, Sicily, and Italy before it was tested in Northwestern Europe. In short, the Mediterranean became the training ground where a generation acquired the rudiments of greatness and where, at the very least, the Allies were able to *éviter le pire*.

A subset of arguments against the Mediterranean option concedes that, while the Mediterranean was beneficial to the Allies insofar as it wore down the Luftwaffe and tied down seven panzer and panzer grenadier divisions that might have intervened in Normandy, the Mediterranean strategy was nevertheless undertaken only because it offered a series of "soft options." "It would be wrong to argue that Mediterranean operations were conducted according to some Allied strategic master plan," Ellis writes. "No such plan ever existed, and throughout the war operations in this theatre were bedeviled by serious disagreements between the Allies about the proper level of commitment there."[20] One result of strategic opportunism, rather than clear planning, according to Graham and Bidwell, was that the Mediterranean and Northwestern Europe became rival rather than complementary theaters: "The failure of Allied grand strategy, as determined by the Americans, was due to treating the two theaters as rivals when they should have been seen as a single, strategic whole," conclude Graham and Bidwell. "The American insistence on the elementary principle of concentration was in reality a rationalization, to conceal misunderstanding, jealousies and rival aims."[21]

The opportunism of Allied Mediterranean strategy was matched with interest by Mussolini and Hitler. Furthermore, the Axis had far more to lose there, and far less to gain, than did the Allies. By miscalculating in June 1940 that Germany had won the war and France and Britain were finished as Mediterranean powers, Mussolini offered London a path to salvation, beyond the distant hope for an internal collapse of Hitler's empire brought about by a strategic bombing offensive and popular insurrection. Mussolini's strategic priorities shifted according to the requirements to shore up his political position in Italy and according to the failure of his generals to achieve success in France, Greece, or Egypt. Field Marshal Kesselring argued correctly that Mussolini's decision for war had been a mistake, because Italy's military inadequacies drew the Germans into the Mediterranean where they had no fundamental interests, thereby complicating German strategic choices and straining its logistical, and one might add operational, capabilities.[22] But the salvation of his ally was only part of Hitler's calculation. Michael Howard notes that the "jugular veins" of British strategic interests in Greece and the Eastern Mediterranean and those of the Germans in the Balkans "ran so close to one another that a struggle for mastery could hardly be avoided."[23] By intervening in the Mediterranean, the German dictator opened a yawning window of vulnerability onto an Axis war machine that was poorly configured to fight in such a geographically and operationally complex theater. If the Allies showed opportunism in exploiting these vulnerabilities, then they were correct to do so.

Hitler's Mediterranean "strategy," therefore, came down to a series of reactions to Mussolini's military embarrassment, was the product of "victory fever," or was forced on him by defeat. The 1941 invasion of the Balkans and Greece (Marita and Herkules, the seizure of Crete), Rommel's strategically barren rampages in the Western Desert, "Tunisgrad," and the decision for forward defense in Italy (Achse) conformed to no vision of the place of the Mediterranean in Germany's overall strategy for winning the war, beyond a vague requirement to defend his ally and the southern flank of Barbarossa. The consequences of poorly considered Axis strategic opportunism in the Mediterranean were that the vital Middle East remained under British control; Malta was still defiant and unconquered; major forces, especially the Luftwaffe, were diverted and weakened at critical periods; Germany's Italian ally was eliminated; and the Allies were given a place and the time to build up their forces, audition their best leaders, strengthen their alliance, gain incremental success, and generally build momentum to deliver the *coup de grâce* to Germany in Northwestern Europe. In short, the Axis created the strategic opportunity that was seized by the Allies. The Mediterranean proved a much stickier tar baby for Hitler than it was for Churchill or Roosevelt. The German official history concludes that the theater's importance was that "it first became evident there how small the aggressors' room for maneuver had become as the war continued its course after the late autumn of 1940 . . . In the words of contemporary observers, in the summer [of 1943] Germany definitely ceased to be the 'hammer' and became the 'anvil.' "[24]

Furthermore, the British, and even the distant Americans, did have strategic interests in the Mediterranean, and a force structure flexible enough, especially when American support kicked in, to operate effectively there. For Churchill, the Mediterranean was the corridor of the British empire, the vital hallway to the Middle East, India, and beyond. And even though Americans grumbled at being drawn into the Mediterranean for the benefit of the "British Empire Machine," in fact, the so-called Marshall Memorandum, drawn up by Eisenhower in 1942, listed the security of the "Middle East–India buttress between the Japanese and the Germans," together with keeping the sea lanes of communication open to Britain and the USSR in the war, as the three major American strategic priorities.[25] The Mediterranean occupied no similar place of importance in Hitler's strategic priorities. On the contrary, he saw it as a distraction and a profligate diversion of limited energy, manpower, and resources, and failed to invest resources there in 1940–42 when he might have achieved some strategic benefit. The Allies, on the other hand, could cover all their strategic bases, especially because they were able to prioritize and sequence their strategic choices. Therefore, the "opportunism" of Mediterranean strategy worked to the benefit of the Allies and to the detriment of the Axis.

The second argument that the Mediterranean and Northwestern Europe were rival, rather than complementary, battlegrounds perpetuates a view of the Mediterranean remaindered from World War I, as a strategic "cul-de-sac,"[26] a dead-end theater that diverted strength from the main front in Northern Europe and deposited Allied expeditionary forces in strategically futile operations like Gallipoli and Salonika. In fact, these World War I analogies were conceived at the time by soldiers who saw Churchill's obsession with drawing Turkey into the alliance, his tireless advocacy of amphibious assaults in the Aegean, Italy, or the Balkans, and his support for a Ljubljana advance into southern Germany as evidence of his desire to recuperate a failed strategy from that earlier war. Debate and tensions certainly existed within and between the Western Allies over whether to engage significant forces in the Mediterranean, as well as when to bolt the Mediterranean for Overlord. On the other hand, an alliance operates as a democracy of sorts, especially when its two major components in the West were themselves democratic nations. Debate was the process through which strategy was constantly reassessed between the Western Allies. The remarkable thing about the Mediterranean is how these debates caused the Western Allies to come up with the right decisions. The compromises forced on the alliance by the requirement to cooperate in the Mediterranean constituted a strength, not a weakness. Argument brought about a balance in strategic aims there, while it required Allied commanders to consider Mediterranean goals within the context of the wider war. The cut and thrust of Allied strategic debates in the Mediterranean, the British official history believes, "brought forth balanced and consistent policies with just enough flexibility to profit from real opportunities."[27] Having achieved the overthrow of Mussolini, cleared the Mediterranean for Lend-Lease, exposed Hitler's southern flank, found their commanders, and built up and trained their forces, the Allies were correct to shift their strategic focus from the Mediterranean to Overlord at the conclusion of Husky. They continued a limited investment in the Mediterranean to pressure the Germans and keep their own army occupied in the winter of 1943–44, but refused to be stampeded by some of the Mediterranean's more passionate advocates into an advance through the Ljubljana Gap into southern Germany. Marshall complained that assets sucked up by the Mediterranean were unavailable for Overlord. Corelli Barnett repeats Marshall's assertion that the Mediterranean tied up more Allied assets than German ones.[28] But the simple truth was that the Allies had more assets than did the Axis, assets that they could not have employed profitably elsewhere before June 1944. Even after Overlord, British ports could not have absorbed more U.S. reinforcements, which would have remained on the sidelines of the European war had the Mediterranean entry point into Europe not existed.[29]

The net result of strategic decisions in the Mediterranean constitute, overall, a story of remarkable alliance cooperation and success, in large part because the peripheral role of the Mediterranean in the war's overall strategy was not in doubt. Michael Howard argued as long ago as 1966 that the real strategic conflict was not so much between British proponents of the Mediterranean and U.S. advocates of Sledgehammer. The Mediterranean was never viewed in London as a substitute for an invasion of Northwestern Europe. Rather, its real benefit was to reinforce Roosevelt's "Europe first" strategy and keep advocates of the primacy of the Pacific at bay.[30] Engagement in the Mediterranean furthered Roosevelt's strategic aim of supporting Churchill's war leadership in Britain, quieting his "America First" enemies and protecting what he saw as the very fabric of American democracy.[31] This also kept his goal of building up an American preponderance in the alliance on track. Sledgehammer would have had to be carried out by British troops in the main. The real issue was when, not whether, to shift the focus of Allied strategy from the "peripheral" to the "main" theater in Northwestern Europe. By June 1944, Roosevelt had built up an American preponderance of forces so that he could dictate the course of the war's closing months. Only then did he judge, correctly as Michael Howard has argued, that the Mediterranean as a peripheral theater had served its purpose and that the time had come to shift the primary effort to the main front. As American preponderance in the alliance increased as the result of Roosevelt's Mediterranean investment, the American president, for better or worse, was able to shape the war's termination to suit his, rather than Churchill's, priorities.

Much of the bad press given the Mediterranean stems from the fact that the Germans retained a perpetual ability to outperform Allied troops with a smaller force investment. German operational and tactical expertise was symbolized by Erwin Rommel, who, until defeated at El Alamein, ran circles around British commanders and thereafter seriously embarrassed American forces at Kasserine. Kesselring orchestrated a brilliant escape from Sicily after fighting a stubborn holding action on the island. He then continued to frustrate the Allied advance up the Italian Peninsula until war's end, despite almost overwhelming Allied firepower and total air supremacy. This book has argued that on the contrary, Rommel's reputation as a military commander is inflated and that his passage through the Mediterranean ultimately benefited the Allies more than the Axis. Rommel's reputation is based on victories gained in 1940 over French B divisions and in 1941 over a succession of second-rate British commanders leading what was, in effect, an inchoate colonial army that simultaneously had to split its limited resources among Greece, Crete, the Middle East, the

Horn of Africa, Cyrenaica, Malta, and Gibraltar. Rommel did not fight particularly well during Crusader in November–December 1942, despite virtual equality of forces. He was inattentive to logistics, underestimated the vital importance of sea power, and cooperated poorly with his Italian allies and even with von Arnim in Tunisia. His most dramatic successes, as in June 1942 at Gazala and Tobruk, relied largely on bluff, surprise, British command mistakes, and poor British mastery of inter-arm cooperation. "Victory," in fact, made his strategic and logistical predicament hopeless.

Ultimately, the Rommel image helped the Allies more than the Axis. "The Champ," a creation of Nazi propaganda, offered Churchill a plausible alibi for the failure of his Mediterranean strategy to pay early dividends. Rommel put a face on the enemy, personalized a distant and apparently inconclusive Mediterranean war, and elevated the Mediterranean in the minds of the British and American public to the status of a major theater. Rommel's victories, especially at Tobruk in June 1942, forced the Allies closer together and precipitated U.S. intervention in the Mediterranean, which helped to make Churchill politically bulletproof. Once Rommel met a British general who had broken the code on his methods, developed a coherent staff system, evolved inter-arm cooperation, and trained his troops to carry out his battlefield concepts, the Desert Fox's victories became a thing of the past. Rommel's defeat at El Alamein marked the coming of age of the Eighth Army and gave Britain a general-hero in Montgomery. It also offered clear evidence of Allied progress toward victory and aborted a nascent stab-in-the-back myth. The bloody nose inflicted by Rommel at Kasserine delivered a serious wake-up call for novice U.S. forces. Hitler's propaganda investment in Rommel reinforced his decision to continue to commit resources to North Africa long after they had ceased to pay dividends.

The Italian campaign especially symbolized the futility and attritional character of a Mediterranean war that tied down over a million Allied personnel, not to mention significant air and naval assets, in what they believed constituted little more than an elaborate sideshow. "Overnight Italy went from German ally to German-occupied country," notes historian David Kennedy. "Now it was about to become a battleground in a grinding war of attrition whose costs were justified by no defensible military or political purpose."[32] Carlo D'Este calls Italy "the longest and bloodiest campaign fought by the Allies in the West during World War II."[33] It is certainly true that the Italian campaign, from the Allied strategic perspective, was informed by much wishful thinking. Nor was it always well executed on the operational and tactical level. Mark Clark's experience as army and army group commander was dearly bought, while the overly mechanized British Eighth Army under Oliver Leese adapted poorly to the challenges of Italian terrain.

That said, however, the Italian campaign, while bitter, frustrating, and difficult, paid considerable strategic dividends for the Allies. Quite apart from the roughly forty German divisions tied down in Italy, Greece, and the Balkans, the major battles fought at Salerno, Cassino, Anzio, and those in the Apennines in the winter of 1944–45 cost the Allies less than half the casualties they absorbed in Northwestern Europe in an Italian campaign that lasted twice as long. Despite the fact that the British and Americans were constantly on the offensive against formidable, well-trained troops fighting from near-impregnable positions, they managed to inflict 536,000 casualties on the Germans—more than Stalingrad and "Tunisgrad" combined—at a cost to themselves of 312,000 casualties. This is less than half the 766,294 casualties suffered in Northwestern Europe in a far shorter campaign.[34] This makes Kesselring's parochial argument that "we won in my sector" ring hollow.[35]

In fact, it was to the Allied advantage to spin out the campaign in Italy, where Hitler continued to invest disproportionate resources in a place where he had other, more economical, options. Hitler would have been far better off had he followed Rommel's advice to withdraw to the Alps in 1943, preserving German manpower for other, more important, fronts. The detrimental effects of Hitler's decision to defend Italy placed further strains on a fragmented German high command unable effectively to coordinate such far-flung fronts.[36] By 1944, for instance, there were 125,000 troops in German uniform fighting partisans in Yugoslavia alone, considered for Hitler's purposes as an extension of the Italian, as well as the Eastern Fronts.[37] German divi-

sions committed to Italy and the Balkans could have made the difference between victory and defeat in Normandy in 1944. So, while
Hitler had other, more urgent tasks for his troops, the Allies had no
better way to utilize their divisions outside the Mediterranean before
June 1944.

None of this is to argue that the Mediterranean contained no pit-
falls for the Allies. Allied operations in the Mediterranean attacked no
German center of gravity, hence the strong commitment of forces
there seemed rather nonsensical to the casual observer. The feeling
among GIs that the North African campaign actually prolonged the
war, was shared by many Tommies. "Gunner Woods is puzzled," wrote
Spike Milligan in May 1943 at the end of the Tunisian campaign. " 'I
don't understand, we're fighting *Germany* yet we're in *Africa* bloody
miles from Germany.' 'That's because the weather's better 'ere,' says
Fildes, 'if you're killed when sun tanned you don't look too bad. Mind
you,' he said, 'up North on the Russian front, the cold preserves the
body so good, they post 'em back to the relatives.' "[38]

Progress in the Mediterranean was attritional, and hence incremental, rather than decisive. But then that was the case in all theaters.
The problem for the Allies was that fighting in the Mediterranean
seemed to progress at a snail's pace, an inconclusive slogging match
similar to that of World War I, that wore down Axis forces at an imper-
ceptible rate for what appeared to be small strategic gain. For this reason, despite the fact that momentum in the Mediterranean shifted in
the Allies' favor from the autumn of 1942, it became difficult for Allied
commanders at the time, and historians since, to measure progress
against an enemy that committed only a fraction of its forces there,
while the Soviets appeared to be doing the heavy lifting on the Eastern
Front. Indeed, when George Greenfield, part of the British contingent
at the November–December 1943 Teheran Conference, proposed a
toast to "El Alamein" in reply to the numerous toasts offered to "the
Battle for Kiev" and "Stalingrad," the contingent of Soviet officers,
who had never heard of El Alamein, looked perplexed and asked how
many Axis divisions had fought in the battle. "To make the Eighth
Army look good, I told a lie, or at least a wild exaggeration," remembered Greenfield. " 'About fifteen.' 'In the Soviet Army, we do not call

that a battle,' " the Soviet officer replied after a moment of reflection. " 'To us, that is a skirmish.' "[39]

The political challenges of fighting in the Mediterranean contrasted with the "pure" warfare of Northern Europe. Allied commanders exhibited understandable impatience with fractured Balkan and Greek politics and with irreconcilable Arab and Jewish ambitions that turned the Middle East into a powder keg. Strategic choices and operational plans had to calculate the possibilities of Spanish or Turkish belligerency, aid resistance groups more interested in fighting their domestic rivals than the Axis, arbitrate a French near–civil war, and negotiate an invasion of Italy with a claque of calculating and pusillanimous former Fascists. Their tasks would have been helped had a more robust civil affairs structure been created to increase Eisenhower's leverage in dealing with elusive characters like Darlan and Badoglio, not to mention de Gaulle in 1944–45, men Eisenhower had to accommodate because he did not want to assume the burden of running their countries. One is also struck by how far the political leadership, beginning with Churchill and Roosevelt, left senior soldiers largely on their own in negotiating the labyrinthine politics of the Mediterranean.

If the Mediterranean was the cauldron of Allied unity, it was also the theater in which the Anglo-American entente became estranged. As the Allies gained the strategic momentum in the war and shifted to the offensive, it became increasingly clear that the Mediterranean was a wasting strategic asset for them. So long as the campaign was fought out on the southern shore of the Mediterranean, where Allied sea and air power could be pitted against Axis land power, the Allies fought at an advantage. Once the battle moved to the northern shore, Allied sea power formed a fragile link to support Allied armies against German forces commanded by very competent generals, using interior lines to fight from strong defensive positions. Nor did the Allied expertise in armored operations gained in North Africa transfer to Italy. In fact, it became far easier for the Germans to adjust to the requirements of defensive warfare than for the Allies to reorganize and restructure their forces for the offensive in Italy. German advantages in Italy were offset somewhat by Allied air power, the ability to carry out amphibious operations that kept the Germans on the qui vive for flanking maneuvers, partisan warfare, and the reluctance of Hitler to withdraw divisions from Italy until March 1945.

Nevertheless, glacial Allied progress in Italy intensified disagreement over strategic priorities as the focus of the war shifted from the Mediterranean to Northwestern Europe. Churchill, as leader of the weaker power in the Western Alliance, was keen to keep alive a theater where Britain could retain a preponderance of influence, enhance its status, and advance its postwar aims. Churchill's attitude combined with the collapse of Italy in September 1943 to perpetuate and intensify the strategic opportunism and wishful thinking that had characterized Mediterranean strategy from the beginning. Ambitious officers like Alexander and Mark Clark, abandoned in a secondary theater with limited resources, were tempted to raise their public profile as well as that of their theater by launching strategically risky operations. This led to Salerno, Cassino, Anzio, Rome, Operation Accolade, and opposition to Anvil in favor of plans to invade Germany through the Ljubljana Gap.

The final downside of the Mediterranean war for the Allies was that victory was achieved at a considerable political price. The disintegration of governmental structures had left the region in a volatile state. France's 1940 collapse and the Allied occupation of North Africa hastened the erosion of French authority there. The 8 May 1945 Moslem rebellion in the town of Sétif in eastern Algeria would be hailed after 1954 by the Algerian National Liberation Front as the first blow against French imperialism in North Africa. Arab nationalism and Moslem fundamentalism made serious advances on the southern and eastern shores of the Mediterranean. Britain's handling of King Farouk had undermined his prestige with a generation of young Egyptian officers, who removed him in 1952. The Libyan regime that replaced Italian authority in Tripolitania and Cyrenaica had roots too shallow to survive. Hitler's "final solution" had catapulted Zionism from a minority to a mainstream ideology among Jewish survivors of the Holocaust. The influx of Jewish refugees from Europe into Palestine accelerated the confrontation between Arab and Jew that had caused conflict since the 1930s. Greece stood on the threshold of civil war, a fate avoided in Yugoslavia only because Tito's bloody repression of his discredited opposition with weapons supplied by the Allies enabled him to triumph in short order. One great irony of the Mediterranean war was that Great Britain, which had fought to preserve its interests there, was now too exhausted to play its traditional role as a stabilizing influence. In any case, independence granted to the Indian subcontinent removed the strategic rationale for Britain's presence in the Mediterranean. With the empire on the wane, America had to assume responsibility for stability in the region, justifying Marshall's fear that, once committed to the Mediterranean, the United States would find it difficult to disengage.

NOTES

PREFACE

1. John Ellis, *Brute Force: Allied Strategy and Tactics in the Second World War* (New York: Viking, 1990), xx, 292.

2. Corelli Barnett, *Engage the Enemy More Closely: The Royal Navy in the Second World War* (London: Hodder and Stoughton, 1991), 689–92.

3. David Kennedy, *Freedom from Fear* (Oxford: Oxford University Press, 1999), 596.

4. "The American insistence on the elementary principle of concentration was in reality a rationalization, to conceal misunderstandings, jealousies and rival aims," write Dominick Graham and Shelford Bidwell. *Tug of War: The Battle for Italy, 1943–45* (New York: St. Martin's, 1986), 404.

5. John Keegan, *The Second World War* (London: Penguin, 1989), 368.

6. Robert W. Love, *History of the US Navy*, vol. 2 (1942–91) (Harrisburg, Pa.: Stackpole, 1992), 87.

7. Williamson Murray and Allan R. Millett, *A War to be Won: Fighting in the Second World War* (Cambridge, Mass.: Harvard University Press, 2000), 374.

INTRODUCTION: A STRATEGIST'S NIGHTMARE

1. Lt. John Mason Brown, USNR, *To All Hands: An Amphibious Adventure* (New York: McGraw-Hill, 1943), 95.

2. Fernand Braudel, *The Mediterranean and the Mediterranean World in the Age of Philip II*, vol. 1 (New York: Fontana/Collins, 1976), 170.

3. Michael Simpson, "Superhighway to the World Wide Web: The Mediterranean in British Imperial Strategy, 1900–45," in John B. Hattendorf, ed., *Naval Policy and Strategy in the Mediterranean: Past, Present and Future* (London: Frank Cass, 2000), 51.

4. D. A. Farnie, *East and West of Suez: The Suez Canal in History, 1854–1956* (Oxford: Clarendon, 1969), 611.

5. Simpson sums up some of the anti-Mediterranean arguments. "Superhighway to the World Wide Web," 68–69. See also the arguments laid out in the Preface of this book.

6. H. P. Wilmott, *The Great Crusade: A New Complete History of the Second World War* (New York: Free Press, 1989), 188–89.

7. Klaus Schmider, "The Mediterranean in 1940–1941: Crossroads of Lost Opportunities?" *War and Society* 15, no. 2 (October 1997): 19.

8. David Fromkin, *A Peace to End All Peace: Creating the Modern Middle East, 1914–1922* (New York: Henry Holt, 1989), 663.

9. Simpson, "Superhighway to the World Wide Web," 57.

10. E. Monroe, *The Mediterranean in Politics* (London: Oxford University Press, 1938), 12, 249; H. Rowan Robinson, *Imperial Defence: A Problem in Four Dimensions* (London: Muller, 1938), 287, quoted in Farnie, *East and West of Suez*, 614–15.

11. Simpson, "Superhighway to the World Wide Web," 58–59.

12. Schmider, "The Mediterranean in 1940–1941," 32–33.

13. F. W. Deakin, *The Brutal Friendship: Mussolini, Hitler and the Fall of Italian Fascism* (New York: Harper and Row, 1962), 275.

14. Schmider, "The Mediterranean in 1940–1941," 35–36.

15. Simpson, "Superhighway to the World Wide Web," 60–61, 52.

16. Ibid., 64.

17. Farnie, *East and West of Suez*, 601.

18. Major General I.S.O. Playfair, *The Mediterranean and the Middle East*, vol. 1, *The Early Successes against Italy (to May 1941)* (London: HMSO, 1954), 27, 75, 79.

19. Schmider, "The Mediterranean in 1940–1941," 35.

20. George Greenfield, *Chasing the Beast: One Man's War* (London: Richard Cohen Books, 1998), 59.

21. Wilmott, *The Great Crusade*, 189–90.

22. Ronald H. Spector, *At War at Sea: Sailors and Naval Combat in the Twentieth Century* (New York: Viking, 2001), 168.

23. Williamson Murray, "British Military Effectiveness in the Second World War," in Williamson Murray and Allan Millett, eds., *Military Effectiveness*, vol. 3, *The Second World War* (Boston: Unwin Hyman, 1990), 110, 114, 118, 121–22.

24. Alan Moorehead, *The March to Tunis: The North African War 1940–1943* (New York: Harper & Row, 1943), 48.

25. See Admiral of the Fleet Viscount Cunningham of Hyndhope, *A Sailor's Odyssey* (London: Hutchinson, 1951).

26. Spector, *At War at Sea*, 183.

27. Nigel Hamilton, *Master of the Battlefield: Monty's War Years, 1942–1944* (New York: McGraw-Hill, 1983), 388–89.

28. Alan F. Wilt, *War from the Top: German and British Military Decision Making during World War II* (Bloomington: Indiana University Press, 1990), 47–48.

29. Jack Greene and Alessandro Massignai, *The Naval War in the Mediterranean, 1940–1943* (London: Chatham, 1998), 139.

30. Playfair, *The Mediterranean and the Middle East*, 1: 9–10, 74–80.

31. K. Feiling, *The Life of Neville Chamberlain* (London: Macmillan, 1946), 273.

32. MacGregor Knox, *Hitler's Italian Allies: Royal Armed Forces, Fascist Regime, and the War of 1940–1943* (Cambridge: Cambridge University Press, 2000), 46.

33. Martin van Creveld argues that logistical problems in North Africa were insoluble even without Malta's role in cutting the maritime communications between Italy and Tripoli. *Supplying War: Logistics from Wallenstein to Patton* (Cambridge: Cambridge University Press, 1977), 181–92. MacGregor Knox faults Italy's inadequate logistical structure and organization, and points out that 83 percent of cargoes shipped to North Africa actually arrived, despite British maritime interdiction. *Hitler's Italian Allies*, 135.

34. Farnie, *East and West of Suez*, 629.

35. Paul Theroux, *The Pillars of Hercules: A Grand Tour of the Mediterranean* (New York: Putnam, 1995), 310.

36. Charles A. Jellison, *Besieged: The World War II Ordeal of Malta, 1940–1942* (Hanover, N.H.: University Press of New England, 1984), 2–3, 10–17, 22–24.

37. Brown, *To All Hands*, 54.

38. For Franco, see André Bachoud, *Franco ou la réussite d'un homme ordinaire* (Paris: Fayard, 1997), 198–201, 204–16, 220–22.

39. E. L. Woodward, *British Foreign Policy in the Second World War* (London: HMSO, 1962), 127, quoted in Farnie, *East and West of Suez*, 625.

40. Farnie, *East and West of Suez*, 598–600, 605–06.

41. Ibid., 634.

42. Peter Mansfield, *The British in Egypt* (New York: Holt, Rinehart and Winston, 1971), 235, 251, 262, 265–68, 271, 274.

43. Farnie, *East and West of Suez*, 632.

44. P. J. Vatikiotis, *The Egyptian Army in Politics: Pattern for New Nations?* (Bloomington: Indiana University Press, 1961), 29–30.

45. Howard M. Sachar, *A History of Israel from the Rise of Zionism to Our Time* (New York: Knopf, 1998), 171, 203.

46. Ibid., 196–226.

47. Farnie, *East and West of Suez*, 627, 632.

48. John Wright, *Libya: A Modern History* (Baltimore: Johns Hopkins University Press), 39–42.

49. General der Flieger a.D. Hellmuth Felmy and General der Artillerie a.D. Walter Warlimont, *World War II German Military Studies*, vol. 13, *German*

Exploitation of Arab Nationalist Movements in World War II (Historical Division, Headquarters United States Army, Europe), 26.

50. Gerhard Schreiber, Bernd Stegemann, and Detlef Vogel, edited by the Militärgeschichtliches Forshungsamt, *Germany and the Second World War*, vol. 3, *The Mediterranean, South-East Europe and North Africa, 1939–1941: From Italy's Declaration of Non-Belligerence to the Entry of the United States into the War* (Oxford: Clarendon, 1995), 758.

51. H. P. Wilmott, *The Barrier and the Javelin: Japanese and Allied Pacific Strategies, February to June 1942* (Annapolis: Naval Institute Press, 1983), 47–52; Weinberg, *A World at Arms*, 324–27.

52. Schmider, "The Mediterranean in 1940–1941," 21, 28; Wilmott, *The Great Crusade*, 188–89.

53. Harold E. Raugh, Jr., *Wavell in the Middle East 1939–1941: A Study in Generalship* (London: Brassey's UK, 1993), 204.

54. Quoted in Raugh, *Wavell in the Middle East*, 203.

55. Farnie, *East and West of Suez*, 632–33.

56. Schrieber et al., *Germany and the Second World War*, 3: 760.

57. Ansel, *Hitler*, 26.

58. Herwig, "The Failure of German Sea Power," 100–01.

59. Israeli historian Martin van Creveld concludes that Hitler probably made his decision for Barbarossa, the attack on the USSR, in late November 1940. Martin van Creveld, *Hitler's Strategy, 1940–1941: The Balkan Clue* (Cambridge: Cambridge University Press, 1973), 180. However, his decision was probably made as early as July. See Schreiber et al., *Germany and the Second World War*, 3: 133.

CHAPTER ONE: 1940: WAR COMES TO THE MEDITERRANEAN

1. Denis Mack Smith, *Mussolini* (New York: Knopf, 1982), 72, 112–13.

2. MacGregor Knox, *Hitler's Italian Allies: Royal Armed Forces, Fascist Regime, and the War of 1940–1943* (Cambridge: Cambridge University Press, 2000), 31–35.

3. Smith, *Mussolini*, 248.

4. Robert Mallett, *The Italian Navy and Fascist Expansionism, 1935–1940* (London: Frank Cass, 1998), 1–2. "Mussolini continued to believe that his imperialist aims were realizable only at the side of Hitler," concludes the German official history of World War II. Several reasons explain why Italian foreign policy appeared at times to be ambivalent. First, unlike his father-in-law, Foreign Minister Ciano wanted to break with Hitler. Second, Mussolini periodically endeavored to demonstrate fits of independence to show he was not entirely dependent on the Germans. Finally, Mussolini feared that Germany and the USSR would divide the Balkans between them. Yet this in no way impacted on Mussolini's pro-German attitude. "Mussolini continued to see the Western democracies as the enemy and Germany as his ally." Gerhard Schreiber,

Bernd Stegemann, and Detlef Vogel, edited by the Militärgeschichtliches Forshungsamt, *Germany in the Second World War*, vol. 3, *The Mediterranean, South-East Europe and North Africa, 1939–1941: From Italy's Declaration of Non-Belligerence to the Entry of the United States into the War* (Oxford: Clarendon, 1995), 16–17, 19, 23.

5. Mallett, *Italian Navy and Fascist Expansion*, 191; F. W. Deakin, *The Brutal Friendship: Mussolini, Hitler and the Fall of Italian Fascism* (New York: Harper and Row, 1962), 5.

6. Smith, *Mussolini*, 243–45, 251.

7. Albert Speer, *Inside the Third Reich* (New York: Macmillan, 1970), 106.

8. Smith, *Mussolini*, 240–41.

9. Schreiber et al., *Germany and the Second World War*, 3: 108.

10. Ibid., 3: 25–39.

11. Ibid., 3: 42.

12. Smith, *Mussolini*, 248.

13. Walter Ansel, *Hitler and the Middle Sea* (Durham, N.C.: Duke University Press, 1972), 14.

14. Knox, *Hitler's Italian Allies*, 16.

15. Smith, *Mussolini*, 239–42.

16. Knox, *Hitler's Italian Allies*, 69–72.

17. Enzo Angelucci and Paolo Matricardi, *Complete Book of World War II Combat Aircraft* (Vercelli, Italy: White Star, 2000), 116–17, 193.

18. Charles A. Jellison, *Besieged: The World War II Ordeal of Malta, 1940–1942* (Hanover, N.H.: University Press of New England, 1984), 10–12, 19–22, 38.

19. Playfair, *The Mediterranean and the Middle East*, 1: 92–97.

20. Reynolds M. Salerno, *Vital Crossroads: Mediterranean Origins of the Second World War, 1935–1940* (Ithaca, N.Y.: Cornell University Press, 2002), 207–09.

21. Smith, *Mussolini*, 254–56.

22. Ibid., 247–48, 251–52; Deakin, *Brutal Friendship*, 12.

23. Schreiber et al., *Germany and the Second Word War*, 3: 247.

24. Ibid., 3: 165–73.

25. Ibid., 3: 173–79.

26. Winston S. Churchill, *The Second World War*, vol. 2, *Their Finest Hour* (Boston: Houghton Mifflin, 1949), 470.

27. Schreiber et al., *Germany and the Second World War*, 3: 266–77.

28. Malett, *The Italian Navy and Fascist Expansionism*, 2.

29. Schreiber et al., *Germany and the Second World War*, 3: 87.

30. Estimates of Italian naval strength vary. *Jane's Fighting Ships 1939* (London: Sampson Low, Marston, 1939), viii, places Italian strength at seven heavy and fourteen light cruisers and 104 submarines.

31. Donald Macintyre, *The Naval War Against Hitler* (New York: Scribner, 1971), 147–50.

32. Schreiber et al., *Germany and the Second World War*, 3: 90; Knox, *Hitler's Italian Allies*, 60–63, 159–61.

33. Admiral Franco Maugeri, *From the Ashes of Disgrace* (New York: Reynal and Hitchcock, 1948), 7.

34. S.W.C. Pack, *The Battle of Matapan* (New York: Macmillan, 1961), 151.

35. Knox, *Hitler's Italian Allies*, 161–62.

36. Macintyre, *Naval War*, 151–52.

37. Playfair, *The Mediterranean and the Middle East*, 1: 150–54, 156–59.

38. Schreiber et al., *Germany and the Second World War*, 3: 256.

39. Macintyre, *Naval War*, 151.

40. Salerno, *Vital Crossroads*, 207.

41. Brian Sullivan, "A Fleet in Being: The Rise and Fall of Italian Sea Power, 1861–1943," *International History Review* 10, no. 1 (February 1988): 119–20.

42. Jack Greene and Alessandro Massignai, *The Naval War in the Mediterranean, 1940–1943* (London: Chatham, 1998), 146. Playfair records thirteen Italian destroyers. *The Mediterranean and the Middle East*, 2: 63.

43. On 26 March, British intelligence sent Enigma decrypts of Luftwaffe and Italian navy signals to Cunningham, together with an intelligence appreciation that he should expect a combined air/naval operation in the waters off southern Greece, although the exact nature of the Axis operation was unclear. F. H. Hinsley, *British Intelligence in the Second World War: Its Influence on Strategy and Operations*, vol. 1 (New York: Cambridge University Press, 1979), 403–06.

44. Pack, *Battle of Matapan*, 158.

45. *http://www.regiamarina.it/*; much of this account is drawn from Pack, *Battle of Matapan*.

46. Greene and Massignai, *Naval War*, 145–60; Playfair, *Mediterranean and the Middle East*, 2: 61–69; Hinsley, *British Intelligence*, 1: 403–06, Schreiber et al., *Germany and the Second World War*, 3: 668–70.

47. Mallett, *The Italian Navy and Fascist Expansionism*, 3, 172–73.

48. Macintyre, *Naval War*, 214–15.

49. That said, however, the Allied combination of Ultra intelligence and radar would probably have inflicted a fate identical to that of the merchant fleet on Italian carriers. See James J. Sadkovich, *The Italian Navy in World War II* (Westport, Conn: Greenwood, 1994), 335. Sadkovich generally presents a favorable assessment of the Italian navy. For a less favorable assessment, see Knox, *Hitler's Italian Allies*, 59–61.

50. Schreiber et al., *Germany and the Second World War*, 3: 90–91.

51. Knox, *Hitler's Italian Allies*, 28.

52. Ansel, *Hitler and the Middle Sea*, 3.

53. See MacGregor Knox, "The Italian Armed Forces, 1940–1943," in Williamson Murray and Allan Millett, eds., *Military Effectiveness*, vol. 3, *The Second World War* (Boston: Unwin Hymann, 1990), 146.

54. Knox, "Italian Armed Forces," 142, 143, 153, 158, 160, 167–68.

55. Schreiber et al., *Germany in the Second World War*, 3: 209–10, 213.

56. Ansel, *Hitler and the Middle Sea*, 19, 21–22, 64–65, 72–73.

57. Schreiber et al., *Germany and the Second World War*, 3: 236–39, 245–46.

58. Arthur J. Marder, *From the Dardanelles to Oran: Studies in the Royal Navy in War and Peace 1915–1940* (London: Oxford University Press, 1974), 226.

59. Ibid., 218–19.

60. Ibid., 228–59, 264–65.

61. Ibid., 272–73.

62. Ibid., 282. For a view of Mers el-Kébir as a tragic misunderstanding, see Philippe Lasterle, "Could Admiral Gensoul have Averted the Tragedy of Mers el-Kébir?" *Journal of Military History*, 67 (July 2003), 835–44.

63. Playfair, *The Mediterranean and the Middle East*, 1: 130–43.

64. Ansel, *Hitler and the Middle Sea*, 12–13.

65. Marder, *From the Dardanelles to Oran*, 279.

66. Ansel, *Hitler and the Middle Sea*, 12–14.

CHAPTER TWO: "THE NORWAY OF THE MEDITERRANEAN"

1. Gerhard Schreiber, Bernd Stegemann, and Detleff Vogel, edited by the Militärgeschichtliches Forshungsamt, *Germany and the Second World War*, vol. 3, *The Mediterranean, South-East Europe and North Africa, 1939–1941* (Oxford: Clarendon, 1995), 133.

2. Winston S. Churchill, *The Second World War*, vol. 2, *Their Finest Hour* (Boston: Houghton Mifflin, 1949), 418.

3. Geoffrey P. Megargee, *Inside Hitler's High Command* (Lawrence: University Press of Kansas, 2000), 88–91.

4. MacGregor Knox, *Hitler's Italian Allies: Royal Armed Forces, Fascist Regime, and the War of 1940–1943* (Cambridge: Cambridge University Press, 2000), 79.

5. Denis Mack Smith, *Mussolini* (New York: Knopf, 1982), 256–57.

6. Schreiber et al., *Germany and the Second World War*, 3: 409.

7. Churchill, *The Second World War*, 2: 618.

8. Admiral Franco Maugeri, *From the Ashes of Disgrace* (New York: Reynal and Hitchcock, 1948), 88–89; F. W. Deakin, *The Brutal Friendship: Mussolini, Hitler and the Fall of Italian Fascism* (New York: Harper and Row, 1962), 43–44; MacGregor Knox, *Mussolini Unleashed, 1939–1941: Politics and Strategy in Fascist Italy's Last War* (Cambridge: Cambridge University Press, 1982), 47.

9. Schreiber et al., *Germany and the Second World War*, 3: 310–16 on Albania, 3: 376–79 on Ciano and the Italian invasion.

10. Ibid., 3: 381.

11. Walter Ansel, *Hitler and the Middle Sea* (Durham, N.C.: Duke University Press, 1972), 43.

12. Schreiber et al., *Germany and the Second World War*, 3: 416–17.

13. David Fromkin, *A Peace to End All Peace: Creating the Modern Middle East 1914–1922* (New York: Henry Holt, 1989), 545–46.

14. Michael Llewellyn Smith, *Ionian Vision: Greece in Asia Minor 1919–1922* (New York: St. Martin's, 1973), 203, quoted in Fromkin, *A Peace to End All Peace*, 541.

15. Mark Mazower, *Inside Hitler's Greece: The Experience of Occupation, 1941–44* (New Haven: Yale University Press, 1993), 11–14; Schreiber et al., *Germany and the Second World War*, 3: 332–39; Louis de Bernières, *Corelli's Mandolin* (New York: Vintage Books, 1994), 25–30.

16. Smith, *Mussolini*, 258.

17. I.S.O. Playfair, *The Mediterranean and the Middle East*, vol. 1, *The Early Successes against Italy (to May 1941)* (London: HMSO, 1954), 227; Schreiber et al., *Germany and the Second World War*, 3: 429–32.

18. Knox, *Hitler's Italian Allies*, 169, 175.

19. Sir David Hunt, *A Don at War* (London: William Kimber, 1966), 19.

20. Eric Newby, *Love and War in the Apennines* (London: Hodder and Stoughton, 1971), 30.

21. Alan Moorehead, *The March to Tunis: The North African War, 1940–1943* (New York: Harper & Row, 1943), 97.

22. MacGregor Knox, "The Italian Armed Forces, 1940–1943," in Williamson Murray and Allan Millett, eds., *Military Effectiveness* vol. 3, *The Second World War* (Boston: Allen & Unwin, 1988), 142. See also Knox, *Hitler's Italian Allies*, 176.

23. Schreiber et al., *Germany and the Second World War*, 3: 92–96.

24. Ugo Cavallero, chief of the Italian high command from December 1940 to January 1943, and Giovanni Messe, who succeeded Rommel in Tunisia in March 1943, count among the exceptions.

25. Carlo Levi, *Christ Stopped at Eboli* (New York: Farrar, Straus and Giroux, 1974), 28–29.

26. George Greenfield, *Chasing the Beast: One Man's War* (London: Richard Cohen Books, 1998), 85–86; Moorehead, *The March to Tunis*, 66–71.

27. MacGregor Knox, *Common Destiny: Dictatorship, Foreign Policy and War in Fascist Italy and Nazi Germany* (Cambridge: Cambridge University Press, 2000), 168–69.

28. David Irving, *The Trail of the Fox: The Life of Field-Marshal Erwin Rommel* (London: Book Club Associates, 1977), 198.

29. A. J. Liebling, *The Road Back to Paris* (New York: Modern Library, 1997), 450.

30. Newby, *Love and War in the Apennines*, 33, 44.

31. Knox, "The Italian Armed Forces, 1940–1943," 27–29; Brian R. Sullivan, "The Italian Soldier in Combat, June 1940–September 1943: Myths, Realities and Explanations," in Paul Addison and Angus Calder, eds., *Time to Kill: The Soldier's Experience of War in the West, 1939–1945* (London: Pimlico, 1997), 182.

32. Churchill, *The Second World War*, 2: 420.

33. Sullivan, "The Italian Soldier in Combat," 193–94, 197–98; Irving, *Trail of the Fox*, 198. In quieter moments, Rommel believed Italian soldiers capable of good performance; however, "Their officers are worthless. Their High Command are traitors."

34. William A. Lessa, *Spearhead Governatore: Remembrances of the Campaign in Italy* (Malibu, Calif.: Undena Publications, 1985), 21.

35. Italian "divisions" were, in reality, mixed brigades, made up of two two-battalion regiments instead of three three-battalion regiments.

36. Christopher F. Foss, *The Encyclopedia of Tanks and Armored Fighting Vehicles* (San Diego: Thunder Bay Press, 2002), 295; Sullivan, "The Italian Soldier in Combat," 185–86.

37. Moorehead, *The March to Tunis*, 71.

38. Lucio Ceva and Giorgio Rochat, "Italy," in I.C.B. Dear and M.R.D. Foot, eds., *The Oxford Companion to World War II* (Oxford: Oxford University Press, 1995), 597.

39. Alan Moorehead, *The Desert War* (London: Penguin, 2001), 56–57.

40. Newby, *Love and War in the Apennines*, 28.

41. Knox, "The Italian Armed Forces, 1940–1943," 152–66, 171–72; Knox, *Hitler's Italian Allies*, 51–58, 145–57; Knox, *Common Destiny*, 165–67; Deakin, *Brutal Friendship*, 12; Schreiber et al., *Germany and the Second World War*, 3: 62–78.

42. Enzo Angelucci and Paolo Matricardi, *Complete Book of World War II Combat Aircraft* (Vercelli, Italy: White Star, 2000), 193.

43. Manfred von Richtofen, "The Red Fighter Pilot," *The War Times Journal*, 1999, http://www.richthofen.com/arcdocs/richt12b.htm.

44. Knox, *Hitler's Italian Allies*, 65–67, 163–67.

45. Richard Overy, *The Air War, 1939–1945* (London, 1980), 41; Rudolfo Gentile, *Storia dell'aeronautica dalle origini ai giorni nostri* (Rome, 1958), 186–93; both quoted in Schreiber et al., *Germany and the Second World War*, 3: 82.

46. Lucio Ceva and Andra Curami, "Air Army and Aircraft Industry in Italy, 1936–1943," in Horst Boog, ed., *The Conduct of the Air War in the Second World War* (New York: Berg, 1992), 106, 111; Knox, "Italian Military Effectiveness," 153–70; Schreiber et al., *Germany and the Second World War*, 3: 67; Moorehead, *The March to Tunis*, 78–85.

47. Ceva and Rochat, "Italy," 597.

48. Schreiber et al., *Germany and the Second World War*, 3: 410–11, 423, for attack plan.

49. Sullivan, "The Italian Soldier in Combat," 189.

50. De Bernières, *Corelli's Mandolin*, 91–97; Playfair, *The Mediterranean and the Middle East*, 1: 228.

51. Hugh Gibson, ed., *The Ciano Diaries, 1939–1943* (Garden City, N.Y.: Doubleday, 1946), 4 December 1940, 318.

52. Playfair, *The Mediterranean and the Middle East*, 1: 238.

53. Churchill, *The Second World War*, 1: 544.

54. Oliver Warner, *Admiral of the Fleet: Cunningham of Hyndhope: The Battle for the Mediterranean* (Athens: Ohio University Press, 1967), 115.

55. Donald Macintyre, *The Naval War Against Hitler* (New York: Scribner, 1971), 159–61.

56. Gibson, *Ciano Diaries*, 309.

57. Playfair, *The Mediterranean and the Middle East*, 1: 235–38.

58. Smith, *Mussolini*, 263–64.

59. Ibid., 259–60.

60. Ibid., 259–61.

61. Playfair, *The Mediterranean and the Middle East*, 1: 223–35, 333–38.

62. Schreiber et al., *Germany and the Second World War*, 3: 448.

63. Playfair, *The Mediterranean and the Middle East*, 1: 165–79.

64. Churchill, *The Second World War*, 2: 433.

65. Moorehead, *The March to Tunis*, 15–16, 28, 57, 188–90.

66. Klaus Schmider, "The Mediterranean in 1940–1941: Crossroads of Lost Opportunities?," *War and Society* 15, no. 2 (October 1997): 25 (note 31).

67. Schreiber et al., *Germany and the Second World War*, 3: 678. Wavell's counter was that he discovered that his local commanders were about to make deplorable mistakes in their tactical dispositions. Harold E. Raugh, Jr., *Wavell in the Middle East, 1939–1941* (London: Brassey's, 1993), 256.

68. Quoted in Raugh, *Wavell in the Middle East*, 248.

69. Lord Carver suggested that Churchill looked upon Wavell as "a rather dumb Scotsman." Ibid., 246, 254, 267–68.

70. Field Marshal Vicount Montgomery of Alamein, *The Path to Leadership* (London: Collins, 1961), 46.

71. Brian Bond, ed., *Chief of Staff: The Diaries of Lt. Gen. Sir Henry Pownall* (London: Leo Cooper, 1974), 2: 95.

72. Moorehead, *The March to Tunis*, 59.

73. Ian Beckett, "Wavell," in John Keegan, ed., *Churchill's Generals* (New York: Grove Weidenfeld, 1991), 71. For other opinions on Wavell's relationship with Churchill see Bernard Fergusson, "Field-Marshal the Ear Wavell," in Michael Carver, ed., *The War Lords* (London: Weidenfeld and Nicolson, 1976), 213–30; Ronald Lewin, *The Chief: Field Marshal Lord Wavell, Commander-in-Chief and Viceroy, 1939–1947* (New York: Farrar, Straus and Giroux, 1980), 13–29; Correlli Barnett, *The Desert Generals* (Bloomington: Indiana University Press, 1983), 76–77.

74. Percival Spear, *A History of India*, vol. 2 (London: Penguin, 1978), 233.

75. Churchill, *The Second World War*, 2: 537.

76. "To modern students of Churchill, he appears a brilliant orator, but one whose reactionary views and wild imagination, whose incessant meddling and irrational enthusiasms made him as much a menace as a source of salvation to a beleaguered Britain," concludes American political scientist Eliot Cohen.

"Indeed, it is fair to say that this is now very much the scholarly view of Churchill." In support of this statement, Cohen lists, in particular, John Charmley, *Churchill: The End of Glory* (New York: Harcourt Brace, 1993); A.J.P. Taylor, ed., *Churchill Revised: A Critical Assessment* (New York: Dial Press, 1968); Robert Blake and William Roger Louis, eds., *Churchill* (New York: Norton, 1993). I thank Eliot Cohen for allowing me to consult the manuscript of his "Supreme Command," from which much of the following argument is taken.

77. "The Prime Minister had no understanding of operational details, nor of logistic constraints and opportunities," concludes the biographer of Alanbrooke, David Fraser. "He pestered Commanders in the field for information and bombarded them with exhortations which went well beyond his responsibilities." David Fraser, *Alanbrooke* (New York: Atheneum, 1962), 532.

78. Field Marshal Lord Alanbrooke, *War Diaries, 1939–1945* (Berkeley: University of California Press, 2001), 447.

79. S. W. Roskill, *Churchill and the Admirals* (New York: William Morrow, 1978), 188.

80. Bernard Fergusson, ed., *The Business of War: The War Narrative of Major-General Sir John Kennedy* (New York, 1958), 115.

81. Winston S. Churchill, *The World Crisis*, vol. 3. *The Grand Alliance* (Boston: Houghton Mifflin, 1950), 194–95.

82. Harold Macmillan, *War Diaries: Politics and War in the Mediterranean, 1943–1945* (New York: St. Martin's, 1984), 295.

83. John Wheeler-Bennett, ed., *Action This Day: Working with Churchill* (London: Macmillan, 1969), 22.

84. Cohen, "Supreme Command," unpublished manuscript.

85. Robin Higham, *Diary of a Disaster: British Aid to Greece, 1940–41* (Lexington: University Press of Kentucky, 1986), 76.

86. Eliot A. Cohen, "Churchill and Coalition Strategy in World War II," in Paul Kennedy, ed., *Grand Strategies in War and Peace* (New Haven: Yale University Press, 1991), 49; see also Matthew Jones, *Britain, the United States and the Mediterranean War, 1942–1944* (New York: St. Martin's, 1996).

87. Churchill, *Painting as a Pastime* (pamphlet), quoted in Cohen, "Supreme Command."

88. Ronald Lewin, *Churchill as Warlord* (London: B. T. Batsford, 1973), 4, 8, 17–18, 42–43, 50.

89. Brooke, *War Diaries*, 451.

90. Raugh, *Wavell in the Middle East*, 204.

91. David Carlton, *Anthony Eden: A Political Biography* (London: A. Lane, 1981), 180.

92. Beckett, "Wavell," 76–77; Churchill, *The Second World War*, 2: 483; W.G.F. Jackson, *The Battle for North Africa 1940–43* (New York: Mason Charter, 1975), 37.

93. The process was complicated by the fact that troops had to be carried

to the Cape in fast liners able to sprint past U-boat ambushes in the Atlantic. Once in Cape Town, however, troops were off-loaded and placed on board slower troop ships for the less hazardous trip up the east coast of Africa. The voyage could take up to six months.

94. Suez, the main port for ships arriving via the Cape route and India, was deficient in docks, lighters, wharf cranes, and a rail-marshaling yard. Ships, therefore, had to be directed to Kantara inside the canal, or past Port Said to Haifa and Alexandria to off-load. Fortunately for the British, the delayed appearance of the Luftwaffe in theater, combined with Axis failure adequately to target the Suez Canal once they did arrive, allowed British infrastructure improvements to proceed virtually unhindered. By the end of 1940, lighter jetties had appeared along the canal, a rail-marshaling yard was under construction at Port Said, and three deep-water berths and two lighter jetties had been completed at Suez.

95. Churchill, *The Second World War*, 2: 500; Schreiber et al., *Germany and the Second World War*, 3: 645.

96. "Strange as it may seem," Churchill remarked in his memoirs of this period, "the Air Force, except in the air, is the least mobile of all the Services. A squadron can reach its destination in a few hours, but its establishment, depots, fuel, spare parts, and workshops take many weeks, and even months, to develop." Churchill, *The Second World War*, 2: 434.

97. The port of Takoradi had to be enlarged to receive an increased volume of shipping, as did an air base that could assemble and transit 120 planes of different types each month. Airfields at Lagos, Kano, Maiduguri, Geneina, Khartoum, and Abu Sueir near Suez had to be improved. Hangers, barracks, and fuel depots had to be built and signaling equipment installed.

98. Churchill, *The Second World War*, 2: 453–54; Playfair, *The Mediterranean and the Middle East*, 1: 244–50, 195–97.

99. Playfair, *The Mediterranean and the Middle East*, 1: 262.

100. Moorehead, *The March to Tunis*, 87.

101. Playfair, *The Mediterranean and the Middle East*, 1: 264, 266.

102. Ibid., 1: 273–74.

103. F. H. Hinsley, *British Intelligence in the Second World War: Its Influence on Strategy and Operations*, vol. 1 (New York: Cambridge University Press, 1979), 375–79, 381.

104. John W. Gordon, *The Other Desert War: British Special Forces in North Africa, 1940–1943* (New York: Greenwood, 1987), 8–67.

105. Hinsley, *British Intelligence*, 1: 379.

106. Moorehead, *The March to Tunis*, 66–71; Playfair, *The Mediterranean and the Middle East*, 1: 267–68.

107. Moorehead, *The Desert War*, 71.

108. Churchill, *The Second World War*, 2: 452.

109. John Connell, *Wavell, Scholar and Soldier* (London: Collins, 1964),

323, quoted in Paul Collier, "The Capture of Tripoli in 1941: 'Open Sesame' or Tactical Folly?" *War & Society* 20, no 1 (May 2002): 89.

110. Hinsley, *British Intelligence*, 1: 381.

111. Playfair, *The Mediterranean and the Middle East*, 1: 282–87; Moorehead, *The March to Tunis*, 84–86.

112. Moorehead, *The Desert War*, 83.

113. Playfair, *The Mediterranean and the Middle East*, 1: 362.

114. Ibid., 1: 287–93; Moorehead, *The March to Tunis*, 88–91.

115. Schreiber et al., *Germany and the Second World War*, 3: 651–52.

116. Hinsley, *British Intelligence*, 1: 379.

117. Schmider, "The Mediterranean in 1940–1941," 22.

118. Churchill, *The Second World War*, 2: 619, 626–27.

119. Churchill, *The Second World War*, vol. 3: 92; Cecil Brown, *Suez to Singapore* (New York: Random House, 1942), 84.

120. Hinsley, *British Intelligence*, 1: 380.

121. Playfair, *The Mediterranean and the Middle East*, 1: 166–67; Knox, *Mussolini Unleashed*, 150–55; *La guerra in Africa orientale, giugno 1940–novembre 1941* (Rome: Ministero della Difensa, Stato Maggiore Esercito, Ufficio Storico, 1952), 32–35.

122. Playfair, *The Mediterranean and the Middle East*, 1: 181–84.

123. Ibid., 1: 429–30.

124. Hinsley, *British Intelligence*, 1: 380–81.

125. Ibid., 1: 381.

126. Playfair, *The Mediterranean and the Middle East*, 1: 439.

127. Ibid., 1: 395.

128. Churchill, *The Second World War*, 3: 83.

129. Moorehead, *The March to Tunis*, 121–22.

130. Ibid., 126.

131. Playfair, *The Mediterranean and the Middle East*, 1: 424–28.

132. Ibid., 1: 447–50.

133. Churchill, *The Second World War*, 3: 67. And indeed, some criticize Wavell for not doing so. See Jackson, *The Battle for North Africa*, 76.

134. I.S.O. Playfair, *The Mediterranean and the Middle East*, vol. 2, *The Germans Come to the Help of Their Ally"* (London: HMSO, 1956), 303–04.

135. Smith, *Mussolini*, 266.

CHAPTER THREE: TACTICAL TRIUMPHS,
STRATEGIC MISJUDGMENTS

1. Alan Moorehead, *The March to Tunis: The North African War, 1940–1943* (New York: Harper and Row, 1943), 184.

2. Ronald Lewin, *Churchill as Warlord* (London: Batsford, 1974), 56. Lewin quotes Asquith's 1916 criticism of Churchill.

3. Gerhard L. Weinberg, *A World At Arms: A Global History of World War II* (Cambridge: Cambridge University Press, 1994), 218–19.

4. W.G.F. Jackson, *The Battle for North Africa, 1940–43* (New York: Mason/Charter, 1975), 70.

5. Gerhard Schreiber, Bernd Stegemann, and Detlef Vogel, edited by the Militärgeschichtliches Forshungsamt, *Germany and the Second World War*, vol. 3, *The Mediterranean, South-East Europe and North Africa, 1939–1941* (Oxford: Clarendon, 1995), 653.

6. I.S.O. Playfair, *The Mediterranean and the Middle East*, vol. 1, *Early Successes against Italy (to May 1941)* (London: HMSO, 1954), 371.

7. Hinsley, *British Intelligence in the Second World War: Its Influence on Strategy and Operations*, vol. 1 (New York: Cambridge University Press, 1979), 359.

8. Playfair, *The Mediterranean and the Middle East*, 1: 384, 387.

9. Indeed, on 24 February 1941, the director of military intelligence for the Middle East warned that "we must be prepared to face the loss of all forces sent to Greece." On the same day, the chiefs of staff predicted that intervention in Greece was "unlikely to have a favourable effect on the war as a whole." Hinsley, *British Intelligence*, 1: 361.

10. Schreiber et al., *Germany and the Second World War*, 3: 653.

11. Jackson, *The Battle for North Africa*, 75.

12. Hinsley, *British Intelligence*, 1: 355–56. Hinsley calls this "a major failure of intelligence at the strategic level." 1: 260.

13. Hinsley, *British Intelligence*, 1: 253–54, 259–60, 347. There seemed to be a clear civil-military split on the issue of German capacity for an advance through Turkey and the Levant. 1: 361–62.

14. Schreiber et al., *Germany and the Second World War*, 3: 766.

15. Churchill, *The Second World War*, vol. 3, *The Grand Alliance* (Boston: Houghton Mifflin, 1950), 95.

16. Schreiber et al., *Germany and the Second World War*, 3: 757.

17. Playfair, *The Mediterranean and the Middle East*, 1: 373. For a discussion of the logistical shortcomings of a British advance on Tripoli, see Paul Collier, "The Capture of Tripoli in 1941: 'Open Sesame' or Tactical Folly?" *War & Society* 20, no. 1 (May 2002): 94–95.

18. Jackson, *The Battle for North Africa*, 76. The First Armoured Brigade Group, the New Zealand Division, and the Sixth Australian Division from Cyrenaica, plus artillery and support troops, were initially sent. The Seventh Australian Division and the Polish Brigade were to follow. By March 1941, 31,000 men were transported to Greece. In all, 58,364 British soldiers were transported to Greece over six weeks. Playfair, *The Mediterranean and the Middle East*, vol. 2, *The Germans Come to the Help of Their Ally* (London: HMSO, 1956), 79, note 104.

19. Playfair, *The Mediterranean and the Middle East*, 1: 384–87; Churchill, *The Second World War*, vol. 2, *Their Finest Hour* (Boston: Houghton Mifflin, 1950), Chapter 6.

20. Moorehead, *The March to Tunis*, 144.

21. Smith, *Mussolini*, 264–65.

22. Playfair, *The Mediterranean and the Middle East*, 2: 74–79.

23. Robert Crisp, *The Gods Were Neutral* (New York: Norton, 1961), 41.

24. Schreiber et al., *Germany and the Second World War*, 3: 451–69.

25. Misha Glenny, *The Balkans: Nationalism, War and the Great Powers 1804–1999* (New York: Viking, 1999), 402–13, 429–36.

26. Churchill, *The Second World War*, 3: 161–63.

27. Schreiber et al., *Germany and the Second World War*, 3: 479–83.

28. Hinsley, *British Intelligence*, 1: 407–09.

29. Ibid., 1: 409.

30. Crisp, *The Gods Were Neutral*, 142–43.

31. Playfair, *The Mediterranean and the Middle East*, 2: 100. It is not clear whether Wilson had been warned by Ultra or whether this was simply intuition.

32. Anthony Heckstall-Smith and Vice-Admiral H. T. Vaillie-Grohman, *Greek Tragedy, 1941* (New York: Norton, 1961), 197–208; Playfair, *The Mediterranean and the Middle East*, 2: 102–03.

33. Playfair, *The Mediterranean and the Middle East*, 2: 82–105.

34. Ibid., 1: 335, 2: 121.

35. Walter Ansel, *Hitler and the Middle Sea* (Durham, N.C.: Duke University Press, 1972), 13, 44, 46, 81.

36. Schreiber et al., *Germany and the Second World War*, 3: 528.

37. Ibid., 3: 530. Other sources place this decision on 25 April.

38. Ansel, *Hitler and the Middle Sea*, 199, 202, 482.

39. Hinsley, *British Intelligence*, 1: 413, 415–17.

40. Schreiber et al., *Germany and the Second World War*, 3: 533.

41. George Greenfield, *Chasing the Beast: One Man's War* (London: Richard Cohen Books, 1998), 56.

42. Playfair, *The Mediterranean and the Middle East*, 5: 807 and note.

43. Dominick Graham and Shelford Bidwell, *Tug of War: The Battle for Italy: 1943–45* (New York: St. Martin's, 1986), 187.

44. Antony Beevor, *Crete: The Battle and the Resistance* (Boulder, Colo.: Westview, 1994), 82–84.

45. Nigel Hamilton, *Master of the Battlefield: Monty's War Years, 1942–1944* (New York: McGraw-Hill, 1983), 238.

46. General Sir John Hackett, "Student: Colonel-General Kurt Student," in Correlli Barnett, ed., *Hitler's Generals* (New York: William Morrow, 1989), 463–79.

47. Christopher Buckley, *Greece and Crete 1941* (London: HMSO, 1952), 121–26.

48. Hinsley, *British Intelligence*, 1: 415–19; Ansel, *Hitler and the Middle Sea*, 193–95.

49. Ansel, *Hitler and the Middle Sea*, 206, 210–18; Schreiber et al., *Germany and the Second World War*, 3: 534–38.

50. Hinsley, *British Intelligence*, 1: 419.

51. Stephen Bungay, *The Most Dangerous Enemy: A History of the Battle of Britain* (London: Aurum, 2000), 52–53, 258.

52. Ibid., 256–57.

53. Beevor, *Crete*, 91–94.

54. Playfair, *The Mediterranean and the Middle East*, 2: 143.

55. Ronald H. Spector, *At War at Sea: Sailors and Naval Combat in the Twentieth Century* (New York: Viking, 2001), 178–84.

56. Student was sentenced to five years' imprisonment after the war for these war crimes, a sentence that he never served. His apologists claim that he did much to thwart more severe measures ordered by Göring, and that the king of Greece had encouraged partisan-led atrocities in a radio broadcast from Cairo on 24 May 1941. Hackett, "Student," 474–75.

57. Martin van Creveld, *Hitler's Strategy, 1940–1941: The Balkan Clue* (Cambridge: Cambridge University Press, 1973), 182–83.

58. J.R.M. Butler, *Grand Strategy*, vol. 2, *September 1939–June 1941* (London: HMSO, 1957), 515–16.

59. Playfair, *The Mediterranean and the Middle East*, 2: 151.

60. Beevor, *Crete*, 227–28.

61. Churchill, *The Second World War*, 3: 234.

62. Cecil Brown, *Suez to Singapore* (New York: Random House, 1942), 40.

63. For this multisided interpretation of the Balkan struggle, see Stevan K. Pavlowitch, "Neither Heroes nor Traitors: Suggestions for a Reappraisal of the Yugoslav Resistance," in Brian Bond and Ian Roy, eds., *War and Society: A Yearbook of Military History* (London: Croom Helm, 1975), 227–30; Kirk Ford, Jr., *OSS and the Yugoslav Resistance, 1943–1945* (College Station: Texas A&M University Press), Chapter 9.

64. Fifty percent of German oil, all its chrome, 60 percent of bauxite, 24 percent of antimony, and 21 percent of copper came from Balkan sources. Paul N. Hehn, *The German Struggle Against Yugoslav Guerrillas in World War II: German Counter-Insurgency in Yugoslavia, 1941–1943* (New York: Columbia University Press, 1979), 4.

65. Mark Wheeler, "Pariahs to Partisans to Power: the Communist Party of Yugoslavia," in Tony Judt, ed., *Resistance and Revolution in Mediterranean Europe, 1939–1948* (London: Routledge, 1989), 124–25.

66. Glenny, *The Balkans*, 500. Glina again became a scene of conflict and slaughter in 1991 when Serbs and Croats battled for control of the town. Franklin Lindsay, *Beacons in the Night: With the OSS and Tito's Partisans in Wartime Yugoslavia* (Stanford, Calif.: Stanford University Press, 1993), 349.

67. Quoted in Glenny, *The Balkans*, 496.

68. Ibid., 495–506.

69. Aleska Djilas, *The Contested Country: Yugoslav Unity and Communist Revolution, 1919–1953* (Cambridge, Mass.: Harvard University Press, 1991), 146.

70. Milovan Djilas, *Wartime* (New York: Harcourt Brace Jovanovich, 1977), 140, 145.

71. Hehn, *The German Struggle Against Yugoslav Guerrillas*, 8.

72. Winston S. Churchill, *The Second World War*, vol. 5, *Closing the Ring* (Boston: Houghton Mifflin, 1951), 461–62; Walter R. Roberts, *Tito, Mihailović and the Allies, 1941–1945* (New Brunswick, N.J.: Rutgers University Press, 1973), 21; Ford, *OSS and the Yugoslav Resistance*, 173–75.

73. Hehn, *The German Struggle Against Yugoslav Guerrillas*, 12–13.

74. Churchill, *The Second World War*, 5: 461.

75. A. Djilas, *The Contested Country*, 149.

76. Churchill, *The Second World War*, 5: 463 and *passim*.

77. Ibid., 5: 462.

78. Lindsay, *Beacons in the Night*, Chapter 8, describes the prototypical Communist method of indoctrination and control of a village.

79. Hehn, *The German Struggle Against Yugoslav Guerrillas*, 12–13.

80. Lindsay complained that the uniform was simply an outward sign of special status accorded a partisan officer corps that claimed special food, shelter, equipment, and privileges that would not have been tolerated in "bourgeois" British and American forces. *Beacons in the Night*, 196.

81. Ibid., 197, 215.

82. Milovan Djilas, *Tito: The Story from Inside* (London: Weidenfeld and Nicolson, 1981), 12–13; M. Djilas, *Wartime*, 222.

83. M. Djilas, *Wartime*, 7–8.

84. Churchill, *The Second World War*, 5: 462–63.

85. M. Djilas, *Wartime*, 93.

86. Kenneth Macksey, *The Partisans of Europe in the Second World War* (New York: Stein and Day, 1975), 138.

87. M. Djilas, *Tito*, 13–15, 57–58.

88. A. Djilas, *The Contested Country*, 165. See M. Djilas, *Wartime*, 143–44 on Tito's sense of betrayal by Stalin.

89. Indeed, Pavlowitch argues that there was a three-way struggle in Yugoslavia between collaboration, resistance as represented by the Chetniks, and Tito's revolution. "Neither Heroes nor Traitors," 335–37.

90. M. Djilas, *Wartime*, 23, 30, 66.

91. Ibid., 114.

92. Hehn, *The German Struggle Against Yugoslav Guerrillas*, 28.

93. M. Djilas, *Wartime*, 324–25.

94. Lindsay, *Beacons in the Night*, 131; on the problems of air drops of supplies see 78, 89, 101, 126, 129–30, 187.

95. Churchill, *The Second World War*, 5: 535.

96. Many of these points are made by Judt, *Resistance and Revolution*, 14, 19–20.

97. The traditional political parties formed EDAM in December 1942 to

serve as the political basis for a resistance organization, but they lacked the techniques of mass mobilization. Haris Valvianos, "The Greek Communist Party," in Judt, *Resistance and Revolution*, 171; Mark Mazower, *Inside Hitler's Greece: The Experience of Occupation, 1941–44* (New Haven: Yale University Press, 1993), 26–27.

98. Mazower, *Inside Hitler's Greece*, 141.

99. Valvianos, "The Greek Communist Party," 170–71.

100. Mazower, *Inside Hitler's Greece*, 106, 138–40.

101. David H. Close, *The Origins of the Greek Civil War* (London: Longman, 1995), 66–67.

102. Although the deportations were carried out by the Germans, it is clear that certain high-placed Greeks profited by taking over Jewish businesses.

103. Mazower, *Inside Hitler's Greece*, 314–15.

104. Valvianos, "The Greek Communist Party," 169.

105. Close, *The Origins of the Greek Civil War*, 98–99.

106. Ibid., 81.

107. Ibid., 70–71, 82–83.

108. Ibid., 78.

109. Charles R. Shrader, *The Withered Vine: Logistics and the Communist Insurgency in Greece, 1945–1949* (Westport, Conn.: Praeger, 1999), 24–27. For the general lack of preparation of Greek officers to undertake guerrilla warfare, both psychologically and by training, see Close, *The Origins of the Greek Civil War*, 67.

110. Mazower, *Inside Hitler's Greece*, 113; Shrader, *The Withered Vine*, 32–33.

CHAPTER FOUR: ROMMEL'S WAR: A PERFECT BATTLEFIELD

1. Alan Moorehead, *The Desert War* (London: Penguin, 2000), 304.

2. Robert Crisp, *Brazen Chariots: An Account of Tank Warfare in the Western Desert, November–December 1941* (New York: Norton, 1960), 159.

3. Ronald Lewin, *The Life and Death of the Afrika Korps* (London: Corgi Books, 1979), 24.

4. *Krieg Ohne Hass* ("War Without Hate") was the title of Rommel's memoir of the desert war. Gerhard Schreiber, Bernd Stegemann, and Detlef Vogel, edited by the Militärgeschichtliches Forshungsamt, *Germany and the Second World War*, vol. 3, *The Mediterranean, South-East Europe and North Africa, 1939–1941* (Oxford: Clarendon, 1995), 767. Schreiber does not subscribe to this interpretation of the desert war as a purely operational phenomenon.

5. Winston S. Churchill, *The Second World War*, vol. 3, *The Grand Alliance* (Boston: Houghton Mifflin, 1950), 200.

6. Lewin, *Life and Death of the Afrika Korps*, 25. "Highly admired by both sides, not merely for his inspirational leadership and skill but also for his charisma and chivalry," writes American historian Martin Blumenson, "Rom-

mel was a throwback to the medieval knight in his personal traits." "Rommel," in Correlli Barnett, ed., *Hitler's Generals: Authoritative Portraits of the Men Who Waged Hitler's War* (New York: William Morrow, 1989), 293. German Major Hans von Luck insisted that the two antagonists in the desert "understood each other. The prevailing atmosphere was one of respect and fair play." *Panzer Commander: The Memoirs of Colonel Hans von Luck* (New York: Dell, 1989), 96. For Rommel's refusal to countenance criminal orders from Hitler, see David Irving, *The Trail of the Fox: The Life of Field-Marshal Erwin Rommel* (London: Book Club Associates, 1977), 5.

    7. Klaus Schmider, "The Mediterranean in 1940–1941: Crossroads of Lost Opportunities?" *War and Society* 15, no. 2 (October 1997): 28, 30.

    8. Irving, *Trail of the Fox*, 6.

    9. Ibid., 67.

    10. Horst Boog, Werner Rahn, Reinhard Stumpf, and Bernd Wegner, *Germany and the Second World War*, vol. 6, *The Global War: Widening of the Conflict into a World War and the Shift of the Initiative, 1941–1943* (Oxford: Clarendon, 2001), 119, 127.

    11. Irving, *Trail of the Fox*, 13–18; Blumenson, "Rommel," 296.

    12. Irving, *Trail of the Fox*, 22.

    13. Ibid., 27.

    14. Jürgen Förster, "Motivation and Indoctrination in the Wehrmacht, 1933–45," in Paul Addison and Angus Calder, eds., *Time to Kill: The Soldier's Experience of War in the West, 1939–1945* (London: Pimlico, 1997), 265.

    15. Irving, *Trail of the Fox*, 22–23.

    16. Ibid., 24.

    17. Förster, "Motivation and Indoctrination in the Wehrmacht," 267.

    18. Jürgen Förster, "The Dynamics of *Volksgemeinschaft*: The Effectiveness of the German Military Establishment in the Second World War," in Williamson Murray and Allan R. Millett, eds., *Military Effectiveness*, vol. 3, *The Second World War* (Boston: Unwin Hyman, 1988), 210.

    19. Irving, *Trail of the Fox*, 26–36.

    20. Ibid., 38–51.

    21. Schreiber et al., *Germany and the Second World War*, 3: 693.

    22. Irving, *Trail of the Fox*, 51–53.

    23. Churchill, *The Second World War*, 3: 200.

    24. Förster, "The Dynamics of *Volksgemeinschaft*," 200, 202, 204, 209.

    25. Irving, *Trail of the Fox*, 22.

    26. Förster, "The Dynamics of *Volksgemeinschaft*," 202.

    27. Irving, *Trail of the Fox*, 67.

    28. Rommel later lamented that had the five army corps and one Luftwaffe corps sent to conquer the Balkans in the spring of 1941, Operation Marita, been given to him, he would have been able to achieve his goals and also made the Balkan campaign unnecessary. Here Rommel overlooks the fact that the Germans and Italians lacked the means to transport so many troops to North

Africa. Also, he would have faced considerably stronger British forces in North Africa, as over 58,000 British troops had been withdrawn from Cyrenaica precisely to deal with the German threat to Greece. Nor was Hitler eager to send troops to North Africa that he intended to use for Barbarossa in June 1941. Schreiber et al., *Germany and the Second World War*, 3: 457–58, 657–58.

29. To criticize Rommel was tantamount to criticizing the German army, which many preferred to see as a band of courageous men ordered into battle by a lunatic leader. Schreiber et al., *Germany and the Second World War*, 3: 693.

30. Irving, *Trail of the Fox*, 54–56, 62.

31. Churchill, *The Second World War*, 3: 200.

32. The Fifth Light Motorized Division included a strong armored reconnaissance unit, a twelve-gun field artillery battery, an antiaircraft unit, and a regiment of two motorized machine-gun battalions, with attached engineers, antitank guns, and armored troop carriers. It contained two tank-hunting battalions (*Panzerjäger*) armed with the formidable 88 mm guns. Its armored regiment consisted of two panzer battalions of 70 light and 80 medium tanks with 50 mm or 75 mm guns. It also had an attached air reconnaissance squadron.

33. Irving, *Trail of the Fox*, 58.

34. Schreiber et al., *Germany and the Second World War*, 3: 654–56; Irving, *Trail of the Fox*, 55–56.

35. I.S.O. Playfair, *The Mediterranean and the Middle East*, vol. 2, *The Germans Come to the Help of Their Ally* (London: HMSO, 1956), 174.

36. Martin van Creveld, *Fighting Power: German and U.S. Army Performance, 1939–1945* (Westport, Conn: Greenwood, 1982), 163.

37. Geoffrey P. Megargee, *Inside Hitler's High Command* (Lawrence: University Press of Kansas, 2000), 231.

38. Förster, "The Dynamics of *Volksgemeinschaft*," 207.

39. Omar Bartov, *Hitler's Army: Soldiers, Nazis and War in the Third Reich* (New York: Oxford University Press, 1991), 117–18.

40. Gerhard Schreiber, "Italy and the Mediterranean in the Power-Political Calculations of German Naval Leaders, 1919–45," in John B. Hattendorf, ed., *Naval Policy and Strategy in the Mediterranean: Past, Present and Future* (London: Frank Cass, 2000), 118, 120.

41. Dennis L. Bark and David R. Gress, *From Shadow to Substance, 1945–1963* (Oxford: Basil Blackwell, 1989), 5, 44, 80–81.

42. Megargee, *Inside Hitler's High Command*, 233.

43. Förster, "The Dynamics of *Volksgemeinschaft*," 204–05.

44. Hitler commanded the army through the Oberkommando der Wehrmacht (OKH) under Wilhelm Keitel. The OKH Operations Branch under Alfred Jodl was Hitler's military staff for formulating strategic goals. Keitel took over the administrative powers of the army high command in December 1941, when Hitler assumed direct command over the army and expanded the OKW Operations Branch. This disaggregated the army high command, taking

away many functions of the Army General Staff. Franz Halder, chief of the Army General Staff, forfeited his function of advising Hitler on the conduct of the war to the chiefs of the Wehrmacht high command and the Wehrmacht operations staff. The Army General Staff was responsible for the Eastern Front, while Jodl's Operations Branch looked after all other theaters, including the Mediterranean. After the Allied landings in North Africa led to Franz Halder's dismissal, Hitler in effect had two rival army chiefs of staff—Jodl and Kurt Zeitzler (replaced in 1944 by Heinz Guderian). Förster, "The Dynamics of *Volksgemeinschaft*," 182; Boog et al., *Germany and the Second World War*, 6: 121, 131.

45. Schreiber, "Italy and the Mediterranean," 126–28.

46. Bernhard R. Kroener, Rolf-Dieter Müller, and Hans Umbreit, *Germany and the Second World War*, vol. 5, *Organization and Mobilization of the German Sphere of Power* (Oxford: Clarendon, 2000), 1001–1139.

47. In 1941 the Germans placed face-hardened steel armor plates on their PzKw III and IV medium tanks. The PzKw IIIs mounted a 5 cm gun from 1941. By the end of 1941, the Germans did away with plates altogether and increased the depth of their frontal armor by 20 mm. A long-barreled 5 cm gun was placed on PzKw IIIs, which began to arrive for the Battle of Gazala in May 1942. The PzKw IV "Special" was given a "long" 7.5 cm gun, which made them an "outstanding good" weapon. Fortunately for the British, only a small number arrived in the summer of 1942. That summer the Germans introduced a "hollow charge" shell for low-velocity antitank weapons. Playfair, *The Mediterranean and the Middle East*, 2: 435–38.

48. The PzKw II was lightly armored and used mainly for reconnaissance. The PzKw IV was a support tank with a 7.5 mm gun that was most effective against infantry. The PzKw III was the workhorse of the Panzergruppe in the desert. Its 5 cm gun fired an armor-piercing shell that could disable a British tank at short range. The Italian light tanks were considered worthless, while the medium M13/40 was slow, armed with a 47 mm gun, and poorly armored. Playfair, *The Mediterranean and the Middle East* (Sept. 1941–Sept. 1942), *British Fortunes Reach Their Lowest Ebb* (London: HMSO, 1960), 27.

49. Christopher F. Foss, ed., *The Encyclopedia of Tanks and Armored Fighting Vehicles* (San Diego: Thunder Bay Press, 2002), 241.

50. Stephen Bungay, *The Most Dangerous Enemy: A History of the Battle of Britain* (London: Aurum Press, 200), 263–67.

51. Richard Overy, *Why the Allies Won* (New York: Norton, 1995), 217–20.

52. Megargee, *Inside Hitler's High Command*, 235.

53. Playfair, *The Mediterranean and the Middle East*, 2: 5.

54. Schreiber et al., *Germany and the Second World War*, 3: 708–09.

55. Greenfield, *Chasing the Beast*, 55, 84.

56. Schreiber et al., *Germany and the Second World War*, 3: 673–75; Irving, *Trail of the Fox*, 76.

57. Irving, *Trail of the Fox*, 66.

58. Boog et al., *Germany and the Second World War*, 6: 553–54.

59. Hans-Otto Behrendt, *Rommel's Intelligence in the Desert Campaign, 1941–1943* (London: William Kimber, 1985), 68–69.

60. B. H. Liddell Hart, ed., *The Rommel Papers* (London, 1953), 107; Irving, *Trail of the Fox*, 69.

61. Harold E. Raugh, Jr., *Wavell in the Middle East, 1939–1941: A Study in Generalship* (London: Brassey's, 1993), 190.

62. Schreiber et al., *Germany and the Second World War*, 3: 676.

63. Playfair, *The Mediterranean and the Middle East*, 2: 2.

64. F. H. Hinsley, *British Intelligence in the Second World War: Its Influence on Strategy and Operations*, vol. 1 (New York: Cambridge University Press, 1979), 390–92; Churchill, *The Second World War*, 3: 197–203.

65. Playfair, *The Mediterranean and the Middle East*, 2: 2–6; Churchill, *The Second World War*, 2: 197, 200–02, Raugh, *Wavell in the Middle East*, 185–86.

66. Hinsley, *British Intelligence*, 1: 392–94.

67. "In the battle," Wavell complained, "[Neame] seemed to me never to have any idea whatever where his troops were, or to make any particular effort to find out." Gambier-Parry he found to be "equally inept," a "complete failure." Raugh, *Wavell in the Middle East*, 256.

68. Playfair, *The Mediterranean and the Middle East*, 2: 32; Raugh, *Wavell in the Middle East*, 188–89.

69. Playfair, *The Mediterranean and the Middle East*, 2: 10.

70. Ibid. 2: 31.

71. Behrendt, *Rommel's Intelligence*, 73; Schreiber et al., *Germany and the Second World War*, 3: 679.

72. Playfair, *The Mediterranean and the Middle East*, 2: 34.

73. Hinsley, *British Intelligence*, 1: 395.

74. Playfair, *The Mediterranean and the Middle East*, 2: 35–37.

75. Ibid., 2: 38–39; Frank Harrison, *Tobruk: The Great Siege Reassessed* (London: Brockhampton, 1991), 39–63.

76. Irving, *Trail of the Fox*, 81–86; Playfair, *The Mediterranean and the Middle East*, 2: 37–39, for attacks on Tobruk.

77. Schreiber et al., *Germany and the Second World War*, 3: 680–86.

78. Ibid., 3: III, 671–72, 686–87.

79. Harrison, *Tobruk*, 86–87.

80. Playfair, *The Mediterranean and the Middle East*, 2: 153–57; Irving, *Trail of the Fox*, 89; Schreiber et al., *Germany and the Second World War*, 3: 716, on supplies actually getting through in 1941.

81. Schreiber et al., *Germany and the Second World War*, 3: 689–94.

82. Alan Moorehead, *The March to Tunis: The North African War, 1940–1943* (New York: Harper and Row, 1965), 142.

83. Playfair, *The Mediterranean and the Middle East*, 2: 157–58, on life in Tobruk; Irving, *Trail of the Fox*, 90.

84. Hinsley, *British Intelligence*, 2: 397.

85. Behrendt, *Rommel's Intelligence*, 82.

86. Hinsley, *British Intelligence*, 1: 398–99; Playfair, *The Mediterranean and the Middle East*, 2: 161–62.

87. Schreiber et al., *Germany and the Second World War*, 3: 699–700.

88. Irving, *Trail of the Fox*, 94–95.

89. David Hunt, *A Don at War* (London: William Kimber, 1966), 95.

90. Lieutenant General Sir Francis Tuker, *Approach to Battle* (London: Cassell, 1963), 14.

91. Churchill, *The Second World War*, 3: 339; Playfair, *The Mediterranean and the Middle East*, 2: 172–73.

92. Behrendt, *Rommel's Intelligence*, 83.

93. Playfair, *The Mediterranean and the Middle East*, 2: 172–74; Churchill, *The Second World War*, 3: 342.

94. Behrendt, *Rommel's Intelligence*, 84–86.

95. Schreiber et al., *Germany and the Second World War*, 3: 702–03. Irving gives a much more optimistic assessment of German success. *Trail of the Fox*, 100–01.

96. Schreiber et al., *Germany and the Second World War*, vol. 3: 704–07; Irving, *Trail of the Fox*, 101.

97. Churchill, *The Second World War*, 3: 343.

98. Raugh, *Wavell in the Middle East*, 203–04.

99. Churchill, *The Second World War*, 3: 250.

100. Churchill, *The Second World War*, 3: 344. Playfair, *The Mediterranean and the Middle East*, 2: 243–46, offers a more favorable assessment of Wavell. Raugh, *Wavell in the Middle East*, 244–50, argues that Wavell was not tired. Churchill was the victim of his own impossible demands.

101. Moorehead, *The March to Tunis*, 210, 212–13.

102. Churchill, *The Second World War*, 3: 135.

103. Nigel Hamilton, *Monty: The Making of a General, 1887–1942* (New York: McGraw-Hill, 1981), 436. In his memoirs, Churchill writes that Auchinleck was his suggestion, to which his senior commanders did not object. Hamilton writes that Auchinleck was the candidate of General Alan Brooke, the commander-in-chief of home forces and future chief of the Imperial General Staff. Ibid., 520.

104. Moorehead believed that one mistake Auchinleck made was to leave his vivacious American wife behind in India, so as better to concentrate on his duties. One unfortunate result was that this deprived Auchinleck of one means to connect with his milieu, and increased his isolation. In the end, not only was Auchinleck defeated by Rommel, but his wife ran off with a fellow officer. Moorehead, *The March to Tunis*, 210–11.

105. Winston S. Churchill, *The Second World War*, vol. 4, *The Hinge of Fate* (Boston: Houghton Mifflin 1950), 458.

106. Before 1932, a select few upper-class Indians were sent to Sandhurst,

to become King's Commissioned Officers, or KCOs. Graduates of Dehra Dun were "Indian Commissioned Officers" (ICOs) who, unlike the KCOs, were not allowed to command British troops. Stephen P. Cohen, *The Indian Army: Its Contribution to the Development of a Nation* (Delhi: Oxford University Press, 1990), 114–19. The venerated "memsahibs" were now expected to socialize with Hindustani-speaking spouses of Indian officers, whom they equated with house servants. As a result, many of the most socially and racially conscious British officers sought sanctuary in a handful of non-Indianizing units. Efforts to limit Indian officer recruitment to the "martial classes"—Punjabi Moslems, Sikhs, Rajputs, Jats, Mahrattas, and Gurkhas—or to the athletically gifted but often intellectually challenged sons of Indian princes or rich zamindar landowners was sidetracked by Indian and British reformers, who insisted that sons of the urban middle classes who scored well in entrance exams, including allegedly "unheroic" Bengalis and Madrassis, be included. Although officers could be assigned to any regiment regardless of their backgrounds, units tended to be segregated according to the Hindu, Sikh, or Moslem recruitment of the soldiers. A military academy was opened at Dehra Dun, which offered training to Indian officers that many considered superior to Sandhurst.

107. Ibid., 139.

108. Ibid., 125–31.

109. Philip Mason, *A Matter of Honor: An Account of the Indian Army, Its Officers and Men* (New York: Penguin, 1976), 511–13; Gerard Douds, "'Matter of Honour': Indian Troops in the North African and Italian Theatres," in Addison and Calder, *Time to Kill*, 115–28; Percival Spear, *A History of India*, vol. 2 (London: Penguin, 1978), 215.

110. Philip Warner, "Auchinleck," in John Keegan, ed., *Churchill's Generals* (New York: Grove Weidenfeld, 1991), 141.

111. Playfair, *The Mediterranean and the Middle East*, 3: xv.

112. Hinsley, *British Intelligence*, 2: 279–80. At this time, the British were able to read only the Luftwaffe intercepts. But even these spoke eloquently about Rommel's supply problems.

113. David French, *Raising Churchill's Army: The British Army and the War against Germany, 1919–1945* (Oxford: Oxford University Press, 2000), 227–30, 264.

114. The expression is Eric Newby's, describing the power structure in his POW camp in Italy. Eric Newby, *Love and War in the Apennines* (London: Hodder and Stoughton, 1971), 37.

115. Playfair, *The Mediterranean and the Middle East*, 3: 285.

116. Moorehead, *The March to Tunis*, 4–5. Montgomery called Auchinleck's chief of staff, General T. Corbett, "the stupidest officer in the Indian army; he has no brains at all." Monty's chief of staff Freddy de Guingand called Corbett "a complete fathead." Churchill was greatly disturbed when told in July 1942 that the "uniquely stupid" Corbett had been designated by Auchinleck to be the new Eighth Army head. Hamilton, *Monty*, 570–71; Nigel Hamilton,

Master of the Battlefield: Monty's War Years, 1941–1944 (New York: McGraw-Hill, 1983), 378.

117. Hamilton, *Master of the Battlefield*, 378.

118. French, *Raising Churchill's Army*, 215, 230–32, 264.

119. Hamilton, *Master of the Battlefield*, 378.

120. Hamilton, *Monty*, 436.

121. One feels that Montgomery probably had Auchinleck in mind when, in November 1942, he denounced "Generals who become depressed when things are not going well, and who lack the drive to get things done, and the moral courage and resolution to see their plan through to the end." In Monty's view, such men were "worse than useless—they are a menace—since any lack of moral courage, or any sign of wavering or hesitation, has very quick repercussions down below. To win battles you require good Commanders in the senior ranks, and good senior staff officers; all of these must know their stuff." Hamilton, *Master of the Battlefield*, 50.

122. Playfair, *The Mediterranean and the Middle East*, 3: 4.

123. Hinsley, *British Intelligence*, 2: 283–85. Under German pressure, the Italians switched to a commercially available Swedish C38 cipher machine, which the British broke with regularity.

124. Ibid., 2: 287–88.

125. Schreiber et al., *Germany and the Second World War*, 3: 712–20, 716 for a chart of tonnage losses for 1941.

126. Panzer divisions, like the Fifteenth and the Twenty-first, consisted of a two-battalion tank regiment, a reconnaissance unit, a machine-gun battalion, a *Panzerjäger* or antitank unit, an engineering battalion, and a three-battalion artillery regiment. Each had a mobile infantry regiment. The Ninetieth Light consisted of seven battalions of infantry. The Ariete Armored Division had three tank battalions, a motorized Bersaliere regiment, and attached artillery and engineers. See Playfair, *The Mediterranean and the Middle East*, 3: 29.

127. Ibid., 3: 435–36.

128. Hinsley, *British Intelligence*, 2: 298–99.

129. Schreiber et al., *Germany and the Second World War*, 3: 725–26. See Hinsley, *British Intelligence*, 2: 290–91, for higher estimates of Axis aircraft.

130. The Thirteenth Corps, the old Western Desert Task Force under Godwin-Austen, contained the New Zealand Division, the Fourth Indian Division, and the First Armoured Division. The Thirtieth Corps under C.W.M. Norrie contained the Seventh Armoured Division, the Fourth Armoured Brigade Group, the First South African Division, and the Twenty-second Guards Brigade. The Seventieth Division and two brigades, including a Polish infantry brigade, held Tobruk.

131. Major General D. Belcham, *All in a Day's March* (London, 1978), 98.

132. Moorehead, *The March to Tunis*, 217, 213.

133. Allegedly the Stuarts got their nickname when one British tank driver, during a test drive, described the tank as a "honey." Crisp, *Brazen Chariots*, 16–

17, 47–48; Schreiber et al., *Germany and the Second World War*, 3: 729; Playfair, *The Mediterranean and the Middle East*, 3: 437.

134. Joint air support control teams were established at each corps and armored division HQ. RAF forward air control officers attached to each brigade could radio the joint air support control team for air support from a bank of aircraft controlled by the Desert Air Force. The flaw in the system was that it would take the planes up to two hours to arrive. Once the planes arrived overhead, the forward air control officers had radio sets that allowed them to communicate directly with the pilots, who in turn could inform the units about enemy positions. Tedder and Coningham also improved the mobility of ground organizations to allow DAF units to follow the ebb and flow of battle in the desert.

135. The Y Service was defective at this stage of the war in direction finding, so that enemy transmitters could not easily be located, and in the interpretation of German signals, which was more difficult than interpreting their "self-explanatory" Italian counterparts. Technical intelligence on German armaments was also improving. Hinsley, *British Intelligence*, 2: 289–90, 293, 295–98.

136. Rommel planned his attack on Tobruk for 23 November. Ibid., 2: 300, 304.

137. Ibid., 2: 294.

138. Behrendt, *Rommel's Intelligence*, 99–100; Playfair, *The Mediterranean and the Middle East*, 3: 21.

139. Playfair, *The Mediterranean and the Middle East*, 3: 102.

140. Moorehead, *The March to Tunis*, 221.

141. In many respects, this willingness to disperse the tanks and the slow realization of the need for inter-arm cooperation was a legacy of the facile early victories over the Italians, which the British were slow to unlearn. French, *Raising Churchill's Army*, 215.

142. Irving argues that it was Rommel's failure to react to the British advance on Gabr Saleh that forced them to push forward, thus splitting their forces. *Trail of the Fox*, 121.

143. The German tactic was for the panzers to advance in a box, with artillery in the middle. When they encountered the British, the box halted and tanks deployed on a broad front to invite an attack by British armor. As the British tanks pressed home their attacks, the panzers withdrew slowly, opening the British to an ambush by antitank guns that had deployed on the flank. Meanwhile, the panzers on the disengaged side of the box would swing around to attack the British from the rear. French, *Raising Churchill's Army*, 218.

144. Crisp, *Brazen Chariots*, 30.

145. Irving, *Trail of the Fox*, 121–22.

146. Harrison, *Tobruk*, 217, 267–68.

147. Hinsley, *British Intelligence*, 2: 306–07.

148. Ibid., 2: 307; Playfair, *The Mediterranean and the Middle East*, 3: 52.

149. Moorehead, *The March to Tunis*, 227–28.

150. This was in part because it was difficult to make sense of the Sigint intercepts and in part because the Germans had overrun the forward air bases, forcing the RAF to retreat and depriving the British of air reconnaissance. Hinsley, *British Intelligence*, 2: 309; Playfair, *The Mediterranean and the Middle East*, 3: 55.

151. Churchill, *The Second World War*, 3: 567–69. Cunningham had allegedly "lost his nerve." French, *Raising Churchill's Army*, 229.

152. Crisp, *Brazen Chariots*, 118–119.

153. French, *Raising Churchill's Army*, 229–30.

154. Crisp, *Brazen Chariots*, 88–89.

155. Ibid., 70–71, 88; Moorehead, *The March to Tunis*, 228–29.

156. Crisp, *Brazen Chariots*, 103.

157. Irving argues that Rommel was forced to return after his corps commanders ordered a retreat against his orders. *Trail of the Fox*, 130–31.

158. Hinsley, *British Intelligence*, 2: 311.

159. Ibid., 2: 321.

160. Churchill, *The Second World War*, 3: 575.

161. Crisp, *Brazen Chariots*, 31.

162. Behrendt, *Rommel's Intelligence*, 141–42.

163. Playfair, *The Mediterranean and the Middle East*, 3: 36–37, 70–71, 76, 102.

164. Moorehead, *The March to Tunis*, 234–35.

165. Churchill, *The Second World War*, 3: 577.

166. Hinsley, *British Intelligence*, 2: 329–30; Irving, *Trail of the Fox*, 142; Boog et al., *Germany and the Second World War*, 6: 636.

167. Moorehead, *The March to Tunis*, 248. For an account of Crusader from the German perspective, see Schreiber et al., *Germany and the Second World War*, 3: 725–52, 715–24.

168. Hinsley, *British Intelligence*, 2: 332–36.

169. Playfair, *The Mediterranean and the Middle East*, 3: 143.

170. German intelligence was aware that the British Seventh Armoured Division had been replaced by the inexperienced First Armoured, while the Indian Fourth had few forward elements in position. It estimated that German superiority would last until 25 January. Encouraged by this intelligence, Rommel decided to attack. Boog et al., *Germany and the Second World War*, 6: 636–37.

171. Hinsley, *British Intelligence*, 2: 337–38.

172. The Axis had lost 21,712 Italian and 14,760 German troops to 17,700 British casualties. The British losses in tanks and vehicles were considerably higher than those of the Germans. Boog et al., *Germany and the Second World War*, 6: 652–53; for the advance across Cyrenaica, see 649–52.

173. Playfair, *The Mediterranean and the Middle East*, 3: 135–54.

CHAPTER FIVE: "THE GREAT KINGDOM OF TERROR"

1. F. H. Hinsley, *British Intelligence in the Second World War: Its Influence on Strategy and Operations*, vol. 1 (New York: Cambridge University Press, 1979), 179–88.

2. Winston S. Churchill, *The Second World War*, vol. 4, *The Hinge of Fate* (Boston: Houghton Mifflin, 1950), 35.

3. Robert O'Neill, "Japan and British Security in the Pacific," and Michael Carver, "Churchill and the Defence Chiefs," in Robert Blake and William Roger Louis, eds., *Churchill: A Major New Assessment of His Life in Peace and War* (New York: Norton, 1993), 288, 369; I.S.O. Playfair, *The Mediterranean and the Middle East*, vol. 3, *British Fortunes Reach Their Lowest Ebb* (London: HMSO, 1960), 200–02.

4. Charles A. Jellison, *Besieged: The World War II Ordeal of Malta, 1940–1942* (Hanover, N.H.: University Press of New England, 1984), 70–74.

5. Ibid., 166–67, 174–82, 242–44; Horst Boog, Werner Rahn, Reinhard Stumpf, and Bernd Wegner, *Germany and the Second World War*, vol. 6, *The Global War: Widening of the Conflict into a World War and the Shift of the Initiative, 1941–1943* (Oxford: Clarendon, 2001), 654–57.

6. Boog et al., *Germany and the Second World War*, 6: 656, states that "many . . . were shot down," but gives no figures.

7. Hinsley, *British Intelligence*, 2: 341–46, 349.

8. Auchinleck's main argument centered upon British inferiority, both qualitative and quantitative, in tanks. Ibid., 2: 350–58.

9. Jellison, *Besieged*, 70–77, 85–86, 94, 103, 127–32, 140–41, 149, 151–52, 157–63, 166–67, 171–73, 175, 179, 183, 189, 202, 213–14, 339; Playfair, *The Mediterranean and the Middle East*, 3: 179, 182–86.

10. Playfair, *The Mediterranean and the Middle East*, 3: 204.

11. Albert Kesselring, *Kesselring: A Soldier's Record* (New York: William Morrow, 1954), 143.

12. Playfair, *The Mediterranean and the Middle East*, 3: 193–95, 219.

13. The Germans were persuaded that an invasion of Malta must be primarily an Italian operation. But the two Axis partners could not agree on a unified plan. Boog et al., *Germany and the Second World War*, 6: 657–60.

14. Hinsley, *British Intelligence*, 2: 360, 366.

15. Boog et al., *Germany and the Second World War*, 6: 668.

16. Alan Moorehead, *The Desert War: The North African Campaign, 1940–1943* (London: Penguin, 2001), 338.

17. Basil Liddell Hart, ed., *The Rommel Papers* (London, 1953), 204.

18. David French, *Raising Churchill's Army: The British Army and the War against Germany, 1919–1945* (Oxford: Oxford University Press, 2000), 248.

19. Playfair, *The Mediterranean and the Middle East*, 3: 216–18.

20. Lumsden of the First Armoured Division and Messervy of the Seventh did not get along, and neither liked the corps commander Norrie. Gott,

commander of the Thirteenth Corps, had his hands full refereeing disputes between his division commanders. French, *Raising Churchill's Army*, 230.

21. Ibid., 235.

22. Boog et al., *Germany and the Second World War*, 6: 671.

23. Hinsley, *British Intelligence*, 2: 367; French, *Raising Churchill's Army*, 231. However, the German official history insists that British intelligence warnings were more fragmentary, and that Rommel's attack occurred before the British could put a system in place to evaluate and disseminate the fruits of the "cracking" of German radio intercepts. Boog et al., *Germany and the Second World War*, 6: 666–67.

24. Moorehead, *The Desert War*, 344.

25. Ibid., 345.

26. Ibid., 351.

27. Kesselring, *Kesselring*, 146.

28. Axis leaders attributed the stiff resistance of the Bir Hacheim garrison to the fact that they were political refugees who fought hard because they expected no quarter. Ciano, *Diaries*, 497 (11 June 1942). The quote from Lieutenant Kämpf is taken from Boog et al., *Germany and the Second World War*, 6: 690, note 139.

29. W.G.F. Jackson, *The Battle for North Africa, 1940–43* (New York: Mason/Charter, 1975), 217–20.

30. Boog et al., *Germany and the Second World War*, 6: 692.

31. Playfair, *The Mediterranean and the Middle East*, 3: 247.

32. Moorehead, *The Desert War*, 371–72.

33. Ibid., 374.

34. For a description of the final siege, see Boog et al., *Germany and the Second World War*, 6: 692–99; Playfair, *The Mediterranean and the Middle East*, 3: 267–76.

35. Moorehead, *The Desert War*, 381.

36. J.A.I. Agar-Hamilton and L.C.F. Turner, *Crisis in the Desert, May–July 1942* (Cape Town: Oxford University Press, 1952), 276. British historian Philip Warner attributes this to a scurrilous rumor begun by Montgomery. Philip Warner, "Auchinleck," in John Keegan, ed., *Churchill's Generals* (New York: Grove Weidenfeld, 1991), 140. However, Auchineck did make plans to withdraw his headquarters to Gaza. Nor did he exude a "backs-to-the-wall" confidence. Playfair, *The Mediterranean and the Middle East*, 3: 333–34. See also Nigel Hamilton, *Monty: The Making of a General, 1887–1943* (New York: McGraw-Hill, 1981), 593–94, 608–09, 635, for Auchinleck's plans to move GHQ to Jerusalem.

37. Alan Moorehead, *The March to Tunis: The North African War, 1940–1943* (New York: Harper and Row, 1965), 353–56.

38. Moorehead, *The Desert War*, 385.

39. Peter Mansfield, *The British in Egypt* (New York: Holt, Rinehart and Winston, 1971), 275–79; D. A. Farnie, *East and West of Suez: The Suez Canal in*

History, 1854–1956 (Oxford: Clarendon, 1969), 628–29; Lukasz Hirszowicz, *The Third Reich and the Arab East* (London: Routledge & Kegan Paul, 1966), 241–42.

40. Churchill, *The Second World War,* 4: 383, 395–96.

41. Shipping losses at Tobruk were 20 percent in August. Martin van Creveld, *Supplying War: Logistics from Wallenstein to Patton* (Cambridge: Cambridge University Press, 1977), 197–99.

42. Churchill, *The Second World War,* 4: 432.

43. Hew Strachan, *The Politics of the British Army* (Oxford: Clarendon, 1997), 161–62.

44. Kenneth S. Davis, *FDR: The War President, 1940–1943* (New York: Random House, 2000), 523, 529–30, 544–45, 553–54.

45. Boog et al., *Germany and the Second World War,* 6: 706.

46. Axis plans to invade Malta were incomplete. Hitler opposed the operation. Who could predict what state the Luftwaffe would be in following an invasion of Malta? Ibid., 6: 713–20.

47. F. W. Deakin, *The Brutal Friendship: Mussolini, Hitler, and the Fall of Italian Fascism* (New York: Harper and Row, 1962), 18–24. Hitler objected that the Italians could not keep Herkules a secret, that Kesselring's plan was too complex for them to carry out, that the Italian navy would turn tail at the first sight of a British warship, leaving the paratroopers stranded, and that Rommel could be supplied via Crete. But Hitler's real problem, according to American historian Walter Ansel, was that he was "water shy." Ansel, *Hitler and the Middle Sea* (Durham, N.C.: Duke University Press, 1972), 477–83. For an overall assessment of the Malta-versus-Egypt debate, see Boog et al., *Germany and the Second World War,* 6: 706–10.

48. Jellison, *Besieged,* 232–34, 252–57. On Pedestal, see Peter Shankland and Anthony Hunter, *Malta Convoy* (New York: Ives Washburn, 1961). Losses of supplies began to go up as soon as the air offensive against Malta was lifted, and reached their peak in August–October 1942, at the time of El Alamein. Boog et al., *Germany and the Second World War,* 6: 834; Gerhard Schreiber, Bernd Stegemann, and Detlef Vogel, edited by the Militärgeschichtliches Forschungsamt, *Germany and the Second World War,* vol. 3, *The Mediterranean, South-East Europe and North Africa, 1939–1941* (Oxford: Clarendon, 1995), 716–17.

49. Boog et al., *Germany and the Second World War,* 6: 720 and notes.

50. Van Creveld, *Supplying War,* 195–96, 198–201.

51. Between June 1940 and January 1943, 80 percent of vehicles, 88 percent of weapons and equipment, 81 percent of "dry cargo," 82 percent of fuel, 86 percent of other cargo, and 91.6 percent of troops reached their destination. Boog et al., *Germany and the Second World War,* 6: 838.

52. Hinsley, *British Intelligence,* 2: 417–24; Ralph Bennett, *Ultra and Mediterranean Strategy* (New York: William Morrow, 1989), 79–80, 137–38, 159–60.

For instance, of seven tankers dispatched to Rommel in August 1942, four were sunk. When Rommel launched his attack on the British position at El Alamein in late July, he had fuel for only 150 miles per troop-transporting vehicle, 250 for other vehicles. Playfair, *The Mediterranean and the Middle East*, 3: 350, 382. Van Creveld counters that at the time of the First Battle of El Alamein, one-third of Rommel's fuel stocks were still at Benghazi. *Supplying War*, 200. "Shipment by sea remained of prime importance where operationally effective supplies—fuel, arms, ammunition—were concerned," concludes the German official history. "What counted was not so much that the supply system as a whole functioned, but that *operationally effective* supplies eventually ran out." Boog et al., *Germany and the Second World War*, 6: 839.

53. Hinsley, *British Intelligence*, 2: 417–21.

54. See Alan J. Levine, *The War Against Rommel's Supply Lines, 1942–1943* (Westport, Conn.: Praeger, 1999), 184–85. See Schreiber et al., *Germany and the Second World War*, 3: 716, for Axis tonnage losses in 1943. American historian Walter Ansel argues that the Allies would never have attempted Torch had Malta not been in their possession. Ansel, *Hitler and the Middle Sea*, 484. For instance, 46 of 53 German transports employed in the Mediterranean were lost in 1941 and 1942. The Italian merchant marine was also devastated. Boog et al., *Germany and the Second World War*, 6: 837.

55. Playfair, *The Mediterranean and the Middle East*, 3: 339, 379–82; Levine, *The War Against Rommel's Supply Lines*, 24.

56. Major General John Harding objected that this battle was merely a "probing operation" on Rommel's part and "far too disjointed" to dignify with the title of "First Alamein." Hamilton, *Monty: The Making of a General*, 592.

57. Boog et al., *Germany and the Second World War*, 6: 712.

58. Behrendt, *Rommel's Intelligence*, 161; Boog et al., *Germany and the Second World War*, 6: 728.

59. British forces at El Alamein consisted of the Second New Zealand and First South African Divisions, both badly battered in previous fighting, the First Armoured Division, two Indian brigades, and heterogeneous combat groups. The Ninth Australian Division was being dispatched to the front. Boog et al., *Germany and the Second World War*, 6: 725.

60. Hinsley, *British Intelligence*, 2: 392–93.

61. Playfair, *The Mediterranean and the Middle East*, 3: 338–39.

62. Kesselring, *Kesselring*, 151.

63. Boog et al., *Germany and the Second World War*, 6: 732.

64. Jackson, *The Battle for North Africa*, 260.

65. Boog et al., *Germany and the Second World War*, 6: 732–40.

66. Hamilton, *Monty: The Making of a General*, 571–72; Playfair, *The Mediterranean and the Middle East*, 3: 367.

67. Playfair, *The Mediterranean and the Middle East*, 3: 369.

CHAPTER SIX: MONTY'S WAR: EL ALAMEIN—
THE UNNECESSARY BATTLE?

1. Nigel Hamilton, *Monty: The Making of a General, 1887–1942* (New York: McGraw-Hill, 1981), 608.

2. Hitler believed that Rommel might swing up from Egypt to lend a hand to German forces in the Caucasus. Mussolini simply wanted to revive his faltering reputation with the seizure of Egypt. Horst Boog et al., *Germany and the Second World War*, vol. 6, *The Global War: Widening of the Conflict into a World War and the Shift of the Initiative, 1941–1943* (Oxford: Clarendon, 2001), 132, 134, 753.

3. David Irving, *The Trail of the Fox: The Life of Field-Marshal Erwin Rommel* (London: Book Club Associates, 1977), 194.

4. Winston S. Churchill, *The Second World War*, vol. 4, *The Hinge of Fate* (Boston: Houghton Mifflin, 1950), 529.

5. Nigel Hamilton, *Master of the Battlefield: Monty's War Years, 1942–1944* (New York: McGraw-Hill, 1983), 172–82, 213, 215.

6. Hamilton, *Monty: The Making of a General*, 511; see 353, 436–37, for Monty's views on German armor. Michael Carver, "Montgomery," in John Keegan, ed., *Churchill's Generals* (New York: Grove Weidenfeld, 1991), 148–53.

7. Martin Blumenson, *The Patton Papers, 1940–1945* (Boston: Houghton Mifflin, 1974), 267.

8. David Irving, *The Trail of the Fox: The Life of Field-Marshal Erwin Rommel* (London: Book Club Associates, 1977), 11, 186–87.

9. Alan Moorehead, *The March to Tunis: The North African War, 1940–1943* (New York: Harper and Row, 1943), 476.

10. Hamilton, *Monty: The Making of a General*, 653.

11. Hamilton, *Master of the Battlefield*, 6, 84, 136–37, 172–74, 264–65, 478–79, 719.

12. Alan Moorehead, *The Desert War: The North African Campaign, 1940–1943* (New York: Penguin, 2001), 576, 579–80 and note.

13. Harold Macmillan, *War Diaries: Politics and War in the Mediterranean, January 1943–May 1945* (New York: St. Martin's Press, 1984), 270.

14. Omar N. Bradley, *A Soldier's Story* (New York: Henry Holt, 1951), 207.

15. Mark W. Clark, *Calculated Risk* (New York: Harper, 1950), 211.

16. General Sir William Jackson, *The Mediterranean and the Middle East*, vol. 6, *Victory in the Mediterranean*, part 3, *November to May 1945* (London: HMSO, 1988), 196–97, 363; Hamilton, *Monty: The Making of a General*, 764–65; Hamilton, *Master of the Battlefield*, 249, 265–66, 322–23, 325–26, 345, 377–80, 466–74; Michael Carver, "Churchill and the Defense Chiefs," in Robert Blake and William Roger Louis, eds., *Churchill* (New York: Norton, 1993), 354.

17. Winston S. Churchill, *The Second World War*, 4: 518.

18. I.S.O. Playfair, *The Mediterranean and the Middle East*, vol. 3, *British Fortunes Reach Their Lowest Ebb* (London: HMSO, 1960), 372.

19. J.R.M. Butler, *Grand Strategy*, vol. 3, part 2 (London, 1964), 419.

20. John Kennedy, *The Business of War: The War Narrative of Major-General Sir John Kennedy* (London, 1957), 198.

21. Quoted in David Rolf, *The Bloody Road to Tunis: Destruction of the Axis Forces in North Africa: November 1942–May 1943* (London: Greenhill Books, 2001), 49.

22. David French, *Raising Churchill's Army: The British Army and the War against Germany, 1919–1945* (New York: Oxford University Press, 2000), 242.

23. French, *Raising Churchill's Army*, 219–28; Hamilton, *Monty: The Making of a General*, 577–80, 630.

24. Hamilton, *Monty: The Making of a General*, 569, 598, 641.

25. Ibid., 587–88, 602–03, 605, 620, 626.

26. Churchill, *The Second World War*, 4: 520.

27. F. H. Hinsley, *British Intelligence in the Second World War: Its Influence on Strategy and Operations*, vol. 2 (New York: Cambridge University Press, 1981), 408, 412–16.

28. Boog et al., *Germany and the Second World War*, 6: 749.

29. Hamilton, *Monty: The Making of a General*, 643.

30. Boog et al., *Germany and the Second World War*, 6: 753.

31. In addition, the British had become more security-conscious as the result of the Fellers revelation. They also began to adopt wireless deception tactics such as frequent frequency changes which made it difficult to identify units. Hans-Otto Behrendt, *Rommel's Intelligence in the Desert Campaign, 1941–1943* (London: William Kimber, 1985), 164, 190–94; Boog et al., *Germany and the Second World War*, 6: 759.

32. Stanley P. Hirshson, *General Patton: A Soldier's Life* (New York: HarperCollins, 2002), 304.

33. Hinsley, *British Intelligence*, 2: 417–21.

34. Hamilton, *Monty: The Making of a General*, 619, 661–63: Irving, *Trail of the Fox*, 189, gives slightly different figures. For fuel problems, see Playfair, *The Mediterranean and the Middle East*, 3: 382; Boog et al., *Germany and the Second World War*, 6: 748–50.

35. Boog et al., *Germany and the Second World War*, 6: 745–48, 757.

36. As opposed to the fifteen days he required. Hinsley, *British Intelligence*, 2: 420.

37. B. H. Liddell Hart, *The Rommel Papers* (New York: Harcourt, Brace, 1953), 277.

38. Boog et al., *Germany and the Second World War*, 6: 761.

39. This followed the loss of the tanker *Pozarica* on 21 August to RAF torpedoes, and the freighter *San Andrea* on 30 August. The loss of the *San Andrea* and the *Abruzzi* caused Rommel to call off his attack. Hinsley, *British Intelligence*, 2: 419–21. Playfair, *The Mediterranean and the Middle East*, 3: 388, writes that it was the sinking of the *Picci Fassio* that convinced Rommel that, even if two other tankers arrived, he would not have petrol before 7 September.

40. Lieutenant General Sir Francis Tuker, *Approach to Battle* (London: Cassell, 1963), 203.

41. Hinsley, *British Intelligence*, 2: 417. The Germans took 1,859 casualties and the Italians 1,051, to 1,750 British casualties, many suffered in the New Zealand Division. The Germans lost 33 guns, 298 vehicles, and 38 tanks destroyed, with large numbers damaged. Playfair, *The Mediterranean and the Middle East*, 3: 390–91.

42. Albert Kesselring, *Kesselring: A Soldier's Record* (New York: William Morrow, 1954), 152.

43. Irving, *Trail of the Fox*, 194.

44. Judging by his memoirs, Rommel was certainly impressed by the intensity of British bombing, which he ranked with poor intelligence and lack of petrol as the major causes of his defeat. Liddell Hart, *The Rommel Papers*, 281, 283–85.

45. Hamilton, *Monty: The Making of a General*, 674.

46. In particular, the sinking by Malta-based Beaufort bombers of the large tanker *San Andrea* on the eve of the battle, and the *Picci Fassio* as Alam Halfa was being fought, coming on top of a fortnight of supply-line disaster for the Axis, sapped Rommel's morale. Hinsley, *British Intelligence*, 2: 417–25. The RAF had destroyed much of the fuel storage depot at Tobruk in attacks in July and on 6 August. For the effectiveness of British attacks, particularly on Rommel's fuel supply, see Alan J. Levine, *The War Against Rommel's Supply Lines, 1942–1943* (Westport, Conn.: Praeger, 1999), 26–27. It was calculated that at the beginning of the 30 August attack, vehicles with troops had enough fuel to travel 150 miles, and those without troops 250 miles. Playfair, *The Mediterranean and the Middle East*, 3: 382.

47. For a description of Alam Halfa, see Irving, *Trail of the Fox*, 188–94; Hamilton, *Monty: The Making of a General*, 669–711; Playfair, *The Mediterranean and the Middle East*, 3: 379–91. The German official history lists Rommel's losses between 30 August and 6 September as 2,910 casualties, of whom 553 had been killed. He had lost 38 German and 11 Italian tanks, 55 guns, and 395 vehicles. Boog et al., *Germany and the Second World War*, 6: 766.

48. Keep the armor concentrated behind a screen of antitank guns on ground the enemy will be forced to attack; infantry in strong positions backed by centrally controlled artillery fire; divisions fight as divisions with definite tasks and clear-cut objectives; don't react to enemy moves or thrusts but stick to the plan; pursue a defeated foe. Hamilton, *Monty: The Making of a General*, 712–13.

49. Kesselring, *Kesselring*, 153–54; Hamilton, *Monty: The Making of a General*, 705–06.

50. Liddell Hart, *The Rommel Papers*, 286, 297–98.

51. A total of 152,000 Axis troops were in Egypt in October 1942. Panzerarmee laid claim to 50,000 Germans and 54,000 Italians. The remainder fell

under navy and Luftwaffe command. These were opposed by 195,000 British-led troops. Boog et al., *Germany and the Second World War*, 6: 775–76.

52. I.S.O. Playfair, *The Mediterranean and the Middle East*, vol. 4, *The Destruction of the Axis Forces in Africa* (London: HMSO, 1966), 20–23.

53. Rommel's northern defenses were held by the Twenty-first Corps, composed of the Bologna and Trento Infantry Divisions backed by the nine-battalion 164th Light Division. The Tenth Corps, made up of the Brescia Infantry Division, the Trieste Motorized Division, and the Ninetieth Light Division (later moved), and the Ramcke Parachute Brigade, occupied the central sector. The southern sector was held by the Twentieth Corps of the Ariete and Littorio Armored Divisions, the Folgore Paratroop Division, and the German Reconnaissance Group. The Afrika Korps was held as a mobile reserve behind the Twentieth Corps with two combat groups in the rear of the Twenty-first Corps. Boog et al., *Germany and the Second World War*, 6: 767.

54. John Ellis argues that the discrepancy in tanks was closer to four to one, presumably because all of the Italian tanks and many of the German ones were obsolete. *Brute Force: Allied Strategy and Tactics in World War II* (New York: Viking, 1990), 263–65. Axis forces: German—two armored divisions, one motorized division, one partly motorized division, one parachute brigade; Italian—two armored divisions, one motorized division, four infantry divisions, one parachute division. Although Rommel was relatively inferior in tanks, he was well supplied with antitank guns. Rommel could also count 350 serviceable aircraft in North Africa, including 80 dive-bombers; 130 long-range bombers based in Greece, Crete, Sicily, and Sardinia were also available, as were 300 transport aircraft. The Fifteenth and Twenty-first Panzer Divisions counted 240 tanks between them, together with 278 Italian tanks. The British would have 1,029 tanks ready for service, including 252 Shermans and 78 of the new Crusader IIIs, with another 1,000 tanks in workshops. Playfair, *The Mediterranean and the Middle East*, 4: 3, 9–10, 29–30. Boog et al., *Germany and the Second World War*, 6: 772, lists Axis tank strength at 234 German and 323 Italian.

55. Hinsley, *British Intelligence*, 2: 436–37.

56. Boog et al., *Germany and the Second World War*, 6: 772.

57. Playfair, *The Mediterranean and the Middle East*, 4: 28; Liddell Hart, *The Rommel Papers*, 298.

58. Hinsley, *British Intelligence*, 2: 427.

59. Irving, *Trail of the Fox*, 201–02. Boog et al., *Germany and the Second World War*, 6: 770–71.

60. Liddell Hart, *The Rommel Papers*, 300.

61. Hinsley, *British Intelligence*, 2: 433, 435–37.

62. Hamilton, *Monty: The Making of a General*, 752, 776–77. Montgomery had had only 9 guns per kilometer of front at Alam Halfa, and 31 at El Alamein. This compared to 92 guns per kilometer of front at the 1916 Battle of the Somme and 161 per kilometer at Vimy Ridge in the following year. Air

power compensated somewhat for the relative paucity of artillery. But it was always a weather-impacted arm. French, *Raising Churchill's Army*, 255–56. Boog et al., *Germany and the Second World War*, 6: 775–76, argues that although the relative strengths of the two forces in Egypt in October 1942 were 152,000 Axis soldiers to 195,000 British-led troops, in effect Rommel could only put 60,000 troops in line, thereby spotting Montgomery a three-to-one superiority.

63. Hamilton, *Monty: The Making of a General*, 761. John Ellis argues that "Clodhopper" would have been a more apt name for Lightfoot. The lanes cleared through the minefields were too narrow for the armor to operate, so that vast traffic jams were created. Forcing tanks through these narrow corridors allowed the Germans to concentrate their antitank guns. However, so insecure was Montgomery that he refused to countenance any criticism of his plan. *Brute Force*, 279–81.

64. Liddell Hart, *The Rommel Papers*, 302.

65. Behrendt argues against the thesis of intelligence surprise, as a British attack was widely expected at any time. *Rommel's Intelligence*, 196–98. Boog et al., *Germany and the Second World War*, 6: 770–71, also argues that signs that an attack was in preparation had been obvious to the Germans since 7 October. German intelligence was divided on where the main thrust would come. Hinsley, *British Intelligence*, 2: 437, argues that Montgomery's preliminary air campaign distracted the Luftwaffe and kept it from detecting British troops concentrations, and hence the Germans were unaware of the site and timing of the offensive.

66. Liddell Hart, *The Rommel Papers*, 306.

67. The armored corps failed to advance because of narrow corridors through the minefields, which restricted movement; mines that remained to be cleared; and German antitank guns. Playfair, *The Mediterranean and the Middle East*, 6: 46–47.

68. Liddell Hart, *The Rommel Papers*, 306.

69. Ibid., 307, 309–10.

70. See Hinsley, *British Intelligence*, 2: 442–43, for Ultra-guided sinkings.

71. Rommel fully expected that the main British thrust would come in the area of Hill 28, not least because he had captured the Supercharger plan. Boog et al., *Germany and the Second World War*, 6: 781–82. And while Montgomery had anticipated that his attack would fall on the Italians, instead it hit a battalion of the Twenty-first Panzer Division that had been left behind to stiffen the Trieste Division. Hinsley, *British Intelligence*, 2: 445.

72. Hinsley, *British Intelligence*, 2: 448.

73. Hamilton refutes Irving's assertion that von Thoma was a traitor. *Monty: The Making of a General*, 846–47. Playfair, *The Mediterranean and the Middle East*, 4: 96–97; Boog et al., *Germany and the Second World War*, 6: 784–85, asserts that von Thoma's headquarters was surrounded early on the morning of 4 November by 150 British tanks and virtually annihilated.

74. Boog et al., *Germany and the Second World War*, 6: 789–90.

75. Churchill, *The Second World War*, 4: 603.

76. Irving, *Trail of the Fox*, 226–28; Hamilton, *Master of the Battlefield*, 118, 123–26.

77. Hamilton, *Monty: The Making of a General*, 776; Hamilton, *Master of the Battlefield*, 4.

78. Official estimates put Axis casualties at El Alamein at 57,000, including POWs. Four hundred fifty Axis tanks were destroyed and left behind, as well as over a thousand artillery pieces. Quoted in Hamilton, *Master of the Battlefield*, 39 note.

79. Liddell Hart, *The Rommel Papers*, Chapter 15, on Rommel's reasons for the defeat.

80. Ellis, *Brute Force*, 281, 283; Ronald Lewin, *Rommel as Military Commander* (London: Batsford, 1968), 170.

81. Churchill, *The Second World War*, 4: 602.

82. French, *Raising Churchill's Army*, 265.

83. Quoted in Hamilton, *Master of the Battlefield*, 15.

84. Ellis, *Brute Force*, 283.

85. Liddell Hart, *The Rommel Papers*, 299, 308; Dominick Graham and Shelford Bidwell, *Fire Power: British Army Weapons and Theories of War, 1904–1945* (London, 1982), 245; Ellis, *Brute Force*, 283.

86. Hinsley, *British Intelligence*, 2: 454.

87. Playfair, *The Mediterranean and the Middle East*, 4: 96–97. Ellis argues that Montgomery was so concentrated on fighting his set-piece battle that he did nothing to prepare for pursuit. Indeed, the way he fought his battle, advancing along narrow, traffic-choked corridors through the minefields, meant that his tanks would filter through too slowly to round up the dazed enemy. In any case, Montgomery feared a counterattack of the sort that had undone his predecessors at the head of the Eighth Army. *Brute Force*, 284–86.

88. Hamilton singles out Herbert Lumsden, whose Tenth Corps was turned into a *corps de chasse* just for the purpose of pursuit, for special, if not exclusive, blame. A flamboyant, immaculately dressed cavalryman who cruised the battlefield in his personal white tank, Lumsden appeared to regard Montgomery as a social inferior. His Tenth Corps had failed to screen the infantry during the "crumbling" phase as Montgomery had planned, and had to be withdrawn. Came time to pursue, Lumsden was slow to move through the gap in the Alamein line made by the infantry, and once he cleared it, he cut himself off from communication with headquarters. On 24 November, Montgomery fired Lumsden and replaced him with Thirteenth Corps commander Brian Horrocks, by which time Rommel was almost to Tripolitania. "In the final analysis Montgomery must bear the blame" for Rommel's escape, Hamilton concludes. "He had not himself assumed direct command of the pursuit, but had entrusted the encirclement of Rommel's rearguard to a Corps Commander who proved unable to control or administer his forces in a battle of maneuver." *Master of the Battlefield*, 37.

89. Ibid., 56.

90. Playfair, *The Mediterranean and the Middle East*, 4: 81–106; Hamilton, *Master of the Battlefield*, 15, 18–26, 28, 37–38, 53–63.

91. Hamilton, *Master of the Battlefield*, 10.

92. Liddell Hart, *The Rommel Papers*, 324.

CHAPTER SEVEN: "FDR'S SECRET BABY"

1. Stanley P. Hirshson, *General Patton: A Soldier's Life* (New York: HarperCollins, 2002), 264; Carlo D'Este, *Eisenhower: A Soldier's Life* (New York: Henry Holt, 2002), 308.

2. Christopher Thorne, *Allies of a Kind: The United States, Britain, and the War against Japan, 1941–1945* (New York: Oxford University Press, 1978), 146–50.

3. "Indeed, in general terms there was a tendency [by the British] to treat the United States not as a distinctively 'foreign' country, but as a rather special and eccentric form of white dominion, possessing an essentially hollow civilization, but capable of being 'educated' by the guiding and paternalistic hands of the British," writes British historian Matthew Jones. "Such images, often amounting to little more than crass generalizations, were strongly ingrained and penetrated many aspects of the relationship." *Britain, the United States and the Mediterranean War, 1942–44* (New York: St. Martin's, 1996), 14.

4. Robert Dalleck, "Roosevelt," in I.C.B. Dear and M.R.D. Foot, eds., *The Oxford Companion to World War II* (New York: Oxford University Press, 1995), 965.

5. John Colville, *Fringes of Power: Ten Downing Street Diaries, 1939–1955* (New York, 1985), 624.

6. Robert E. Sherwood, *Roosevelt and Hopkins: An Intimate History* (New York, 1948), 363–64. Matthew Jones argues that the relationship was solidified by shared enthusiasms, especially for naval matters. *Britain, the United States and the Mediterranean War*, 8.

7. Eliot A. Cohen, "Churchill and Coalition Strategy in World War II," in Paul Kennedy, ed., *Grand Strategies in War and Peace* (New Haven: Yale University Press, 1991), 52.

8. Robert Dallek, *Franklin D. Roosevelt and American Foreign Policy, 1932–1945* (New York: Oxford University Press, 1995), 350.

9. Churchill had no memory of meeting Roosevelt in 1918, which upset the president even more. Warren F. Kimball, "Wheel within a Wheel: Churchill, Roosevelt, and the Special Relationship," in Roger Blake and William Roger Louis, eds., *Churchill* (New York: Norton, 1993), 293, 297–98.

10. Harold Macmillan, *The Blast of War, 1939–45* (London, 1967), 158–59.

11. "We will have more trouble with Great Britain after the war than we are having with Germany now," he predicted. W. F. Kimball, ed., *Churchill and*

Roosevelt: The Complete Correspondence (Princeton, N.J.: Princeton University Press, 1984), 3: 535.

12. Kenneth S. Davis, *FDR: The War President, 1940–1943: A History* (New York: Random House, 2000), 3–14, 414, 544–45, 552–53.

13. Westley F. Craven and James L. Cate, *The Army Air Forces in World War II*, vol. 2, *Europe: Torch to Pointblank* (Chicago: University of Chicago Press, 1950), 41.

14. Davis, *FDR*, 553.

15. Ibid., 545.

16. D'Este, *Eisenhower*, 290.

17. Kimball, "Wheel within a Wheel," 306.

18. Jones, *Britain, the United States and the Mediterranean War*, 17–18.

19. Ibid., 42.

20. Dallek, *Franklin D. Roosevelt and American Foreign Policy*, 351–52. Roosevelt also knew that the blame for the delay of Sledgehammer/Roundup would fall on the British. John Lamberton Harper, *American Visions of Europe* (Cambridge: Cambridge University Press, 1996), 86–87.

21. Arthur Bryant, *The Turn of the Tide: A History of the War Years Based on the Diaries of Field-Marshal Lord Alanbrooke, Chief of the Imperial General Staff* (Garden City, N.Y.: Doubleday, 1957), 454.

22. Allan R. Millett, "The United States Armed Forces in the Second World War," in Williamson Murray and Allan R. Millett, eds., *Military Effectiveness*, vol. 3, *The Second World War* (Boston: Unwin Hyman, 1988), 56.

23. Eric Larrabee, *Commander in Chief: Franklin Delano Roosevelt, His Lieutenants, and Their War* (New York: Touchstone, 1988), 139.

24. Stephen E. Ambrose, *The Supreme Commander: The War Years of Dwight D. Eisenhower* (New York: Doubleday, 1970), 109.

25. Robert O. Paxton, *Parades and Politics at Vichy: The French Officer Corps under Marshal Pétain* (Princeton, N.J.: Princeton University Press, 1966), 323–31.

26. D'Este, *Eisenhower*, 228.

27. Ibid., 280.

28. Ibid., 173, 254–55, 303, 306–07.

29. Paul Fussell, *Doing Battle: The Making of a Skeptic* (Boston: Little, Brown, 1996), 221, 296–97.

30. D'Este, *Eisenhower*, 415–17, 420–21.

31. Stephen Ambrose, *Eisenhower: Soldier, General of the Army, President-Elect, 1890–1952* (New York: Simon and Schuster, 1983), 214.

32. Nigel Hamilton, *Master of the Battlefield: Monty's War Years, 1941–1944* (New York: McGraw-Hill, 1983), 211, 272.

33. Jones, *Britain, the United States and the Mediterranean War*, 33.

34. Martin Blumenson, *The Patton Papers, 1940–1945* (Boston: Houghton Mifflin, 1974), 263, 283, 289.

35. Jones, *Britain, the United States and the Mediterranean War*, 89.

36. Bryant, *The Turn of the Tide*, 454–55; Ambrose, *Eisenhower*, 219, 238.

37. D'Este, *Eisenhower*, 437.

38. Macmillan, *War Diaries*, 259–60.

39. D'Este, *Eisenhower*, 423.

40. Jones, *Britain, the United States and the Mediterranean War*, 237–38.

41. Ibid., 24–25.

42. Thorne, *Allies of a Kind*, 133.

43. "[Eisenhower] is completely sold out to the British," George Patton complained in March 1943. "I hope the press at home get on to it." Blumenson, *The Patton Papers*, 211.

44. Carlo D'Este, *Patton: A Genius for War* (New York: HarperCollins, 1995), 555.

45. Anthony Samson, *Macmillan: A Study in Ambiguity* (London, 1967), 61.

46. Ambrose, *Eisenhower*, 186, 219, 238.

47. Omar N. Bradley, *A Soldier's Story* (New York: Henry Holt, 1951), 31.

48. Bryant, *The Turn of the Tide*, 453.

49. Omar N. Bradley and Clay Blair, *A General's Life: An Autobiography by General of the Army Omar N. Bradley* (New York: Simon and Schuster, 1983), 136.

50. Alan Moorehead, *The Desert War: The North African Campaign, 1940–1943* (London: Penguin, 2001), 482.

51. Jones, *Britain, the United States and the Mediterranean War*, 28, 33; D'Este, *Eisenhower*, 422–23.

52. A. J. Liebling, *The Road Back to Paris* (New York: Modern Library, 1997), 354.

53. Moorehead, *The Desert War*, 483.

54. I.S.O. Playfair, *The Mediterranean and the Middle East*, vol. 4, *The Destruction of the Axis Forces in Africa* (London: HMSO, 1966), 124.

55. Harry C. Butcher, *Three Years with Eisenhower* (London: Heinemann, 1946), 47–51. Both the joint planning staff and the joint intelligence staff argued that Russian resistance at Stalingrad and in the Caucasus tied down Axis troops that could have intervened against Gibraltar and thus precluded the certainty of an Axis victory on the Eastern Front, which Franco required before he would intervene. F. H. Hinsley, *British Intelligence in the Second World War: Its Influence on Strategy and Operations*, vol. 2 (New York: Cambridge University Press, 1981), 473–74.

56. Butcher, *Three Years with Eisenhower*, 91; Dalleck, *Franklin Roosevelt and American Foreign Policy*, 363; Davis, *FDR*, 670–71.

57. Indeed, Juin had originally been considered by Murphy as a candidate for Giraud's job, but was rejected because, unlike Giraud, as a condition for his release from a German POW camp Juin had agreed not to take up arms against the Reich. For his part, Juin considered the pledge meaningless, as it had been coerced. Davis, *FDR*, 682.

58. Indeed, the West Point class of 1915, which included both Eisenhower and Bradley, became known as "the class the stars fell on" because it produced so many generals.

59. Larrabee, *Commander in Chief*, 5.

60. Millett, "The United States Armed Forces in the Second World War," 73.

61. Lee Kennett, *G.I.: The American Soldier in World War II* (New York: Scribner, 1987), 21–22; Millett, "The United States Armed Forces in the Second World War," 74.

62. Kennett, *G.I.*, 38.

63. Winston S. Churchill, *The Second World War*, vol. 4, *The Hinge of Fate* (Boston: Houghton Mifflin, 1950), 386.

64. Hamilton, *Master of the Battlefield*, 177.

65. Fussell, *Doing Battle*, 172.

66. Millett, "The United States Armed Forces in the Second World War," 60–61, 66–67, 69, 72, 73–75, 83.

67. Horst Boog, Werner Rahn, Reinhard Stumpf, and Bernd Wegner, *Germany and the Second World War*, vol. 6, *The Global War: Widening of the Conflict into a World War and the Shift of the Initiative, 1941–1943* (Oxford: Clarendon, 2001), 791–92.

68. Ibid., 6: 139–40.

69. Henri Michel, *François Darlan* (Paris: Hachette, 1993), 281–82.

70. Hinsley, *British Intelligence*, 2: 477–82.

71. Indeed, the French had begun to evacuate civilian dependents from Dakar on 4 November in anticipation of an Allied strike against French West Africa. Paxton, *Parades and Politics at Vichy*, 330.

72. Playfair, *The Mediterranean and the Middle East*, 4: 135–36.

73. Stanley Sandler, *"Cease Resistance: It's Good For You": A History of U.S. Army Combat Psychological Operations* (no place or publisher, 1999), 49.

74. Playfair, *The Mediterranean and the Middle East*, 4: 137–51, 155.

75. Christine Levisse-Touzé, *L'Afrique du Nord dans la guerre, 1939–1945* (Paris: Albin Michel, 1998), 259.

76. Quoted in Jones, *Britain, the United States and the Mediterranean War*, 31.

77. The occupation of Tunis and of southern France were seen by Hitler as complementary operations, designed to eliminated power vacuums in the Mediterranean and stabilize the situation there. Boog et al., *Germany and the Second World War*, 6: 793–94.

78. Ambrose, *Eisenhower*, 210–11.

79. Spike Milligan, *"Rommel?" "Gunner Who?" A Confrontation in the Desert* (London: Michael Joseph, 1974), 45.

80. He believed that seven Axis divisions would be able to push the Allies back to Suez. Boog et al., *Germany and the Second World War*, 6: 794.

81. James H. Doolittle, *I Could Never Be So Lucky Again* (New York: Bantam, 1991), 326.

82. Ambrose, *The Supreme Commander*, 113–16; Moorehead, *The Desert War*, 478.

83. Gerhard Weinberg, *A World At Arms* (New York: Cambridge University Press, 1994), 432.

84. George E. Melton, *Darlan: Admiral and Statesman of France* (Westport, Conn.: Praeger, 1998), 163–65. According to Melton, these attempts were never followed up because they were sent through his son, Alain, who fell ill with polio, and because the pro-Gaullist French working with Murphy refused to have anything to do with Darlan. For his part, Darlan did not think the Allies yet capable of invading.

85. Paxton, *Parades and Politics at Vichy*, 343.

86. The different outcomes in Morocco and Algeria compared with Tunisia can be explained by the presence of Allied troops in the former. Estéva, receiving contradictory orders from Algiers, elected to follow clear orders from Vichy to fight the Anglo-Americans. The ground commander, General Georges Barré, felt too weak to oppose the Axis forces on his own and opted for resistance only on 15 November as Allied troops crossed into western Tunisia. Paxton, *Parades and Politics at Vichy*, 363–71. In 1945 Estéva was court-martialed and sentenced to life imprisonment. He was released in 1950 and died the following year.

87. Melton, *Darlan*, 178.

88. D'Este, *Eisenhower*, 354, 356.

89. Ambrose, *The Supreme Commander*, 125.

90. D'Este, *Eisenhower*, 418.

91. The option of taking over the direction of French North Africa was unavailable to the Allied commander for at least three reasons: the United States had been slow to address the question of the government of occupied territories because of disputes between the War Department and State Department over whether civil affairs should be a military or a civilian enterprise. Second, FDR was slow to relinquish his belief that "Military Government was a repulsive notion, associated with imperialism, dollar diplomacy, and other aspects of our behavior we have abandoned." W. Miller, ed., *Arms and the State* (New York, 1958), 124. Finally, civil affairs military government had been given low priority by a U.S. Army concentrating on getting combat units up and running. Better the French continue to administer their possessions, so that Ike could concentrate on the fighting. "Had there been an extensive Allied Military Government apparatus in place ready to take over the civil governance of French North Africa," writes the historian of U.S. civil affairs Stanley Sandler, "the whole Darlan Deal might not have been necessary." SHAEF (Supreme Headquarters Allied Expeditionary Force) had created a civil affairs "French Unit" in June 1942. However, this was destined to be the embryo of a military government of mainland France behind Sledgehammer, and seems never to have been destined for French North Africa. Stanley Sandler, *Glad to See Them*

Come and Sorry to See Them Go: A History of U.S. Army Tactical Civil Affairs/ Military Government, 1775–1991 (no place, publisher, or date), 171–73, 190. Despite the Darlan deal, the Allies found that they had to assume the economic direction of French North Africa, setting exchange rates, paying the salaries of French civil servants, and supplying the civilian population with food. Levisse-Touzé, *L'Afrique du Nord dans la guerre*, 264–67.

92. Dallek, *Franklin D. Roosevelt and American Foreign Policy*, 364–65. American diplomat George Kennan complained that Roosevelt gave soldiers far too much freedom to make diplomatic decisions in the war. John Lamberton Harper, *American Visions of Europe* (Cambridge: Cambridge University Press, 1996), 193.

93. Bradley, *A Soldier's Story*, 32. For his part, Eisenhower never acknowledged that he had been naive; he insisted that he had entered into an arrangement with Darlan with his eyes wide open. Ambrose, *The Supreme Commander*, 126.

94. Sandler, *"Cease Resistance,"* 50.

95. Dallek, *Franklin D. Roosevelt and American Foreign Policy*, 366.

96. Liebling, *The Road Back to Paris*, 344.

97. Jones, *Britain, the United States and the Mediterranean War*, 75.

98. Ambrose, *The Supreme Commander*, 128–31.

99. Eisenhower's justifications included: Roosevelt had forbidden him to work with de Gaulle, and Giraud had proved honest but inept; Darlan represented the legal regime recognized by the French military; Vichy's anti-Semitic policies made the government acceptable to Moslems (Darlan had cleverly played on Eisenhower's fear of a Moslem revolt); the Allies lacked the capability to take over the administration of North Africa; Allied forces needed to move rapidly toward Tunisia and he needed to secure his rear; the Allied strategic goal was to gain France as an ally, not to govern a conquered country; and Darlan had arranged for the occupation of Dakar by the Allies. Davis, *FDR*, 691–92.

100. Ambrose, *Eisenhower*, 208–09.

101. Jones, *Britain, the United States and the Mediterranean War*, 75–76.

102. The law excluding Jews from the liberal professions was withdrawn on 5 December 1942, but their "reintegration" proceeded on a case-by-case basis. Jews were excluded from the mobilization order of 24 November 1942, and instead integrated into a special *Corps franc d'Afrique*. Giraud allowed Jews to volunteer for military service on an individual basis. A 2 June 1941 law that prohibited Jews from becoming officers or NCOs in the French army still stood. Nor could Jews acquire "veteran" status that qualified them for a pension. Only gradually were Jews reintegrated into the administration. Demands by nationalist leader Ferhat Abbas that Moslems be given full citizenship rights in return for participation in the war effort were also rejected. Levisse-Touzé, *L'Afrique du Nord dans la guerre*, 269–70.

103. Playfair, *The Mediterranean and the Middle East*, 4: 191; see also 158–64.

104. Dallek, *Franklin D. Roosevelt and American Foreign Policy*, 365.

105. Jones, *Britain, the United States and the Mediterranean War*, 95.

106. Davis, *FDR*, 693–97.

107. Jones, *Britain, the United States and the Mediterranean War*, 76, 95.

108. J. Harvey, *The War Diaries of Oliver Harvey* (London, 1978), 14 November 1942.

109. Jones, *Britain, the United States and the Mediterranean War*, 72.

110. Boog et al., *Germany and the Second World War*, 6: 141.

111. Moorehead, *The Desert War*, 481–82.

112. Ambrose, *Eisenhower*, 207.

113. Davis, *FDR*, 705.

114. Mark Clark, *Calculated Risk* (New York Harper, 1950), 130.

115. Ambrose, *The Supreme Commander*, Chapter 8; Davis, *FDR*, 701–09.

116. Moorehead, *The Desert War*, 478.

117. Hervé Coutau-Bégarie and Claude Huan, *Darlan* (Paris: Fayard, 1989), 684.

118. Ambrose, *Eisenhower*, 440–41; Jones, *Britain, the United States and the Mediterranean War*, 76–80.

119. John Ellis, *Brute Force: Allied Strategy and Tactics in the Second World War* (London: Viking, 1990), 293.

120. Ambrose, *Eisenhower*, 207.

121. Ibid., 214–15, 219.

122. Boog et al., *Germany and the Second World War*, 6: 140–41; David Rolf, *The Bloody Road to Tunis: Destruction of the Axis Forces in North Africa: November 1942–May 1943* (London: Greenhill Books, 2001), 87.

123. Hamilton, *Master of the Battlefield*, 10. By the end of 1942, 70 percent of German air assets were concentrated in the Mediterranean, the Reich, and Western Europe. Boog et al., *Germany and the Second World War*, 6: 627.

124. Denis Mack Smith, *Mussolini* (New York: Knopf, 1986), 277, 285.

125. F. W. Deakin, *The Brutal Friendship: Mussolini, Hitler and the Fall of Italian Fascism* (New York: Harper and Row, 1962), 28.

126. Boog et al., *Germany and the Second World War*, 6: 137, 143.

127. Deakin, *The Brutal Friendship*, 274.

CHAPTER EIGHT: TUNISIA: "THE VERDUN OF
THE MEDITERRANEAN"

1. Horst Boog, Werner Rahn, Reinhard Stumpf, and Bernd Wegner, *Germany and the Second World War*, vol. 6, *The Global War: Widening of the Conflict into a World War and the Shift of the Initiative, 1941–1943* (Oxford: Clarendon, 2001), 813.

2. F. W. Deakin, *The Brutal Friendship: Mussolini, Hitler and the Fall of Italian Fascism* (New York: Harper and Row, 1962), 282.

3. Albert Kesselring, *Kesselring: A Soldier's Record* (New York: William Morrow, 1954), 165.

4. Boog et al., *Germany and the Second World War*, 6: 794.

5. I.S.O. Playfair, *The Mediterranean and the Middle East*, 4, *The Destruction of the Axis Forces in Africa* (London: HMSO, 1966), 170–71, 268, 393, 395.

6. Denis Mack Smith, *Mussolini* (New York: Knopf, 1986), 277, 287–90; F. W. Deakin, *The Brutal Friendship: Mussolini, Hitler and the Fall of Italian Fascism* (New York: Harper and Row, 1962), 145, 147.

7. Kesselring, *Kesselring*, 174.

8. F. H. Hinsley, *British Intelligence in the Second World War*, vol. 2 (New York: Cambridge University Press, 1981), 576–77; B. H. Liddell Hart, *The Rommel Papers* (New York: Harcourt, Brace, 1953), 404.

9. David Rolf, *The Bloody Road to Tunis: Destruction of the Axis Forces in North Africa: November 1942–May 1943* (London: Greenhill Books, 2001), 53–54.

10. Alan Moorehead, *The Desert War: The North African Campaign, 1940–1943* (New York: Penguin, 2000), 594.

11. Rolf, *Bloody Road to Tunis*, 87.

12. The Axis could expect 60,000 to 70,000 tons of supplies each month as opposed to the 150,000 required to carry out offensive operations. Playfair, *The Mediterranean and the Middle East*, 4: 189–90, 240–41, 274, 289; Smith, *Mussolini*, 282.

13. Kesselring, *Kesselring*, 171.

14. Lee Kennett, *G.I.: The American Soldier in World War II* (New York: Scribner, 1987), 200.

15. Playfair, *The Mediterranean and the Middle East*, 4: 174–76; Stephen E. Ambrose, *The Supreme Commander: The War Years of Dwight D. Eisenhower* (New York: Doubleday, 1970), 164.

16. Moorehead, *The Desert War*, 508.

17. Omar N. Bradley and Clay Blair, *A General's Life: An Autobiography by General of the Army Omar N. Bradley* (New York: Simon and Schuster, 1983), 153.

18. Playfair, *The Mediterranean and the Middle East*, 4: 171, 239.

19. R. J. Overy, *The Air War, 1939–1945* (New York: Stein and Day, 1980), 44–45.

20. Hinsley, *British Intelligence*, 574.

21. The RAF in the Western Desert had been reorganized from July 1941 by Air Chief Marshal Sir Arthur Tedder, the air officer commanding what came to be known as the Desert Air Force. Each corps and armored division HQ had a joint Air Support Control, linked to brigades through Forward Air Support

Links that radioed requests for air support, and, through direct radio links with the attacking planes, directed aircraft toward their targets. This system was also used to disseminate RAF tactical reconnaissance reports. David French, *Raising Churchill's Army: The British Army and the War against Germany, 1919–1945* (New York: Oxford University Press, 2000), 237–38.

22. Playfair, *The Mediterranean and the Middle East*, 4: 182–83, 189–90.

23. All of this hinged, in von Arnim's view, on a constant flow of supplies and the capture of Malta. Rolf, *Bloody Road to Tunis*, 64–65.

24. Samuel W. Mitcham, Jr., "Arnim: General of Panzer Troops Hans-Jürgen von Arnim," in Correlli Barnett, ed., *Hitler's Generals: Authoritative Portraits of the Men Who Waged Hitler's War* (New York: Quill/William Morrow, 1989), 343.

25. Liddell Hart, *Rommel Papers*, 401.

26. Kesselring, *Kesselring*, 176.

27. The Panzerarmee Afrika had been renamed the German-Italian Panzer Army on the eve of El Alamein. For a description of Rommel's retreat, see Boog et al., *Germany and the Second World War*, 4: 807–21.

28. Playfair, *The Mediterranean and the Middle East*, 4: 268–70; David Irving, *The Trail of the Fox: The Life of Field-Marshal Erwin Rommel* (London: Book Club Associates, 1977), 241–42; Rolf, *Bloody Road to Tunis*, 88–89.

29. I thank Alan Wilt for this observation.

30. Carlo D'Este, *Eisenhower: A Soldier's Life* (New York: Henry Holt, 2002), 228.

31. Ibid., 406.

32. Ambrose, *Supreme Commander*, 161–63; Stephen E. Ambrose, *Eisenhower: Soldier, General of the Army, President-Elect, 1890–1952* (New York: Simon and Schuster, 1983), 220–21; Matthew Jones, *Britain, the United States and the Mediterranean War, 1942–44* (New York: St. Martin's, 1996), 49–53.

33. Rolf, *Bloody Road to Tunis*, 83–84.

34. Ibid., 41, 67, 226.

35. Nigel Hamilton, *Master of the Battlefield: Monty's War Years, 1942–1944* (New York: McGraw-Hill, 1983), 378–79; Nigel Hamilton, *Monty: The Making of a General, 1887–1942* (New York: McGraw-Hill, 1981), 173.

36. Quoted in Rolf, *Bloody Road to Tunis*, 33.

37. D'Este, *Eisenhower*, 376, 398.

38. Rolf, *Bloody Road to Tunis*, 287.

39. Bradley and Blair, *A General's Life*, 134. An intermediary headquarters established at Constantine under General Lucien K. Truscott was regarded as no more than a "post office." Playfair, *The Mediterranean and the Middle East*, 4: 270.

40. "Patton was a notorious and outspoken Anglophobe, worse even than Fredendall, if that were possible," wrote Omar Bradley. Bradley and Blair, *A General's Life*, 137; Ambrose, *Eisenhower*, 223, 227; Rick Atkinson, *An Army at*

Dawn: The War in North Africa, 1942–1943 (New York: Henry Holt, 2002), 272–74.

41. Quoted in Stanley P. Hirshson, *General Patton: A Soldier's Life* (New York: HarperCollins, 2002), 307.

42. Ambrose, *Supreme Commander*, 171.

43. Hirshson, *General Patton*, 349.

44. Playfair, *The Mediterranean and the Middle East*, 4: 282.

45. Liddell Hart, *Rommel Papers*, 394.

46. Irving, *Trail of the Fox*, 242–43.

47. Ultra decrypts had revealed that Messe was to replace a sick Rommel, who was to be repatriated to Europe. The Germans had also tightened their security procedures. Nor did the Allies in North Africa, unlike in the Middle East command, initially have a mechanism for intercepting Enigma traffic and sending it to Bletchley for decrypting. Changes in the Allied command structure also confused the intelligence picture. Anderson lacked adequate staff and communications to process intelligence. Some important signals remained undecrypted. Hinsley, *British Intelligence*, 2: 580–90.

48. Liddell Hart, *Rommel Papers*, 400.

49. Ibid., 401.

50. Carlo D'Este, *World War II in the Mediterranean, 1942–1945* (Chapel Hill, N.C.: Algonquin Books, 1990), 21.

51. George F. Howe, *Northwest Africa: Seizing the Initiative in the West* (Washington, D.C.: Department of the Army, 1957), 460; this view is supported by Sir Basil Liddell Hart, *A History of the Second World War* (London, 1970), 406; Kesselring, *Kesselring*, 180–81.

52. Irving, *Trail of the Fox*, 241–52.

53. Liddell Hart, *Rommel Papers*, 398, 400–01.

54. Mitcham, "Arnim," 347.

55. Playfair, *The Mediterranean and the Middle East*, 4: 300–02.

56. Howe, *Northwest Africa: Seizing the Initiative in the West*, 470.

57. Nigel Nicolson, *Alex: The Life of Field Marshal Earl Alexander of Tunis* (London: Pan Books, 1976), 211.

58. Bradley and Blair, *A General's Life*, 134; Hamilton, *Master of the Battlefield*, 215–16; Rolf, *Bloody Road to Tunis*, 146–47.

59. D'Este, *Eisenhower*, 423.

60. Playfair, *The Mediterranean and the Middle East*, 4: 304.

61. Ambrose, *Eisenhower*, 225–27.

62. Bradley and Blair, *A General's Life*, 130.

63. Liddell Hart, *Rommel Papers*, 404, 406–07.

64. After all, the faltering of novice troops in combat was not a peculiarly U.S. malady. The Fifty-sixth (British) Division, introduced into the well-oiled machine of the vaunted Eighth Army, "fell into some disorder" in their first combat against Axis forces north of Enfidaville in the final days of the Tunisian

campaign. In the process, they forfeited two hills hard won by New Zealand troops in earlier attacks. Playfair, *The Mediterranean and the Middle East*, 4: 443.

65. Rolf, *Bloody Road to Tunis*, 149.

66. Mark Clark, *Calculated Risk* (New York: Harper, 1950), 167, 169.

67. Winston S. Churchill, *The Second World War*, vol. 3, *The Grand Alliance* (Boston: Houghton Mifflin, 1950), 607.

68. R. L. Crimp, *Diary of a Desert Rat* (London: Leo Cooper, 1971), 179–80; quoted in Rolf, *Bloody Road to Tunis*, 256.

69. Quoted in Hamilton, *Master of the Battlefield*, 220–21.

70. Moorehead, *The Desert War*, 578–79.

71. Clark, *Calculated Risk*, 167.

72. Stanley Sandler, *"Cease Resistance: It's Good For You": A History of U.S. Army Combat Psychological Operations* (no place or publisher, 1999), 54.

73. Kennett, *G.I.*, 124–26.

74. Peter Schrijvers, *The Crash of Ruin: American Combat Soldiers in Europe During World War II* (New York: New York University Press, 1998), 36, 37, 39, 262.

75. Schrijvers. *Crash of Ruin*, 41–45, 116–19, 155.

76. The most notorious was the tiff between George Patton and the New Zealander, Air Marshal Sir Arthur Coningham, over the absence of air support for Second Corps. Coningham complained that Patton was trying to use "the air force as an alibi for lack of success on the ground." Patton insisted that his troops had been insulted and demanded an apology. Martin Blumenson, *The Patton Papers, 1940–1945* (Boston: Houghton Mifflin, 1974), 207–10.

77. "I feel that I must respectfully call General Alexander's attention to the fact that in the United States Army we tell officers what to do, not how to do it, that to do otherwise suggests lack of confidence in the officer," Patton objected when in March 1943 the British sent a detailed operation plan to Second Corps. "I feel that, for the honor and prestige of the U.S. Army, I must protest." Blumenson, *Patton Papers*, 200.

78. Bradley and Blair, *A General's Life*, 137. Eisenhower had originally designated Mark Clark for the task. But the ambitious Clark refused to surrender command of the Fifth Army. Ambrose, *Eisenhower*, 237.

79. Hirshson, *General Patton*, 234–35, 249.

80. Bradley and Blair, *A General's Life*, 98.

81. Field Marshal Lord Alanbrooke, *War Diaries, 1939–1945* (Berkeley: University of California Press, 2001), 360–61.

82. Hirshson, *General Patton*, 700.

83. Ambrose, *Supreme Commander*, 174–75; Ambrose, *Eisenhower*, 225–27; Playfair, *The Mediterranean and the Middle East*, 4: 303–05, 313.

84. Hirshson, *General Patton*, 314.

85. Second Corps consisted of the First, Ninth, and Thirty-fourth Infantry Divisions and the First Armored Division, the Thirteenth Field Artillery

Brigade, and seven battalions of the First Tank Destroyer Group. Howe, *Northwest Africa: Seizing the Initiative in the West*, 546.

86. Omar N. Bradley, *A Soldier's Story* (New York: Henry Holt, 1951), 43–45.

87. Blumenson, *Patton Papers*, 188–89, 203; Carlo D'Este, *Patton: A Genius for War* (New York: HarperCollins, 1995), 463.

88. Rolf, *Bloody Road to Tunis*, 158.

89. Playfair, *The Mediterranean and the Middle East*, 4: 239–51; Alan J. Levine, *The War Against Rommel's Supply Lines, 1942–1943* (Westport, Conn.: Praeger, 1999), 136–43; Rolf, *Bloody Road to Tunis*, 88.

90. James H. Doolittle, *I Could Never Be So Lucky Again* (New York, Bantam, 1991), 327.

91. Kesselring, *Kesselring*, 178.

92. Hamilton, *Master of the Battlefield*, 56, 198.

93. Playfair, *The Mediterranean and the Middle East*, 4: 306–13.

94. Howe, *Northwest Africa: Seizing the Initiative in the West*, 552; Rolf, *Bloody Road to Tunis*, 172, 183.

95. Bradley and Blair, *A General's Life*, 146.

96. Hinsley, *British Intelligence*, 2: 597.

97. Hamilton, *Master of the Battlefield*, 152–71; Bradley and Blair, *A General's Life*, 146.

98. Rolf, *Bloody Road to Tunis*, 256.

99. Hamilton, *Master of the Battlefield*, 183–95.

100. The close support role of the Desert Air Force was the work of thirty-six-year-old Battle of Britain fighter ace Air Vice Marshal Harry Broadhurst, who replaced Coningham, promoted to air-officer-commanding allied tactical air forces. Broadhurst had abandoned Coningham's priority, which had been to detail fighters to escort bombers. Hamilton, *Master of the Battlefield*, 199–203.

101. Nicolson, *Alex*, 216–17.

102. Moorehead, *The Desert War*, 548–59.

103. Kesselring, *Kesselring*, 185.

104. Hamilton, *Master of the Battlefield*, 221–26. On the campaign, see ibid., 183–203; Playfair, *The Mediterranean and the Middle East*, 4: 315–68; Howe, *Northwest Africa: Seizing the Initiative in the West*, 564–77; Rolf, *Bloody Road to Tunis*, 216.

105. Bradley, *A Soldier's Story*, 153.

106. Levine, *The War Against Rommel's Supply Lines*, 83–84, 148, 159–60, 167.

107. Levine says that the Axis lost 506 ships, of which 170 were over 500 tons. The Italians admitted to only 79 merchant ships lost "at sea." Another Italian source owns up to 243 ships sunk. *The War Against Rommel's Supply Lines*, 180. Playfair, *The Mediterranean and the Middle East*, 4: 368, 422–24. Supplies were supplemented by an additional 8,000 tons brought in by air in March and

3,000 in April. 416–19. However, the food situation did not seem to be too bad. At the surrender, the Allies found enough food in Axis stores to feed the POWs. Hinsley, *British Intelligence*, 2: 614.

108. Rolf, *Bloody Road to Tunis*, 229–30.

109. Sandler, *"Cease Resistance,"* 54.

110. Playfair, *The Mediterranean and the Middle East*, 4: 393–95; 444–45 for a list of officers leaving Tunisia. Levine, *The War Against Rommel's Supply Lines*, 177.

111. Hamilton, *Master of the Battlefield*, 232–33; Rolf, *Bloody Road to Tunis*, 222.

112. Hirshson, *General Patton*, 331.

113. Ambrose, *Eisenhower*, 237.

114. D'Este, *Eisenhower*, 404.

115. Bradley and Blair, *A General's Life*, 145; Howe, *Northwest Africa: Seizing the Initiative in the West*, 599.

116. Playfair, *The Mediterranean and the Middle East*, 4: 401–05.

117. Hinsley, *British Intelligence*, 2: 612–13.

118. Bradley and Blair, *A General's Life*, 157; Howe, *Northwest Africa: Seizing the Initiative in the West*, 609–43.

119. Playfair. *The Mediterranean and the Middle East*, 4: 443.

120. Moorehead, *The Desert War*, 607.

121. Ibid., 612.

122. Spike Milligan, *Monty: His Part in My Victory* (London: Penguin, 1978), 16–17.

123. In fact, only 632 officers and men were evacuated in the last days of the campaign. Hinsley, *British Intelligence*, 2: 614.

124. Bradley and Blair, *A General's Life*, 158.

125. Hamilton, *Master of the Battlefield*, 229–41; Playfair, *The Mediterranean and the Middle East*, 4: 446–47.

126. These included 18,221 U.S.; 16,180 French; 23,545 British First Army; and 12,395 British Eighth Army; Howe, *Northwest Africa: Seizing the Initiative in the West*, 675. Playfair, *The Mediterranean and the Middle East*, vol. 4, gives these figures: British First Army, 25,742; Eighth Army, 12,618; Second Corps, 18,221; French, 19,439.

127. This scenario is laid out by Rolf, *Bloody Road to Tunis*, 288.

128. John Ellis, *Brute Force* (London: Viking, 1990), 306.

129. Bradley and Blair, *A General's Life*, 159.

130. Thirty-two German, Romanian, Hungarian, and Italian divisions were annihilated and a further sixteen virtually ceased to exist as a result of Stalingrad. The Soviets also claimed 12,000 German guns captured or destroyed, 3,500 tanks, and 3,000 aircraft. Above all, the Red Army had come of age. Richard Overy, *Why the Allies Won* (London: Norton, 1995), 84.

131. British official history records 238,243 POWs, while the Americans claim 275,000. Playfair, *The Mediterranean and the Middle East*, 4: 460.

132. Levine argues that the Axis lost 2,422 planes in Tunisia. *The War Against Rommel's Supply Lines*, 181. Playfair gives lower figures. *The Mediterranean and the Middle East*, 4: 460.

133. Gerhard Weinberg, *A World At Arms: A Global History of World War II* (New York: Cambridge University Press, 1995), 446–47; Howe, *Northwest Africa: Seizing the Initiative in the West*, 676–77.

134. Hinsley, *British Intelligence*, 3: 80.

135. Ronald Lewin, *Ultra Goes to War: The Secret Story* (London: Hutchinson, 1978), 314.

136. Deakin, *The Brutal Friendship*, 120–21, 134–41, 285–87.

137. Rolf, *Bloody Road to Tunis*, 275, 282.

CHAPTER NINE: HUSKY: "ONE CONTINENT REDEEMED"

1. Winston S. Churchill, *The Second World War*, vol. 4, *The Hinge of Fate* (Boston: Houghton Mifflin, 1950), 799.

2. Arthur Bryant, *The Turn of the Tide: A History of the War Years Based on the Diaries of Field-Marshal Lord Alanbrooke, Chief of the Imperial General Staff* (Garden City, N.Y.: Doubleday, 1957), 449.

3. The arguments for Brimstone are that Sardinia was poorly defended, and Corsica would have fallen rapidly after Sardinia. Once these islands on the flank of Italy had been seized, the Allies would not have been obliged to invade the mainland at Salerno at the limit of air range from Sicily, but instead could have invaded farther up the coast. For a summary of these arguments, see Carlo D'Este, "What If the Allies Had Invaded Sardinia and Corsica Instead of Sicily in 1943?" in Harold C. Deutsch and Dennis E. Showalter, eds., *What If? Strategic Alternatives of WWII* (Chicago: Emperor's Press, 1997), 128–30.

4. Bryant, *The Turn of the Tide*, 456; Philip Ziegler, *Mountbatten* (New York: Knopf, 1985), 203.

5. On 30 April 1943 a British submarine dumped a body near Huelva on the Spanish coast, where the German consul was known to be a spy. The cadaver, allegedly the victim of an air crash, was dressed in the uniform of a Royal Marine. Attached to its wrist was an attaché case carrying a letter to General Alexander that gave the impression that the objective of the next Allied attack would be Greece. Ultra intercepts on 14 May revealed that the Germans had sent reinforcements to Greece, the Balkans, and Sardinia based on their reading of the intelligence in the attaché case. Churchill, in Washington for the Trident Conference, received the message: "MINCEMEAT swallowed whole." For a discussion of Mincemeat, see E. Montagu, *The Man Who Never Was* (London, 1953).

6. Deakin, *The Brutal Friendship: Mussolini, Hitler and the Fall of Italian Fascism* (New York: Harper and Row, 1962), 350.

7. I.S.O. Playfair, *The Mediterranean and the Middle East*, vol. 4, *The Destruction of the Axis Forces in Africa* (London: HMSO, 1966), 263–66.

8. Alan F. Wilt, *War From the Top: German and British Decision Making During World War II* (Bloomington: Indiana University Press, 1990), 199.

9. Playfair, *The Mediterranean and the Middle East*, 4: 263; Bryant, *The Turn of the Tide*, 451.

10. C.J.C. Molony, *The Mediterranean and the Middle East*, vol. 5, *The Campaign in Sicily 1943 and the Campaign in Italy 3rd September 1943 to 31st March 1944* (London: HMSO, 1973), 3, 6–9.

11. Nigel Hamilton, *Master of the Battlefield: Monty's War Years, 1942–1944* (New York: McGraw-Hill, 1983), 245–46.

12. Albert N. Garland and Howard McGaw Smyth, *Sicily and the Surrender of Italy* (Washington, D.C.: Office of the Chief of Military History, 1965), 420.

13. Molony, *The Mediterranean and the Middle East*, 5: 15.

14. Martin Blumenson, *The Patton Papers, 1940–1945* (Boston: Houghton Mifflin, 1974), 237.

15. Garland and Smyth, *Sicily and the Surrender of Italy*, 421.

16. Molony, *The Mediterranean and the Middle East*, 5: 24–25.

17. Hamilton, *Master of the Battlefield*, 288.

18. Denis Mack Smith, *Mussolini* (New York: Knopf, 1982), 281–82.

19. F. H. Hinsley, *British Intelligence in the Second World War*, vol. 3 (New York: Cambridge University Press, 1984), 77.

20. Horst Boog, Werner Rahn, Reinhard Stumpf, and Bernd Wegner, *Germany and the Second World War*, vol. 6, *The Global War: Widening of the Conflict into a World War and the Shift of the Initiative, 1941–1943* (Oxford: Clarendon, 2001), 138.

21. Deakin, *The Brutal Friendship*, 367, 371, 377.

22. Hinsley, *British Intelligence*, 3: 80.

23. Albert Kesselring, *Kesselring: A Soldier's Record* (New York: William Morrow, 1954), 191. This is essentially the argument made by D'Este, "What If the Allies Had Invaded Sardinia?"

24. Dominick Graham and Shelford Bidwell, *Tug of War: The Battle for Italy, 1943–45* (New York: St. Martin's, 1986), 38.

25. Carlo D'Este, *Patton: A Genius for War* (New York: HarperCollins, 1995), 203.

26. Kesselring, *Kesselring*, 193.

27. Molony, *The Mediterranean and the Middle East*, 5: 41.

28. By 17 July, Hube was in tactical control of all German forces while von Senger was technically liaison officer with the Italian Sixth Army. Molony, *The Mediterranean and the Middle East*, 5: 92.

29. Allied aircraft numbered 3,462 (2,510 serviceable). Ibid., 5: 46–47.

30. Kesselring, *Kesselring*, 193–95.

31. Molony, *The Mediterranean and the Middle East*, 5: 42.

32. "Our last doubts about the objective of the invasion were removed,"

Kesselring insisted. *Kesselring*. 195. But British intelligence showed Axis opinion still divided on the possible Allied objectives. Hinsley, *British Intelligence*, 3: 79. See also Hamilton, *Master of the Battlefield*, 287; Carlo D'Este, *Bitter Victory: The Battle for Sicily, 1943* (New York: Dutton, 1988), 214–16. On Eisenhower's role in Corkscrew, over the objections of Tedder and Cunningham, see Carlo D'Este, *Eisenhower: A Soldier's Life* (New York: Henry Holt, 2002), 429–31.

33. Only two U.S. warships, one British hospital ship, and seven merchant vessels were lost to Axis air attack. Five U.S. warships, six British warships, one British hospital ship, and seven merchant vessels were damaged. Molony, *The Mediterranean and the Middle East*, 5: 99–100, 173.

34. Hinsley, *British Intelligence*, 3: 80.

35. Molony, *The Mediterranean and the Middle East*, 5: 42–43; Carlo D'Este, *World War II in the Mediterranean, 1942–1945* (Chapel Hill, N.C.: Algonquin Books, 1990), 50. Kesselring defended the scattering about of men and supplies as the only way to protect them against air attack and a breakdown of communications. *Kesselring*, 193; for his orders to his divisional commanders, see 194.

36. Hamilton, *Master of the Battlefield*, 286–88.

37. Omar N. Bradley, *A Soldier's Story* (New York: Henry Holt, 1951), 133; Molony, *The Mediterranean and the Middle East*, 5: 83–84, 86–87; D'Este, *World War II in the Mediterranean*, 51–53; D'Este, *Eisenhower*, 433; Stanley P. Hirshson, *General Patton: A Soldier's Life* (New York: HarperCollins, 2002), 366–67.

38. Molony, *The Mediterranean and the Middle East*, 5: 66, 68.

39. Kesselring, *Kesselring*, 196.

40. Molony, *The Mediterranean and the Middle East*, 5: 84–85; Bradley, *A Soldier's Story*, 131.

41. Bradley, *A Soldier's Story*, 130.

42. Molony, *The Mediterranean and the Middle East*, 5: 91.

43. Kesselring, *Kesselring*, 196–98.

44. Garland and Smyth, *Sicily and the Surrender of Italy*, 213.

45. Hinsley, *British Intelligence*, 3: 90–92.

46. Kesselring, *Kesselring*, 197, 199.

47. Mauldin was referring to Italy in general. But the quote fits the occasion. William Mauldin, *Up Front* (Cleveland: World, 1945), 64.

48. Smith, *Mussolini*, 278, 282, 285, 290, 292–98.

49. Kesselring, *Kesselring*, 205–06.

50. Elena Agarossi, *A Nation Collapses: The Italian Surrender of September 1943* (Cambridge: Cambridge University Press, 1999), 55–57.

51. Molony, *The Mediterranean and the Middle East*, 5: 122.

52. Kesselring, *Kesselring*, 207.

53. Hamilton, *Master of the Battlefield*, 303; Nigel Nicolson, *Alex: The Life of Field Marshal Earl Alexander of Tunis* (London: Pan Books, 1987), 241.

54. Garland and Smyth, *Sicily and the Surrender of Italy*, 209.

55. Molony, *The Mediterranean and the Middle East*, 5: 88–89; Garland and Smyth, *Sicily and the Surrender of Italy*, 209.

56. Carlo D'Este, *World War II in the Mediterranean*, 63; D'Este, *Patton*, 516.

57. Omar N. Bradley and Clay Blair, *A General's Life: An Autobiography by General of the Army Omar N. Bradley* (New York: Simon and Schuster, 1983), 189.

58. Molony, *The Mediterranean and the Middle East*, 5: 110–11.

59. Hinsley, *British Intelligence*, 3: 93.

60. Hamilton, *Master of the Battlefield*, 307.

61. Ibid., 308, 312.

62. Alexander's biographer argues that by pitting Montgomery and Patton in bitter competition to be the first to reach Messina, Alexander actually made sense of his plan to take the island. Nicolson, *Alex*, 241. But the British official history contends that Alexander was simply insensitive to Patton's feeling of being slighted. Molony, *The Mediterranean and the Middle East*, 5: 109.

63. Molony, *The Mediterranean and the Middle East*, 5: 89.

64. Bradley and Blair, *A General's Life*, 188–89. Patton was also in the doghouse after the massacre of seventy-three Italian POWs by a captain and a sergeant of the Forty-fifth Division. Their defense was that Patton's bloodthirsty speeches delivered to U.S. troops before the invasion had cautioned against taking prisoners, and so constituted a direct order. D'Este, *Patton*, 509–11, 515.

65. Ladislas Farago, *Patton: Ordeal and Triumph* (London: Arthur Baker, 1966), 170–71.

66. Kesselring, *Kesselring*, 198.

67. Hamilton, *Master of the Battlefield*, 321.

68. Robert Capa, *Slightly Out of Focus* (New York: Henry Holt, 1947), 106–07.

69. Richard Tregaskis, *Invasion Diary* (New York: Random House, 1944), 22.

70. Peter Schrijvers, *The Crash of Ruin: American Combat Soldiers in Europe During World War II* (New York: New York University Press, 1998), 122; Tregaskis, *Invasion Diary*, 23–24, 62–63.

71. Edward K. Rodgers, *Doughboy Chaplain* (Boston: Meador, 1945), 112.

72. The U.S. official history concludes that Alexander gave in because he realized that "if he waited too long Patton would probably say, 'To hell with this,' and push out anyway." Garland and Smyth, *Sicily and the Surrender of Italy*, 236. Patton's chief of staff also withheld from his commander Alexander's directive ordering Patton to seize Petralia to cut off Axis troops still in western Sicily. Hamilton, *Master of the Battlefield*, 321–23.

73. Bradley, *A Soldier's Story*, 142.

74. Farago, *Patton*, 176.

75. D'Este, *Patton*, 525.

76. Molony, *The Mediterranean and the Middle East*, 5: 173–74.

77. Terry Allen was relieved as division commander "without prejudice" and returned to the States, eventually to command the 104th Division in Northern Europe. However, it was felt that Allen had mishandled the battle by underestimating German strength and then committing his troops piecemeal to the fight. Garland and Smyth, *Sicily and the Surrender of Italy*, 323–47. Bradley complained that Allen was too temperamental, had developed an unhealthy rivalry with his assistant division commander, Ted Roosevelt, and that the unit had developed an excess of "self-pity and pride" which had undermined discipline and made it reluctant to subordinate itself to larger battle plans. Bradley, *A Soldier's Story*, 154–55. In *A General's Life*, 195, Bradley insisted that the First Division under Allen tried to operate "as an undisciplined, independent army, unresponsive to my wishes."

78. "We had fought the entire campaign with an acute shortage of artillery ammunition," Bradley complained after Messina was taken, "forced on one occasion to stop fighting and send every truck we had to the rear to bring up ammo. We had been compelled to lay our own lines of communication to the Seventh Army, when it was their responsibility to lay lines to us. Army had failed to establish any sort of reliable operating procedures with our air forces. We had had little or no direct air support, had often been bombed or strafed by our own planes, and could not get anyone to carry out proper photo reconnaissance over enemy positions. Patton did not give a damn about these details, and his attitude was reflected by his staff." Bradley and Blair, *A General's Life*, 199.

79. For the slapping incidents, see Hirshson, *General Patton*, 385–88; Farago, *Patton*, 183, 186–87.

80. Naval Task Force 88 consisted of 2 cruisers, 14 destroyers, 14 MTBs, and 19 landing craft (2 LSTs, 10 LCIs, and 7 LCTs), plus some smaller escort vessels. Garland and Smyth, *Sicily and the Surrender of Italy*, 320.

81. Bradley, *A Soldier's Story*, 158–59.

82. Garland and Smyth, *Sicily and the Surrender of Italy*, 357, 366.

83. For an account of the Brolo operation, see Garland and Smyth, *Sicily and the Surrender of Italy*, 388–405.

84. Molony, *The Mediterranean and the Middle East*, 5: 181.

85. Garland and Smyth, *Sicily and the Surrender of Italy*, 378–79; Hinsley, *British Intelligence*, 3: 96–99.

86. Nicolson, *Alex*, 247.

87. Garland and Smyth, *Sicily and the Surrender of Italy*, 380–81.

88. Oliver Warner, *Admiral of the Fleet Cunningham of Hyndhope: The Battle for the Mediterranean* (Athens: Ohio University Press, 1967), 211–12.

89. Molony, *The Mediterranean and the Middle East*, 5: 167–68; Hamilton, *Master of the Battlefield*, 347–49.

90. Garland and Smyth, *Sicily and the Surrender of Italy* 426–31; D'Este, *Patton*, 541.

91. D'Este, *Eisenhower*, 438.

92. Tregaskis, *Invasion Diary*, 64.

93. Schrijvers, *The Crash of Ruin*, 51–53.

94. The opening of the Mediterranean released 225 merchant vessels. A merchant ship sailing from Liverpool to Alexandria saved ninety days on a return trip over the Cape of Good Hope route. Men and supplies could reach India in 20 percent less time. The increase in the volume of Allied shipping in the Mediterranean also increased losses, however, as convoys, some numbering up to 129 ships, were vulnerable to attack by nearly a thousand Axis planes that remained in the Mediterranean in October 1943. The opening of the Mediterranean and the surrender of the Italian fleet also allowed the Allies to release many of their warships to other theaters. I.S.O. Playfair, *The Mediterranean and the Middle East*, vol. 5 (London: HMSO, 1973), 357, 359, 363, 371–72. For Lend-Lease Percentages for Arctic and Persian routes, see I.C.B. Dear and M.R.D. Foot, eds. *The Oxford Companion to World War II* (Oxford: Oxford University Press, 1995), 46, 874.

95. Four of the six American divisions that fought in Sicily would transfer to Normandy: the First and Ninth Infantry, Second Armored, and Eighty-second Airborne. The Third and Forty-fifth Divisions would fight in Italy and subsequently in Operation Anvil, the August 1944 Riviera invasion.

96. Bradley and Blair, *A General's Life*, 200.

97. Matthew Jones, *Britain, the United States and the Mediterranean War, 1942–44* (New York: St. Martin's, 1996), 64.

98. S. E. Morison argues that a bold thrust of cruisers and destroyers up the strait could have cut off the German escape. *History of United States Naval Operations in World War II*, 15 vols. (New York: Oxford University Press, 1948–62), 9: 216–17.

99. D'Este, *Eisenhower*, 423, 437.

100. David French, *Raising Churchill's Army: The British Army and the War against Germany, 1919–1945* (Oxford: Oxford University Press, 2000), 264.

101. Hamilton, *Master of the Battlefield*, 377–78.

102. Ibid., 270. "[Alexander] may order you to carry out some crazy plan," Montgomery told U.S. Fifth Army commander Mark Clark at Salerno. "If he does, just tell him to go to hell." Quoted in John Ellis, *Cassino: The Hollow Victory: The Battle for Rome, January–June 1944* (New York: McGraw-Hill, 1984), 23.

103. Hamilton, *Master of the Battlefield*, 371.

104. Garland and Smyth, *Sicily and the Surrender of Italy*, 423.

105. Bradley, *A Soldier's Story*, 159.

106. D'Este, *Eisenhower*, 440.

107. A lesser general, D'Este insists, would have been fired. But Eisenhower and Marshall both valued Patton's reputation as "a fighter." D'Este, *Eisenhower*, 442.

108. On Bradley's mistakes in Northwestern Europe, see ibid., 563, 569–70, 580, 592–93, 597.

109. Hirshson, *General Patton*, 409–13.

110. Molony, *The Mediterranean and the Middle East*, 5: 67.

111. Garland and Smyth, *Sicily and the Surrender of Italy*, 421; Bradley, *A Soldier's Story*, 150–52.

112. Garland and Smyth, *Sicily and the Surrender of Italy*, 423.

113. Many of the landing craft used in the July amphibious invasion had to be withdrawn for repair and to prepare for the follow-up invasion of Italy. Molony, *The Mediterranean and the Middle East*, 5: 181.

114. Kesselring, *Kesselring*, 196.

115. Ibid., 199.

116. Ibid., 194.

CHAPTER TEN: "THE MEDITERRANEAN YEAR"

1. Matthew Jones, *Britain, the United States and the Mediterranean War, 1942–44* (New York: St. Martin's, 1996), 138–39.

2. Winston S. Churchill, *The Second World War*, vol. 4, *The Hinge of Fate* (Boston: Houghton Mifflin, 1950), 799.

3. Field Marshal Lord Alanbrooke, *War Diaries, 1939–1945* (Berkeley: University of California Press, 2001), 442–43, 462–63.

4. Michael Howard, *The Mediterranean Strategy in the Second World War* (New York: Praeger, 1968), 69–71.

5. Winston S. Churchill, *The Second World War*, vol. 5, *Closing the Ring* (Boston: Houghton Mifflin, 1951), 52; Howard, *The Mediterranean Strategy*, 54, 70. This was the view of the Joint War Plans Committee of the U.S. Joint Chiefs of Staff in July 1943. Albert N. Garland and Howard McGaw Smyth, *Sicily and the Surrender of Italy* (Washington, D.C.: Office of the Chief of Military History, Department of the Army, 1965), 435.

6. Mark Mazower, *Dark Continent: Europe's Twentieth Century* (New York: Vintage, 1998), 225–27.

7. On 3 August the JIC predicted that Germany would be able to send to Italy no more than four divisions, which would have the task of extricating those already there and then fall back to the Alps. The British chiefs of staff were unconvinced by this intelligence prediction, however. Instead, they expressed the hope that the Germans would reinforce Italy and the Balkans and so relieve pressure on Russia. F. H. Hinsley, *British Intelligence in the Second World War*, vol. 3 Part 1 (New York: Cambridge University Press, 1984), 103.

8. Richard Tregaskis, *Invasion Diary* (New York: Random House, 1944), 73.

9. Alanbrooke, *War Diaries*, 451.

10. Ronald Lewin, *Churchill as Warlord* (London: Batsford, 1974), 203.

11. At the conclusion of Husky, nineteen British or British-controlled divisions, four U.S., and four French divisions remained in the Mediterranean. I.S.O. Playfair, *The Mediterranean and the Middle East*, vol. 5 (London: HMSO, 1973), 194.

12. Howard, *The Mediterranean Strategy*, 40; Garland and Smyth, *Sicily and the Surrender of Italy*, 440.

13. Howard, *The Mediterranean Strategy*, 44; Lewin, *Churchill as Warlord*, 217.

14. Alanbrooke, *War Diaries*, 459. Furthermore, any operation against the Dodecanese as a prelude to an attack on the Balkans must be preceded by the reconquest of Crete, which would push back any attack on the Balkans into late 1943 at the earliest. Playfair, *The Mediterranean and the Middle East*, 5: 191. On Churchill's vision of how to exploit Mediterranean opportunities, see Churchill, *The Second World War*, 5: 57–58.

15. Nigel Hamilton, *Master of the Battlefield: Monty's War Years, 1942–1944* (New York: McGraw-Hill, 1983), 257–58.

16. Playfair, *The Mediterranean and the Middle East*, 5: 194.

17. Churchill, *The Second World War*, 5: 83.

18. Hinsley, *British Intelligence*, 3: Part 1, 107.

19. Lewin, *Churchill as Warlord*, 201. To get a firmer grip on the Mediterranean, Churchill proposed that Brooke step down as commander-designate for Overlord in favor of Eisenhower. In return, Alexander would succeed Eisenhower as supreme commander in the Mediterranean. Churchill wrote that Brooke took the news of his demotion "with soldierly dignity." *The Second World War*, 5: 85. In fact, Brooke was crushed by the prospect of finishing the war without a major combat command. Alanbrooke, *War Diaries*, 441–42. See also Howard, *The Mediterranean Strategy*, 38–40; Garland and Smyth, *Sicily and the Surrender of Italy*, 435–40.

20. Ralph S. Mavrogordato, "Hitler's Decision on the Defense of Italy," in Kent Roberts Greenfield, ed., *Command Decisions* (Washington, D.C.: Center for Military History, 1990), 309–10.

21. This was the argument of Walter Warlimont, *Inside Hitler's Headquarters, 1939–45* (London: Weidenfeld and Nicolson, 1964), 386–87.

22. Albert Kesselring, *Memoirs* (London: Kimber, 1953), 267.

23. Mavrogordato, "Hitler's Decision on the Defense of Italy," 318–20.

24. Howard, *The Mediterranean Strategy*, 41–43; Garland and Smyth, *Sicily and the Surrender of Italy*, 452–53, 469–70.

25. Kenneth Macksey, *Kesselring: German Master Strategist of the Second World War* (London: Greenhill Books, 2000), 173.

26. Ernest F. Fuller, *The Mediterranean Theater of Operations: Cassino to the Alps* (Washington, D.C.: Center for Military History, U.S. Army, 1977), 535.

27. David Kennedy, *Freedom from Fear* (Oxford: Oxford University Press, 1999), 596.

28. *The Diaries of Robert Bruce Lockhart, 1935–1965* (London, 1980), 1: 220, quoted in Elena Agarossi, *A Nation Collapses: The Italian Surrender of September 1943* (Cambridge: Cambridge University Press, 1999), 38.

29. Churchill, *The Second World War*, 5: 126–27.

30. Fuller, *The Mediterranean Theater of Operations*, 536.

31. Warlimont, *Inside Hitler's Headquarters*, 387.

32. Howard, *The Mediterranean Strategy*, 44.

33. Carlo D'Este, *Eisenhower: A Soldier's Life* (New York: Henry Holt, 2002), D'Este, *Eisenhower*, 446.

34. Agarossi, *A Nation Collapses*, 130.

35. German casualties in Italy were 434,646, of which 48,067 were killed and 214,048 missing. The Allies took 312,000 casualties. Fuller, *The Mediterranean Theater of Operations*, 545.

36. Agarossi, *A Nation Collapses*, 37.

37. Ibid., 14, 41; Garland and Smyth, *Sicily and the Surrender of Italy*, 444.

38. Agarossi, *A Nation Collapses*, 13, 16–17, 33–34, 36.

39. Churchill, *The Second World War*, 5: 102.

40. Harold Macmillan, *War Diaries: Politics and War in the Mediterranean, January 1943–May 1945* (New York: St. Martin's, 1984), 220.

41. Agarossi, *A Nation Collapses*, 34, 42–49, 51.

42. Richard Lamb, *War in Italy, 1943–1945: A Brutal Story* (New York: St. Martin's, 1993), 12.

43. Macmillan, *War Diaries*, 220, 399.

44. Although German divisions on the peninsula amounted to only one incomplete panzer grenadier division in central Italy, two armored divisions in the south, and elements of a paratroop division in Tuscany, German divisions from France and the Balkans could have quickly reinforced. F. W. Deakin, *The Brutal Friendship: Mussolini, Hitler and the Fall of Italian Fascism* (New York: Harper and Row, 1962), 483–84.

45. Albert Kesselring, *Kesselring: A Soldier's Record* (New York: William Morrow, 1954), 203, 205.

46. Deakin, *The Brutal Friendship*, 495.

47. Kesselring, *Kesselring*, 210.

48. Agarossi, *A Nation Collapses*, 52–53, 59–60, 73; Garland and Smyth, *Sicily and the Surrender of Italy*, 440–41, 445.

49. Garland and Smyth, *Sicily and the Surrender of Italy*, 444–45, 475.

50. Castellano's problem, as Churchill noted, was to attempt "to carry out a major and cardinal operation of the war from a subordinate position." Winston S. Churchill, *The Second World War*, vol. 2, *Their Finest Hour* (Boston: Houghton Miffin, 1949), 15.

51. Agarossi, *A Nation Collapses*, 65–68, 72, 75–76; Garland and Smyth, *Sicily and the Surrender of Italy*, 447–50, 457–58.

52. Garland and Smyth, *Sicily and the Surrender of Italy*, 477.

53. The Allies had been assured by General Zanussi, sent to Lisbon on 25 August, that Italian forces would defend Rome against the Germans at all costs. Increasing German reinforcement of the peninsula caused Eisenhower to believe that the cooperation of Italian forces might make the difference between success and failure of Avalanche. Ibid., 464–65.

54. Ibid., 458–60, 478.

55. Tregaskis, *Invasion Diary*, 107.

56. D'Este, *Eisenhower*, 451.

57. Memoria 44, an operations order setting out Italian resistance, had been sent out by chief of the Army General Staff General Roatta to Italian generals between 2 and 5 September. But these orders were essentially defensive and were never implemented because of confusion and indecision in the Italian high command. On 8 September, Roatta ordered three divisions in Rome to resist German incursions into Rome, but not to prevent their departure. When German units began to attack Italian forces, Ambrosio, chief of the *Commando Supremo*, interpreted these attacks as German attempts to secure their line of retreat. Everyone deferred to Badoglio, who refused to make a decision. Garland and Smyth, *Sicily and the Surrender of Italy*, 481, 491–92, 512–15.

58. This was in part because at Cassibili on 31 August Clark and Smith had promised a total of at least fifteen divisions in the invasion of Italy. For this reason, Badoglio continued to insist that the Allies bore moral responsibility for the Italian collapse. Ibid., 478–79, 542.

59. Agarossi, *A Nation Collapses*, 97, 101–02; Garland and Smyth, *Sicily and the Surrender of Italy*, 528–30.

60. Agarossi, *A Nation Collapses*, 111–12; Garland and Smyth, *Sicily and the Surrender of Italy*, 535.

61. Agarossi, *A Nation Collapses*, 100–01.

62. Michael Howard, *Grand Strategy*, vol. 4, *August 1942–September 1943* (London: HMSO, 1972), 270.

63. Ronald Lewin is very critical of the American refusal to support Accolade, suggesting that it would have diverted significant German troops at little cost to the Allies. *Churchill as Warlord*, 222–23. But the Americans had no interest in opening yet another front in the Mediterranean when they had barely enough troops to hold their own in Italy. Eliot Cohen compares Accolade to British intervention in Syria and Iraq in 1941, an example of Churchill's willingness to move rapidly to gain cheap victories on the margins of a global conflict before his enemy could preempt his options and do more damage. Eliot Cohen, "Churchill and Coalition Strategy," in Paul Kennedy, ed., *Grand Strategies in War and Peace* (New Haven: Yale University Press, 1991), 62–63. However, the Germans were very distant from the Levant in 1941 and unable to intervene. In the Dodecanese in 1943, the Germans were in a far more advantageous position, especially after the Americans refused to help.

64. Howard, *Grand Strategy*, 4: 381.

65. Playfair, *The Mediterranean and the Middle East*, 5: 532–59; John Ehrman, *Grand Strategy*, vol. 5, *August 1943–September 1944* (London: HMSO, 1956), 88–103. For a detailed discussion of Accolade, see Jeffrey Holland, *The Aegean Mission: Allied Operations in the Dodecanese* (New York: Greenwood, 1988).

66. Kenneth Strong. *Intelligence at the Top* (London, 1968), 127.

67. This was also a step in the transformation of AFHQ into a "branch ministry of defense" rather than a military headquarters. Nevertheless, Wilson's

position as Supreme Allied Commander Mediterranean (SACMED) was undermined by his association with the Dodecanese operation. Oliver Leese, commander of the Eighth Army in Italy, referred to Wilson as the "Island Princess." Jones, *Britain, the United States and the Mediterranean War*, 111–12, 117, 161.

68. Agarossi, *A Nation Collapses*, 81–99.

69. Garland and Smyth, *Sicily and the Surrender of Italy*, 542.

70. Ibid., 544–48.

71. Deakin, *The Brutal Friendship*, 95, 99, 101, 253.

72. Churchill confessed that "the Balkans and especially Yugoslavia never left my thoughts" from the summer of 1943. Churchill, *The Second World War*, 5: 463.

73. Stevan K. Pavlowitch, "Neither Heroes nor Traitors: Suggestions for a Reappraisal of the Yugoslav Resistance," in Brian Bond and Ian Roy, eds., *War and Society: A Yearbook of Military History* (London: Croom Helm, 1975), 233–34.

74. Milovan Djilas, *Wartime* (New York: Harcourt Brace Jovanovich, 1977), 202–03, 327; Franklin Lindsay, *Beacons in the Night: With the OSS and Tito's Partisans in Wartime Yugoslavia* (Stanford, Calif.: Stanford University Press, 1993), 31.

75. M. Djilas, *Wartime*, 216.

76. Paul N. Hehn, *The German Struggle Against Yugoslav Guerrillas in World War II: German Counter-Insurgency in Yugoslavia, 1941–1943* (New York: Columbia University Press, 1979), 3, 9.

77. M. Djilas, *Wartime*, 225–28.

78. Ibid., 220, 224.

79. Lindsay, *Beacons in the Night*, 136, 195.

80. M. Djilas, *Wartime*, 301–02.

81. When the Soviets complained about the negotiations, Tito replied that they were confined to the exchange of wounded. Ibid., 380.

82. David Pryce-Jones, *Evelyn Waugh and His World* (Boston: Little, Brown, 1973), 145, 161.

83. M. Djilas, *Wartime*, 93.

84. Aleska Djilas, *The Contested Country: Yugoslav Unity and the Communist Revolution, 1919–1953* (Cambridge, Mass.: Harvard University Press, 1991), 147.

85. M. Djilas, *Wartime*, 328.

86. Churchill, *The Second World War*, 5: 466.

87. Walter R. Roberts, *Tito, Mihailović and the Allies, 1941–1945* (New Brunswick, N.J.: Rutgers University Press, 1973), 149–51, 229; Hehn, *The German Struggle Against the Yugoslav Guerrillas*, 15. During 1944 the Western Allies delivered 100,000 rifles, 50,000 light machine guns and submachine guns, 1,280 mortars, 324,000 mortar bombs, 636,000 grenades, and 97 million rounds of small-arms ammunition to the partisans, as well as radios, uniforms, and boots. Fitzroy Maclean, *Eastern Approaches* (London: Jonathan Cape, 1949), 461.

88. Lindsay, *Beacons in the Night*, 42, 74–75.

89. Churchill claimed that twenty-five German divisions were tied down in Yugoslavia and Greece, a number that he admitted was disputed by Stalin. Churchill, *The Second World War*, 5: 467. Some of these "German" divisions were made up of former Soviet and Italian POWs, and Bosnian Moslems, among whom desertion became a problem for the Germans. For German troop strength, see *German Antiguerrilla Operations in the Balkans (1941–1944)* (Washington, D.C.: Department of the Army Pamphlet No. 20-243, 1954), 49, 53.

90. Mihailović stayed in the background so as publicly to maintain his anti-German stance. The British mission finally left the Chetniks in May 1944. Roberts, *Tito, Mihailović and the Allies*, 157, 197, 225.

91. Charles R. Shrader, *The Withered Vine: Logistics and the Communist Insurgency in Greece, 1945–1949* (Westport, Conn.: Praeger, 1999), 32–33.

92. Ibid., 28; Mark Mazower, *Inside Hitler's Greece: The Experience of Occupation, 1941–44* (New Haven: Yale University Press, 1993), 145–52.

93. Churchill, *The Second World War*, 5: 538.

94. Mazower, *Inside Hitler's Greece*, 113, 129, 133–37; Shrader, *The Withered Vine*, 23.

95. David H. Close, *The Origins of the Greek Civil War* (London: Longman, 1995), 113.

96. Ibid., 89.

97. Mazower, *Inside Hitler's Greece*, 324–39; Close, *Origins of the Greek Civil War*, 88–91.

98. *German Antiguerrilla Operations in the Balkans*, 73–78; Close, *Origins of the Greek Civil War*, 100.

99. Mazower, *Inside Hitler's Greece*, 155, 161–86, 216, 227–29.

100. Churchill, *The Second World War*, 5: 535. Mazower, Ibid., 144: Pound notes with "Greece" and "Bulgaria" were printed and large amounts of drachmas were purchased in Cairo. Greek troops at Alexandria were put through amphibious training. Michael Howard, *British Intelligence in the Second World War*, vol. 5, *Strategic Deception* (New York: Cambridge University Press, 1990), 86–87.

101. Hinsley, *British Intelligence*, 3: 106.

102. Playfair, *The Mediterranean and the Middle East*, 5: 204; Stephen Ambrose, *Eisenhower: Soldier, General of the Army, President-Elect, 1890–1952* (New York: Simon and Schuster, 1983), 256.

103. Nor were German plans for the withdrawal from Sardinia revealed. Hinsley *British Intelligence*, 3: 107–09.

104. Ibid., 3: 109–10.

105. Churchill, 4: 527.

106. Carlo D'Este, *Eisenhower: A Soldier's Life* (New York: Henry Holt, 2002), 280, 287, 306–07.

107. Stanley P. Hirshson, *General Patton: A Soldier's Life* (New York: HarperCollins, 2002), 261, quoting General Jacob Devers.

108. Ibid., 299.

109. D'Este, *Eisenhower*, 455.

110. Tregaskis, *Invasion Diary*, 113.

111. Martin Blumenson and James L. Stokesbury, *Masters of the Art of Command* (Boston: Houghton Mifflin, 1975), 183, 190–91.

112. Omar N. Bradley and Clay Blair, *A General's Life: An Autobiography by General of the Army Omar N. Bradley* (New York: Simon and Schuster, 1983), 204.

113. Ambrose, *Eisenhower*, 226. Clark thereby unwittingly opened the way for Patton to make his reputation. Blumenson and Stokesbury, *Masters of the Art of Command*, 186–87. Brooke had a different take on this incident: according to the CIGS, Eisenhower exiled Clark to Morocco after the "unscrupulous" Clark, in an attempt to wrest control of the entire Tunisian front from the British, incited Giraud to refuse to place French troops under British command. "Through this action Ike greatly rose in my estimation," Brooke wrote. Alanbrooke, *War Diaries*, 356.

114. Hirshson, *General Patton*, 417–18.

115. John Ellis, *Cassino: The Hollow Victory: The Battle for Rome, January–June 1944* (New York: McGraw-Hill, 1984), 23. For a general assessment of Clark's character, see Dominick Graham and Shelford Bidwell, *Tug of War: The Battle for Italy, 1943–1945* (New York: St. Martin's, 1986), 36–37.

116. Instead Patton was retained in Sicily as a replacement commander should Clark falter or become a casualty. Martin Blumenson, *Patton: The Man Behind the Legend, 1885–1945* (New York: William Morrow, 1985), 214. Eisenhower's justification for selecting Clark to head Avalanche was that he "is the ablest and most experienced officer we have in planning of amphibious operations . . . In preparing the minute details of requisitions, landing craft, training of troops and so on, he has no equal in our Army." Bradley seemed to think that he was the designated substitute as Fifth Army commander should Clark fail. Omar N. Bradley, *A Soldier's Story* (New York: Henry Holt, 1951), 204–05.

117. Forrest Pogue, "General of the Army Omar Bradley," in Field Marshal Sir Michael Carver, ed., *The War Lords: Military Commanders of the Twentieth Century* (Boston: Little, Brown, 1976), 543.

118. Monty was being repaid in his own coin for assigning the Seventh Army a secondary role in the invasion of Sicily. Hamilton, *Master of the Battlefield*, 345–46.

119. Blumenson, *Patton*, 175–76.

120. Ambrose, *Eisenhower*, 237, 263, 274; Ellis, *Cassino*, 475–76.

121. Graham and Bidwell, *Tug of War*, 55.

122. Indeed, it is arguable that the initial Allied plan for Husky—to land the American forces on the northwestern tip of the island—might have proven more profitable. Palermo could have been seized earlier as a logistical base and as a position for an early thrust along the north coast toward Messina.

123. Bradley, *A Soldier's Story*, 204.

124. Kesselring, *Kesselring*, 221.

125. Robert Wallace, *The Italian Campaign* (Chicago: Time-Life Books, 1981), 55.

126. Carlo D'Este, *World War II in the Mediterranean, 1942–1945* (Chapel Hill, N.C.: Algonquin Books, 1990), 91; Graham and Bidwell call Eisenhower's premature announcement "one of the few political miscalculations of his military career," for at least two reasons. First, it triggered Operation Achse, the German takeover of Italy, which "had the very consequence Eisenhower wished to avoid, as his bold move was based on the hopes of active collaboration of the Italians." A second consequence of Eisenhower's announcement was that it caused the Allied troops standing off Salerno to expect a rapturous Italian welcome. *Tug of War*, 39–40. Leaving aside Eisenhower's role in the Darlan deal, the problem with this verdict is that it fails to consider the likely consequences of Eisenhower's failure to make the announcement. The Allied commander suspected that Badoglio and the king were backsliding on their promise to exit the war, a suspicion that Italian documents show to have been fully justified. Eisenhower's announcement forced their hand, although it did not cause them to make preparations to defend themselves against a likely German reaction. In any case, the news had already been released by Reuters. Agarossi, *A Nation Collapses*, 94–95. Therefore, "active Italian collaboration" appears *never* to have been in the cards, with or without German intervention.

127. Much German energy was put into securing Rome. In the south, OKW temporarily wrote off Kesselring, while Tenth Army commander Heinrich von Vietinghoff, without firm orders, did not know whether to defend the coast or wrap up the Italians. He decided to do the latter. "Indeed, but for the distraction at Rome, von Vietinghoff's reaction [at Salerno] could have been quicker and more violent at the outset and blessed with far-reaching results," concludes British historian Kenneth Macksey. Macksey, *Kesselring*, 176–78. For his part, Kesselring complained, "Unfortunately the work of disarming the Italians and storing away arms, munitions and material in safety occupied more time and men than I liked in view of the tactical developments at Salerno." Kesselring, *Kesselring*, 224.

128. Rommel's and Kesselring's troops were not even in contact. Kesselring, *Kesselring*, 222.

129. Bruce Cutler, *Seeing the Darkness: Naples, 1943–1945* (Kansas City: BkMk Press of UMKC, 1998), 6.

130. Ibid., 18–19.

131. Norman Lewis, *Naples '44* (London: Collins, 1978), 13.

132. Ibid., 18.

133. Ibid., 16, 18.

134. Ambrose, *Eisenhower*, 263.

135. Alanbrooke, *War Diaries*, 452.

136. Quoted in Wallace, *The Italian Campaign*, 61.

137. Lewis, *Naples, 44*, 17.

138. Cutler, *Seeing the Darkness*, 21.
139. Kesselring, *Kesselring*, 225.
140. Mavrogordato, "Hitler's Decision on the Defense of Italy," 305–06.
141. Graham and Bidwell, *Tug of War*, 91.
142. The refusal was on the part of veterans of the Fiftieth Northumbrian and Fifty-first Highland who had been left behind when their divisions were repatriated to England. They, too, expected to be sent home, and were loath to be assigned to other units in Italy. The mutiny was defused by McCreery, who persuaded 500 to report to their new assignments. The remainder were returned to North Africa for court martial. Three sergeants, judged to be ringleaders, were sentenced to death, but were reintegrated into units and allowed to earn their rehabilitation. Ibid., 92–94.
143. Ambrose, *Eisenhower*, 265.
144. D'Este, *Eisenhower*, 455.
145. Graham and Bidwell, *Tug of War*, 117–18.
146. Ibid., 92–100.

CHAPTER ELEVEN: THE INCOMPLETE VICTORY

1. Albert Kesselring, *Kesselring: A Soldier's Record* (New York: William Morrow, 1954), 229–30.
2. Ultra intelligence began to give indications as early as 1 October 1943 that Kesselring and Hitler intended to make a fight for Rome. However, Luftwaffe intercepts passed on to Churchill indicated that the Germans were preparing a withdrawal from Italy. F. H. Hinsley, *British Intelligence in the Second World War: Its Influence on Strategy and Operations*, vol. 3, part 1 (New York: Cambridge University Press, 1984), 173–77. See also Dominick Graham and Shelford Bidwell, *Tug of War: The Battle for Italy, 1943–1945* (New York: St. Martin's, 1986), 126–27.
3. The German Tenth Army in January–February 1944 consisted of two corps. The Fourteenth Panzer Corps was made up of the Forty-fourth, Seventy-first, and Ninety-fourth Infantry Divisions, the Fifth Mountain Division, and the Third, Fifteenth, and Ninetieth Panzer Grenadier Divisions. The Seventy-sixth Panzer Corps, which did not participate in the early fighting, was composed of the 305th and 334th Infantry Divisions, the First Parachute Division, and the Twenty-sixth Panzer Division.
4. By May 1944 the Fourteenth Army would consist of two corps: the First Parachute Corps, made up of the Sixty-fifth Infantry, Fourth Parachute, and Third Panzer Grenadier Divisions; and the Seventy-sixth Panzer Corps, made up of the 362d, 715th, and Hermann Göring Panzer Divisions.
5. I.S.O. Playfair, *The Mediterranean and the Middle East*, vol. 4, *The Campaign in Sicily 1943 and the Campaign in Italy 3rd September 1943 to 31st March 1944* (London: HMSO, 1973), 571–77, 584.

6. Ibid., 4: 588.

7. Michael D. Doubler, *Closing with the Enemy: How GIs Fought the War in Europe, 1944–1945* (Lawrence: University Press of Kansas, 1994), 24.

8. your stonk is your American way of winning your war
   your stonk is when you take your whole production, Rock Island
   Arsenal '42, or whatever arsenal
   in South Carolina, South Dakota, no difference
   you throw it at the krauts from six to eight a.m.
   maybe add a naval stonk to your stonk being the really
   big suckers that take out the little towns on the mountainsides
   anyhow you stonk, you stonk the shit out of them

Bruce Cutler, *Seeing in the Darkness: Naples 1943–1945* (Kansas City: BkMk Press of UMKS, 1998), 12.

9. In addition to photo reconnaissance, which gave excellent tactical intelligence and which reached its highest potential in Italy, high-grade Sigint and Army Y Service tracked the location and movement of German units, including those of the Luftwaffe, their strength and supply situation. Collaboration with SIM, the Italian Secret Service, gave the Allies an important human intelligence (Humint) capability in Italy, especially around Rome. Humint was increased as SOE helped to organize the Italian resistance movement from autumn 1943. Hinsley, *British Intelligence*, 3(1): 177–81 and notes.

10. By February 1944, Leese's command would group the Canadian First Corps, composed of the Canadian First (Infantry) Division and the Canadian Fifth Armoured Division; the Thirteenth Corps, made up of the Seventy-eighth Division and the Indian Eighth Division; and the Polish Second Corps, made up of the Third Carpathian Division. The Indian Fourth Division was held in reserve. The New Zealand First Division under the experienced Bernard Freyberg was transferred to the Fifth Army in February and combined with the Indian Fourth and eventually the Seventy-eighth Infantry Division to create the New Zealand Corps. (The Seventh Armoured Division and the Fiftieth and Fifty-first Infantry Divisions had been repatriated to England.) For the First Battle of Cassino, Mark Clark's U.S. Fifth Army, which occupied the line running from the mouth of the Garigliano north to Monte Cassino, was a mixed Anglo-American force of four corps. On the left flank bordering the Tyrrhenian Sea, the Tenth Corps under McCreery was composed of the British Fifth, Fifty-sixth, and British Forty-sixth Divisions and the 201st Guards Brigade. The U.S. Second Corps under Major General Geoffrey Keyes, composed of the Thirty-fourth and Thirty-sixth Infantry Divisions, the First Armored Division, and the Italian First Motorized Group, were to the right of the Tenth Corps. The French Expeditionary Corps (CEF) under General Alphonse Juin, composed of the Algerian Third and Moroccan Second Divisions, rounded out the Fifth Army ranged before the Gustav line. The Sixth Corps designated for Anzio included the British First and U.S. Third Infantry Divisions and the First Special

Service Force with the Forty-fifth U.S. Division in reserve. The Fifty-sixth Division was transferred to Anzio between 3 and 18 February 1944.

11. Nigel Hamilton, *Master of the Battlefield: Monty's War Years, 1942–1944* (New York: McGraw-Hill, 1983), 46, 461.

12. Harold Macmillan, *War Diaries: Politics and War in the Mediterranean, January 1943–May 1945* (New York: St. Martin's, 1984), 389, 528–29.

13. Graham and Bidwell, *Tug of War,* 94.

14. Field Marshal Lord Alanbrooke, *War Diaries, 1939–1945* (Berkeley: University of California Press, 2001), 582.

15. This was not a huge liability in Italy. But it led to embarrassment in Burma in July 1945 when Leese was relieved as commander-in-chief of Allied land forces in Southeast Asia after he tried unsuccessfully to fire the popular and successful General, later Field Marshal, William Slim from command of the Fourteenth Army. Graham and Bidwell, *Tug of War,* 253–54; General William Jackson, *The Mediterranean and the Middle East,* vol. 6, *Victory in the Mediterranean,* part 2, *June to October 1944* (London: HMSO, 1987), 360–63. For a more favorable, though less penetrating, assessment of Leese, see Michael Craster, "Cunningham, Ritchie and Leese," in John Keegan, ed., *Churchill's Generals* (New York: Grove Weidenfeld, 1991), 214–21.

16. Stanley Sandler, *Glad to See Them Come and Sorry to See Them Go: A History of U.S. Army Tactical Civil Affairs/Military Government, 1775–1991* (no place, publisher, or date), 178.

17. Mark W. Clark, *Calculated Risk* (New York: Harper and Row, 1950), 214–15.

18. Macmillan, *War Diaries,* 354.

19. Churchill had fixed the lira at 400 to the pound, which made economic recovery difficult, in an attempt to discourage Italian economic competition. Paul Ginsborg, *A History of Contemporary Italy: Society and Politics, 1943–1988* (London: Penguin, 1990), 40.

20. Sandler, *Glad to See Them Come,* 177.

21. The greatest success was probably in its reconstruction of the rudiments of a court system based on rules of evidence and "reasonable doubt." C.R.S. Harris, *Allied Military Administration of Italy, 1943–1945* (London: HMSO, 1957), 369. Harold Macmillan praised AMGOT in Naples for restoring a badly damaged infrastructure in record time—water, sanitation, telephone service, the port, clearing booby traps, and burying the dead. *War Diaries,* 269.

22. Not only were personnel below average, but the real problem was that AMGOT had no plan. The top layers of the organization were dominated by lawyers who saw their mission as a narrow one of keeping the rear areas secure, rather than creating a public administration capable of getting society working again. George C. S. Benson and Maurice Neufel, "American Military Government in Italy," in Carl J. Frederich, ed., *American Experiences in Military Government in World War II* (New York: Reinhart, 1948), 119–121.

23. This included selling ration cards, driver's licenses, etc. Sandler, *Glad to See Them Come*, 184.

24. Only 3.4 percent of goods for sale in Naples were available in the form of rations for the population. Ginsborg, *A History of Contemporary Italy*, 37.

25. Norman Lewis, *Naples '44* (London: Collins, 1978), 84.

26. Grain was shipped from Reggio to Sicily, which caused food shortages in Reggio. Allied forces stationed on Sardinia to prepare the invasion of Corsica, 150,000 troops, ate up the food stocks on that island. Harris, *Allied Military Administration of Italy*, 46, 70, 84–87, 102, 373, 417; Macmillan, *War Diaries*, 331.

27. Harris, *Allied Military Administration of Italy*, 368.

28. Lewis, *Naples '44*, 157.

29. Cutler, *Seeing the Darkness*, 28, 31, 32; Cutler's poems are based on descriptions found in Lewis, *Naples '44*, 51–53.

30. Macmillan, *War Diaries*, 389.

31. Ginsborg puts the proportion of merchandise stolen at 60 percent. *A History of Contemporary Italy*, 37.

32. Matthew Jones, *Britain, the United States and the Mediterranean War, 1942–44* (New York: St. Martin's, 1996), 144.

33. Lewis claims that the Genoveses' influence extended to the upper echelons of the AMGOT, to the point that mayors appointed by the AMGOT to replace ousted Fascists were able to hijack aid distributed through municipal halls. *Naples '44*, 75. See also Ginsborg, *A History of Contemporary Italy*, 36. Scotland Yard was brought in to investigate Allied personnel thought to be complicit in the thefts, which had reached "alarming proportions." But only a few small fry were ever charged. Macmillan, *War Diaries*, 386–87.

34. Lewis, *Naples '44*, 86, 134–39.

35. Harris, *Allied Military Administration of Italy*, 428.

36. Lewis, *Naples '44*, 25, 56–57, 96.

37. Harris, *Allied Military Administration of Italy*, 427.

38. Lewis, *Naples '44*, 101.

39. Macmillan, *War Diaries*, 354.

40. Cutler, *Seeing the Darkness*, 43.

41. Sandler, *Glad to See Them Come*; Ginsborg, *A History of Contemporary Italy*, 40–41.

42. Joseph Heller served as a first lieutenant and bombardier with the 488th Squadron of the Twelfth Air Force. Stephen W. Potts, *Catch-22: Antiheroic Antinovel* (Boston: Twayne, 1989), 8; Sanford Pinsker, *Understanding Joseph Heller* (Columbia: University of South Carolina Press, 1991), 10, 12, 21.

43. World War I novels have been described as concerned with "the plunge of civilization into this abyss of blood and horror." They are about embittered idealism. World War II novels, by contrast, seldom protest the necessity of the war, although they fail to see it as noble. In this respect *Catch-22* is a throwback to the novels of the 1920s, which depict military bureaucracies using soldiers as cannon fodder. Pinsker, *Understanding Joseph Heller*, 15–17.

44. Constance Denniston, "The American Romance-Parody: A Study of Purdy's *Malcolm* and Heller's *Catch-22*," in Green D. Wyrick, ed., *The American Novel: Two Studies, Emporia State Research Studies* 14, no. 2 (December 1965): 52–55. See also Robert Brustein, "The Logic of Survival in a Lunatic World," 31, and Les Standiford, "Novels into Film: *Catch-22* as Watershed," 230, both in James Nagel, ed., *Critical Essays on Joseph Heller* (Boston: G. K. Hall, 1984).

45. John Ellis, *Cassino: The Hollow Victory: The Battle for Rome, January–June 1944* (New York: McGraw-Hill, 1984), 90–91, 93.

46. In this battle fought in Flanders, the British artillery barrage shattered an intricate system of dikes, causing the battlefield to flood, so that some of the attacking British troops drowned.

47. In fact, Leese concluded that the Eighth Army was too weak to mount an offensive before mid-February 1944. I.S.O. Playfair, *The Mediterranean and the Middle East*, vol. 5, *The Campaign in Sicily, 1943, and the Campaign in Italy, 3rd September 1943 to 31 March 1944* (London: HMSO, 1973), 597.

48. Ellis, *Cassino*, 51–52.

49. Graham and Bidwell, *Tug of War*, 297–98. Peter Schrijvers, *The Crash of Ruin: American Combat Soldiers in Europe During World War II* (New York: New York University Press, 1998), 45–47.

50. Juin put a stop to Gaullist "kidnapping" of Armée d'Afrique soldiers for Gaullist units in 1943, while assuring erstwhile Vichy loyalists that they would not be purged. Robert Paxton, *Parades and Politics at Vichy: The French Officer Corps under Marshal Pétain* (Princeton, N.J.: Princeton University Press, 1966), 416.

51. André Martel, *Histoire militaire de la France*, vol. 4, *De 1940 à nos jours* (Paris: Presses universitaires de France, 1994), 201.

52. Graham and Bidwell, *Tug of War*, 127–29.

53. Different assessments occurred depending on whether one counted short-term or long-term German capability to rush reinforcements to Anzio. Hinsley, *British Intelligence*, 3(2): 184–85.

54. Playfair, *The Mediterranean and the Middle East*, 5: 579–81, 589, 771–74.

55. Ibid., 5: 645–47.

56. Martin Blumenson, "General Lucas at Anzio," in Kent Roberts Greenfield, ed., *Command Decisions* (Washington, D.C.: Center for Military History, 1990), 327; Carlo D'Este, *World War II in the Mediterranean, 1942–1945* (Chapel Hill, N.C.: Algonquin Books, 1990), 131.

57. Blumenson, "Lucas at Anzio," 333.

58. Forty DUKWs and nineteen 105 mm howitzers had been lost. No battalion had arrived on the beaches on time. Clark, *Calculated Risk*, 268–69.

59. Lucas's diary, quoted in Graham and Bidwell, *Tug of War*, 137.

60. D'Este, *World War II in the Mediterranean*, 132.

61. It was to Lucas that Bradley passed on his growing discontent over Patton's conduct in Sicily and over the poor performance of Seventh Army headquarters. Omar Bradley and Clay Blair, *A General's Life* (New York: Simon and Schuster, 1983), 185, 199.

62. Graham and Bidwell, *Tug of War*, 155.

63. Bradley and Blair, *A General's Life*, 190.

64. Playfair, *The Mediterranean and the Middle East*, 5: 649, 751–52.

65. Clark, *Calculated Risk*, 306.

66. Both Alexander and Clark realized that the Mediterranean had been shoved to the back burner of Allied priorities. Their only hope to return to the mainstream of Allied endeavors was to seize Rome and take the Fifth Army to southern France to "be part of the great adventure of Overlord." Graham and Bidwell, *Tug of War*, 132–33.

67. Omar N. Bradley, *A Soldier's Story* (New York: Henry Holt, 1951), 297.

68. Playfair, *The Mediterranean and the Middle East*, 5: 643–45.

69. Graham and Bidwell, *Tug of War*, 138–40.

70. D'Este, *World War II in the Mediterranean*, 132.

71. Hinsley, *British Intelligence*, 3(1): 186; Kesselring, *Kesselring*, 231.

72. Graham and Bidwell attribute Clark's inflexibility to his stubborn adherence to his plan, his dislike of "feather-duster" McCreery, and his competitive resentment of the British. *Tug of War*, 145–46. While these were certainly major factors in Clark's decision, one real problem was that in Clark's mind as well as those of the Germans, the Liri Valley was the key to the German position. Route 7, which followed a tortuous course along the coast until it reached the Anzio Plain south of Rome, was considered an inferior path to Rome.

73. Clark, *Calculated Risk*, 269.

74. Robert Wallace, *The Italian Campaign* (Chicago: Time-Life Books, 1981), 116, quoted in Ellis, *Cassino*, 103–04.

75. Clark's justification was that the Thirty-sixth had to be made to attack again to take pressure off Lucas at Anzio. *Calculated Risk*, 277–79; Playfair, *The Mediterranean and the Middle East*, 5: 609–20. For a good description of the attack, see Ellis, *Cassino*, Chapter 5.

76. Playfair, *The Mediterranean and the Middle East*, 5: 627–28.

77. For the French performance, see Lieutenant Colonel Georges Boulle, *Le Corps Expéditionnaire Français en Italy (1943–1944)*, vol. 1, *La campagne d'hiver* (Paris: Imprimerie Nationale, 1971), 80–132. The Fourteenth Panzer Corps counted 6,444 casualties. Playfair, *The Mediterranean and the Middle East*, 5: 629, 636.

78. See Graham and Bidwell, *Tug of War*, Chapter 10.

79. Service Historique de l'Armée de Terre (SHAT), Château de Vincennes, 10P 56, 26 January, 8 & 13 February 1944.

80. Kesselring, *Kesselring*, 230, 233.

81. This was in part because German air reconnaissance had virtually ceased to exist, while agents' reports "were inaccurate and misleading." Pre-

vious alerts had proved false and only tired the troops. Kesselring, *Kesselring*, 231–32.

82. Hinsley, *British Intelligence*, 3(1): 186–87.

83. For his part, Kesselring argued that Clark should have delayed Shingle until he was certain that his offensive on the Garigliano had made sufficient progress "to make possible local coordination in a kind of encirclement . . . to turn our Tenth Army's right flank." Kesselring's second nightmare was that Lucas would make a dash for Rome, where the appearance of American troops might provoke a popular insurrection that the Germans, their hands full containing the Allied offensive, would prove unable to manage. Kesselring, *Kesselring*, 232.

84. Playfair, *The Mediterranean and the Middle East*, 5: 663.

85. Kesselring, *Kesselring*, 233.

86. Ibid., 234.

87. Martin Blumenson argues that Lucas came close to breakout at this point, but was dissuaded from persisting by Allied intelligence overestimates of German troop strength. "Lucas at Anzio," 344.

88. Kesselring, *Kesselring*, 234.

89. This included the Sixty-fifth, Seventy-first, and 715th Infantry Divisions, the Hermann Göring Division, the Third Panzer Grenadier Division, the Twenty-sixth Panzer Division, and the Fourth Parachute Division. Hinsley, *British Intelligence*, 3(1): 188.

90. The British First Division, U.S. First Armored Division, U.S. Third and Forty-fifth Divisions, British 168th Infantry Brigade, First Special Service Force, and Third Infantry Brigade. On 10 February, Templer's British Fifty-sixth Division and the 167th and 168th Brigades joined the beachhead. See Playfair, *The Mediterranean and the Middle East*, 5: 723–24, for the Allied order of battle.

91. Hinsley, *British Intelligence*, 3(1): 189–91.

92. Ibid., 3(1): 192–93.

93. The Twenty-ninth Panzer Grenadiers or the Twenty-sixth Panzers would have broken the Allied position, he believed. Kesselring, *Kesselring*, 235–36.

94. Hinsley, *British Intelligence*, 3(1): 196–97.

95. Playfair, *The Mediterranean and the Middle East*, 5: 752–56; Kesselring, *Kesselring*, 236; Hinsley, *British Intelligence*, 3(1): 197.

96. Wallace, *The Italian Campaign*, 139. Eisenhower briefly thought of placing Patton in charge of Sixth Corps. Stanley P. Hirshson, *General Patton: A Soldier's Life* (New York: HarperCollins, 2002), 433.

97. Winston S. Churchill, *The Second World War*, vol. 5, *Closing the Ring* (Boston: Houghton Mifflin, 1951), 487, 493.

98. Hinsley, *British Intelligence*, 3(1): 190.

99. Wallace, *The Italian Campaign*, 137.

100. Playfair, *The Mediterranean and the Middle East*, 5: 697–704.

101. Freyberg insisted on a wide flanking maneuver rather than a direct assault on Monastery Hill. Among the arguments against this course of action can be counted the fact that he lacked the mules to maintain even one division more than a few miles beyond the roadhead; the element of surprise was missing; German defenses were too strong to be easily overcome; and he lacked the troops to resist the inevitable German counterattacks. Playfair, *The Mediterranean and the Middle East*, 5: 706–77.

102. Wallace, *The Italian Campaign*, 145.

103. Quoted in Graham and Bidwell, *Tug of War*, 215.

104. Although Alan Brooke cited this as evidence of Freyberg's "weakness," he conceded that the New Zealand Division had taken its fair share of casualties in North Africa and that Freyberg was under pressure from his government to avoid heavy losses. Alanbrooke, *War Diaries*, 536.

105. Graham and Bidwell, *Tug of War*, 219.

106. C.J.C. Molony, *The Mediterranean and the Middle East*, vol. 6, part I, *1 April to 4 June 1944* (London: HMSO, 1984), 5, 9.

107. Kesselring, *Kesselring*, 236–37.

108. Playfair, *The Mediterranean and the Middle East*, 5: 780–81.

109. Ellis, *Cassino*, 286.

110. Jackson, *The Mediterranean and the Middle East*, 6(2): 68.

111. At the time, the Twelfth Air Force greatly exaggerated its success. Graham and Bidwell argue that Strangle would have been more effective had it focused on preventing troop transfers between the Gustav line and Anzio. *Tug of War*, 231–33. For a more complete assessment, see Playfair, *The Mediterranean and the Middle East*, 5: 810–16, 6: 36–45; F. M. Sallager, *Operation Strangle* (Santa Monica,: Calif. Rand Corporation, 1972), 19, quoted in Ellis, *Cassino*, 280–82.

112. Fifteenth Army Group headquarters was split between a logistics section in Algiers, a field HQ at Taranto, and a tactical HQ operating out of railway carriages near Naples. Harding organized a proper headquarters at Caserta, near Naples. Graham and Bidwell *Tug of War*, 241, 245.

113. Alanbrooke, *War Diaries*. 539, 584, 613, 633, 646.

114. The Germans called it the von Senger line, which was ironic as von Senger had objected strenuously that it was defective in conception. Molony, *The Mediterranean and the Middle East*, 6(1): 181–84.

115. Graham and Bidwell, *Tug of War*, 247.

116. Hinsley, *British Intelligence*, 3(1): 200; Kesselring, *Kesselring*, 238–39.

117. Kesselring, *Kesselring*, 240–41.

118. This complicated command and control. The Canadians also insisted on having their own command structure separate from that of the British, which complicated operations.

119. W. Anders, *An Army in Exile* (London: Macmillan, 1949), 174.

120. Ellis, *Cassino*, 318.

121. Alexander and Macmillan were plotting to remove Clark as head of

the Fifth Army after his failed Cassino offensives. Macmillan, *War Diaries*, 404–05 and note. See Graham and Bidwell, *Tug of War*, 250–51, for a particularly damning assessment of Clark's state of mind on the eve of Diadem.

122. Graham and Bidwell argue that it was like putting a "half-nelson on a grizzly bear." *Tug of War*, 247.

123. Archives Historique de la Guerre, Château de Vincennes, 10P 56, 8 May 1944. Graham and Bidwell argue that Valmontone was "simply the center of gravity of a potentially critical area. It was not, as Clark seemed to argue, a spot where the 6th Corps would stand on the Via Casilina like so many traffic policemen ordering the stream of German fugitives pouring up it to halt. From there, the whole front of Army Groups 'C' could be disarticulated, by not only the 6th Corps but by all the Allied forces available." *Tug of War*, 248.

124. D'Este, *World War II in the Mediterranean*, 168–69.

125. Ellis, *Cassino*, 327, 329.

126. R.L.V.B. French, *History of the 17/21 Lancers, 1922–59* (London: Macmillan, 1962), 165, quoted in Ellis, *Cassino*, 305.

127. Molony, *The Mediterranean and the Middle East*, 6(1): 104.

128. Kesselring, *Kesselring*, 241–42.

129. Hinsley, *British Intelligence*, 3(1): 202.

130. Ibid., 3(1): 203.

131. Ibid., 3(1): 204–07.

132. SHAT, 10P 56, 15 April 1944. Juin insisted that the British did not know how to handle mules well, because, *"Les animaux ne comprenent pas anglais."* Molony, *The Mediterranean and the Middle East*, 6(1): 294.

133. Ellis, *Cassino*, 274–75.

134. R. Chambé, *L'Epopée française d'Italie 1944* (Paris: Flammarion, 1952), 144.

135. Hinsley, *British Intelligence*, 3(1): 202.

136. Playfair, *The Mediterranean and the Middle East*, 5: 624.

137. The British First and Fifty-sixth Divisions were understrength, short of tanks and artillery, and lacked replacements because manpower priority was assigned to Overlord. Therefore, they were held back at London's request.

138. Kesselring, *Kesselring*, 244.

139. Lucian Truscott, *Command Missions* (New York: Dutton, 1954), 375.

140. Ernest F. Fisher, Jr., *The United States Army in World War II: The Mediterranean Theater of Operations: Cassino to the Alps* (Washington, D.C.: Center of Military History, 1993), 165–66.

141. Clark advanced four arguments for modifying Buffalo. First, intelligence told Clark that the Germans had already placed two divisions at Valmontone, and he expected further reinforcement there. Therefore, Sixth Corps's chances of successfully blocking Route 6 were significantly diminished. Second, even if Truscott took Valmontone, he would leave his line of communications dangerously exposed to attack by German forces on the Alban Hills. Third, the seizure of Valmontone would not have cut off the Tenth Army, as

there were plenty of other escape routes open to Kesselring. This was especially true because the leisurely pursuit of the retreating Germans by the Eighth Army gave Kesselring plenty of time to study other options. Indeed, most of Tenth Army escaped by routes other than Route 6. Fisher, *Cassino to the Alps*, 163–64, 199, 221.

142. John North, ed., *Memoirs, Field Marshal Alexander of Tunis, 1939–45* (New York: McGraw-Hill), quoted in Nigel Nicholson, *Alex: The Life of Field Marshal Earl Alexander of Tunis* (London: Pan Books, 1976), 296.

143. Churchill, *The Second World War*, 5: 607.

144. D'Este, *World War II in the Mediterranean*, 176–77.

145. Fisher, *Cassino to the Alps*, 178; Molony, *The Mediterranean and the Middle East*, 6(1): 226.

146. Clark's defense was that he had promised to send a column toward Valmontone, *and* to capture Rome, and that was what he did. Furthermore, once Alexander understood that he did not object. Nicolson, *Alex*, 293–95; Clark, *Calculated Risk*, 350–52, 357–58; D'Este, *World War II in the Mediterranean*, 175. Although he admitted that Alexander was upset by his actions, Clark insisted that he had never deliberately tried to deceive him. Although Clark admitted that "I was probably over sensitive to indications that practically everybody else was trying to get into the act [of being the first to Rome]," he made it clear to the Fifteenth Army Group commander that Rome was a prize that the Fifth Army had earned, and that Alexander had no right to tell him how to dispose of his army. He feared that Alexander wanted to delay his arrival in Rome so that the British could claim equal share in its capture. Fisher, *Cassino to the Alps*, 171. The U.S. official history also points out that as Second Corps and the CEF were closing in on Valmontone from the south, he could reinforce troops there and even cut Route 6 farther south. It was Alexander who prevented this because he wanted to keep Route 6 open so that the Eighth Army could advance on Rome. However, when Alexander was told of Clark's intent on the morning of 26 May, he did not object. Fisher, *Cassino to the Alps*, 171–73.

147. Indeed, John Ellis argues, somewhat in Clark's defense, that the entire concept of Diadem was flawed because it was simply not possible to cut off the German advance. Each individual failure contributed to the general failure of the plan. *Cassino*, 444–47, 458–63.

148. Graham and Bidwell argue that Clark misunderstood, deliberately or otherwise, that Valmontone was not a spot where Sixth Corps could stand "like so many traffic policemen ordering the stream of German fugitives pouring up it to halt," but "a center of gravity of potentially critical areas [from which] the whole front of the Army Group 'C' could be disarticulated, by not only the 6th Corps but by all the Allied forces available." *Tug of War*, 248.

149. Ibid., 343.

150. The OKW war diary for the Tenth and Fourteenth Armies recorded 38,024 casualties from 10 May to 10 June 1944. Although of these only 2,127 were

killed, the number may have been higher because the Germans did not include *Hilfswillige* or *HiWis*, mainly Red Army POWs who volunteered to serve in the German forces, in their tallies. In addition, Kesselring had lost half of the tanks in the Tenth and Fourteenth Armies, and 300 guns. Fisher, *Cassino to the Alps,* 222–23.

151. Clark, *Calculated Risk,* 366.

152. Carlo D'Este, *Eisenhower: A Soldier's Life* (New York: Henry Holt, 2002), 531.

153. Clark, *Calculated Risk,* 370.

CHAPTER TWELVE: THE MEDITERRANEAN ROAD TO
FRANCE'S RESURRECTION, 1940–45

1. Marshal Jean de Lattre de Tassigny, *The History of the First French Army* (London: George Allen and Unwin, 1952), 520.

2. Ibid., 506–09, 513, 517–23.

3. Nigel Hamilton, *Master of the Battlefield*, vol. 2, *Monty's War Years, 1942–1944* (New York: McGraw-Hill, 1983), 163, 183.

4. George Greenfield, *Chasing the Beast: One Man's War* (London: Richard Cohen Books, 1998), 83–84.

5. Stephen E. Ambrose, *The Supreme Commander: The War Years of Dwight D. Eisenhower* (Garden City, N.Y.: Doubleday, 1970), 154.

6. Hamilton, *Master of the Battlefield*, 164–66.

7. Marcel Vigneras, *United States Army in World War II: Special Studies: Rearming the French* (Washington, D.C.: U.S. Government Printing Office, 1957), 34.

8. I.S.O. Playfair, *The Mediterranean and the Middle East*, vol. 5, *The Campaign in Sicily, 1943, and the Campaign in Italy, 3rd September 1943 to 31 March 1944* (London: HMSO, 1973), 593, 603.

9. Norman Lewis, *Naples '44* (London: Collins, 1978), 143, 147–48.

10. André Lanquetot, *Un hiver dans les Abruzzes*, (Vincennes: SHAT, 1991), 23,

11. Ibid., 63.

12. I.S.O. Playfair, *The Mediterranean and the Middle East*. vol. 4, *The Destruction of the Axis Forces in Africa* (London: HMSO, 1966), 159.

13. Dean Acheson in particular relied on France to take a leadership role in postwar Europe. John Lamberton Harper, *American Visions of Europe* (Cambridge: Cambridge University Press, 1996), 289.

14. Jean Lacouture, *De Gaulle: The Rebel, 1890–1944* (New York: Norton, 1990), 368.

15. Roosevelt feared that French West Africa and Casablanca might be used as bases to attack the Western Hemisphere. Harper, *American Visions of Europe,* 84.

16. Ibid., 90–91, 114–15.

17. Jean Lacouture, *De Gaulle*, vol. 1, *Le Rebelle, 1890–1944* (Paris: Editions du Seuil, 1984), 684.

18. Much of this paragraph is taken from Lacouture, *De Gaulle: Le Rebelle*, 1: 682–85.

19. André Martel, *Leclerc: Le soldat et la politique* (Paris: Albin Michel, 1998), 138, 145–49.

20. Reeva S. Simon, *Iraq Between the Two World Wars: The Creation and Implementation of a Nationalist Ideology* (New York: Columbia University Press, 1986), 130.

21. Harold E. Raugh, Jr., *Wavell in the Middle East, 1939–1941* (London: Brassey's, 1993), 203.

22. I.S.O. Playfair, *The Mediterranean and the Middle East*, vol. 2, *The Germans Come to the Help of Their Ally (1941)* (London: HMSO, 1956), 185.

23. The Turkish offer seems to have been an ambivalent one, according to Tarbush, *The Role of the Military in Politics*, 179.

24. Majid Khadduri, *Independent Iraq, 1932–1958* (Oxford: Oxford University Press, 1960), 229.

25. The only reason Churchill did not fire Wavell was that the prime minister did not want to appear to be scapegoating Wavell for Churchill's decision to defend Greece. Raugh, *Wavell in the Middle East*, 212.

26. Gerhard Schreiber, Bernd Stegemann, and Detlef Vogel, edited by the Militärgeschichtliches Forshungsamt, *Germany and the Second World War*, vol. 3, *The Mediterranean, South-East Europe and North Africa, 1939–1941* (Oxford: Clarendon, 1995), 591–605. Furthermore, at this critical juncture, they had no way to communicate with the mufti, as the Arab radio operator, trained in Vienna and returned to Iraq with a transmitter, promptly forgot how to use it. Khadduri, *Independent Iraq*, 229.

27. In the "Paris Protocols" signed by Darlan and Otto Abez, the German ambassador in Paris, on 27 May 1941, Darlan, eager to extract concessions from the Germans, actually offered more assistance than the Germans had requested, including allowing U-boats access to French West African ports and purging the French administration of men hostile to Germany. Hervé Coutau-Bégarie and Calude Huan, *Darlan* (Paris: Fayard, 1989), 395–98.

28. Approximately four trains got through to Baghdad before the British blew the bridge at Tel Kotchek. Khadduri, *Independent Iraq*, 232–33.

29. Playfair, *The Mediterranean and the Middle East*, 2: 186.

30. Ibid., 177–97; Raugh, *Wavell in the Middle East*, 211–16.

31. An estimated 180 were killed. "Sandstorm," www.martinkramer.org.

32. Playfair, *The Mediterranean and the Middle East*, 2: 177–97; Raugh, *Wavell in the Middle East*, 211–16.

33. Henri Lerner, *Catroux* (Paris: Albin Michel, 1990), 180–81.

34. Raugh, *Wavell in the Middle East*, 216–21.

35. Schreiber et al., *Germany and the Second World War*, 3: 617–18.

36. Raugh, *Wavell in the Middle East*, 221–22.

37. British "treachery" over Syria and Lebation continued to envenom relations between de Gaulle and the British beyond the war's end, this explains why many Jewish refugees destined for Palestine from 1945 were able to embark on ships like the *Exodus* at Marseilles.

38. Christine Levisse-Touzé, *L'Afrique du Nord dans la guerre, 1939–1945* (Paris: Albin Michel, 1998), 134–35.

39. The Vichy casualties include those who deserted to the Free French. Playfair, *The Mediterranean and the Middle East*, 2: 222. For the post-Exporter defections, see Douglas Porch, *The French Foreign Legion* (New York: Harper-Collins, 1991), 474–79.

40. Robert Paxton, *Parades and Politics at Vichy: The French Officer Corps under Marshal Pétain* (Princeton, N.J.: Princeton University Press, 1966), 133.

41. Levisse-Touzé, *L'Afrique du Nord dans la guerre*, 175.

42. Lacouture, *De Gaulle: The Rebel*, 369.

43. Ambrose, *Supreme Commander*, 24, 100.

44. Lacouture, *De Gaulle: The Rebel*, 339.

45. Jon Latimer, *Alamein* (Cambridge, Mass.: Harvard University Press, 2002), 195.

46. Hamilton, *Master of the Battlefield*, 184.

47. André Martel, *Histoire militaire de la France*, vol. 4, *De 1940 à nos jours* (Paris: Presses Universitaires de France, 1994), 122.

48. Hamilton, *Master of the Battlefield*, 163.

49. Martel, *Leclerc*, 211.

50. On 8 May 1943, Jean Moulin united the diverse groups of the French resistance behind de Gaulle. Levisse-Touzé, *L'Afrique du Nord dans la guerre*, 313.

51. André Lanquetot, *1943–1944: Un hiver dans les Abruzzes* (Vincennes: SHAT, 1991), 24.

52. Shortly before the invasion, the code name became Dragoon. However, to avoid confusion, the Riviera invasion will be referred to as Anvil.

53. Jeffrey J. Clark and Robert Ross Smith, *Riviera to the Rhine* (Washington, D.C.: Center of Military History, 1993), 5–7.

54. Churchill, *The Second World War*, vol. 5, *Closing the Ring* (Boston: Houghton Mifflin, 1951), 356–57; Dominick Graham and Shelford Bidwell, *Tug of War: The Battle for Italy, 1943–1945* (New York: St. Martin's, 1986), 129–30. Clark and Smith trace the ups and downs of Anvil. *Riviera to the Rhine*, 9–22.

55. C.J.C. Molony, *The Mediterranean and the Middle East*, vol. 6, part 1, *1st April to 4 June 1944* (London: HMSO, 1984), 312–13, 319–20; John Ehrman, *Grand Strategy*, vol. 5, *August 1943–September 1944* (London: HMSO, 1956), 239–41, 249; Michael Howard, *The Mediterranean Strategy in the Second World War* (New York: Praeger, 1968), 58–59.

56. Howard, *The Mediterranean Strategy*, 60.

57. Clark and Smith, *Riviera to the Rhine*, 561–63.

58. Molony, *The Mediterranean and the Middle East*, 6(1): 330–31; Ehrman, *Grand Strategy*, 5: 250–51, 258; Matthew Jones, *Britain, the United States and the Mediterranean War, 1942–44* (New York: St. Martin's, 1996), 155, 167–78.

59. Mark Clark, *Calculated Risk* (New York: Harper and Brothers, 1950), 368.

60. Graham and Bidwell, *Tug of War*, 318.

61. SHAT, 10P 10, CEF, le Bureau. Martel, *Histoire militaire de la France*, 201, gives lower figures.

62. Peter Schrijvers, *The Crash of Ruin: American Combat Soldiers in Europe During World War II* (New York: New York University Press, 1998), 46.

63. For an overview of the French resistance, see André Martel, "La Résistance: 'Aux Armes, Citoyens,'" in Martel, ed., *Histoire militaire de la France*, vol. 4, *De 1940 à nos jours*, 131–74; Douglas Porch, *The French Secret Services: A History of French Intelligence from the Dreyfus Affair to the Gulf War* (New York: Farrar, Straus and Giroux, 1995), Chapters 8–10.

64. Tony Judt, ed., *Resistance and Revolution in Mediterranean Europe, 1939–1948* (London: Routledge, 1989), 1–2, 9–10.

65. Charles de Gaulle, *The War Memoirs of Charles de Gaulle*, vol. 3, *Salvation, 1944–1946* (New York: Simon and Schuster, 1960), 38.

66. Raoul Salan, *Mémoires: Fin d'un empire*, vol. 1, *Le sens d'un engagement* (Paris: Presses de la Cité, 1970), 125.

67. Clark and Smith, *Riviera to the Rhine*, 144–70.

68. Ibid., 197–98.

69. Omar N. Bradley and Clay Blair, *A General's Life: An Autobiography by General of the Army Omar N. Bradley* (New York: Simon and Schuster, 1983), 210.

70. Carlo D'Este, *Eisenhower: A Soldier's Life* (New York: Henry Holt, 2002), 483.

71. Clark and Smith, *Riviera to the Rhine*, 24, 562, 574–77.

72. Field Marshal Lord Alanbrooke, *War Diaries, 1939–1945* (Berkeley: University of California Press, 2001), 624.

73. Clark and Smith, *Riviera to the Rhine*, 225–29, 254–57, 291.

74. Quoted in Anthony Clayton, *Three Marshals of France: Leadership after Trauma* (London: Brassey's, 1992), 116.

75. Jean Lacouture, *De Gaulle*, vol. 2, *La politique, 1944–1959* (Paris: Editions du Seuil, 1985), 63–64.

76. Vigneras, *Rearming the French*, 319–23.

77. Salan, *Mémoires*, 1: 133.

78. Vigneras, *Rearming the French*, 338.

79. De Gaulle, *War Memoirs*, 3: 35–36.

80. Martel, *Histoire militaire de la France*, 4: 234.

81. Alanbrooke, *War Diaries*, 625; Robert Aron, *Histoire de la libération de*

France, juin 1944–mai 1945 (Paris: Fayard, 1959), 664–66; Jean-Pierre Roux, *La France de la quatrième république: L'ardeur et la nécessité, 1944–1952* (Paris: Editions du Seuil, 1980), 21–25.

82. Jean Lattre de Tassigny, *History of the First French Army* (London: George Allen and Unwin, 1952), 171–72.

83. De Lattre, *History of the First French Army*, 170–71; Lacouture, *De Gaulle*, 2: 63–65; Clark and Smith, *Riviera to the Rhine*, 355–56.

84. De Lattre, *History of the First French Army*, 171.

85. Vigneras, *Rearming the French*, 337.

86. De Lattre noted that in the last week of September, the five reinforced divisions of his French First Army had received 8,715 tons of supplies compared to almost 19,000 tons for the three-division Seventh Army. For their part, the Americans pointed out that the French had neglected to create an adequate logistical infrastructure, while inexperienced French staffs were unable to predict French logistical needs with any accuracy. Devers resolved the debate when he intervened to increase the logistical allocations to de Lattre. Clark and Smith, *Riviera to the Rhine*, 299–301. The inability to coordinate U.S. and French efforts was also tied to supply problems. Ibid., 310.

87. The mouth of the Schelde Estuary had been cleared of Germans by 3 November, thereby opening the shipping channel to Antwerp. However, it would take several weeks to get the harbor into shape. For de Gaulle's diversion of troops from de Lattre, see ibid., 358–59.

88. For slightly more conservative figures, see ibid., 431.

89. De Lattre, *History of the First French Army*, 284.

90. Lacouture, *De Gaulle*, 2: 65.

91. Vigneras, *Rearming the French*, 323.

92. Eisenhower's argument was that a Seventh Army crossing of the Rhine would have exposed the flank of Patton's Third Army. Nevertheless, the official history calls Eisenhower's decision "difficult to understand." Clark and Smith, *Riviera to the Rhine*, 439–45, 563. For his part, Patton sided with Devers, believing his flank was perfectly safe. Martin Blumenson, *The Patton Papers, 1940–1945* (Boston: Houghton Mifflin, 1974), 583.

93. Lacouture, *De Gaulle*, 2: 64.

94. Paul Fussell, *Doing Battle: The Making of a Skeptic* (Boston: Little, Brown, 1996), 129–30.

95. Ibid., 131–32, 141.

96. Lacouture, *De Gaulle*, 2: 76; Clark and Smith, *Riviera to the Rhine*, 496–97, 511–12, 527.

97. Of 8,000 U.S. casualties, only 500 were killed. French casualties were probably twice that. Clark and Smith, *Riviera to the Rhine*, 556–57.

98. De Lattre, *History of the First French Army*, 399.

99. Ibid., 480–81.

100. Clark and Smith, *Riviera to the Rhine*, 561–63.

CHAPTER THIRTEEN: CASSINO WITHOUT THE MONASTERY:
CRACKING THE GOTHIC LINE

1. Matthew Jones, *Britain, the United States and the Mediterranean War, 1942–44* (New York: St. Martin's, 1996), 207.

2. Martin Blumenson, *Mark Clark* (New York: Congdon and Weed, 1984), 224, 226.

3. Albert Kesselring, *Kesselring: A Soldier's Record* (New York: William Morrow, 1954), 250.

4. Kesselring, *Kesselring*, 246–49. Kesselring, Fourteenth Army commander von Mackensen, and Maelzer, military governor of Rome, were tried after the war for war crimes related to these reprisals.

5. Many of these units were stationed in coastal defense to guard against amphibious landings. On 27 June, Hitler's directive calling for a stand on the Pisa-Rimini line was decrypted by Allied intelligence. F. H. Hinsley, *British Intelligence in the Second World War: Its Influence on Strategy and Operations*, vol. 3, part 2 (New York: Cambridge University Press, 1988), 313, 316.

6. The Germans referred to this as the Green line. It began life in August 1943 before the Allied invasion of Italy as a trace of primitive defensive positions reconnoitered by Rommel and scratched out by the Todt Organization. Ernest F. Fisher, Jr., *The United States Army in World War II: The Mediterranean Theater of Operations: Cassino to the Alps* (Washington, D.C.: Center of Military History, United States Army, 1993), 299–300.

7. General Sir William Jackson, *The Mediterranean and the Middle East*, vol. 6, *Victory in the Mediterranean*, part 2, *June to October 1944* (London: HMSO, 1987), 15–23.

8. Graham and Bidwell credit the idea for Olive to Thirteenth Corps commander Lieutenant General Sir Sidney Kirkman. Dominick Graham and Shelford Bidwell, *Tug of War: The Battle for Italy, 1943–1945* (New York: St. Martin's, 1986), 348. A successful offensive along the Adriatic coast would also put the British in a better position to realize Churchill's goal of advancing into Slovenia and joining up with Soviet forces in Romania, although how far this influenced Alexander's decision is unclear. Fisher, *Cassino to the Alps*, 304–05.

9. Fisher, *Cassino to the Alps*, 308.

10. The weaknesses of the Rimini sector of the Gothic line were lack of depth, the fact that many positions were laid out along roads, which allowed the artillery to register, and the fact that air superiority and domination of high ground gave the British good observation. Jackson, *The Mediterranean and the Middle East*, 6(2): 239.

11. William Jackson, "Mine Warfare," in I.C.B. Dear and M.R.D. Foot, *The Oxford Companion to World War II* (Oxford: Oxford University Press, 1995), 751–52.

12. Kesselring feared that American forces in southern France would surge over the Alps, link up with Italian partisan bands, and pry the Germans out of the

Ligurian coast and the Po Valley. He shifted the Ninetieth Panzer Grenadiers to guard the Alps, thus forfeiting his reserve. Kesselring, *Kesselring*, 255–56.

13. General Devers and the planners at AFHQ did express concerns. But General Maitland Wilson approved Olive on 6 August Fisher, *Cassino to the Alps*, 305, 310.

14. Jackson, *The Mediterranean and the Middle East*, 6(2): 119–48, 155; Graham and Bidwell, *Tug of War*, 348; Blumenson, *Mark Clark*, 226.

15. Hinsley, *British Intelligence*, 3(2): 336.

16. Field Marshal Lord Alanbrooke, *War Diaries, 1939–1945* (Berkeley: University of California Press, 2001), 613.

17. One reason why McCreery was able to make good progress was that von Vietinghoff, standing in for an injured Kesselring, accepted a British advance as the necessary price to pay for keeping reserves on the Fifth Army front at Bologna. Hinsley, *British Intelligence*, 3(2): 351.

18. Fisher, *Cassino to the Alps*, 411. Eventually fifteen companies of Italian troops were employed to herd 3,900 mules.

19. Hinsley, *British Intelligence*, 3(2): 340–42.

20. Ibid., 3(2): 342–44.

21. Mark Clark, *Calculated Risk* (New York: Harper, 1950), 396.

22. Kesselring, *Kesselring*, 265.

23. Fisher, *Cassino to the Alps*, 370–73.

24. Clark, *Calculated Risk*, 402.

25. Fisher, *Cassino to the Alps*, 410; Hinsley, *British Intelligence*, 3(2): 357–58.

26. Kesselring, *Kesselring*, 258.

27. Jackson concludes that these were spurious arguments, as the Germans were forced to export coal to keep Italian industry going, and lacked the transport to import products and foodstuffs from Italy. *The Mediterranean and the Middle East*, 6(2): 422–24. See also General Sir William Jackson, *The Mediterranean and the Middle East*, vol. 6, *Victory in the Mediterranean*, part 3, *November 1944 to May 1945* (London: HMSO, 1988), 154–55.

28. Kesselring, *Kesselring*, 262–63.

29. Hinsley, *British Intelligence*, 3(2): 349.

30. Kesselring, *Kesselring*, 254–55.

31. Ibid., 259.

32. Jackson, *The Mediterranean and the Middle East*, 6(2): 300–06, 360–63, 373–77. For the performance of the Canadians, especially their low number of POWs, see ibid., 6(3): 163.

33. Ibid., 6(3): 149–50.

34. Graham and Bidwell, *Tug of War*, 377.

35. Clark, *Calculated Risk*, 396–97.

36. Graham and Bidwell, *Tug of War*, 379–80; Blumenson, *Mark Clark*, 229–33.

37. Jones, *Britain, the United States and the Mediterranean War*, 190–91.

38. Misha Glenny, *The Balkans: Nationalism, War and the Great Powers*,

1804–1999 (New York: Viking, 1999), 522; Winston S. Churchill, *The Second World War*, vol. 5, *Closing the Ring* (Boston: Houghton Mifflin, 1951), 468.

39. Walter R. Roberts, *Tito, Mihailović and the Allies, 1941–1945* (New Brunswick, N.J.: Rutgers University Press, 1973), 183.

40. Milovan Djilas, *Wartime* (New York: Harcourt Brace Jovanovich, 1977), 352–53.

41. Ibid., 401.

42. Glenny, *The Balkans*, 532: M. Djilas, *Wartime*, 415–16.

43. Franklin Lindsay, *Beacons in the Night: With the OSS and Tito's Partisans in Wartime Yugoslavia* (Stanford, Calif.: Stanford University Press, 1993), 141.

44. Roberts, *Tito, Mihailović and the Allies*, 285.

45. Hinsley, *British Intelligence*, 3(2): 287, 295–302.

46. David H. Close, *The Origins of the Greek Civil War* (London: Longman, 1995), 81.

47. Haris Valvianos, "The Greek Communist Party," in Tony Judt, ed., *Resistance and Revolution in Mediterranean Europe, 1939–1948* (London: Routledge, 1987), 170–81; Charles R. Shrader, *The Withered Vine: Logistics and the Communist Insurgency in Greece, 1945–1949* (Westport, Conn.: Praeger, 1999), 32–36.

48. Valvianos, "The Greek Communist Party," 181–84; Close, *Origins of the Greek Civil War*, 108–09.

49. Mark Mazower, "The Cold War and the Appropriation of Memory: Greece after Liberation," in Istvan Deak, Jan T. Gross, and Tony Judt, eds., *The Politics of Retribution in Europe* (Princeton: Princeton University Press, 2000), 213.

50. Jackson, *The Mediterranean and the Middle East*, 6(3): 148.

51. Fisher, *Cassino to the Alps*, 373.

52. Ibid., 359; Jones, *Britain, the United States and the Mediterranean War*, 210.

53. Fisher, *Cassino to the Alps*, 392.

54. Jones, *Britain, the United States and the Mediterranean War*, 211–12.

55. Kesselring, *Kesselring*, 268.

56. David W. Ellwood, *Italy 1943–1945* (New York: Holmes and Meier, 1985), 157, 159.

57. Kesselring, *Kesselring*, 269.

58. Ellwood, *Italy 1943–1945*, 155–57.

59. Ibid., 159–60.

60. Paul Ginsborg, *A History of Contemporary Italy: Society and Politics, 1943–1988* (London: Penguin, 1990), 20–22.

61. Kesselring, *Kesselring*, 275.

62. Ginsborg, *A History of Contemporary Italy*, 70.

63. Kesselring, *Kesselring*, 271–72.

64. There was a fear that the resisters who survived the winter would be among the most militant. Jackson, *The Mediterranean and the Middle East*, 6(3): 413. See also Ellwood, *Italy 1943–1945*, 163.

65. Ellwood, *Italy 1943–1945*, 177.

66. Jackson, *The Mediterranean and the Middle East*, 6(3): 145.

67. Ellwood, *Italy 1943–1945*, 199–200.

68. Ginsborg, *A History of Contemporary Italy*, 45–47.

69. David Travis, "Communism and Resistance in Italy, 1943–1948," in Tony Judt, ed., *Resistance and Revolution in Mediterranean Europe, 1939–1948* (London: Routledge, 1989), 106.

70. A realistic estimate according to the German commander was 5,000 German soldiers killed and 7,000–8,000 missing, presumed killed, or kidnapped. His own intelligence put the figures much higher. Kesselring, *Kesselring*, 272.

71. Jackson, *The Mediterranean and the Middle East*, 6(3): 413–15.

72. Travis, "Communism and Resistance in Italy," 91.

73. Fisher, *Cassino to the Alps*, 417.

74. Kesselring, *Kesselring*, 265.

75. Hinsley, *British Intelligence*, 3(2): 694–96.

76. A fourth division, the 710th Infantry, was ordered to the Eastern Front in April 1945. Ibid., 3(2): 691, 697–702.

77. Many of the trains were carrying coal from Germany to keep Italian industry running. Fisher, *Cassino to the Alps*, 440.

78. Jackson, *The Mediterranean and the Middle East*, 6(3): 155.

79. Fisher, *Cassino to the Alps*, 441.

80. Jones, *Britain, the United States and the Mediterranean War*, 209–10, 227.

81. Fisher, *Cassino to the Alps*, 449, 443. Opinion was divided on this possibility, especially as neither photo reconnaissance nor Sigint revealed any preparations to retire to the Alps. Hinsley, *British Intelligence*, 3(2): 711–18.

82. Hinsley, *British Intelligence*, 3(2): 693; Jackson, *The Mediterranean and the Middle East*, 6(3): 237.

83. Jackson, *The Mediterranean and the Middle East*, 6(3): 152.

84. Hinsley, *British Intelligence*, 3(2): 694, 704.

85. Jackson, *The Mediterranean and the Middle East*, 6(3): 238–39, 241–45; Hinsley, *British Intelligence*, 3(2): 702–03, 714, 737–38.

86. Fisher, *Cassino to the Alps*, 446.

87. The ration strength of the Eighth Army in the spring of 1945 was 632,980, compared to 266,883 for the Fifth Army. Jones, *Britain, the United States and the Mediterranean War*, 228.

88. Lucian K. Truscott, *Command Missions* (New York: Dutton, 1959), 478–79.

89. Branden Little, "The Marine Corps, Industrial Entrepreneurship, and Victory in the Pacific, 1898–1945," master's thesis (Monterey, Calif.: Naval Postgraduate School, 2002), 3–7.

90. Hinsley, *British Intelligence*, 3(2): 707–09.

91. Ibid., 3(2): 705.

92. Quoted in Robert Wallace, *The Italian Campaign* (Chicago: Time-Life Books, 1981), 188–89.

93. Harold Macmillan, *War Diaries: The Mediterranean, 1943–1945* (New York: St. Martin's, 1984), 741.

94. Clark, *Calculated Risk*, 434.

95. Macmillan, *War Diaries*, 743.

96. Ibid.

97. Clark, *Calculated Risk*, 440.

98. Stanley P. Hirshson, *General Patton: A Soldier's Life* (New York: HarperCollins, 2002), 636.

99. Roberts, *Tito, Mihailović and the Allies*, 321.

100. Mazower, "The Cold War and the Appropriation of Memory," 215.

101. Ibid.

102. Shrader, *The Withered Vine*, 39–48; Valvianos, "The Greek Communist Party," 186–97.

103. John Ellis, *Brute Force: Allied Strategy and Tactics in the Second World War* (New York: Viking, 1990), 342.

104. For casualty figures, see Jackson, *The Mediterranean and the Middle East*, 6(3): 335.

105. Kesselring, *Kesselring*, 267.

106. David Kennedy, *Freedom from Fear* (Oxford: Oxford University Press, 1999), 596.

107. John Keegan, *The Second World War* (London: Penguin, 1989), 362, 368.

108. Jackson, *The Mediterranean and the Middle East*, 6(3): 351.

109. Table adopted from Graham and Bidwell, *Tug of War*, 401. A slightly different set of figures can be found in John Ellis, *Brute Force*, 319. Graham and Bidwell make the point that number of divisions is not a perfect indicator of troop strength, as many of the German divisions were understrength. In July 1944, Army Group C numbered 411,000 troops; in 1945, 439,000. In the last year of the war, the Fifth Army counted 359,565 and the Eighth Army 190,000. The division figures do not include independent brigades, artillery assigned to corps or army level, or logistical infrastructure, which was far more elaborate on the Allied side. In all, Allied strength in theater was 1,677,000 men. Fisher makes the point that U.S. divisions in particular had larger overstrength and deeper replacement pools in the closing months of the war than did the Germans, or even the Eighth Army. *Cassino to the Alps*, 458.

110. Graham and Bidwell, *Tug of War*, 402.

111. Fisher, *Cassino to the Alps*, 536.

112. Ibid., 535–36.

113. U.S. Army estimates of German casualties were 434,646, including 48,067 killed, 172,531 wounded, and 214,048 missing. Graham and Bidwell, *Tug of War*, 403.

114. Carlo D'Este, *Eisenhower: A Soldier's Life* (New York: Henry Holt, 2002), 446, 452.

115. Allied casualties in Northwestern Europe were 766,294. Graham and Bidwell, *Tug of War*, 403.

116. Lindsay, *Beacons in the Night*, 86–87.

117. Churchill, *The Second World War*, 5: 552.

118. Jackson, *The Mediterranean and the Middle East*, 6(3): 360.

119. On this point, Graham and Bidwell disagree. *Tug of War*, 404.

120. Kesselring, *Kesselring*, 267.

121. Graham and Bidwell, *Tug of War*, 403; Jackson, *The Mediterranean and the Middle East*, 6(3): 352–56; Fisher, *Cassino to the Alps*, 538–39; Michael Howard, *The Mediterranean Strategy in the Second World War* (New York: Praeger, 1968), 66–67.

122. Jackson, *The Mediterranean and the Middle East*, 6(3): 356.

CONCLUSION: THE PIVOTAL THEATER

1. Michael Simpson, "Superhighway to the World Wide Web: The Mediterranean in British Imperial Strategy, 1900–45," in John B. Hattendorf, ed., *Naval Policy and Strategy in the Mediterranean: Past, Present and Future* (London: Frank Cass), 64.

2. John Ellis, *Brute Force: Allied Strategy and Tactics in the Second World War* (New York: Viking, 1990), xx.

3. Robert W. Love, *History of the U.S. Navy*, vol. 2 (1942–91) (Harrisburg, Pa.: Stackpole, 1992), 87.

4. John Keegan, *The Second World War* (London: Penguin, 1989), 368.

5. Ellis, *Brute Force*, 292–93, 289.

6. Dominick Graham and Shelford Bidwell, *Tug of War: The Battle for Italy, 1943–1945* (New York: St. Martin's, 1986), 403.

7. Jeffrey J. Clark and Robert Ross Smith, *Riviera to the Rhine* (Washington, D.C.: Center of Military History, 1993), 197–98.

8. Corelli Barnett, *Engage the Enemy More Closely: The Royal Navy in the Second World War* (London: Hodder and Stoughton, 1991), 692.

9. Horst Boog, Werner Rahn, Reinhard Stumpf, and Bernd Wegner, *Germany and the Second World War*, vol. 6, *The Global War: Widening of the Conflict into a World War and the Shift of the Initiative, 1941–1943* (Oxford: Clarendon, 2000), 118, 120.

10. Martin van Creveld, *Hitler's Strategy, 1940–1941: The Balkan Clue* (Cambridge: Cambridge University Press, 1973), 12–13, 180–83.

11. Elena Agarossi, *A Nation Collapses: The Italian Surrender of September 1943* (Cambridge: Cambridge University Press, 1999), 127; Boog et al., *Germany and the Second World War*, 6: 118.

12. R. J. Overy. *The Air War, 1939–1945* (New York: Stein and Day, 1980), 45–46.

13. Boog et al., *Germany and the Second World War*, 6: 119; Ellis, *Brute Force*, xx.

14. Winston S. Churchill, *The Second World War*, vol. 4, *The Hinge of Fate* (Boston: Houghton Mifflin, 1950), 799.

15. I.S.O. Playfair, *The Mediterranean and the Middle East*, vol. 4, *The Destruction of the Axis Forces in Africa* (London: HMSO, 1966), 460. John Ellis puts Axis losses in North Africa at 266,000 dead, missing, and POWs. John Ellis, *World War II: A Statistical Survey* (New York: Facts on File, 1993), 255.

16. Ellis, Ibid., 255.

17. Ellis, *Brute Force*, xx.

18. James H. Doolittle, *I Could Never Be So Lucky Again* (New York: Bantam, 1991), 374.

19. Carlo D'Este, *Eisenhower: A Soldier's Life* (New York: Henry Holt, 2002), 290.

20. Ellis, *Brute Force*, xx, 289, 292–93.

21. Graham and Bidwell, *Tug of War*, 403.

22. Albert Kesselring, *Kesselring: A Soldier's Record* (New York: William Morrow, 1954), 267.

23. Michael Howard, *The Mediterranean Strategy in the Second World War* (New York: Praeger, 1968), 11.

24. Gerhard Schreiber, Bernd Stegemann, and Detlef Vogel, edited by the Militärgeschichtliches Forshungsamt, *Germany and the Second World War*, vol. 3, *The Mediterranean, South-East Europe and North Africa, 1939–1941* (Oxford: Clarendon, 1995), 767.

25. D'Este, *Eisenhower*, 300.

26. Barnett, *Engage the Enemy More Closely*, 692.

27. General Sir William Jackson, *The Mediterranean and the Middle East*, vol. 6, *Victory in the Mediterranean*, part 3, *November 1944 to May 1945* (London: HMSO, 1988), 356.

28. Barnett, *Engage the Enemy More Closely*, 369.

29. Ernest F. Fuller, *The Mediterranean Theater of Operations: Cassino to the Alps* (Washington, D.C.: Center of Military History, United States Army, 1977), 536.

30. Howard, *The Mediterranean Strategy*, xi, 69.

31. Kenneth S. Davis, *FDR: The War President, 1940–1943* (New York: Random House, 2000), 523, 529–30, 544–45, 553–54.

32. David Kennedy, *Freedom from Fear* (Oxford: Oxford University Press, 1999), 596.

33. D'Este, *Eisenhower*, 446.

34. Graham and Bidwell, *Tug of War*, 403. Ellis, *A Statistical Survey*, 255–56.

35. Fuller, *Cassino to the Alps*, 540.

36. Boog et al., *Germany and the Second World War*, 6: 138.

37. Van Creveld, *Hitler's Strategy*, 176.

38. Spike Milligan, *Monty: His Part in My Victory* (New York: Penguin, 1978), 29. Schrijvers, *The Crash of Ruin*, 120.

39. George Greenfield, *Chasing the Beast: One Man's War* (London: Richard Cohen Books, 1998), 133–34.

SELECTED BIBLIOGRAPHY

Addison, Paul, and Angus Calder, eds. *Time to Kill: The Soldier's Experience of War in the West, 1939–1945*. London: Pimlico, 1997.

Agarossi, Elena. *A Nation Collapses: The Italian Surrender of September 1943*. Cambridge: Cambridge University Press, 1999.

Alanbrooke, Field Marshal Lord. *War Diaries, 1939–1945*. Berkeley: University of California Press, 2001.

Ambrose, Stephen E. *The Supreme Commander: The War Years of Dwight D. Eisenhower*. New York: Doubleday, 1970.

———. *Eisenhower: Soldier, General of the Army, President-Elect, 1890–1952*. New York: Simon and Schuster, 1983.

Anders, W. *An Army in Exile*. London: Macmillan, 1949.

Angelucci, Enzo, and Paolo Matricardi. *Complete Book of World War II Combat Aircraft*. Vercelli, Italy: White Star, 2000.

Ansel, Walter. *Hitler and the Middle Sea*. Durham, N.C.: Duke University Press, 1972.

Atkinson, Rick. *An Army at Dawn: The War in North Africa, 1942–1943*. New York: Henry Holt, 2002.

Bachoud, André. *Franco ou la réussite d'un homme ordinaire*. Paris: Fayard, 1997.

Barnett, Correlli, ed. *Engage the Enemy More Closely: The Royal Navy in the Second World War*. London: Hodder and Stoughton, 1991.

——— *Hitler's Generals: Authoritative Portraits of the Men Who Waged Hitler's War*. New York: William Morrow, 1989.

Bartov, Omar. *Hitler's Army: Soldiers, Nazis and War in the Third Reich*. New York: Oxford University Press, 1991.

Beevor, Antony. *Crete: The Battle and the Resistance*. Boulder, Colo.: Westview, 1994.

Behrendt, Hans-Otto. *Rommel's Intelligence in the Desert Campaign, 1941–1943*. London: William Kimber, 1985.

Belcham, Major General D. *All in a Day's March*. London: William Collins & Co., 1978.

Bernières, Louis de. *Corelli's Mandolin*. New York: Vintage, 1994.

Blake, Roger, and William Roger Louis. *Churchill*. New York: Norton, 1993.

Blumenson, Martin. *The Patton Papers, 1940–1945*. Boston: Houghton Mifflin, 1974.

———. *Mark Clark*. New York: Congdon and Weed, 1984.

———. *Patton: The Man Behind the Legend, 1885–1945*. New York: William Morrow, 1985.

Blumenson, Martin, and James L. Stokesbury. *Masters of the Art of Command*. Boston: Houghton Mifflin, 1975.

Bond, Brian, ed. *Chief of Staff: The Diaries of Lt. Gen. Sir Henry Pownall*. London: Leo Cooper, 1974.

Bond, Brian, and Ian Roy, eds. *War and Society: A Yearbook of Military History*. London: Croom Helm, 1975.

Boog, Horst, ed. *The Conduct of the Air War in the Second World War*. New York: Berg, 1992.

Boog, Horst, Werner Rahn, Reinhard Stumpf, and Bernd Wegner. *Germany and the Second World War*. 6 vols. Oxford: Oxford University Press, 1991–2001.

Boulle, Lieutenant Colonel Georges. *Le Corps Expéditionnaire Français en Italy (1943–1944)*. Vol. 1, *La campagne d'hiver*. Paris: Imprimerie Nationale, 1971.

Bradley, Omar N. *A Soldier's Story*. New York: Henry Holt, 1951.

Bradley, Omar N., and Clay Blair. *A General's Life: An Autobiography by General of the Army Omar N. Bradley*. New York: Simon and Schuster, 1983.

Braudel, Fernand. *The Mediterranean and the Mediterranean World in the Age of Philip II*. New York: Collins, 1976.

Brown, Cecil. *Suez to Singapore*. New York: Random House, 1942.

Brown, Lt. John Mason. *To All Hands: An Amphibious Adventure*. New York: McGraw-Hill, 1943.

Bryant, Arthur. *The Turn of the Tide: A History of the War Years Based on the Diaries of Field-Marshal Lord Alanbrooke, Chief of the Imperial General Staff*. Garden City, N.Y.: Doubleday, 1957.

Butcher, Harry C. *Three Years with Eisenhower*. London: William Heinemann, 1946.

Carlton, David. *Anthony Eden: A Political Biography*. London: A. Lane, 1981.

Carver, Field Marshal Sir Michael. *The War Lords: Military Commanders of the Twentieth Century*. Boston: Little, Brown, 1976.

Chambé, R. *L'Epopée française d'Italie 1944*. Paris: Flammarion, 1952.

Charmley, John. *Churchill: The End of Glory*. New York: Harcourt Brace, 1993.

Churchill, Winston S. *The Second World War*. 6 vols. Boston: Little, Brown, 1948–55.

Clark, Jeffrey J., and Robert Ross Smith. *Riviera to the Rhine*. Washington, D.C.: Center of Military History, 1993.

Clark, Mark. *Calculated Risk*. New York: Harper, 1950.

Clayton, Anthony. *Three Marshals of France: Leadership after Trauma*. London: Brassey's, 1992.

Close, David H. *The Origins of the Greek Civil War*. London: Longman, 1995.

Cohen, Stephen P. *The Indian Army: Its Contribution to the Development of a Nation*. Delhi: Oxford University Press, 1990.

Colville, John. *Fringes of Power: Ten Downing Street Diaries, 1939–1955*. New York: W. W. Norton & Co., 1985.

Connell, John. *Wavell, Scholar and Soldier*. London: Collins, 1964.

Coutau-Bégarie, Hervé, and Claude Huan. *Darlan*. Paris: Fayard, 1989.

Crisp, Robert. *Brazen Chariots: An Account of Tank Warfare in the Western Desert, November–December 1941*. New York: Norton, 1960.

——. *The Gods Were Neutral*. New York: Norton, 1961.

Cunningham of Hyndhope, Admiral of the Fleet Viscount. *A Sailor's Odyssey*. London: Hutchinson, 1951.

Cutler, Bruce. *Seeing the Darkness: Naples, 1943–1945*. Kansas City: BkMk Press of the University of Missouri at Kansas City, 1998.

Dallek, Robert. *Franklin D. Roosevelt and American Foreign Policy, 1932–1945*. New York: Oxford University Press, 1995.

Davis, Kenneth S. *FDR: The War President*. New York: Random House, 2000.

Deakin, F. W. *The Brutal Friendship: Mussolini, Hitler and the Fall of Italian Fascism*. New York: Harper and Row, 1962.

Dear, I.C.B., and M.R.D. Foot. *The Oxford Companion to World War II*. New York: Oxford University Press, 1995.

de Gaulle, Charles. *The War Memoirs of Charles de Gaulle*. Vol. 3, *Salvation, 1944–1946*. New York: Simon and Schuster, 1960.

de Lattre de Tassigny, Marshal Jean. *The History of the First French Army*. London: George Allen and Unwin, 1952.

D'Este, Carlo. *Bitter Victory: The Battle for Sicily, 1943*. New York: Dutton, 1988.

——. *World War II in the Mediterranean, 1942–1945*. Chapel Hill, N.C.: Algonquin Books, 1990.

——. *Patton: A Genius for War*. New York: HarperCollins, 1995.

——. *Eisenhower: A Soldier's Life*. New York: Henry Holt, 2002.

Djilas, Aleska. *The Contested Country: Yugoslav Unity and Communist Revolution, 1919–1953*. Cambridge, Mass.: Harvard University Press, 1991.

Djilas, Milovan. *Wartime*. New York: Harcourt Brace Jovanovich, 1977.

——. *Tito: The Story from Inside*. London: Weidenfeld and Nicolson, 1981.

Doolittle, James H. *I Could Never Be So Lucky Again*. New York: Bantam, 1991.

Doubler, Michael D. *Closing with the Enemy: How GIs Fought the War in Europe, 1944–1945*. Lawrence: University Press of Kansas, 1994.

Ehrman, John. *Grand Strategy*. Vol. 5, *August 1943–September 1944*. London: HMSO, 1956.

Ellis, John. *Cassino: The Hollow Victory: The Battle for Rome, January–June 1944*. New York: McGraw-Hill, 1984.

———. *Brute Force: Allied Strategy and Tactics in the Second World War*. New York: Viking, 1990.

Ellwood, David W. *Italy 1943–1945*. New York: Holmes and Meier, 1985.

Farnie, D. A. *East and West of Suez: The Suez Canal in History, 1854–1956*. Oxford: Clarendon, 1969.

Feiling, K. *The Life of Neville Chamberlain*. London: Macmillan, 1946.

Felmy, General der Flieger a.D. Hellmuth, and General der Artillerie a. D. Walter Warlimont. *World War II: German Military Studies*. Vol. 13, *German Exploitation of Arab Nationalist Movements in World War II*. Historical Division, Headquarters United States Army, Europe.

Fergusson, Bernard, ed. *The Business of War: The War Narrative of Major-General Sir John Kennedy*. New York, William Morrow, 1958.

Ford, Kirk, Jr. *OSS and the Yugoslav Resistance, 1943–1945*. College Station: Texas A&M University Press, 1992.

Fraser, David. *Alanbrooke*. New York: Atheneum, 1962.

Frederich, Carl J., ed. *American Experiences in Military Government in World War II*. New York: Reinhart, 1948.

French, David. *Raising Churchill's Army: The British Army and the War against Germany, 1919–1945*. New York: Oxford University Press, 2000.

Fuller, Ernest F. *The Mediterranean Theater of Operations: Cassino to the Alps*. Washington, D.C.: Center of Military History, 1977.

Fussell, Paul. *Doing Battle: The Making of a Skeptic*. Boston: Little, Brown, 1996.

Garland, Albert N., and Howard McGaw Smyth. *Sicily and the Surrender of Italy*. Washington, D.C.: Office of the Chief of Military History, 1965.

German Antiguerrilla Operations in the Balkans (1941–1944). Department of the Army Pamphlet No. 20-243. Washington, D.C.: Department of the Army, August 1954.

Gibson, Hugh, ed. *The Ciano Diaries, 1939–1943*. Garden City, N.Y.: Doubleday, 1946.

Ginsborg, Paul. *A History of Contemporary Italy: Society and Politics, 1943–1988*. London: Penguin, 1990.

Glenny, Misha. *The Balkans: Nationalism, War and the Great Powers, 1804–1999*. New York: Viking, 1999.

Gordon, John W. *The Other Desert War: British Special Forces in North Africa, 1940–1943*. New York: Greenwood, 1987.

Graham, Dominick, and Shelford Bidwell. *Fire Power: British Army Weapons and Theories of War, 1904–1945*. London: Allen and Upwin, 1982.

———. *Tug of War: The Battle for Italy, 1943–1945*. New York: St. Martin's, 1986.

Greene, Jack, and Alessandro Massignai. *The Naval War in the Mediterranean, 1940–1943*. London: Chatham, 1998.

Greenfield, George. *Chasing the Beast: One Man's War*. London: Richard Cohen Books, 1998.

Greenfield, Kent Roberts, ed. *Command Decisions*. Washington, D.C.: Center for Military History, 1990.

Hamilton, Nigel. *Monty: The Making of a General, 1887–1942.* New York: McGraw-Hill, 1981.

———. *Master of the Battlefield: Monty's War Years, 1942–1944.* New York: McGraw-Hill, 1983.

Harper, John Lamberton. *American Visions of Europe.* Cambridge: Cambridge University Press, 1996.

Harris, C.R.S. *Allied Military Administration of Italy, 1943–1945.* London: HMSO, 1957.

Harvey, J. *The War Diaries of Oliver Harvey.* London, 1978.

Hattendorf, John B., ed. *Naval Policy and Strategy in the Mediterranean: Past, Present and Future.* London: Frank Cass, 2000.

Heckstall-Smith, Anthony, and Vice-Admiral H. T. Vaillie-Grohman. *Greek Tragedy 1941.* New York: Norton, 1961.

Hehn, Paul N. *The German Struggle Against Yugoslav Guerrillas in World War II: German Counter-Insurgency in Yugoslavia, 1941–1943.* New York: Columbia University Press, 1979.

Higham, Robin. *Diary of a Disaster: British Aid to Greece, 1940–41.* Lexington: University Press of Kentucky, 1986.

Hinsley, F. H., et al. *British Intelligence in the Second World War: Its Influence on Strategy and Operations.* 3 Vols. New York: Cambridge University Press, 1979–88.

Hirshson, Stanley P. *General Patton: A Soldier's Life.* New York: HarperCollins, 2002.

Holland, Jeffrey. *The Aegean Mission: Allied Operations in the Dodecanese.* New York: Greenwood, 1988.

Howard, Michael. *The Mediterranean Strategy in the Second World War.* New York: Praeger, 1968.

———. *British Intelligence in the Second World War,* Vol. 5, *Strategic Deception.* New York: Cambridge University Press, 1990.

Howe, George F. *Northwest Africa: Seizing the Initiative in the West.* Washington, D.C.: Department of the Army, 1957.

Hunt, Sir David. *A Don at War.* London: William Kimber, 1966.

Irving, David. *The Trail of the Fox: The Life of Field-Marshal Erwin Rommel.* London: Book Club Associates, 1977.

Jackson, W.G.F. *The Battle for North Africa, 1940–43.* New York: Mason/Charter, 1975.

Jellison, Charles A. *Besieged: The World War II Ordeal of Malta, 1940–1942.* Hanover, N.H.: University Press of New England, 1984.

Jones, Matthew. *Britain, the United States and the Mediterranean War, 1942–1944.* New York: St. Martin's, 1996.

Judt, Tony, ed. *Resistance and Revolution in Mediterranean Europe, 1939–1948.* London: Routledge, 1989.

Keegan, John, ed. *Churchill's Generals.* New York: Grove Weidenfeld, 1991.

Kennedy, David. *Freedom from Fear.* Oxford: Oxford University Press, 1999.

Kennett, Lee. *G.I.: The American Soldier in World War II*. New York: Scribner, 1987.

Kesselring, Albert. *Kesselring: A Soldier's Record*. New York: William Morrow, 1954.

Kimball, W. F., ed. *Churchill and Roosevelt: The Complete Correspondence*. Princeton: Princeton University Press, 1984.

Knox, MacGregor. *Hitler's Italian Allies: Royal Armed Forces, Fascist Regime, and the War of 1940–1943*. Cambridge: Cambridge University Press, 2000.

Lacouture, Jean. *De Gaulle*. Vol. 1, *Le Rebelle, 1890–1944*. Paris: Editions du Seuil, 1984.

Lamb, Richard. *War in Italy, 1943–1945: A Brutal Story*. New York: St. Martin's, 1993.

Lanquetot, André. *Un hiver dans les Abruzzes*. Vincennes: SHAT, 1991.

Larrabee, Eric. *Commander in Chief: Franklin Delano Roosevelt, His Lieutenants, and Their War*. New York: Touchstone, 1988.

Lerner, Henri. *Catroux*. Paris: Albin Michel, 1990.

Lessa, William A. *Spearhead Governatore: Remembrances of the Campaign in Italy*. Malibu, Calif.: Undena Publications, 1985.

Levi, Carlo. *Christ Stopped at Eboli*. New York: Farrar, Straus and Giroux, 1974.

Levine, Alan J. *The War Against Rommel's Supply Lines, 1942–1943*. Westport, Conn.: Praeger, 1999.

Levisse-Touzé, Christine. *L'Afrique du Nord dans la guerre, 1939–1945*. Paris: Albin Michel, 1998.

Lewin, Ronald. *Churchill as Warlord*. London: B.T. Batsford, 1973.

———. *The Life and Death of the Afrika Korps*. London: Corgi Books, 1979.

Lewis, Norman. *Naples '44*. London: Collins, 1978.

Liddell Hart, B. H., ed. *The Rommel Papers*. New York: Harcourt, Brace, 1953.

Liebling, A. J. *The Road Back to Paris*. New York: Modern Library, 1997.

Louis, William Roger, ed. *Churchill*. New York: Norton, 1993.

Luck, Major Hans von. *Panzer Commander: The Memoirs of Colonel Hans von Luck*. New York: Dell, 1989.

Macintyre, Donald. *The Naval War Against Hitler*. New York: Scribner, 1971.

Macksey, Kenneth. *The Partisans of Europe in the Second World War*. New York: Stein and Day, 1975.

———. *Kesselring: German Master Strategist of the Second World War*. London: Greenhill Books, 2000.

Macmillan, Harold. *The Blast of War, 1939–45*. London, 1967.

———. *War Diaries: Politics and War in the Mediterranean, 1943–1945*. New York: St. Martin's, 1984.

Mallett, Robert. *The Italian Navy and Fascist Expansionism, 1935–1940*. London: Frank Cass, 1998.

Mansfield, Peter. *The British in Egypt*. New York: Holt, Rinehart and Winston, 1971.

Marder, Arthur J. *From the Dardanelles to Oran: Studies in the Royal Navy in War and Peace, 1915–1940*. London: Oxford University Press, 1974.

Martel, André. *Histoire militaire de la France*. Vol. 4, *De 1940 à nos jours*. Paris: Presses Universitaires de France, 1994.

———. *Leclerc: Le soldat et la politique*. Paris: Albin Michel, 1998.

Mason, Philip. *A Matter of Honor: An Account of the Indian Army, Its Officers and Men*. London: Penguin, 1976.

Maugeri, Admiral Franco. *From the Ashes of Disgrace*. New York: Reynal and Hitchcock, 1948.

Mauldin, William. *Up Front*. Cleveland: World, 1945.

Mazower, Mark. *Inside Hitler's Greece: The Experience of Occupation, 1941–44*. New Haven: Yale University Press, 1993.

———. *Dark Continent: Europe's Twentieth Century*. New York: Vintage, 1998.

Megargee, Geoffrey P. *Inside Hitler's High Command*. Lawrence: University Press of Kansas, 2000.

Melton, George E. *Darlan: Admiral and Statesman of France*. Westport, Conn.: Praeger, 1998.

Michel, Henri. *François Darlan*. Paris: Hachette, 1993.

Milligan, Spike. *"Rommel?" "Gunner Who?" A Confrontation in the Desert*. London: Michael Joseph, 1974.

———. *Monty: His Part in My Victory*. London: Penguin, 1978.

Montagu, E. *The Man Who Never Was*. Oxford, 2001.

Moorehead, Alan. *The March to Tunis: The North African War, 1940–1943*. New York: Harper and Row, 1943. Reissued as *The Desert War*. London: Penguin, 2000.

Murray, Williamson. *The War in the Air, 1914–45*. London: Cassell, 1999.

Murray, Williamson, and Allan Millett. *Military Effectiveness*. Vol. 3, *The Second World War*. Boston: Unwin Hyman, 1990.

Nagel, James, ed. *Critical Essays on Joseph Heller*. Boston: G. K. Hall, 1984.

Nicolson, Nigel. *Alex: The Life of Field Marshal Earl Alexander of Tunis*. London: Pan Books, 1976.

Overy, R. J. *The Air War, 1939–1945*. New York: Stein and Day, 1980.

———. *Why the Allies Won*. New York: Norton, 1995.

Pack, S.W.C. *The Battle of Matapan*. New York: Macmillan, 1961.

Paxton, Robert O. *Parades and Politics at Vichy: The French Officer Corps under Marshal Pétain*. Princeton: Princeton University Press, 1966.

Pinsker, Stanford. *Understanding Joseph Heller*. Columbia: University of South Carolina Press, 1991.

Playfair, Ian Stanley. *The Mediterranean and the Middle East*. 6 vols. London: HMSO, 1954–88.

Potts, Stephen W. *Catch-22: Antiheroic Antinovel*. Boston: Twayne, 1989.

Pryce-Jones, David. *Evelyn Waugh and His World*. Boston: Little, Brown, 1973.

Raugh, Harold E., Jr., *Wavell in the Middle East, 1939–1941: A Study in Generalship*. London: Brassey's, 1993.

Roberts, Walter R. *Tito, Mihailović and the Allies; 1941–1945.* New Brunswick, N.J.: Rutgers University Press, 1973.

Rodgers, Edward K. *Doughboy Chaplain.* Boston: Meador, 1945.

Rolf, David. *The Bloody Road to Tunis: Destruction of the Axis Forces in North Africa: November 1942–May 1943.* London: Greenhill Books, 2001.

Roskill, S. W. *Churchill and the Admiral.* New York: William Morrow, 1978.

Roux, Jean-Pierre. *La France de la quatrième république: L'ardeur et la nécessité, 1944–1952.* Paris: Editions du Seuil, 1980.

Sachar, Howard M. *A History of Israel from the Rise of Zionism to Our Time.* New York: Knopf, 1998.

Sadkovich, James J. *The Italian Navy in World War II.* Westport, Conn: Greenwood, 1994.

Salan, Raoul. *Mémoires: Fin d'un empire.* Vol. 1, *Le sens d'un engagement.* Paris: Presses de la Cité, 1970.

Salerno, Reynolds M. *Vital Crossroads: Mediterranean Origins of the Second World War, 1935–1940.* Ithaca, N.Y.: Cornell University Press, 2002.

Samson, Anthony. *Macmillan: A Study in Ambiguity.* London, 1967.

Sandler, Stanley. *Glad to See Them Come and Sorry to See Them Go: A History of U.S. Army Tactical Civil Affairs/Military Government, 1775–1991.* No place, publisher, or date.

Schmider, Klaus. "The Mediterranean in 1940–1941: Crossroads of Lost Opportunities?" *War and Society* 15, no. 2 (October 1997).

Schrijvers, Peter. *The Crash of Ruin: American Combat Soldiers in Europe during World War II.* New York: New York University Press, 1998.

Sherwood, Robert E. *Roosevelt and Hopkins: An Intimate History.* New York: Harper, 1948.

Shrader, Charles R. *The Withered Vine: Logistics and the Communist Insurgency in Greece, 1945–1949.* Westport, Conn.: Praeger, 1999.

Smith, Denis Mack. *Mussolini.* New York: Knopf, 1982.

Spector, Ronald H. *At War at Sea: Sailors and Naval Combat in the Twentieth Century.* New York: Viking, 2001.

Speer, Albert. *Inside the Third Reich.* New York: Macmillan, 1970.

Strong, Kenneth. *Intelligence at the Top.* London: Cassell, 1968.

Sullivan, Brian. "A Fleet in Being: The Rise and Fall of Italian Sea Power, 1861–1943." *International History Review* 10, no. 1 (February 1988).

Taylor, A.J.P., ed. *Churchill Revised: A Critical Assessment.* New York: Dial Press, 1968.

Theroux, Paul. *The Pillars of Hercules: A Grand Tour of the Mediterranean.* New York: Putnam's, 1995.

Thorne, Christopher. *Allies of a Kind: The United States, Britain, and the War against Japan, 1941–1945.* New York: Oxford University Press, 1978.

Tregaskis, Richard. *Invasion Diary.* New York: Random House, 1944.

Truscott, Lucian K. *Command Missions.* New York: Dutton, 1959.

Tuker, Lieutenant General Sir Francis. *Approach to Battle*. London: Cassell, 1963.

van Creveld, Martin. *Hitler's Strategy, 1940–1941: The Balkan Clue*. Cambridge: Cambridge University Press, 1973.

———. *Supplying War: Logistics from Wallenstein to Patton*. Cambridge: Cambridge University Press, 1977.

———. *Fighting Power: German and U.S. Army Performance, 1939–1945*. Westport, Conn.: Greenwood, 1982.

Vatikiotis, P. J. *The Egyptian Army in Politics: Pattern for New Nations?* Bloomington: Indiana University Press, 1961.

Vigneras, Marcel. *United States Army in World War II: Special Studies: Rearming the French*. Washington, D.C.: U.S. Government Printing Office, 1957.

Warlimont, Walter. *Inside Hitler's Headquarters, 1939–45*. New York: Praeger, 1964.

Weinberg, Gerhard. *A World at Arms: A Global History of World War II*. Cambridge: Cambridge University Press, 1994.

Wheeler-Bennett, John, ed. *Action This Day: Working with Churchill*. London: Macmillan, 1969.

Wilmott, H. P. *The Barrier and the Javelin: Japanese and Allied Pacific Strategies, February to June 1942*. Annapolis, Md.: Naval Institute Press, 1983.

——— *The Great Crusade: A New Complete History of the Second World War*. New York: Free Press, 1989.

Wilt, Alan F. *War from the Top: German and British Military Decision Making during World War II*. Bloomington: Indiana University Press, 1990.

Woodward, E. L. *British Foreign Policy in the Second World War*. London: HMSO, 1962.

Wright, John. *Libya: A Modern History*. Baltimore: Johns Hopkins University Press, 1982.

Ziegler, Philip. *Mountbatten*. New York: Knopf, 1985.

Zurcher, Erik J. *Turkey: A Modern History*. London: I. B. Tauris, 1998.

INDEX

Index

Index

Index

Index

Gazala, Battle of, 232, 265–73, 275, 291, 327, 583, 678
Genoa, 139, 649
Genovese crime family, 518
Gensoul, Admiral Marcel Bruno, 63, 64–65
George II, King of Greece, 77, 78, 189, 484–85, 633
George VI, King of England, 263
German intelligence, 213–14, 225, 233, 242, 549, 622
El Alamein and, 302, 307
Germany:
  Allied air attacks inside, 291, 430, 456, 544
  alliance with Italy, see Italy, alliance with Germany
  assessment of German armed forces, 209–17
  economy of, 214–15
  French forces enter, 611–12
  Jews and, see Jews, Germany and
  surrender of, 459, 563–64, 643
  see also Hitler, Adolf; individual battles and military figures
Gerow, General Leonard, 395
Ghost Division, The (Rommel), 204
Giant II, 468, 475, 488, 659
Gibraltar, 12, 14, 16–17, 19, 24, 48, 59–60, 71, 139, 335
  Torch and, 343, 348, 350
Giogo Pass, 624, 625
Giraud, General Henri, 343–44, 350, 358, 365, 366, 382, 465, 563, 582, 586, 594
Gneisenau, 258
Godfroy, Admiral René-Emile, 63
Godwin-Austin, Major General, 98, 108
Goebbels, Joseph, 500
Golden Square, 573, 574, 578
Göring, Hermann, 159, 163, 165, 173, 175, 214, 216, 407
Gort, General Lord, 264, 282
Gothic line, 618, 621, 638, 646, 658
  cracking the, 616–30
Gott, General William "Strafer," 231, 255, 289, 293
Graham, Dominick, 591, 662, 673
Grandi, Dino, 465
Grapeshot, Operation, 639–40, 643–49, 658
Graziani, Marshal Rodolfo, 39, 45–46, 71–72, 75, 78, 84, 87, 90, 92, 98, 102, 130, 617
  Compass offensive against, 108, 114, 115, 118, 126, 127, 128
Grazzi, Emanuele, 91
Greece, 67, 68, 99, 104, 108, 124–25, 139, 175, 224, 231, 235, 413, 631, 632–34, 635, 651–53, 666, 681
  Churchill's decision to aid, 27, 140–46, 671

Civil War in, 485, 653, 682
evacuation of British troops from, 155
Marita, 121, 139, 143–56, 158, 174, 657, 674
Mussolini's attack on, 72–79, 89–98, 108, 114, 147
postwar, 453, 615, 630, 658
the resistance in, 188–95, 421, 480–85, 632–34, 651–53, 658, 667
surrender to Germany, 154–55
Greek Communist Party (KKE), 188–89, 192, 194, 195, 633, 652, 653
Greenfield, Captain George, 218, 564, 680
Greyhound, 54
Guadalcanal, 289, 359
Guam, 614
Guderian, Heinz, 508
Gustav line, 507, 508, 511, 512, 521–23, 526, 527, 528, 530, 534, 539, 541, 544–49, 555, 560, 658
Guzzoni, General Alfredo, 423, 425, 427, 428
Gymnast, see Torch, Operation
Gypsies, 179

Halder, General Franz, 28, 199, 206, 228, 230, 234
Halfaya Pass, 228, 232, 233, 249, 253, 256
Hamburg, firestorm in, 430
Hamilton, Niger, 323, 368, 433–34
Hanke, Karl-August, 202, 204–205
Harding, Field Marshal A. R., 117, 546–51, 635
Harding, General Sir John, 298
Harmon, Major General Ernest, 383, 522
Harvey, Oliver, 365
Hassan Saby Pasha, 42
Havlock, 55
Haw Haw, Lord, 231, 500
Heller, Joseph, 520
Herkules, 264, 281, 282, 283–84, 667, 674
Hermes, 66
Hewitt, Vice-Admiral H. K., 496
Heydrich, Reinhard, 258, 273
Himmler, Heinrich, 202, 643
Hitler, Adolf, 68, 257, 291, 411, 484, 608, 656
  airborne forces and, 164–65
  assassination attempt of July 1944, 213, 614
  Barbarossa's importance to, see Barbarossa, Operation
  Crete and, 157–59, 264
  death of, 650
  defense of North Africa and, 369, 370, 371
  described, 36–37
  Dodecanese and, 473
  fall of Tobruk and calling off of Herkules, 281, 282, 283–84
  Franco and, 59–60, 71, 139

Index

Index

Index

Monte Cassino, *see* Cassino (Monte Cassino)
Monte Castellone, 540, 541
Monte Grandi, 625–26
Montélimar, 597
Montenegro, 177, 180
Montgomery, Field Marshall Bernard, 5, 11, 101, 109, 199, 208, 347, 368, 375, 390, 456, 505, 509, 589, 599, 635, 670–71
Alexander and, 293, 297, 298, 408, 410, 447, 546
Anderson and, 382–83
Auchinleck and, 237, 241, 293
Avalanche and, 468, 486, 487, 491, 505
Churchill and, 289, 293, 312, 318
described, 292–96, 404
Eisenhower and, 339, 340
El Alamein and, 84, 117, 300–24, 564, 582–83, 678
Freyberg and, 162
Gaullist units and, 564, 582–86
Husky and, 417, 418–19, 420, 431–36, 438, 442–44, 446, 447–48
Italian campaign and, 509, 527
named head of Eighth Army, 289, 292
Tunisia and, 401–406, 410–11, 413, 417, 560
Moorehead, Alan, 10, 80, 82, 86, 99, 101, 119–20, 134, 135, 139, 196, 236, 240, 243, 255–56, 342, 365, 376, 411
on Battle of Gazala, 269
on Crusader, 247, 249, 250–51, 254
on fall of Tobruk, 274–75, 276, 277
on Montgomery, 295, 296
Morocco, 60, 291, 336, 343, 360, 367
Morshead, Major General L. J., 224, 226, 230
Moslem Brotherhood, 21, 573
Moulin, Jean, 593
Mountbatten, Lord "Dickie," 416
Mulhouse, 606
Munich conference of 1938, 164
Murphy, Audie, 610
Murphy, Robert, 341, 343, 365, 366
Murrow, Edward R., 362
Mussolini, Benito, 31–36, 68, 301–302, 358, 368–69, 371–72, 412
aborted triumphal entry into Cairo, 282, 288
described, 31–35
execution of, 649
fall of Tobruk and, 281
Greek invasion and, 72–79, 89–98, 147
Hitler and, 28, 31, 36–39, 74–75, 97, 380, 408, 429–30, 466, 496, 673–74
invasion of Malta and, 264–65
loss of East Africa, 137–38
Malta and, 42–43
overthrow and arrest of, 414, 430, 439, 444, 445, 458, 463, 464–66, 666, 676

"parallel war," 38–46, 79
purpose for entering WWII, 36, 39
relationship with Italian military, 80–81
rescue by Germans, 470, 496
Sicilian invasion and, 421, 428, 429
Tunisia and, 370
view of Mediterranean, 5, 35–36
see also Italy
Myer, Colonel C. W., 480, 481

Nahas Pasha, Egyptian Prime Minister, 615
Nairobi, 134
Naples, 503, 515–21
Narvik expedition, 98–99, 236
National Committee for the Liberation of Upper Italy (CLNAI), 637, 638, 639
National Liberation Front (EAM) of Greece, 192–94, 480–83, 485, 632–33, 634, 651, 652, 658
National Popular Liberation Army (ELAS), 192–95, 480–83, 485, 632, 634, 651, 652, 653, 658
National Republican Greek League (EDES), 188, 190–91, 193, 480, 632–33, 634, 651
Neame, Lieutenant General Philip, 221–22, 223, 669
Nedíc, General Milan, 178, 180, 181
Nehring, General Walter, 304, 354–55, 356
Nelson, 87
Neretva River, battle on the, 477–78
Neubacher, Hermann, 634
New Britain, 544
Newby, Eric, 80, 82–83, 86
New Caledonia, 571
New Guinea, 544
New York Times, The, 464
New Zealand, 175
Nicholson, Bridgadier Cameron, 386
Nicosia, 439
Noguès, General Auguste, 363
Nordwind, Operation, 609–10
Normandy:
    collapse of German defenses in, 596–97
    invasion of, *see* Overlord
Northwest African Tactical Air Force, 400
Norway:
    Narvik expedition, 98–99, 236
    resistance in, 543
Nouguès, General Auguste, 352

Ochsenhkopf (Oxhead), Operation, 398–99
O'Connor, General Richard, 87, 113, 128, 222, 223
    Compass and, 117, 118, 123, 126–27, 140, 145
    described, 110

Index

ILLUSTRATION CREDITS

Grateful acknowledgment is made to the following for permission to reproduce the maps: to the Department of History, United States Military Academy, for maps of the Mediterranean Basin, North Africa 1940 (Graziani's advance and Wavell's offensive; Rommel's first offensive), The Balkans 1941, Crete 1941, North Africa 1940 (Auchinleck's offensive; Rommel's second offensive), Gazala and vicinity—Libya (Initial Dispositions), Gazala and vicinity—Libya (decisive German-Italian breakout), North Africa 1941 (pursuit to Tunisia; the Allied Invasion), Allegria-Tunisia 1942, Tunisia 1942 (the race for Tunisia; Axis initiative), Central Tunisia 1943, Tunisia 1942 (situation 22 April and operations since 26 February 1943; final Allied offensive), Sicily 1943 (Allied plan for the invasion of Sicily), Sicily 1943 (Italo-German counterattack and Allied advance), Southern Italy 1944, Anzio-Cassino Area 1943 (attempts to cross Rapido and Gargiliano rivers), Anzio-Cassino area 1943 (situation 18 May 1944 and advance in Operation Diadem), Southern France 1944, Northwestern Europe 1944, Southeastern France and Eastern France and the Low Countries 1944, Northern Italy 1944 (Allied advance to Gothic Line), northern Italy 1944 (Allied plan of attack); to Frank Martini for the maps of the campaign in East Africa, and the Middle East; *History of the Second World War: The Mediterranean and the Middle East II*, by I.S.O. Playfair, Her Majesty's Stationary Office (HMSO), for the map of the radius of action of aircraft from Malta 1941; *History of the Second World War: The Mediterranean and the Middle East III*, by I.S.O. Playfair, HMSO, for the maps of Tobruk and the battle of Alam El Halfa; *Greece and Crete 1941*, by Christopher Buckley, HMSO, for the map of Maleme; *War and Revolution in Yugoslavia 1941–1945: The Chetniks*, by Jozo Tomasevich, copyright © 1975 by the Board of Trustees of the Leland Stanford Jr. University, used with permission of Stanford University Press, www.sup.org, for the map of Eastern Europe; *Inside Hitler's Greece: The Experience of Occupation, 1941–44*, by Mark Mazower, Copyright © 1993 by Mark Mazower, Yale University Press, for the map of the zones of occupation in Greece 1941; *Decisive Battles of the 20th Century*, eds. Noble Frankland and Christopher Dowling, David McKay Publishing, for the map of the Eighth

Army attack and X Corps breakthrough; *U.S. Army in World War II: Mediterranean Theater of Operations: Northwest Africa: Seizing the Initiative in the West*, by George F. Howe, Office of the Chief of Military History, Department of the Army, for the maps of the first Allied drive on Tunisia, Mareth and Chott positions; *The Italian Navy in World War II*, by Marc Antonio Bragadin, A Naval Institute Publication, for the map of the "Death Route"; *U.S. Army in World War II: Mediterranean Theater of Operations: Salerno to Cassino*, by Martin Blumenson, Office of the Chief of Military History, Department of the Army, for the map of invasion plans in 1943; *The West Point Atlas of American Wars*, Vol II 1900–1953, ed. Vincent J. Esposito, Praeger Publishers, copyright © T. E. Griess, for the map of Salerno: the German counterattack.

Grateful acknowledgment is made to the following for permission to reproduce the images: *U.S. Army in World War II: Mediterranean Theater of Operations: Northwest Africa: Seizing the Initiative in the West*, by George F. Howe, Office of the Chief of Military History, Department of the Army, for the images of Erwin Rommel, of Eisenhower and Clark with Jean François Darlan, of U.S. troops in the Kasserine Pass, of Juergen von Arnim, of Anderson and Bradley in Tunisia, and of the Siebel ferry in Tunisia; *History of the Second World War: The Mediterranean and the Middle East III*, by I.S.O. Playfair, HMSO, for the image of the crippled tanker *Ohio*; *History of the Second World War: The Mediterranean and the Middle East IV*, by I.S.O. Playfair, HMSO, for the images of the Axis airfield in Tripolitania, and of Montgomery interviewing Messe; *U.S. Army in World War II: Pictorial Record, The War Against Germany and Italy: Mediterranean and Adjacent Areas*, ed. Kent Roberts Greenfield, Office of the Chief of Military History, Department of the Army, for the images of the sixty-ton "Tiger" tank, of the American solider examining a mine, of the German POWs, of Monte Cassino, and of the Fifth Army entering Rome; *U.S. Army in World War II: Mediterranean Theater of Operations: Salerno to Cassino*, by Martin Blumenson, Office of the Chief of Military History, Department of the Army, for the image of the troops cheering at the news of Italy's surrender; the U.S. Army for the images of the M13/40 tank, of the American Spitfire, of the LSTs loading supplies, of retreating German troops, of the U.S. B-24 "Liberators," of the French North African troops, of Tito and Churchill, and of Anvil meets Overlord.